The Ecology of the Rocky Shores of Sherkin Island

A Twenty-Year Perspective

Gillian Bishop

This book is dedicated
to the memory of
Eileen Murphy
1941–1979

Co-founder of Sherkin Island Marine Station

Published by
Sherkin Island Marine Station,
Sherkin Island, Co. Cork, Ireland

Typeset and Layout by Susan Murphy Wickens
Drawings by Charlotte Leeder and Audrey Murphy
Photography by Pete Atkinson, Terry Farnell, Paul Kay, Daphne Pochin Mould, Robbie Murphy, Iain Watts and from the Murphy Family Archives
Printed by City Print Ltd, Victoria Cross, Cork, Ireland.

Cover photographs by Paul Kay and Robbie Murphy:
Kinish Narrows, Sherkin Island, Co. Cork, Ireland;
Actinothoë sphyrodeta; Gillian Bishop

ISBN: 1 870492 37 4 – Hardback
ISBN: 1 870492 57 9 – Softback

Printed on 50% recycled paper

AN ROINN COMHSHAOIL, OIDHREACHTA AGUS RIALTAIS ÁITIÚIL
DEPARTMENT OF THE ENVIRONMENT, HERITAGE AND LOCAL GOVERNMENT

We thank the Department of Environment, Heritage & Local Government for their support in the printing of this book.

Foreword

This book is built upon exceptional and inspired effort going back to 1975. Year by year, volunteer biologists, scientific advisors and practical helpers have contributed to Sherkin Island Marine Station's rocky shore monitoring programme, which by international standards is now outstanding because of its scope and longevity. We are indebted to Dr Gillian Bishop for distilling an enormous amount of data, so that the programme's findings together with background information and interpretation can be brought to a wide audience. In this book there is something for everyone. Students and teachers (whether at school or university) will find much that is relevant to biological studies and fieldwork projects, and whilst the monitoring results are from southwest Cork, the information on species and on general principles is relevant for the whole of Ireland.

For researchers, it is a key to the huge data bank maintained at the Marine Station. For any member of the general public with an interest in marine biology, it is a way of exploring more deeply the fascinating dynamism of shore life. For environmental scientists, it elucidates long-term natural fluctuations and trends in the abundance and distribution of species. This helps provide a framework for interpreting perceived industrial or other human influences on the marine environment.

Notwithstanding the significance of this book, it is not the final word because the monitoring programme continues! It is a milestone.

Dr Jenifer M Baker
Shrewsbury, UK

PREFACE

In 1975, my late wife, Eileen and I founded Sherkin Island Marine Station to monitor the diverse and fascinating marine life of Roaringwater Bay. One of the first projects undertaken was to establish a number of rocky shore sites for investigation and in the first year 17 sites were selected by six volunteer biologists. The number of sites was increased to over 60 by 1981 and seven of the selected sites were monitored monthly and the remainder annually.

In our pioneering enthusiasm we were perhaps naive and innocent enough to expect that state grants and commercial sponsorship would be forthcoming for what, we believed, was a very worthwhile venture. To our great disappointment such support did not materialise and we were faced with the difficult dilemma to either abandon our quest or continue against the odds. The latter course we took with some trepidation, acutely aware of our parental responsibilities to our young family, and not knowing what the future had in store. We lived on a wing and a prayer. Eileen was a tower of strength and inspiration in those difficult times; she never wavered in her commitment and offered encouragement and support when it was needed most. Our family, collectively and individually, made huge personal sacrifices, without hesitation or regret; this has continued to be the case to the present day. I am proud of what we have achieved and it stands as a perpetual memorial to Eileen who passed from this life in 1979. I have dedicated this book to her memory.

Our Marine station is now in its 28th year of productivity. We manage two of the largest and most comprehensive monitoring programmes of their kind in Europe - the phytoplankton and rocky shore. However, collecting this information is not enough. I have been criticised, often, for not publishing our data. My response has been that a single "snapshot" or a week's worth of pictures of a site's resources lacks appreciation of the events and natural cycles that can colour and enhance the picture. The snapshot view of our environment is totally irrelevant to me. I know from the information provided by our continuous sampling, that long-term monitoring is a must. And, the verification of that is the description and understanding of our rocky shores that is presented in the following pages. This information is offered to guide the use of the coastal zone far into the future.

When I decided it was time to have this book written, I knew only one person who had the ability to paint a meaningful picture of our rocky shore natural history using the monitoring data. That person is Gillian Bishop, the Station's first marine biologist. She possessed vision, common sense and enthusiasm in 1975. Over the years she has lost none of those wonderful qualities. However, I was slightly apprehensive about asking her because I knew the drafting would take a long time and need many trips to Sherkin from her home in Scotland. When I asked, she readily agreed although I suspect that many times since, she has wondered why. Her family and professional commitments make her time precious, indeed. My brief to Gillian was to bring out the facts and make sure that all the readers; lay and scientific, young and old, alike, could understand the nature of the bounty and story of our coastal waters. I did not want a book that would be solely facts and statistics. The marine environment is for all, not a select few. It must be monitored and protected and to do that, it is necessary that everyone understand that these gifts are provided from our Maker and that we share the responsibility for passing them on to our children. Gillian has been faithful to her brief, she has set the standard and ground rules for the books and reports of Sherkin data that will follow this one. Beyond receiving full marks for her writing, my family and I treasure her friendship and admire, greatly, her dedication and integrity.

Of course, this book could never have been written but for the many volunteer biologists that have come to Sherkin Island Marine Station. They should be immensely proud of their achievements, as we are. These budding biologists live a Spartan existence at the Station. The early years were especially so. I imagine many found me uncompromising, demanding and difficult in my pursuit of getting the job done properly and these would be mild words from some of them. However, I often hear that the working ethic foundations laid during their time at Sherkin have helped many of them in their careers.

I am very grateful to all the landowners who have given the Marine Station access to the sites. They have made the survey possible. To those people who have helped me with advice and support, I thank you for getting our Marine Station through the many crises we have endured. I have a wonderful richness of friends - the most precious of gifts.

Finally, I was blessed in life to have had a wonderful companion, friend, wife and mother of our children. We had the same vision and belief in ourselves. Even after Eileen's death, she has continued to guide and watch out for me from that place beyond. To my seven children Matty, Michael, Susan, Mark, Robbie, Peter and Audrey, who from a very early age were involved in the workings of the Station, I owe a debt I can never repay. Without my gang there could be no Marine Station. Their father has made life difficult for them by being obsessed with learning and educating rather than more "practical" matters. In this instance, I must recognise especially, my daughter Susan. Without her dedication to producing this book, we could not have achieved our goal.

The book reveals and highlights that the rocky shore cannot be taken for granted. Algae and animals must be monitored to understand the complexities of their environment. Anything less is an insult to nature. We must educate both ourselves and others by collecting long-term knowledge. This will give us, if we are prepared to record the changes, great rewards in our understanding of the rocky shore.

Matt Murphy
Director, Sherkin Island Marine Station

ACKNOWLEDGEMENTS

My thanks to all the volunteer biologists who have participated in the rocky shore survey, from the early days of the very first Marine Station surveys in 1975. Thanks especially to those who were part of the early discussions on data handling and who have helped with data analysis and production of graphs, including Claire Browne, Tim Budd, Jane Clark, Maxine Egerton, Kate Falcous, Terry Farnell, Richard Hatch, Julie Hunter, Talei Jackson, Leslie Mahon, Karen Mould, Ben Sampson and Sangeeta Taylor. Many of the Station's volunteers have made a valuable contribution to the book by spending tedious hours checking spellings, latin names, data points etc. and I am truly grateful for their dedication. It is impossible to name everyone but I hope that each of the "bods" realises the enormity of their contribution to the book and the survey as a whole. We are also grateful to the islanders whose land we tramped across to access the shores. Without their assistance there would be no survey.

I feel the book is far more readable thanks to the superb drawings of Charlotte Leeder and Audrey Murphy. These, together with the photographs taken by Pete Atkinson, Terry Farnell, Paul Kay, Daphne Pochin Mould, Robbie Murphy, Iain Watts and from the Murphy Family archives, have brought the shores, species and Marine Station to life.

I thank all those who generously gave of their time in reading the final draft of the book, verifying facts and offering constructive criticism. Their wider perspectives have been a constructive force in developing some issues further, thus making the text more complete. These are John Akeroyd, Jenny Baker, Brian McK Bary, Rev Denis Collin, Michéal Corduff, Michael Courtney, John Costello, Mark Costello, Terry Farnell, Natalie Frost, Michael Guiry, John Hartley, Cliff Hilliard, Niamh Hunt, Dave Jackson, Mike Johnston, John Joyce, Lucy Kay, Brendan Keenan, Alex Kirby, Paddy Leahy, Sheila Liggins, Dan Linehan, Michael Ludwig, Ian Maclean, Tom McSweeney, Karen Mould, Robbie Murphy, David Nichols, Liam O'Regan, Tony Toole, Ian Townend, Jane Twelves, Katherine Walshe, Barney Whelan and E. Williamson.

Thank you to An Coiste Téarmaíochta, and particularly to Fidelma Ní Ghallchobhair, for assistance with the Irish names. City Print have done a superb job in bringing the book to print and we are grateful for their care and commitment throughout.

The rocky shore survey would not exist were it not for Matt Murphy's inspired insight into the value of such a programme back in 1975. Without his drive and passion the data would never have been collected to such high standards.

My very special thanks to Matt's family, Matty, Michael, Susan, Mark, Robbie, Peter and Audrey for the countless hours of their growing up that were willingly sacrificed to the Marine Station. More recently to Michael, Robbie and Audrey for their practical help and support with a million things, from transporting me and other biologists in vans and boats, to checking data and discussing ideas. Particular thanks to Susan, for her infinite skill and patience with the design, layout, editing and incisive criticism of the text. Her drive for clarity and consistency and refusal to accept second best has turned the book into something far bigger than originally envisaged. The time she has given to our task has often encroached upon her own family and I hope that her young sons Eoin and Eric will one day read the words they 'helped' to put on the page. My heartfelt thanks to all the Murphy family for welcoming me into their home year upon year, and lastly to my own family for putting up with my repeated disappearances to Sherkin to work on "The Book"! I hope that Hannah, Esther and Alexander may one day share my love of the Island's rocky shores.

It has been a pleasure and privilege to work in such a beautiful location which the Irish government has recently proposed as a candidate Special Area of Conservation. This is in recognition of habitat and species richness and I am proud that the work of Sherkin Island Marine Station can contribute to a deeper understanding of the ecology of Roaringwater Bay.

Gillian Bishop

The common brittlestar *Ophiothrix fragilis* amongst sponges on the lower shore.

CONTENTS

Appendices

Glossary

Highlight Boxes

Plates

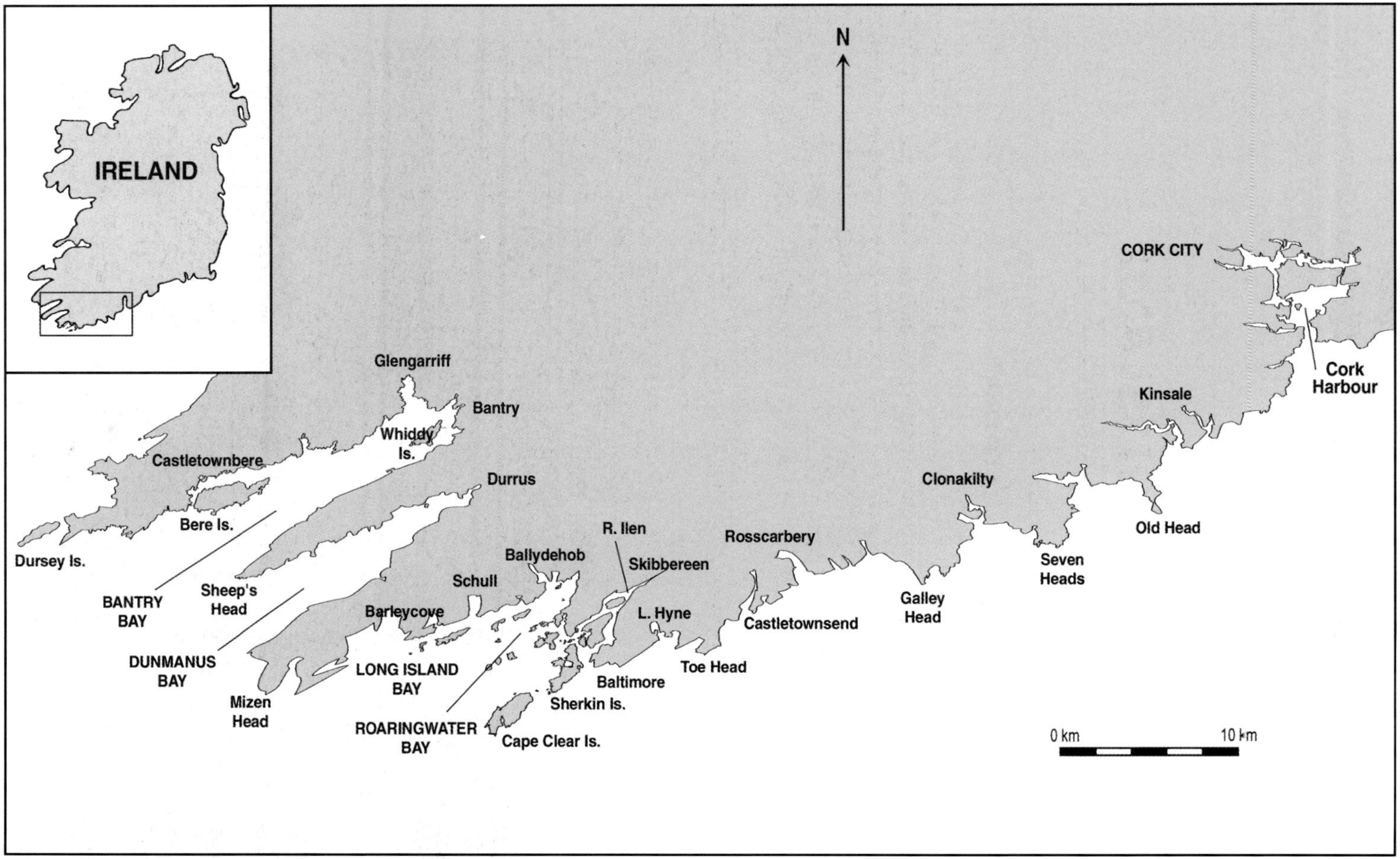

Southwest Ireland, from Cork Harbour to Bantry Bay, Co. Cork.

Chapter One

Sherkin Island

Sherkin Island Marine Station

In October 1974 the oil tanker *Universe Leader* spilled approximately 2,600 tonnes of Kuwait crude oil into the waters of Bantry Bay. Three months later, in January 1975, a second spill of about 460 tonnes of heavy fuel oil occurred. Seashore monitoring sites, located and described by Crapp (1973), had already been established in Bantry Bay shortly after the oil transhipment facility opened on Whiddy Island in 1969. These sites were re-surveyed following the two accidents in order to establish whether any damage had occurred to the intertidal flora and fauna (Baker *et al.*, 1981).

At Sherkin these incidents focussed attention on the fact that the clear Atlantic waters

Figure 1.1 An aerial view of Sherkin Island Marine Station, looking west.

of Long Island Bay and Roaringwater Bay had no similar industrial threat hanging over them and as such should be described and studied in order to record naturally occurring changes in the marine plant and animal communities. And so, in summer 1975, the first transects were established and surveyed on Sherkin and several other islands and mainland shores within Roaringwater Bay. By 1981 the survey had developed the meticulous and robust methodology which is described in Chapter 3. This and additional rocky shore surveys have developed and grown geographically and continue to this day. The original aim of the survey was to standardise the recording of a limited number of animals and plants over a long period in order to detect fine changes in populations. Such changes have indeed been found; they are real – and present a fascinating picture. The Marine Station has thus been prompted to broaden its remit and attempt to understand the environmental cues operating on Sherkin's rocky shores.

When the Marine Station began work in 1975, its location, facilities and ethos attracted various universities from Britain and the Netherlands to bring students to the Station for field trips. These further stimulated the direction of the Marine Station's programme and various recording and monitoring programmes developed simultaneously with the rocky shore survey. These now cover a wide range of subjects including plankton, seaweeds, rock pools, benthos, sedimentary shores, sponges, terrestrial flora, insects, otters and birds. The Station holds an annual conference and occasional workshops and produces an environmental newspaper *Sherkin Comment.* Together with its environmental competition and programme of talks for primary schools, the Marine Station now reaches a wide audience within Ireland. A complete publications list is given at the back of the book.

The seashore survey data are now complemented by the climate data that have been collected at the Station and within this book the first attempt to draw on this data has been made. The rocky shore is a complex and dynamic habitat, influenced by many environmental factors. The rocks themselves vary from being hard, soft, smooth or creviced, which offer different surfaces that suit different combinations of animals and plants. Water temperatures, air temperature, wind strength, wind direction and rainfall all play their part in determining which species colonise, survive, thrive and reproduce on the shore and for this reason they are briefly described in this chapter.

LOCATION

When asked where Sherkin Island is, my reply is usually "the second island inshore from the Fastnet". It is here that the coast of Ireland changes character from the relatively open bays and narrow harbours between Cork and Baltimore Harbour, becoming more rugged with many dramatic, long-fingered inlets extending westward from Roaringwater Bay.

Together, Baltimore Harbour, Sherkin Island and Cape Clear Island form the southern boundary of Long Island Bay and Roaringwater Bay, with Mizen Head lying at the very end of its northwest coast.

The islands of Roaringwater Bay are too numerous for all to bear names, and many are just rocky outcrops. The large ones are named and some of them are inhabited,

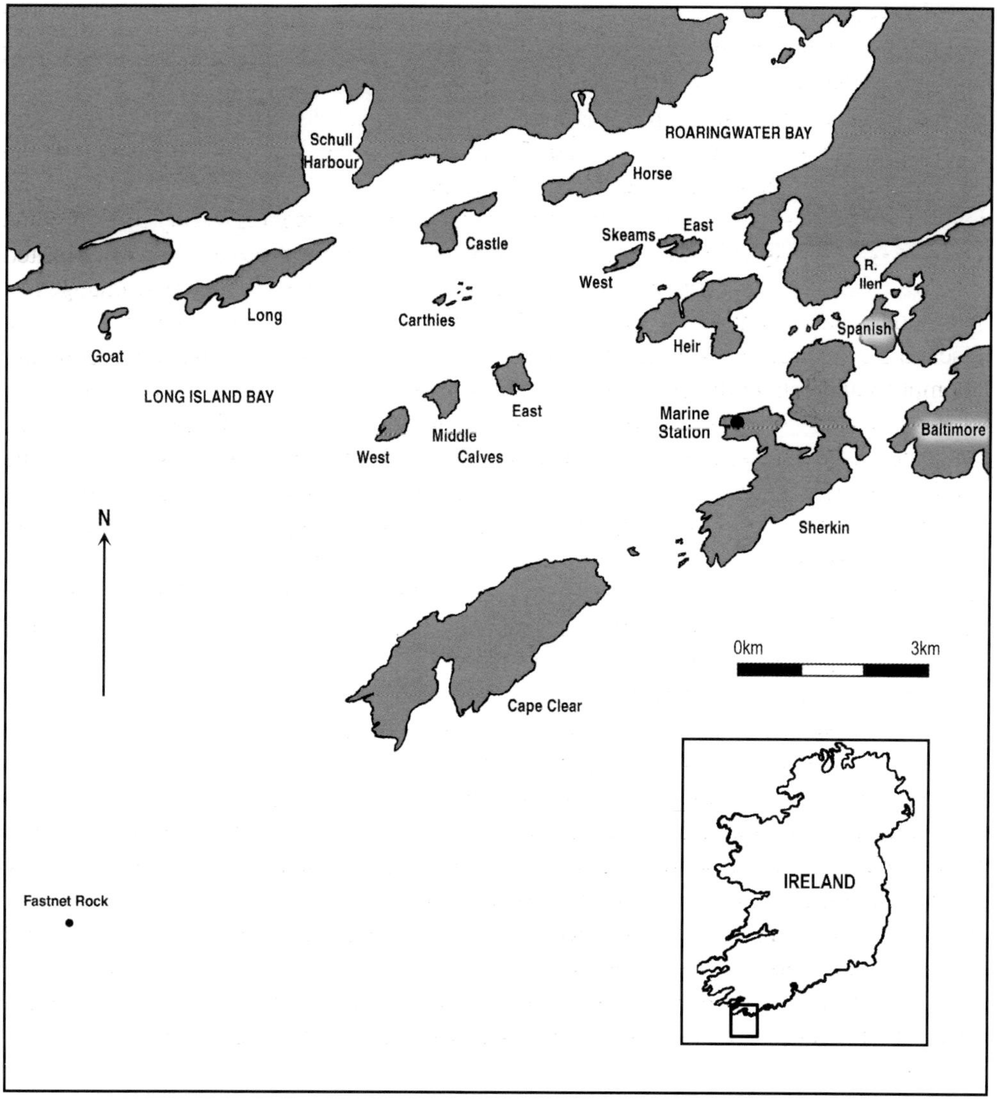

Figure 1.2 Roaringwater Bay, Co. Cork.

whilst many of the smaller ones are probably only visited once a year – by the marine scientists of Sherkin Island Marine Station. Sherkin and Cape Clear are the two largest islands and both are inhabited by independent islanders who mostly farm and fish. Cape Clear Island is well-known as a Gaeltacht (Irish speaking) area and for its long-established bird observatory, where hundreds of bird lovers come to watch for the spring and autumn migrants. Sherkin Island has a smaller population (approximately 110) with the privately funded Sherkin Island Marine Station perched on its northwest headland.

The outer bay – Long Island Bay – is fully exposed to the long Atlantic swell, which sometimes brings harbour porpoise, Risso's dolphin, killer whale, minke whale and white-sided dolphin for brief visits. In recent years there have also been sightings from Cape Clear Island of humpback whales (see *Irish Naturalists' Journal* 'Cetacean Notes'). The inner bay – Roaringwater Bay – is much more sheltered and during the 1980s became a focus for mussel farming which has flourished throughout the survey years.

GEOLOGY

The rocks of Sherkin Island are Old Red Sandstone of the Lower Devonian period. Along the tip of the northeast peninsula and southwestern tip of the island the sandstones are of the Castlehaven Formation, but the majority of the island rocks bask in the glory of bearing their own name "The Sherkin Formation". Not all red sandstones are red! The Sherkin Formation consists of drab grey and green sandstones interbedded with grey, green and pale purple mud/stones. It is a distinct zone within the West Cork Sandstone Formation and can be traced from Cape Clear Island to Rosscarbery, forming part of the Rosscarbery Anticline.

Although there are early geological descriptions of the area (Jukes, 1861) and the relatively recent recognition of a distinct geological unit (Coe & Selwood, 1968), it was Graham & Reilly (1972) who gave the Sherkin rocks the specific geological term "Formation". The ecology of rocky shores from both formations – Castlehaven and Sherkin – is presented in this book.

When the Rosscarbery Anticline formed, as a result of folding of the earth's crust, the Sherkin Formation rocks were thrust to the surface and subsequent erosion has formed

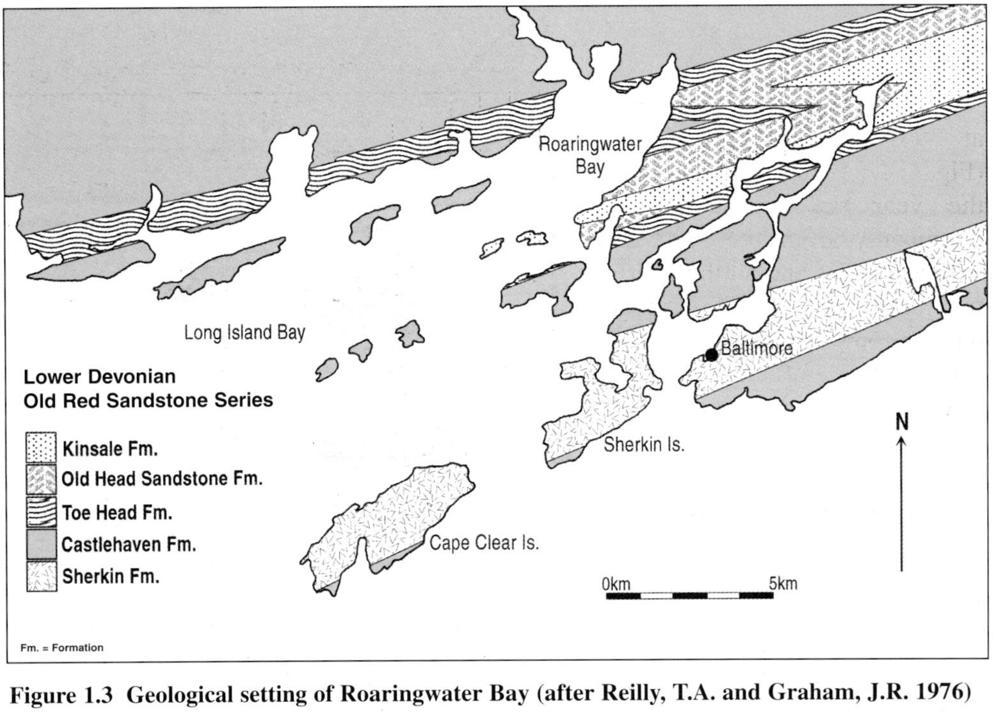

Figure 1.3 Geological setting of Roaringwater Bay (after Reilly, T.A. and Graham, J.R. 1976)

them into the landscape we know today. Shores within both the Sherkin and Castlehaven Formations have a broadly similar physical appearance of near-vertical jagged layers of rocks, which easily shear and break when exposed to storm conditions. This jagged surface offers a large area of relatively sheltered micro-habitat in the crevices within the lee of the rock strata. The relative similarity of the geology throughout Sherkin provides a baseline to the habitats that enables comparisons to be drawn with regard to other variables.

CLIMATE

The Irish climate is strongly influenced by the Gulf Stream current washing the area and moderating both winter and summer temperatures. Situated at a latitude of 51°28'N 9°25'W, Sherkin has a minimum daylength of 7 hours (December) and a maximum of 16.5 hours (June). Sherkin's climate is dominated by the maritime influence of the Atlantic Ocean. The island receives the full force of Atlantic weather fronts as they hit the south and west coasts of Ireland. During the autumn and winter low pressure systems dominate with associated frontal rainfall, whereas in the spring and summer high pressure is common.

The collection of meteorological data at Sherkin Island Marine Station has been ongoing since 1972 and the Marine Station is one of Ireland's daily recording stations for the national meteorological office, Met Éireann. Data on wind, air temperatures, sunshine, rainfall, wet periods, dry spells and sea temperatures are presented in Figures 1.4 to 1.12.

Wind

Wind measurements are recorded at 0900 GMT. The wind rose (Figure 1.4) shows that throughout the year the wind was predominantly from the southwest, with westerlies and northwesterlies fairly common also. The strongest winter gales were from the southwest. March, April and May often comprise many days of light, northeast and easterly winds. The number of days of gales per year ranged from eight to 44, with an average of 25 days.

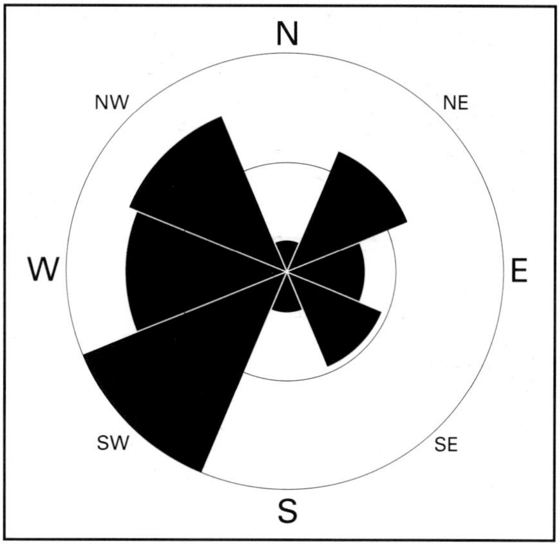

Figure 1.4 Wind rose showing frequency of wind direction for the years 1981–2000 as recorded at Sherkin Island Marine Station.

Air Temperatures

The air temperatures at Sherkin Island, recorded daily at the Marine Station over the 20-year period, have ranged from a minimum of 5.8°C (1987) to a maximum of 26.5°C (1995).

Mean maximum temperatures of 23.9°C and 22.4°C occurred during July and August respectively. In some years however, maximum temperatures have occurred in April (1993), May (1997, 2000), June (1981, 1986, 1988, 1992) and even September (1991). Extremely low minimum temperatures occurred in 1985, 1987, 1997 and 1998 (Figure 1.5). Maximum and minimum temperatures are likely to have a role in controlling animal and plant survival, growth and reproduction (Orton, 1920; Southward, 1953; Holme, 1963; Holme, 1967; Bowman & Lewis, 1977).

Figure 1.6 shows the number of days per year with temperatures of 21°C and over. Those years which were particularly warm were 1983, 1989 and 1995.

Sherkin Island experiences very little frost. Between 1981 and 2000 an average of only six days per year (122 days in the 20-year period) were recorded with air temperatures below 0°C. These occurred primarily during January and February, but occasionally in March, April, October, November and December.

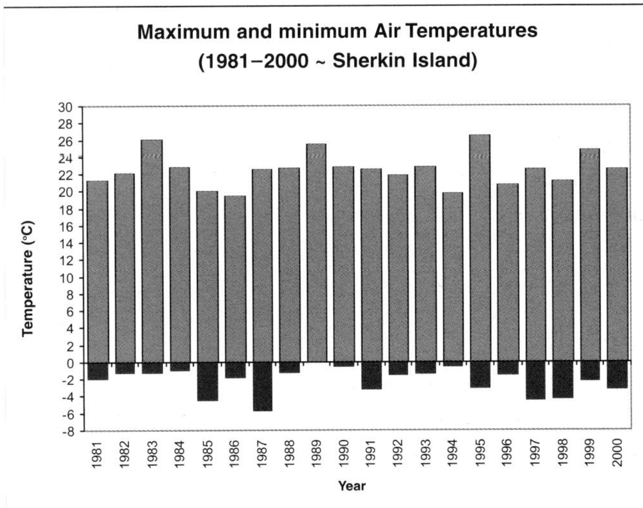

Figure 1.5

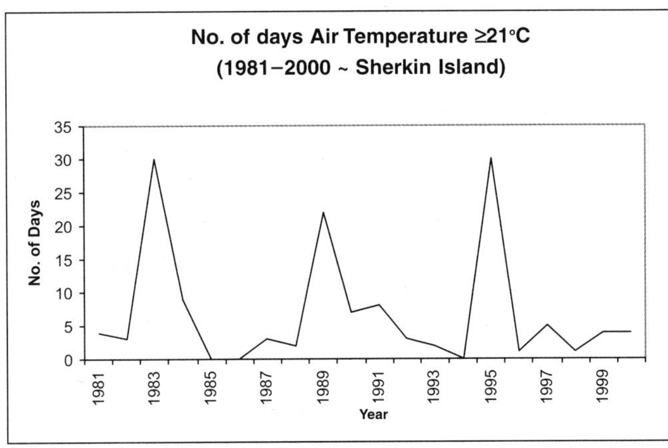

Figure 1.6

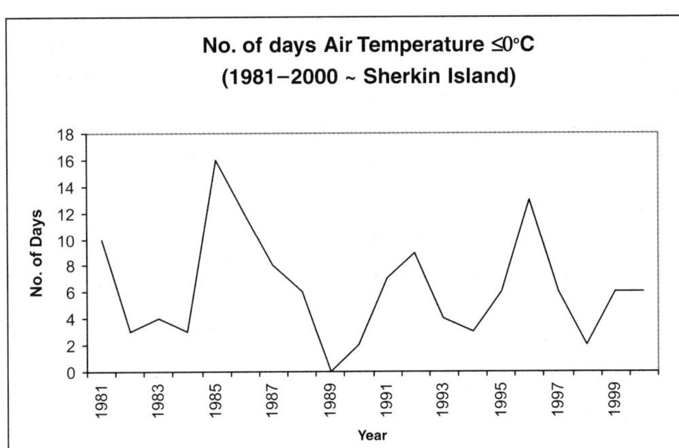

Figure 1.7

Figure 1.7 shows the yearly variation of the number of days when temperatures were zero or below. Years with a higher than average number of below zero days were 1981, 1985, 1986, 1987, 1991, 1992 and 1996.

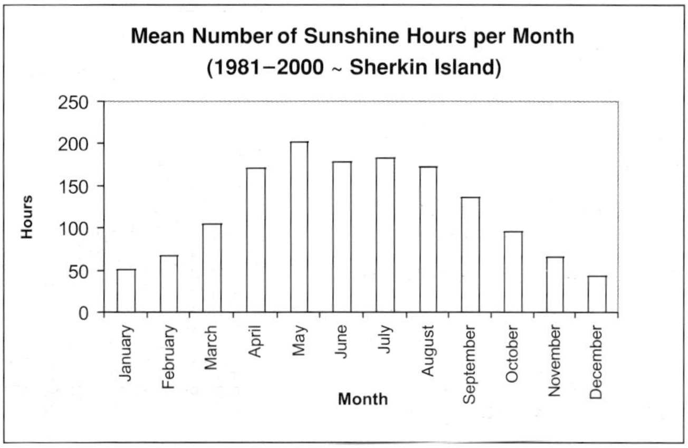

Figure 1.8

Sunshine

The number of hours of sunshine per 24 hours has been recorded daily since 1974. Although maximum air temperatures usually occurred in July and August, the month of May had the highest number of sunshine hours (average 205 hours) (Figure 1.8). Through June, July and August the number of hours fell slowly; for a total of five months, April to August, the mean number of sunshine hours remained above 150 per month.

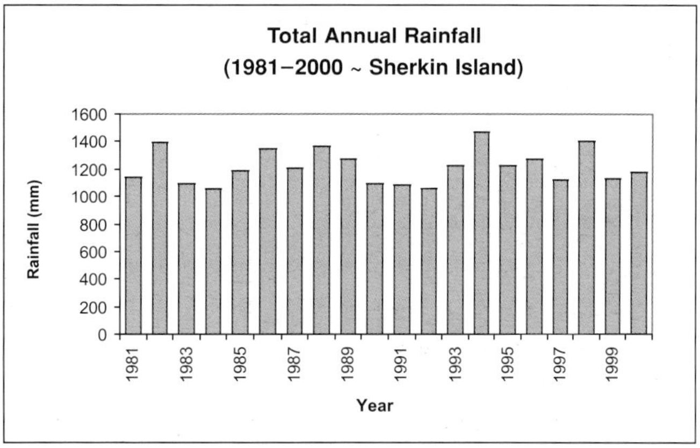

Figure 1.9

Rainfall

In general much of the rainfall in Ireland is made up of falls of low intensity over relatively long periods. At Sherkin Island Marine Station, rainfall data (total per 24 hours) have been recorded continuously since 1972. The average number of raindays per year on the island was 207. (A 'rainday' = 0.2 mm or more

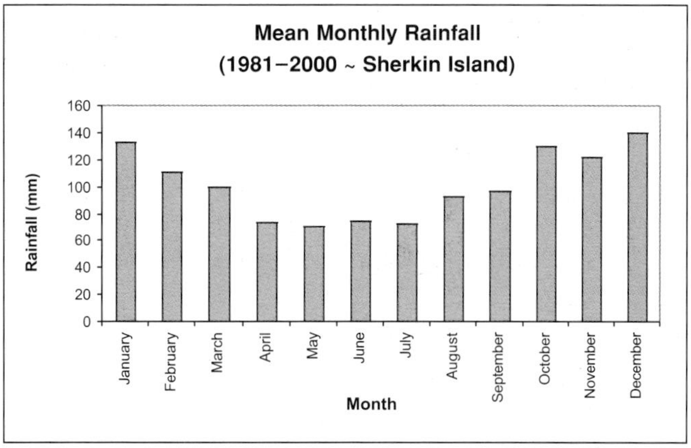

Figure 1.10

falling in a 24 hour period). Palmer (1986) summarises data from 1973–1984, but data from 1985 to date remain unpublished. During the 20-year period 1981–2000 Sherkin's average annual rainfall was 1218 mm. This varied from a minimum of 1000 mm in 1984 to a maximum of 1467 mm in 1994, which represents an increase of almost 50%. The years 1982, 1986, 1988, 1994 and 1998 were exceptionally wet (Figure 1.9).

As one would expect in the temperate maritime climate of Ireland, rainfall distribution on Sherkin throughout the year was uneven (Figure 1.10). Here the wettest months were usually December and January with an average of 137 mm, while April to July were by contrast quite dry (< 80 mm per month). May was the driest month with an average of 60 mm.

Wet Periods and Dry Spells

Prolonged periods of extreme weather will influence the seashore environment and are likely to be more important to the upper shore communities than to those of the lower shore.

The Sherkin Island Rocky Shore Survey developed during the end of a relatively dry period (1972–76) with below-average rainfall and a number of dry spells (Palmer, 1986). In 1976 four dry spells were recorded between April and September. Seven years later, in 1983, there was an absolute drought from mid July to mid August; the following year 1984 saw an exceptionally long dry spell (7th June–7th July).

Sea Temperatures

Temperatures at the sea surface change with the seasons, but do not fluctuate as widely as air temperatures. Both surface (Figure 1.11) and depth profile temperatures are recorded at Sherkin between April and October. Surface temperature at the mid Sherkin Island/Heir Island site was warmest in August (an average of 15.1°C) (Figure 1.12). Over the 20-year period, 1981–2000, August surface temperatures have ranged from 10.5°C (1986) to 19.5°C (2000) and for September from 12.5°C (1992) to 17.5°C (1991).

Analysis of early August surface temperatures shows that 11 years in particular were high (1981, 1982, 1983, 1984, 1989, 1990, 1994, 1995, 1997, 1998, 1999) with temperatures of 15°C or higher.

Late August/early September temperatures with particularly high values (16°C or more) occurred in 1981, 1983, 1987, 1991, 1995, 1999 and 2000. Surface temperatures were particularly low (lower than 13°C) in 1985, 1996 (early August) and 1998 (mid to late August). Minimum surface temperatures occur in February

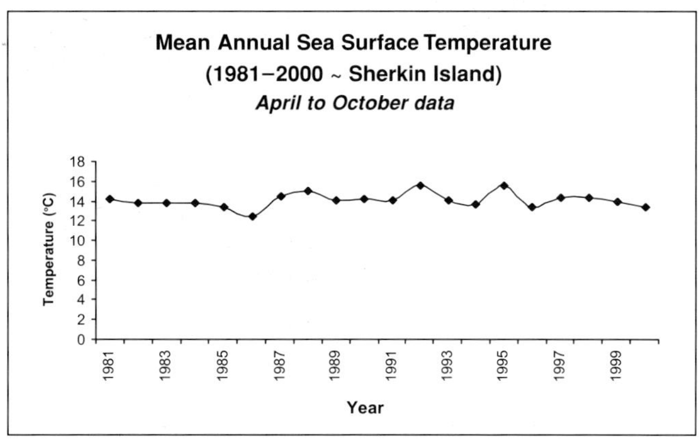

Figure 1.11

and do not fall below 7°C in Ireland (Lee & Ramster, 1981) but no data have yet been collected on the Heir Island/Sherkin Island site during the winter months.

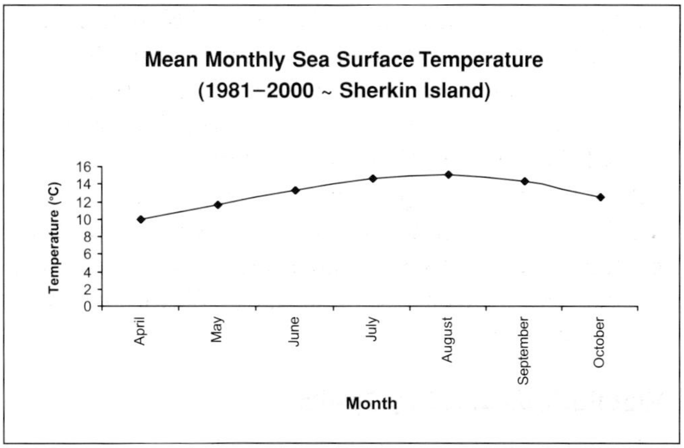

Figure 1.12

HYDROGRAPHY

Tides, currents, winds and waves all influence the shore, both in their constancy and their extremes. The flow tide that approaches the Irish coast from the west-southwest, divides offshore from Dingle Bay and it is the southeasterly component, flowing down to the Mizen Head that affect the shores of Roaringwater Bay. The tidal range within Roaringwater Bay varies from a mean neap range of 1.5 m to a spring range of 3.1 m.

In common with most of the inlets of SW Ireland, the waters of Baltimore Harbour and Long Island Bay are less than 50 m deep (Figure 1.13). The 50 m depth contour lies very close to the headlands of Dursey Head, Mizen Head and Cape Clear, crossing the

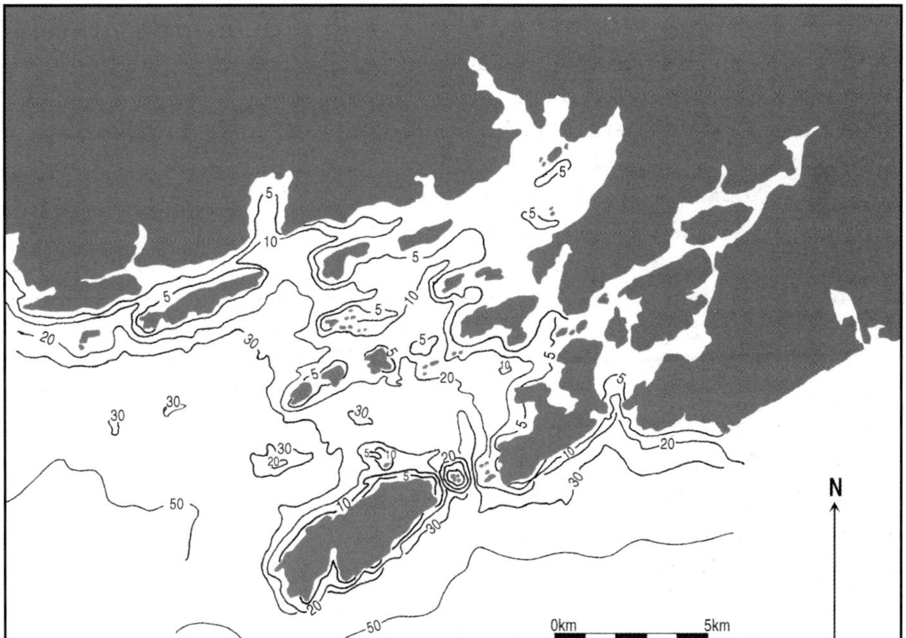

Figure 1.13 Hydrography of Roaringwater Bay, showing contour depths in metres.

mouths of the bays. It then parallels the eastern edge of Cape Clear Island, coming closest to Sherkin about half a mile off the southwestern tip of the island.

Along the western coast of Sherkin the 20 m depth contour is quite close (200 m) to Sherkin Point and about ¾ mile offshore at Drolain Point where the slope is gentler. From Drolain Point around the northern shores of Sherkin the waters offshore are shallow – all within the 10 m depth contour. The eastern shores of Sherkin border the very shallow (< 5 m) waters of Baltimore Harbour, which is a very wave-sheltered environment, but there are strong tidal flows through the southern and northern entrances of the harbour.

The eastern and northern coasts of Sherkin thus have considerable wave attenuation, with moderate attenuation off the western headlands and least along the southeast coastline. However, a funnelling of water movement from the eastern part of the outer Long Island Bay in through the narrowing channel and up to the mouth of the River Ilen tends to create fast currents and a choppy sea. The largest waves occur on spring tides when the wind has been in the southwest for a number of days. Offshore wave heights of 1.5 m to 3 m occur in summer when southwesterly are less common, but during winter the southwesterlies help to create offshore wave heights of 1.3 m to 5.5 m (BODC, 1998).

Chapter Two

The Rocky Shore Environment

Today there is a wealth of knowledge and literature about rocky seashores and the rocky shores of Ireland and Britain. This has been built up from the work of early Victorian naturalists who tended to concentrate on descriptions of the physical nature of individual shores together with lists of the species found there. Gosse, for example, inspired many people with books such as "A Naturalist's Rambles on the Devonshire Coast" written in 1853 and "Tenby: A Seaside Holiday" written in 1856. Taxonomy – the description and naming of species – was a thriving field of study during this period of discoveries and many key works on different animal groups were written in the late nineteenth century. Hincks (1868), for example, wrote about hydroids and ectoprocts and Gosse (1860) wrote about British sea anemones and corals.

Opportunities for travel to a wide variety of shores however were probably limited, hence the extremes of shore types and conditions were often not fully appreciated. Nowadays we have the benefit of information from offshore islands such as St Kilda and Rockall whose Atlantic rocky shores are extremely exposed to wave action (Powell, 1957). These truly represent shore conditions at the harshest end of the spectrum and contrast strongly with the very sheltered shores found at the head of sea lochs and marine inlets.

During the 1940s and 1950s biologists working from the UK Marine Laboratories of Plymouth, Oban, the Isle of Man, Millport and St. Andrews began to look at the ecology of rocky shores around them and some also started experimental work in the field. Names such as Burrows, Crisp, Lewis, Moore, Southward and Stephenson should all be familiar to today's students of marine biology, and some of their key works are referenced in this book. Lewis (1964), Stephenson & Stephenson (1972) and Barnes & Hughes (1982) give excellent and wide-ranging accounts of rocky shore ecology and to the non-biologist reader books such as "Sealife of Britain and Ireland" (Wood, 1988) are a stimulating introduction. In Ireland, Lough Hyne (near Baltimore, Co. Cork) was the main focus of early marine ecological study by Renouf (1931) and others. Further survey and experimental work was conducted there by Bristol University (Ebling *et al.*, 1960, 1962; Kitching, 1967; Kitching & Thain, 1983) and Little *et al.* (1992) carried out a limited intertidal study comparing abundance of 39 species in 1990/91 with 1955 records. Further north, the Clare Island Survey, Co. Mayo, was first carried out in the early 1900s (Royal Irish Academy, 1915) and a follow-up survey was carried out in the 1990s under the auspices of the Royal Irish Academy (Myers, 2002).

Other more recent studies in Ireland (excluding Sherkin studies) relate to the presence of the oil transhipment terminal in Bantry Bay, where 40 monitoring sites were selected and described (Crapp, 1973) and re-assessed after two oil pollution incidents in 1975 (Baker *et al.,* 1981). The ecology of four of the same sites was subsequently studied over a three-year period (Myers *et al.,* 1978, 1980a, 1980b; Cross & Southgate 1983).

In Britain, a Rocky Shore Surveillance Group based at the Wellcome Marine Laboratory in Robin Hood's Bay, Yorkshire, investigated the long-term fluctuations of some common intertidal species, particularly the barnacle *Semibalanus balanoides* (Kendall *et al.,* 1982, 1985) and the common limpet *Patella vulgata* (Lewis & Bowman, 1975). Lewis (1975) stems from the work of this group.

Another Coastal Surveillance Unit, based at University College North Wales, Bangor, was set up to monitor the natural fluctuations of rocky shore communities. This work continued for nine years and is reported by Jones *et al.* (1979, 1981, 1982 and 1983).

Just as in Ireland, rocky shore monitoring programmes were set up around oil terminals in Milford Haven (Moyse & Nelson-Smith, 1963), Shetland (Hiscock, 1983) and Orkney (Baxter *et al.*, 1985), where pollution incidents were expected. In Shetland the programme of qualitative estimates of species abundance made over a six-year period (1976–81) (Hiscock, 1983) was reduced to a continuing programme, still ongoing in 2000, of expert annual surveillance, which involves a combination of qualitative visual assessments and photography of key species.

In Orkney, quantitative annual shore surveys of intertidal fauna and flora have been complemented by studies on the population structures of individual species of limpet (Baxter *et al.*, 1985; Jones & Baxter, 1985).

In this context of rocky shore surveys, work from the Sherkin Island Marine Station is geographically far-ranging, long-term and not based around any source of potential marine pollution.

VERTICAL ZONATION

European marine biologists of the late nineteenth and early twentieth centuries realised that animals and plants do not occur randomly on the seashore; discussions on zonation began. Two factors were quickly recognised as being important in determining which species live on any particular shore and whereabouts on the shore they are found:

- the amount of time that animals and plants spend uncovered by the tide (emersion) and
- the degree of exposure to wave action on the shore.

However it is the much later books by Lewis (1964), "The Ecology of Rocky Shores" and the Stephensons (1972), "Life Between the Tidemarks on Rocky Shores", which are held as modern classics.

One of the first patterns to be recognised by every student is the distinct zonation of large brown seaweeds – the wracks and kelps – which is very conspicuous on moderately exposed rocky shores. Four species of wrack are found in a sequence from

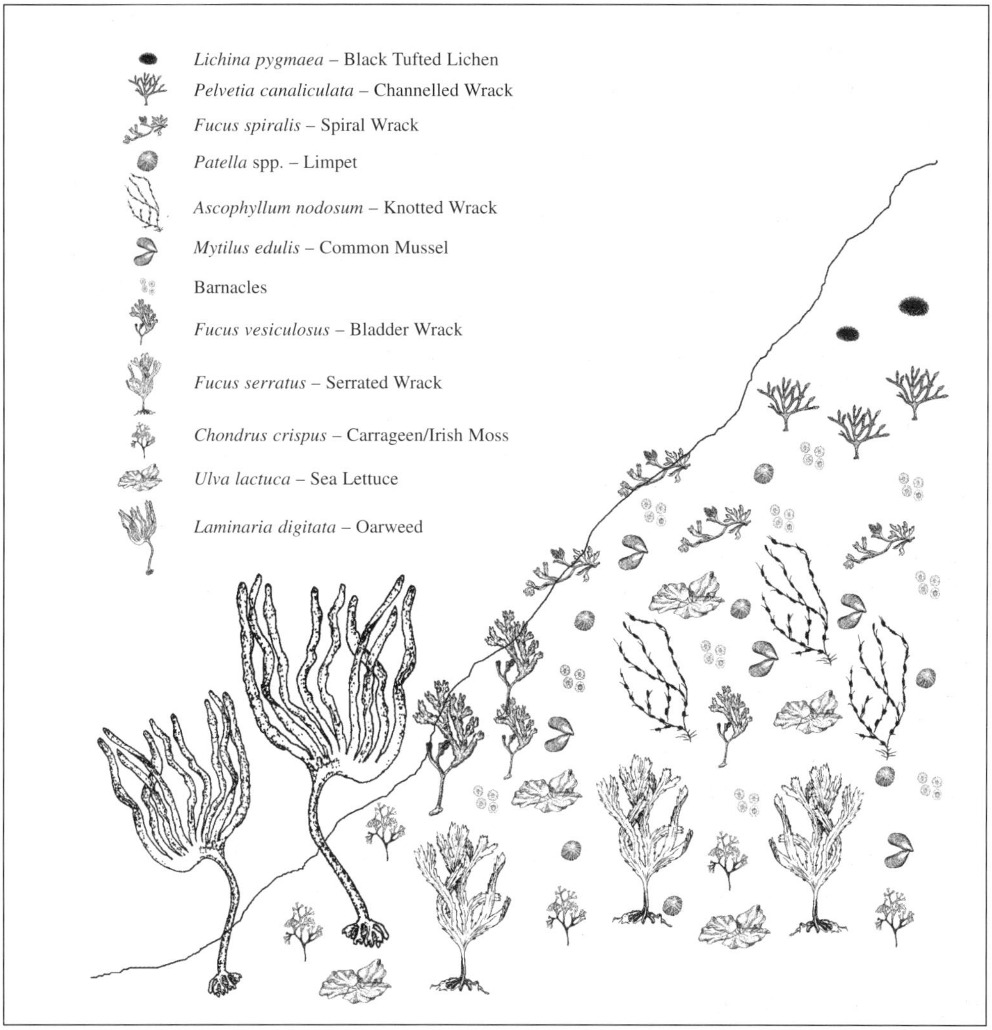

Figure 2.1 Stylised drawing of species distribution on a moderately exposed shore.

channelled wrack *Pelvetia canaliculata* on the upper shore down through spiral wrack *Fucus spiralis*, bladder wrack *F. vesiculosus* and finally serrated wrack *F. serratus* on the lower shore. During low spring tides the kelp plant oarweed *Laminaria digitata* is also exposed. Figure 2.1 illustrates this zonation in the highly visual manner adopted by many marine ecologists today, which combines stylised drawing of species with their abundance and vertical distribution over the shore together with the shore profile.

This particular pattern only really holds true for shores which are moderately exposed to wave action, and within the pattern there can be wide variation amongst associated species. As conditions become more extreme, so the assemblage of species on the shore changes to reflect either the increasing or decreasing exposure to wave action.

WAVE EXPOSURE

Comparatively few species tolerate or thrive in extreme shelter or extreme exposure. Such shores therefore are considered to be "stable" and are reasonably predictable in their species composition and balance of numbers.

Some species, such as dabberlocks *Alaria esculenta,* are abundant only in wave-beaten places while others, such as knotted wrack *Ascophyllum nodosum* are commonest in sheltered areas. Some species have varieties which only occur in very extreme conditions. Bladder wrack *Fucus vesiculosus* for example is very common and found in greater or lesser abundance on most rocky shores – sheltered, moderate and exposed – however it has a bladderless form called *F. vesiculosus* f. *evesiculosus*, which occurs only on very exposed shores. At the other end of the exposure range, a free-living form of *Ascophyllum nodosum* called *A. nodosum* ecad. *mackayi* is found only at the inner ends of marine inlets where the waters are very still.

The degree of wave action affecting a shore depends on wind speed and duration, together with the distance of open water over which the wind blows. This is known as the fetch and can be worked out from charts and maps. Shores which face the open Atlantic, e.g. Mizen Head and other headlands of West Cork, are frequently subjected to pounding waves which have travelled for hundreds of miles, whereas shores along Ireland's Irish Sea coast face a far smaller fetch. In comparison the latter may have a more diverse fauna and flora. The northwest and southwest coasts of Sherkin are more exposed than the northeast Sherkin coast which faces Baltimore Harbour; this latter coast however is only moderately sheltered compared with the almost land-locked shores of Lough Hyne which lies 5½ miles east of Baltimore on the mainland coast.

Although it is useful to measure the aspect and fetch of a shore, another tool which helps to categorise rocky shores is the biologically-defined exposure scale devised by Ballantine (1961) (Appendix 5). This is based on the observations that the communities of plants and animals change as the degree of wave exposure changes. He defines eight grades of exposure according to the abundance of the various key plant and animal groups (barnacles, limpets, winkles, topshells, kelps, wracks, other seaweeds and lichens).

Based on the work of Crisp & Southward (1958) in the English Channel, Ballantine also defines a five-point scale of abundance (Abundant, Common, Frequent, Occasional, Rare) for each of the above plant and animal criteria. Although Ballantine created his exposure scale for shores in Pembrokeshire, and it should really only be used on shores of relatively uniform bedrock, it nevertheless serves as a useful reference in other localities. Crapp (1973) used it in Bantry Bay, although not without difficulties due to the distribution of species differing slightly between the two geographical areas. Crapp also expanded the abundance scale into seven points, by adding the categories Superabundant and Extremely Abundant. Lewis (1964) included a more general five point biological exposure scale, which can be more safely applied to the whole of Ireland and Britain. However, on Sherkin it was felt that it would be useful to adopt similar criteria to the earlier Bantry Bay work of Crapp. These worked successfully and are now used extensively along the Co. Cork coastline.

INTERTIDAL ZONES

In order to understand how the Sherkin shores are structured, they have been divided into three zones: the Upper, Middle and Lower Shores – a practice applied worldwide by Stephenson and Stephenson (1972) and adopted by many marine biologists. The three zones are quite different in terms of environmental conditions, and in consequence the plant and animal communities tend to be structured by different elements.

The **Upper Shore** is covered by seawater for a maximum of three to four hours every 12 hours during spring tides and is permanently uncovered during neap tides. Animals and plants may be exposed to air for several days at a time. Only a small number of species can tolerate such harsh physical conditions and each shows adaptations to enable it to do so. For example, the perennial seaweeds of the upper shore are channelled wrack *Pelvetia canaliculata* and spiral wrack *Fucus spiralis*. *Pelvetia* has a channelled stipe and when it dries out the edges of the plant fold inward to form a cylinder, whereas when *F. spiralis* dries out the fronds tend to roll round and form spirals – giving rise to their common names. The folding and rolling reduce the surface area open to the drying air and are adaptations for conserving moisture. The abundance of those plants is probably controlled by periodic winter storms which physically tear them from the rocks, leaving spaces for fresh colonisation. The only common animal is the small periwinkle *Melarhaphe neritoides* which grazes on the ephemeral green algae and diatoms which we notice initially as a "furriness" at the top of the shore. *M. neritoides* can withdraw inside its shell and has various physiological adaptations to surviving without seawater for long periods of time. These are not shared by the other littorinid snails, which as a consequence cannot survive at such a high level on the shore.

The **Lower Shore** is the opposite extreme. The rocks at this tidal level are covered by seawater throughout the entire period of neap tides, and are only uncovered for a maximum of four hours during the lowest spring tides. The zone is usually rich in

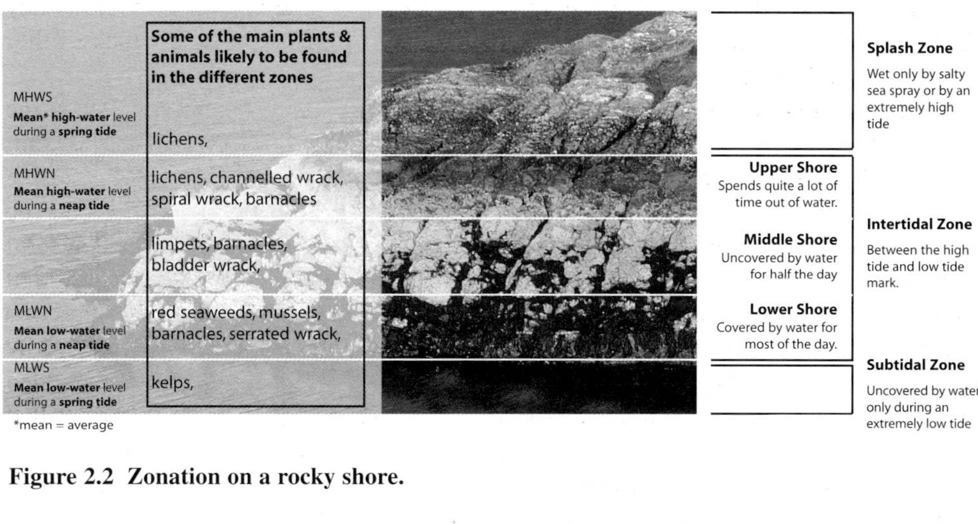

Figure 2.2 Zonation on a rocky shore.

species, many of which continue down to sublittoral levels. A dense canopy of large brown algae – fucoids or laminarians – protects the underlying animals and plants from drying out when exposed to air.

The **Middle Shore** is the main part of the intertidal zone, referred to as "eulittoral" by Lewis (1964), where animals and plants are subjected to immersion by seawater for four to eight hours every tidal cycle, i.e. twice a day. It is this variability of habitat which underpins the variability of the animal and plant communities present.

Additional Influences on the Shores of Sherkin

Many other physical factors have an influence on rocky shore biology, contributing to whether species thrive or fail.

Sea and Air Temperatures

Most marine species can live within a wide range of temperatures, but have a critical temperature requirement for breeding. Breeding of the small periwinkle *Melarhaphe neritoides* occurs from autumn to spring (Graham, 1988) but in different localities the breeding period can be shorter than this. For example March/April in Britain (Graham, 1971) and December to April in southwest Britain (Lebour, 1947) where more detailed records are available. A southern species (i.e. one whose main geographical distribution is to the south of Ireland) such as the limpet *Patella depressa* may not reproduce successfully at the northern limit of its range because temperatures are not sufficiently high for a long enough period at the critical time of year. Southern intertidal species will benefit from warm sea and/or air temperatures during the critical point of their breeding cycle, and northern species will thrive in colder conditions. In the barnacle species *Semibalanus balanoides* the critical phase of the reproductive cycle is the late autumn just before fertilisation takes place. Barnes (1963) showed that a four- to six-week period of air temperatures less than 10°C and day length of less than 12 hours is critical for the final development of eggs and sperm.

Aspect

Aspect is also important. On a south- or west-facing shore (typically) the strongest winds will be warm ones, whereas on a northeast facing shore they will be much colder. The greatest cooling by evaporation occurs when air temperatures are high. In prolonged spells of very hot sunshine, several of the more delicate species of algae can suffer from desiccation – hence the habitat preference of most for moist, sheltered situations beneath a canopy of wracks or in the lee of boulders. In warm weather they may also survive better on north-facing shores, which have less direct sunlight. High cliffs also provide shade.

Water Currents

Reproductive success is influenced not only by sea and air temperatures, but by winds and currents which determine whether planktonic larvae settle on suitable shores. Many of the common rocky shore animals do have planktonic larvae, for example limpets, barnacles, mussels, the edible periwinkle *Littorina littorea* and the small periwinkle *Melarhaphe neritoides*.

For many species there are minimal densities of adults below which the population cannot maintain itself without being re-populated from other localities. Sherkin's western shores lie very close to the strong current running between Sherkin and Cape Clear and this may either bring larvae to the shore from further along the mainland coast, or alternatively sweep away the locally produced planktonic larvae. The main tidal flow and residual current sweeps in an easterly direction from Mizen Head, across the mouth of Roaringwater Bay, along the southern shore of Sherkin and eastwards up the mainland coast.

UNPREDICTABLE EVENTS

In the 20 years of the survey, together with the six pilot years 1975–80, no major unpredictable events appear to have affected the shores of Sherkin. However various factors that can potentially stress the balance of the island's rocky shore environment are outlined below.

Climate Episodes

In addition to the weather data routinely collected at Sherkin, major climatic events between 1981 and 2000 have been noted.

A hurricane (Force 12 on the Beaufort Scale) occurred in October 1987. Since storms are known to affect the seashore by tearing larger wracks and kelps from the rocks, the 1988 records of algal abundance were analysed in relation to this factor. However there was no conclusive evidence as both increases and decreases in the wracks and kelps occurred in 1988. Furthermore some of the declines noted were part of a more widespread decrease.

Figure 2.3 Rough seas at Drolain Point, Sherkin Island.

Phytoplankton Blooms

Phytoplankton blooms occur naturally in spring as a response to increased nutrients in the water. Red tides, an example of this phenomenon, occur occasionally and can have lethal effects on seashore organisms (Cross & Southgate, 1980; Leahy, 1980). Of special interest is the dinoflagellate *Karenia mikimotoi* (known earlier as *Gyrodinium aureolum*) which, from time to time is responsible for "red tides" around the coast of S.W. Ireland (Jenkinson & Connor, 1980; Roden *et al.*, 1980. When densities rise above a certain threshold, other organisms in the vicinity can be affected, either by physical clogging of the gills or by toxins released by the phytoplanktonic organisms. The potentially lethal implications for farmed fish and shellfish are well-known, but there are also possible consequences to benthic and seashore plants and animals. The two major red tides recorded by the Station in Roaringwater Bay were in 1978 and 1979 (Leahy, 1980; Roden *et al.*, 1980; Roden *et al.*, 1981). Since then, although not warranting the title of "red tide", Sherkin Island Marine Station's phytoplankton survey has shown that large numbers of *K. mikimotoi* were present in the water column on numerous occasions, although no obvious widespread deleterious effects were found. In 2000 for example, an outbreak of *K. mikimotoi* affected shores on the north side of Roaringwater Bay (Rubio *et al*, 2000).

Pollution Incidents

In November 1986 the cargo ship *Kowloon Bridge* ran aground on the Stag Rocks, off Toe Head in West Cork (about eight miles east of Sherkin). The impact of the oil pollution (fuel oil) from this incident was qualitatively assessed on 34 shores within Roaringwater Bay. Oiling of shores around Sherkin was not severe, but localised and sporadic (Baker, 1987 a,b,c); oil lumps (< 10 cm diameter) were found scattered throughout the area. The rocky shores of Sherkin were not affected in any way.

Seaweed Harvesting

Although no seaweed harvesting is known to occur on Sherkin, species of wrack and carrageen are commonly collected in Ireland. When harvesting occurs, the growth and abundance of others species is also affected, as areas of space are created on the shore. Initially the removal of plants takes away both cover and food for animal species and the number of grazing animals is likely to fall. New algal growth brings subsequent repeated increases in the grazing populations.

Periwinkle Harvesting

Harvesting of edible periwinkles *Littorina littorea* for food occurs spasmodically on some of the sheltered shores of Sherkin Island. Almost total removal of the edible periwinkle population on a particular stretch of shore is usual in these circumstances.

Organic Enrichment

The land around Roaringwater Bay is sparsely populated and much of it is used for rough grazing. The 20-year survey period has seen an increase in housing around the main populated areas, for example Baltimore, and on Sherkin itself. Recent sewage inflow to Roaringwater Bay from Cork County Council plants and outfalls suggest increases of up to 100% over the May to September period when holiday homes are occupied.

ROCKY SHORE BIOLOGY

The brown algae of the classic zonation pattern are the VISUAL DOMINANTS on moderate and sheltered shores, but on exposed shores these are replaced by barnacles and mussels. The main components of a rocky shore can be listed as follows:

- **GROUND COVER**
- **GRAZERS**
- **PREDATORS**

In addition to these three main components, there are secondary components – the epiflora and epifauna (plants and animals growing on other plants/animals) and infauna (animals living inside sediment, crevices or kelp holdfasts). The organisms of these groups are often (but not always) small in size, not immediately obvious and often not so readily identifiable in the field, e.g. amphipod crustaceans.

Although the visual dominants together comprise few species, they comprise most of the biomass (organic bulk) on a shore. In contrast the secondary components represent a low biomass but can consist of a large number of species. The majority of species selected for analysis in the Sherkin data are visual dominants.

GROUND COVER

Ground cover consists of suspension-feeding animals, such as barnacles and mussels, or algae. Algae can be present either as a turf of close-cropped small plants, such as carrageen, or a canopy of larger plants whose stipes are held vertically when covered by the tide, thus allowing other species to grow beneath their fronds. Most of the rock surface is usually covered – there are very few open spaces on a rocky shore! In the splash zone, lichens often cover a large percentage of the rock surface, though this can depend on the rock type and orientation. Horizontal or gently sloping surfaces are more readily colonised than vertical faces of easily fractured sedimentary rocks, as found on Sherkin. On sheltered and moderately exposed shores the brown algae (mainly fucoids) form a canopy which allows a rich understorey of red algal species to develop. As conditions become more exposed the density of red algae increases or dominates and this is also true for vertical rock faces.

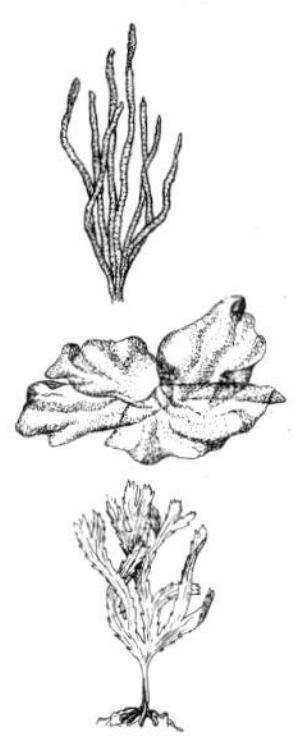

i) Algae (Seaweeds)

Just as in open fields or woodland clearings, on the shore there are aquatic plant species which tend to be the first to invade "bare space". These early colonisers are mostly the green seaweeds such as gut weed *Enteromorpha* spp., sea lettuce *Ulva lactuca* and *Blidingia* spp., but some red algae such as dulse *Palmaria palmata* also fulfil this role. Like terrestrial annual plants, most of the green algae are also short-lived – ephemeral – and are found in the late spring and summer months. The major exception to this is the dark green and wiry seaweed *Cladophora rupestris*. Again like terrestrial plants, some algae are biennial. Perhaps the most obvious example of this is the thong weed *Himanthalia elongata* which appears as "buttons" the first year, from which long fronds grow in the second year. Many seaweeds however are long-lived (perennial) and understandably the most conspicuous and common ones have acquired common English or Irish names. Typical algal species of the canopy and understorey are listed in Figure 2.4.

ii) Barnacles

Chthamalus stellatus, *C. montagui*, *Semibalanus balanoides* and *Elminius modestus* are the four common barnacle species of SW Ireland's shores. It is interesting that the genera have very different large-scale distribution patterns. *S. balanoides* is a northern species which is found throughout Ireland and Britain (Sherkin, at 51° 28' N, lies within this distribution). *Chthamalus* is a southern Mediterranean genus which has colonised Ireland and the British Isles on the warm Gulf Stream current.

Chthamalus montagui reaches higher on the shore than *C. stellatus*; both species reach higher up the shore than *S. balanoides*

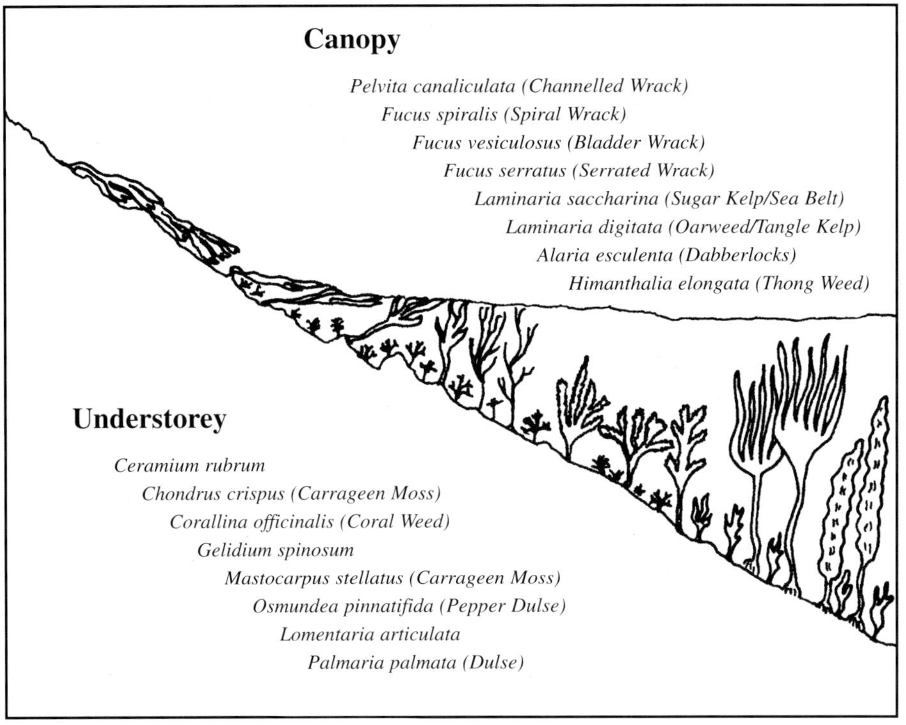

Figure 2.4 Stylised drawing of the large brown seaweeds of the canopy layer, with the smaller seaweeds (such as the reds listed above) living in the understorey beneath for protection.

and their densities increase in more wave-exposed situations. It was only in 1976 that two species of *Chthamalus* were recognised (Southward, 1976); prior to that all occurrences of *Chthamalus* were identified and recorded as *C. stellatus*.

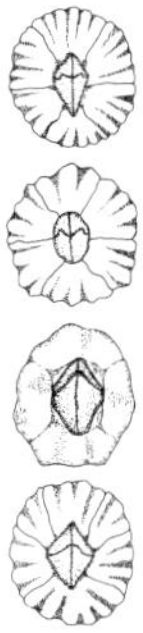

Elminius modestus is a relative newcomer to the shores of Ireland. It is a non-native, southern species – the "Australasian barnacle" – and was first recorded in Ireland in Cork Harbour in 1954 (Crisp & Southward, 1959). Successful reproduction and subsequent settlement has resulted in a spread of the species along the coasts (Egerton, 1999). The process of introduction was accelerated by increasing numbers of cargo ships entering Irish waters from more southerly latitudes. The first record in Roaringwater Bay was at Schull Harbour in 1966, and by 1972 it was recorded as common throughout the Bay (Crapp, 1973). Abundance in Roaringwater Bay between 1990 and 2000 is reported by Egerton (1999).

iii) Mussels

The common mussel *Mytilus edulis* is most often dominant on exposed shores. Here, much of a mussel's energy is spent withstanding the physical forces of heavy wave swell and breaking surf, at the expense of growth. The large masses of *Mytilus* thus characteristically comprise small individuals. Large mussels are usually associated with rocky outcrops in very sheltered conditions where fine sediments are deposited and the water is often turbid.

GRAZERS

The most common groups of grazing molluscs of the rocky shore are winkles, topshells and limpets. Additionally, in the lower shore there are chitons, but they are usually few in number and therefore rated as secondary components of the community. On some shores, though not evident on Sherkin, the sea urchins *Psammechinus miliaris* and *Echinus esculentus* are common in this zone as well. Where common, their grazing activities can be a significant controlling factor in algal species abundance and diversity. In southwest Ireland the black sea urchin *Paracentrotus lividus* is generally common and can dominate the lower shore and larger rock pools.

i) Winkles

Four species of littorinid or winkles have long been recognised as common on rocky shores, where they occupy restricted zones. These are the small periwinkle *Melarhaphe neritoides* of the upper shore, the rough periwinkle *Littorina saxatilis* straddling the upper and middle shores, and the flat periwinkle *L. obtusata* and edible

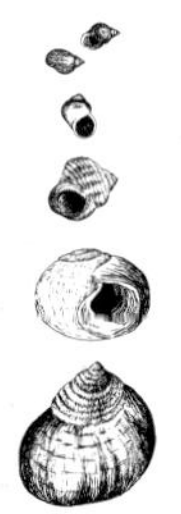

periwinkle *L. littorea* of the middle and lower shores. Another tiny littorinid *L. neglecta* characteristically lives in empty barnacle shells in the middle shore and its distribution, although strongly correlated with barnacle abundance, is also controlled by the age structure of barnacles together with the abundance and predator pressure from the dogwhelk *Nucella lapillus*. *L. littorea* and *L. saxatilis* feed on both the larger algae and micro-algal films present on rocks. *L. obtusata* live and feed on the fucoid algae and their epiphytes.

ii) Topshells

The five common topshell species are all found on Sherkin, but the dominant species are either purple topshell *Gibbula umbilicalis* or grey topshell *G. cineraria*. The painted topshell *Calliostoma zizyphinum* occurs on the lower shore at extreme low tides, but only in low densities; and a fourth species *Osilinus lineatus* is scarce on the Sherkin transects since it is more often found on shores of stable boulders than unbroken bedrock. *G. magus* is rarely recorded on Sherkin.

iii) Limpets

Two species of limpet *Patella vulgata* and *P. aspera* occur in southwest Ireland; *P. aspera* is found on moderate and exposed shores whereas *P. vulgata* occurs on rocky shores of all exposures. However, it can be difficult to distinguish between the two species in the field without constantly removing individuals from the rock surface and inspecting their undersides. They have been recorded together as *Patella* spp. in the Sherkin programme. A third species, *P. depressa*, is a southern species and occurs rarely on the west coast of Ireland. It has never been found on Sherkin.

Grazing limpets feed on sporeling fucoids rather than larger plants. Early work by Knight & Parke (1950) showed that once fucoid algae have grown to a length of 30–50 mm, they are no longer vulnerable to direct grazing by limpets and begin to flourish, but on exposed and moderately exposed shores it is limpet grazing which limits seaweed growth.

Limpets change sex as they age, starting as males and later becoming females. Females release eggs which are fertilised in the water. Once hatched, the larvae remain in the plankton for several weeks before they settle in crevices and shallow pools. The larvae are only about 0.2 mm long when they settle but are not visible to the naked eye until about 2–3 mm long.

PREDATORS

As in any other ecosystem, the rocky shore community has various predatory species including fish, seabirds, dogwhelks, starfish and crabs. There are also human predators collecting mussels and periwinkles from the seashore (although no mussels are collected on Sherkin). Of these fish, seabirds and humans have not been considered in this survey as we have concentrated on the more permanent invertebrate shore residents.

The dogwhelk *Nucella lapillus* can be found throughout the lower and middle shores. An ebbing tide reveals dense clusters of dogwhelks in crevices and between barnacles, but when covered by the tide they disperse to feed voraciously on barnacles and mussels. The common starfish *Asterias rubens* and the shore crab *Carcinus maenas* tend to be restricted to the lower shore where they can remain fairly wet at low tide underneath boulders or a canopy of algae. They feed predominantly on mussels, dogwhelks and other gastropods.

Breeding in dogwhelks is most prolific in spring when the vase-shaped egg capsules are found in crevices and other sheltered places. Each contains up to 1000 eggs. Only 25–30 live to become juveniles and the remainder act as nourishment for those that develop successfully. Dogwhelks do not reach sexual maturity for two to five years.

ADDITIONAL SPECIES

A wide variety of additional, less conspicuous species (secondary components) are found mostly towards the bottom of the intertidal zone, or in rock pools and under boulders. They are the ones which cannot tolerate drying out; many are sublittoral species at the highest part of their distribution range when found in the intertidal zone. They include sponges, sea firs, sea anemones, sea mats and crabs.

Species Interactions

Biological interactions control many aspects of the appearance of a shore, by limiting the spread of various species. For example, on the upper shore interspecific (between species) competition is the most important element controlling the lower limit of the fucoid alga *Pelvetia canaliculata*. Experiments by Schonbeck & Norton (1980) show that *Pelvetia* grows more slowly than *Fucus spiralis* when reared in laboratory cultures and on the shore. If *Pelvetia* germinates in the *F. spiralis* zone it will grow, but only if *F. spiralis* is removed, as both species are competing for the same space. Both need high light levels to grow and will not grow in the shade of another plant. Thus *Pelvetia*, which can be described as a stress-tolerant species, is excluded from an optimal habitat by a less hardy but competitively superior species (Colwell & Fuentes, 1975) because of its slower growth rate.

On the lower shore there are several controlling factors. Physical factors play an important part in species that have a slow growth rate and cannot tolerate living under a shade of canopy. Grazing is also a structuring factor, but it is predators which play an important role on the lower shore. For example, the shore crab *Carcinus maenas* will eat the mussel *Mytilus edulis*. In an experiment by Jancke (1990) on a sheltered rocky shore, *Fucus serratus* no longer settled and grew on the lower shore because he had doubled the number of winkles, thereby increasing the grazing pressure. However when shore crabs were introduced, *F. serratus* soon flourished because the mussels were excluded from the rock surfaces thus creating space for the sporelings. Some sporelings were able to develop as there were more than sufficient numbers to support the grazing winkles.

At the same site the middle shore was dominated by mussels, fucoids and the winkle *Littorina littorea*. When *L. littorea* was excluded, the canopy of *Fucus* spp. increased continuously and reached total (as opposed to the typical 20%) cover within two years. Also the mussels and bare rock surfaces became overgrown by the green alga *Ulva pseudocurvata*. The two structural elements at work here are the grazing of *L. littorea* and the competition for space between mussels and algae *Fucus* spp.

On Sherkin no experimental manipulation of the rocky shore habitat has been carried out. The aim of the survey has always been to describe natural variation on the shores over time. Chapters 4, 5, 6 and 7 present data on the visually dominant shore species, i.e. the main ground cover species, grazers and predators. A brief summary of trends at each site over the 20-year period is given. Chapter 8 discusses the seasonal and annual variation recorded, with observations of apparent physical or biological relationships.

Chapter Three

The Sherkin Island Marine Station Rocky Shore Survey

Sherkin Island Marine Station's rocky shore surveys of West Cork developed gradually from 1975 to stretch over 700 miles of indented coastline, from Cork Harbour to Bantry Bay. In 2000 they comprised 152 marked monitoring sites as described on the following pages. The majority of sites (145) are surveyed annually by a team of Sherkin Island Marine Station biologists.

Sherkin Island – Monthly Survey

The remaining seven sites of the 152 form Sherkin's monthly sampling programme. These sites are part of the original project piloted in 1975 and have developed into the largest data set at the Station. The value of such a long-term data set has inspired the writing of this book, which focuses on the analysis and discussion of the data from the seven sites.

The sites were chosen to reflect a range of exposure to wave action. They comprise the very exposed shore of Poulacurra, the exposed shore of Drolain Point, the moderately exposed shores of Globe Rocks, Horseshoe Harbour and Reenahoe, and the sheltered shores of Kinish Narrows East and Kinish Narrows West. The map opposite shows their locations.

Six of the seven shores lie on rocks of the Sherkin Formation; the seventh, Reenahoe, is on the adjacent upper (slightly younger) Castlehaven exposure. At Poulacurra the boundary line between these two formations can be clearly seen (see p. 4).

The seven sites on Sherkin Island are surveyed monthly between April and October, during the growing season. Survey work began in 1975 and by 1981 well-defined methods and standards were in place. Data spanning 20 years from 1981–2000 therefore form the basis of this book. This is the first comprehensive publication of the results, though some preliminary findings were reported by Bishop (1998).

While the monthly programme developed the same standards and very similar techniques were used to expand the geographical range of the work. The Station currently runs a programme of five additional annual surveys. These are described on the following pages.

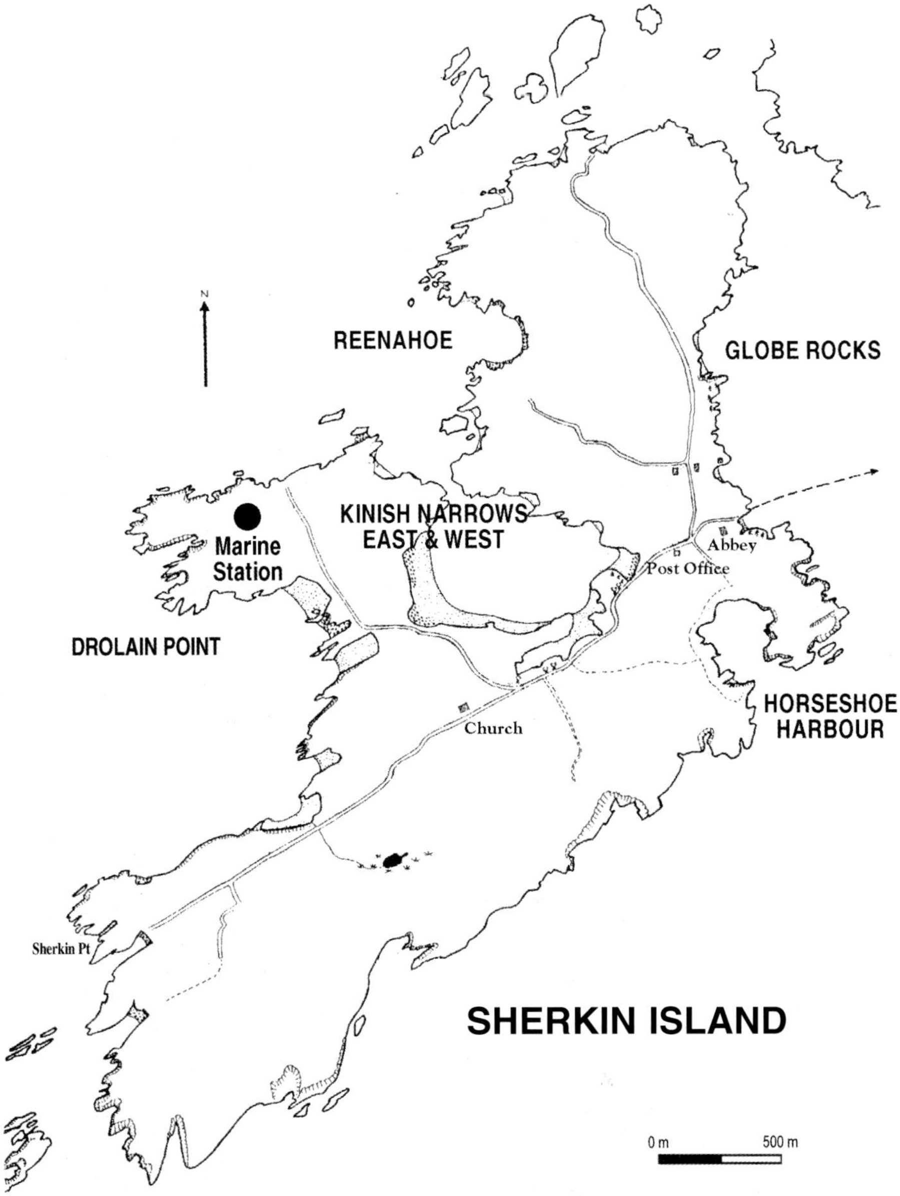

Figure 3.1 Sherkin Island showing general location of the seven monthly sampling sites.

ANNUAL SURVEYS

Roaringwater Bay

Roaringwater Bay has 62 sites which are surveyed annually (Falcous *et al*, 2001). These include the 19 sites on Sherkin Island. Twenty nine sites are located on the various islands (excluding Sherkin) and 14 are on the mainland coast from the mouth of the River Ilen to Mizen Head.

Figure 3.2 Sherkin Island Marine Station Survey Areas.

There are 19 marked sites on Sherkin Island that are surveyed annually by the Marine Station. Data have been collected since 1975 and have been reported in Hunter (1997), Egerton (1998), Jackson *et al.* (2001) and Migus & Moore (2002). More detailed studies have been made for certain site locations and are described by Kowalik & Gupta (2000a&b). The sites are quite separate from the seven monthly sites and are not reported in this book.

Dunmanus Bay

This survey has been running since 1981 (Layden & Lane, 1984; Taylor & Hunter, 1996; Clark *et al.*, 1997; Egerton *et al.,* 1998; Ratcliff, 1999; Browne *et al*, 2001a). Eight sites of varying wave exposure and aspect are monitored annually. They range from exposed to very sheltered.

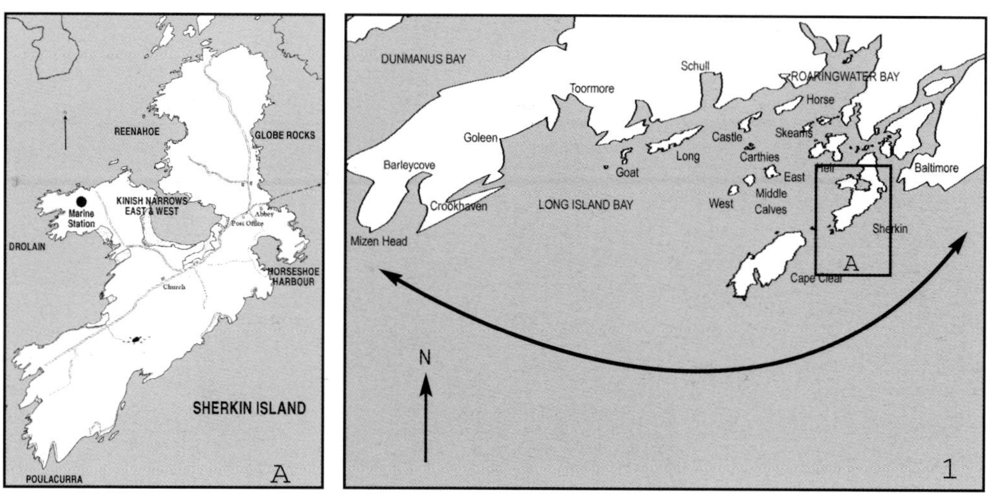

Sherkin Island survey area (19 sites) **Roaringwater Bay survey area (43 sites)**

Figure 3.3

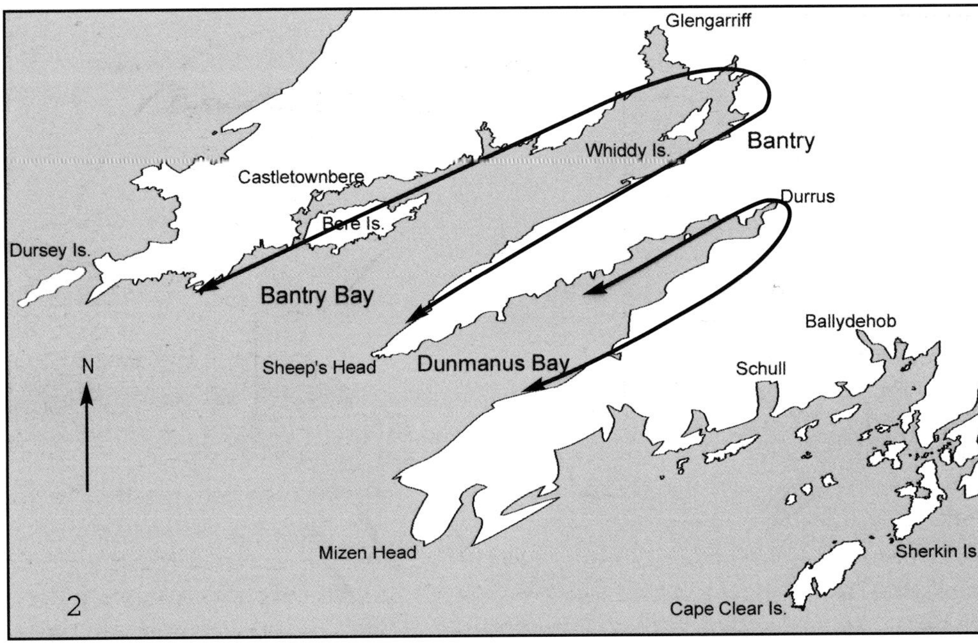

Figure 3.4 **Bantry Bay (18 sites) and Dunmanus Bay (8 sites) survey areas**

Bantry Bay

Eighteen rocky shore sites are surveyed annually by the Marine Station. The majority of the sites were set up in 1995 and are reported in Taylor & Hunter (1996), Clark *et al.*(1997), Egerton *et al.*(1998), Clark (1999) and Edwards *et al.*(2001).

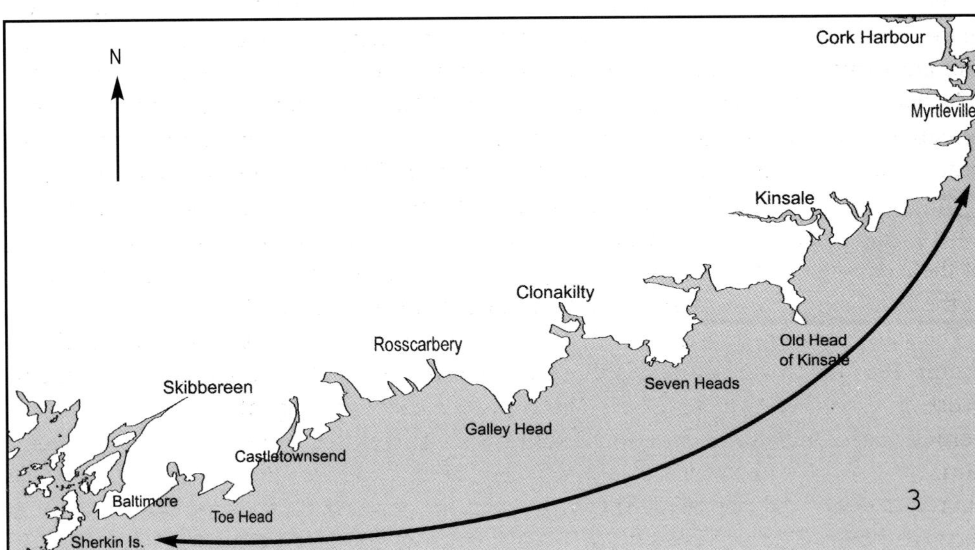

Figure 3.5 **East of Baltimore survey area (30 sites)**

East of Baltimore

Between Baltimore and Myrtleville Bay, near Cork Harbour, a total of 30 rocky shore sites have been surveyed annually since 1995. Ten of these are located within the relatively sheltered inlets and 20 are on the open coast (Taylor & Hunter, 1996; Clark *et al.*, 1997; Egerton *et al.*, 1998; Clark, 1999; Browne *et al.*, 2001b).

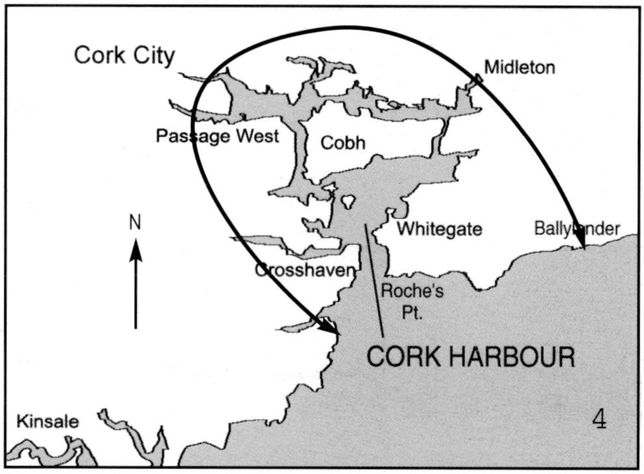

Figure 3.6 **Cork Harbour survey area (27 sites)**

Cork Harbour

Twenty seven sites in Cork Harbour and east to Ballylander are surveyed annually. These were set up in 1995 and are located throughout the 125 miles of coast within and just outside the harbour, so that a range of wave exposures are sampled. The data are reported in Taylor & Hunter (1996), Clark *et al.* (1997), Egerton *et al.* (1998), Bolger-Hynes (1999), Clark (1999) and Falcous *et al.* (2001). Studies on the barnacle *Elminius modestus* in Cork Harbour are reported in Egerton (1999).

MONTHLY SURVEY METHODOLOGY

The seven monthly sites, which are surveyed April to October, are permanently marked at the top of the transect. The transects run perpendicular to the water's edge and are surveyed from the top marker (station 1) at vertical intervals of 30 cm to low tide. The number of stations per shore varies up to a maximum of 17; however it is not possible to record data at the lowest stations at every visit due to weather and tide. In order to standardise the analysis, results were used from only the stations where data were always available. The individual sites, as presented here, have between nine and 14 stations, with the more exposed shores having a greater number of stations because of the larger areas of upper shore and splash zones. A shore profile for each site is given at the beginning of each site description in Chapters 4, 5, 6 and 7.

The stations were originally located and established using a cross-staff level (Nelson-Smith, 1967) with the height of the leg fixed at one tenth of the tidal range, i.e. 30 cm. Working from the bottom of the shore this enables sighting of each station 30 cm vertically above the previous one. At some of the shores, e.g. Poulacurra, there is a long horizontal distance between stations, whereas the shores at Kinish Narrows are both very short and steep, with very little horizontal distance between each station. Each station is then permanently marked but if the mark should be dislodged the whole exercise can easily be repeated. There are detailed site maps and photographs for each transect which greatly assist locating the transects for new workers each year. The sites were deliberately chosen to reflect different exposures to wave action and are therefore distributed over the whole island. At Kinish Narrows the opportunity was taken to establish two sites in close proximity, with similar wave exposure but differing aspects. The line of the transect is selected to run over uniform bedrock where possible, avoiding rock pools, gullies and outcrops.

Figure 3.7 Layout of typical transect line with tape measure and quadrats.

FIELD EQUIPMENT

The following items are used for routine surveying:

1. Photographs, site diagrams and shore profiles
2. 0.25 m^2 quadrat (0.5 m x 0.5 m)
3. Perspex marker boards and pencils
4. Tape measure
5. Sampling jars
6. Hand lens and forceps
7. Crosstaff } *used for re-marking where necessary*
8. Cement & sand }

RECORDING FREQUENCY

Monthly sites are surveyed during the first spring tides of each month from April until October. In the winter months the lower shore stations are often not safe to work and therefore the consistency of the data would be affected. Another important factor is the prohibitive cost of funding a longer field season.

Times and heights of low water are calculated from the *South of Ireland Tide Tables of Cork City and Cobh*. A tidal cycle matches a lunar cycle, with the largest (spring) tides occurring during the full moon and new moon, and the smallest tides (neap) occuring in the intervening weeks of the waxing and waning half moons. Throughout the survey sampling is only carried out on spring tides with a low water height of less than 0.8 m.

RECORDING METHOD

Because the transect stations are permanently marked, the survey teams revisit the same precise areas each month. Recording of species present is made within two adjacent 0.25 m^2 quadrats at each station, with the top right or top left hand corner of the quadrat touching the station marker (Figure 3.7, 3.8). Abundance of species is recorded as either percentage cover (algae and ground cover animals such as mussels and barnacles) or number per quadrat (most animal species).

The area inside the quadrat is viewed as a two-dimensional plane, and surfaces are viewed from above only. Where deep cracks, crevices or vertical rock faces are encountered, it must be remembered that stations are located at 30 cm vertical intervals and therefore flora and fauna below this depth are ignored. Rock pools are also ignored. Rocks and stones are left unturned and disturbance kept to a minimum within the quadrat area. However where a canopy structure exists it is moved aside and percentage cover for each layer is estimated independently, so that in many cases the total cover may exceed 100%.

Most animal densities are given as direct counts per 0.25 m^2 quadrat. Dense aggregations such as barnacles, mussels, bryozoans, sponges and tube worms are recorded as percentage cover. In order to obtain more accurate density figures, additional counts of some of these species are made in the central 10 cm x 10 cm square (no./dm^2). These include barnacles, the tiny winkle *Melarhaphe neritoides*, the rough periwinkle *Littorina saxatilis* and the worms *Pomatoceros triqueter* and *Spirorbis* spp. Barnacles are further split into genus/species to find the ratio of barnacle species within a square decimetre (dm^2). When counting dm^2 numbers, the quadrat is as close to the rock surface as possible.

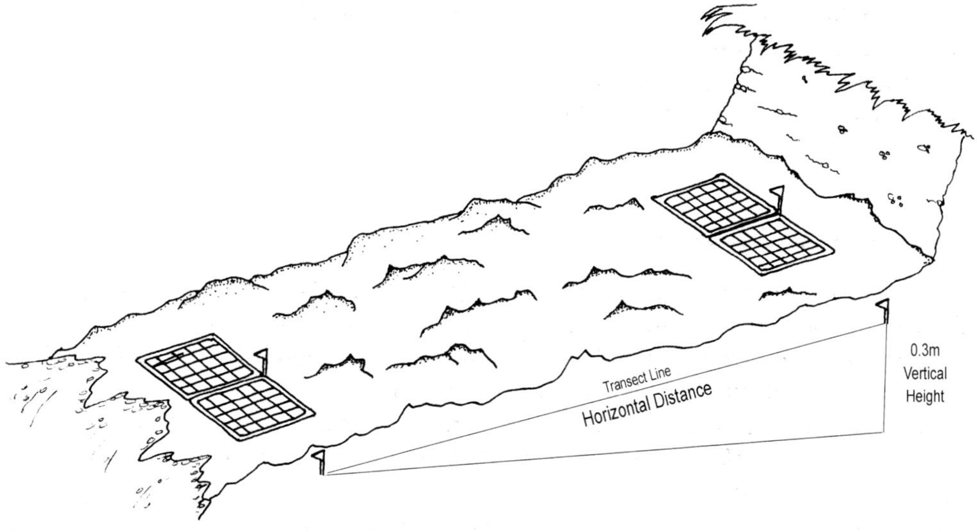

Figure 3.8 Stylised drawing of transect line, perpendicular to the water's edge, showing left and right quadrats .

WORKER VARIATION

Surveys are carried out by a team of up to six people who usually and preferentially work one site per pair per tide. At the beginning of each sampling year (April) great care is taken to ensure that the methodology is maintained, e.g. correct placement of quadrats at stations in relation to the station marker; careful estimation of percentage cover; accurate species identification. Only after rigorous training are biologists allowed to survey shores independently. The estimation of percentage cover is notoriously difficult to standardise; however, familiarisation with the percentage area charts and photographs all help to reduce variation between workers. Human error is bound to occur in any survey but we have systematically endeavoured to minimise this possibility. An important aid for the recorder is that the 50 x 50 cm quadrat is divided into 25 10 x10 cm squares, each representing 4% of the total quadrat area (Figure 3.9). Samples are returned to the lab for identification where field recognition is difficult. Often a seashore biologist returns for a second year's survey which gives the new team a head start in sampling methods and identification skills. However, written instructions together with photographs, location diagrams and shore profiles exist for every site and provide an excellent introduction for new volunteers. Identification skills improve over the season and each person usually develops or has an existing preference for certain groups or phyla.

Figure 3.9 Quadrat showing 25 x 10 cm squares (each square is 1 dm^2).

NOTES ON SPECIES IDENTIFICATION

Barnacles

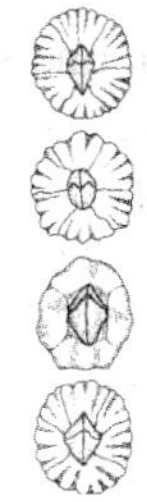

For measuring percentage cover of barnacles within the quadrat, all barnacle species have been lumped together and recorded as "barnacles" and "barnacle spat". Within the central decimetre of the quadrat, the relative proportions of the three common species, *Semibalanus balanoides*, *Chthamalus montagui* and *Chthamalus stellatus* are recorded.

Winkles

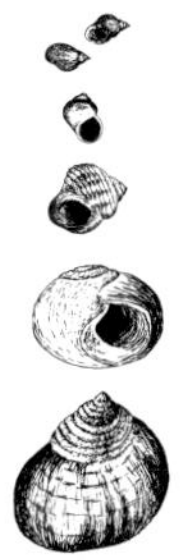

The taxonomy of winkles has been recorded as *Littorina obtusata*, *L. littorea*, *L. neglecta*, *Melarhaphe neritoides* and *L. saxatilis*. The taxonomy of *L. obtusata* and *L. saxatilis* is difficult (James, 1968; Heller, 1975; Raffaelli, 1982) and at the Marine Station we have followed the practice of the Ray Society (Reid, 1996).

Since the survey began, species names of certain littorinids have changed: *Littorina obtusata* has been subdivided into *L. obtusata* (found on *Ascophyllum* and *Fucus vesiculosus*) and *L. mariae* (found on *Fucus serratus*). At Sherkin we have continued to combine the recording of both these species as *L. obtusata*. *L. saxatilis* is known as *L. saxatilis* aggregate. It was deemed to be a group containing six species *L. saxatilis, L. neglecta, L. nigrolineata, L. arcana, L. tenebrosa* and *L. rudis*. We have recorded *L. neglecta* which inhabits empty barnacle shells, but have combined all other variants.

Mussels

Two species of mussel occur in southwest Ireland, *Mytilus edulis* and *Mytilus galloprovincialis*. However they are not easy to distinguish in the field. Work by Gosling (1984) questions whether *M. galloprovincialis* is actually a separate species and therefore mussels at Sherkin have been recorded as *M. edulis*.

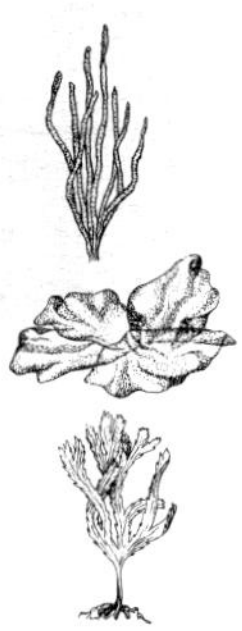

Algae

Many algal species have undergone name changes since 1975. The Marine Station has, since 1997, followed "The Species Directory of the Marine Fauna and Flora of the British Isles and Surrounding Seas" (Howson & Picton, 1997). However a number of taxa have a complex and unresolved taxonomy, in which case the appropriate expert opinion has been followed, e.g. the red seaweed *Ceramium rubrum*.

DATA ANALYSIS

Until 1991 all the seashore data were entered into notebooks; however, 1992 heralded the arrival of computers at the marine station and subsequent data were entered immediately into a seashore database. Paper copies of all computer entries are still maintained. During 1992, when the database was set up, all previous years' records were also entered. Data from the first few years of surveying (1975–80) were not always easy to transcribe into the database, due to lack of standardisation and use of abundance categories (e.g. abundant, common, frequent). Since 1981 data have been recorded as percentage cover or numbers of animals per quadrat. Analysis for the present study has been carried out on results from 1981–2000. Use of the program Microsoft Excel™ enables sorting by species, phylum, date or station, and the subsequent calculation of mean density values.

For each species, the means and standard errors were calculated for station, monthly and annual data. In Chapters 4, 5, 6 and 7 key species at each of the seven sites are described using the following three graph formats:

- Distribution down the shore
- Monthly variation
- Annual variation.

For two species, *Littorina obtusata* and *L. saxatilis,* counts were made within two different quadrat sizes (0.25m^2 and dm^2 - see p. 31). Ideally counts in both quadrat sizes should have been made for each species but in practice data were recorded for only one of these quadrat sizes in some months (primarily during the years 1985 and 1991). Data analysis and the resulting graphs for these two species use only the 0.25m^2 quadrat data. Although this sampling error distorts the results of the middle years of the survey (by having a mean calculated from fewer samples), we felt it important to include data for these particular species as they are important grazers on the shore and it is better to have a cautious picture of variation than none at all.

PRESENTATION OF SHORE DATA

The shore sites are presented in order of decreasing wave exposure, with the very exposed Poulacurra shore as Chapter 4, the exposed shore at Drolain Point as Chapter 5, the moderately exposed shores of Horseshoe Harbour, Globe Rocks and Reenahoe as Chapter 6 and the sheltered shores of Kinish Narrows East and Kinish Narrows West as Chapter 7. Because there are differences in the physical environment at each site the community structures differ. In order to begin to understand the complex shoreline communities, the data were screened for continuity of species present. The final selection of species presented here reflects this process and enables identification of the key species and their more meaningful analysis. Some appear only once, e.g. the kelp *Laminaria digitata* and the topshell *Gibbula cineraria*, while some are discussed for most or all of the seven sites, e.g. the wrack *Fucus serratus*, barnacles, limpets and dogwhelks.

Because of tidal restrictions inherent in accessing the lowest stations, information regarding those stations has not been included in the discussion. Thus at each site up to three of the lower stations were excluded from calculations. However that information remains part of the long-term data set and continues to be supplemented as a matter of course during the sampling. The species recorded from the lower stations are presented in Appendix 4.

SPECIES PRESENTED GRAPHICALLY

Descriptions are given on the following pages for the 26 species which are presented graphically in Chapters 4, 5, 6 and 7. The species are listed in the functional categories described on p. 19. Site names in brackets, in the section below, indicate where each particular species has been analysed.

ALGAE

CANOPY LAYER

BROWN ALGAE

The common wracks and thong weed *Himanthalia elongata* are part of the fucoid group and are some of the most conspicuous seaweeds on the shore. Related species, found less frequently on the Sherkin rocky shores are *Bifurcaria bifurcata* and *Cystoseira* spp. These are much smaller plants, as are most of the remaining brown algae found on Sherkin. *Fucus* spp. in the species list refers to young plants where the species cannot be identified. Very young growth is therefore not reflected in the graphs.

Channelled Wrack
Pelvetia canaliculata
Caisíneach

(Drolain Point, Globe Rocks – pp. 71, 93)

Channelled wrack *Pelvetia canaliculata* is the brown fucoid seaweed found highest up the shore around Mean High Water Neaps (MHWN - Figure 2.2, p. 15). It can exploit the often dry habitat due to its thick, hard, rubbery fronds and channelled stipe, which helps it to conserve water. Olive-green when wet, the species becomes very dark – almost black – when it dries out.

Spiral Wrack
Fucus spiralis
Casfhearmainn

(Globe Rocks, Horseshoe Harbour, Reenahoe, Kinish Narrows East, Kinish Narrows West – pp. 94, 113, 136, 166, 184)

Spiral wrack *Fucus spiralis* is a brown fucoid seaweed found typically in a band on the upper shore but below the

Pelvetia zone. Each frond has a midrib and is slightly twisted and completely lacking any air bladders. This distinguishes it from bladder wrack *Fucus vesiculosus,* which grows slightly below *Fucus spiralis* on the shore.

Bladder Wrack
Fucus vesiculosus
Feamainn bhoilgíneach

(Globe Rocks, Horseshoe Harbour, Reenahoe, Kinish Narrows East, Kinish Narrows West – pp. 95, 114, 137, 167, 185)

Bladder wrack *Fucus vesiculosus* is a brown fucoid seaweed which forms a band on the middle shore, typically between the spiral wrack *Fucus spiralis* and the serrated wrack *Fucus serratus,* but there can be considerable overlap between the species. The fronds have a midrib and air bladders – often paired.

Knotted/Egg Wrack
Ascophyllum nodosum
Feamainn bhuí

(Reenahoe, Kinish Narrows East, Kinish Narrows West – pp. 138, 168, 186)

Knotted wrack *Ascophyllum nodosum* is a brown fucoid seaweed usually found on sheltered shores, especially where mud or silt accumulates amongst rocks and boulders. It is found on the lower and middle shore. The fronds can grow very long and normally develop a single air bladder each year. The small red seaweed *Polysiphonia lanosa* can nearly always be found growing in dark tufts on the fronds of *Ascophyllum nodosum.*

Serrated/Toothed Wrack
Fucus serratus
Míoránach

(Drolain Point, Globe Rocks, Horseshoe Harbour, Reenahoe, Kinish Narrows East, Kinish Narrows West – pp. 72, 96, 115, 139, 169, 187)

Serrated wrack *Fucus serratus* is a brown fucoid seaweed forming a band on the lower shore. It has a midrib but no air bladders and a distinctive serrated edge to the frond. Small brown tufts of another brown seaweed *Elachista fucicola* are usually found growing on its fronds.

Thong Weed
Himanthalia elongata
Ríseach

(Poulacurra, Drolain Point, Horseshoe Harbour – pp. 51, 73, 116)

Thong weed *Himanthalia elongata* is found on the lower shore. It is related to the fucoid seaweeds but is in a different family. The plant is usually biennial, with "buttons" appearing one year and the strap-like fronds the following year, which develop from the button-shaped holdfast. New plants often form very dense patches on the lower shore.

Dabberlocks
Alaria esculenta
Láracha

(Poulacurra – p. 52)

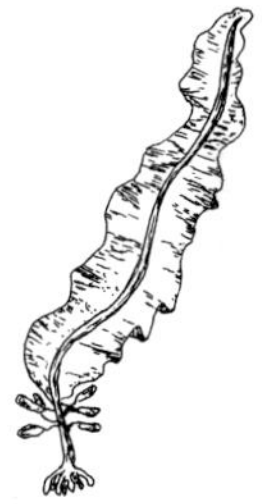

Dabberlocks *Alaria esculenta* is a large brown seaweed related to the kelps which grows on the lower shore in exposed sites. It has a large distinct midrib and a translucent membranous green/brown frond, which is often ripped and may appear feather-like. Reproductive bodies (wings) are present at the base of the stipe.

Oarweed/Tangle Kelp
Laminaria digitata
Coirleach

(Poulacurra – p. 53)

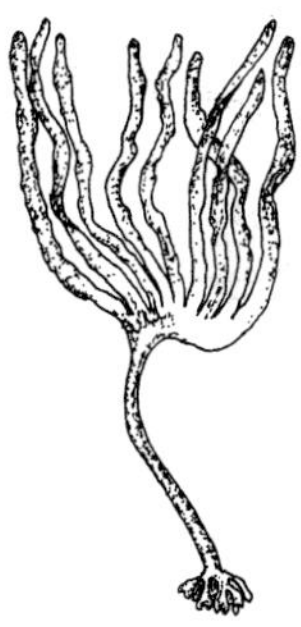

Oarweed *Laminaria digitata* is one of the kelps which grows subtidally and up into the extreme lower shore. The frond is tough, leathery, slimy and divided. The flexible stipes can be seen bending over as they emerge at the low spring tides.

UNDERSTOREY

RED ALGAE

Ceramium spp.

(Reenahoe – p. 140)

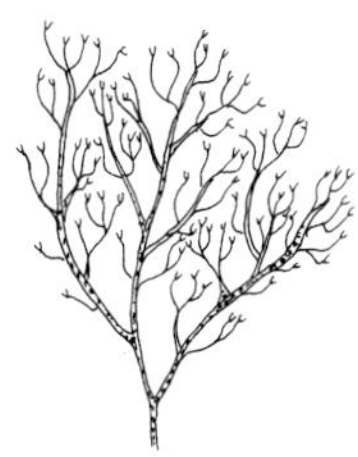

Ceramium spp. are small filamentous red seaweeds found in the understorey. Many species are found on Sherkin (see p. 131), and identification of individual species is only possible by detailed microscopic examination. This group can be recognised in the field by the tightly rolled tips of the fronds that resemble tiny pincers, or by colour banding of the filaments.

Carrageen/Irish Moss
Chondrus crispus
Cosáinín (carraige)

(Drolain Point, Reenahoe – pp. 74, 141)

A small red seaweed found on the lower shore. It has simple, forked-branching fronds that can either be flattened or curled in appearance, depending on environmental conditions. Known as carrageen/Irish moss, *Chondrus crispus* is collected as a food. It can be part of the understorey on more sheltered shores or form a turf on more exposed shores. It is dark brownish-red in colour, often changing to olive-green at the tips. Under the water, the tips of the female fronds often have a purple/blue shine known as iridescence.

Carrageen/Irish Moss
Mastocarpus stellatus
Clúimhín cait

(Poulacurra, Drolain Point, Globe Rocks, Horseshoe Harbour, Reenahoe – pp. 54, 75, 97, 117, 142)

Mastocarpus stellatus is superficially similar to *Chondrus crispus*, hence both species being traditionally called carrageen. However it has a channelled frond, similar to that of the wrack *Pelvetia canaliculata*, and often has small outgrowths from the flat face of the frond. These are reproductive bodies and these characteristics help to distinguish *Mastocarpus* from *Chondrus crispus*.

Gelidium spp.

(Reenahoe – p. 143)

Gelidium spp. are small red seaweeds found in the understorey. They have an upright frond with side-branching, that may be regular or irregular depending on the species. The various species have different growth forms, from small and flattened, to spiny, wiry and filamentous and can resemble one another very closely. They grow either in solitary tufts or dense mats under large algae.

Lomentaria articulata

(Horseshoe Harbour, Reenahoe – pp. 118, 144)

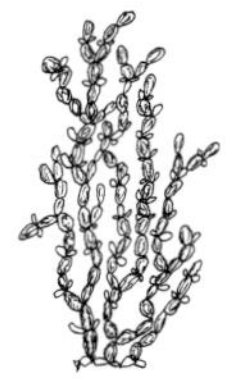

A small red, smooth and shiny seaweed of the middle and lower shore understorey. The branched fronds are hollow, tubular and regularly constricted into obvious segments. Branches grow out from the constrictions. This species, generally quite small, is easily recognised and common on shores.

Pepper Dulse

Osmundea pinnatifida
Míobhán

(Poulacurra, Globe Rocks, Horseshoe Harbour, Reenahoe – pp. 55, 98, 119, 145)

Pepper dulse *Osmundea pinnatifida* is a small red seaweed with flattened thick fleshy fronds which have small blunt-ended branches. Its colour changes from purple/red in winter and spring to yellow in summer. It grows as a turf on exposed shores and grows larger in the understorey on more sheltered shores. The common name derives from its peppery taste.

GREEN ALGAE

Gut Weed

***Enteromorpha* spp.**
Líneáil ghorm

(Drolain Point, Reenahoe, Kinish Narrows East, Kinish Narrows West – pp. 76, 146, 170, 188)

Gut weed is a group of species (*Enteromorpha* spp.) with delicate hollow fronds. The weed looks like guts or intestines, hence the name of one species, *Enteromorpha intestinalis*. It can be found at any level on the shore, but mostly in the shelter of rock pools or canopy species to prevent it from drying out. It is often associated with fresh water input on the upper shore due to its tolerance of very low salinity and is known as an "ephemeral" species because of its relative abundance during the summer months, but absence during the winter.

Sea Lettuce

Ulva lactuca
Glasán

(Drolain Point – p. 77)

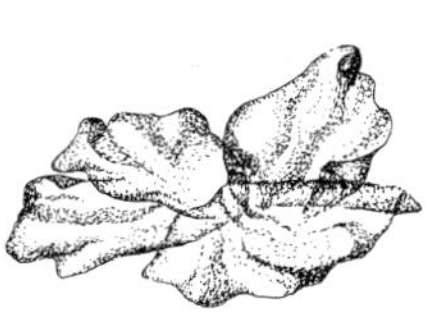

The green seaweed known as sea lettuce Ulva lactuca has bright green, thin flattened fronds which arise from a small narrow stipe. It grows attached to rocks or other seaweeds at any level on the shore, but is restricted to a sheltered habitat beneath the canopy seaweeds or in rockpools. This is also an "ephemeral" species.

ANIMALS

GROUND COVER

Barnacles

Semibalanus balanoides, Chthamalus stellatus, Chthamalus montagui, Elminius modestus
Giúrainn

(Poulacurra, Drolain Point, Globe Rocks, Horseshoe Harbour, Reenahoe, Kinish Narrows East, Kinish Narrows West – pp. 56, 78, 99, 120, 147, 171, 189)

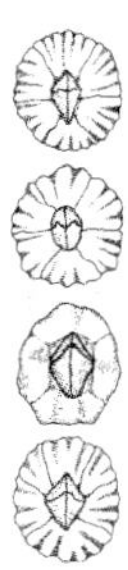

The barnacle is a small crustacean, with four or six calcareous plates which rigidly attach to the rock surface. When covered by the tide, tiny "feathery" legs extend from the open central plates to feed by trapping small planktonic organisms. Barnacles may be seen individually when cover is sparse, or as newly settled spat, but they are usually seen as a continuous cover over the rock surface. There are two periods of settlement of barnacle larvae from the plankton, an early one of *Semibalanus balanoides* in spring and a later one of *Chthamalus* spp. in early autumn. Barnacle spat and juveniles are important food sources for many species of vertebrates and invertebrates.

Common/Blue Mussel

Mytilus edulis
Diúilicín

(Poulacurra, Drolain Point, Horseshoe Harbour, Reenahoe – pp. 58, 80, 149)

The common/blue mussel *Mytilus edulis* is a bivalve mollusc attached to the rock surface by strong byssus threads. Dark blue/black in colour, it can occur singly, in clumps in crevices or in large numbers covering extensive rock faces on exposed shores. In this situation individuals tend to be smaller in size. Mussels are filter feeders, feeding on small planktonic organisms when covered by seawater.

GRAZERS

The grazers described from the Sherkin shore communities are all single-shelled gastropod molluscs.

Grey Topshell

Gibbula cineraria

Faochán Mhuire glas

(Reenahoe – p. 150)

The grey topshell *Gibbula cineraria* lacks the green tint of the closely related purple topshell *Gibbula umbilicalis* and cannot live quite as high on the shore. Like *G. umbilicalis*, it feeds on algae and reproduces similarly in the spring time.

Purple/Flat Topshell

Gibbula umbilicalis

Faochán Mhuire corcra

(Horseshoe Harbour, Reenahoe – pp. 122, 151)

The purple/flat topshell *Gibbula umbilicalis* has a silvery green-grey shell with purple stripes. It is a grazer of the middle or lower shore, feeding on seaweeds. It lays single eggs which are fertilised externally to produce planktonic larvae. These settle low on the shore and the young gradually move upwards to where the adults are mainly distributed.

Edible Periwinkle

Littorina littorea

Gioradán

(Horseshoe Harbour, Reenahoe, Kinish Narrows East, Kinish Narrows West – pp. 123, 152, 173, 191)

The edible periwinkle *Littorina littorea* is Ireland's largest winkle species. Found mainly on the middle and lower shore of moderate and sheltered shores, it reproduces in spring when juveniles settle from the plankton in crevices and amongst barnacles. The edible periwinkle grazes the rocks for algal particles, eating diatoms, young algae and the surface layers of older algae. It appears to prefer the green seaweeds *Ulva* and *Enteromorpha* and apparently avoids the rough fucoids. Edible periwinkle are collected from the shore occasionally for food, a fact to be taken into account when considering shore ecology.

Flat Periwinkle
Littorina obtusata
Faocha leathan

(Drolain Point, Globe Rocks, Horseshoe Harbour, Reenahoe, Kinish Narrows East, Kinish Narrows West – pp. 81, 101, 124, 153, 174, 192)

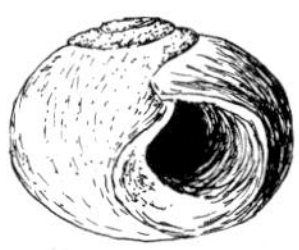

The flat periwinkle *Littorina obtusata* is found on the middle and lower shore amongst fucoid seaweeds where it shelters. It is therefore sparse or absent on the more exposed shores due to lack of suitable habitat. It grazes the surfaces of wracks and kelps for food. It can be vivid orange and yellow, or dull brown/green in colour. In spring it lays eggs in thin, flat sheets of jelly that are attached to the fucoids. The eggs hatch in three or four weeks.

Rough Periwinkle
Littorina saxatilis
Faocha gharbh

(Poulacurra, Globe Rocks, Reenahoe, Kinish Narrows East, Kinish Narrows West – pp. 59, 102, 154, 175, 193)

The rough periwinkle *Littorina saxatilis* is found mainly on the upper and middle shore of moderate and exposed shores. It can be found sheltering in large numbers in crevices. It is much larger than the small periwinkle and has a rough, ridged shell of varying colour which is sometimes striped. Breeding occurs throughout the year.

Small Periwinkle
Melarhaphe neritoides
Faocha bheag

(Poulacurra, Drolain Point, Horseshoe Harbour – pp. 60, 82, 125)

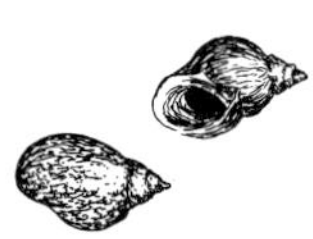

The small periwinkle *Melarhaphe neritoides* is indeed Ireland's smallest periwinkle species and resembles black grape pips sitting in empty barnacle shells or rock crevices. It is found on the upper shore and splash zone, living the highest on the shore of all the winkle species. It feeds on black lichens and algal detritus. Splash zone individuals time their spawning to coincide with high spring tides. After fertilisation, larvae spend about three weeks in the plankton before settling low on the shore and migrating upwards. Individuals are known to live for at least five years.

Limpet
Patella spp.
Bairneach

(Poulacurra, Drolain Point, Globe Rocks, Horseshoe Harbour, Reenahoe, Kinish Narrows East, Kinish Narrows West - pp. 61, 83, 103, 126, 155, 176, 194)

The limpet *Patella* spp. has a cone-shaped grey-white shell, that firmly attaches itself to the rock during low tide, but moves around when covered by seawater or when uncovered at night, to scrape rock and algal surfaces for food (diatoms and juvenile algae).

Limpets are fairly long-lived and each individual always occupies the same "home patch" on the shore. When the tide goes out it returns to this "home patch", where it clamps itself very tightly to the rock to help prevent desiccation when out of the water on hot days. Limpets have planktonic larvae which settle onto the rocks on the shore in the late autumn and winter.

PREDATOR

Dogwhelk
Nucella lapillus
Cuachma chon

(Poulacurra, Drolain Point, Globe Rocks, Horseshoe Harbour, Reenahoe, Kinish Narrows East, Kinish Narrows West - pp. 62, 84, 104, 127, 156, 177, 195)

The dogwhelk *Nucella lapillus* is a key predator of the rocky shore. It is a very robust gastropod mollusc with a thick shell which it retreats into as the tides goes out or when dislodged by rough seas. It moves up and down the shore to find optimum shelter and food. Dogwhelks eat barnacles and mussels, but are known to prefer mussels. They secrete acid to soften the shell and then drill a hole through which the soft parts of the animal can be extracted and eaten. In between feeding they spend long periods resting.

Chapter Four

Very Exposed Shores

Poulacurra

Poulacurra lies at the southwestern tip of Sherkin along a coastline exposed to persistent swell and heavy wave action (Figure 4.1). A large sea swell is often present on calm days. The shore faces south and is exposed to the long fetch of the North Atlantic Ocean. It is open to wave action between 170° and 190°. Offshore the water quickly deepens: by 250 m offshore it is 20 m deep and is down to a depth of 30 m by 400 m distance from the coast. These depths allow significant wave sizes to reach the shore. Using Ballantine's 1961 scale (see Appendix 5), the shore is classified as very exposed.

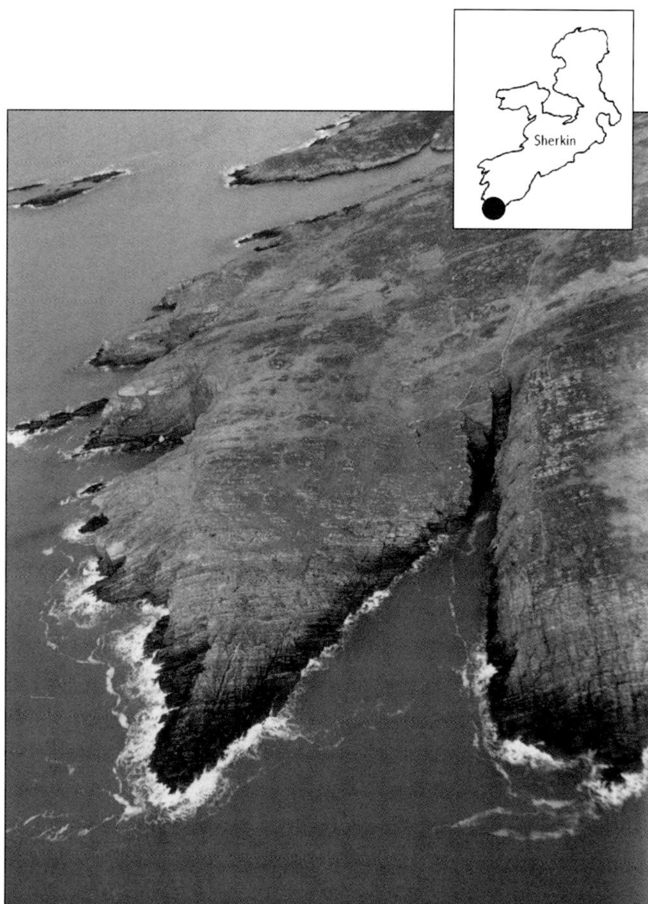

Figure 4.1 Poulacurra inlet from the south.

The east side of the cove comprises vertical cliffs 33 m high, which are heavily fissured. The terrestrial vegetation ends abruptly where the steep slope becomes a vertical face colonised by a rich lichen flora. The orange crusting lichen *Caloplaca marina* was present but not particularly common, and the black tar lichen *Verrucaria maura* dominated over a very wide band. Beneath this, a narrow middle shore band of barnacles dominated and then a lower shore band of encrusting red algae.

The west side of the cove slopes steeply into the sea and is backed by rough grassland. It is accessible with care. The middle shore comprises a wide bedrock platform with rock pools. Above and below this the shore zones are compressed by the steepness of the profile.

The horizontal distance of the transect perpendicular to the shore at Poulacurra is 20.5 m and the vertical height is 4.8 m, giving a gradient of 0.23. Fourteen stations are always recorded, although on a good spring tide, when there is no swell, an extra three stations can be worked. Stations 1–6 form the upper shore, stations 7–10 the middle shore and station 11 and below the lower shore. Station 1 is 6.25 m above chart datum.

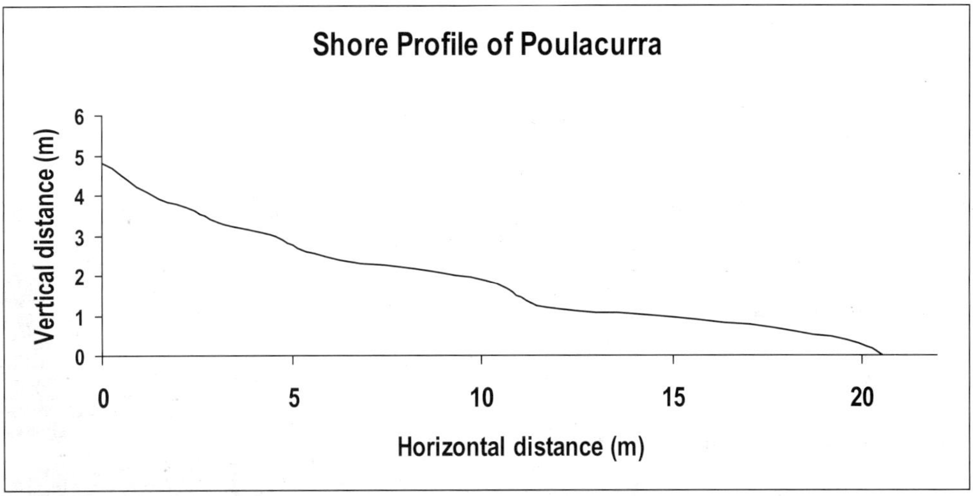

Figure 4.2 A cross-section of the shore from top to bottom showing the varying gradient of the Poulacurra transect.

VISUAL DOMINANTS

The midshore was dominated by a barnacle/mussel mosaic, with a virtual absence of wracks (fucoids).

The lower shore rock was dominated by species of red encrusting algae Lithothamnia and had a rich understorey of red foliose and filamentous algae. Floating above this was a canopy of *Laminaria digitata*, *Himanthalia elongata* and *Alaria esculenta*.

Highlight on Seaweed Species

Dabberlocks *Alaria esculenta* is a large brown seaweed characteristically found on wave-exposed shores. Of the seven shores described in this book, it occurs consistently only at Poulacurra. The strong flexible cartilaginous fronds have an adaptation to survive the physical abrasion generated on wave-exposed shores. Other seaweeds show different characteristics for adaptation to these conditions. These include much-branched and inrolled fronds to hold water and minimise evaporation as seen in channelled wrack *Pelvetia canaliculata* and carrageen moss *Mastocarpus stellatus*. The membranous parts of plants are often torn and broken by the force of winter storms. In response, many plants are able to produce new growth from the frond tips or margins after being damaged.

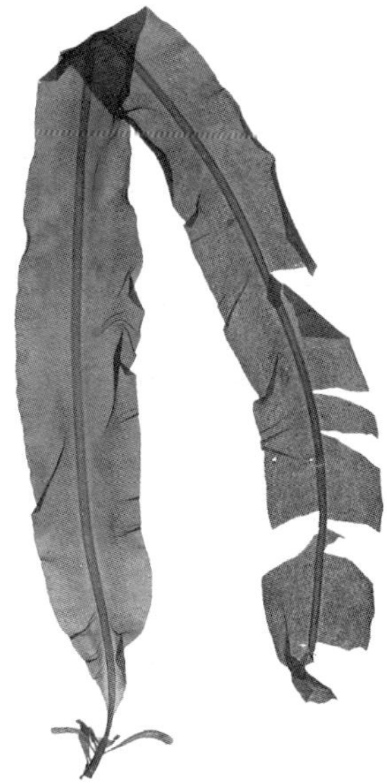

Dabberlocks – *Alaria esculenta*

The **carrageen moss *Mastocarpus stellatus*** is a tough red seaweed of the family Gigartinaceae. Its fronds are flattened but channelled and tending to inroll, a characteristic which helps conserve moisture. The fronds are branched dichotomously i.e. divided into two. The species occurs on the lower shore on all seven transect sites, but is prominent at Poulacurra where there is no fucoid canopy. Its hardiness enables it to thrive in this exposed environment.

Carrageen Moss – *Mastocarpus stellatus*

ALGAE

Although the middle and upper shore zones were animal-dominated, a few red seaweeds were prominent on the lower middle and lower shore. These were pepper dulse *Osmundea pinnatifida* and carrageen moss *Mastocarpus stellatus* which can tolerate the harsh environment at Poulacurra. Others, such as the very thin purple laver *Porphyra umbilicalis,* can also thrive in these exposed conditions. These three species were more abundant in the early 1980s as compared to 1987–2000.

Porphyra was the most spasmodic in its presence/absence and in many years occupied less than 1% cover per quadrat. A more usual figure was 3% cover, and records from pilot work before 1980 showed an unusually large amount of *Porphyra* was present in 1978 (18% cover). *Osmundea pinnatifida* – a small red fleshy plant – was also consistently found at under 5% cover.

Mastocarpus stellatus – a larger, tougher plant than *Osmundea* – was mostly recorded at just under 1% in the early survey years (1981–1985), but since then fell to below 0.4% between 1987 and 1991 and was very sparse from 1992 onwards.

In total 83 algal species were recorded from the transect, plus 27 taxa identified to genus only. The majority were found on the lower shore where they form understorey beneath the *Himanthalia/Alaria* canopy. This number of species represents the lowest algal diversity of all seven Sherkin monthly sites.

Brown Algae

A total of 24 taxa of brown algae were recorded at Poulacurra, 17 of which have been identified to species level. Wracks were virtually absent from the Poulacurra shore, with only a single entry for *Pelvetia canaliculata* in 1992. The species recorded almost every year were: *Alaria esculenta*, Ectocarpaceae, *Laminaria digitata* and *Scytosiphon lomentaria*. *Himanthalia elongata* and *Ralfsia verrucosa* often occurred (eight years and ten years respectively) and the remaining species were all recorded in fewer than eight years. *Himanthalia* was not recorded after 1989.

Red Algae

Seventy taxa of red algae were recorded, 56 to species level. As well as the dominant species usually recorded (*Corallina officinalis*, Lithothamnia, *Mastocarpus stellatus*, *Osmundea pinnatifida*, *Chondrus crispus*, *Hildenbrandia rubra*, *Lomentaria articulata*, *L. clavellosa*, *Porphyra umbilicalis*, *Polysiphonia* spp., *Ceramium* spp. and *Hildenbrandia* spp.) a number of species were present for 10–15 of the 20 years. These are *Callithamnion* spp., *Ceramium rubrum*, *C. shuttleworthianum* and *Palmaria palmata*.

Green Algae

Sixteen taxa of green algae were recorded at Poulacurra, 10 of which have been identified to species level. Of the green algae at Poulacurra, only two, *Ulva lactuca* and *Enteromorpha* spp., were recorded every year. *Cladophora* was often present, being recorded as either *Cladophora* spp. or *C. rupestris* in 15 of the 20 years. *Chaetomorpha* was present in 11 years (either as *Chaetomorpha* spp. or *C. linum*). *Spongomorpha* spp. and *S. arcta* were recorded only between 1988 and 1996. Other species listed were only recorded during two or three years.

Lichens

Only six lichen species were identified on the Poulacurra transect, three of which were present most or every year(s) (*Lichina pygmaea*, *Verrucaria maura* and *V. mucosa*). *Lichina confinis* was recorded in seven of the 20 years, *Lecanora atra* for three years and *Caloplaca marina* was recorded only once (1993).

Animals

A total of 86 animal taxa were recorded at Poulacurra, 67 of which were identified to species level. The majority were found in small numbers on the lower shore and were often noted below the lowest station of the transect. They were therefore only recorded in months when tides were exceptionally low. In this virtually sublittoral habitat are found the three common seashore sponges *Halichondria panicea*, *Hymeniacidon sanguinea* and *Myxilla incrustans*, together with two sea slugs which feed on them – *Archidoris pseudoargus* and *Runcina coronata*.

A small number of edible crabs, shore crabs, starfish and brittlestars were found amongst the red algal understorey and the seaweeds themselves were sometimes colonised by bryozoans and hydroids. The three most commonly recorded sea mat were

Highlight on Snails and Sea Slugs (Gastropods and Nudibranchs)

Sea slug – *Archidoris pseudoargus*

As well as the five mollusc species which always occur and form part of the dominant structure of the Poulacurra shore (*Littorina saxatilis, Melarhaphe neritoides*, *Mytilus edulis*, *Nucella lapillus* and *Patella* spp.) a number of species were recorded less frequently. These include the sea slugs – *Aeolidia papillosa*, *Archidoris pseudoargus* and *Runcina coronata*; sea snails – *Buccinum undatum*, *Calliostoma zizyphinum*, *Gibbula cineraria*, *Hinia reticulata*, *Littorina obtusata*, *L. neglecta;* and the mussel *Modiolus barbatus*. The scarcity of most of these was most likely related to the lack of algae and hence a lack of the required food and shelter. Sea slugs have no external shell to protect their soft bodies, which is one reason why they are found amongst the damp seaweed habitat of the lowest stations on the shore.

Highlight on Anemones (Cnidarians)

Gem Anemone – *Aulactinia verrucosa*

The Poulacurra shore had a wide variety of anemones, with *Actinia equina*, *Sagartia elegans* and *Urticina felina* recorded most years and *Aulactinia verrucosa* being fairly common. Less frequently found were *Actinothoë sphyrodeta*, *Anemonia viridis*, *Anthopleura thallia*, *Cereus pedunculatus*, *Corynactis viridis* and *Sagartia troglodytes*. The daisy anemone *Cereus pedunculatus* is more usually found with its column buried in trapped muddy sand particles with only the mouth and tentacles showing. The other species listed above are found mostly in crevices, overhangs and amongst kelp holdfasts in the lowest stations. The common beadlet anemone *Actinia equina* also occurs on more exposed open rock surfaces.

Electra pilosa, *Membranipora membranacea* and *Umbonula* spp., each of which was recorded in eight or nine of the survey years. All other sea mats were recorded in four or fewer years only.

None of the six hydroid taxa recorded (*Dynamena pumila*, *Obelia geniculata*, *Plumularia setacea, Haliclystus auricula, Tubularia larynx* and *Coryne* sp.), were present every year; *Dynamena pumila* was the most common.

In addition to the dominant barnacle species, a small number of other crustaceans were occasionally found at Poulacurra. A variety of amphipods (*Talitrus saltator*; *Caprella linearis*), isopods (*Idotea granulosa*) and crabs (*Carcinus maenas*; *Cancer pagurus*) occurred amongst the seaweeds at the very bottom of the shore, and at the highest levels those animals adapted to the drier upper shore habitats (the isopod *Ligia oceanica* and the tiny insect *Lipura maritima*).

Very small numbers of the Australasian barnacle *Elminius modestus* were found in five years (1992, 1995, 1998, 1999, 2000).

Species analysed for Poulacurra, their place in the food chain and the shore ecology (Predatory pathway ——▶ Grazing pathway ••••••▶)

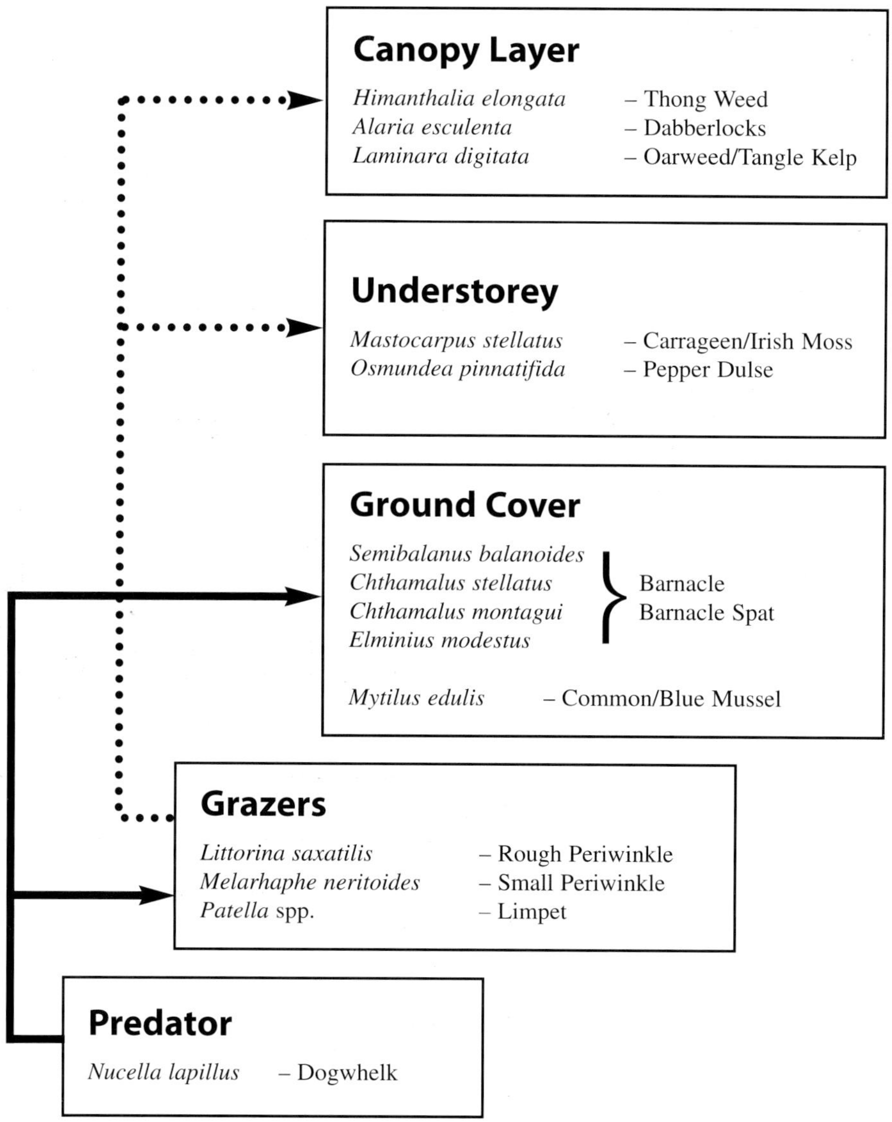

POULACURRA

CANOPY LAYER

Thong Weed
Himanthalia elongata
Ríseach

The thong weed *Himanthalia elongata* occupied a band on the lower middle shore (stations 9–13).

Its growth was very sparse and there were noticeable density peaks of the young buttons in May, and an October peak of adult growth.

Although recorded in the early years of sampling, *Himanthalia elongata* was absent from the transect after 1989. There was a single year, 1984, when cover was denser than average (1.8%), but otherwise when present it occupied less than 0.5% of the rock cover.

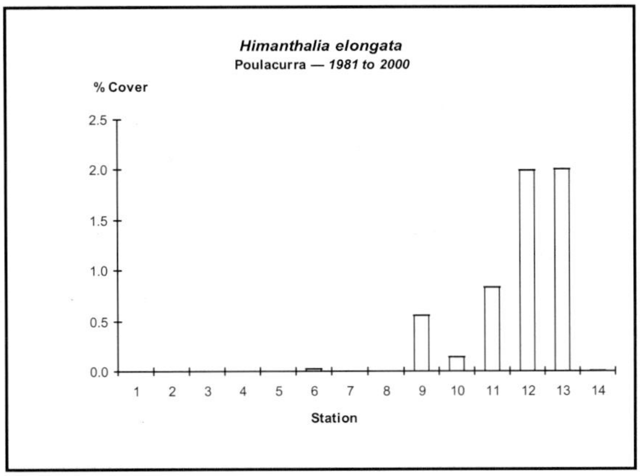

Figure 4.3

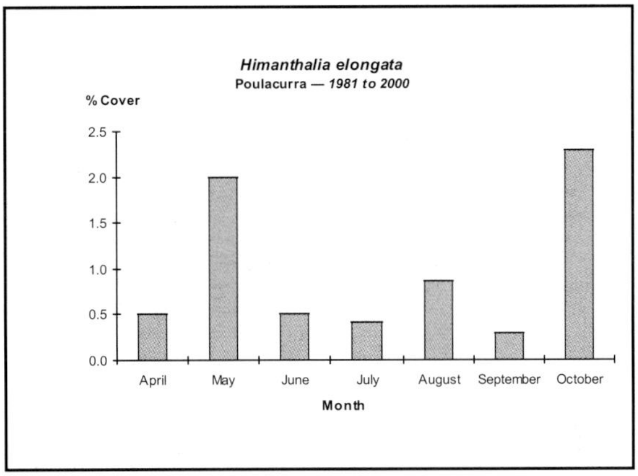

Figure 4.4

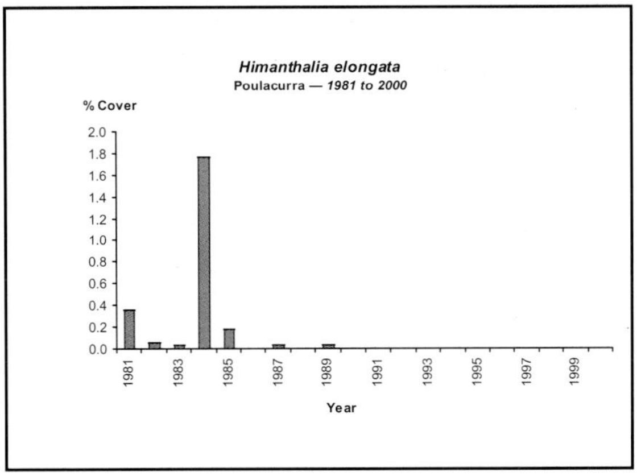

Figure 4.5

POULACURRA

CANOPY LAYER

Dabberlocks
Alaria esculenta
Láracha

Dabberlocks *Alaria esculenta* was intermittently present on the Poulacurra transect. The species covered a wider vertical range than perhaps would be expected, being found on the middle to lower shore, from station 9 to station 14; it is interesting to note that the records from the upper limit of its range (stations 9 and 11) were restricted to the years 1983–85.

There appeared to be some seasonality, with a fourfold increase in May, decreased cover in June/July, and a second increase in August. It then declined in the autumn.

Between 1981 and 2000 it was present in 11 years on the transect. However it is evident from Appendix 4 that it was also present at lower levels observed during extremely low tides, for nine additional years. As a contribution to ground cover, *Alaria esculenta* plays but a small part, only accounting for a low percentage of the lower shore rock cover within its range. In 1983 and 1991 this figure was much higher, but the species was absent or very sparse throughout the 1990s.

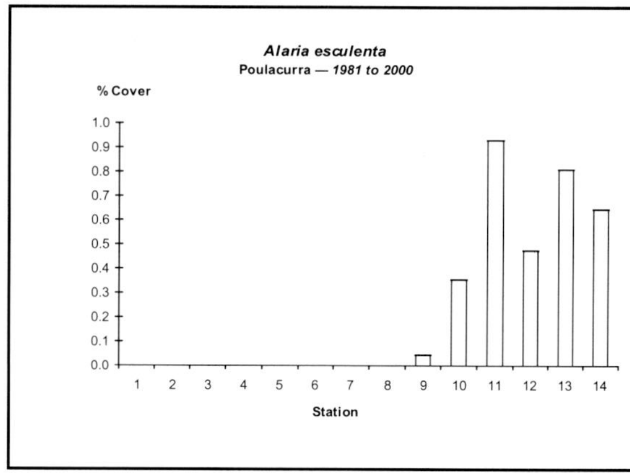

Figure 4.6

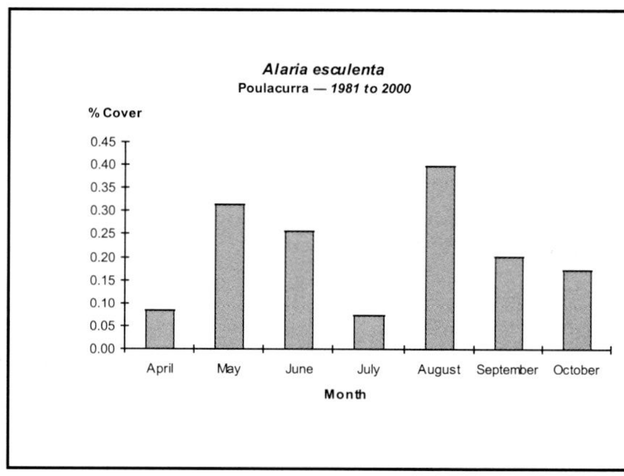

Figure 4.7

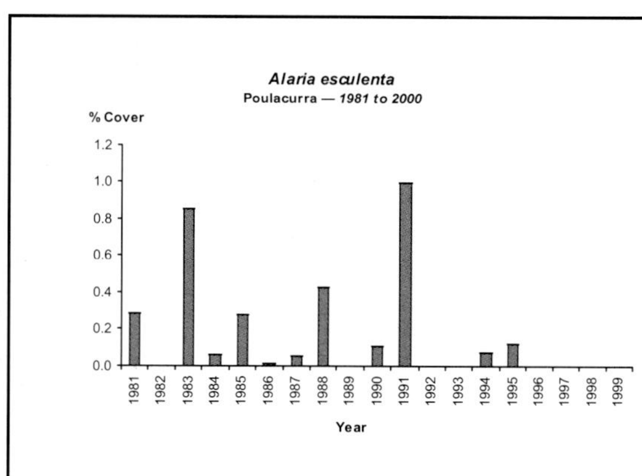

Figure 4.8

POULACURRA

CANOPY LAYER

Oarweed/Tangle Kelp
Laminaria digitata
Coirleach

Small quantities of the kelp species oarweed *Laminaria digitata* were present on the middle and lower shore, but occupied only 3–5% cover per quadrat.

This species showed a small seasonal increase in cover, with abundance dropping markedly after September.

Over the 20 years of sampling the species was much more abundant in the 1980s than in the 1990s with 1988 showing the highest density (8%). By contrast, the kelp was very sparse in the early 1990s and absent from 1996 onwards.

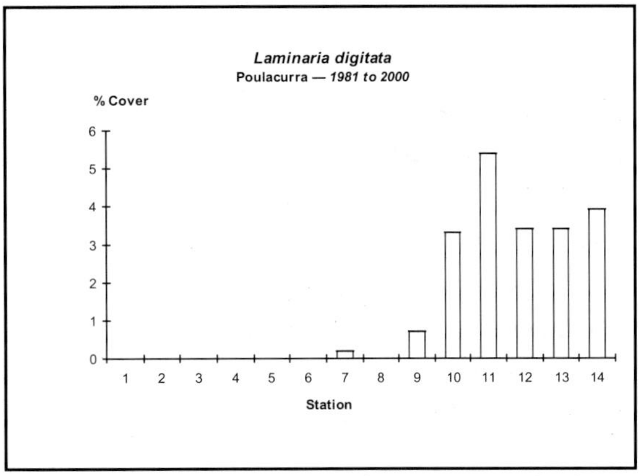

Figure 4.9

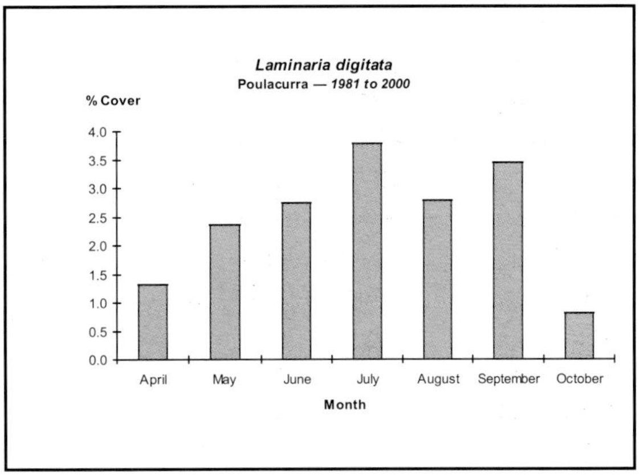

Figure 4.10

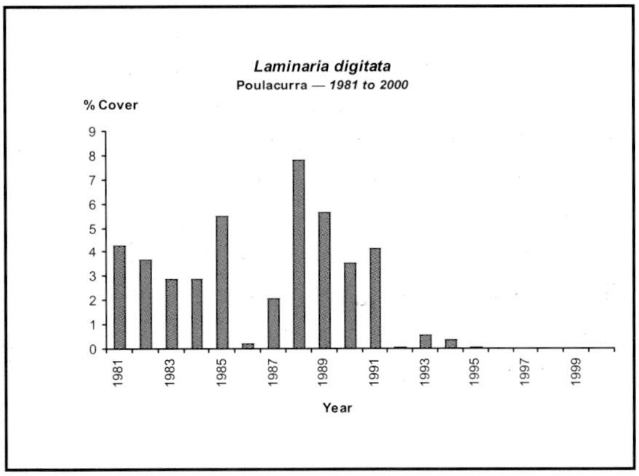

Figure 4.11

POULACURRA

UNDERSTOREY

Carrageen/Irish Moss
Mastocarpus stellatus
Clúimhín cait

The carrageen moss *Mastocarpus stellatus* was present in the understorey in very small amounts. It was found between stations 9 and 14, with most plants living at station 11. Throughout the 20 years the maximum mean cover was just under 1%.

Seasonal variation was present, with almost twice as much presence in June and August as in the spring and autumn months. The July figure was surprisingly low (0–12%).

An overall decline in abundance took place in three stages. The relatively more abundant cover in 1981–85 was reduced to an absence in 1986, followed by five years of abundance of > 0.4% per quadrat. After 1991 *Mastocarpus stellatus* was very scarce – an occasional plant only – or absent.

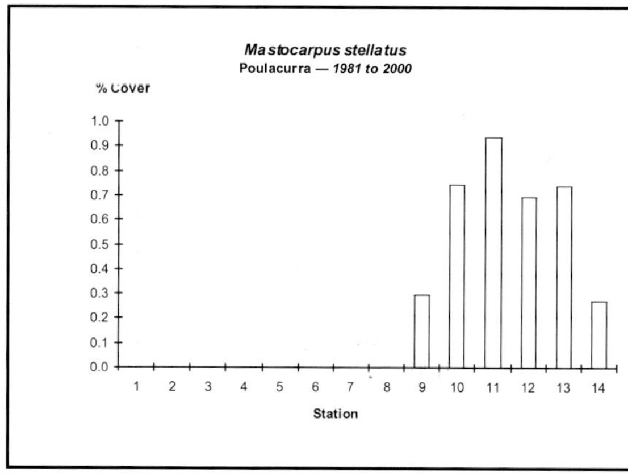

Figure 4.12

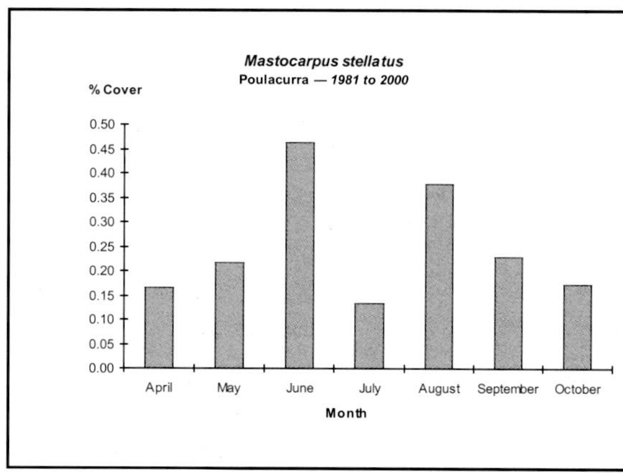

Figure 4.13

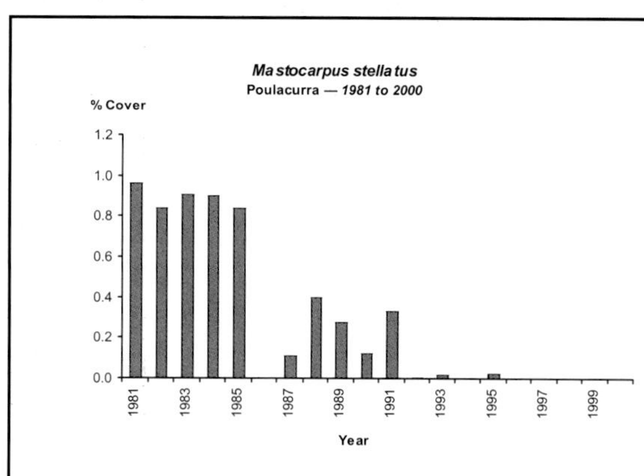

Figure 4.14

POULACURRA

UNDERSTOREY

Pepper Dulse
Osmundea pinnatifida
Míobhán

The red seaweed pepper dulse *Osmundea pinnatifida* occurred on the lower shore primarily between stations 9 and 14, with occasional plants higher up the shore. Cover was always very sparse though, never reaching more than 0.5% cover per quadrat.

There was an increase in abundance in May and June, then a decrease in July. From late July to October, there was a small but steady increase, but the amount present in October was never as much as in early summer.

The varying abundance between 1981 and 2000 appeared to be cyclical. Three cycles were evident, of varying length: 1981–86, 1986–93 and 1993–2000. Levels were consistently low throughout the last cycle, with a small peak in 1995.

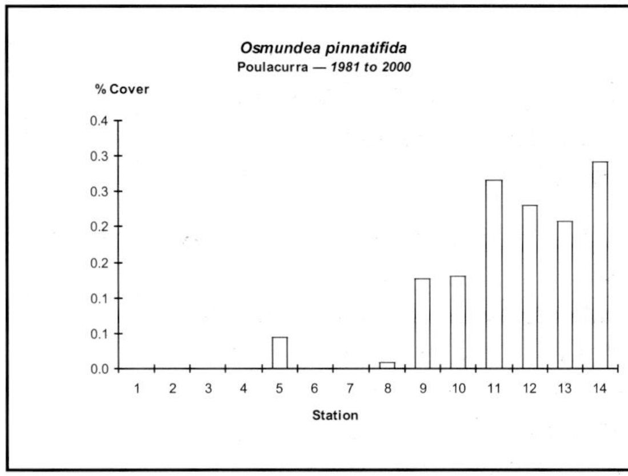

Figure 4.15

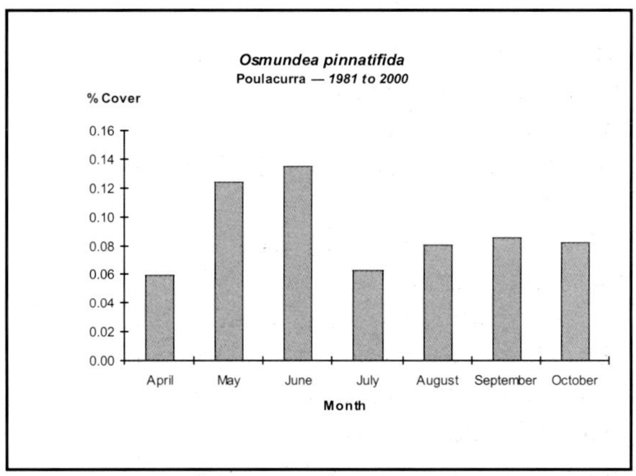

Figure 4.16

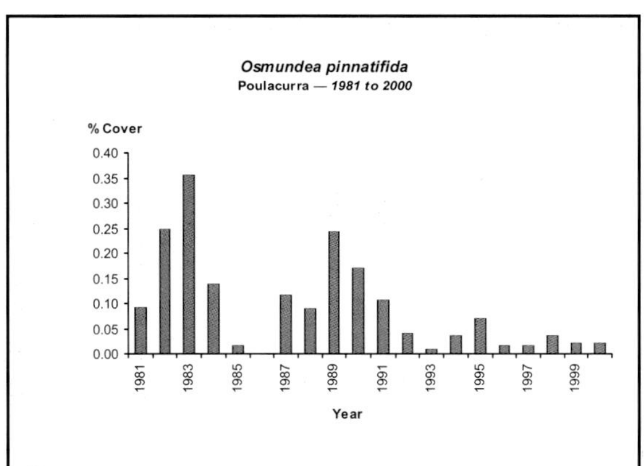

Figure 4.17

POULACURRA

GROUND COVER

Barnacles

Semibalanus balanoides
Chthamalus stellatus
Chthamalus montagui
Elminius modestus

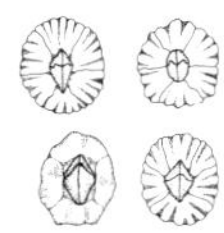

Giúrainn

Barnacles were part of the dominant ground cover at Poulacurra and were recorded from all but the highest station. Cover of 30% per quadrat or more was found throughout the middle shore and the upper part of the lower shore (stations 5–13), with the peak density (50%) occurring at station 11.

There was noticeable seasonality, with lowest cover recorded during April and a steady level of about 30% from May through to October.

Over the 20-year sampling period barnacles showed three phases of change. Cover was at its lowest in 1981 and 1991, and there were two years (1989 and 1990) when cover was exceptionally high. The steady increase seen during 1981–84 was maintained for two further years (1985 and 1986), fell back in 1987, then increased noticeably in 1988 and 1989 to a peak of 64%. This was more or less maintained the following year. 1991 however recorded a large fall in cover to 14% and throughout the 1990s levels stayed relatively low at between 16% and 25%. This pattern is similar to that seen at the other sites (e.g. see p.78, 99, 120).

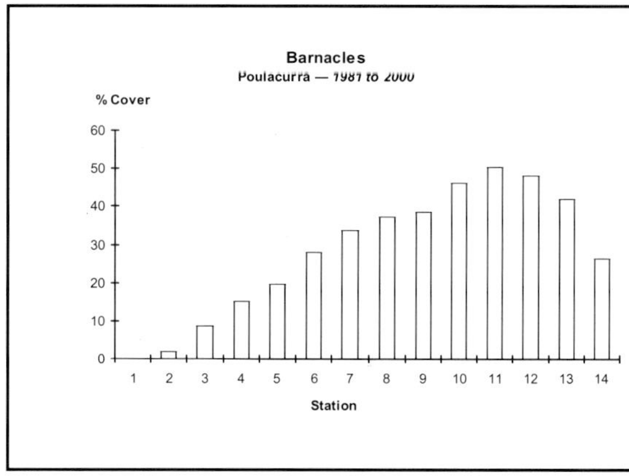

Figure 4.18

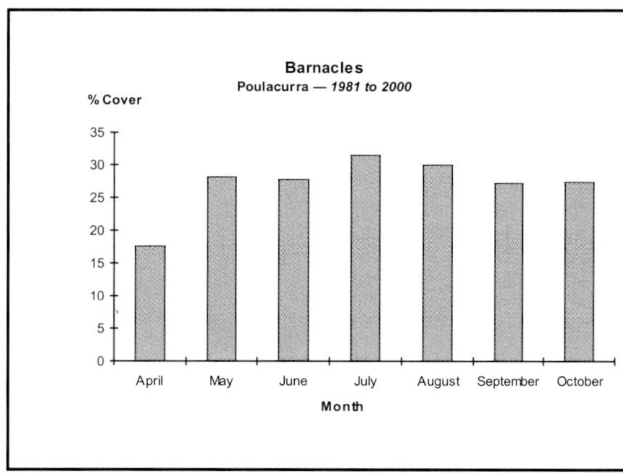

Figure 4.19

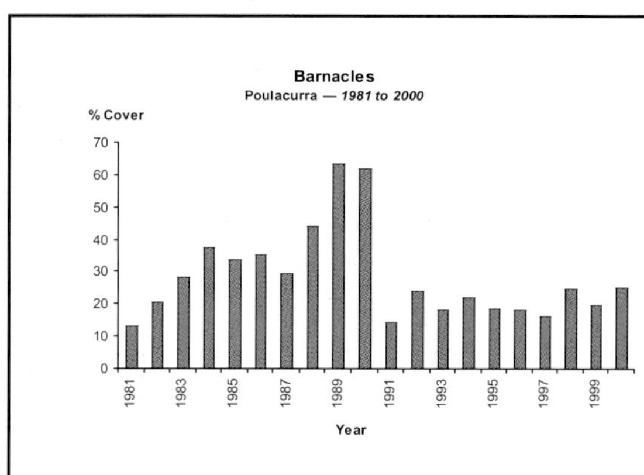

Figure 4.20

POULACURRA

GROUND COVER

Barnacle Spat
Síol giúrainn

Barnacle spat were most concentrated at station 10, though they had a fairly wide distribution from station 3 to station 14.

There were two distinctive peaks of occurrence, an early short-lived one in May (*Semibalanus balanoides*) and a second one which was sustained through August, September and October (*Chthamalus* spp.).

Barnacle spat did not appear to achieve successful settlement every year at Poulacurra, and there were five years when no spatfall was recorded in the 1980s. The recorded density varied quite considerably from less than 10/dm^2 in 1983 to a maximum of 54/dm^2 in 1991.

The relationship between density of spat observed and the fluctuations of density in the adult population is not immediately apparent. For example, the highest spat density was observed in 1991, which was the year that showed a crash in the adult population. The subsequent years 1992–94 saw low but increasing spat densities, while the adult population was also slowly increasing from the 1991 minimum.

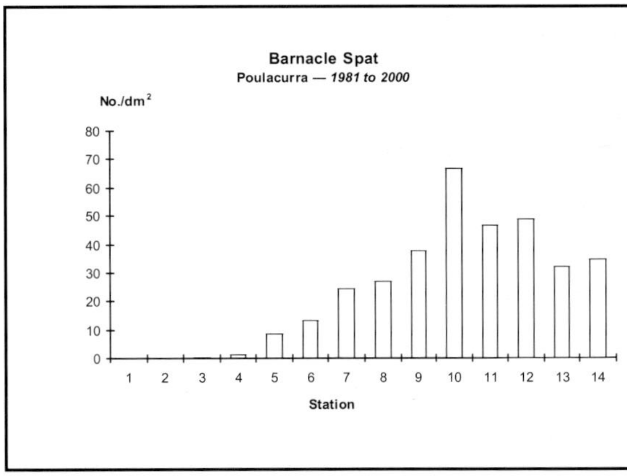

Figure 4.21

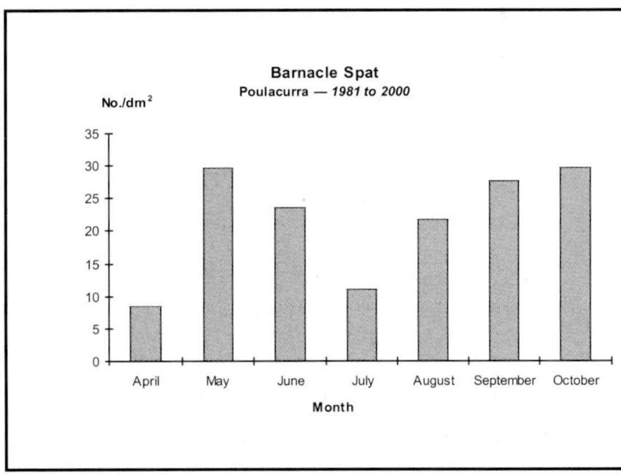

Figure 4.22

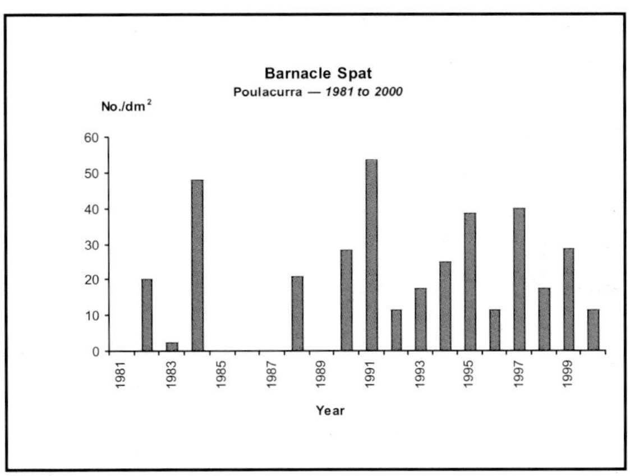

Figure 4.23

POULACURRA

GROUND COVER

Common/Blue Mussel
Mytilus edulis
Diúilicín

Common mussel *Mytilus edulis* was present throughout the shore transect with the exception of station 1. The densest band lay across stations 9–14 in the lower middle to lower shore.

There was a steady seasonal increase in cover from April to June. This level of mussel cover was then maintained until the autumn.

Over the 20-year recording period the mean annual density over the entire transect fluctuated considerably, with a noticeable decrease in mussels in 1990 and onwards. The variation can be described as four cycles: 1981–86, 1986–91, 1991–97 and from 1997–2000. The maximum cover (19.5% per quadrat) was recorded in 1989, and followed by a drastic reduction to 5% and 2% in 1990 and 1991 respectively. The third cycle built up to a smaller peak of around 9% and mussels were steady at approximately 5% from then on. It may be that between 1991 and 2000 there was only a single cycle, but this is difficult to determine.

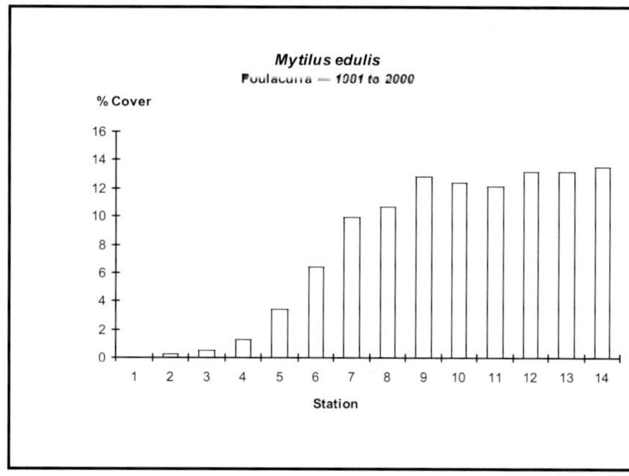

Figure 4.24

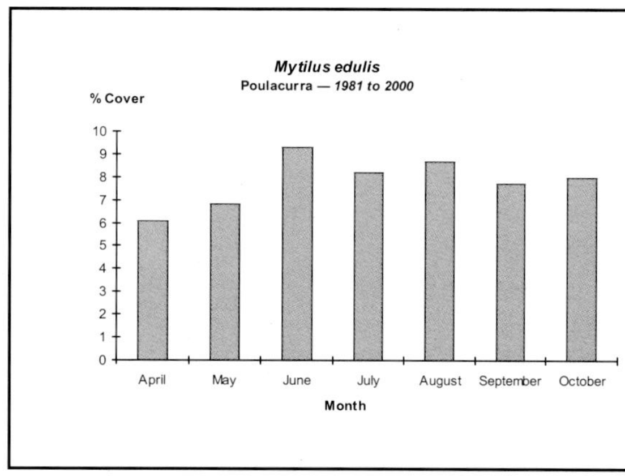

Figure 4.25

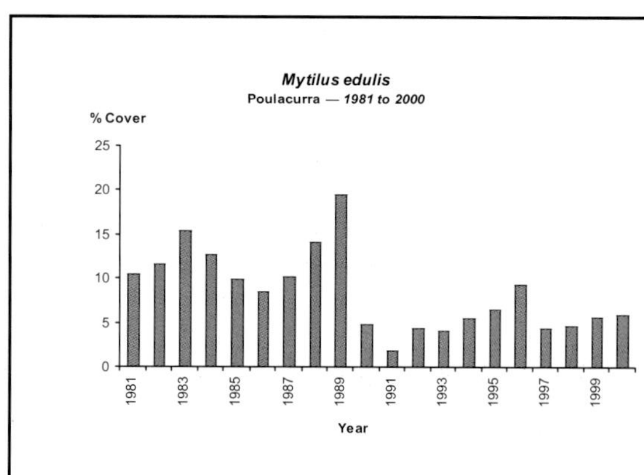

Figure 4.26

POULACURRA

GRAZERS

Rough Periwinkle
Littorina saxatilis
Faocha gharbh

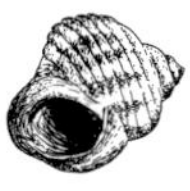

The rough periwinkle *Littorina saxatilis* was found predominantly on the upper shore (station 1–6) and in lower numbers (2 per quadrat or fewer) on the middle and lower shore.

L. saxatilis was always most plentiful during May, June, July and August, although there was an obvious decrease in numbers from July through to October. This decline was partly due to animals being displaced from the rocks by rough seas. The higher April/May numbers as compared to October, show that migration onto the shore and movement up the shore from deeper water occurred. This is most likely to take place in the spring.

Numbers were very variable during the 20 years of survey. In two separate years densities were relatively high (1982 and 1985), while in all other years densities were less than 6 per quadrat. During 1988, 1990 and 1991, *Littorina saxatilis* was present on the shore but individuals were only counted in a dm^2 rather than in a 0.25 m^2 quadrat (see p. 34). The most conspicuous pattern was the consistently low number recorded during the 1990s.

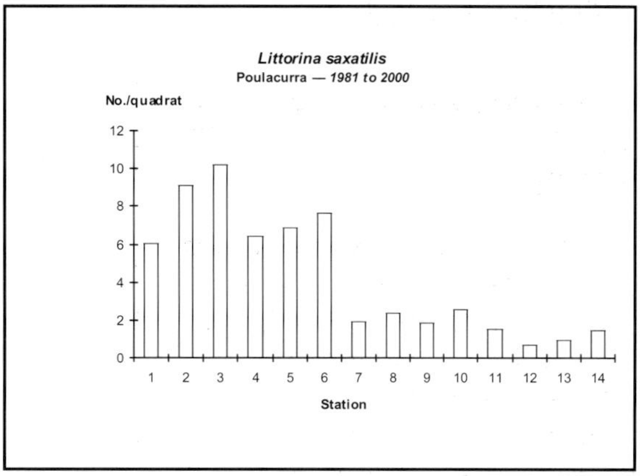

Figure 4.27

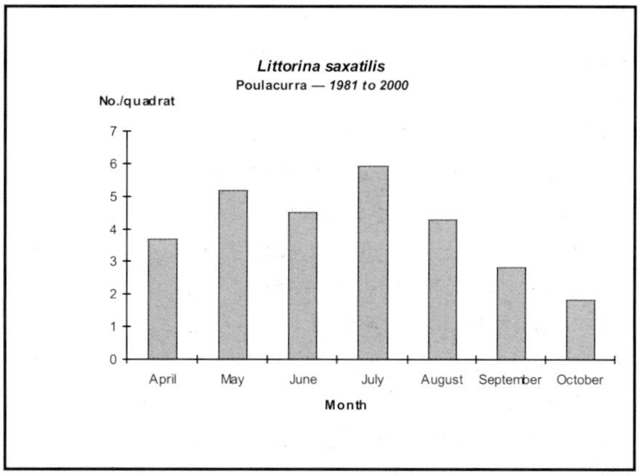

Figure 4.28

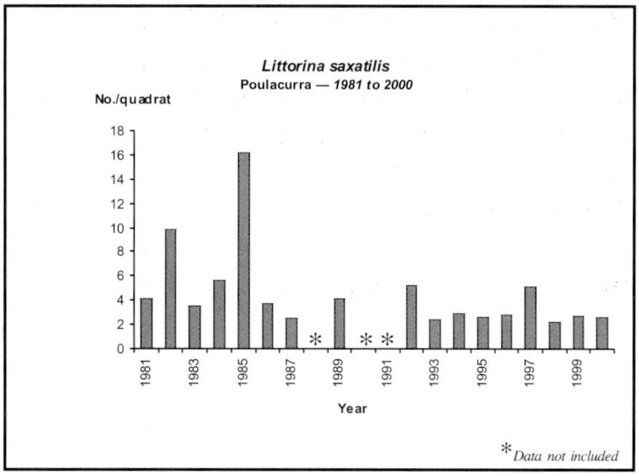

Figure 4.29

POULACURRA

GRAZERS

Small Periwinkle
Melarhaphe neritoides
Faocha bheag

Small periwinkle *Melarhaphe neritoides* was present in very large numbers in the upper stations (2–6) and throughout the remainder of the shore in decreasing numbers.

Numbers recorded in April (95/dm^2) were consistently higher than other months (*ca.* 47/dm^2).

Considerable variation was recorded over the 20-year period. In general, densities were lower in the 1980s as compared to the 1990s. However two years in particular showed high densities: 1986 (100/dm^2) and 1992 (100/dm^2). In 1986 a peak in numbers of *Melarhaphe neritoides* was also seen at Drolain Point (p. 82), where a similar pattern of larger population numbers occurred in the 1990s.

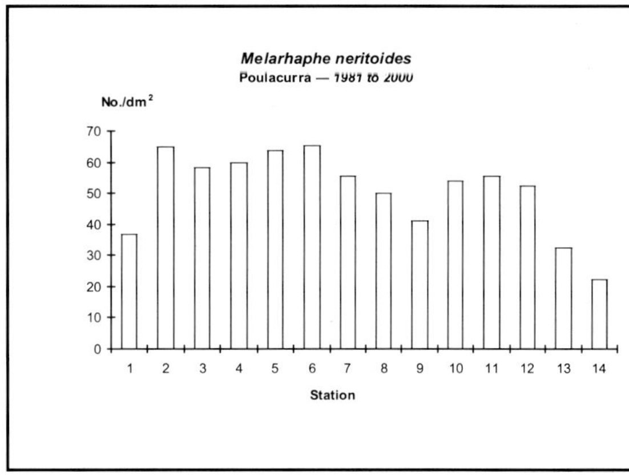

Figure 4.30

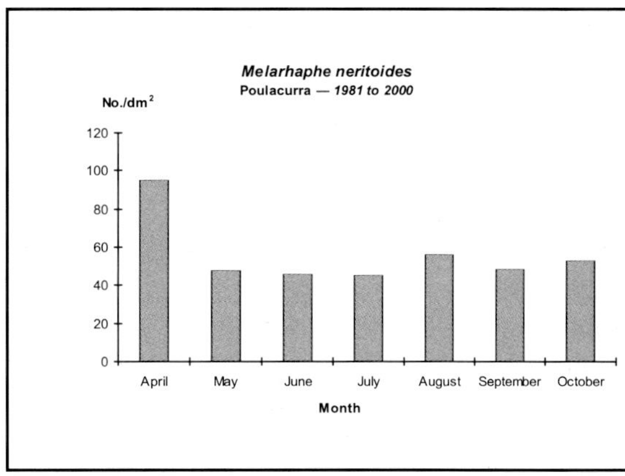

Figure 4.31

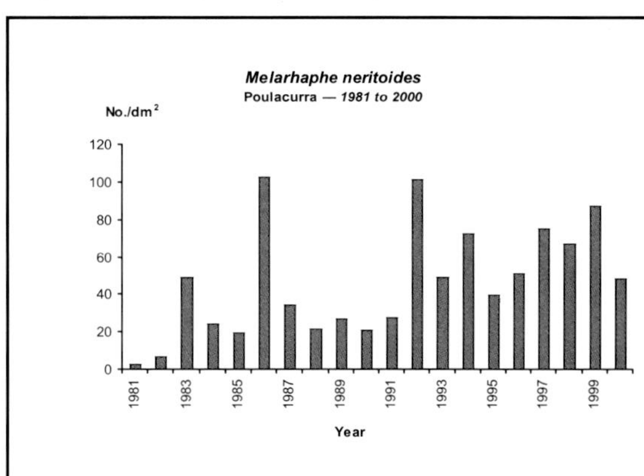

Figure 4.32

POULACURRA

GRAZERS

Limpet
Patella spp.
Bairneach

Limpets *Patella* spp. were present in all but the highest two stations (1 and 2). They reached a maximum density of about 48 per quadrat at station 11. This is within the main distribution zone of mussels (stations 9–14).

The number recorded in April was consistently lower than any other month.

Between 1981 and 2000 the mean density over the whole range fluctuated between 12 (1995) and 45 per quadrat (1982). There is no strong pattern evident in the variation. The 1982 peak value was followed by 12 years when the population remained fairly steady (around 25 per quadrat) with one or two years (1984 and 1990) when numbers rose a little. There was a gradual increase from the minimum density recorded in 1995 until 1999.

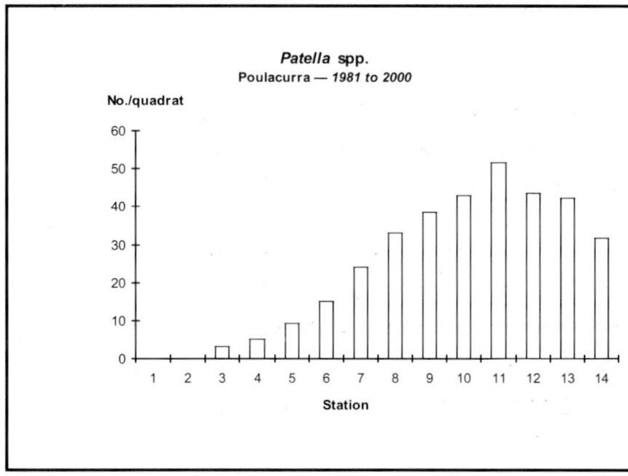

Figure 4.33

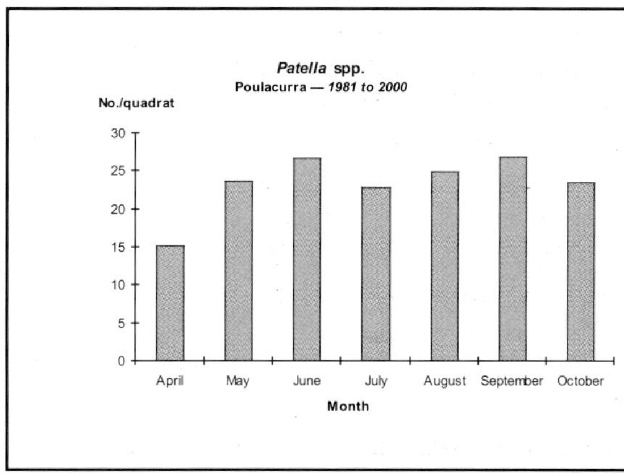

Figure 4.34

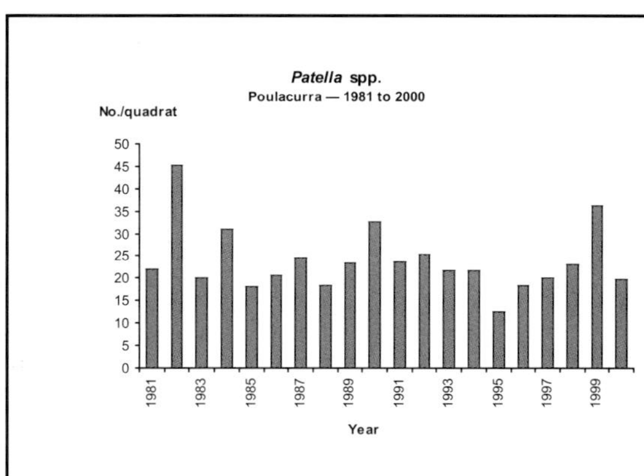

Figure 4.35

POULACURRA

PREDATOR

Dogwhelk
Nucella lapillus
Cuachma chon

The dogwhelk *Nucella lapillus* was common at Poulacurra between stations 7 and 14, and was found in very small numbers on the upper shore (stations 3–6). Within its main range, the maximum density was 5.5 per quadrat.

Numbers were slightly higher during May to August than in the spring and early autumn.

Between 1981 and 2000, dogwhelks were recorded every year. Numbers were exceptionally high in 1982 (5.25 per quadrat) but more usually fluctuated between 0.5 and 3.1 per quadrat. The population appeared to be unaffected in 1989–1991 by declining barnacles and mussels, but the sharp drop in population numbers in 1993 was perhaps a delayed response to loss of these species. The recovery in 1994 was very strong.

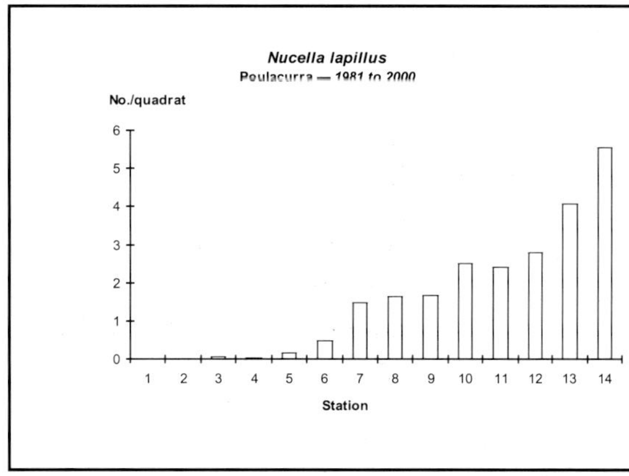

Figure 4.36

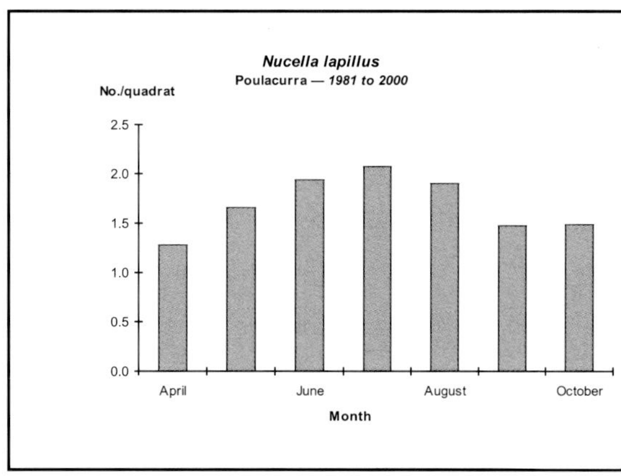

Figure 4.37

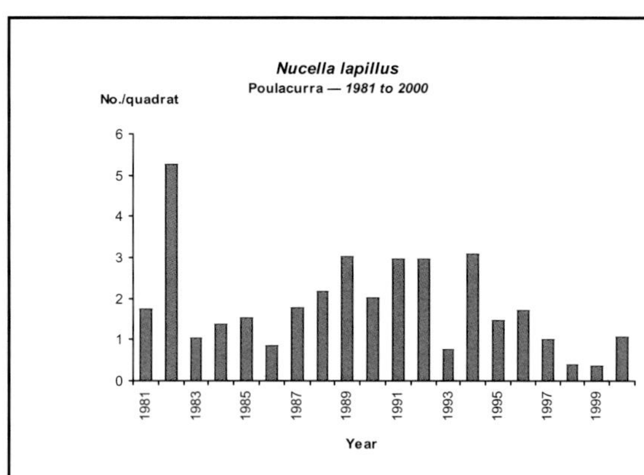

Figure 4.38

Trends for Poulacurra 1981–2002

Of the 10 species analysed at Poulacurra all showed conspicuous changes over the 20 years.

On the upper shore the rough periwinkle *Littorina saxatilis* maintained steady numbers with the exception of the population increases during 1982 and 1985. Small periwinkle *Melarhaphe neritoides* population numbers were much higher in the 1990s as compared to 1980s.

On the middle shore, mussels decreased significantly after 1990 and the population remained sparse. Numbers of barnacles also decreased significantly after 1990 and thereafter maintained a low level of percentage cover. Numbers of limpets *Patella* spp. fluctuated. They did not show a decrease from 1991 onwards, but did decline in 1995 and increased to a peak in 1999.

On the middle to lower shore dogwhelk *Nucella lapillus* numbers fluctuated, but there was a distinctly large isolated population increase in 1982.

On the lower shore dabberlocks *Alaria esculenta* was scarce or absent after 1992, but prior to this was often present at low percentage cover. *Nucella lapillus* was very dense in 1982, when *Alaria* was absent.

Chapter Five

EXPOSED SHORES

DROLAIN POINT

Figure 5.1 Drolain Point from the northwest.

Drolain Point is the northwest point of Sherkin Island and the shore is exposed to wind and wave action from a moderate angle (Figure 5.1). Although Cape Clear Island protects Drolain Point from weather through 210°–235°, wind and waves between 193°–210° come through the channel between Cape Clear Island and Sherkin Island;

between 235° and 265° the shore is fully exposed to the long Atlantic fetch entering Roaringwater Bay. The transect is south-facing so prevailing wave attacks arrive at an angle. The shore is composed of vertically fissured bedrock which is very friable.

The horizontal distance of the transect across the shore is 7.65 m and the vertical height 4.5 m. The resultant profile is very steep, with an overall gradient of 0.59. Fourteen stations are worked regularly and on a good low spring tide 16 stations can be recorded. The splash zone is very extensive where the steepness of the shore is particularly pronounced. Stations 1–6 form the upper shore, stations 7–10 the middle shore and station 11 and below the lower shore. Station 1 is 5.7 m above chart datum.

The shore is classified as exposed on the Ballantine (1961) exposure scale.

VISUAL DOMINANTS

There was much bare rock in the upper shore due to frequent fracturing of the friable rock faces in rough winter seas. The colourful band of yellow and orange lichens *Xanthoria parietina* and *Caloplaca marina* in the splash zone reached down to station 1, then the next five stations of the transect were colonised only by occasional barnacles and occasional large patches of the black tar lichen *Verrucaria maura*.

The middle shore was dominated by a barnacle/mussel/limpet community. Stations 7, 8 and 9 were covered primarily by barnacles and mussels, whereas the lower stations 10–12 usually had a higher proportion of barnacles/limpets.

The lower shore showed more variety of species. It is here that red algae flourish beneath the protective canopy of the brown alga *Himanthalia elongata.* Prominent species were *Chondrus crispus*, *Corallina officinalis*, *Osmundea pinnatifida*, Lithothamnia, *Lomentaria articulata* and *Mastocarpus stellatus.*

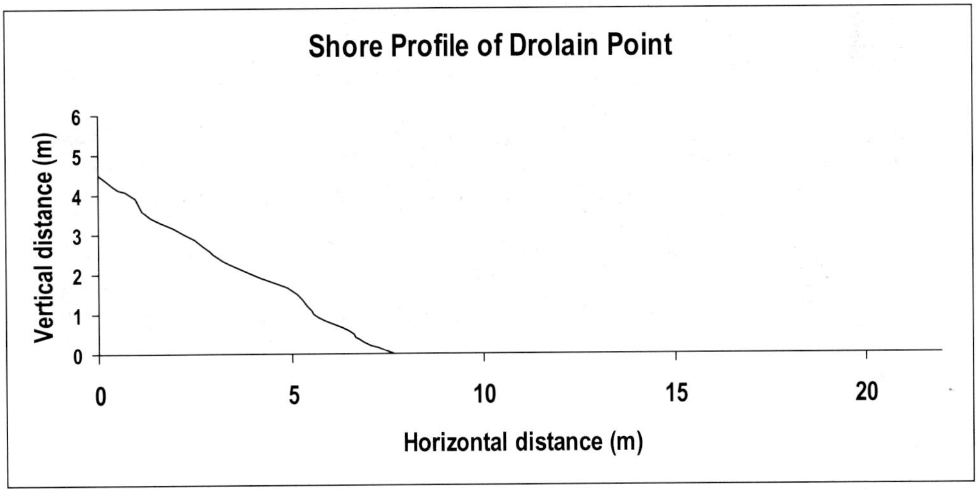

Figure 5.2 A cross-section of the shore from top to bottom showing the steep gradient of the Drolain Point transect.

ALGAE

Although dominated by a mussel/barnacle/limpet community, a total of 99 algal species were identified on the Drolain Point shore, together with a further 28 taxa identified to genus only. Channelled wrack *Pelvetia canaliculata* was present every year, though its growth was far from luxurious; and serrated wrack *Fucus serratus* was present in all years but 1981. The wracks of the middle shore – spiral wrack *F. spiralis* and bladder wrack *F. vesiculosus* – were more patchy, with very little *F. spiralis* and *F. vesiculosus* being recorded in only seven years. The majority of algal records came from the lower shore, where the physical abrasion caused by wave action is much reduced and where the development of a canopy creates a more sheltered habitat colonised by red algae.

Brown algae

Twenty nine brown algal taxa were recorded from the transect, comprising 23 species and six identified to genus only. The dominant species were *Himanthalia elongata* and *Laminaria digitata*, which together form the canopy at low water and beneath which the smaller seaweeds flourish. Other frequently occurring species were *Dictyota dichotoma,* Ectocarpaceae, *Fucus serratus, Leathesia difformis, Pelvetia canaliculata* and *Scytosiphon lomentaria*. They did not form a dominant part of the shore community because each was present only as a small number of plants. *Alaria esculenta* – typical of exposed shores – occurred only in April 1983, June 1986 and June 1987. The wrack *Ascophyllum nodosum*, usually associated with wave-sheltered conditions, was found in August and September 1989 – an interesting one-off occurrence. *Spongonema tomentosum,* recorded only in May and September 1990, grows epiphytically on *Himanthalia elongata.*

Red Algae

A total of 60 species of red algae were recorded together with 15 taxa identified to genus only.

The species recorded almost every year were mostly typical of exposed rocky shores, namely *Chondrus crispus*, *Corallina officinalis*, *Osmundea pinnatifida*, Lithothamnia and *Mastocarpus stellatus*. *Lomentaria articulata*, also common, occurs on both sheltered and exposed shores. In all years *Porphyra umbilicalis* was present – a species which is associated with exposed shores; other species usually present were *Ceramium rubrum*, *Hildenbrandia* spp. and *Ceramium* spp., which are found across a broad range of sheltered to exposed shores.

Green Algae

Twenty three taxa of green algae were recorded at Drolain Point, 16 of which were identified to species. The majority of records (86%) come from stations 7–14. Densities of all species were consistently low (< 5% cover per quadrat), as plants were restricted to the few small pools on the middle shore and to the rock surface beneath the canopy on the lower shore.

Highlight on Seaweed Species

Filamentous Red Algae I

Plants such as the red seaweeds *Ceramium, Griffithsia, Polysiphonia* and *Callithamnion* are filamentous, and many comprise a dense mass of individual fine "hairs". Others have a slightly thicker, filiform axis with branches, which may or may not be filamentous. Those without filamentous branches include *Lomentaria articulata, Nemalion helminthoides, Dumontia contorta, Laurencia hybrida* and *L. obtusa*. Those species with filamentous branches include *Plumaria elegans* and *Heterosiphonia*. *Plumaria elegans* occurs on the lower shore on vertical rock faces and overhangs.

Lomentaria articulata

Polysiphonia sp.

Polysiphonia

Polysiphonia is a very large genus of filamentous red seaweed. Twenty five species are known to occur around Ireland and Britain (Howson & Picton, 1997), 12 of which have been recorded at Drolain Point:

P. atlantica	*P. fucoides*
P. brodiei	*P. harveyi*
P. denudata	*P. lanosa*
P. elongata	*P. nigra*
P. fibrata	*P. simulans*
P. fibrillosa	*P. stricta*

P. denudata will continue to be diligently searched for at Drolain Point and other Sherkin sites, since this is not a common species and is more usually known from Southern England. *P. simulans* is also rarely recorded.

Coralline Algae

Coralline algae can be free-living, branched and knobbly as, for example, the maërl that is harvested for fertiliser; they can completely cover small stones or can be erect with jointed fronds. While no maërl has been recorded on any of the seven transects, it occurs sublittorally in Roaringwater Bay in large living beds. Encrusting red algae are common on stones, in rock pools and on exposed shores, such as Poulacurra, amongst barnacles and mussels. Lithothamnia is a major component of the shore at Poulacurra and Drolain Point. Of the erect coralline algae, only *Corallina officinalis* is recorded on Sherkin; it is most common at Globe Rocks, Horseshoe Harbour and Reenahoe.

The mean number of taxa recorded each year was six, three of which were present almost every year: *Cladophora rupestris, Enteromorpha* spp. and *Ulva lactuca.*

Those rarely recorded were: *Bryopsis hypnoides, Chaetomorpha mediterranea, Cladophora albida, C. laetevirens, C. sericea, Derbesia marina, Enteromorpha linza, Rhizoclonium tortuosum, Spongomorpha aeruginosa and Urospora* spp.

LICHENS

Of the eight species of lichen recorded at Drolain Point, *Caloplaca marina, Lichina confinis, L. pygmaea, Verrucaria maura* and *V. mucosa* were recorded virtually every year, whereas *Lecanora atra* and *Xanthoria parietina* were more spasmodic in their appearance. *Ochrolechia parella* was recorded in only five years.

Highlight on Amphipods and Isopods (Crustaceans)

Amphipods and isopods are in the crustacean class Eumalacostraca and comprise many species. All amphipods have a laterally flattened body. Of the amphipods, *Amphithoe rubricata*, sandhopper *Talitrus saltator* and ghost shrimp *Caprella linearis* were found infrequently at Drolain Point.

Sandhoppers – *Talitrus saltator*

Amphithoe rubricata and *Talitrus. saltator* are both gammarids, a common group of amphipods with over 250 species; whereas *Caprella linearis* is in a small group know as the skeleton shrimps due to their very thin bodies whose paired legs are reduced or absent. *C. linearis* lives amongst bushy clumps of hydroids, bryozoans and red algal turfs and tends to be slow moving. By contrast, *T. saltator* is usually found on sandy beaches amongst the debris of the strand line, jumping when disturbed. *A. rubricata* is a very widespread species around Ireland and Britain. It builds a tube or nest out of algal fragments that are cemented together by a secretion from some of its legs (called pereopods). These tubes are attached to seaweeds or the undersides of stones.

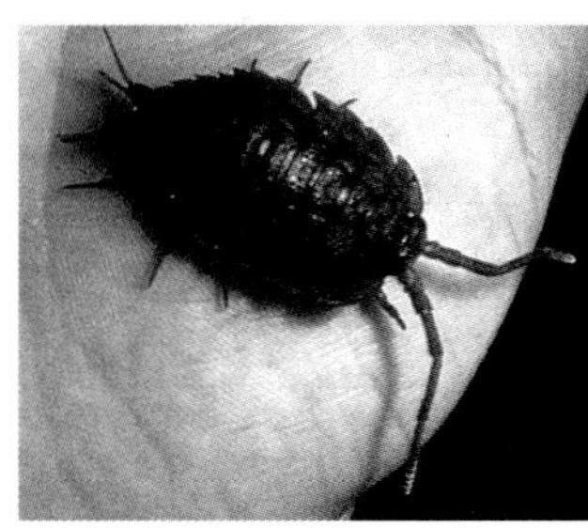

Sea slater – *Ligia oceanica*

Isopods are small, dorso-ventrally flattened crustaceans resembling terrestrial woodlice. The two species recorded at Drolain Point are *Idotea baltica,* which lives and scavenges among the fucoids on the lower shore, and the sea slater *Ligia oceanica* which scavenges in the splash zone.

ANIMALS

A total of 91 animal taxa were recorded at Drolain Point with 72 being identified to species level. Species which occurred most years include: the anemones *Actinia equina*, *Aulactinia verrucosa*, *Cereus pedunculatus* and *Sagartia elegans*, the polychaete worms *Pomatoceros triqueter* and *Eulalia viridis*, the sponges *Halichondria panicea* and *Myxilla incrustans*, the gastropod mollusc *Calliostoma zizyphinum*, the common shore crab *Carcinus maenas*, and the bryozoan *Electra pilosa*.

The tiny insect *Lipura maritima* and the sea slater *Ligia oceanica* were common most years on the upper shore and splash zone, whereas the species of anemones, worms, sponges, crabs and gastropod molluscs listed above were found in the damp crevices of the lower shore.

There were fewer bryozoan and cnidarian taxa than recorded for the slightly more exposed Poulacurra, but more crustacea (18 as compared to 15) and mollusca (25 as compared to 20) taxa.

Only one hydroid species was recorded for Drolain Point (*Dynamena pumila*) as compared with the seven species which were recorded from the seaweeds in the lower stations at Poulacurra.

Carcinus maenas was recorded in eight different years, whereas the edible crab *Cancer pagurus* and the hermit crab *Pagurus bernhardus* were only infrequently found.

The Australasian barnacle *Elminius modestus* was recorded in nine of the twenty years 1981–2000, and a small number of amphipod and isopod species (*Amphithoe rubricata*, *Caprella linearis*, *Idotea baltica* and *Talitrus saltator*) were recorded occasionally.

Species analysed for Drolain Point, their place in the food chain and the shore ecology (Predatory pathway ——► Grazing pathway ••••••►)

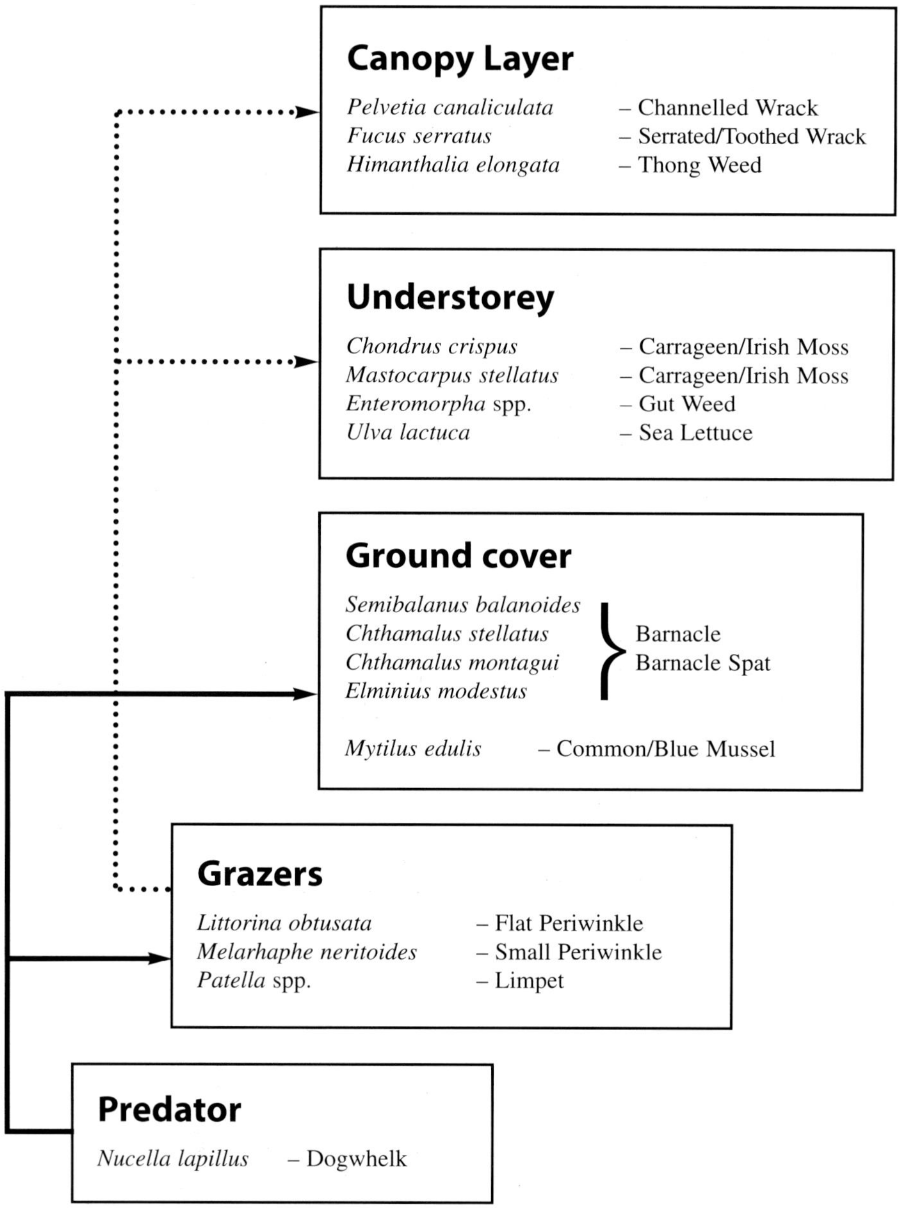

DROLAIN POINT

CANOPY LAYER

Channelled Wrack
Pelvetia canaliculata
Caisíneach

Channelled wrack *Pelvetia canaliculata* occurred very sparsely on the upper shore. Most plants occurred at stations 5, 6, and 7, but the overall cover was still very low (less than 1% per quadrat).

It had a very variable presence throughout the year. A general increase from April to August was interrupted by the low cover recorded in June. September and October were similarly low.

Over the 20 years, 1981–2000, percentage cover never exceeded 1.2%. However, there was a marked difference between the mean value of 1981–90 (*ca.* 0.4%) and 1991–2000 (0.1%), when *Pelvetia canaliculata* abundance was much lower. There was a major decrease in abundance from 1990 to 1991 and recovery never really occurred.

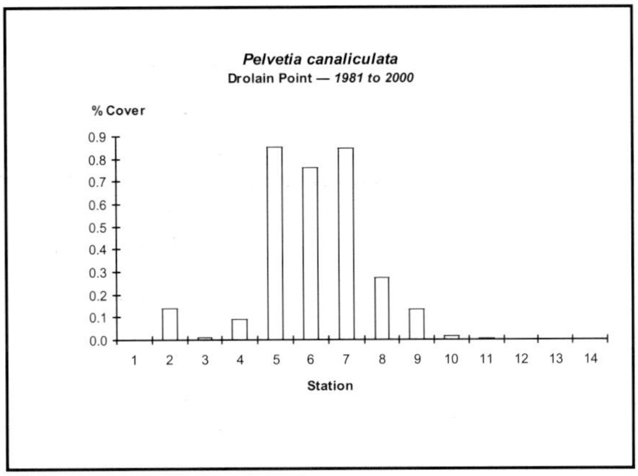

Figure 5.3

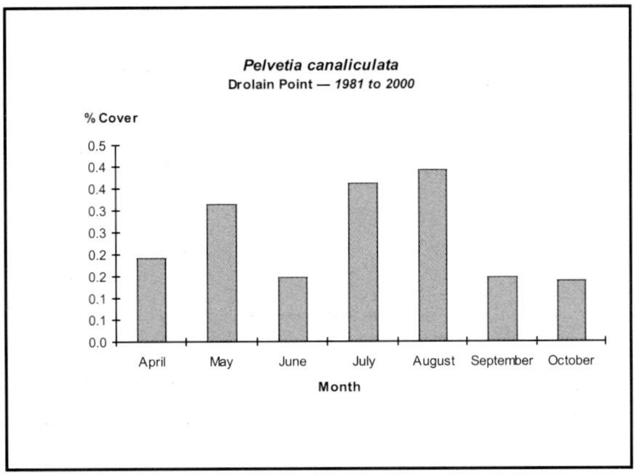

Figure 5.4

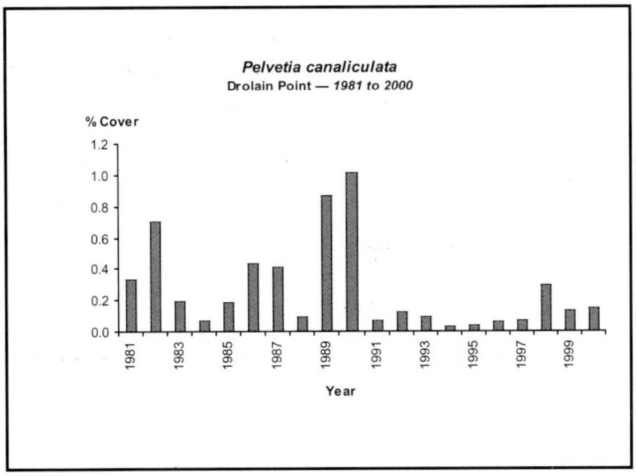

Figure 5.5

DROLAIN POINT

CANOPY LAYER

Serrated/Toothed Wrack
Fucus serratus
Míoránach

Serrated wrack *Fucus serratus* was very sparse at Drolain Point. It occurred at stations 9–14 and occupied less than 1% cover per quadrat.

There was a seasonal trend – an increase which peaked in August, then declined during September and October.

From 1988–92 there was an overall increase in cover from less than 0.3% to 1.5%. 1993 saw an abrupt decline to virtually no plants. In every year between 1993 and 2000, there were very few plants (< 0.2%) with the exception of a single year, 1998, when 0.9% cover was recorded.

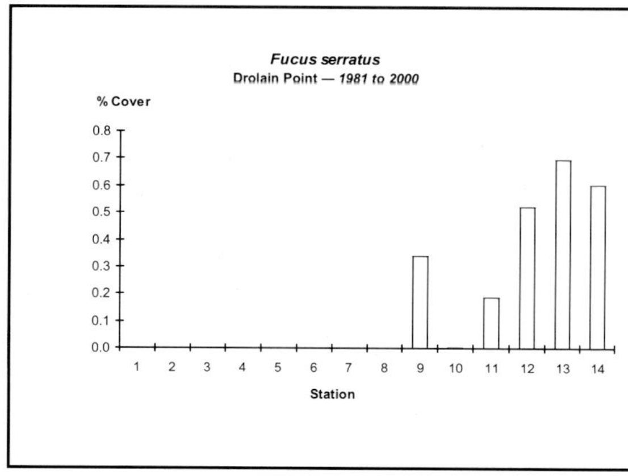

Figure 5.6

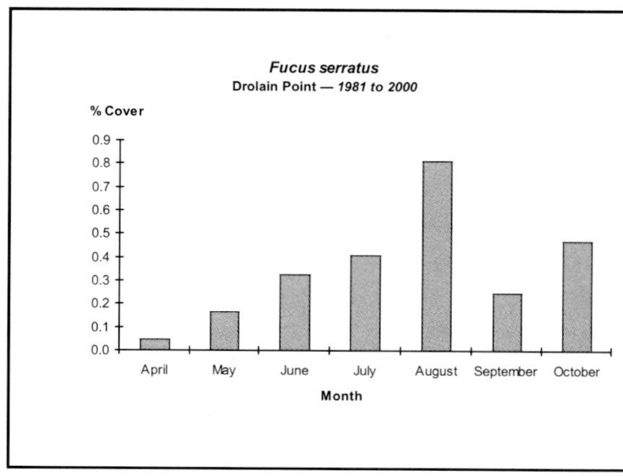

Figure 5.7

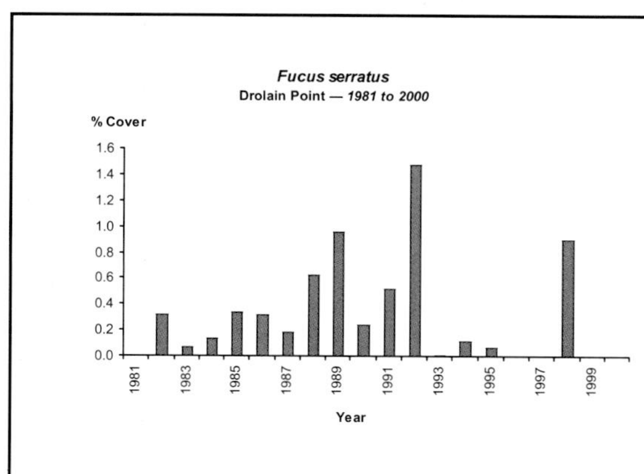

Figure 5.8

DROLAIN POINT

CANOPY LAYER

Thong Weed
Himanthalia elongata
Ríseach

The main zone for thong weed *Himanthalia elongata* was from stations 12–14. A few plants occurred on the middle shore but growth did not progress well at this level.

On a seasonal basis *Himanthalia elongata* cover fluctuated within a narrow range of 0.35% to 0.9%.

Over the 20-year period of recording, three years in particular stood out as having higher than average cover of this species: 1982, 1991 and 1992. There was a general trend of decrease for 1983, 1984 and 1985, followed by a rise and fall until 1988 and a general increase from 1988–92. After 1992 the amount of *Himanthalia elongata* on the shore crashed and the species remained very sparse (< 0.1%) until it disappeared in 2000.

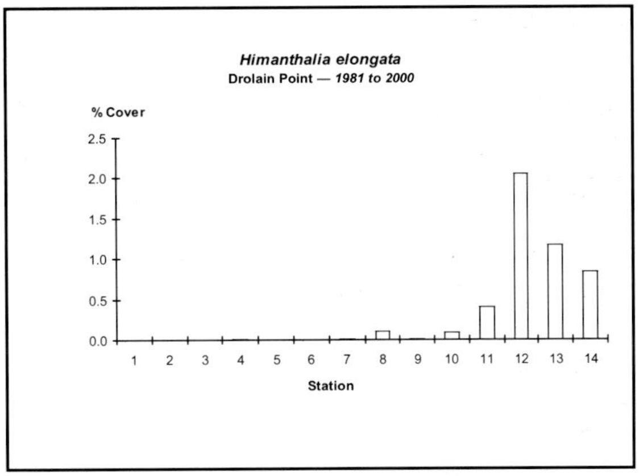

Figure 5.9

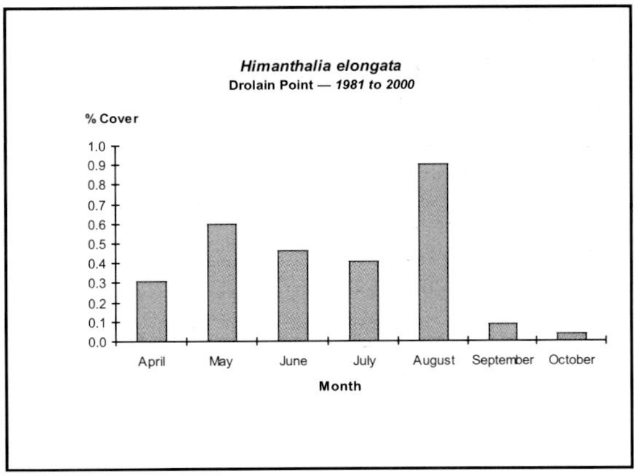

Figure 5.10

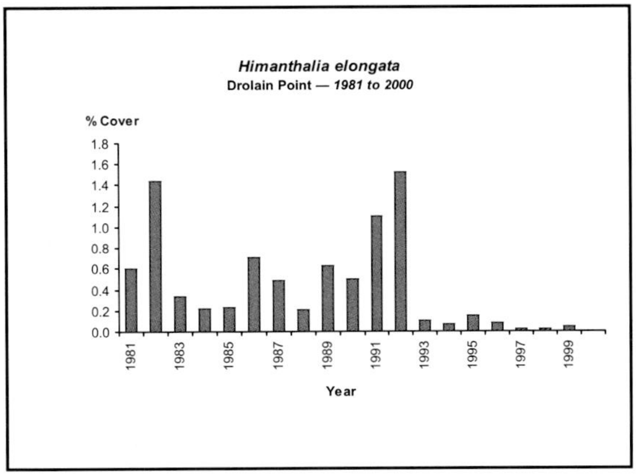

Figure 5.11

DROLAIN POINT

UNDERSTOREY

Carrageen/Irish Moss
Chondrus crispus
Cosáinín (carraige)

The red turf-forming alga carrageen moss *Chondrus crispus* was found low on the shore at Drolain Point mainly between stations 11 and 14, although occasional plants were found at stations 8, 9 and 10.

It was most prolific during the early summer – April, May, June – and then declined to a very low percentage cover in August and September. There was a small increase in plant cover during October.

Density between 1981 and 2000 was predominantly very low, and no specimens at all were found in 1981, 1984, 1994, 1995 and 1997. However abundance was, by comparison, dramatically high in 1983 (1.9%) and 1989 (1.6%).

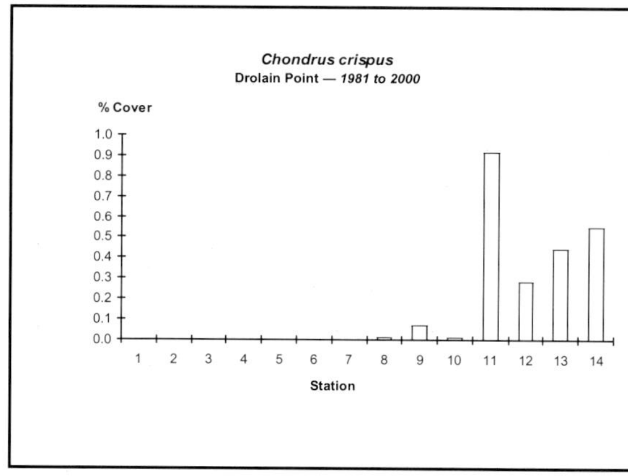

Figure 5.12

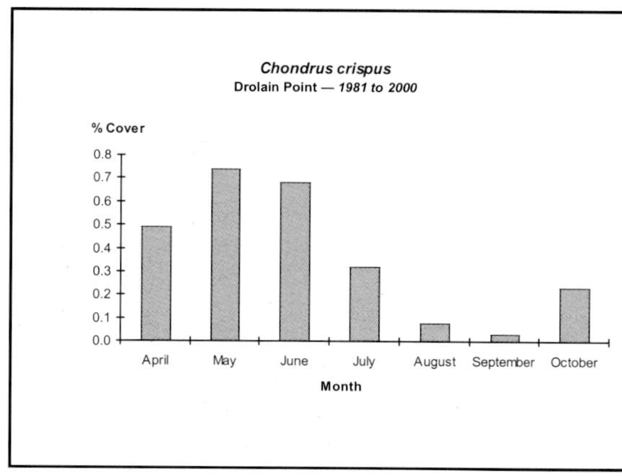

Figure 5.13

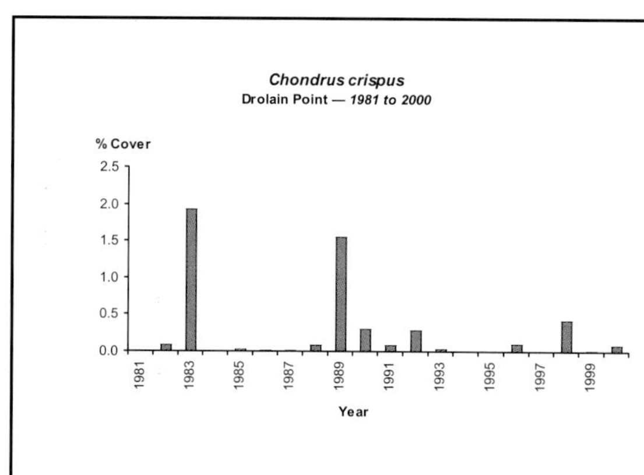

Figure 5.14

DROLAIN POINT

UNDERSTOREY

Carrageen/Irish Moss
Mastocarpus stellatus
Clúimhín cait

Like the other species collected as carrageen moss *Chondrus crispus*, *Mastocarpus stellatus* also occurred on the lower shore at stations 11–14, with occasional plants found higher (stations 7–10) and the species peaked at station 12.

Monthly density values were always below 1% per quadrat and varied little after the low April values had risen to 0.6% in May.

Over the 20 years 1981–2000 there have been two distinct phases of abundance. *Mastocarpus* showed an overall trend of increase from 1981–89, followed by a lower abundance from 1990–92. Between 1993 and 2000 only occasional plants were found, with densities amounting to < 0.1%.

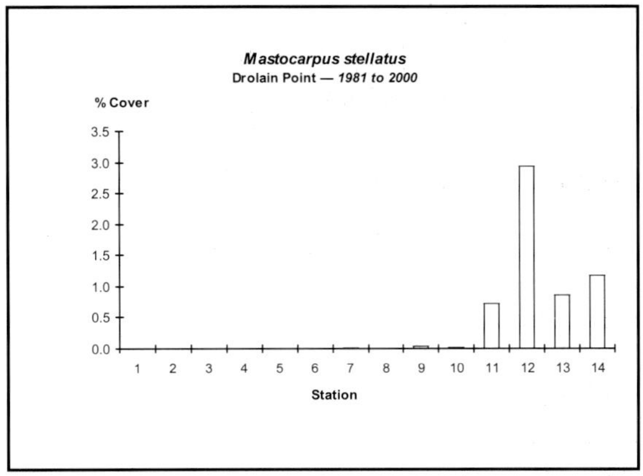

Figure 5.15

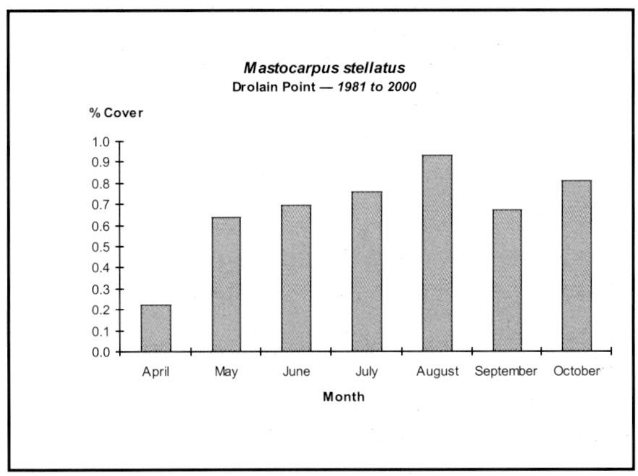

Figure 5.16

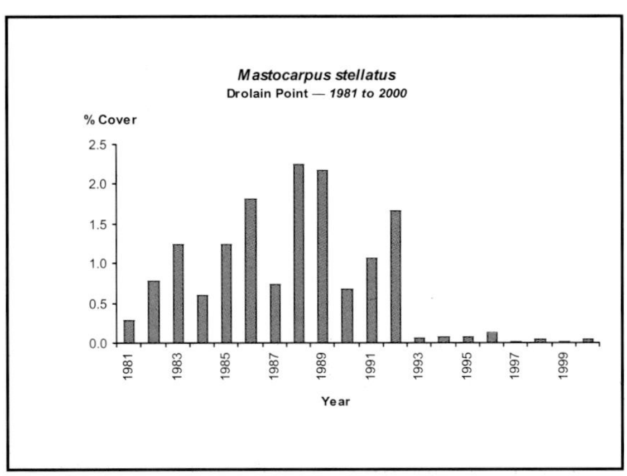

Figure 5.17

DROLAIN POINT

UNDERSTOREY

Gut Weed
Enteromorpha spp.
Líneáil ghorm

Gut weed *Enteromorpha* spp. was found mainly on the middle and lower shore at stations 6–14, although isolated plants occurred throughout the upper stations also.

Although this green seaweed was generally scarce, and never exceeded 1.4% cover per quadrat, there was variation through the year, increasing to a summer peak in June, July and August, then decreasing noticeably in September and October.

The 20-year period appeared to show three cycles of abundance for *Enteromorpha*. When recording started in 1981 cover was in fact at its maximum (at 0.9%). The next five years each showed a decrease down to 0.35% in 1986, followed by another peak of around 0.8% in 1987. Continuous decline was then recorded until 1994 (0.1%), but was followed by three years of increase to a 1997 peak (0.7%). This was followed again by three years of decreasing cover.

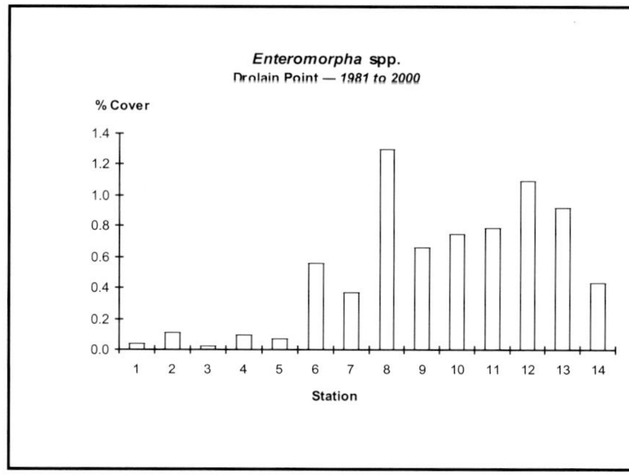

Figure 5.18

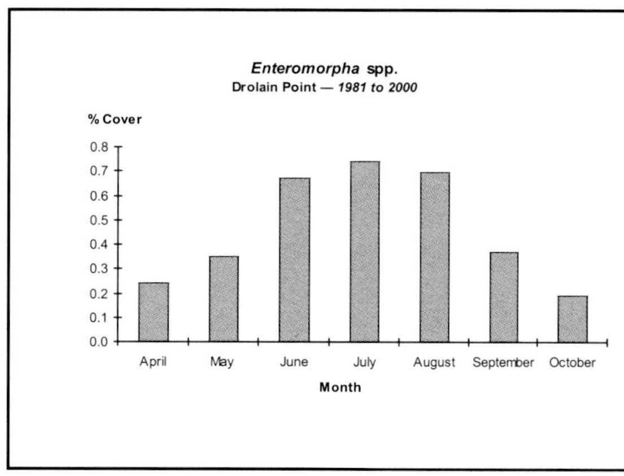

Figure 5.19

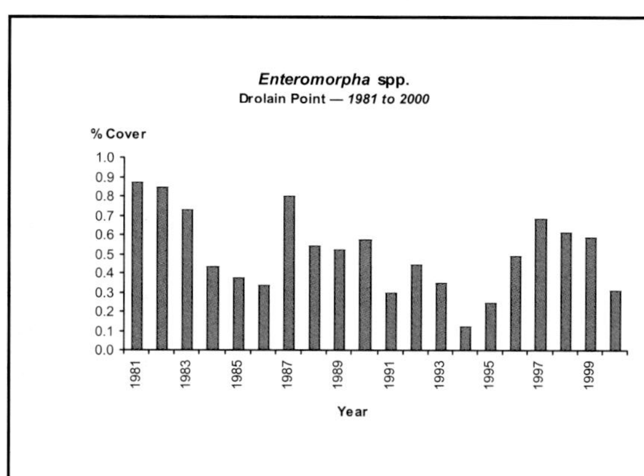

Figure 5.20

DROLAIN POINT

UNDERSTOREY

Sea Lettuce
Ulva lactuca
Glasán

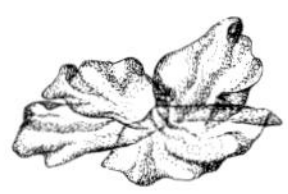

Although sea lettuce *Ulva lactuca* had been recorded in almost every station at Drolain Point, the predominant range was stations 10 to 13, with maximum cover of *ca.* 1.2% per quadrat occurring at station 10 on the lower part of the middle shore.

It was one of the species which showed a general decline in cover through the year, from peak April values (0.6%) to minimum values in October (0.2%). Within this pattern May showed an unexpected low value also.

Over the long-term, *Ulva lactuca* cover was varied; 1981–86 showed an overall decrease despite an exceptionally high cover in 1983; 1987–89 were consistently around 0.5% followed by low values around 0.1% in 1990 and 1991. 1992 saw the highest value (0.45%) of the 1990s, with an overall decrease thereafter.

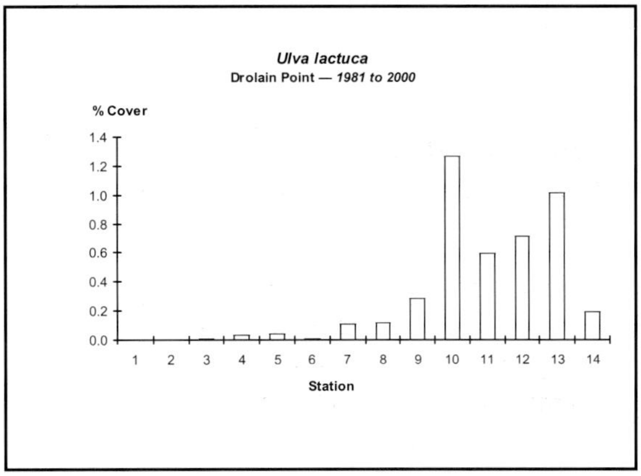

Figure 5.21

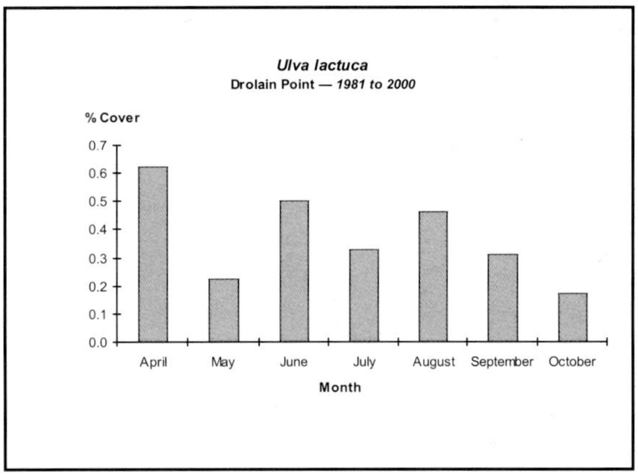

Figure 5.22

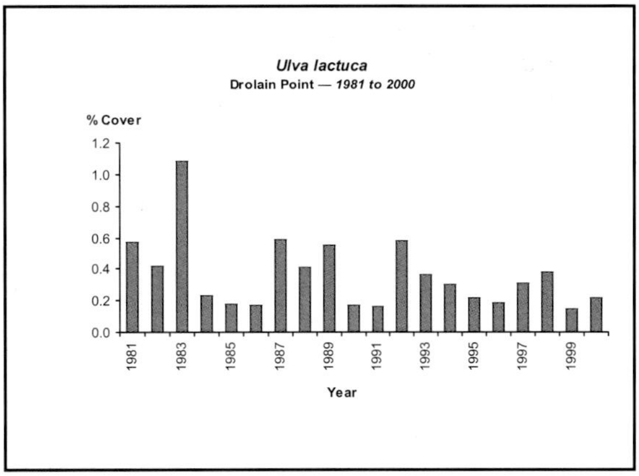

Figure 5.23

DROLAIN POINT

GROUND COVER

Barnacles

Semibalanus balanoides
Chthamalus stellatus
Chthamalus montagui
Elminius modestus
Giúrainn

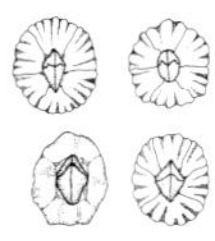

Barnacles were a major component of the dominant cover between stations 7 and 12, but their abundance peaked at stations 9–11 on the lower shore.

There was a small seasonal rise from around 33% cover per quadrat in April to 39% in May, and subsequent months showed no variation from this.

Barnacle cover increased throughout the 1980s from 12% in 1981 to 63% in 1990. A marked fall in cover was recorded in 1991 and a further reduction occurred in 1992. Percentage cover remained at the 1992 level for the rest of the decade. This pattern is similar to that for barnacles at the other sites (see p. 56, 99, 120).

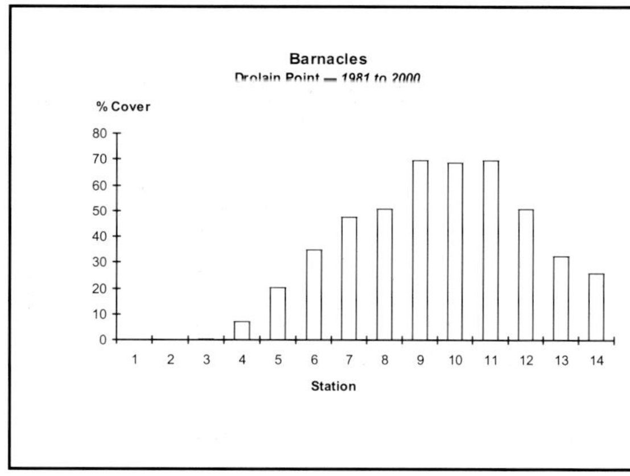

Figure 5.24

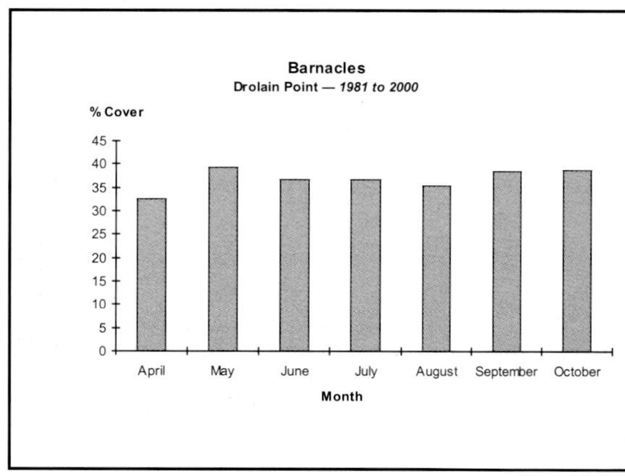

Figure 5.25

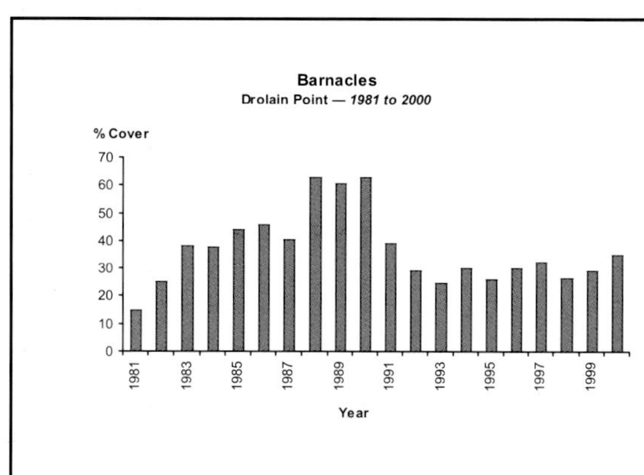

Figure 5.26

DROLAIN POINT

GROUND COVER

Barnacle Spat
Síol giúrainn

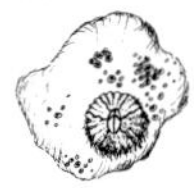

Spat were present over a wide range of the shore (stations 4–14). However the bulk of the spatfall occurred at stations 10–12, which was within the main distribution of the adult population.

The mean density per month ranged from 16/dm² to 65/dm² with the highest no./dm² being recorded in May. There was also a definite but smaller peak in September.

Between 1981 and 2000 barnacle spat were almost always recorded, but were absent from transect in 1981, 1984 and 1985. 1997 was an outstanding year when a density of 120/dm² was recorded. Spatfall was relatively good in 1997 at other sites also (e.g. Poulacurra p. 57; Globe Rocks p. 100; Horseshoe Harbour p. 121).

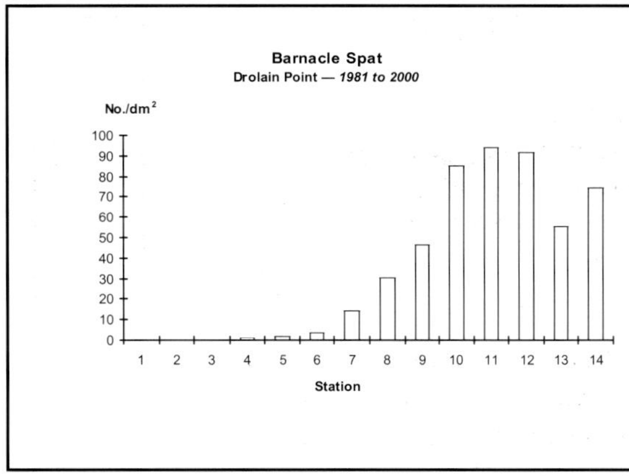

Figure 5.27

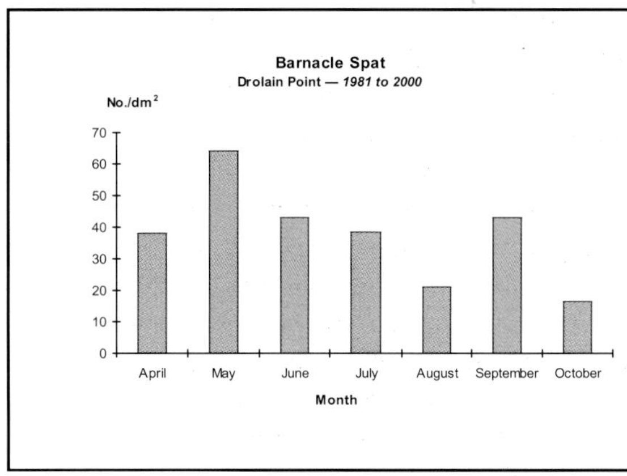

Figure 5.28

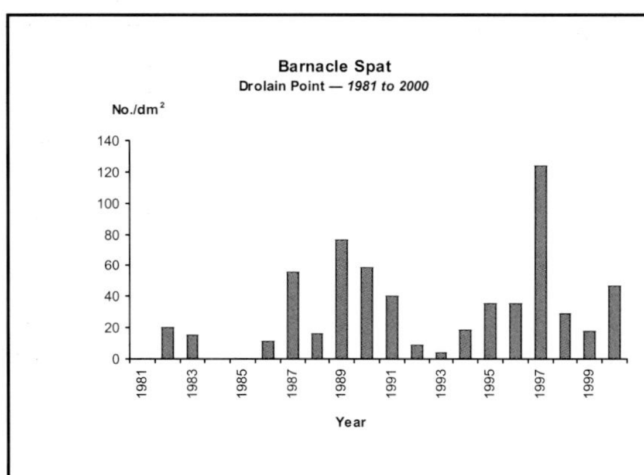

Figure 5.29

DROLAIN POINT

GROUND COVER

Common/Blue Mussel
Mytilus edulis
Diúilicín

The common mussel *Mytilus edulis* was present over much of the shore from station 5 down to station 14, with maximum density occurring at station 8 in the upper middle shore, and the bulk of the population occurring between stations 7 and 12. Records from the highest stations of occurrence (5 and 6) were made during June and July.

Cover varied little over the year. There was a small drop in density in July and August. However September and October densities were similar to those of April, May and June.

There was a general decline in abundance of *Mytilus edulis* at Drolain Point, from around 7% in the 1980s to less than 2.5% for much of the 1990s (1990–97). It has been interesting to record the relatively marked increase in cover in 1999 (5.7%) and 2000 (7%). In one particular year, 1986, mussels were unusually abundant, being almost double the general average for the years 1981–89. The large decline in 1990 and 1991 was similar to the mussel decline recorded at Poulacurra (see p. 58).

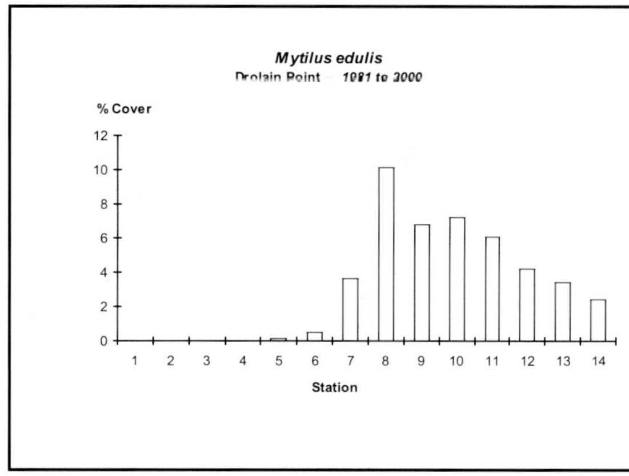

Figure 5.30

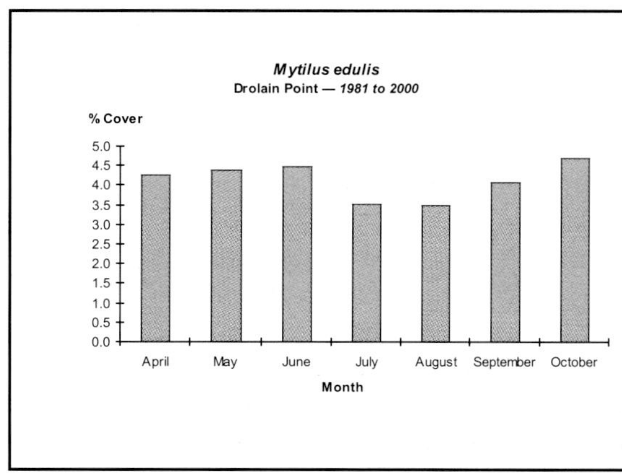

Figure 5.31

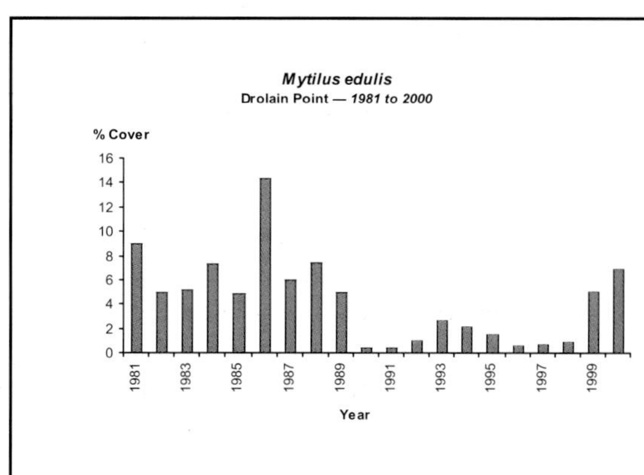

Figure 5.32

DROLAIN POINT

GRAZERS

Flat Periwinkle
Littorina obtusata
Faocha leathan

All five winkle species were recorded at Drolain Point: the flat *Littorina obtusata*, the edible *L. littorea*, the small *Melarhaphe neritoides*, the rough *Littorina saxatilis* and *L. neglecta*. *Littorina obtusata* was found mainly on the upper and middle shores, with maximum numbers at stations 6, 7, and 8. Only occasional individuals were recorded from stations 10 and below and it is likely that these animals were displaced from their "preferred" range by wave action.

There was marked seasonal variation in *Littorina obtusata*, with numbers in April almost ten times higher than during subsequent months. This suggests either that large numbers did not survive beyond April, or that downward migration took place. This is likely to have been a mechanism to avoid desiccation during the summer months, since the available intertidal algal habitat at Drolain Point was very limited.

Littorina obtusata was recorded in only 11 of the 20 years, and its density was very low (< 1 per quadrat) in all but one of these years, 1987, when it reached almost 6 per quadrat. Data were recorded consistently throughout the survey, thus the scarcity of animals is a real phenomenon (see p. 34).

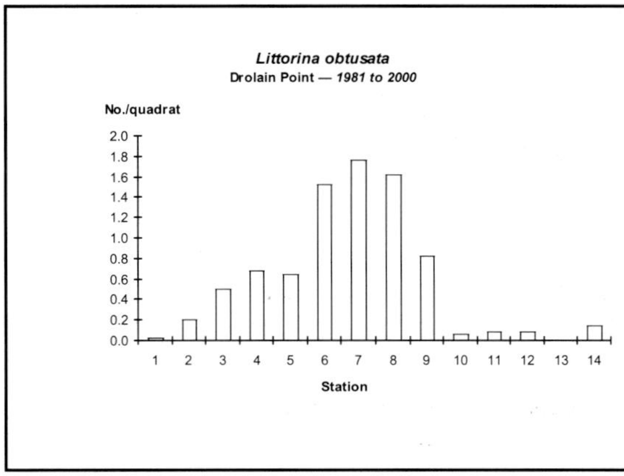

Figure 5.33

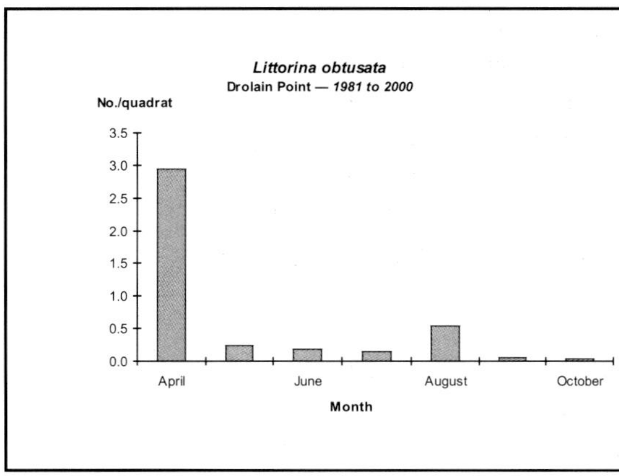

Figure 5.34

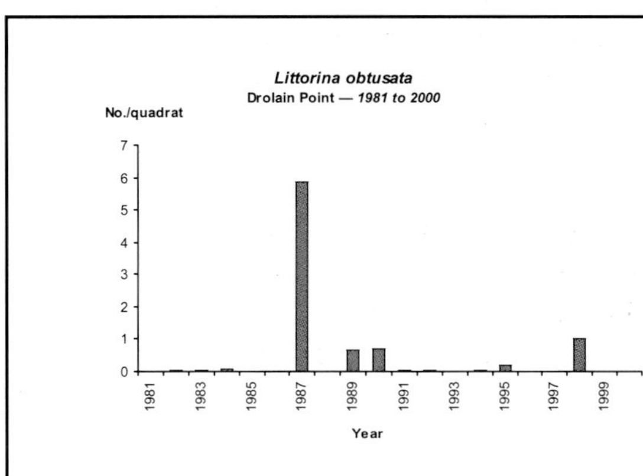

Figure 5.35

DROLAIN POINT

GRAZERS

Small Periwinkle
Melarhaphe neritoides
Faocha bheag

Numbers of the small periwinkle *Melarhaphe neritoides* peaked at stations 4–7 on the upper and middle shore, although they occurred along the entire transect.

Monthly variation was very small. There was a small drop in numbers during June and relatively high numbers in October

Melarhaphe neritoides was recorded every year between 1981 and 2000, but numbers fluctuated considerably. In the early 1980s numbers were only 1 or 2/dm^2, but from then on were usually 10/dm^2 or higher. There appear to have been two cycles of abundance, the first lasting from 1983–89, with peak numbers occurring during 1986; and the second from 1989–98, with peak numbers in 1996. Although the trend of increase from 1989–95/96 was slow and steady, the decline in numbers was not so regular. Within two years, numbers had halved (in 1998), only to rise abruptly the following year, 1999, to a third peak value of approximately 34/dm^2. Numbers in 2000 were down by about a third to approximately 25/dm^2.

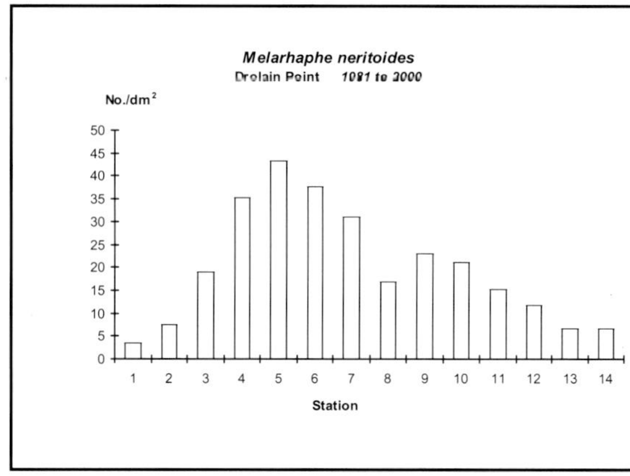

Figure 5.36

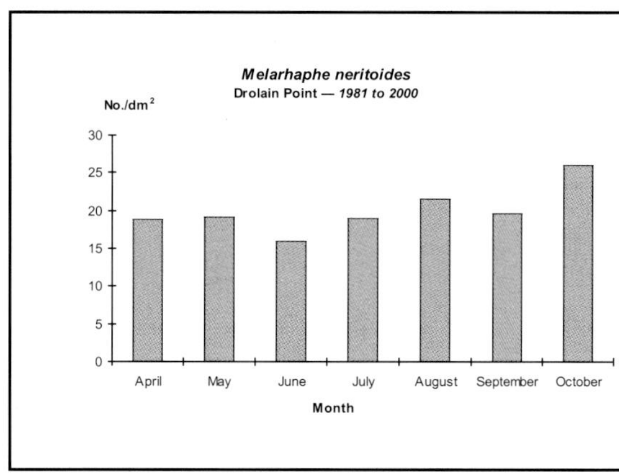

Figure 5.37

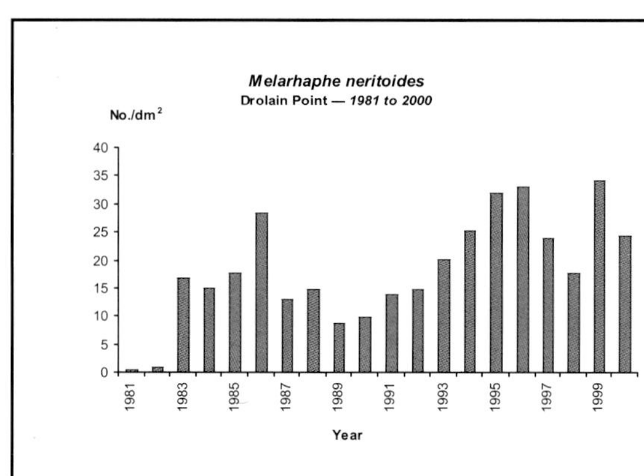

Figure 5.38

Channelled wrack *Pelvetia canaliculata,* a characteristic brown seaweed of the upper shore.

Channelled wrack *Pelvetia canaliculata* gets its name from the channelled appearance of the stipe and branches.

Spiral wrack *Fucus spiralis*, usually found on the upper shore in moderately and sheltered habitats.

Bladder wrack *Fucus vesiculosus*, often a dominant middle shore species.

A sheltered rocky shore at Kinish Narrows, Sherkin Island.

Knotted wrack *Ascophyllum nodosum* with the red seaweed *Polysiphonia* sp. growing on fronds.

Distinctive saw-like edge on the fronds of serrated wrack *Fucus serratus*.

Thong weed *Himanthalia elongata* floating on sea surface at mid tide. Inset: *Himanthalia* “buttons”.

Dabberlocks *Alaria esculenta*, showing the midrib and “wings” on the stipe.

Oarweed *Laminaria digitata* exposed at low tide.

Ceramium spp., a common red seaweed amongst the kelp holdfasts.

Zonation patterns on a steep moderately exposed rocky shore, with kelps and wracks on the lower shore and barnacles dominating the middle shore.

Gelidium spp., a red seaweed of the understorey.

Carrageen moss *Chondrus crispus.*

Mastocarpus stellatus, also known as carrageen moss, common on exposed shores.

Lomentaria articulata, a small red seaweed showing the characteristic branching and segmented structure.

Pepper dulse *Osmundea pinnatifida*, common amongst mussels on moderate and exposed shores.

Luxurious growth of gut weed *Enteromorpha* spp. on a sheltered shore.

The hollow tube-like fronds of *Enteromorpha* spp.

Bright green, flattened fronds of sea lettuce *Ulva lactuca*.

A cluster of mussels *Mytilus edulis* attached to the rocks by byssus threads.

Large numbers of small mussels creating a 'turf' of ground cover.

The fringed siphons of mussels as they filter-feed.

Mussels and barnacles dominating an exposed shore.

Barnacles; small numbers of *Semibalanus balanoides* amongst the predominant *Chthamalus stellatus*.

Australasian barnacle – *Elminius modestus*

Chthamalus spp. and spat.

Grey topshell *Gibbula cineraria.*

Purple topshell *Gibbula umbilicalis.*

Edible periwinkles *Littorina littorea* grazing the rocks of the lower shore.

Flat periwinkle *Littorina obtusata* on *Fucus* frond.

Rough periwinkle *Littorina saxatilis,* showing the typical ridges on the shell.

Small periwinkle *Melarhaphe neritoides* clustered in a crevice on the upper shore.

Limpets *Patella* spp. firmly anchored to the rock surface at low tide.

A rare glimpse of the foot, antennae and shell marginal tentacles of a limpet.

A key predator on the shore – the dogwhelk *Nucella lapillus* amongst its prey.

The vase-shaped eggs of the dogwhelk.

DROLAIN POINT

GRAZERS

Limpet
Patella spp.
Bairneach

The limpet *Patella* spp. occurred over much of the shore, from station 4 down to station 14, though the majority of individuals occurred at stations 7 down to 14, and numbers peaked at station 10.

Seasonal variation occurred with densities ranging from 31.5 per quadrat in April to slightly higher (40.6 per quadrat) in June. The general trend was one of very gradual increase and decrease through the year.

Annual mean density varied between 23.5 and 60.7 animals per quadrat, with relative peaks occurring in 1982, 1984, 1990 and 1999. The overall mean for the 20-year period was around 30 per quadrat and the population never fell below 20 per quadrat. Peak limpet densities at Poulacurra coincided in 1982 and 1999. (p. 61).

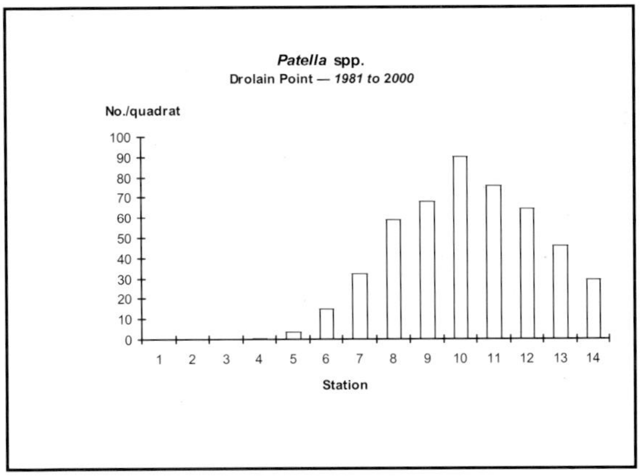

Figure 5.39

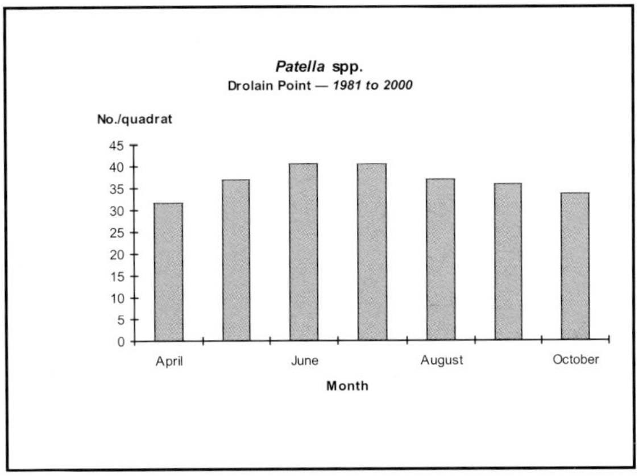

Figure 5.40

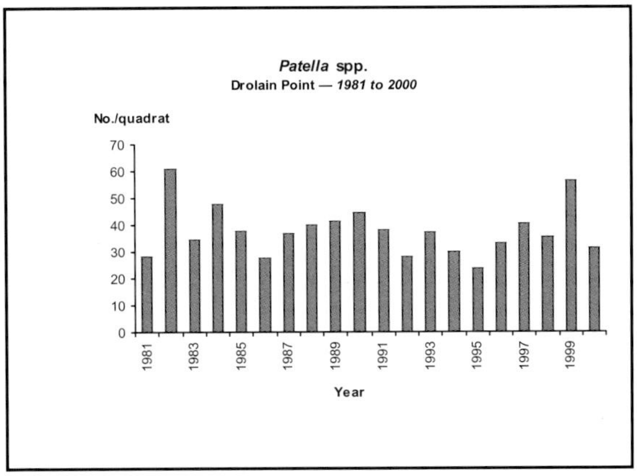

Figure 5.41

DROLAIN POINT

PREDATOR

Dogwhelk
Nucella lapillus
Cuachma chon

The main distribution zone of the predatory dogwhelk *Nucella lapillus* was between stations 7 and 10, with very low numbers also present up to station 5 and decreasing numbers below station 11.

Numbers were higher in the months of April and May (1.7 per quadrat) and subsequently decreased throughout the summer to a minimum in October (0.9 per quadrat).

Over the 20-year period the population changed considerably. For the first 10 years, 1981–90, numbers were generally around 2 per quadrat, although numbers peaked in 1989 at 3.1 per quadrat and then decreased sharply until 1991. The population then remained small (< 1 per quadrat) up until 2000.

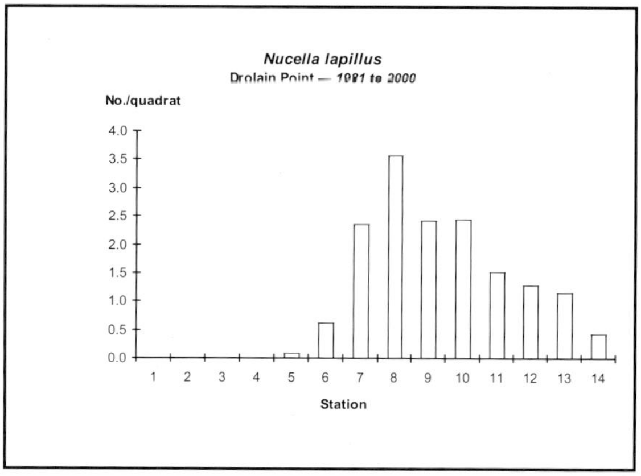

Figure 5.42

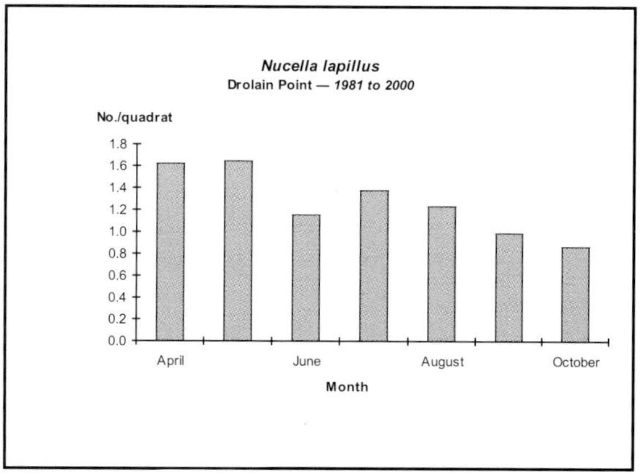

Figure 5.43

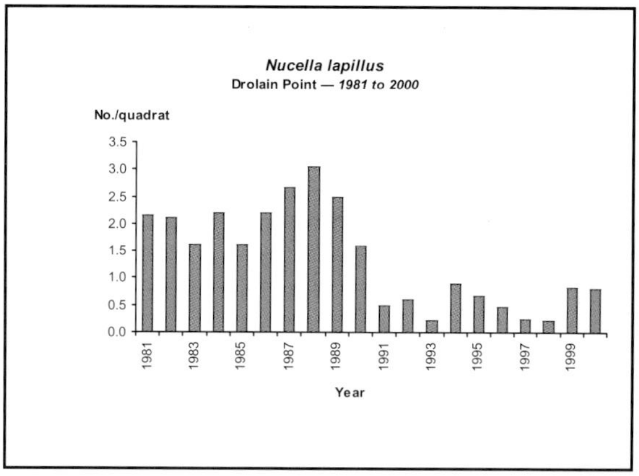

Figure 5.44

TRENDS FOR DROLAIN POINT 1981–2000

The 14 species analysed at Drolain Point all showed considerable variation in abundance over the 20-year period. Some appeared to have cycles of rise and fall, e.g. *Enteromorpha* spp. and *Melarhaphe neritoides*; others showed a marked difference in population size between the first and second ten years, e.g. *Mastocarpus stellatus, Mytilus edulis* and *Nucella lapillus*.

On the upper shore channelled wrack *Pelvetia canaliculata* cover was generally thicker in the 1980s than in the 1990s. This was most obvious in 1981, 1982, 1989 and 1990 when small periwinkles *Melarhaphe neritoides* were less abundant. *Melarhaphe neritoides* numbers were higher during the 1990s when *Pelvetia* was sparse. Even though flat periwinkles *Littorina obtusata* tend to live amongst the *Pelvetia*, their numbers have always been low at Drolain Point. The population explosion in 1987 was not sustained into 1988 – a year when *Pelvetia* was significantly low in cover.

On the middle and lower shore there was an increase in percentage cover of barnacles from 1981 to 1990, followed by a large loss of barnacles in 1991. The low density then remained stable during the 1990s. The good spatfall in 1997 had no apparent effect on the adult population in subsequent years. The mussel *Mytilus edulis* population was also much smaller throughout the 1990s, having fallen significantly from 1989–90. Dogwhelk *Nucella lapillus* numbers were very low after 1991, although numbers had started to decline in 1988, prior to the decline in mussels and barnacles. Limpets *Patella* spp. showed no dramatic sustained change in abundance over the 20 years; the isolated peaks in 1982 and 1999 bore no relation to the cover of any algal species.

On the lower shore, where the distribution of sea lettuce *Ulva lactuca* and limpets overlap, there was likewise no consistent relationship between their two annual graphs. However there was one occurrence when the limpet population was exceptionally dense in 1982, declining in 1983, a year in which *Ulva* showed a large increase. With the exception of 1998, serrated wrack *Fucus serratus* was absent or very sparse from 1993 onwards; so too were thong weed *Himanthalia elongata* and the two carrageens *Chondrus crispus* and *Mastocarpus stellatus*. *Chondrus* had in fact only shown an increase in two separate years (1983 and 1989) whereas *Mastocarpus* was relatively rich for the first 12 years and was absent or sparse from 1993.

Several of the trends noted above show good correlation to trends at Poulacurra, for example barnacles and mussels declined between 1989 and 1991, Irish Moss declined in the 1990s, and there was an increase in small periwinkles at both sites in the 1990s. Although limpet cycles were not very conspicuous at either site, the years of peak and trough abundance were the same.

Chapter Six

Moderately Exposed Shores

Globe Rocks

Figure 6.1 Globe Rocks from the east, showing Kinish Harbour behind.

Globe Rocks lies on the east coast of Sherkin (Figure 6.1). The shore faces southeast and lies in the sheltered, shallow waters of Baltimore Harbour. However, the site displays all the characteristics of a moderately exposed rocky shore, even though it is not directly open to oceanic swell or southwesterly winds. This is due mainly to the considerable wave energy which is refracted and focussed at the harbour entrance between Baltimore and Sherkin Island. The waves sweep along the site rather than perpendicular to it.

The gently sloping shore comprises bedrock of the Sherkin formation whose strata lie in an almost vertical plane and are heavily fissured. The many crevices form a refuge habitat for the mobile grazers and predators. There are no boulders overlying the rock. Since the survey began, the physical nature of the lower shore has changed and the modified profile as shown below has a steep lower shore zone. This was caused by a piece of rock splitting off. With the more gentle profile of the earlier years, an additional two stations were surveyed, but these were lost.

The horizontal distance of the transect across the shore is 8.49 m and the vertical distance is 2.7 m., giving a gradient of 0.32. Ten stations are usually recorded, with up to 13 (in the early years) on good low spring tides. Stations 1–4 form the upper shore, stations 5–8 the middle shore and station 9 and below the lower shore. Station 1 is 4.3 m above chart datum.

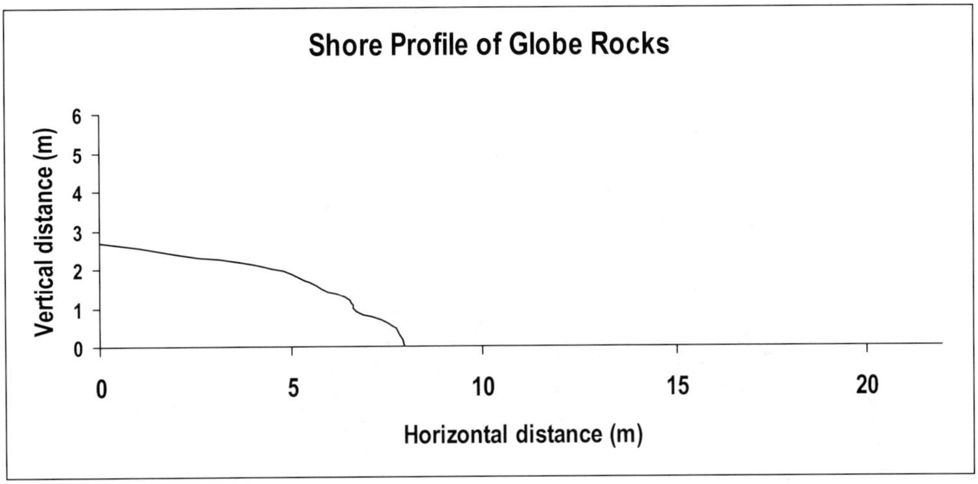

Figure 6.2 A cross-section of the shore from top to bottom showing the gently sloping upper zone and steeper lower zone of the Globe Rocks transect.

VISUAL DOMINANTS

In the splash zone lichen cover was poor, despite the fact that species diversity was high and 12 species were recorded; large areas of bare rock were present.

Beneath this the upper shore had occasional channelled wrack *Pelvetia canaliculata* plants but was dominated by barnacles. There was no appreciable fucoid cover here and spiral wrack *Fucus spiralis* was very sparse on the upper shore. This was most likely due to the vertical rock faces presented by the fractured rock strata. Fucoid density was minimal until almost halfway down the shore.

The middle shore was barnacle dominated with associated limpets, dogwhelks and occasional clumps of small mussels.

The lower shore was fucoid dominated, with oarweed *Laminaria digitata* also present from station 8 downward.

ALGAE

The algal community on the middle and lower shore was moderately developed. A total of 99 species were recorded, with a further 22 taxa identified to genus only.

Highlight on Seaweed Species

Ephemeral Green Algae

The various species of the algae *Enteromorpha* are quite variable in shape. However they are distinguished from *Ulva* by their hollow, cylindrical structure as compared to the single flat layer of cells of the frond of *Ulva*. *Ulva* and *Enteromorpha* are quite closely related, being in the same family (Ulvaceae). Five species of *Enteromorpha* were recorded at Globe Rocks (and Kinish Narrows East). *E. intestinalis* was the most frequently recorded, with *E. compressa* occurring occasionally. *E. muscoides* and *E. prolifera* were each recorded in a single year.

Ulva lactuca was one of about four species of green algae commonly recorded on the Sherkin shores. *Prasiola stipitata* and *Blidingia minima* grow on the upper shore, but many of the green algae are likely to be found at any level. They were always present in very small amounts, for example isolated plants.

Several species of green seaweed, such as *Spongomorpha aeruginosa* and *Derbesia marina,* grow epiphytically.

Gut Weed – *Enteromorpha intestinalis*

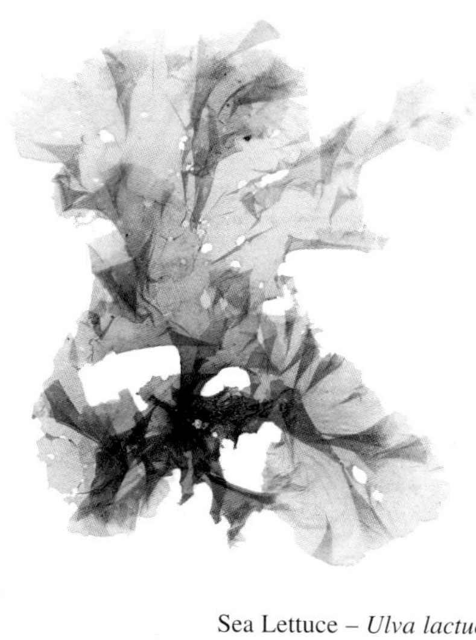

Sea Lettuce – *Ulva lactuca*

Brown Algae

A total of 24 taxa of brown algae were recorded from Globe Rocks, 19 of which were identified to species level. The most commonly occurring smaller plants – which are not so visible as the wracks – include *Cladostephus spongiosus* and various epiphytes such as *Elachista fucicola, Ectocarpus siliculosus, Leathesia difformis* and *Spongonema tomentosum.*

Red Algae

Sixty four species of red algae were recorded on the transect, with an additional ten taxa identified to genus only. Many of these species, for example *Plumaria plumosa,* were present as small plants under the wracks and kelp in the bottom two stations.

Ceramium rubrum and *C. shuttleworthianum* were the most common species of *Ceramium* present, although a total of nine *Ceramium* species have been found in all. Eleven species of *Polysiphonia* were also recorded, the most common being *Polysiphonia lanosa.*

Of the large foliose species growing epiphytically on kelp (*Nitophyllum punctatum, Palmaria palmata, Polysiphonia* spp., *Rhodomela confervoides, Rhodymenia pseudopalmata*) only *Palmaria palmata* was common.

Green Algae

Twenty three taxa of green algae were recorded at Globe Rocks, with 16 recorded to species level. These include two species of *Chaetomorpha* (*C. linum* and *C. mediterranea*), four species of *Cladophora* (*C. albida, C. hutchinsiae, C. rupestris* and *C. sericea*) and five species of *Enteromorpha* (*E. compressa, E. intestinalis, E. linza, E. prolifera* and *E. muscoides*). All were short-lived on the shore in the summer months. Sea lettuce *Ulva lactuca* was the only green algal species recorded every year.

Lichens

Although the splash zone was very compressed at Globe Rocks, 12 species of lichen were recorded. As well as the common and dominant *Caloplaca marina, Lecanora atra, Lichina pygmaea, Verrucaria maura, V. mucosa* and *Xanthoria parietina,* there were occasional records of *Caloplaca thallincola*, a recent (1999) record of *Haematomma ventosum, Ochrolechia parella* in several years and one record of *Ochrolechia frigida. Ramalina siliquosa* was also commonly recorded.

Animals

A total of 111 animal taxa were recorded at Globe Rocks, 93 being identified to species level. Sea mats were well represented (12 species) and nine species of sea squirt were found, which is several more than at the more exposed shores of Poulacurra (three species) and Drolain Point (five species). Seven anemone species occurred in the small rock pools and damp crevices beneath the algal canopy on the lower shore. These were

Highlight on Lichens

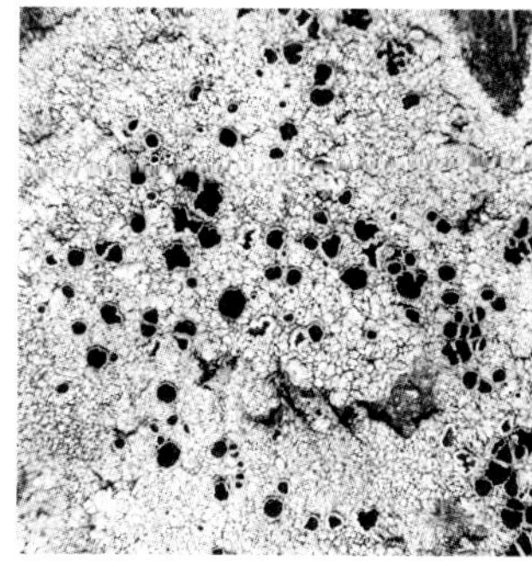
Black Shields – *Lecanora atra*

Lichens, part alga and part fungus, are responsible for the bright colours of the splash zone. Yellow *Xanthoria parietina*, orange *Caloplaca marina*, grey *Lecanora atra* and black *Verrucaria maura* were found on all our seven shores to a greater or lesser extent; greater on the exposed and very exposed shores and lesser elsewhere, such as at Globe Rocks. The black tufts of *Lichina pygmaea* were also noticeable at Globe Rocks, present from the top to the middle of the shore. A huge number of tiny animals live amongst its fronds and holdfasts – young periwinkles, small isopods, insect larvae and mites. The lichen is probably a food source for them all. Although not recorded on the Sherkin sites, a common species associated with *Lichina pygmaea* is the tiny bivalve *Lasaea rubra*, which uses the plant for shelter only.

Actinia equina (recorded every year), *Anemonia viridis, Aulactinia verrucosa, Cereus pedunculatus, Corynactis viridis, Urticina felina* and *Sagartia elegans*. Other cnidaria found in one or two years only were *Alcyonium digitatum* (1984) and *Coryne muscoides* (1983). With the exception of *Dynamena pumila*, hydroids were not common, the only records being *Laomedea flexuosa* (1984) and *Obelia geniculata* (1997).

There was an interesting range of crab species, all recorded occasionally, with *Pirimela denticulata, Necora puber, Pinnotheres pisum, Xantho incisus* and *Porcellana platycheles* in addition to the more easily recognised *Carcinus maenas, Cancer pagurus* and the hermit crab *Pagurus bernhardus*.

As well as the winkies, mussels and dogwhelks, which were consistently present at Globe Rocks, a number of other mollusc species were recorded occasionally. These included the top shells *Calliostoma zizyphinum* (1983–89, 1991, 1993, 1997 and 1998), *Gibbula cineraria* (1987, 1988, 1990–93, 1996, 1997 and 1999), *Gibbula umbilicalis* (unrecorded only in 1982–84 and 1988) and two species of dogwhelk *(Hinia incrassata* and *H. reticulata*).

Highlight on Topshells, Bivalves and other Molluscs

Purple Topshell – *Gibbula umbilicalis*

Topshells are conical in shape and often very beautiful. They are in the same molluscan group as limpets even though their outer shell shapes are completely different. Each topshell species has characteristic reddish or purple markings on its shell of grey, green or yellow and pink, and beneath these markings all have a layer of mother-of-pearl which can clearly be seen around the mouth and on older shells. They all have a horny operculum, which can close off the mouth when the animal withdraws completely into the shell. All are grazers and browse off algae on rock surfaces or the fronds of larger algae. The grey topshell *Gibbula cineraria* and the painted topshell *Calliostoma zizyphinum* occur on the lower shore, whereas the purple topshell *G. umbilicalis* is found on the middle and lower shore. Both *G. cineraria* and *Calliostoma* continue into the sublittoral. The long gelatinous ribbons of eggs laid by this topshell have occasionally been recorded on the shore.

There were occasional records on the lower shore of the saddle oyster *Anomia ephippium*, the sea slug *Archidoris pseudoargus* (known as the sea lemon) and the blue-rayed limpet *Helcion pellucidum*. The sea lemon is associated with and feeds on the breadcrumb sponge *Halichondria panicea* and only ventures onto the shore in summer. In winter it retreats to deeper water. The blue-rayed limpet is associated with kelp stipes and holdfasts, often migrating onto the fronds in summer months.

The saddle oyster is a bivalve, although it is difficult to see both valves. The upper valve is cemented to the rocks by hard, chalky byssus threads and the lower valve is pressed tightly to the rocks.

Species analysed for Globe Rocks, their place in the food chain and the shore ecology (Predatory pathway ——► Grazing pathway ••••••►)

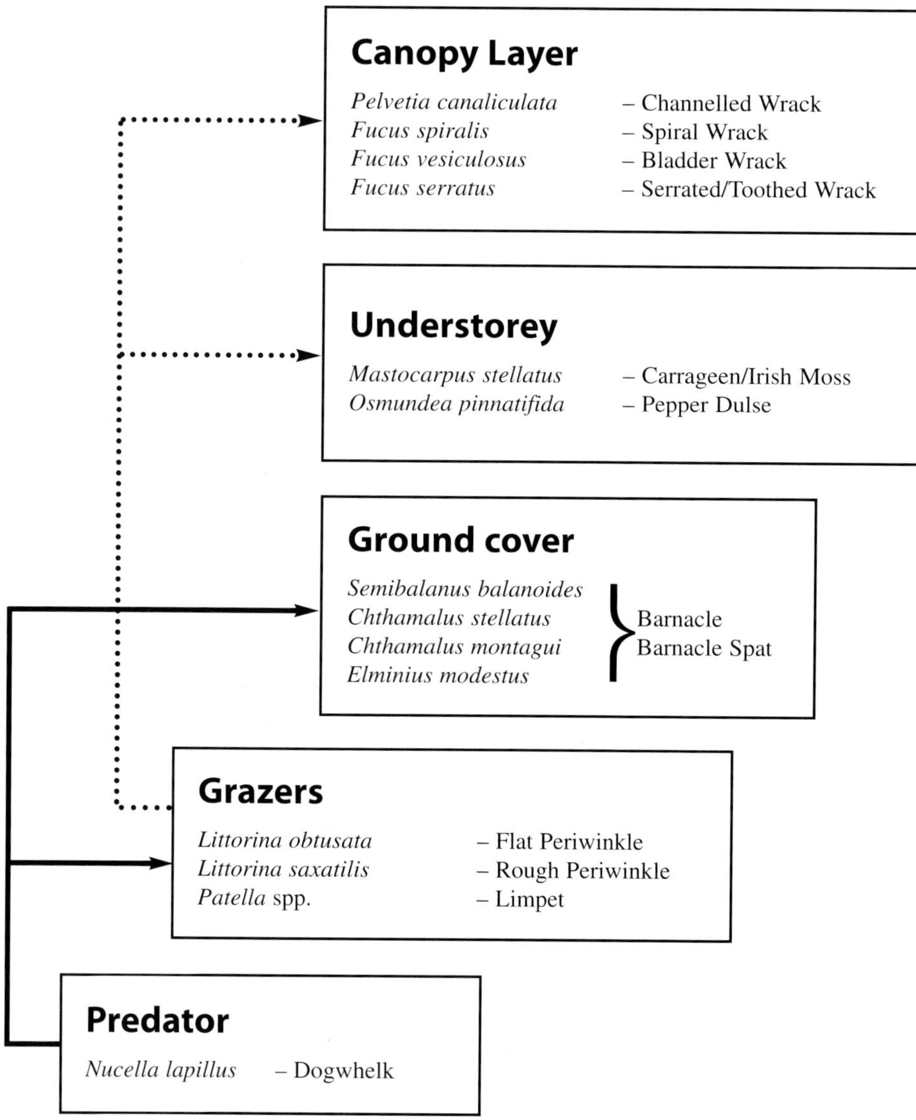

GLOBE ROCKS

CANOPY LAYER

Channelled Wrack *Pelvetia canaliculata* Caisíneach

Channelled wrack *Pelvetia canaliculata* occurred primarily at stations 3 and 4 on the upper shore where it formed a narrow band, never reaching more than 4.5% cover per quadrat.

There was a small increase in cover in May followed by a steady reduction month by month until October. The decline from August to September was the most marked.

1983 was an exceptionally good year for the *Pelvetia canaliculata* population, when percentage cover almost doubled from the 1981 and 1982 level. A sharp decline was recorded in 1984 and cover throughout 1984/85 was exceptionally low at less than 0.5%. For the nine-year period 1986–94 the species fluctuated between 1% and 2% cover, with even lower levels (< 0.5%) being observed after this. Similar low levels for *Pelvetia* were recorded at Drolain Point throughout the 1990s (see p.71).

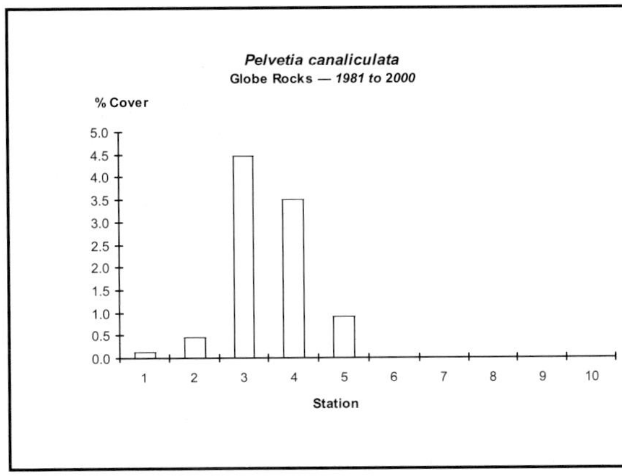

Figure 6.3

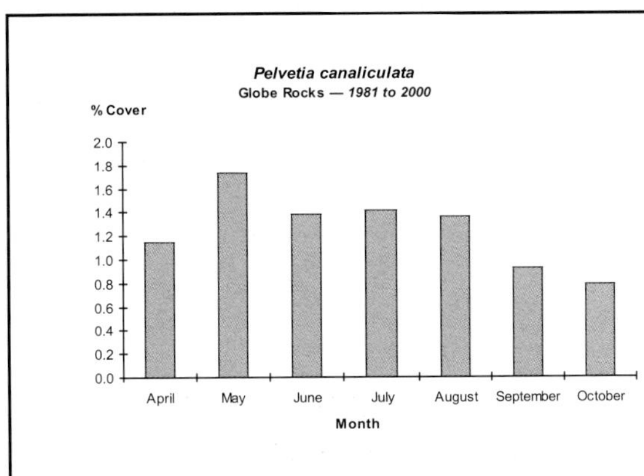

Figure 6.4

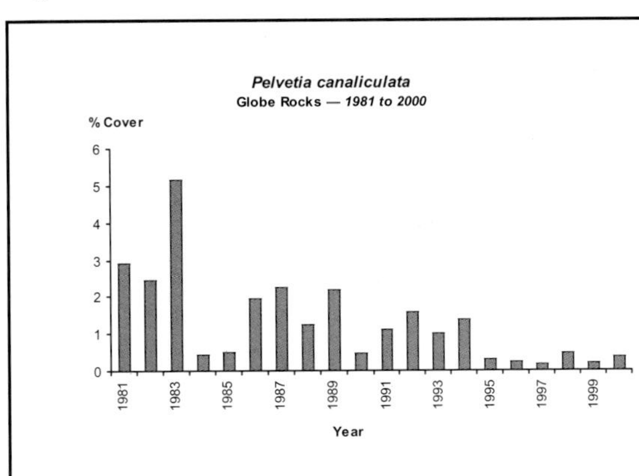

Figure 6.5

GLOBE ROCKS

CANOPY LAYER

Spiral Wrack
Fucus spiralis
Casfheamainn

Spiral Wrack *Fucus spiralis* was found in every quadrat on the transect; however plants at stations 1–5 were very small. The species occurred primarily at stations 6–10 with a pronounced peak density at station 6 on the mid shore.

From spring through to early autumn percentage cover varied, with a maximum of 1.4% in July. Cover in August fell significantly to 0.5% and remained low into the autumn months.

Over the survey period there were good and bad years with 1988 showing an exceptionally high percentage cover at 3.5%. In all other years cover was 1% or less. It was absent in 1982 and very sparse in 1981, 1984, 1986 and 1999.

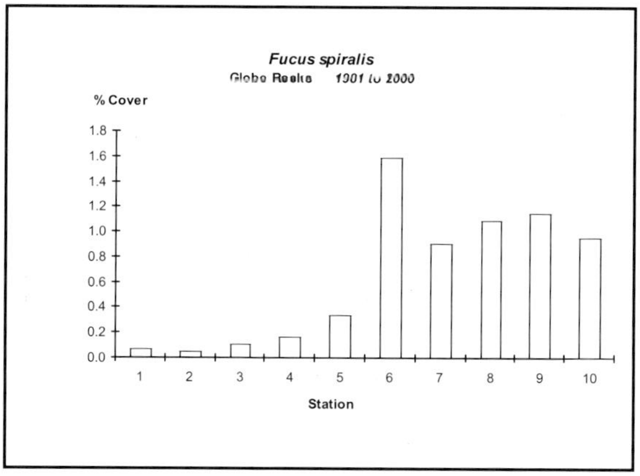

Figure 6.6

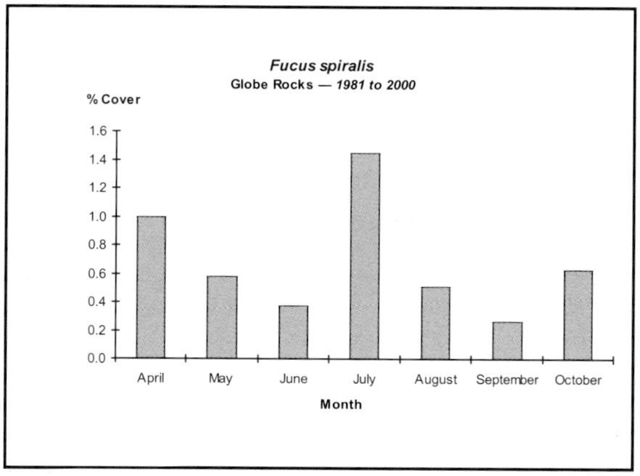

Figure 6.7

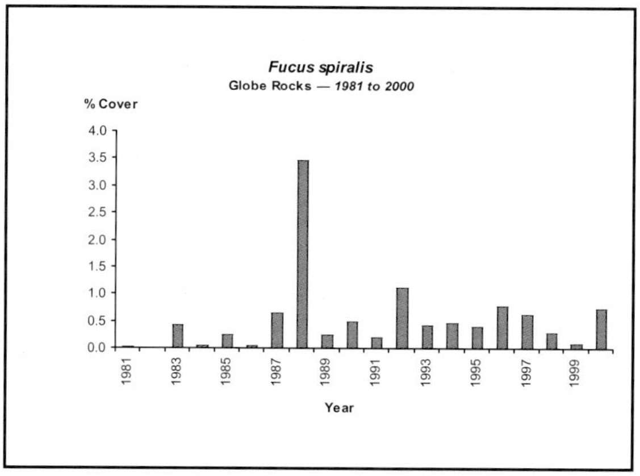

Figure 6.8

GLOBE ROCKS

CANOPY LAYER

Bladder Wrack
Fucus vesiculosus
Feamainn bhoilgíneach

Bladder wrack *Fucus vesiculosus* formed part of the dominant cover on the lower middle and lower shore. It occurred mainly at stations 6–10 and its distribution peaked at station 9. There were a few isolated plants in the upper shore quadrats (3, 4 and 5) and it was also recorded occasionally below the lowest point of the transect.

There was a marked seasonal variation as it appeared to increase to a peak in September, then fell away in October.

Until 1997 density of *Fucus vesiculosus* accounted for only a very small percentage cover of the rock (≤ 1% per quadrat). There was a significant isolated increase in 1989, followed by very low (< 0.3%) level each year until 1994 when cover again reached 0.5%. This level was sustained for 3 years and was followed by a big increase during 1997 (doubling) only to fall back the following year. 1999 saw a significant increase to 1.5% and a further large increase in the year 2000 up to 3.5% cover. This represents more than a fivefold increase over the general level of 1981–96.

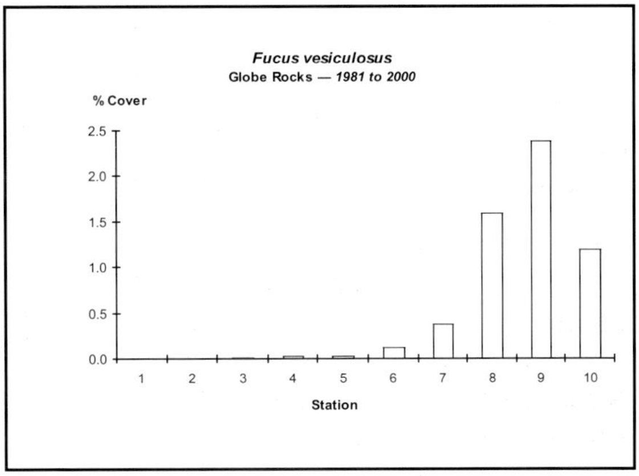

Figure 6.9

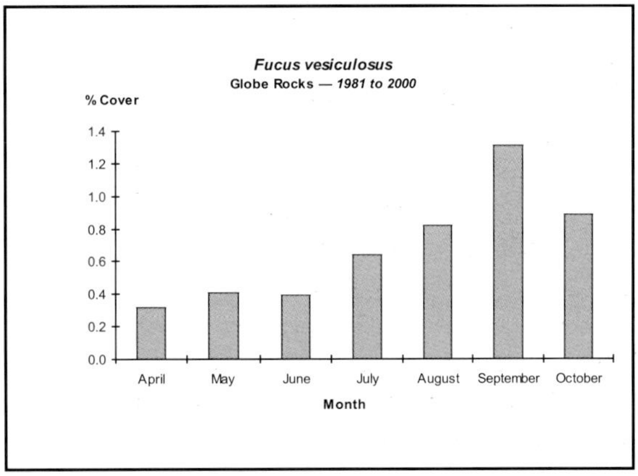

Figure 6.10

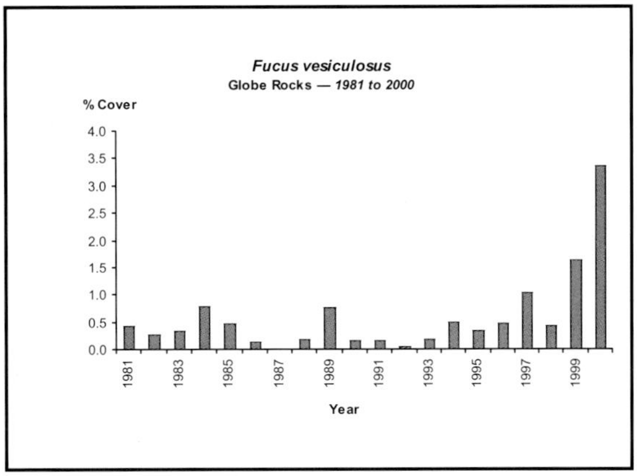

Figure 6.11

GLOBE ROCKS

CANOPY LAYER

Serrated/Toothed Wrack
Fucus serratus
Mioránach

The distribution of serrated wrack *Fucus serratus* was broadly similar to that of bladder wrack *F. vesiculosus* at Globe Rocks, being present from stations 7–10 with occasional plants at stations 5 and 6. It also occurred in the lowest stations (11, 12 and 13) which were not recorded every year. Maximum density was at station 10.

Fucus serratus showed little variation in density from spring through to autumn, with a slight decrease in May, a marked increase in cover in June, and no significant differences between the other months.

However, considerable annual variation was recorded. *Fucus serratus* was consistently less abundant on the shore in the 1990s than in the 1980s, and there was an overall trend of reduction in cover between 1988 and 2000. Cover was at its maximum in 1984 at 17%. There were exceptionally large decreases from 1985–86, 1989–90 and 1991–92. After 1995 the overall mean cover was just under 5%, but there was a trend of decrease evident in the six years 1995–2000.

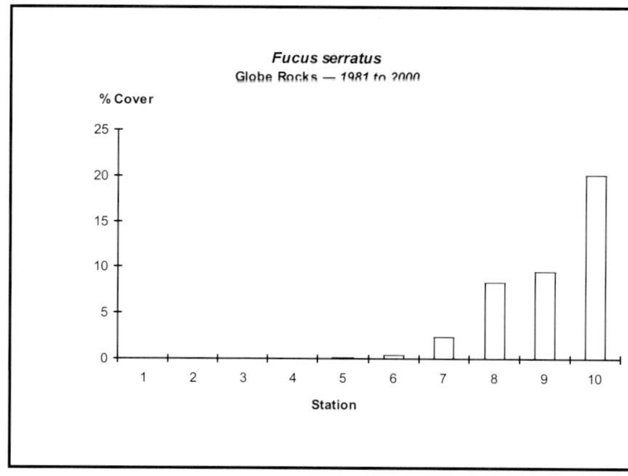

Figure 6.12

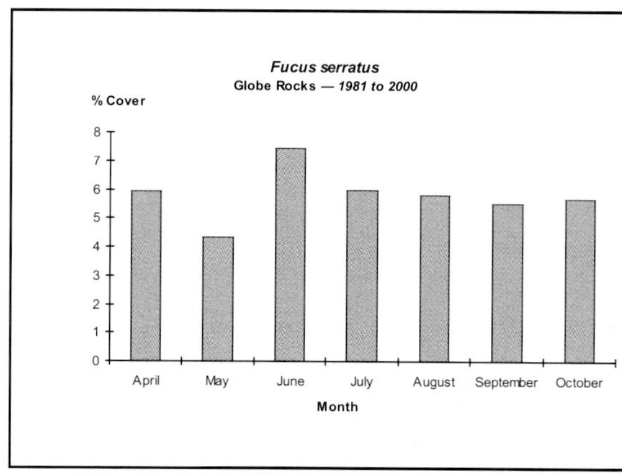

Figure 6.13

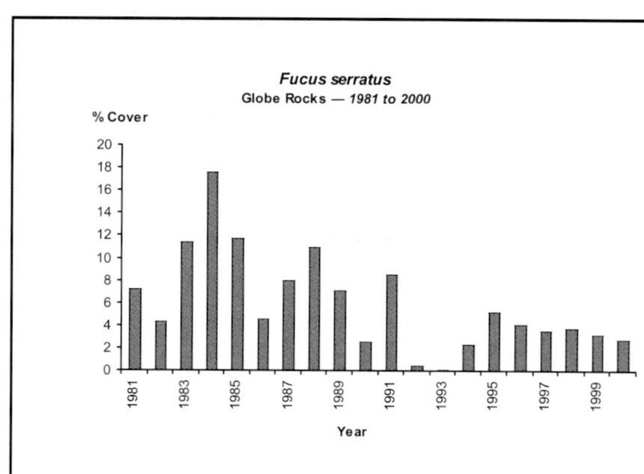

Figure 6.14

GLOBE ROCKS

UNDERSTOREY

Carrageen/Irish Moss
Mastocarpus stellatus
Clúimhín cait

The carrageen moss *Mastocarpus stellatus* occurred primarily on the lower shore with its maximum abundance at station 10. When tides allowed access to stations 11–14 the species was often recorded at this level. On the middle shore at stations 4–7, there were a few isolated plants which amount to < 1% cover per quadrat.

The abundance of *Mastocarpus stellatus* varied a little through thc year, the main change being the increase in cover from April through to June and a drop in July.

Mastocarpus stellatus was present in the understorey throughout the survey, but the number of plants varied. Cover increased steadily from 1981–85 and then crashed dramatically to just a few isolated plants during 1986 and 1987. Growth and cover were relatively prolific in 1988 and 1989, but from then on were consistently low at 2% or less. Like the wrack *Fucus serratus,* there was a general decline between 1986 and 2000.

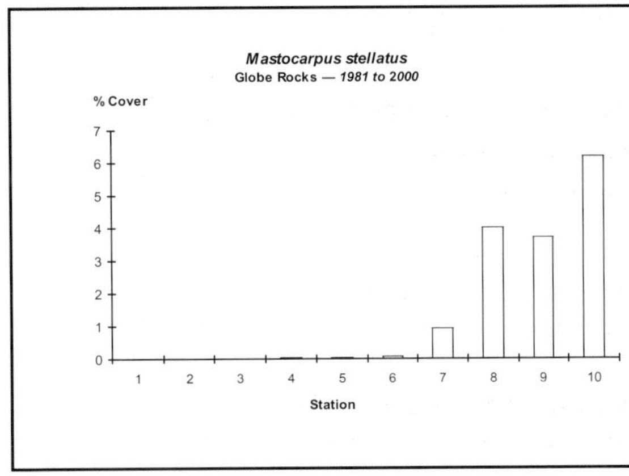

Figure 6.15

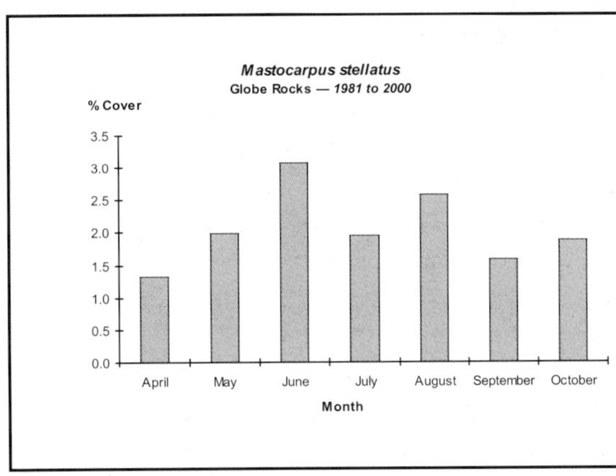

Figure 6.16

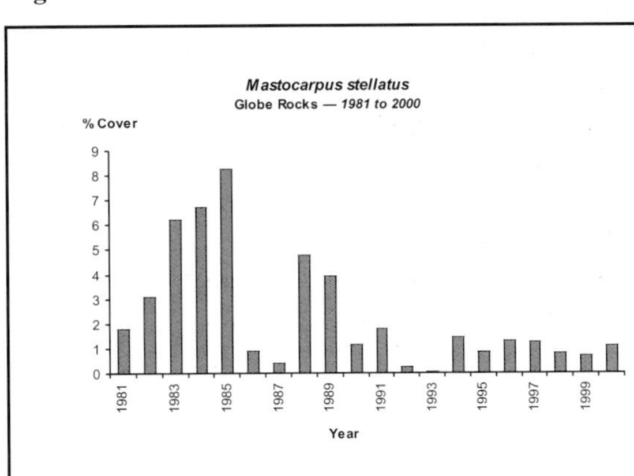

Figure 6.17

GLOBE ROCKS

UNDERSTOREY

Pepper Dulse
Osmundea pinnatifida
Míobhán

Common beneath the fucoids, the range of pepper dulse *Osmundea pinnatifida* was from station 4 to station 10, with maximum levels of 5% per quadrat at stations 8, 9 and 10.

There was little seasonal variation, the only significant difference in cover being an increase from July to August.

Long-term variation in cover was recorded with *Osmundea pinnatifida* exceptionally abundant in 1986 and 1987. Prior to this it occupied about 2–5% cover per quadrat, and in general it was at about 2% cover (or less) between 1988 and 1999. However there were exceptionally few plants present during 1991, 1992 and 1993; and in the year 2000 there was a relatively large increase in density to 3%.

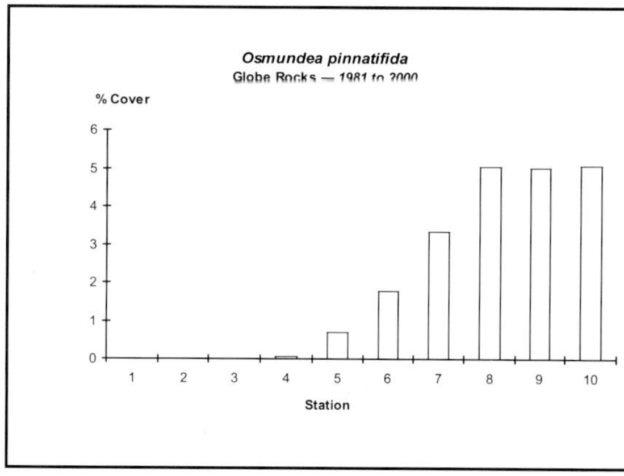

Figure 6.18

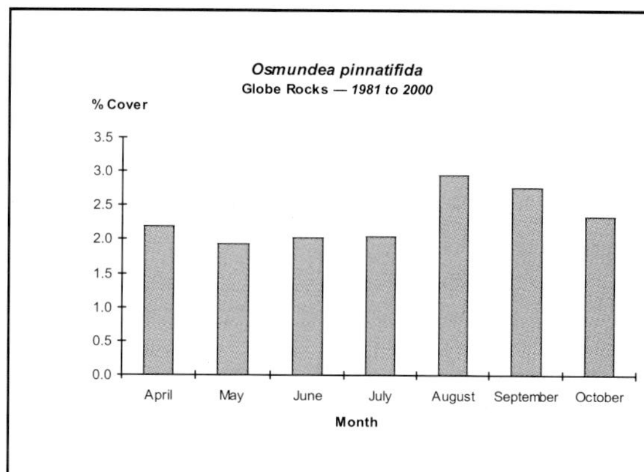

Figure 6.19

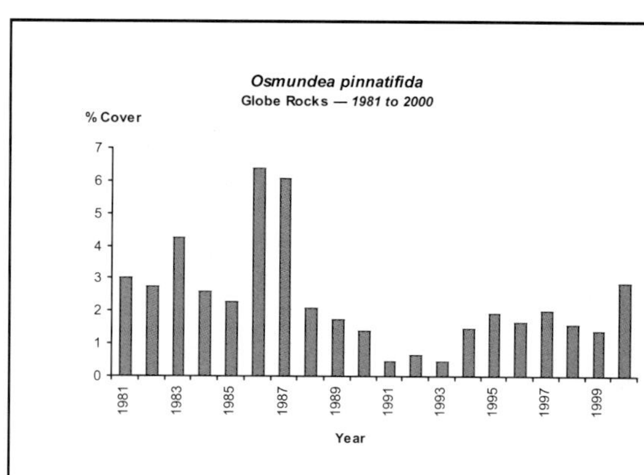

Figure 6.20

GLOBE ROCKS

GROUND COVER

Barnacles

Semibalanus balanoides
Chthamalus stellatus
Chthamalus montagui
Elminius modestus
Giúrainn

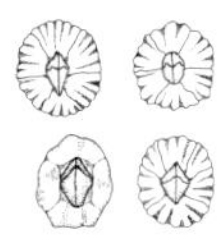

Barnacles formed the dominant ground cover over the upper and middle shores at Globe Rocks despite the fact that there was always a certain amount of bare rock visible in the upper shore stations. Present from station 1 down to station 10, their density peaked at station 6 at almost 80% cover per quadrat. Between stations 5 and 9 barnacles attained more than 50% cover and visually dominated the middle shore.

Month by month variation was not significant – the mean monthly figure varied from 36% in April to 40–44% in most other months.

Annual variation was however more pronounced: from the lowest recorded annual density of 17% in 1981, a major increase occurred during 1984, and a further steady increase was seen until 1986 (62%); 1987 saw a fall in numbers followed by a fairly steady rise to just over 60% in 1990. The following year, 1991, there was a huge drop in cover to 25%, followed by a rise to 37% the following year, and after that barnacle density climbed steadily to the 2000 figure of 49% cover.

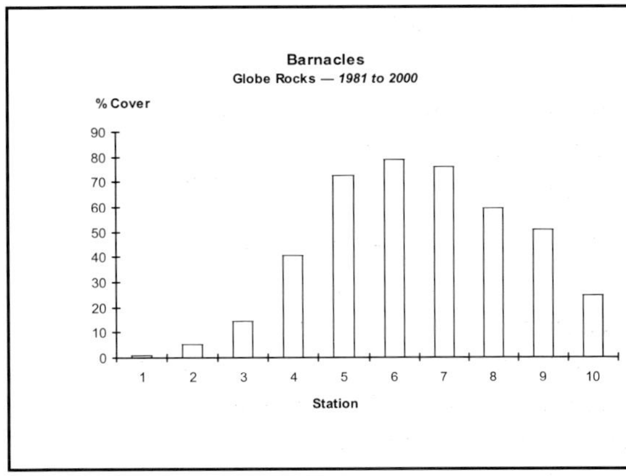

Figure 6.21

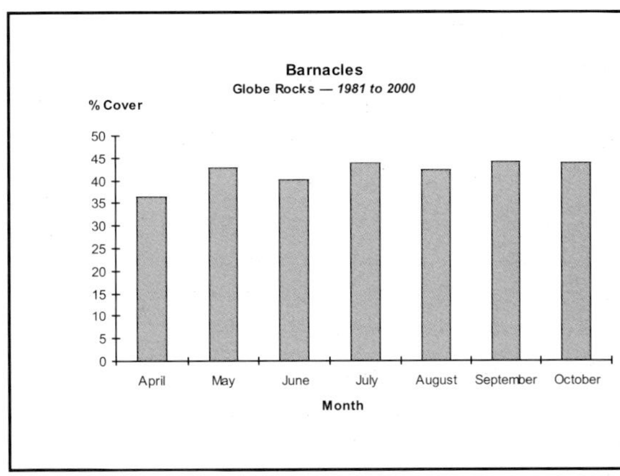

Figure 6.22

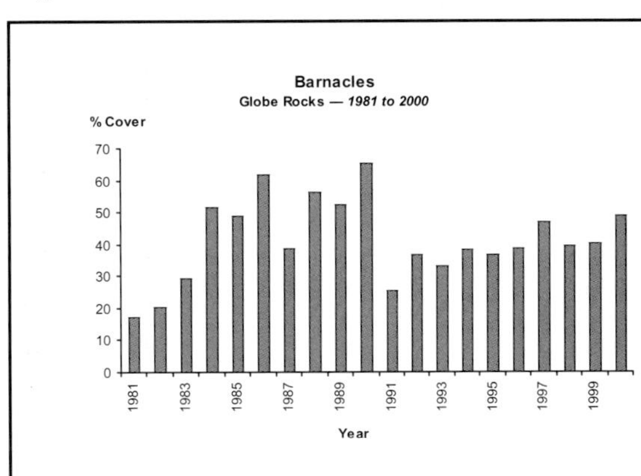

Figure 6.23

GLOBE ROCKS

GROUND COVER

Barnacle Spat
Síol giúrainn

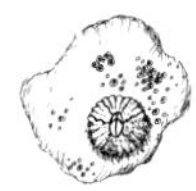

Barnacle spat were not recorded in the highest stations (1 and 2) and presented in small clusters at stations 3 and 4. Density then increased markedly from stations 5 to 8 over the middle shore zone, until the spat were found in their highest numbers on the lower middle and lower shore, with a maximum of 142/dm² at station 8.

As expected, abundance was seasonal with highest numbers occuring in April (147/dm²) and a second smaller peak in August (85/dm²). Apart from this there was an overall decrease following the April spatfall.

Although barnacle spat were deliberately searched for during surveys, there were two years, 1984 and 1985, when no spatfall was recorded at Globe Rocks. Spat were similarly absent at Poulacurra in 1985 (p. 57) and Drolain Point in 1984 and 1985 (p. 79). Spatfall in other years was variable in density. Numbers were generally ≤ 100/dm², but higher densities were recorded in two separate years – 1981 and 1997 – with 1981 showing a hugely successful spatfall (*ca.* 472/dm²). In the same year, by contrast, there was no spatfall recorded at the two more exposed sites of Poulacurra and Drolain Point.

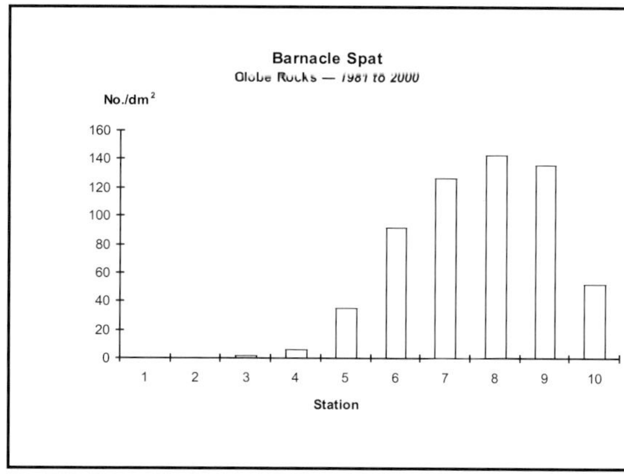

Figure 6.24

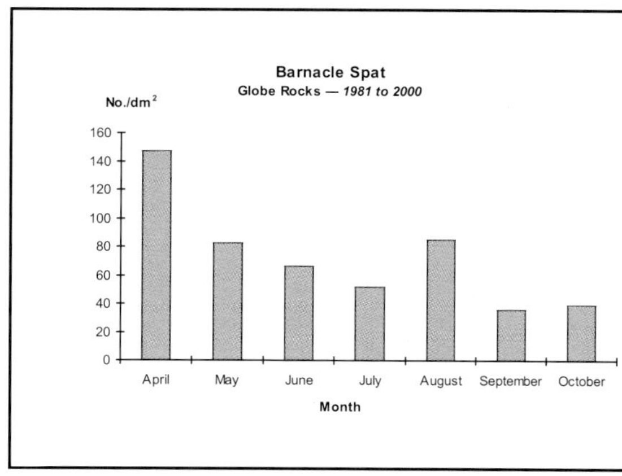

Figure 6.25

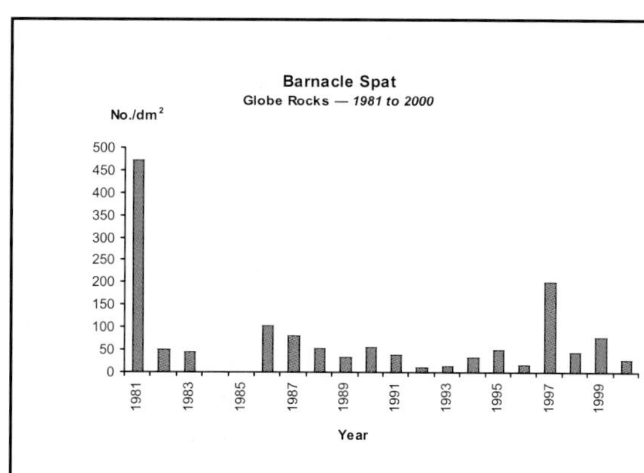

Figure 6.26

GLOBE ROCKS

GRAZERS

Flat Periwinkle
Littorina obtusata
Faocha leathan

Although the flat periwinkle *Littorina obtusata* was not abundant at Globe Rocks, it occurred from station 5 to station 10. The majority of animals were found on the lower shore at stations 8–10.

Numbers were low in April and May, and then there was a significant increase during June followed by another in August when the maximum number of 1.76 per quadrat was reached. Numbers decreased again in September and October.

Over the 20-year period the *Littorina obtusata* population fluctuated greatly. Numbers increased hugely from 1982 to 1983, to a maximum of 2 per quadrat. A slow decrease in numbers over 1984 and 1985 culminated in a crash in 1986 when very few animals were found and density was only 0.22 per quadrat. Further crashes occurred in 1988 and 1990, despite the population increases of 1987 and 1989. In 1991 the population was relatively high (1.26 per quadrat), but again this figure was not sustained and the population crashed in 1992. With the exception of 1998, an eight-year trend of steady increase was then observed.

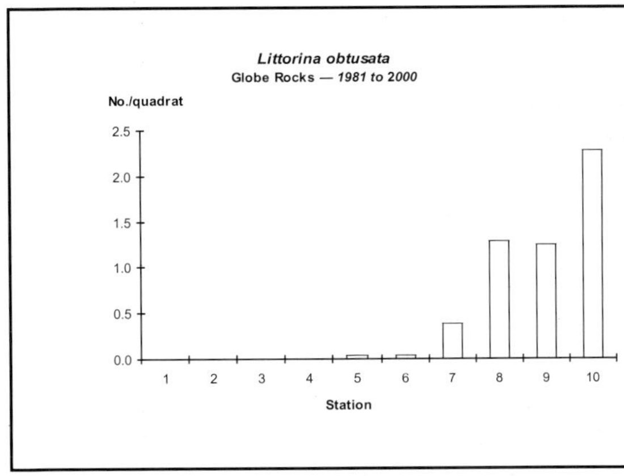

Figure 6.27

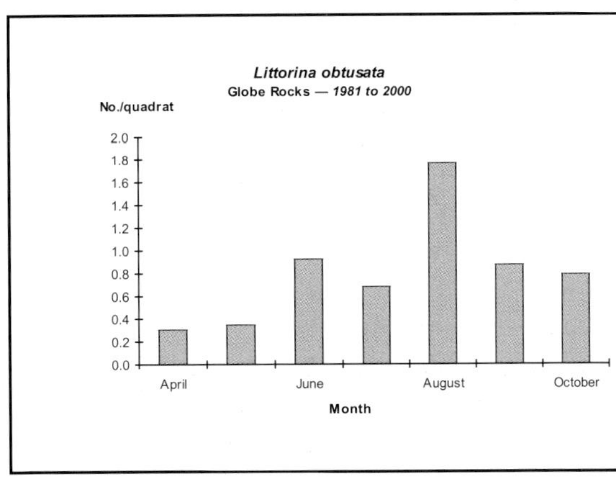

Figure 6.28

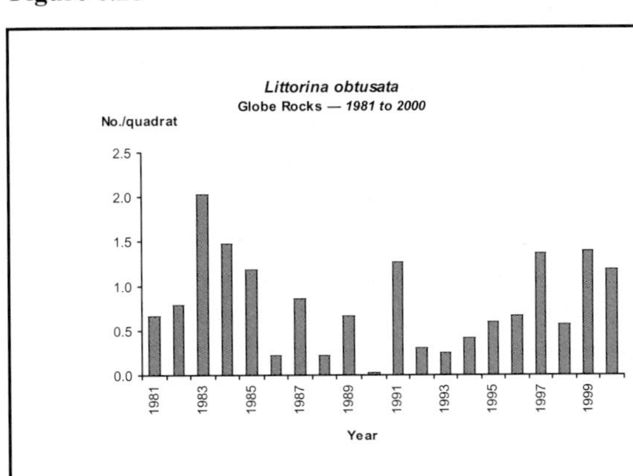

Figure 6.29

GLOBE ROCKS

GRAZERS

Rough Periwinkle
Littorina saxatilis
Faocha gharbh

An important grazer of the upper shore, the rough periwinkle *Littorina saxatilis* was present in very large numbers at Globe Rocks, with a maximum of 100 per quadrat and a mean value of approximately 30 per quadrat. It was found among thrift *Armeria maritima* at station 1, peaked at station 2 and 3 and then decreased in density down to station 10. The peak density at station 3 coincided with the peak density of the wrack *Pelvetia canaliculata*.

Numbers of *Littorina saxatilis* appeared to fall in the summer, with low densities (33 and 29 per quadrat) during June and July. Numbers rose again in August and September, and fell in October.

The population showed irregular variation over the 20 years of the survey. With a mean value of approximately 32 per quadrat, there were two years of huge population increase (1984 and 1992). *Littorina saxatilis* was actually present on the shore in 1986–88 and 1991, but the data are incompatible and cannot be included in Figure 6.32 (see p. 34).

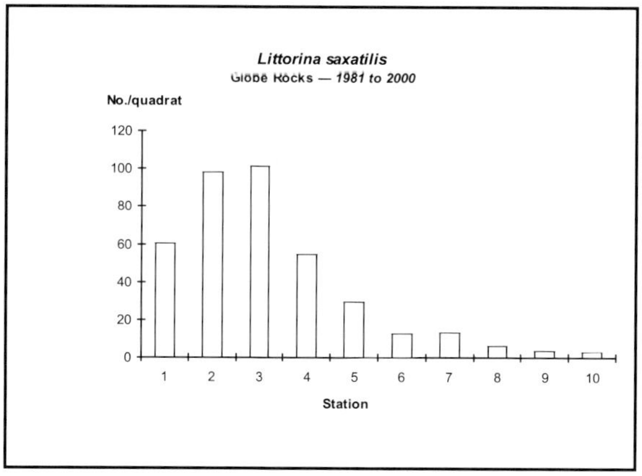

Figure 6.30

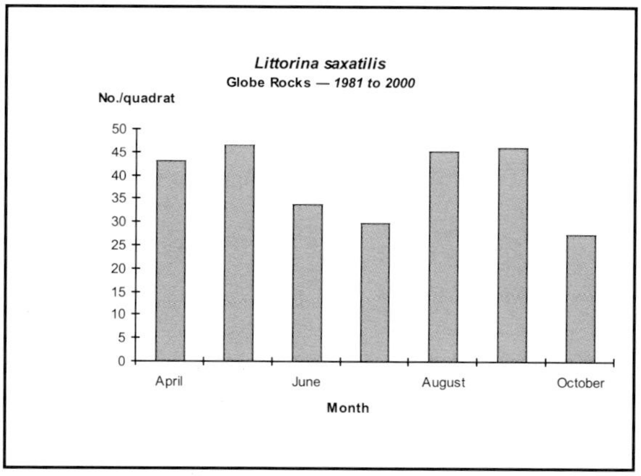

Figure 6.31

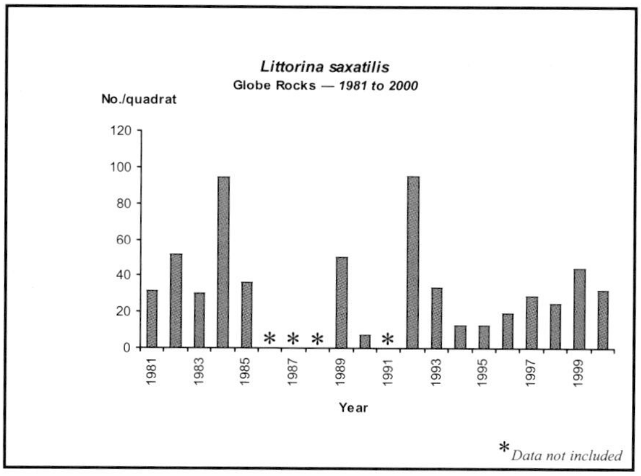

Figure 6.32

GLOBE ROCKS

GRAZERS

Limpet
Patella spp.
Bairneach

Limpets *Patella* spp. were common at Globe Rocks, occurring between stations 2 and 10, but were very sparse on the upper shore, reaching a maximum of 45 per quadrat at station 8. By station 10, where wracks (*Fucus* spp.) were most dense, numbers of limpets had reduced to approximately 20 per quadrat.

There was no significant variation from month to month with the monthly mean being 24 per quadrat – this implies that juveniles either did not settle or that adult losses were balanced by juveniles adding to the population. It is also likely that losses occurred during the winter months when surveying was not carried out.

Annual variation was present on a small scale. From 1990–2000 the overall mean density was approximately 26 per quadrat as compared to 20 per quadrat throughout the previous decade.

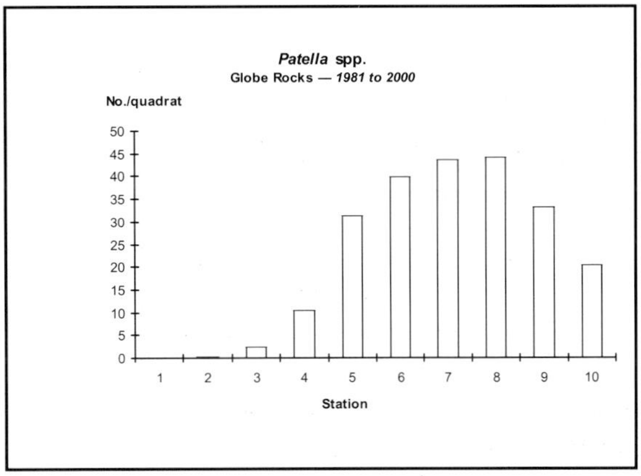

Figure 6.33

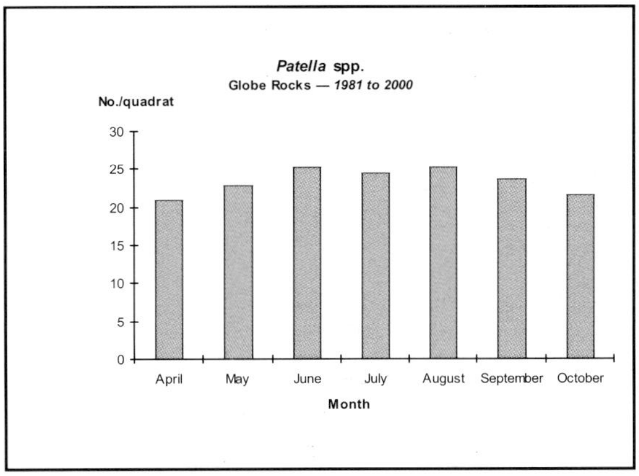

Figure 6.34

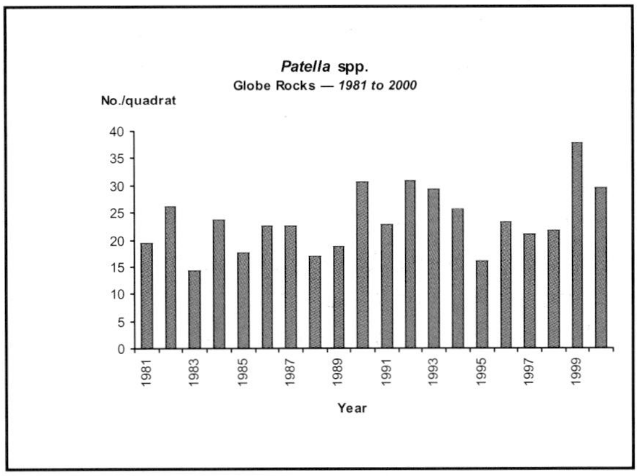

Figure 6.35

GLOBE ROCKS

PREDATOR

Dogwhelk
Nucella lapillus
Cuachma chon

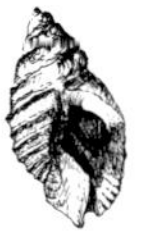

The dogwhelk *Nucella lapillus* was recorded in every quadrat from station 3 down the shore, but the majority of animals were on the middle shore at stations 7–8. Peak numbers were found at station 8 (1.3 per quadrat).

There was a general decrease in animals from spring through to autumn; the April density of 0.86 per quadrat was halved to 0.43 per quadrat by October.

Although present on the shore every year, there was significant annual variation. Apart from 1985, numbers during the early years between 1981 and 1987 were very much higher than the period 1988–2000. In 1988–95 density was consistently around 0.26 per quadrat. This was followed by a doubling of density in 1996 and a trend of increase up to the year 2000.

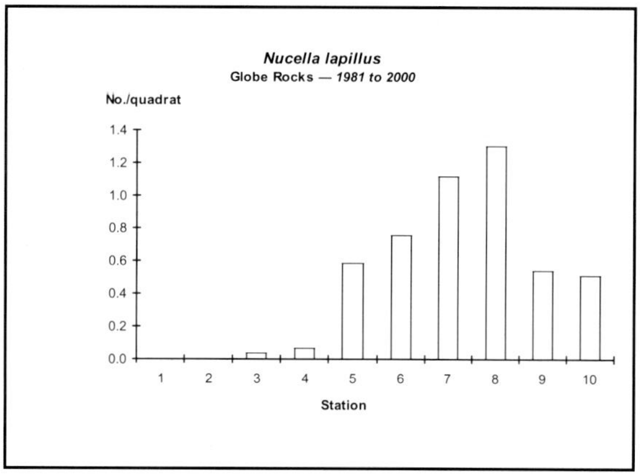

Figure 6.36

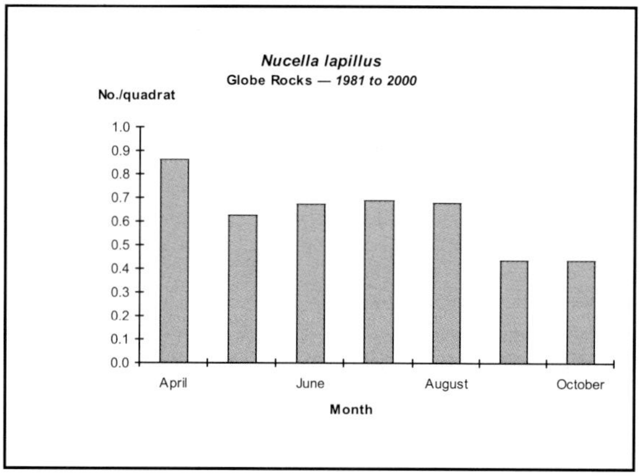

Figure 6.37

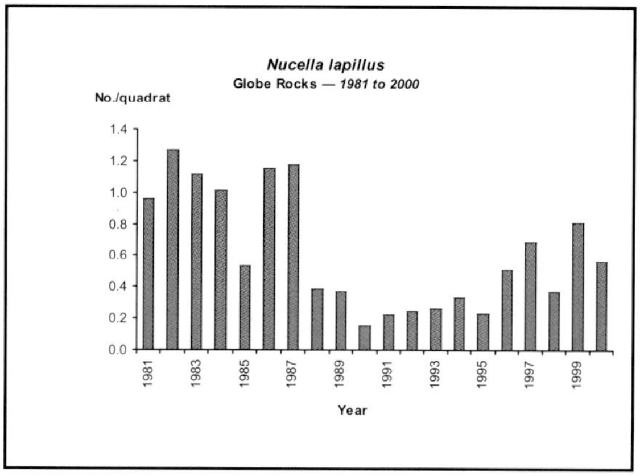

Figure 6.38

TRENDS FOR GLOBE ROCKS 1981–2000

Of the 12 species analysed at Globe Rocks, none has remained constant in its abundance throughout the 20-year survey period.

On the upper shore, channelled wrack *Pelvetia canaliculata* declined in cover from relatively high levels at the start of the survey, through intermediate cover in 1986–94 and very sparse amounts for the period 1995–2000. The rough periwinkle *Littorina saxatilis*, living amongst *Pelvetia,* had similarly larger numbers at the beginning of the survey and was present in moderate numbers during the years of *Pelvetia* scarcity. Its population peaks of 1984 and 1992 were not sustained and although the period 1985–1991 has to be treated with caution for this species, the fall in population numbers after 1992 is reliable.

On the middle shore, cover of bladder wrack *Fucus vesiculosus* increased significantly in the 1990s, while the barnacle population recovered slightly from a marked decline in 1991 to remain steady at half the density it attained in the late 1980s. This pattern is similar to those seen in the barnacle populations of Poulacurra (p. 56) and Drolain Point (p. 78). Limpet *Patella* spp. numbers were slightly higher in the 1990s than the 1980s, but showed less variation in general than all other species analysed.

On the lower shore between 1984 and 1993, serrated wrack *Fucus serratus* declined from its overall maximum cover; similarly the flat periwinkle *Littorina obtusata* declined from its peak in 1983 to its minimum in 1990. The wrack was then very sparse in the 1990s, whereas numbers of *Littorina obtusata* increased in this period. Carrageen moss *Mastocarpus stellatus* and pepper dulse *Osmundea pinnatifida* were also far less abundant in the 1990s. The dogwhelk *Nucella lapillus* population was much larger in the 1980s than in the 1990s, but fell dramatically in 1988. Their slow rate of increase in the 1990s was similar to that of *Littorina obtusata.*

HORSESHOE HARBOUR

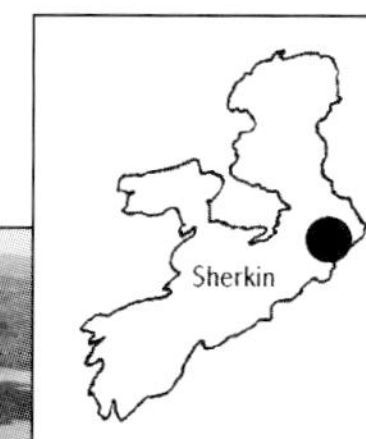

Figure 6.39 Horseshoe Harbour from the south, with Baltimore Harbour to the right.

Horseshoe Harbour is a beautiful natural shallow harbour on the southeast coast of Sherkin (Figure 6.39). The mouth is moderately narrow, but not sufficient to constrict water flow or create any "rapids" or eroding habitats through hydraulic restrictions. Although sheltered from the prevailing southwesterly winds, the harbour is open to winds from the east-southeast quarter round to the south, and there is a considerable fetch from the southeast. This has the effect of creating a slightly more wave-exposed habitat than at Globe Rocks, which lie just inside Baltimore Harbour.

Just outside the harbour mouth the water shelves steeply to 20 m, and down to 30 m depth a further 200 m beyond this. Thus there is little attenuation of wave action before the waves travel through the opening.

The transect site is on the southwestern shore of the harbour, facing northeast. The land behind the shore is covered with rough grass vegetation and rises fairly steeply to about 15 m.

The shore comprises bedrock with vertical fissures, and there are no overlying boulders.

The shore slopes gently with a gradient of 0.273. It spans 11.0 m horizontally and 3.0 m vertically. Ten stations are usually recorded. Stations 1–4 fall in the upper shore, stations 5–8 in the middle shore and stations 9–10 in the lower shore. Station 1 is 4.2 m above chart datum.

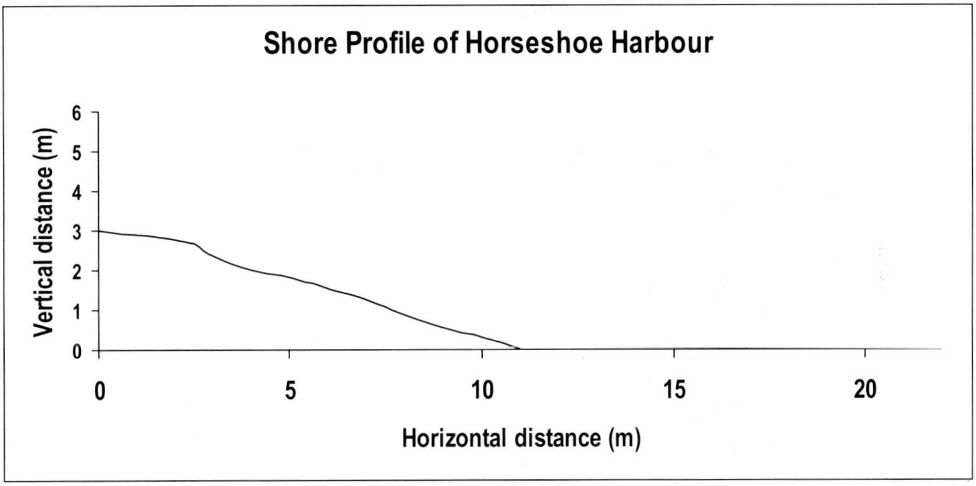

Figure 6.40 A cross-section of the shore from top to bottom showing the gentle gradient of the Horseshoe Harbour transect.

VISUAL DOMINANTS

The splash zone was narrow and not particularly rich in lichen cover. There was a continuous narrow band of black tar lichen *Verrucaria maura* and yellow, orange and grey lichens were sparse. Barnacles dominated the upper and middle shore with associated dogwhelks. This community gave way to a moderately dense band of algae – mainly thong weed *Himanthalia elongata* – on the lower stations. Dabberlocks *Alaria esculenta* was never recorded. In the early years of the survey occasional plants of the wrack *Ascophyllum nodosum* occurred. Zonation of the large brown seaweeds was well defined, with consistent recordings of *Pelvetia canaliculata, Fucus spiralis, F. serratus* and *Laminaria digitata*. *F. vesiculosus,* however, was not often recorded.

ALGAE

On the lower shore, and especially beneath the fucoid canopy, a rich diversity of seaweeds was recorded over the 20 years of surveying. This comprised 144 taxa, with 118 of these identified to species.

Brown Algae

A total of 26 brown algae were recorded to species level, with a further three to genus only. The most frequent (apart from the fucoids and laminarians) were *Dictyota dichotoma,* Ectocarpaceae, *Leathesia difformis, Ralfsia verrucosa* and *Scytosiphon lomentaria.* Several ephiphytic species also occurred.

Highlight on Seaweed Species

Epiphytic red algae

Several species of red seaweed grow on other seaweeds and kelp stipes in particular provide a good habitat for such species as *Palmaria palmata, Phycodrys rubens, Membranoptera alata* and *Polysiphonia* spp. Others seaweeds occur equally on rock or other plant species.

Plocamium cartilagineum

Plocamium cartilagineum is a common red understorey species of the order Plocamiales. Its characteristic one-sided branchlets are very beautiful. The plant is usually flattened in one plane. It is found on the lower shore on rocks or kelp stipes and in rock pools.

Dulse or sheep's weed *Palmaria palmata* is an example of a plant with flattened fronds that have no midrib. The fronds split into wedge-shaped sections and there are often a lot of very small new bladelets towards the base. It grows on rocks and also epiphytically on other algae, especially kelp stipes.

Dulse – *Palmaria palmata*

Red Algae

The Horseshoe Harbour shore was very rich in red algae. A total of 75 species were identified with an additional 13 taxa being identified to genus only.

Those occuring regularly included *Catenella caespitosa, Ceramium rubrum, Chondrus crispus, Corallina officinalis, Cryptopleura ramosa, Dumontia contorta, Gastroclonium ovatum, Gelidium spinosum, Hildenbrandia rubra, Lomentaria articulata, Mastocarpus stellatus, Membranoptera alata, Osmundea pinnatifida, Palmaria palmata, Plocamium cartilagineum* and *Plumaria plumosa*. Most are small and live beneath the wracks on the lower shore where they are protected from exposure to air.

Green Algae

Of the 17 species of green algae recorded, most were found infrequently. These include *Bryopsis plumosa, Chaetomorpha linum, Codium bursa, Derbesia marina Enteromorpha muscoides, E. linza* and *Spongomorpha aeruginosa.* A further ten algae were recorded to genus only.

The regularly occurring green algae were *Cladophora rupestris, Codium tomentosum, Enteromorpha* spp. and *Ulva lactuca. Chaetomorpha* spp. were often recorded in the 1990s, but only recorded twice – as *Chaetomorpha linum* – during the 1980s.

LICHENS

Although the splash zone was narrow and the lichen flora was not particularly well developed at the Horseshoe Harbour site, the seven common species were all present and recorded most years. These were *Caloplaca marina, Lecanora atra, Lichina confinis, L. pygmaea, Verrucaria maura, V. mucosa* and *Xanthoria parietina. Ochrolechia parella* and *Ramalina siliquosa* were also present in certain years.

ANIMALS

A total of 124 taxa were identified at Horseshoe Harbour, 100 to species level.

Bryozoa were well represented, as were crustacea, mollusca, cnidaria and fish.

Eight species of crab included the common shore crab *Carcinus maenas*, the edible crab *Cancer pagurus*, the velvet swimming crab *Necora puber*, hermit crabs *Pagurus bernhardus* and the small crabs *Pinnotheres pisum*, *Pirimela denticulata*, *Porcellana platycheles* and *Pisidia longicornis*. These were found amongst the holdfasts and rich understorey in the two lowest stations of the lower shore. The squat lobster *Galathea squamifera* was also recorded here (in 1992).

Horseshoe Harbour was relatively rich in fish species although only the shanny *Lipophrys pholis* was recorded more than once.

Amphipods included *Caprella linearis*, the gammarids *Sphaeroma rugicauda* and *Talitrus saltator*, and the isopod *Idotea granulosa*. On the upper shore the sea slater *Ligia oceanica* occurred most years.

Highlight on Spiny Skinned Animals – Brittlestars, Starfish, Sea Urchins (Echinoderms)

Echinoderms are unique in the marine environment, having a body shape based on the symmetry of five (pentamerous). This applies to all five classes: feather stars, sea stars (starfish), brittlestars, sea urchins and sea cucumbers. Often colourful, beautiful and found in a wide range of habitats from the seashore to deep waters, there are but few examples recorded on Sherkin's seashores.

Common Starfish – *Asterias rubens*

Starfish are carnivores. *Asterias rubens* feeds mainly on bivalves and is well known for prising the valves apart with its arms, then pushing its stomach out to digest the soft tissues of the bivalve.

Brittlestars are mostly sublittoral animals and only occasional individuals are found on the shore, well hidden under seaweeds, in crevices and overhangs where they stay moist. *Ophiothrix fragilis* is often amongst kelp holdfasts in the lowest stations. A brittlestar's arms are indeed brittle and may get caught or trapped and become detached. If this happens close to the central disc, the arm can be regenerated. *Ophiothrix fragilis* and the black brittlestar *Ophiocomina nigra* both occur widely around Sherkin and huge populations are known to occur in Roaringwater Bay (Gupta, 2000). They are scavengers, feeding on dead or decaying plants and animals.

The common edible sea urchin *Echinus esculentus* is occasionally recorded on Sherkin's shores, whereas the purple sea urchin *Paracentrotus lividus* is absent from the seven monthly sites despite being common in southwest Ireland. Both are key species in the sublittoral; the voracious grazing of a dense population can create a very sparse understorey in the kelp forest known as "urchin barrens". Observations of *Echinus esculentus* on the shore are generally more common in the spring; this is thought to be associated with an upward spawning migration.

Although echinoderms were not abundant in either species or numbers, the common starfish *Asterias rubens* was usually recorded and in one or two years there were records in the lowest station of the black sea cucumber *Holothuria forskali*, the edible sea urchin *Echinus esculentus* and the common brittlestar *Ophiothrix fragilis*. While *Holothuria* and *Echinus* are essentially sublittoral animals, *Ophiothrix fragilis* occurred on many shores amongst seaweeds and under boulders on the lower shore.

The Horseshoe Harbour site had the richest diversity of bryozoans amongst the seven shores described in this book. Those recorded most years were the sea mats *Electra pilosa*, *Flustrellidra hispida* and *Membranipora membranacea*. *Alcyonidium hirsutum* and *Umbonula* spp. were fairly frequent. Other species recorded for a maximum of three years included *Bowerbankia imbricata*, *Cellepora pumicosa*, *Schizoporella unicornis* and *Scrupocellaria* spp.

A fairly wide range of recorded molluscs included *Alvania cancellata, Bittium reticulatum*, *Tectura virginea*, *Tonicella rubra* and *Trivia arctica*. Two species of nudibranch (sea slug) were also recorded, the sea lemon *Archidoris pseudoargus* and *Jorunna tomentosa*.

Of the winkles, *Littorina obtusata* and *L. littorea* were usually present, but these species were absent from the transect in 1994, with *L. littorea* also absent in 1991. *L. saxatilis* and *Melarhaphe neritoides* were recorded every year, in contrast to *Littorina neglecta,* which was recorded only in the years 1981–85.

As well as the dogwhelk *Nucella lapillus*, three other whelk species occurred at Horseshoe Harbour. The European sting winkle *Ocenebra erinacea* was recorded in ten different years. The thick-lipped whelk *Hinia incrassata* was recorded in 13 years and the netted whelk *H. reticulata* eight years.

Highlight on Fish (Osteichthyes)

Shanny – *Lipophrys pholis*

Blennies are one of the most common shore fish. Of the three species which are generally common, the shanny *Lipophrys pholis* has been found at four of the Sherkin shores, while the related butterfish *Pholis gunnellus* occurs at Reenahoe and Kinish Narrows East. Horseshoe Harbour had the widest variety of fish species, with various pipefish species also recorded – the worm pipefish *Nerophis lumbriciformis*, the straight-nosed pipefish *N. ophidion* and the lesser pipefish *Syngnathus rostellatus*. The shanny is well camouflaged amongst the lower shore seaweeds with its yellow/green blotchy colouring. It is an important shore predator, using its sharp teeth to feed on barnacles and bivalves. Pipefish are found on shores with little water movement – they are plankton feeders and are very interesting in that after the female lays eggs, the male then carries them until they hatch. In *Nerophis* the eggs are glued on the underside of the body, but *Syngnathus* has a special pouch similar to that of seahorses.

Species analysed for Horseshoe Harbour, their place in the food chain and the shore ecology (Predatory pathway ——► Grazing pathway ·······►)

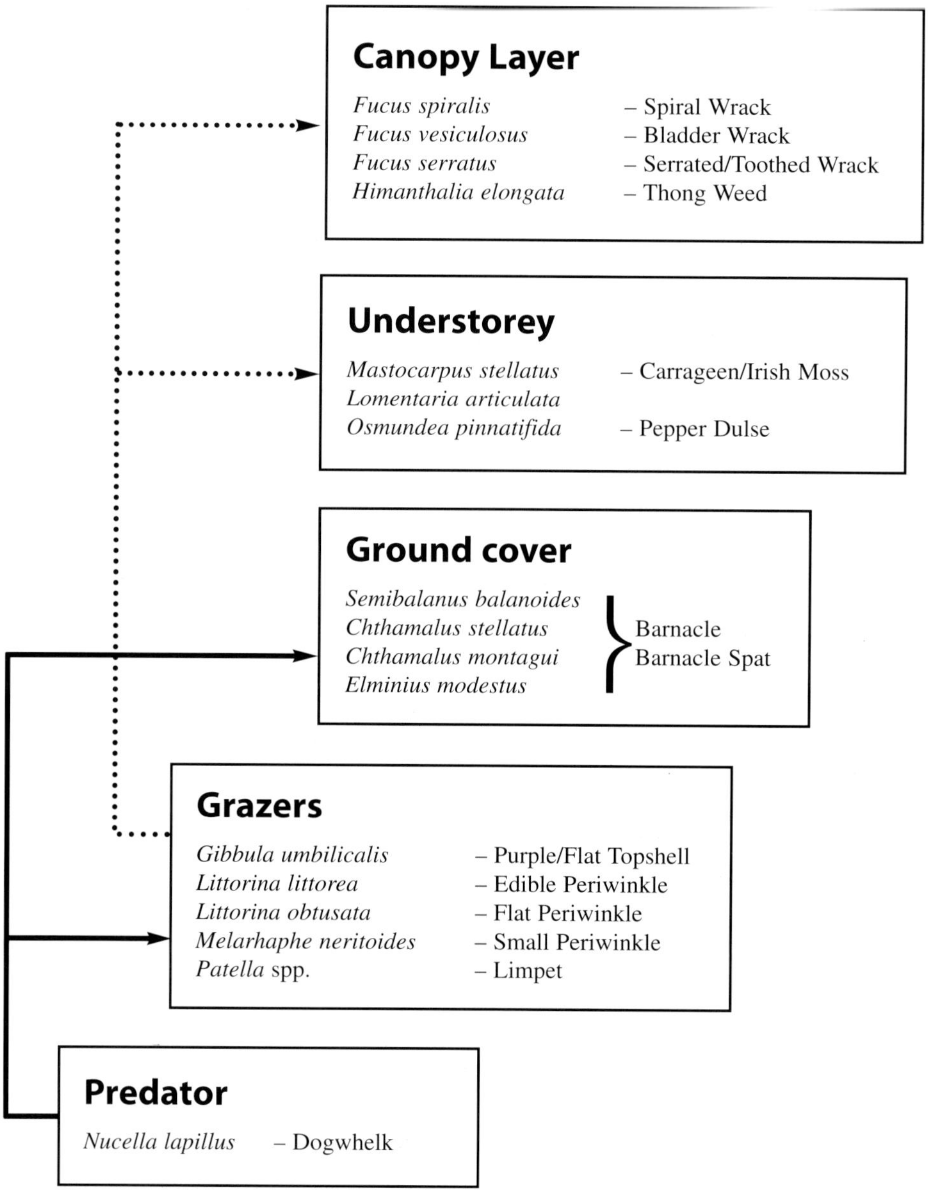

HORSESHOE HARBOUR

CANOPY LAYER

Spiral Wrack
Fucus spiralis
Casfheamainn

The spiral wrack *Fucus spiralis* is an upper shore plant and was found primarily at stations 1–4, with the highest percentage cover occurring at stations 2 (13% per quadrat) and 3 (6%). Occasional plants were recorded in several other stations, though it was noted that these were often young plants unlikely to thrive at the lower tidal levels.

Species cover increased almost threefold from April to May but there was little difference in the abundance of *Fucus spiralis* in all other months, apart from the major decline in October.

It has been of huge interest that this species was recorded in any abundance only during the first three years of the survey. After 1984 it was absent or present in very small quantities (< 0.5% cover).

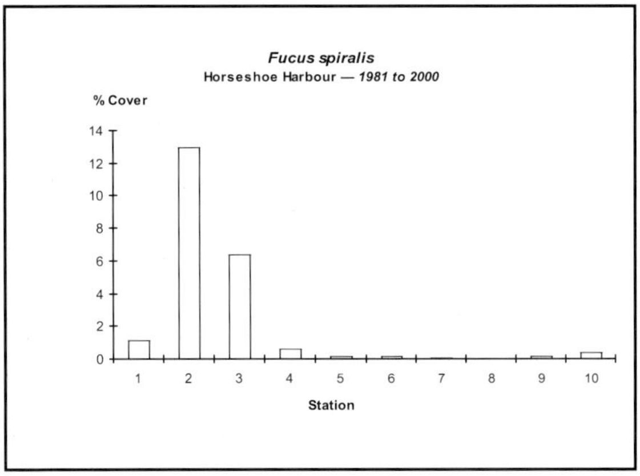

Figure 6.41

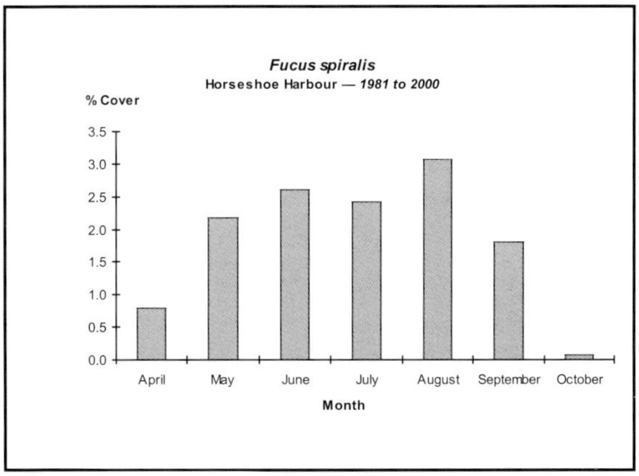

Figure 6.42

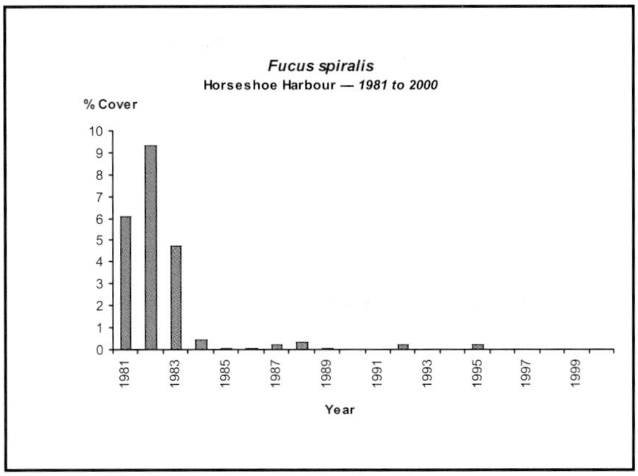

Figure 6.43

HORSESHOE HARBOUR

CANOPY LAYER

Bladder Wrack
Fucus vesiculosus
Feamainn bhoilgíneach

The highest density of bladder wrack *Fucus vesiculosus* occurred at station 3 (9% per quadrat) and the species then decreased in abundance down the shore to minimal levels (< 0.5%) at stations 8 and 9.

Unlike *F. spiralis*, the densest growth was found in April, and this reduced to approximately 3% for the rest of the year. October saw only occasional plants.

Fucus vesiculosus was only recorded during 1981–84. Throughout these four years percentage cover decreased from 7% to < 0.5% and it was not present on the shore for the last 16 years of the survey period.

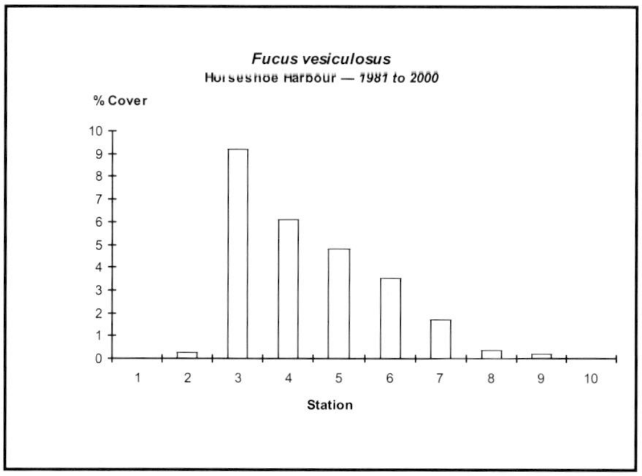

Figure 6.44

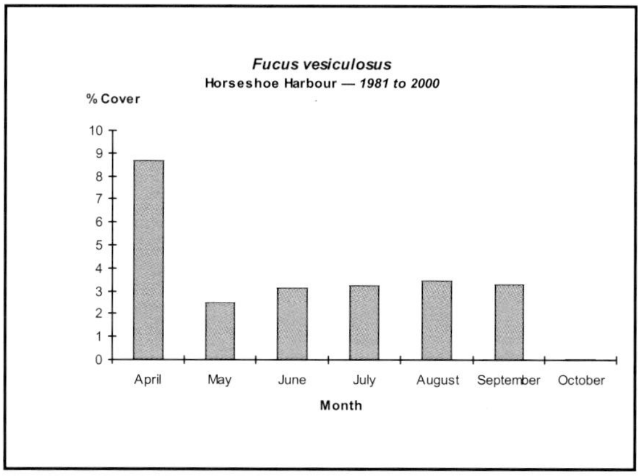

Figure 6.45

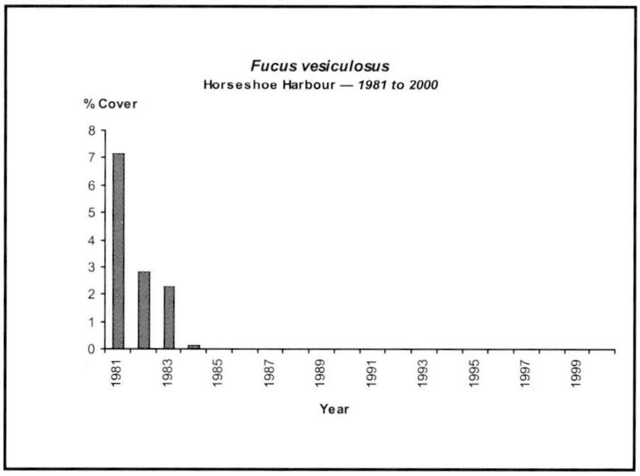

Figure 6.46

HORSESHOE HARBOUR

CANOPY LAYER

Serrated/Toothed Wrack
Fucus serratus
Míoránach

Serrated wrack *Fucus serratus* occurred on the middle and lower shore, with maximum cover at stations 8 (3% per quadrat) and 9 (2.75%).

Fucus serratus cover almost doubled from April to September and, like the other *Fucus* species, October recorded a large decrease in cover.

Fucus serratus was more prolific than *F. spiralis* and *F. vesiculosus*, being recorded in 17 out of the 20 years. However it too had decreased considerably from 1981–84 and maintained sparse cover until 1997. During 1998, 1999 and 2000 the species was absent from the transect.

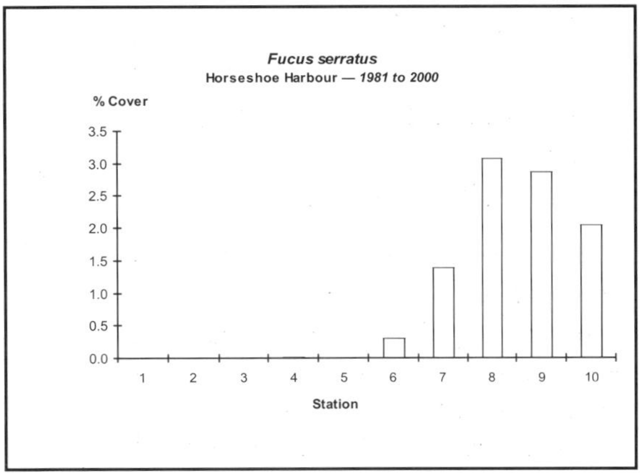

Figure 6.47

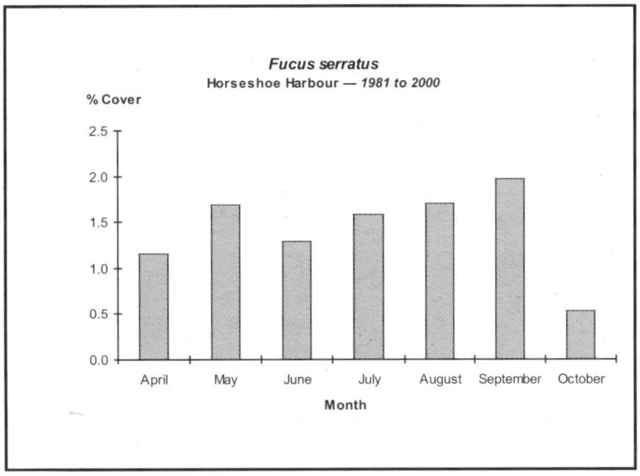

Figure 6.48

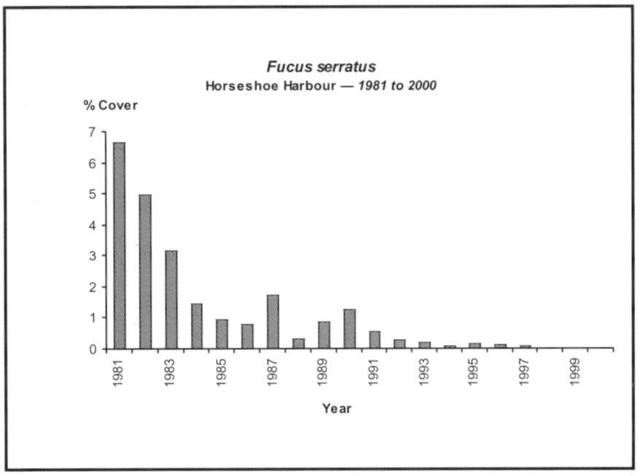

Figure 6.49

HORSESHOE HARBOUR

CANOPY LAYER

Thong Weed
Himanthalia elongata
Ríseach

Thong weed *Himanthalia elongata* occurred on the lower shore from station 7 to station 10, where it was most common.

Growth increased from May to July, then declined through to October. There was a fivefold increase in the amount present on the shore in April (0.4% per quadrat) to May (2.1%).

At the beginning of the survey period *Himanthalia* was at approximately 4.5% cover. It then climbed spasmodically to reach a maximum level of 9.8% in 1989. 1990 and 1991 levels were again low, between 2% and 3%, and from 1992 onwards *Himanthalia* was very scarce at 1% or less.

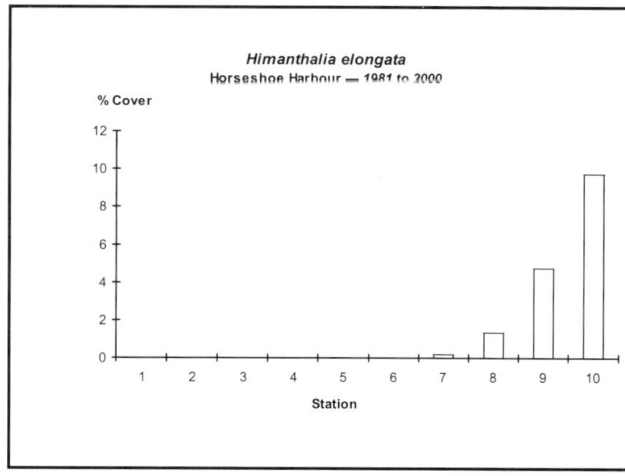

Figure 6.50

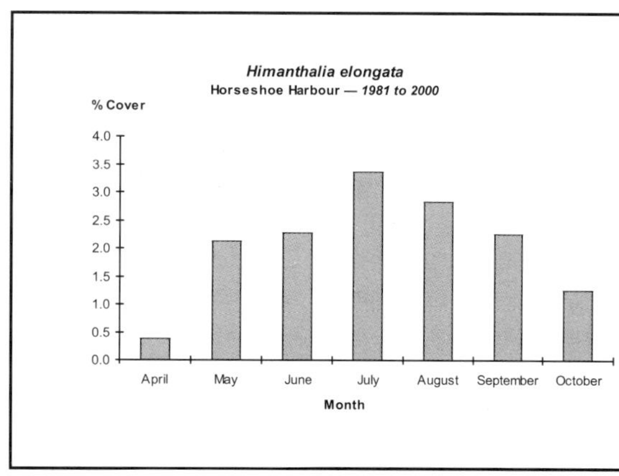

Figure 6.51

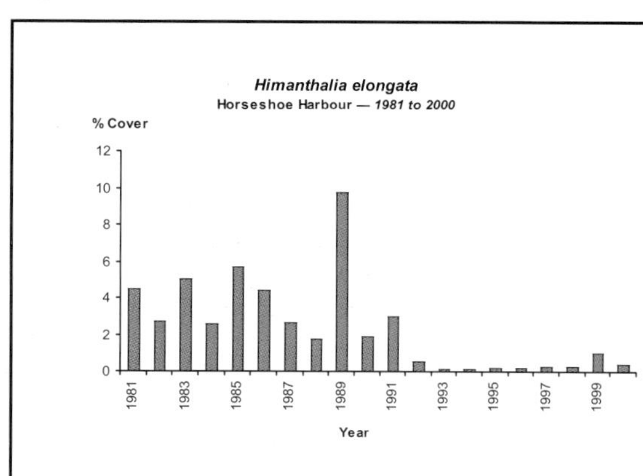

Figure 6.52

HORSESHOE HARBOUR

UNDERSTOREY

Carrageen/Irish Moss
Mastocarpus stellatus
Clúimhín cait

The red alga *Mastocarpus stellatus,* one of the species commonly known as carrageen moss, formed a turf on the middle and lower shores, with the thickest cover found at station 10, and over 90% of the total cover lying between stations 7 and 10.

Seasonal variation was evident in this species, with significant growth from April to May and a steady decrease in cover from May through to September. There followed a large decrease from September to October. Occasional surveys carried out in January and February showed very little cover (< 0.5%). Growth slows down in October as day length shortens and temperatures drop, and some loss of older plants probably occurred, torn off the rocks by rough seas. Good growth conditions return in the late spring when the May increase was observed.

There was a considerable amount of annual variation but the species was more abundant in the 1980s than during the 1990s. A large decrease was recorded from 1988 to 1991. From 1992 onwards *Mastocarpus stellatus* occupied less than 1% of the rock cover.

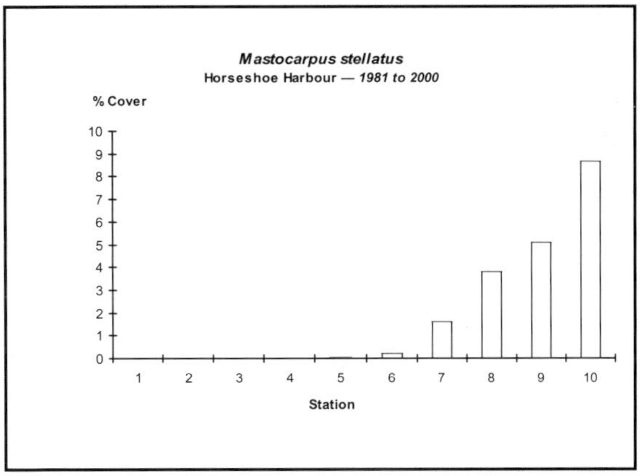

Figure 6.53

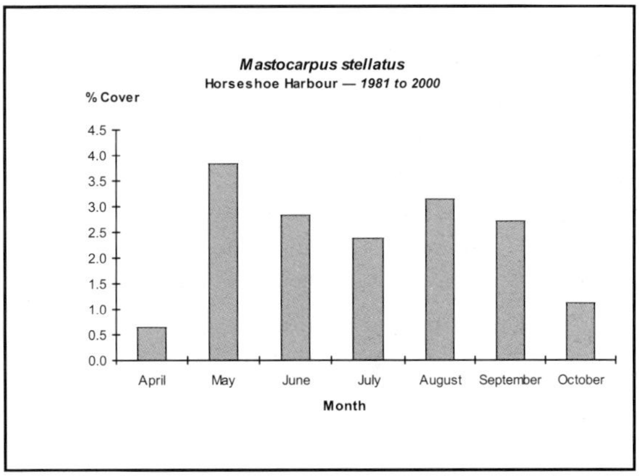

Figure 6.54

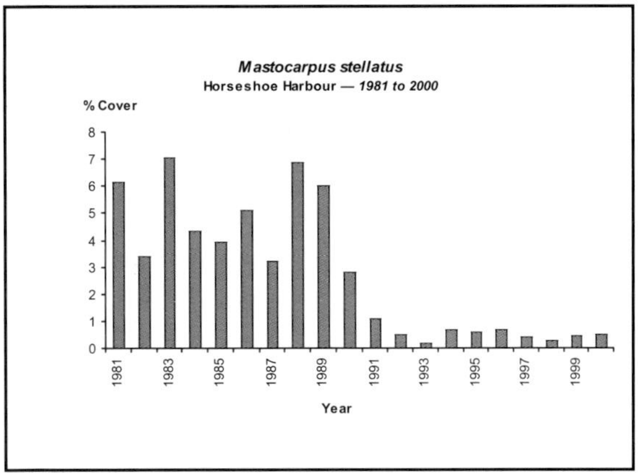

Figure 6.55

HORSESHOE HARBOUR

UNDERSTOREY

Lomentaria articulata

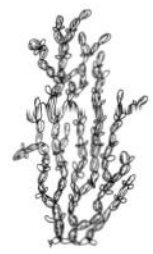

Lomentaria articulata is a red seaweed commonly found in the understorey on the lower shore, though usually in scattered patches totalling only a small percentage of the rock cover. At Horseshoe Harbour, its distribution was centred around station 9, from where plants were found up to station 6 and down to station 10. Occasional plants also occurred as high up the shore as station 3. These were in crevices which remain constantly damp.

During the year *L. articulata* was more abundant in April, May and June (*ca.* 2% per quadrat) than at the end of the growing season – by October it had declined to only 0.4% cover.

Abundance over the years fluctuated considerably. There was a distinct recurring pattern evident in 1983–92 which consisted of a rapid increase in cover followed by two consecutive years of decline. Between 1991 and 2000, the species has never occupied more than 0.6% rock cover.

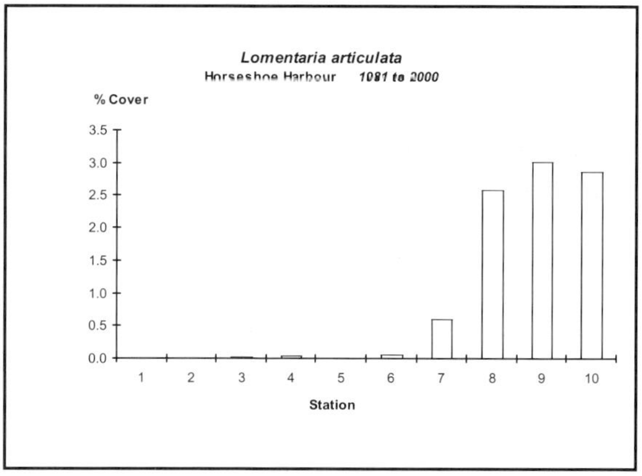

Figure 6.56

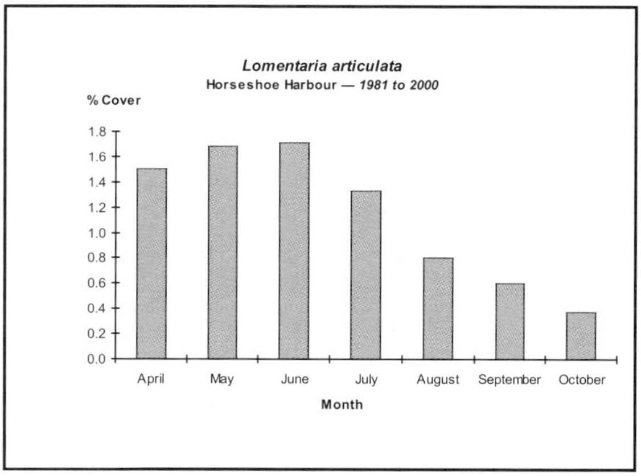

Figure 6.57

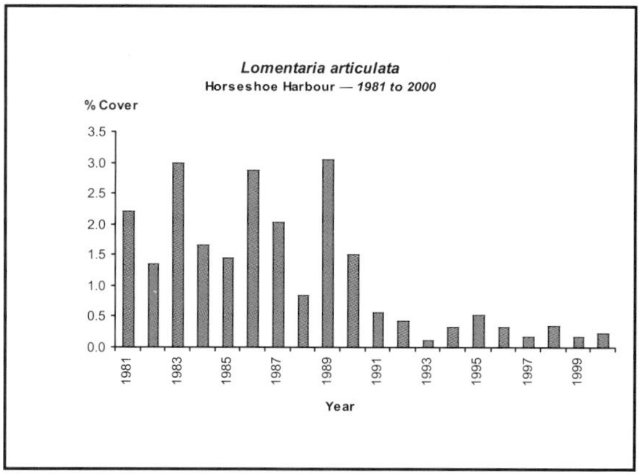

Figure 6.58

HORSESHOE HARBOUR

UNDERSTOREY

Pepper Dulse
Osmundea pinnatifida
Míobhán

The red algae Pepper dulse *Osmundea pinnatifida* had a middle shore distribution growing primarily beneath the wrack *Fucus serratus*, but reaching its peak density at station 7 where *F. serratus* only accounted for 1.5% cover per quadrat.

In a similar way to *Lomentaria articulata* and *Mastocarpus stellatus*, *Osmundea pinnatifida* growth was most prolific in April and May. It then showed a small but steady decrease in cover through to October.

In common with the ground cover algal species at Horseshoe Harbour, *Osmundea pinnatifida* was less abundant from 1988 than during the first seven years of the survey. Overall cover fell from a mean of just under 6% between 1981 and 1987 to approximately 1.8% over the 13 years 1988–2000.

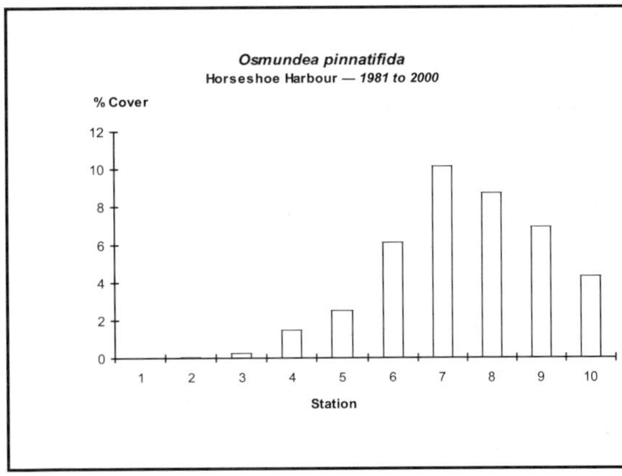

Figure 6.59

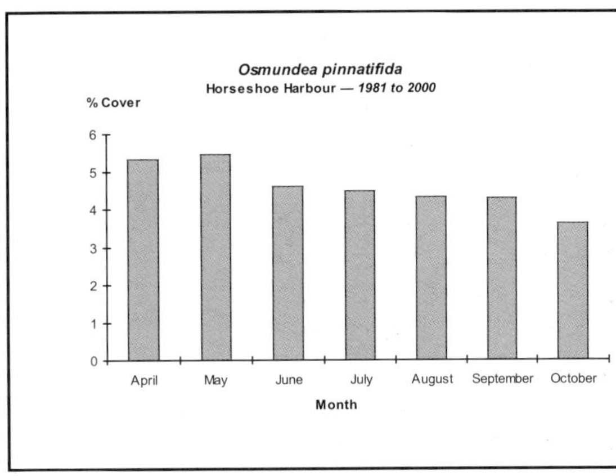

Figure 6.60

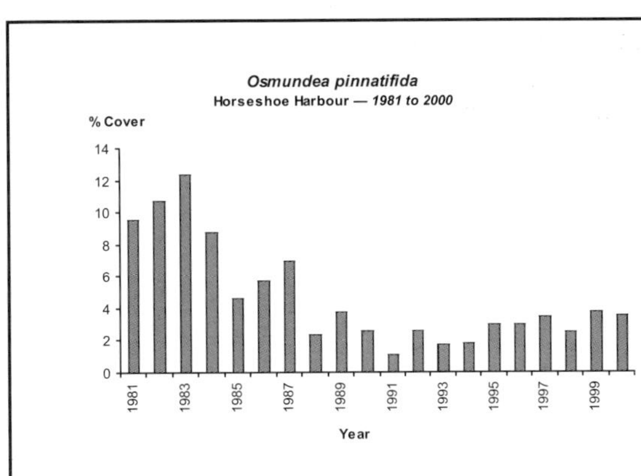

Figure 6.61

HORSESHOE HARBOUR

GROUND COVER

Barnacles

Semibalanus balanoides
Chthamalus stellatus
Chthamalus montagui
Elminius modestus
Giúrainn

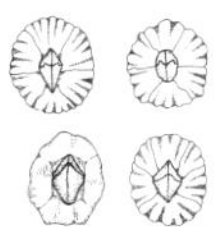

Barnacles were present over most of the shore, peaking at station 5 where percentage cover was just under 70% per quadrat. In the main part of their range, stations 4–9, barnacles comprised over 40% of the total cover on the shore. Thus in the moderately exposed shores they were a very important part of the dynamic structure of the shore community.

Cover was more abundant during June to October than in April and May. The main increase occurred from May to June.

The 20 years survey period showed major differences between the first 10 years, 1981–90, when cover steadily increased, and the 1990s during which cover remained at a steady level of approximately 22%. In the intermittent year – 1991 – there was a huge crash from 50% in 1990 to 7.5% in 1991. 2000 showed an increase to 30%. This pattern is similar to the one seen at other sites on Sherkin (p. 56, p. 78, p. 99).

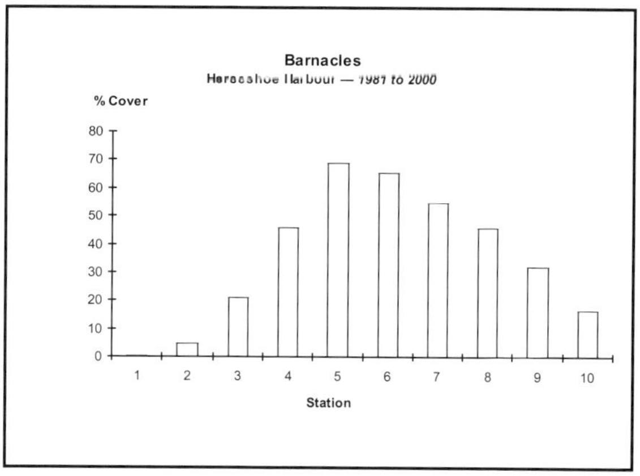

Figure 6.62

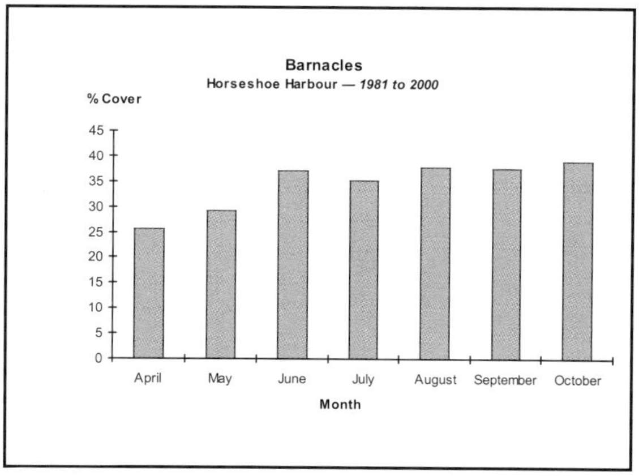

Figure 6.63

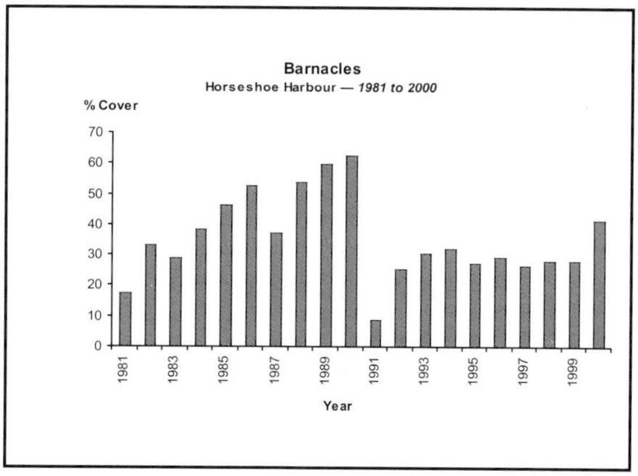

Figure 6.64

HORSESHOE HARBOUR

GROUND COVER

Barnacle Spat
Síol giúrainn

Barnacle spat were found throughout the same range as the adults with the exception of the highest stations (1 and 2). Maximum density was approximately 130/dm^2 at stations 7 and 8.

The major spatfall occurred in April in Horseshoe Harbour, with a smaller rise in spat numbers during September and October. August numbers were distinctly low.

Abundance of spat was very variable over the 20 years. 1988, 1991 and 1997 were three years with particularly good spatfalls; there were also years when no spatfall was recorded at all (1985, 1987 and 1990). These years of abundance and absence appear to bear no relationship to the annual fluctuations of the adult population. For example, there was no corresponding large increase in the adult cover in 1988 nor the year following, 1989. However the fact that there was no spatfall in 1990 may have contributed to the crash in the adult population of 1991. Despite the fact that the adult barnacle population was much lower in the 1990s than the 1980s, the general spatfall levels showed no difference in the two decades.

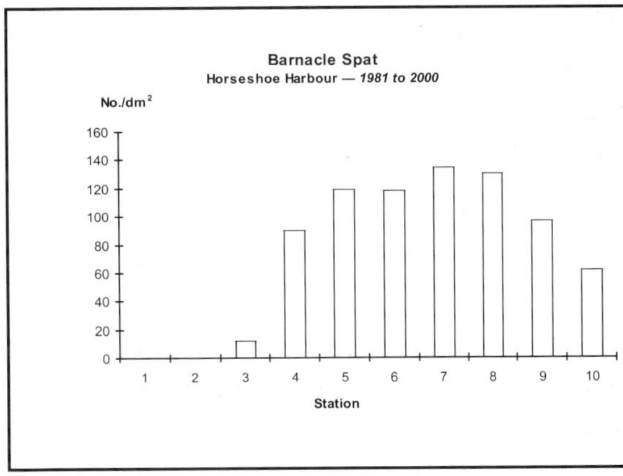

Figure 6.65

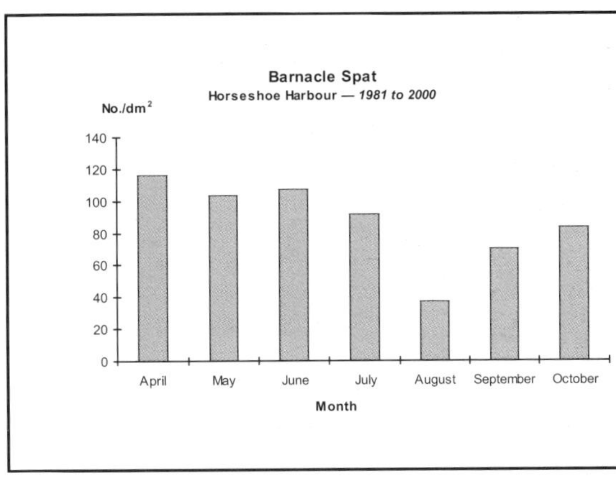

Figure 6.66

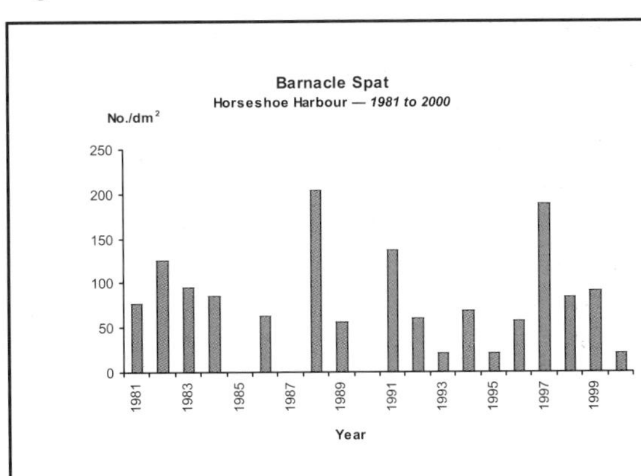

Figure 6.67

HORSESHOE HARBOUR

GRAZERS

Purple/Flat Topshell
Gibbula umbilicalis
Faochán Mhuire corcra

The purple topshell *Gibbula umbilicalis* was found primarily at stations 8–10 on the lower middle shore, although individuals occur in all but the highest shore levels. Its main habitat was amongst the wrack *Fucus serratus* and *Himanthalia elongata*, on the lower shore.

Numbers doubled in May and then steadily reduced to approximately 0.12 per quadrat in October.

The population was larger throughout the 1980s compared to most of the 1990s. However at the end of a seven-year period of low numbers, there were large increases in 1999 and again in 2000. The absences noted in 1983 and 1991 are also separated by a seven-year period.

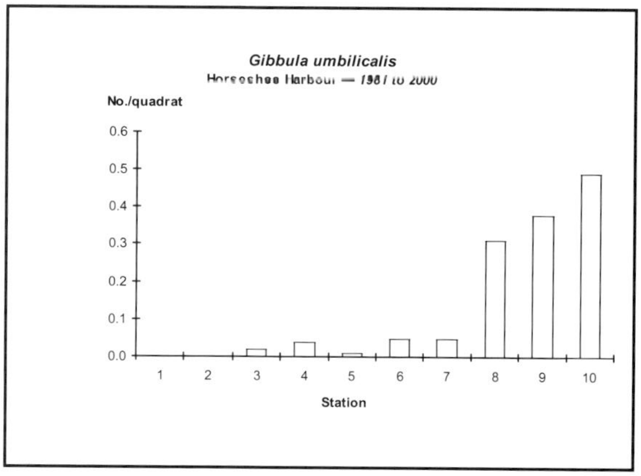

Figure 6.68

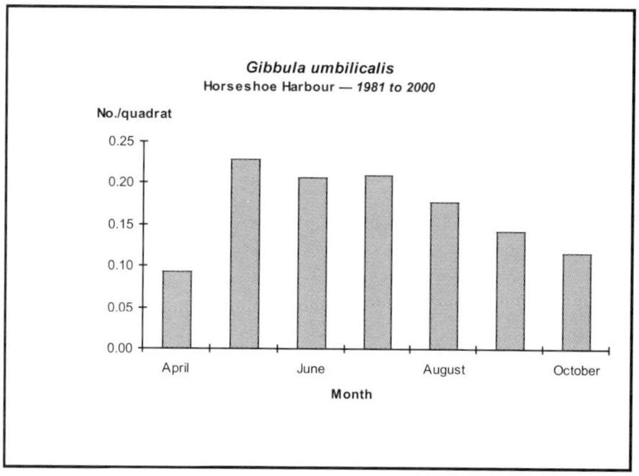

Figure 6.69

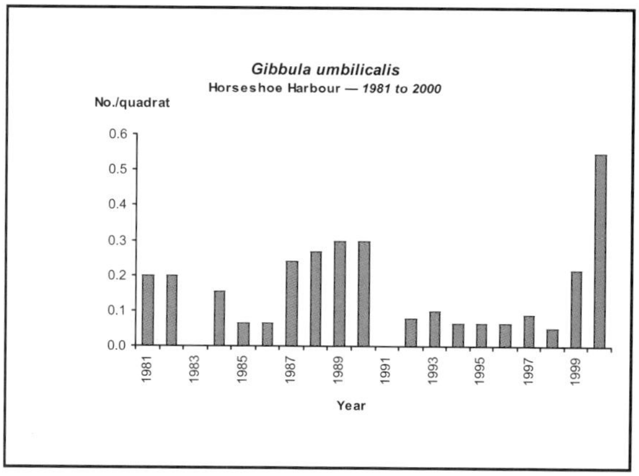

Figure 6.70

HORSESHOE HARBOUR

GRAZERS

Edible Periwinkle
Littorina littorea
Gioradán

The edible periwinkles *Littorina littorea* were most concentrated high on the shore at station 2, with a scatter of individuals between stations 1 and 4. Occasional individuals were found in each of the lower stations (5–10).

Littorina littorea numbers showed a huge increase in May from the overwintering shore population. However, they decreased in June and by July were back to a low density of around 0.1 per quadrat.

The very sparse population of *Littorina littorea* at Horseshoe Harbour has been a consistent characteristic of this shore, though there is a single exception to this and data from 1998 show that isolated events can occur; in this case the short-lived population explosion in 1998. It is not evident whether this was caused by migration into the transect area from adjacent areas or from successful reproduction.

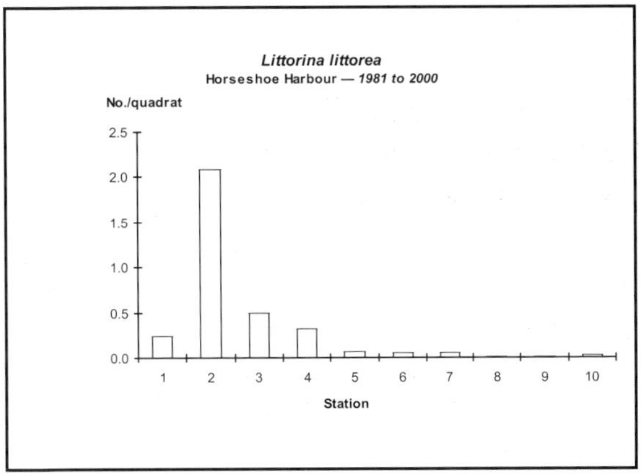

Figure 6.71

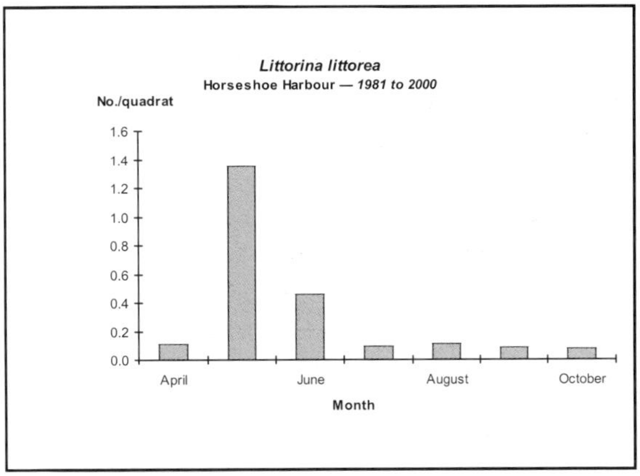

Figure 6.72

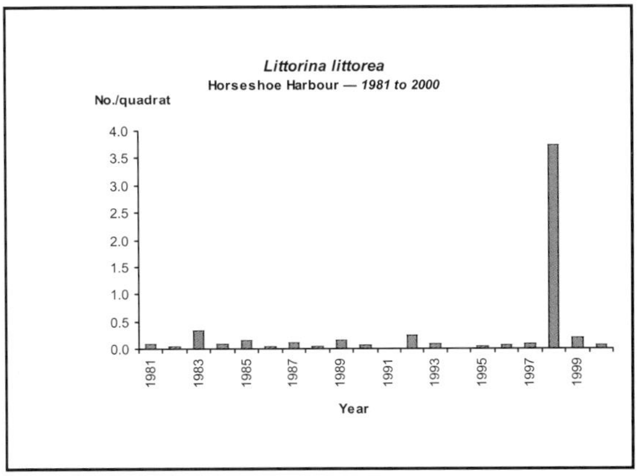

Figure 6.73

HORSESHOE HARBOUR

GRAZERS

Flat Periwinkle
Littorina obtusata
Faocha leathan

Flat periwinkle *Littorina obtusata* lives amongst fucoids, scraping the surface of the seaweed for its food. Although *L. obtusata* occurred throughout the intertidal zone, it is not surprising that there were two density peaks: stations 2 and 3 high on the shore and stations 7–10 in the lower middle shore. These mirror the peak densities of the wracks – *Fucus spiralis* and *F. vesiculosus* at stations 2 and 3 respectively, and *F. serratus* at stations 7–10.

There was considerable seasonal variation in density, with numbers at their lowest during April, followed by a huge increase in May. Numbers remained fairly steady through the early summer, with a fall in numbers in August to 0.4 per quadrat. During the winter a large loss of animals must occur to account for the low April densities.

Annual variation in density followed a broadly similar pattern to that of the fucoid cover. The period from 1981–89 showed an overall decline in the population, and with the exception of 1998, this low level continued up to the year 2000. Data were recorded consistently throughout the survey, thus the contrast between the population size between the 1980s and 1990s is real (see p. 34).

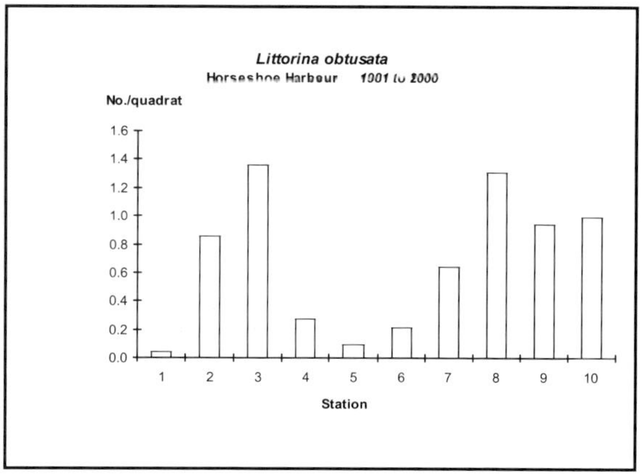

Figure 6.74

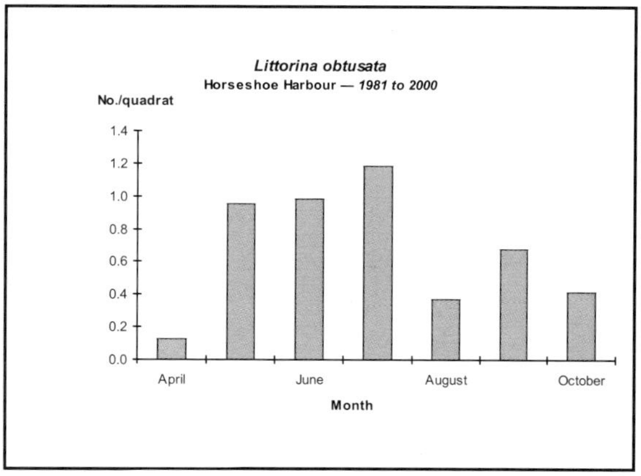

Figure 6.75

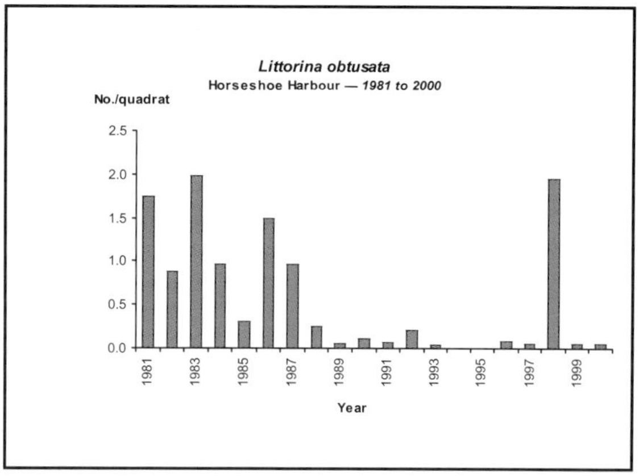

Figure 6.76

HORSESHOE HARBOUR

GRAZERS

Small Periwinkle
Melarhaphe neritoides
Faocha bheag

Small periwinkle *Melarhaphe neritoides* was found on the upper and middle shores, with the bulk of the population occurring at stations 2–5. These quadrats comprised up to 10% *Fucus vesiculosus*, up to 12% *F. spiralis* and between 5% and 70% barnacle cover per quadrat. The periwinkles sit mainly within empty barnacle shells and bare rock crevices.

Melarhaphe neritoides was one of the few species which was more abundant on the shore in spring than summer. It showed a peak in May, then remained at between 12% and 20% from June to October.

It is also one of the few species at Horseshoe Harbour which was more abundant after 1990 as compared with the previous decade. Numbers peaked in 1998 at 63/dm² and declined in 1999 and 2000.

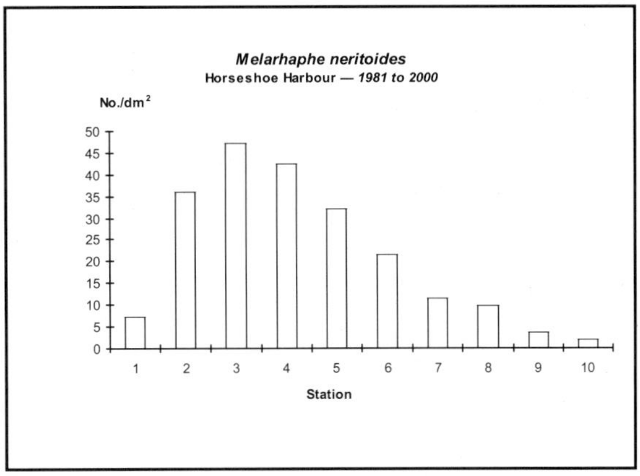

Figure 6.77

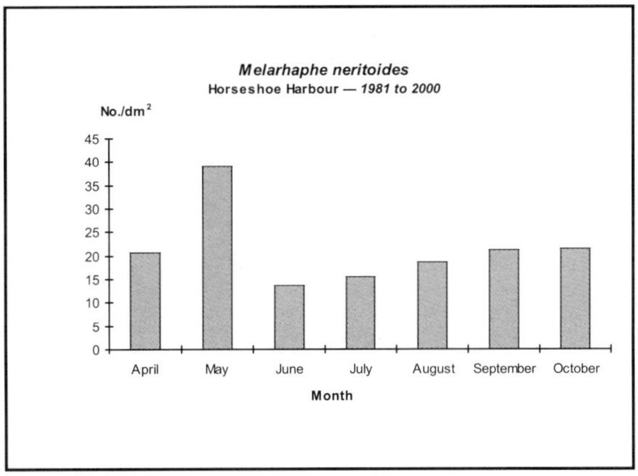

Figure 6.78

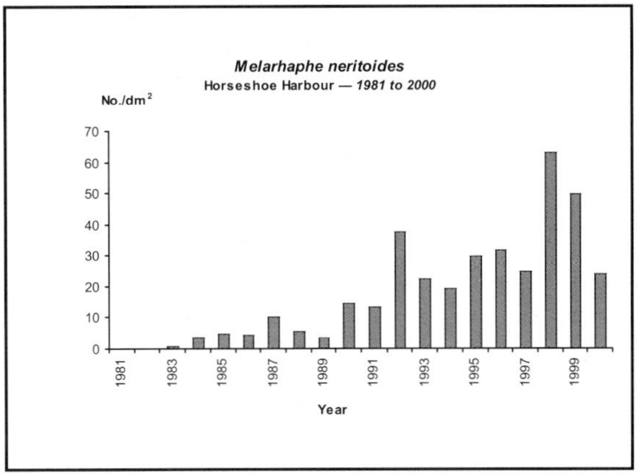

Figure 6.79

HORSESHOE HARBOUR

GRAZERS

Limpet
Patella spp.
Bairneach

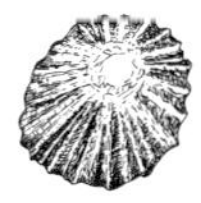

The limpet *Patella* spp. was found over most of the shore at Horseshoe Harbour. Maximum density (80–100 per quadrat) was found on the middle shore at stations 6, 7 and 8.

Seasonal variation was very limited, with a variation in population numbers only occurring from April to May.

There was a general trend of population increase throughout the survey. Within this trend there was variation, with years of increase often followed by two or three years when numbers declined. For example, the increase in 1984 was followed by two years of decline (1985 and 1986); likewise 1992, which had increased by approximately 50% from 1991, was followed by three years of decline (1993, 1994 and 1995). The population declines rarely drop below 40 per quadrat, which suggests that this might be the optimum carrying capacity of the habitat.

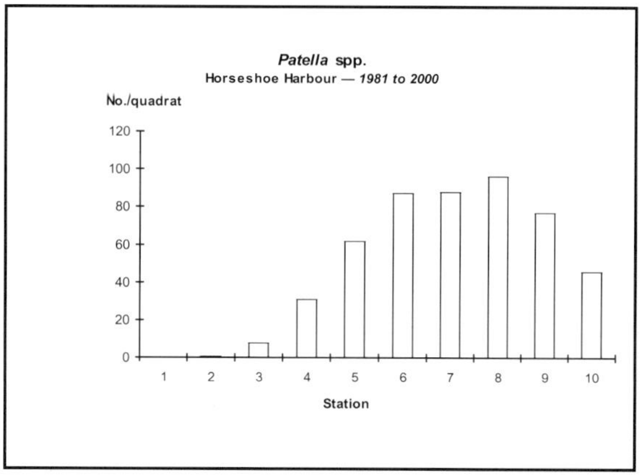

Figure 6.80

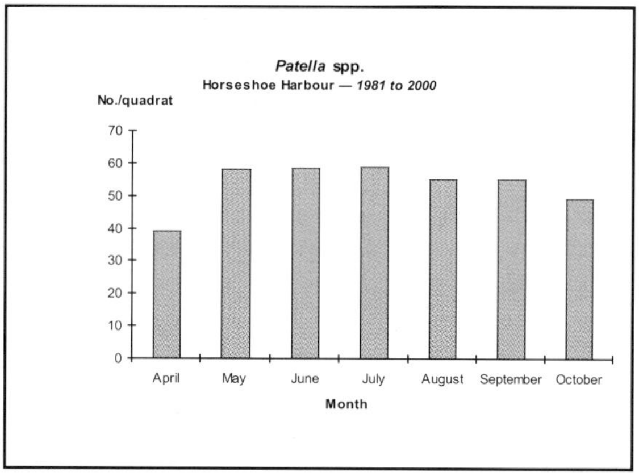

Figure 6.81

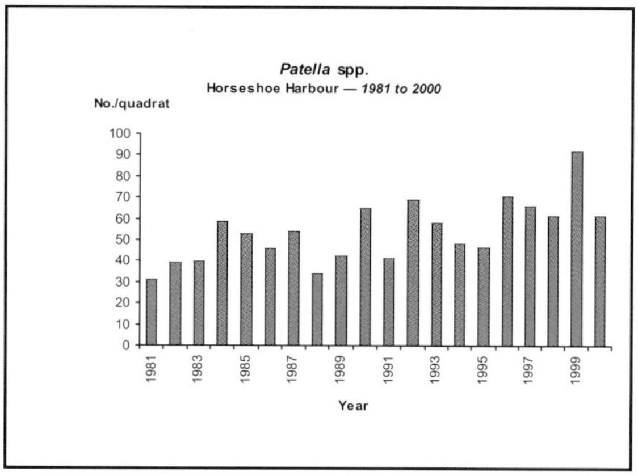

Figure 6.82

HORSESHOE HARBOUR

PREDATOR

Dogwhelk
Nucella lapillus
Cuachma chon

Dogwhelks *Nucella lapillus* had a wide distribution on the shore with maximum numbers at stations 5–8.

Nucella lapillus showed distinct seasonal variation, with higher numbers in May, June and July. Although the decrease in August and September was not continued into October, some occasional additional winter sampling revealed that January and February numbers were significantly lower, and the shore population increase occurred over the period March/April/May.

Nucella lapillus was at a much lower density in the 1990s than for most of the preceding decade. The moderate density of 1981 (1.8 per quadrat) increased steadily for the next three years.

Between 1987 and 1991 there was an overall trend of decreasing numbers, though this was not steady. Throughout the 1990s the density of dogwhelks was never more than 1 per quadrat.

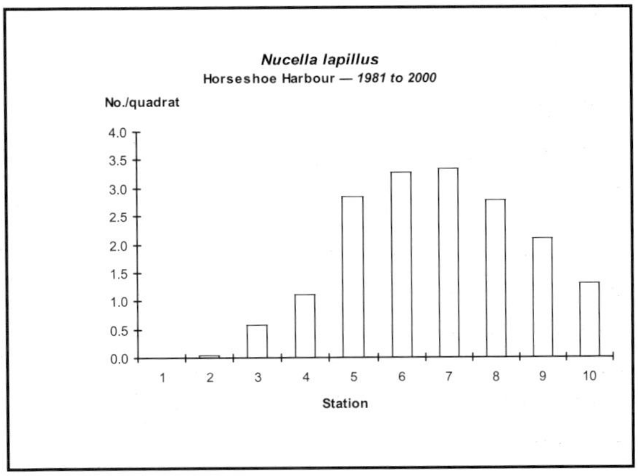

Figure 6.83

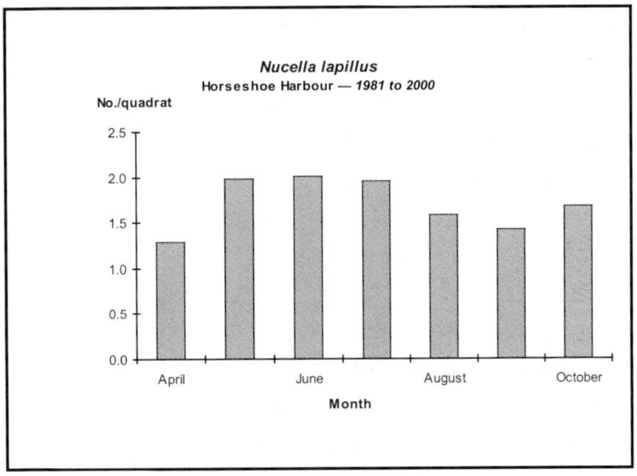

Figure 6.84

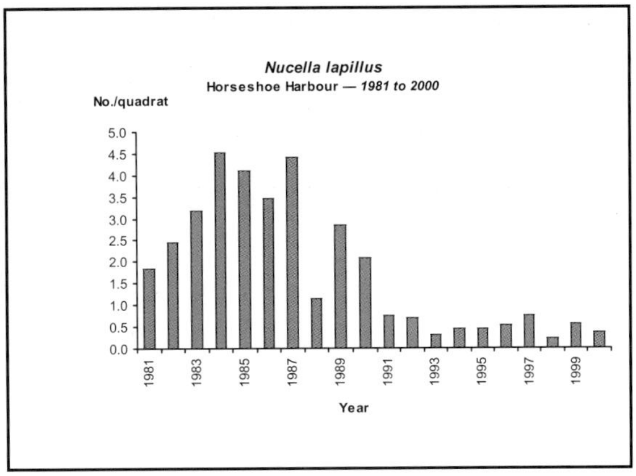

Figure 6.85

TRENDS FOR HORSESHOE HARBOUR 1981–2000

Of the 15 species described in detail for Horseshoe Harbour, all varied in abundance over the 20-year period. The species most consistent in population size was the limpet *Patella* spp.

On the upper shore, the spiral wrack *Fucus spiralis* and bladder wrack *Fucus vesiculosus* were both present and dominant in 1981–83, then noticeably absent or very sparse from 1984 onwards. Neither species thrived on the Horseshoe Harbour transect. Barnacles, which extend into the upper shore, slowly increased their dominance during the 1980s. Flat periwinkles *Littorina obtusata* were also absent or sparse for much of 1988 onwards, though prior to that their relatively high numbers were sustained for several years after the wracks had disappeared. Small periwinkles *Melarhaphe neritoides* gradually increased throughout the 20-year period, having been unrecorded in the first three years.

On the middle shore barnacles increased in dominance until 1990, and then the population crashed in 1991. Recovery the following year was to just half the previous abundance, and this level was maintained in the 1990s. Although relatively consistent, *Patella* numbers were slightly higher in the 1990s than in the 1980s. *Littorina obtusata,* present on both middle and upper shore, was absent or sparse in the 1990s. Dogwhelks *Nucella lapillus* also declined in number during the 1990s.

On the lower shore, the abundance of virtually every species analysed declined in the 1990s. This included the purple topshell *Gibbula umbilicalis*, the seaweeds *Himanthalia elongata, Lomentaria articulata, Mastocarpus stellatus, Osmundea pinnatifida* and the dogwhelk *Nucella lapillus*. Serrated wrack *Fucus serratus* was already declining in the 1980s and remained very sparse in the 1990s.

Although *Himanthalia* and *Fucus serratus* were both very sparse throughout the 1990s, *Himanthalia* remained generally steady or increased in cover during the 1980's, while *Fucus serratus* was continually declining.

REENAHOE

Figure 6.86 Reenahoe looking west, with Drolain Point on the middle left of photograph.

Reenahoe lies on the west coast of the northeast "arm" of Sherkin (Figure 6.86). The transect faces south-southwest. Although with apparently little protection from the southwesterly Atlantic fetch, there are several offshore islets and rocks which break the incoming waves, and there is very shallow water offshore (< 5 m) for approximately 300 m, followed by approximately 1 km of water depth of 5–10 m. These factors combine to render the shore less exposed to wave action than both Poulacurra and Drolain Point.

Of the seven Sherkin Monthly sites, Reenahoe is the only one lying on the younger

Castlehaven rocks. The bedding planes are nearly vertical, with the edges lying along an axis parallel to the water's edge. This structure creates myriad fissures and crevices which afford protection to the mobile animals such as crabs, winkles and whelks and a sheltered environment for newly settled juveniles of many species. There are no boulders overlying the rock.

The horizontal distance of the transect across the shore is 14.3 m and the vertical distance 3.0 m. The resulting profile is a gentle slope of gradient 0.21. Ten stations are usually recorded, with an additional four stations accessible on extremely low spring tides. Stations 1–4 fall in the upper shore, stations 5–8 in the middle shore, and stations 9–10 the lower shore. Station 1 is 4.0 m above chart datum.

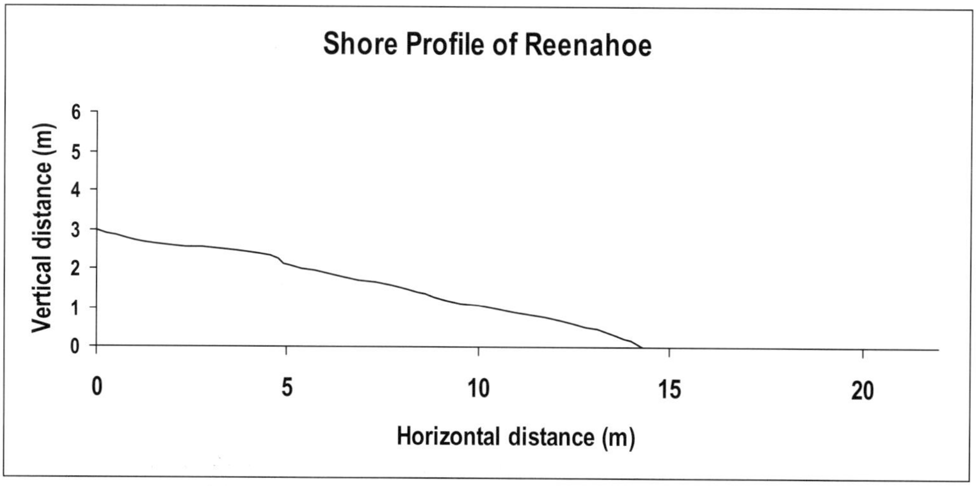

Figure 6.87 A cross-section of the shore from top to bottom showing the gentle gradient of the Reenahoe transect.

VISUAL DOMINANTS

Behind the shore the land is very low-lying with grass, gorse and other scrub vegetation. A narrow splash zone below has a rich development of lichens. The upper middle shore was dominated by barnacles with occasional spiral wrack *Fucus spiralis*, and the diversity of algal species appeared around station 6, peaking at the bottom of the middle shore. Knotted wrack *Ascophyllum nodosum*, associated with wave-shelter, was always present but occupied a small percentage of the rock cover, and often with plants tattered by wave-action. The lower shore had a fairly sparse canopy of the kelps *Laminaria digitata* and *L. saccharina,* with a few *Himanthalia* plants. There was little development of *Fucus*.

Highlight on Seaweed Species

Filamentous Red Algae II

Heterosiphonia plumosa is in the same taxonomic order of red algae (Ceramiales) as *Polysiphonia* and *Ceramium*, but all three are in different families. *Heterosiphonia plumosa* has a feathery appearance with alternate branches from the main stem. These, in turn, divide into sub-branches and very fine branchlets. It grows on rocks or other seaweeds on the lower shore and in shallow water. It was not common on Sherkin but has been recorded at each of the seven sites. It is likely to be more common in shallow water.

Heterosiphonia plumosa

The genus *Ceramium* has a very complex taxonomy and there are many *Ceramium* species found on the northeast Atlantic coasts. Those identified on the Sherkin sites were:

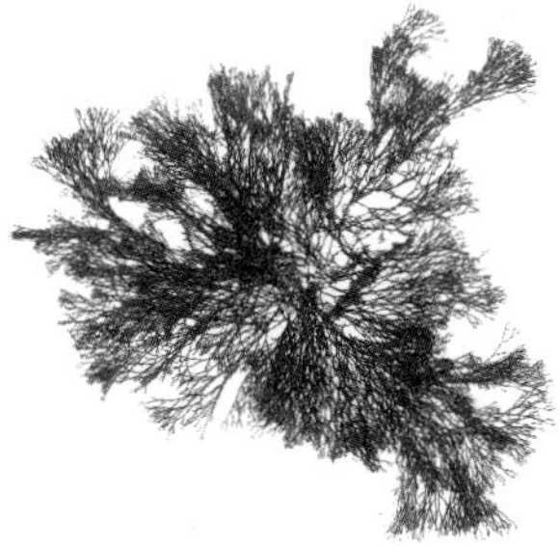

Ceramium spp.

C. botryocarpum
C. ciliatum
C. cimbricum
C. deslongchampii
C. diaphanum
C. echionotum
C. flaccidum
C. gaditanum
C. pallidum
C. rubrum
C. shuttleworthianum
C. siliquosum
C. strictum

The different species are identified by presence or absence of spines and by the structure of the spines. At present the taxonomy of the genus is not stable. Spines are absent from *Ceramium rubrum* and from *C. strictum*, but whereas *C. rubrum* is widespread, *C. strictum* is found mainly on sheltered shores and was noticeably absent from the transect at Poulacurra. Of all these species the most common appears to be *C. shuttleworthianum* which thrives on wave-exposed shores, but was also found on the sheltered shores of Kinish Narrows East and West.

ALGAE

Reenahoe had a fairly diverse range of algal species present, totalling 106 species with a further 24 taxa identified to genus only.

Brown algae

Twenty eight taxa of brown algae were recorded, 23 to species level. Five of these were recorded for one or two years only and were therefore not common, e.g. *Asperococcus fistulosus* and *Halopteris filicina*. *Asperococcus* was usually present in the summer months only. Four species were recorded for three or four years only: *Colpomenia peregrina, Ectocarpus siliculosus, Spongonema tomentosum* and *Scytosiphon lomentaria*. *Chorda filum, Dictyota dichotoma* and the remaining 12 species were regarded as common at Reenahoe. These included the smaller plants of *Cladostephus spongiosus, Elachista fucicola, Leathesia difformis* and *Ralfsia verrucosa,* as well as the dominant fucoids and laminarians. Both *Laminaria digitata* and *L. saccharina* were recorded in the lowest station.

The large brown canopy seaweed *Alaria esculenta* (a species characteristic of very exposed coasts) was never recorded, but *Himanthalia elongata* (which is more typical of slightly less exposed rocky shores) was recorded in 10 of the 20 years.

Red Algae

A total of 81 red algal taxa were recorded, with 70 being identified to species level. Those fairly consistently recorded each year were *Audouinella* spp., *Ceramium* spp., *Chondrus crispus, Corallina officinalis, Dumontia contorta, Gelidium spinosum, Hildenbrandia* spp., Lithothamnia, *Lomentaria articulata, Mastocarpus stellatus, Membranoptera alata, Osmundea pinnatifida, Plumaria plumosa* and *Polysiphonia lanosa*. Forty species were recorded during four years or fewer, and other species present for six or seven years include *Cryptopleura ramosa, Cystoclonium purpureum, Lomentaria clavellosa, Osmundea hybrida* and *Rhodothamniella floridula.*

The increased number of red seaweed species in comparison to other Sherkin shores reflects the somewhat wider variety of habitats present. *Furcellaria lumbricalis, Gracilaria gracilis* and *Rhodothamniella floridula* are all species which tolerate a covering of sand on the rock around their stipes and holdfasts. There was also a moderate development of red algae growing epiphytically on kelp stipes, e.g. *Membranoptera alata*, *Polysiphonia* spp. and *Palmaria palmata*.

Green algae

Thirteen species of green algae were recorded for Reenahoe, with an additional eight taxa identified to genus only.

The most frequently recorded species were *Cladophora rupestris, Cladophora* spp., *Enteromorpha* spp. and *Ulva lactuca*. Other species commonly found were *Chaetomorpha* spp., *E. compressa, E. intestinalis, Spongomorpha arcta. Codium tomentosum* was fairly common in the earlier years of the survey but was not found after 1991.

Those species recorded during only one or two years include other species of *Cladophora* (*C. albida*, C. *hutchinsiae* and *C. sericea)* – together with *Derbesia marina, Enteromorpha linza* and *Urospora* spp.

LICHENS

The black tufted growths of *Lichina pygmaea* were very prominent on the upper and upper middle shore at Reenahoe, standing out amongst the pale barnacles. Above this there was quite a rich development of lichen species. A total of 17 taxa were recorded including three species of *Caloplaca* (*C. ferruginea, C. marina* and *C. thallincola*) and two species of *Ochrolechia* (*O. frigida* and *O. parella*), with *O. parella* being the most frequent. *Haematomma ventosum* was recorded in 1999 only and *Rhizocarpon geographicum* was found in 1989, the only record of this on Sherkin.

ANIMALS

A total of 135 taxa were recorded at Reenahoe, of which 112 were recorded to species level.

The range of bryozoa was similar to that found at Globe Rocks.

A good range of molluscs occurred, though with the exception of winkles, most occurred in relatively few years. Species included *Alvania cancellata, Anomia ephippium, Bittium reticulatum, Calliostoma zizyphinum* and *Epitonium clathrus.* Nudibranchs (sea slugs) included the sea lemon *Archidoris pseudoargus* and *Jorunna tomentosa.*

The number of echinoderm species was relatively high and included the cushion star *Asterina gibbosa* and the brittle stars *Ophiocomina nigra* and *Ophiothrix fragilis*.

Sponges were also relatively rich in the number of species recorded on the Reenahoe shore. Ten species were recorded although only one, breadcrumb sponge *Halichondria panicea* occurred every year and another two, *Hymeniacidon sanguinea* and *Myxilla incrustans,* were found most years. Other species such as *Clathrina coriacea*, *Cliona celata*, *Grantia compressa*, *Hemimycale columella*, *Hymeniacidon perleve*, *Ophlitaspongia seriata* and *Oscarella lobularis* were recorded for a maximum of three years only.

Hydroids were not particularly rich. Apart from *Dynamena pumila*, which was present every year, there were only occasional records of *Clava multicornis*, *Coryne* sp., *Laomedea flexuosa, Obelia geniculata* and *Sertularella polyzonias*.

Annelid records were mainly of the calcareous tubeworms *Pomatoceros* and *Spirorbis*. Only *S. rupestris* and *S. spirorbis* were noted. Species associated with sediments were occasionally noted, e.g. *Amphitritides gracilis, Cirratulus cirratus, Cirriformia tentaculata, Eulalia viridis, Lanice conchilega, Nephtys hombergi* and *Perinereis cultrifera. Lanice,* which has a very characteristic tube coated with sand grains, is a sedentary tube-dwelling species. Others, including *Eulalia viridis, Nephtys hombergi and Perinereis cultrifera,* move freely through sediments and amongst seaweeds.

Highlight on Sponges (Porifera)

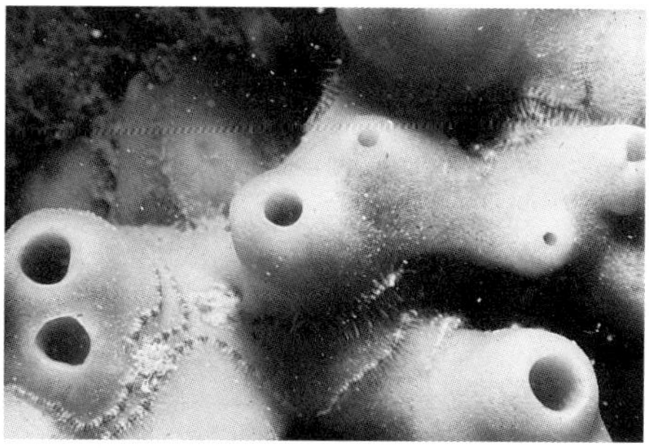
Breadcrumb Sponge – *Halichondria panicea*

Sponges are a large phylum with many species. They have interesting shapes and great beauty when viewed under the microscope due to their structural spicules.

Two classes of sponges occur in Irish waters – those with calcareous spicules (Calcarea) and those with spicules of horny spongin and/or silica (Demospongia). While sponges found on the shore are usually small, for example the purse sponge *Grantia compressa* and small patches of *Leucosolenia botryoides* (both Calcarea), those occurring beneath low water can be massive (up to 50 cm in diameter), for example *Cliona celata* and *Suberites carnosus*. The latter are in the class Demospongia, together with the breadcrumb sponge *Halichondria panicea* and *Hymeniacidon perleve* – both of which are common shore species. All occur in permanently damp habitats and therefore are most frequently found in the lowest stations, in overhangs, amongst algal holdfasts and in crevices.

Of the 22 crustacean taxa recorded, seven are crabs. Hermit crabs *Pagurus bernhardus*, common shore crabs *Carcinus maenas* and edible crabs *Cancer pagurus* were all common in the lowest two stations, and there were occasional records of *Xantho incisus* and the pea crab *Pinnotheres pisum*. Isopods were relatively diverse with *Dynamena bidentata* and *Idotea granulosa* occurring as well as the common sea slater *Ligia oceanica*.

The range of bryozoa was similar to that found at Globe Rocks, with the sea mats *Electra pilosa, Flustrellidra hispida* and *Membranipora membranacea* recorded almost every year. *Alcyonidium* spp. were recorded in a good number of years with both *A. gelatinosum* and *A. hirsutum* present equally.

The number of echinoderm species (five) was the highest found throughout the seven shores and included the common starfish *Asterias rubens*, the cushion star *Asterina gibbosa* and the three species of brittle stars *Amphiura brachiata, Ophiocomina nigra,* and *Ophiothrix fragilis*. *Amphiura brachiata* and *Ophiocomina nigra* were both found amongst the sediment pockets in the lowest stations.

Species analysed for Reenahoe, their place in the food chain and the shore ecology (Predatory pathway ——► Grazing pathway ••••••►)

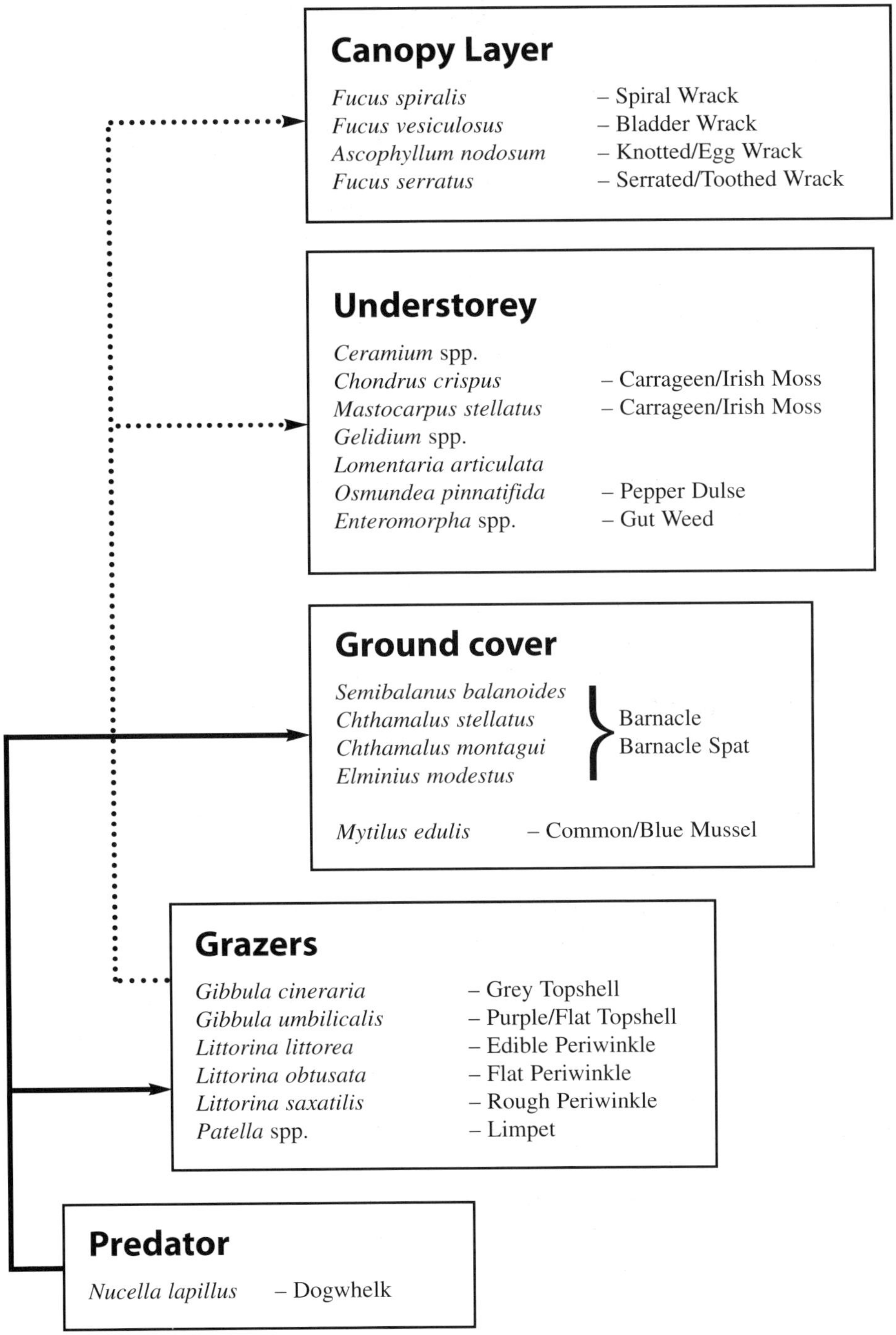

REENAHOE

CANOPY LAYER

Spiral Wrack
Fucus spiralis
Casfheamainn

Spiral wrack *Fucus spiralis* was found mainly on the upper and middle shore at stations 4–7, but did not grow at all luxuriously and formed only approximately 3% to 4% cover per quadrat. Occasional plants were found both higher and lower on the shore.

Variation month by month was only noticeable with the decrease from May to June.

The mean annual cover was always ≤ 6%, but varied considerably. From 1981–89 the amount of *Fucus spiralis* on the shore rose steadily. From 1989–90 it crashed from almost 6% down to less than 0.5% cover. With the exception of 1996 when 4% was recorded, cover remained very low (< 2%) throughout the 1990s and was unrecorded in 1993.

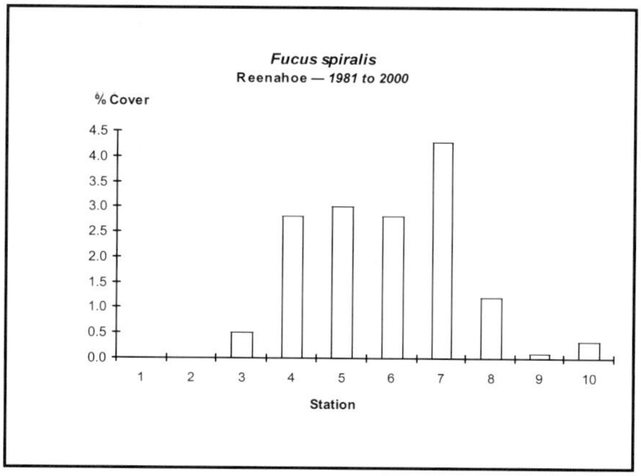

Figure 6.88

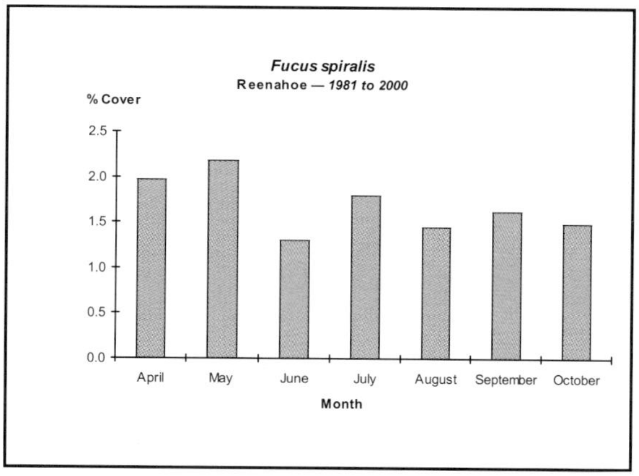

Figure 6.89

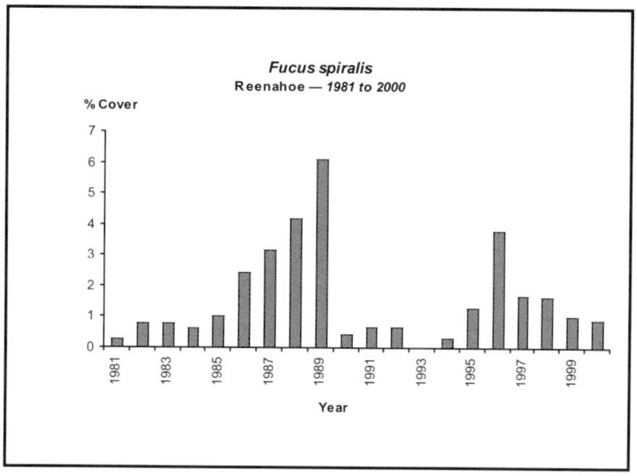

Figure 6.90

REENAHOE

CANOPY LAYER

Bladder Wrack
Fucus vesiculosus
Feamainn bhoilgíneach

Bladder wrack *Fucus vesiculosus* flourished best at stations 6, 7 and 8 on the middle and lower shore. A few plants survived higher up (stations 3–5), and a few in the lowest stations (9 and 10).

Fucus vesiculosus density was lowest in April and May, but there was a marked increase during June (up to 8% per quadrat) and this growth was maintained until October.

The amount varied annually over the 20 years, with four cycles, each lasting six or seven years. 1984, 1989, 1990 and 1995, with intermediate patterns of rise and fall. Densest cover was recorded during 1986–87 and 1998–99. The peak of the intermittent cycle (1989–95) was lower (< 10%) and was sustained over the three-year period 1991–93.

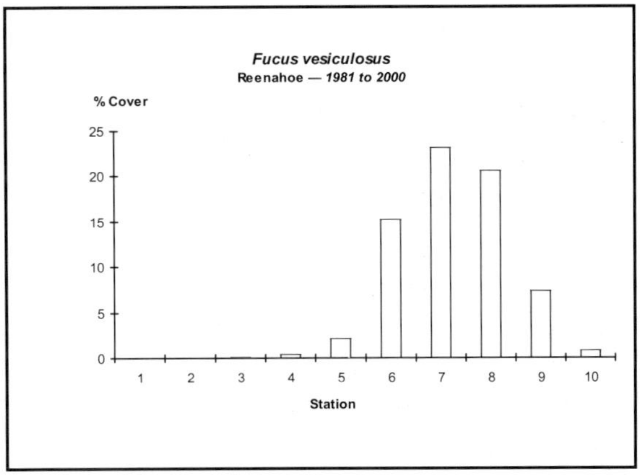

Figure 6.91

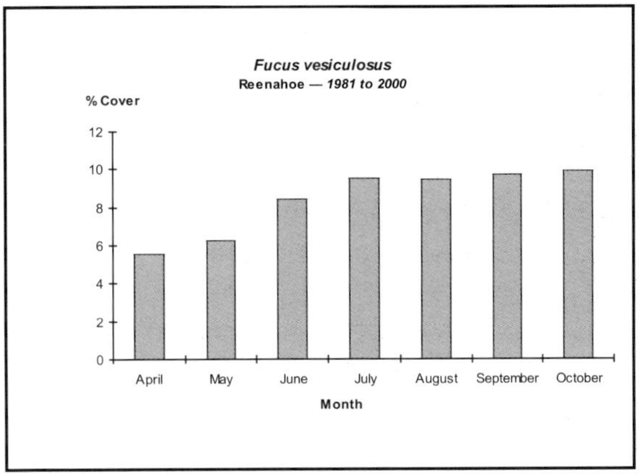

Figure 6.92

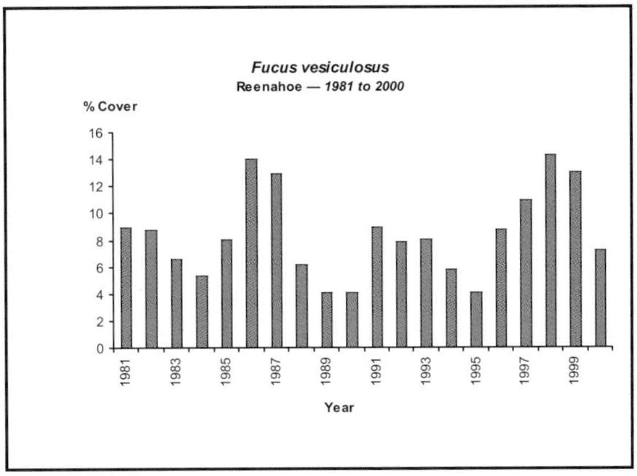

Figure 6.93

REENAHOE

CANOPY LAYER

Knotted/Egg Wrack
Ascophyllum nodosum
Feamainn bhuí

Knotted wrack *Ascophyllum nodosum* is characteristic of sheltered shores where it grows luxuriously and often dominates the canopy layer entirely. On the Reenahoe shore conditions were less than ideal for it. The majority of plants grew at stations 6–9, and occasional plants were recorded at stations 5 and 10.

There was a fairly constant percentage cover in May–September (*ca.* 5–6% per quadrat) but much lower cover in April and October, at the beginning and end of the growing season. Maximum growth took place in the lengthening days of spring.

There was a definite decrease in the amount of *Ascophyllum nodosum* cover after 1985. The first four years of the survey showed 9–15% cover. This figure dropped steeply in 1985 to 7.5% and cover then remained fairly constant at ≤ 5% for 15 years.

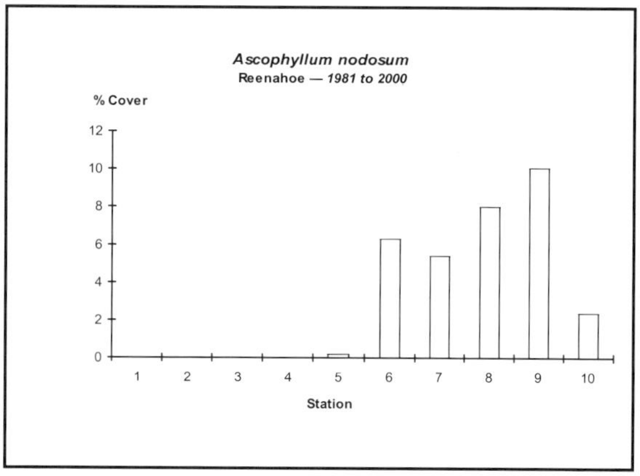

Figure 6.94

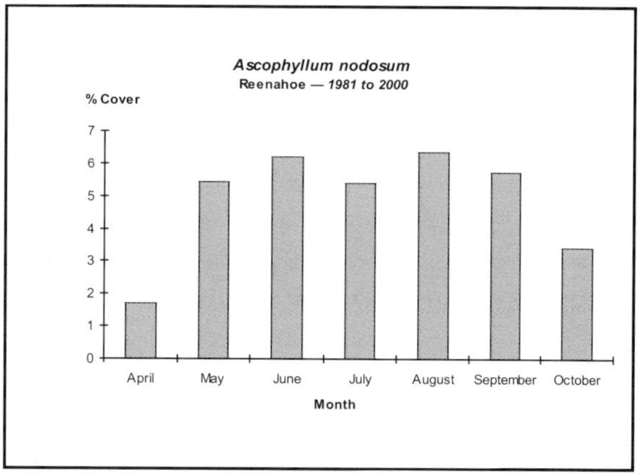

Figure 6.95

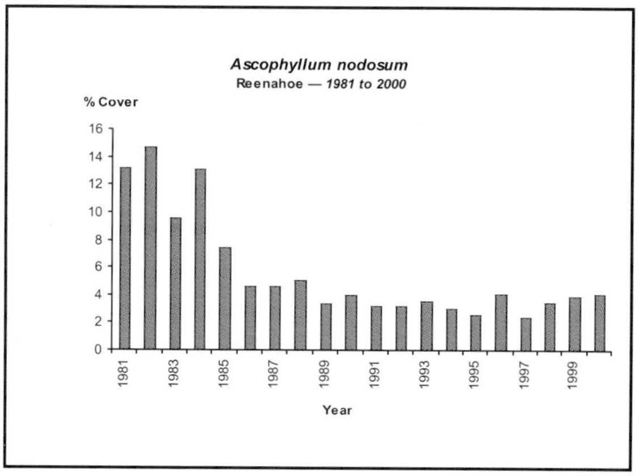

Figure 6.96

REENAHOE

CANOPY LAYER

Serrated/Toothed Wrack
Fucus serratus
Míoránach

The lower shore serrated wrack *Fucus serratus* was recorded from stations 5–10 peaking at stations 9 and 10. It grew much more luxuriantly than the other two *Fucus* species, reaching an overall mean peak of approximately 43% cover per quadrat.

Cover appeared to be consistently low during April, but almost doubled to reach 20% during May. This density was maintained through June and July, and there was a small increase in cover in August, followed by decreasing cover in the autumn. However, October abundance was much greater than in April.

Annual variation occurred although there was no obvious pattern to the recorded increases and decreases. The overall trend might be described as one of cyclical increase and decrease over a six- or seven-year period. The lowest densities were recorded in 1987, 1992 and 1997.

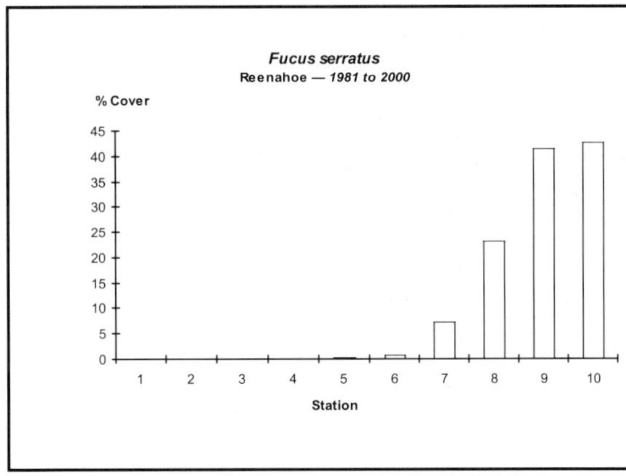

Figure 6.97

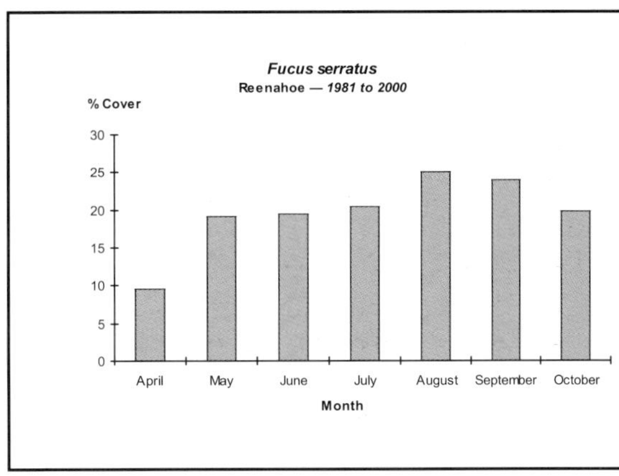

Figure 6.98

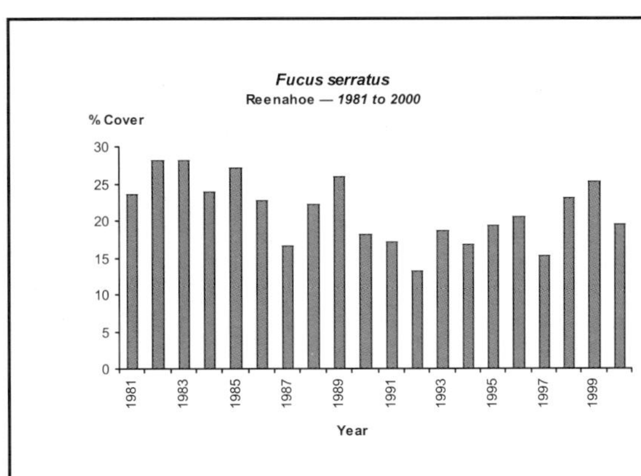

Figure 6.99

REENAHOE

UNDERSTOREY

Ceramium spp.

Part of the understorey, *Ceramium* spp. occurred sparsely over most of the shore (stations 4–10) and was relatively dense at stations 9 and 10.

Monthly variation was present, with extremely low levels recorded in April, followed by a large increase in May, which was sustained until September. October had the highest annual percentage cover at 1.4% per quadrat.

Although the mean annual density was always low (< 2%), densities during isolated years (1983, 1986, 1989, 1995 and 1997) were relatively higher at 0.5–2.0% as opposed to the more commonly seen figures of < 0.25%.

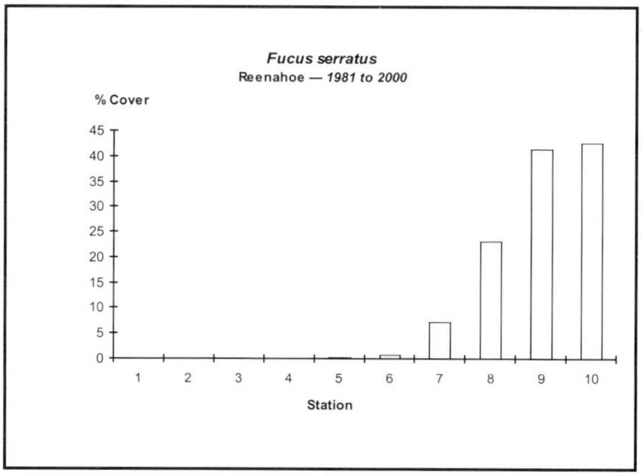

Figure 6.97

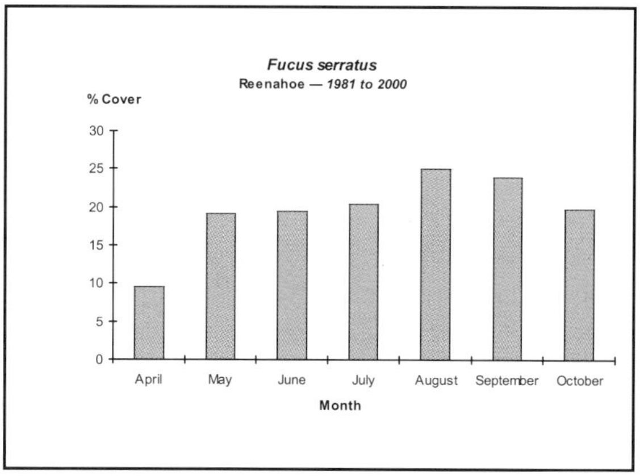

Figure 6.98

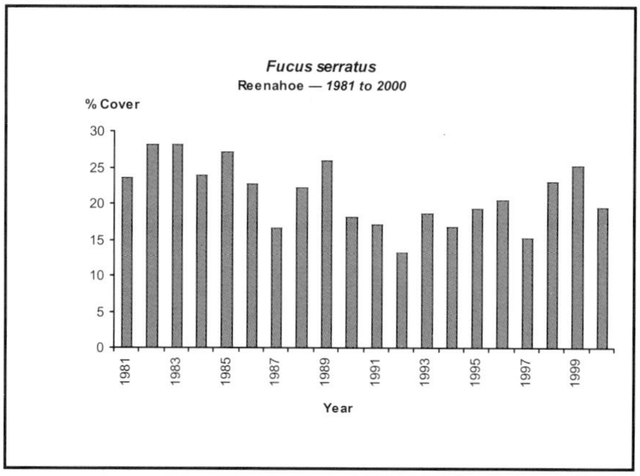

Figure 6.99

REENAHOE

UNDERSTOREY

Carrageen/Irish Moss
Chondrus crispus
Cosáinín (carraige)

The carrageen moss *Chondrus crispus* species followed a similar distribution pattern to the other carrageen *Mastocarpus stellatus*. *C. crispus* occurred from station 5 down to 10, and like *M. stellatus* peaked at station 9. However it was far less common on the Reenahoe shore than *M. stellatus* and occupied only 2–5% cover per quadrat of the shore within its main range.

Monthly variation occurred, with an increase during May. Density appeared to fall slightly during the middle of the summer (July) but plants increased again in August and October.

In many years the overall mean cover was < 2%, however there was a cycle of rise and fall from 1984–95 which peaked very dramatically during 1989. After the 1995 minimum, there was an overall increase in abundance in 1999 and 2000.

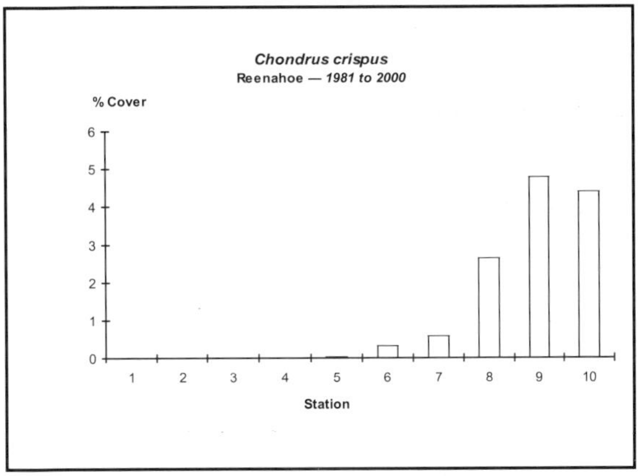

Figure 6.103

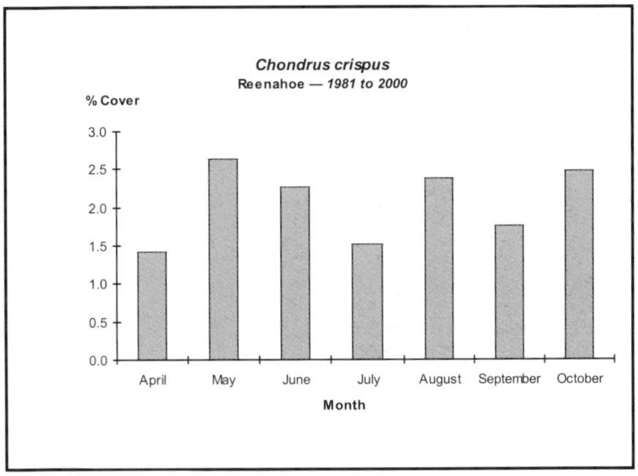

Figure 6.104

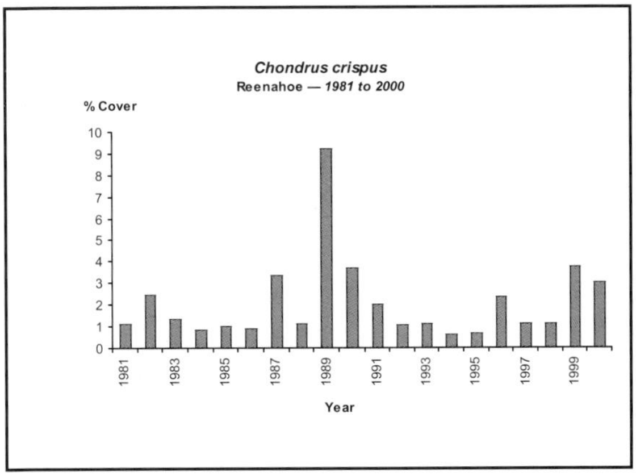

Figure 6.105

REENAHOE

UNDERSTOREY

Carrageen/Irish Moss
Mastocarpus stellatus
Clúimhín cait

The other carrageen *Mastocarpus stellatus* was present from station 5 down to station 10, and carried on growing into the sublittoral. Its main zone was on the lower shore where it peaked at 14% cover per quadrat at station 10.

There was no significant month by month variation in density.

This red seaweed species was present every year and there were trends of increase and decrease in annual density. The small amount recorded in 1981 (1%) increased significantly during 1982 (to 8%) and this was sustained for three years (1982–84). A significant decrease occurred in 1985, which was followed by a trend of increase for the three succeeding years. The period 1989–93 showed a five-year trend of decreasing quantity. This was followed by a cycle of increase to 1995 and a decrease to 1998. During the last two years of the survey presented here (1999 and 2000) percentage cover rose again.

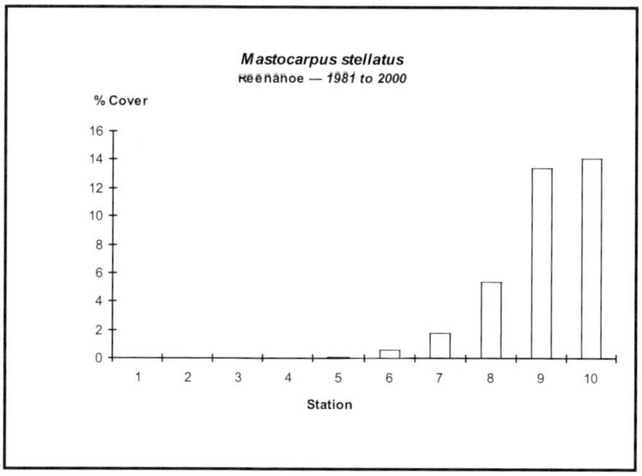

Figure 6.106

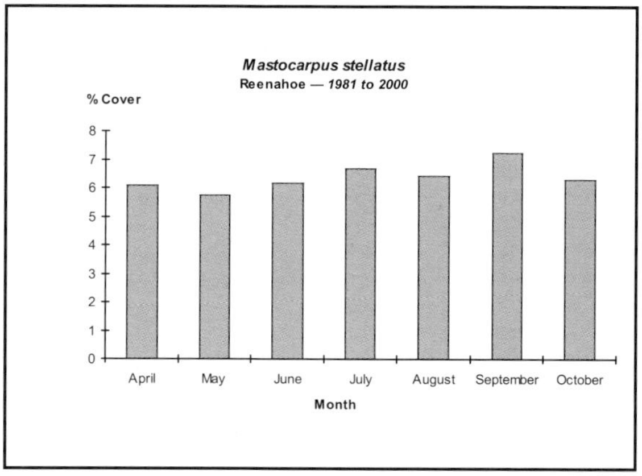

Figure 6.107

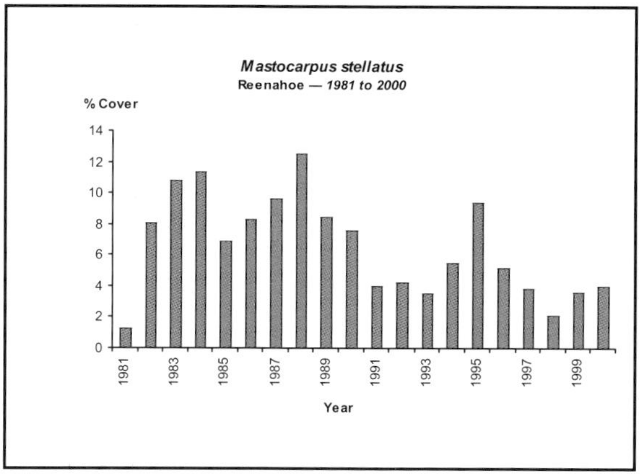

Figure 6.108

REENAHOE

UNDERSTOREY

Gelidium spp.

Gelidium spp. occupied a fairly wide range on the shore. The bulk of the distribution lay between stations 5 and 10, but occasional plants were recorded as high up the shore as station 2.

Monthly variation was seen only in the increase in cover from May to June, and this level was maintained until October.

Annual variation was evident, although not regular, and the most conspicuous years were 1982, 1990 and 1996 when density was relatively high, and 1988 when *Gelidium* was exceptionally sparse on the shore (< 0.05% cover per quadrat). The peak values recorded in 1990 and 1996 were isolated periods of abundance and were not preceded by any trend of general increase.

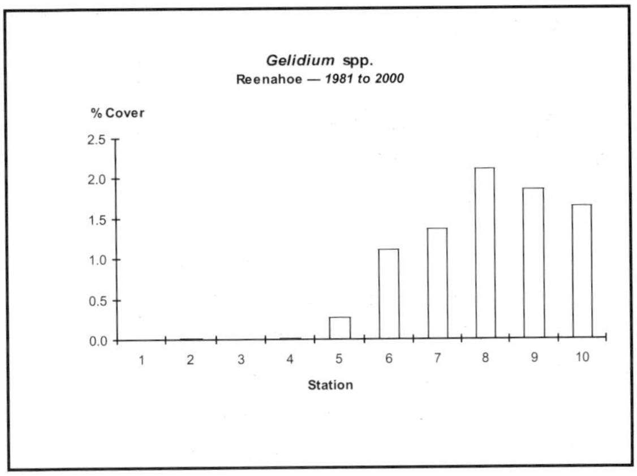

Figure 6.109

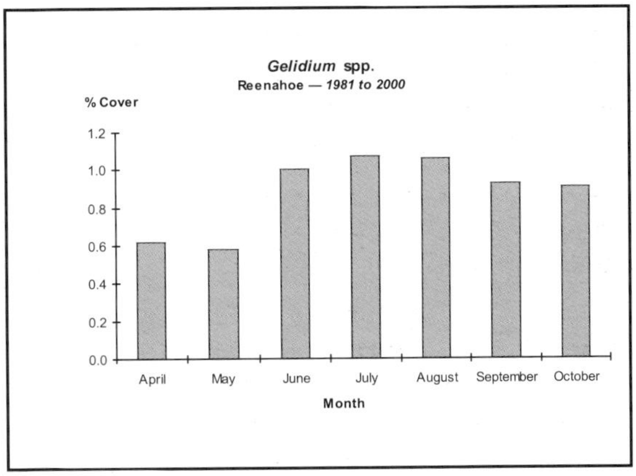

Figure 6.110

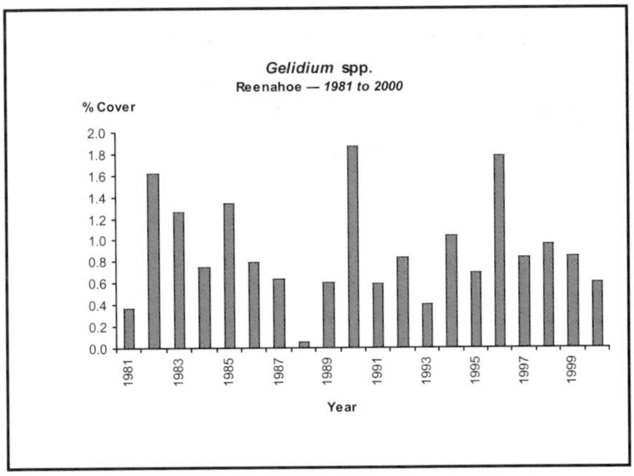

Figure 6.111

REENAHOE

UNDERSTOREY

Lomentaria articulata

Lomentaria articulata occurred on the middle and lower stations (6–10), but it was most common at stations 8 and 9.

Monthly variation was evident, with a trend of increase from April to June. From July to October density remained significantly lower than the June maximum.

Abundance over the 20 years has fluctuated in irregular cycles. A steady rise and fall was noted from 1981–85 and from 1985–91. During the early 1990s this pattern was not so obvious, but amounts of *Lomentaria* decreased significantly during 1996–98.

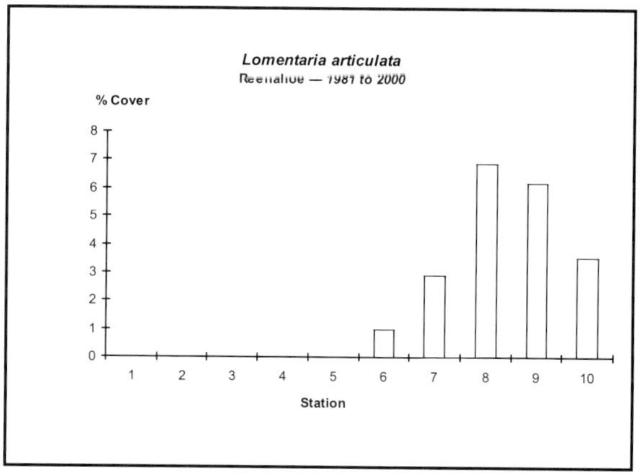

Figure 6.112

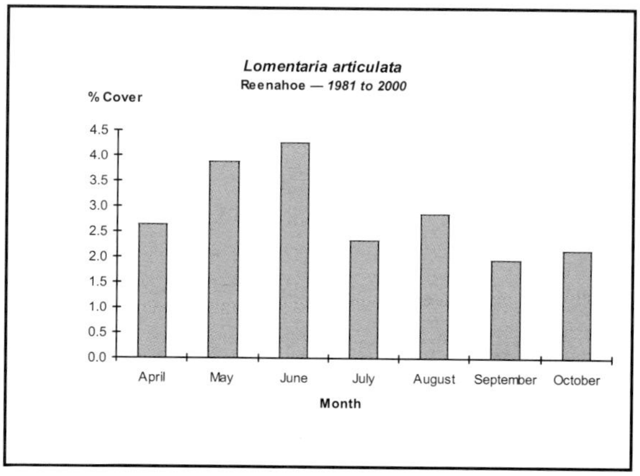

Figure 6.113

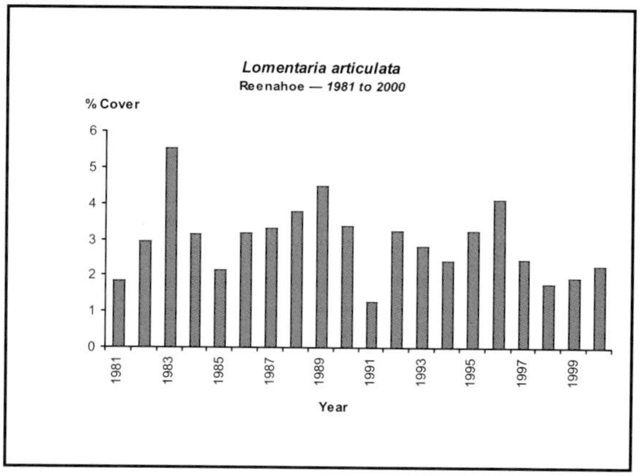

Figure 6.114

REENAHOE

UNDERSTOREY

Pepper dulse
Osmundea pinnatifida
Míobhán

The small red algae pepper dulse *Osmundea pinnatifida* occupied a higher zone on the shore than the carrageen mosses, occurring from station 3 to station 10. Its peak distribution was on the middle shore at stations 6 and 7 where densities of 15% cover per quadrat were recorded.

There was no significant monthly variation.

Annual variation has occurred. Between 1981 and 1991 there were two cycles of abundance whose peaks (in 1983 and 1989) were separated by intervening years of steady decline and increase. After the 1991 low, this pattern was not evident and mean density was consistently around 5% cover.

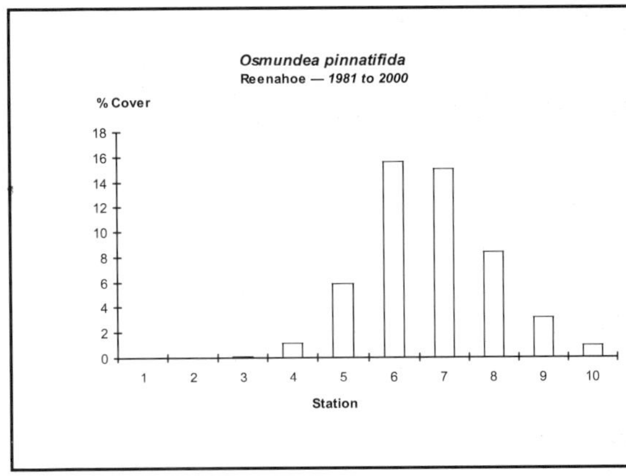

Figure 6.115

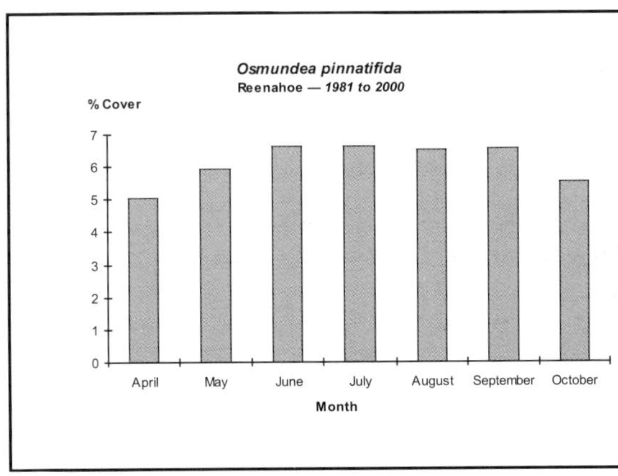

Figure 6.116

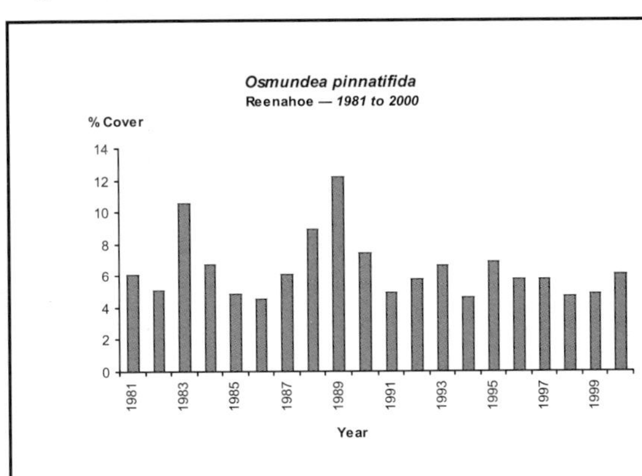

Figure 6.117

REENAHOE

UNDERSTOREY

Gut Weed
Enteromorpha spp.
Líneáil ghorm

The several species of the green alga gut weed *Enteromorpha* were graphed as one (*Enteromorpha* spp.), and occurred over most of the shore, with the maximum percentage cover at station 9.

It is well known to be a short-lived genus with maximum growth during the summer months, and the monthly variation in cover recorded at Reenahoe supports this. There was very little on the shore in April, a small increase in May, followed by a noticeable flush of green during June. Consecutive months then showed a trend of decreasing cover.

Although usually present in small amounts at Reenahoe, there has been some considerable variation over the years. The mean figure for % cover was much higher during four years in particular: 1987, 1988, 1994 and 1996. However it was noted that the amount present on the shore each month in 1987 was extremely variable, with some months having up to 5% cover per quadrat and others virtually nothing.

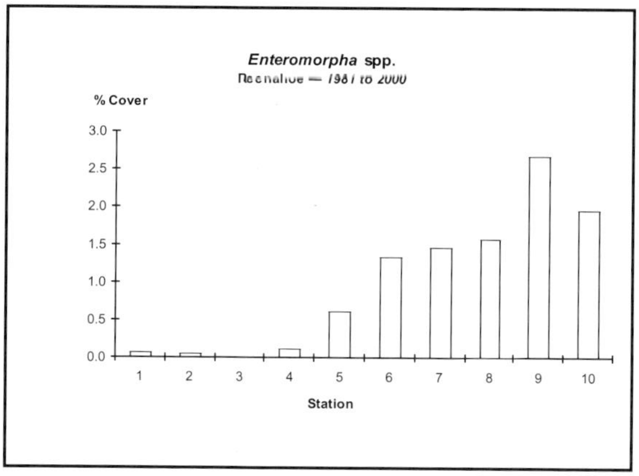

Figure 6.118

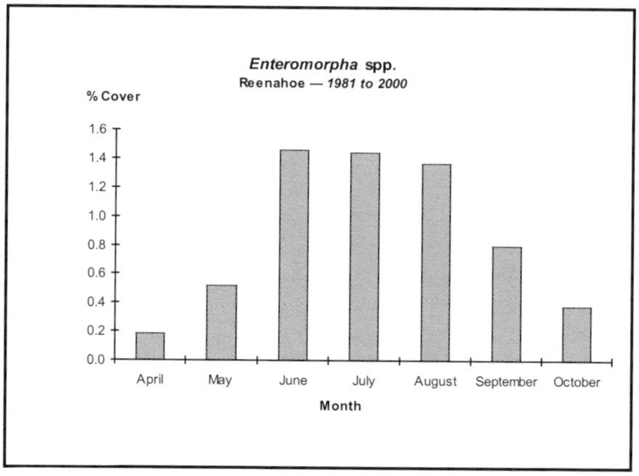

Figure 6.119

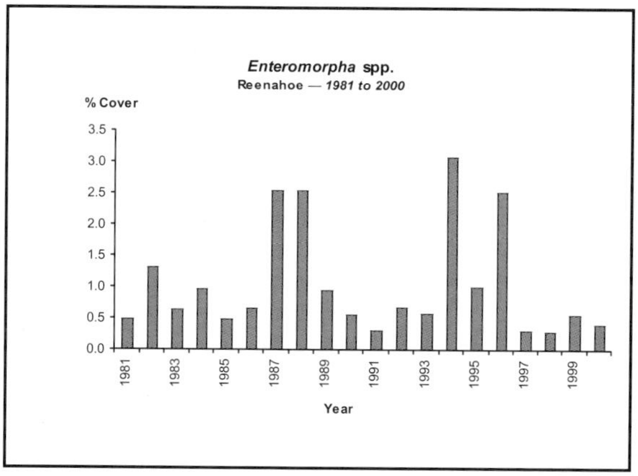

Figure 6.120

The exposed southwest headland of Sherkin Island showing the deep cleft of Poulacurra on the lower right.

Actinothoë sphyrodeta on bryozoan covered rock.

A thick growth of the green seaweed *Chaetomorpha rupestris*.

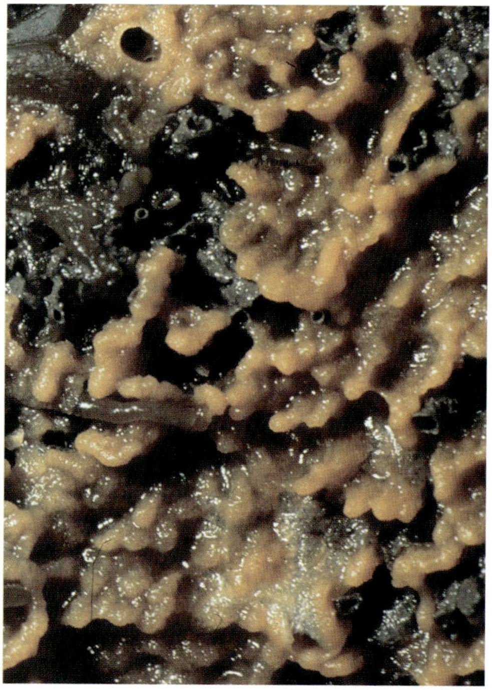

Lobes of the orange encrusting sponge *Myxilla incrustans*.

Clearly visible polyps on the delicate branches of a Plumularian hydroid.

Sherkin Island Marine Station sitting above the exposed coastline of Drolain Point.

Rough seas and swell on the shores of Drolain Point.

Painted topshell *Calliostoma zizyphinum.*

Coralline red alga *Corallina officinalis*, common in rock pools.

Extended column and tentacles of beadlet anemone *Actinia equina*, with marginal beads clearly showing.

The moderately sheltered shores at Globe Rocks on the east coast of Sherkin Island.

Snakelocks anemone *Anemonia viridis.*

Dahlia anemone *Urticina felina*, usually found in crevices and overhangs on the lower shore.

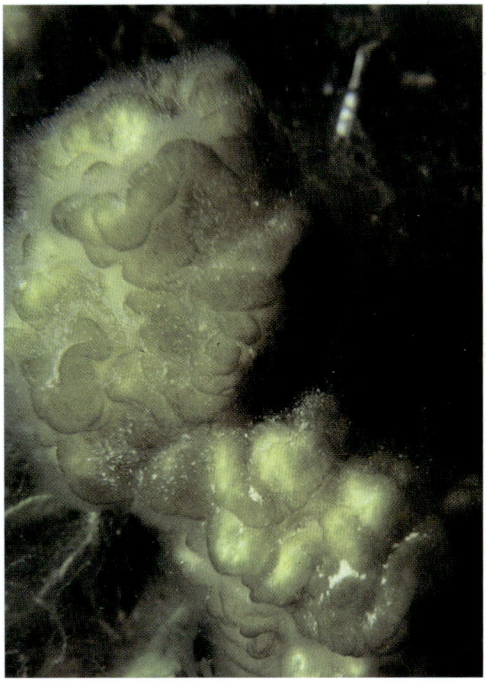

The globular shape of the brown *Leathesia difformis*, which grows on other seaweeds.

The beautiful colours of the jewel anemone *Corynactis viridis* can be seen at extreme low water.

Hermit crab *Pagurus bernhardus* showing the typical unequal development of the pincers, which enables it to retreat into its borrowed shell.

Panorama of Sherkin Island, with Horseshoe Harbour in the foreground and Kinish Harbour behind.

The conspicuous olive-green fronds of the seaweed velvet horn *Codium tomentosum.*

Shanny *Lipophrys pholis*, often camouflaged among rocks on the lower shore.

Velvet swimming crab *Necora puber*, one of the more mobile shore predators, found at low water.

Common edible sea urchin *Echinus esculentus*, an important sublittoral grazer, not often found on the shore.

Moderately exposed shores around Reenahoe, Sherkin Island.

Rich growth of dulse *Palmaria palmata* amongst *Fucus serratus* on the lower shore.

Spirorbid tubeworms, common on fronds of wracks and rock surfaces.

The squat shape of the cushion star *Asterina gibbosa*, on encrusting bryozoans.

Common brittle star *Ophiothrix fragilis*, found singly on the lower shore, but in large clusters sublittorally.

A view from the south of the narrow channel separating Kinish Narrows West and East, Sherkin Island.

Light bulb tunicate *Clavelina lepadiformis*, a colonial sea squirt found at extreme low water and below.

Encrusting red seaweed Lithothamnia.

Rocky shore on a low spring tide, with exposed kelp and barnacle covered rocks.

The white jelly-like mass of the colonial sea squirt *Botryllus schlosseri*, with delicate branched hydroids growing through.

The common starfish *Asterias rubens*, a predator of bivalves and other molluscs on the lower shore.

The laterally flattened bodies of the sandhopper *Talitrus saltator.*

Orange leafy lichen *Xanthoria parietina*, a common lichen in the splash zone.

Dorsal plates of the coat-of-mail chiton *Lepidochitonia cinerea.*

Sea lemon *Archidoris pseudoargus* laying its characteristic jelly-like coil of eggs.

Delicate hydroid colonies of *Dynamena pumila*, which often grow on shells and seaweed.

Calcareous tube worm *Pomatoceros triqueter* (long) and *Spirorbis* (coiled) on rock surface.

The brittle, upright branches of sea ivory *Ramalina siliquosa*, a lichen of the splash zone.

Blue rayed limpet *Helcion pellucidum* on kelp frond, with colonial sea mat *Membranipora membranacea.*

REENAHOE

GROUND COVER

Barnacles

Semibalanus balanoides
Chthamalus stellatus
Chthamalus montagui
Elminius modestus
Giúrainn

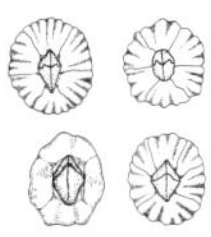

Barnacles formed a dense band between stations 3 and 7 on the upper and upper middle shore where they were visually dominant. As the percentage cover decreased from 15% per quadrat below station 7, so bladder wrack *Fucus vesiculosus* and serrated wrack *F. serratus* began to dominate. The highest barnacle density was reached at station 5.

Monthly variation was evident. From a fairly low mean monthly percentage cover in April and May (< 6%) there was a steady increase through the summer to a maximum of 18% in September.

Annual variation was pronounced. With the exception of one year, 1987, the mean annual figure rose throughout the 1980s from a minimum of 2% in 1981 to a peak of 44% in 1990. Numbers fell dramatically over the winter of 1990 to give an annual mean of 3% at the end of 1991. For the next decade cover remained at a consistently low level (≤ 5%).

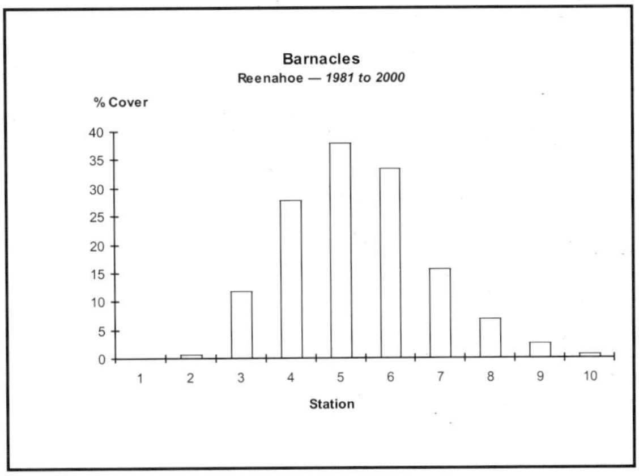

Figure 6.121

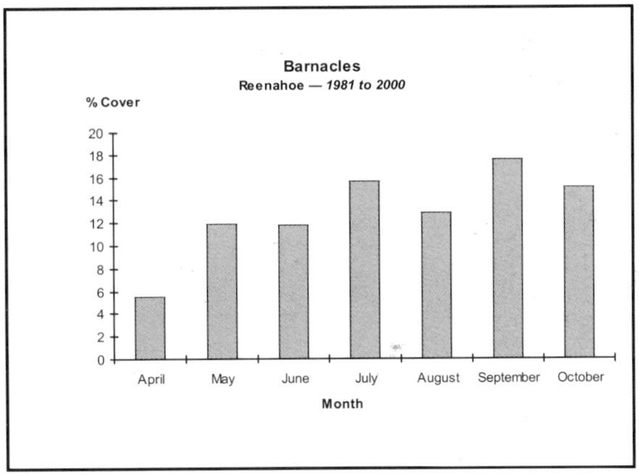

Figure 6.122

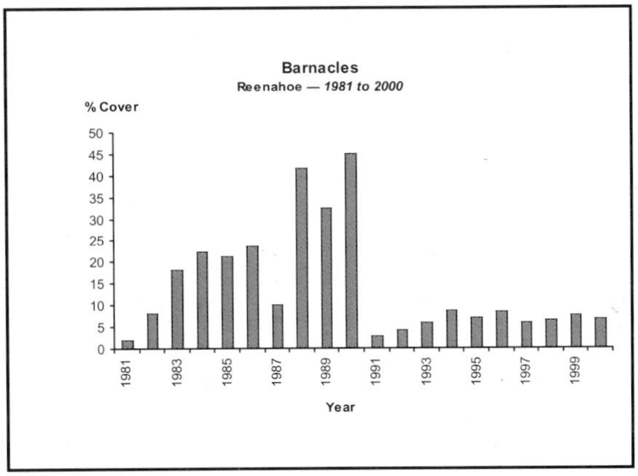

Figure 6.123

REENAHOE

GROUND COVER

Barnacle Spat
Síol giúrainn

The band of spat settlement was fairly wide and lay between stations 3 and 10, with numbers peaking at just over 55/dm² at station 6.

Settlement of *Semibalanus balanoides* generally occurs in May, but at Reenahoe numbers were at a maximum during April. Abundance declined steadily to low September levels (5/dm²). There was no increase in numbers noted in August or September which would correspond with the settlement period of *Chthamalus* spp.

Settlement was erratic over the 20-year period. 1985 was the only year when none was recorded, but 1984, 1993 and 1999 saw very little spatfall. The most prolific years were 1994 and 1997.

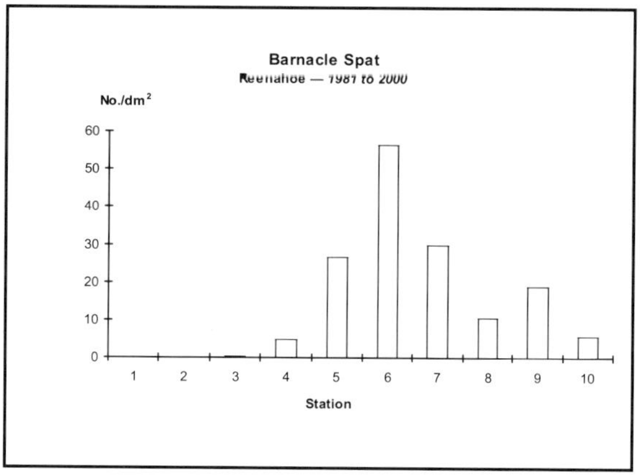

Figure 6.124

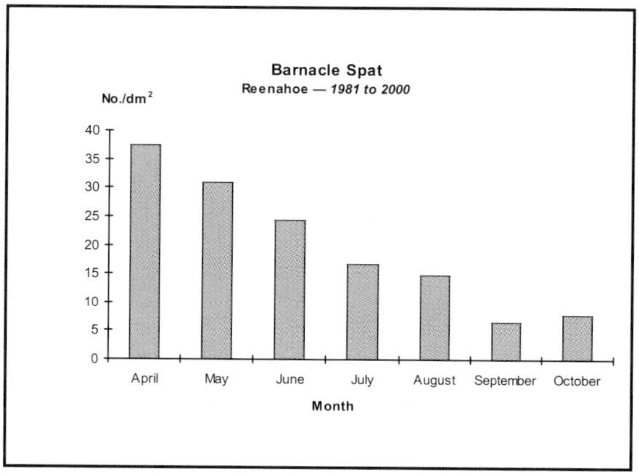

Figure 6.125

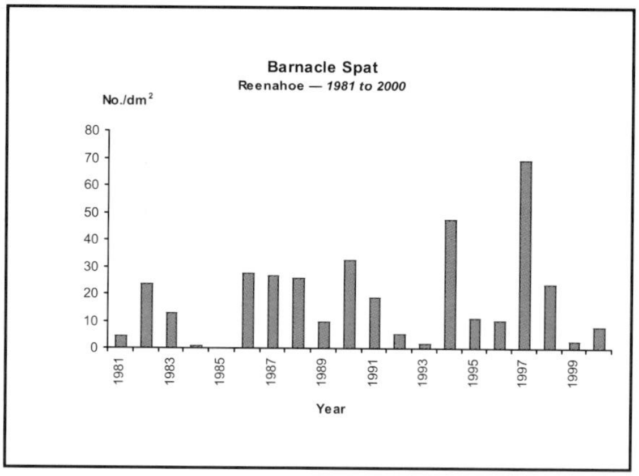

Figure 6.126

REENAHOE

GROUND COVER

Common/Blue Mussel
Mytilus edulis
Diúilicín

A few common mussels *Mytilus edulis* were always present amongst the barnacles at Reenahoe between stations 3 and 10, but the species did not form an important element of the shore community as it accounted for less than 1% cover of the rock surface.

There was a relatively large increase in abundance in May, but this was not maintained into the summer, and was not a constant feature every year. There was, in fact, very large variation about the May mean of 0.8%.

During one year only was there any exception to the low cover (< 0.5% per quadrat) and that was in 1982 when density rose eight-fold. This was due primarily to the huge increase in numbers in May as mentioned above.

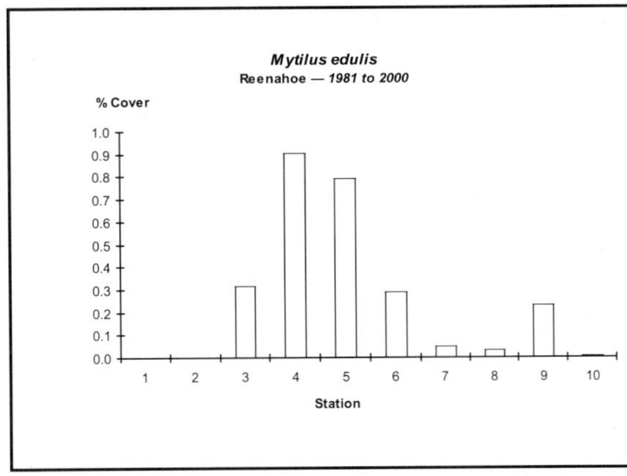

Figure 6.127

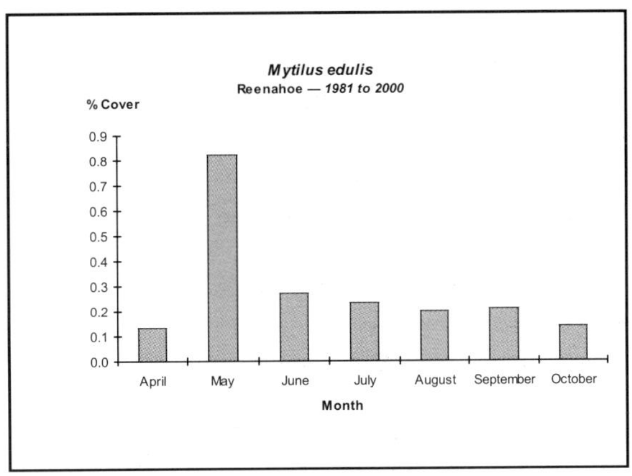

Figure 6.128

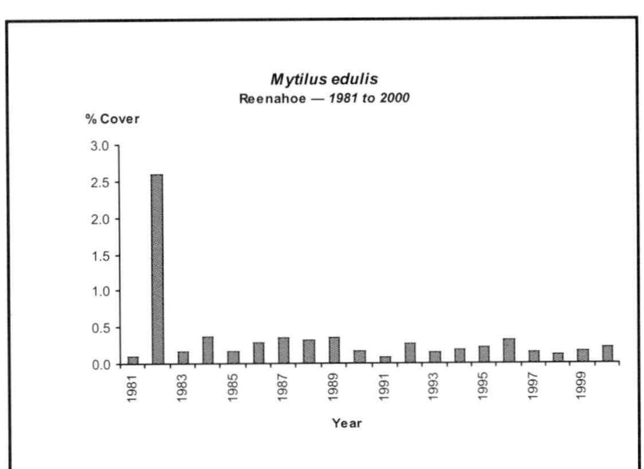

Figure 6.129

REENAHOE

GRAZERS

Grey Topshell
Gibbula cineraria
Faochán Mhuire glas

The grey topshell *Gibbula cineraria* followed a broadly similar distribution pattern to the purple topshell *G. umbilicalis.* It was present at stations 3–10, but its main range extended to stations 9 and 10. Numbers were much smaller, with a maximum density of just under 0.7 per quadrat as compared with 2.8 per quadrat for the purple topshell.

The grey topshell showed insignificant monthly variation. Although the mean number in June was twice that of April, there was wide variation around this figure.

The annual variation is interesting; in one year, 1987, numbers rose dramatically from less than 0.2 per quadrat to 1.0 per quadrat, but unlike the purple topshell, whose numbers continued to rise from a fairly low level in 1987, the grey topshell's success in 1987 was short-lived. It was then unrecorded for two consecutive years and present as a small or moderate population for most other years. Another exceptional year was 1999 when numbers rose to approximately 0.7 per quadrat.

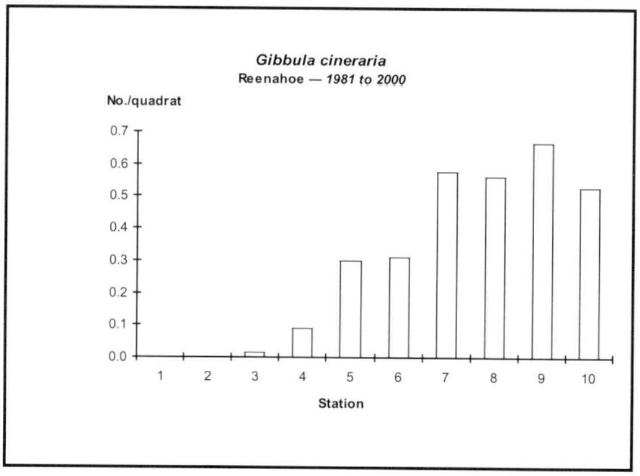

Figure 6.130

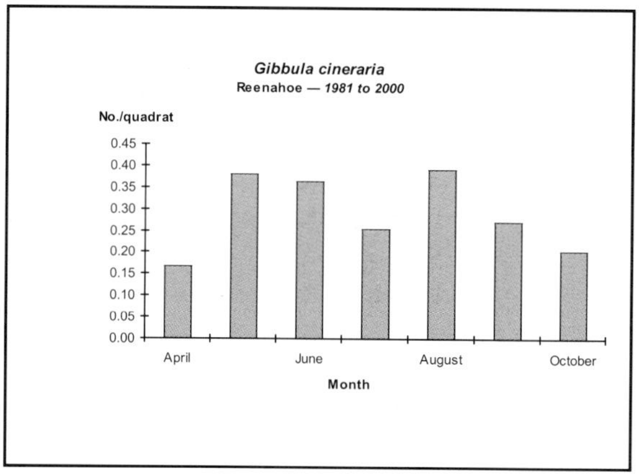

Figure 6.131

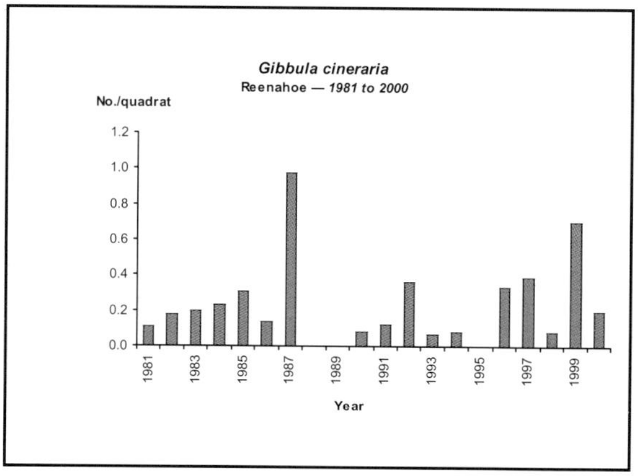

Figure 6.132

REENAHOE

GRAZERS

Purple/Flat Topshell
Gibbula umbilicalis
Faochán Mhuire corcra

The purple topshell *Gibbula umbilicalis* was distributed from station 4 to station 10, with occasional records from station 3. The majority of animals were found on the middle shore at stations 5–8 and numbers peaked at 2.8 per quadrat at station 7.

The monthly mean was approximately 1.2 per quadrat, and this did not vary significantly over the sampling season, although there was a very small increase in June.

There was an overall trend of increasing numbers throughout the 20-year period. The annual mean density rose from about 0.4 per quadrat during 1981 to a maximum of 1.8 per quadrat in 1999. Numbers dropped the following year, 2000. Two years in particular, 1990 and 1991, sustained values above the average trend.

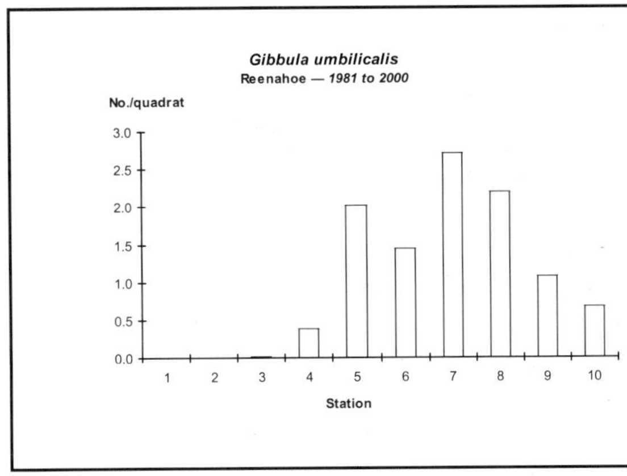

Figure 6.133

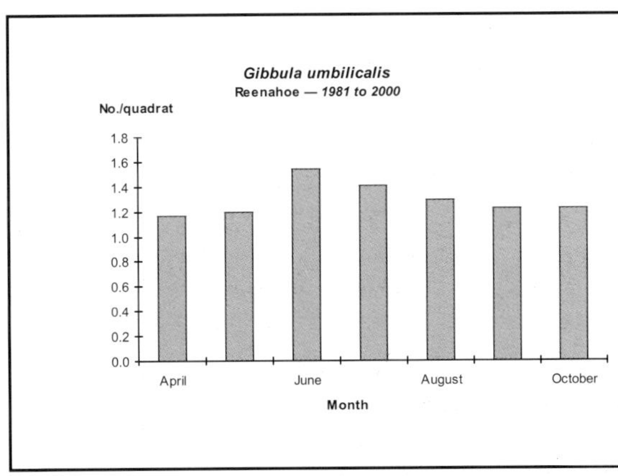

Figure 6.134

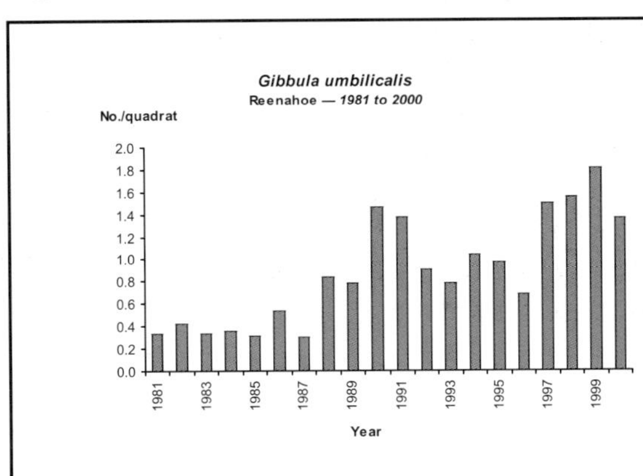

Figure 6.135

REENAHOE

GRAZERS

Edible Periwinkle
Littorina littorea
Gioradán

The edible periwinkle *Littorina littorea* occurred in far smaller numbers than the rough periwinkle *L. saxatilis* but was found over the entire shore. The majority of individuals were found between station 3 and station 8, and numbers peaked at station 4 at approximately 2.7 per quadrat.

There were no significant increases or decreases in numbers from month to month, but there was a gradual decrease from June to October.

At the beginning of the survey numbers were high, however there was a decline from 1983–86. There was then a sharp increase, followed by two years of gentle decline. This pattern was repeated from 1990–96 and suggests that recruitment of juveniles was intermittent and was most successful in the years 1987, 1990, 1997 and 2000.

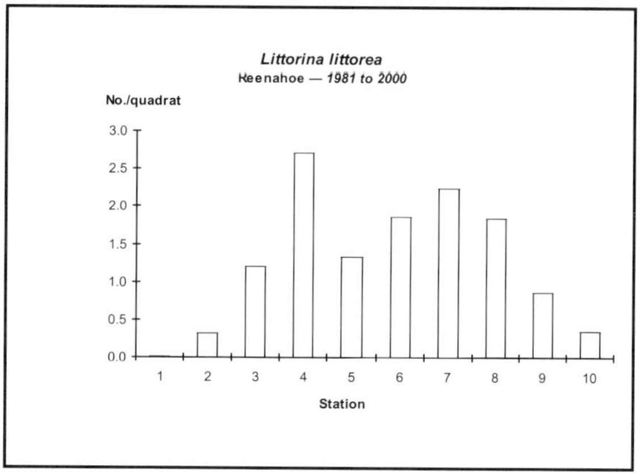

Figure 6.136

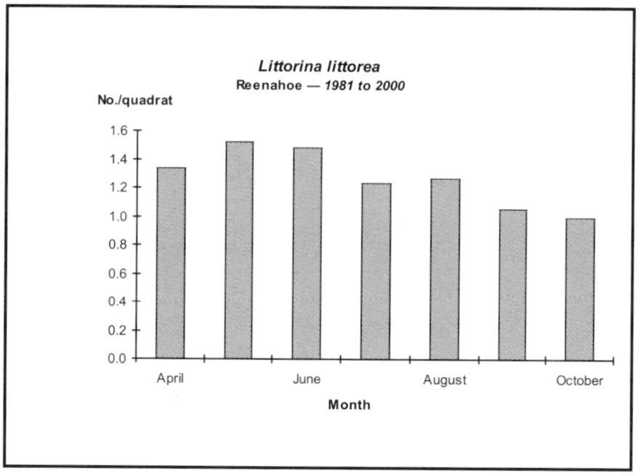

Figure 6.137

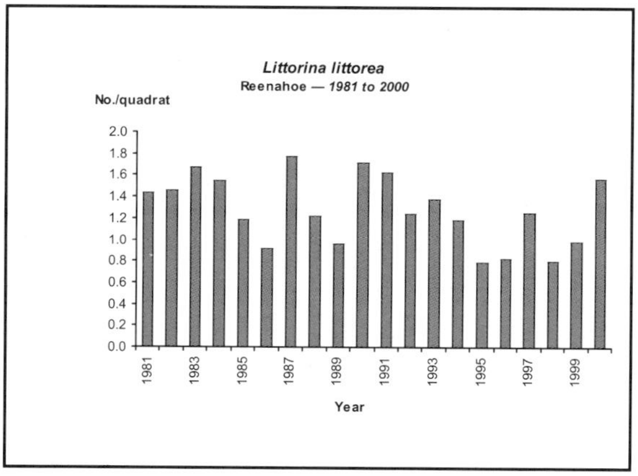

Figure 6.138

REENAHOE

GRAZERS

Flat Periwinkle
Littorina obtusata
Faocha leathan

The range of the flat periwinkle *Littorina obtusata* extended from stations 3 to 10, with a peak of approximately 8 per quadrat at station 9. Thus its density was far greater than that of the edible periwinkle *Littorina littorea*.

Monthly variation was present, with a steady increase in numbers from April (< 1 per quadrat) to August (7 per quadrat) and then back to 4 and 3 per quadrat in September and October respectively.

Annual variation was quite pronounced with possibly four cycles of rise and fall in numbers. 1983, 1987, 1991 and 1999 stand out with exceptionally high mean annual densities. The period 1983–86 showed a gradual fall in numbers, followed by a sharp increase during 1987. This was short-lived and numbers were low again the following year, 1988. A more gradual increase over the next two years to 6 per quadrat was followed by an irregular decrease to about 1 per quadrat during 1994. The population then increased fairly steadily for four years, with a large increase in 1999, and a similarly large fall in numbers in 2000.

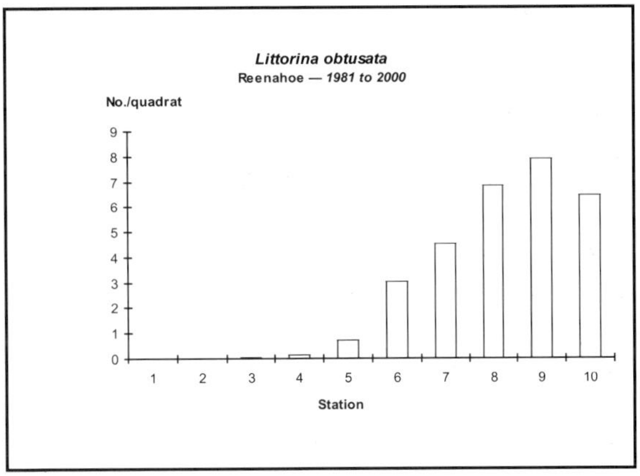

Figure 6.139

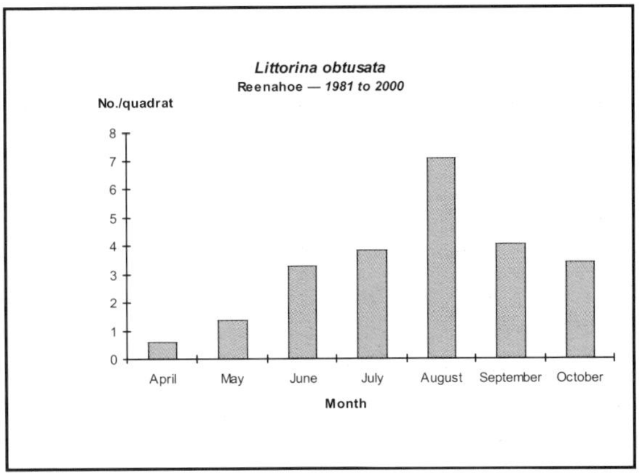

Figure 6.140

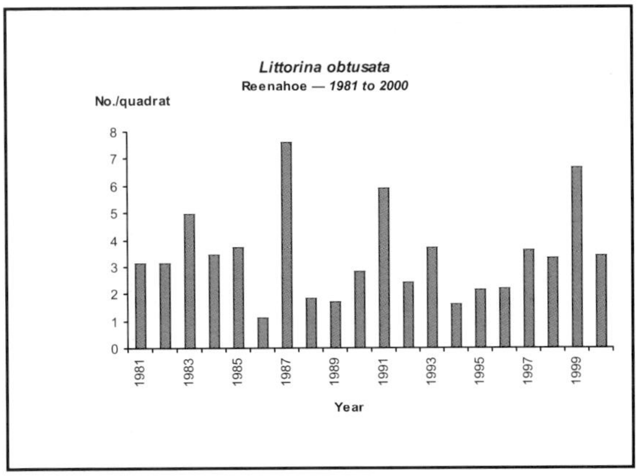

Figure 6.141

REENAHOE

GRAZERS

Rough Periwinkle
Littorina saxatilis
Faocha gharbh

Rough periwinkle *Littorina saxatilis* was found throughout the shore, but its numbers were concentrated within stations 2–5, with the maximum density of almost 45 per quadrat occurring at the bottom of the upper shore at station 3.

Monthly variation was only apparent in the August increase in numbers. Numbers of rough periwinkles fell away again during September.

There was annual variation in rough periwinkle numbers, with the general population level at around 16 per quadrat or less. A large increase in numbers was recorded in 1987 (34 per quadrat) but it is not known whether the population fell to a low level the following year, 1988, or whether it took two years to reach the 1989 low count. However as noted on p. 34 the data between 1985 and 1991 are incomplete for this species and the high mean of 1987 may be exaggerated.

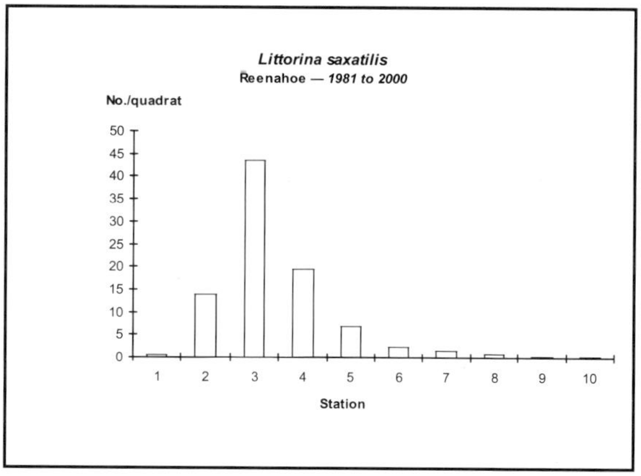

Figure 6.142

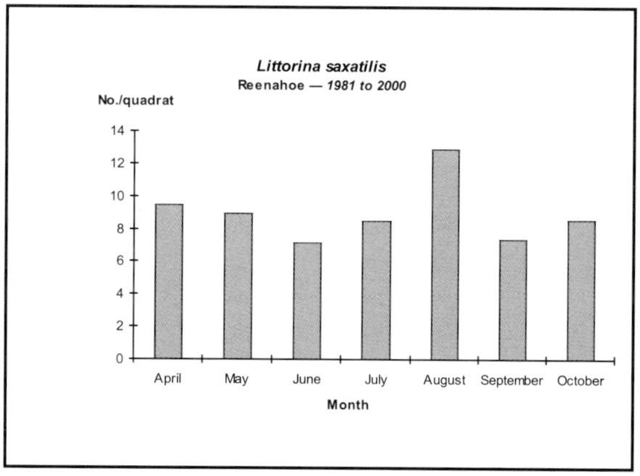

Figure 6.143

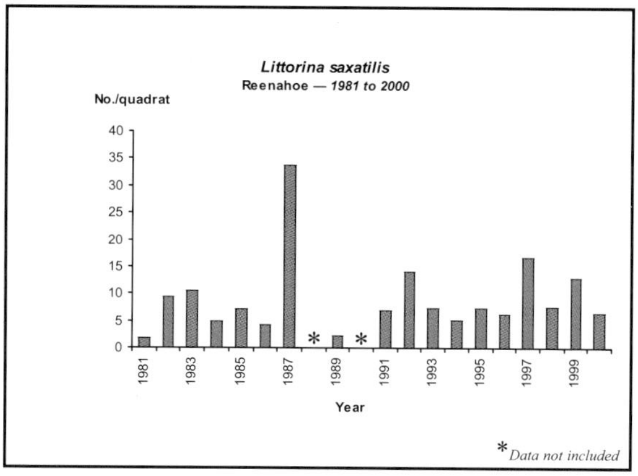

Figure 6.144

REENAHOE

GRAZERS

Limpet
Patella spp.
Bairneach

Limpets *Patella* spp. followed a similar distribution pattern to the barnacles and were the co-dominant species on the upper and upper middle shore. The majority were found between stations 4 and 8, and the maximum density of 52 per quadrat occurred at station 5.

There was, however, a slightly lower number in April and October than in the months May–September.

Annual variation was more evident in the early years, 1981–91, than the last ten years when density was fairly constant at approximately 18 per quadrat. Limpets were below this average density in 1985 and 1986. In 1982 and 1999 numbers were significantly higher at 33 and 30 per quadrat respectively. A consistent mean implies that any recruitment of juveniles to the population is balanced by loss of other individuals – either due to predation, natural death, or being dislodged during storms.

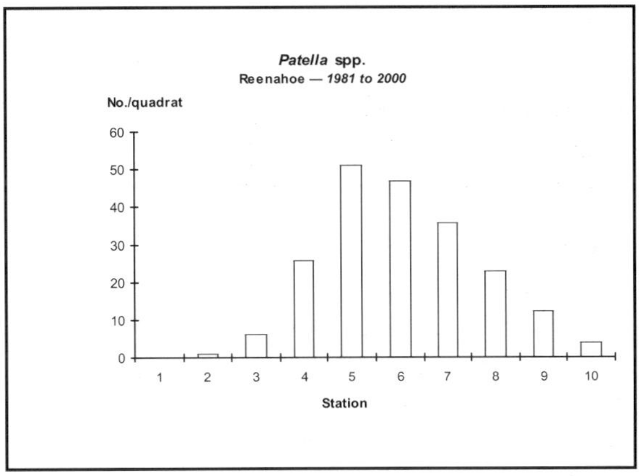

Figure 6.145

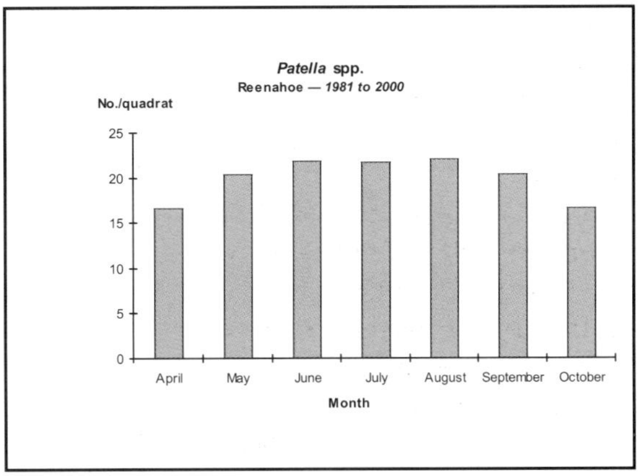

Figure 6.146

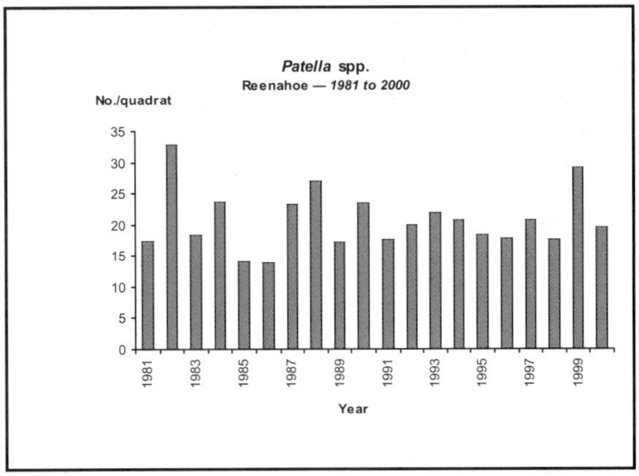

Figure 6.147

REENAHOE

PREDATOR

Dogwhelk
Nucella lapillus
Cuachma chon

The dogwhelk *Nucella lapillus* was the main predator on the shore. It was present in small numbers over much of the shore, from station 3 to station 10. The majority were found at stations 6–8 on the lower middle shore, and numbers peaked at station 7.

There was a small increase in numbers from April through to June which might support the theory of upward migration during the early part of the year. There was also an increase from August through to October.

The annual variation in density was very mixed. There were abrupt increases from one year to the next in 1981–82, 1985–86 and 1995–96, and a sharp decline in numbers in 1992–93. The overall population mean for the 20-year period was around 0.4 per quadrat. The years that are markedly higher or lower than this are 1986 (high) and 1993 (low).

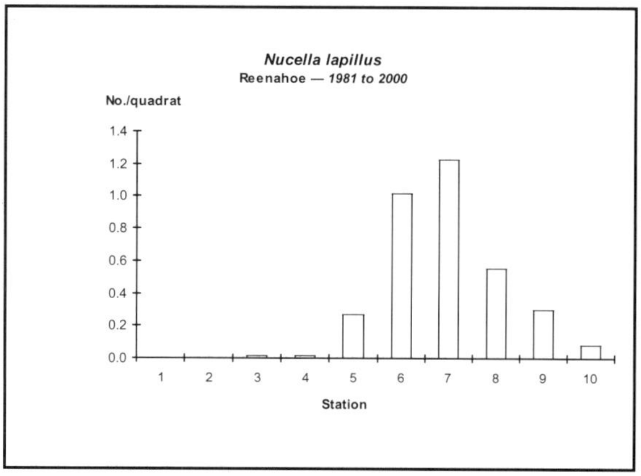

Figure 6.148

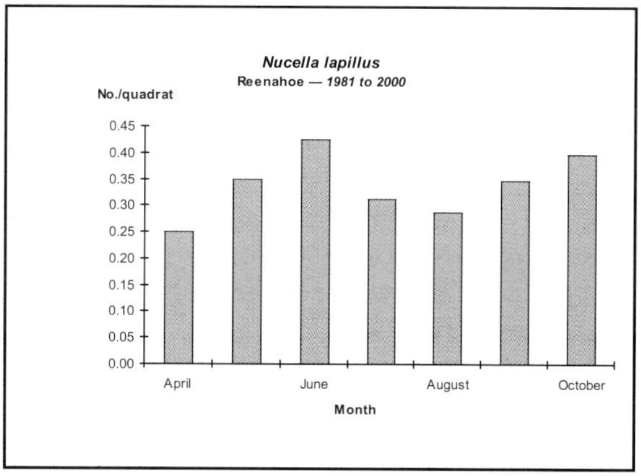

Figure 6.149

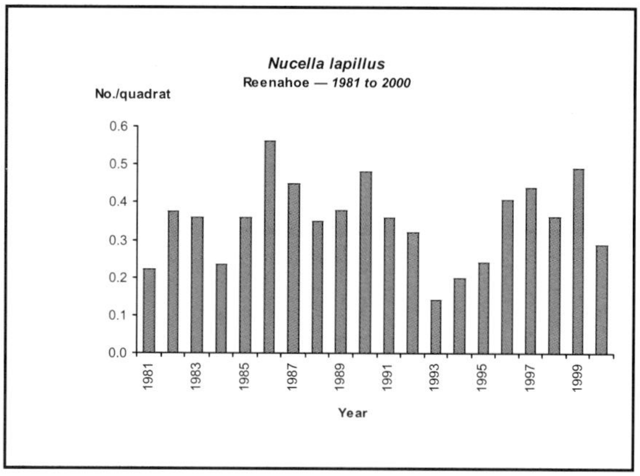

Figure 6.150

TRENDS FOR REENAHOE 1981–2000

Twenty one species were analysed for Reenahoe, and all showed variation in abundance. Limpet *Patella* spp. numbers varied the least over the 20-year period.

On the upper and middle shore spiral wrack *Fucus spiralis* abundance increased in the last half of the 1980s, but the species was virtually absent for the following six-year period. Mussels *Mytilus edulis* were consistently sparse at Reenahoe, but had a big increase in numbers for a single year 1982. Numbers of rough periwinkle *Littorina saxatilis* varied at a low level with the exception of 1987 when a large increase was recorded.

On the middle shore, barnacles increased through the 1980s to become the dominant ground cover in 1988–90. They then crashed dramatically in 1991 and remained at a very low density throughout the 1990s. Algal cover was dominated by knotted wrack *Ascophyllum nodosum* in the early 1980s. However it declined and from 1986 onwards cover remained at a third of its earlier level. Bladder wrack *Fucus vesiculosus* increased in the late 1980s as *Ascophyllum* declined; it was consistently the more common wrack on the middle shore through the 1990s. There were four years in which gut weed *Enteromorpha* spp. was significantly more abundant (1987, 1988, 1994, 1996). The only animal species to increase in the middle shore during the 1990s was the purple topshell *Gibbula umbilicalis*. Edible periwinkle *Littorina littorea* declined through the early 1990s but had started to increase at the end of the decade.

On the lower shore serrated wrack *Fucus serratus* was the dominant cover, but declined slightly over the 20 years. In the understorey *Gelidium* spp. and the carrageen *Chondrus crispus* were both low but steady, with the exception of a few years of increase. These were 1990 and 1996 for *Gelidium*, and 1989 for *Chondrus*. The other carrageen *Mastocarpus stellatus* was less abundant during the 1990s than the 1980s, although it increased noticeably in 1995. *Lomentaria articulata* fluctuated cyclically in a fairly regular manner, apart from 1983 which showed very high abundance, and 1991 when abundance was very low. *Ceramium* spp. was always present in very small amounts but was richer in 1983, 1986, 1989, 1995 and 1997. Of the grazers on the lower shore, the grey topshell *Gibbula cineraria* had good years in 1992, 1996, 1997 and 1999 and an excellent year in 1987, after which it was unrecorded for two years. The flat periwinkle *Littorina obtusata* had exceptionally abundant years in 1987, 1991, 1993 and 1999. Dogwhelk *Nucella lapillus* numbers fluctuated up and down steadily, falling to a minimum in 1993, but increasing in numbers for the remainder of the 20-year period.

Chapter Seven

Sheltered Shores

Kinish Narrows East & West

Figure 7.1 Kinish Harbour from the northwest, showing Kinish Narrows East (left) and Kinish Narrows West (right) at the mouth.

Kinish Harbour is a very shallow marine inlet with a muddy sand seabed (Figure 7.1). The entrance is on the north side of the island and is narrow, approximately 55 m at low tide. The shores either side of the entrance are of fissured bedrock, with the fissures running perpendicular to the water's edge. There are no overlying boulders.

There is a survey site on each side of the channel. Both shores are protected from wave action by the northwest "arm" of Sherkin Island, and by the fact that water depths are very shallow (< 5 m) for large distances off the coast. Kinish Narrows East is exposed to waves with a longer fetch than the Kinish Narrows West shore. Waves breaking directly onto Kinish Narrows West come from a northerly direction and have only crossed the Heir Island/Sherkin Island channel. The majority of waves breaking

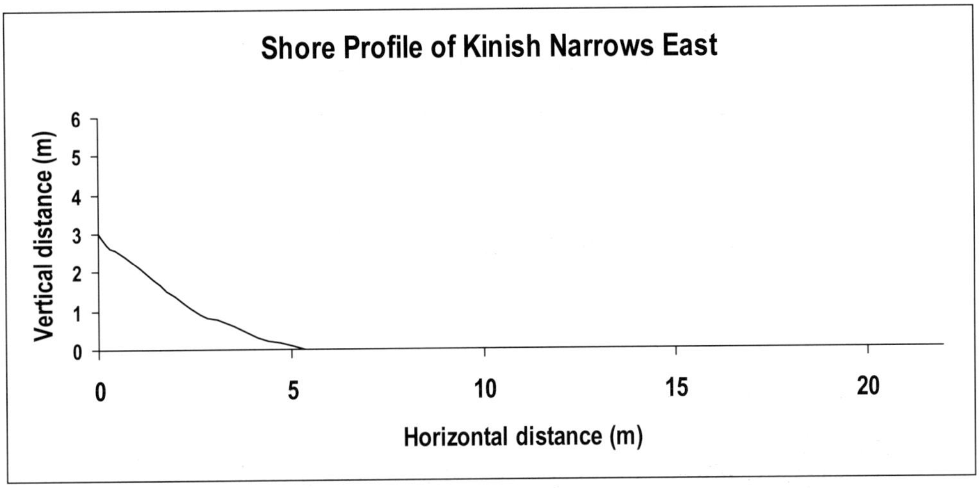

Figure 7.2 A cross-section of the shore from top to bottom showing the steep gradient of the Kinish Narrows East transect.

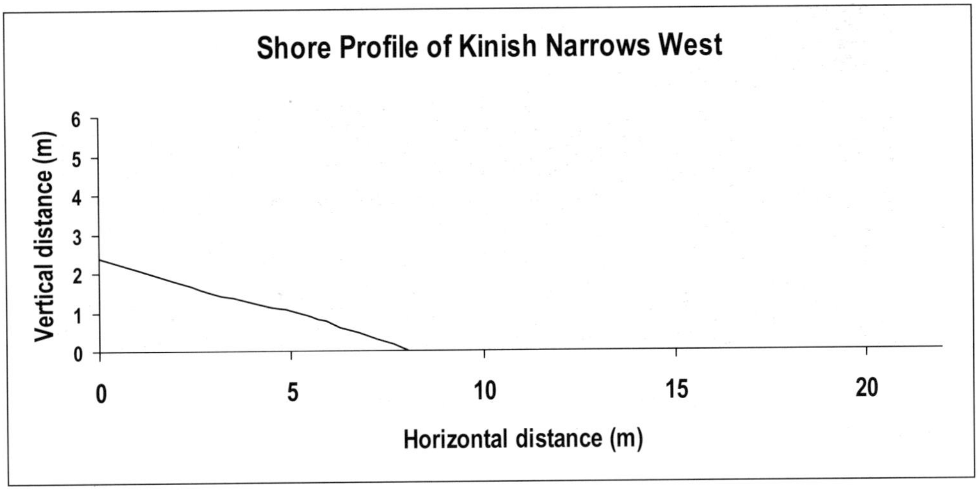

Figure 7.3 A cross-section of the shore from top to bottom showing the more gentle gradient of the Kinish Narrows West transect.

onto the Kinish Narrows East shore have travelled from the line of islands in the centre of Roaringwater Bay. A few will have come back through the gap between East Calf and Heir Islands, which is a short fetch in comparison to those of Poulacurra, Drolain Point, Horseshoe Harbour and Reenahoe.

Behind both shores the ground is low-lying with grass, heather and gorse vegetation. Kinish Narrows East has a vertical height of 3.0 m and a horizontal distance of 5.4 m, giving a gradient of 0.56. Kinish Narrows West has a vertical height of 2.4 m and a horizontal distance of 8.1 m, giving a gradient of 0.30, which is much more gentle than Kinish Narrows East. One of the reasons that the two sites were chosen for sampling was to determine whether the variation in gradient affects the number of species, or diversity of species. The second reason was that the aspect of the shores are different. The number of stations at both sites is smaller than present in the exposed and moderately exposed shores, with ten always recorded at Kinish Narrows East, and nine at Kinish Narrows West. The reduction of stations at the latter is due to the compressed splash zone. Here the band of black tar lichen *Verrucaria maura* was very narrow and there was little development of the orange lichens, *Caloplaca marina* and *Xanthoria parietina*. At Kinish Narrows East, stations 1–4 fall in the upper shore, stations 5–8 in the middle shore and stations 9–10 the lower shore. Station 1 is 4.2 m above chart datum.

At Kinish Narrows West, stations 1–3 fall in the upper shore, stations 4–7 in the middle shore and stations 8–9 the lower shore. Station 1 is 3.9 m above chart datum.

KINISH NARROWS EAST

VISUAL DOMINANTS

Kinish Narrows East had a rich development of wrack on the middle and lower shore, with barnacles dominating the upper middle shore.

ALGAE

Kinish Narrows East was rich in algae with a total of 132 taxa recorded, 109 of which were identified to species. The shore appeared to show more diversity than Kinish Narrows West.

Brown algae

Twenty three species of brown algae were recorded from Kinish Narrows East, with a further 5 taxa recorded to genus only. As well as the fucoids and laminarians, some smaller plant species were fairly regularly recorded, such as Ectocarpaceae and *Leathesia difformis*. Others found infrequently were *Cladostephus spongiosus, Elachista fucicola* and *Scytosiphon lomentaria*.

Highlight on Seaweed Species

Red Seaweeds of the Understorey

Dilsea carnosa

Beneath the kelps and wracks, the understorey is often rich in red algae, whose shapes vary hugely. *Dilsea carnosa* is in the same order of red seaweeds as the carrageen *Mastocarpus stellatus* but its structure is very different and it cannot live in the exposed situations favoured by *M. stellatus*. It is found in shallow water and on the extreme lower shore, usually at stations that can be worked only on very low spring tides. It was not recorded at Poulacurra, Reenahoe and Kinish Narrows West, although it was found at Kinish Narrows East, Drolain Point, Globe Rocks and Horseshoe Harbour. It has a flattened frond with no midrib, which is either simple or often torn into sections.

Furcellaria lumbricalis was most often recorded from Reenahoe and Kinish Narrows East and was absent from the transects on the exposed shores of Poulacurra and Drolain Point. A red seaweed of the order Gigartinales, it has stiff filiform stems and forked regular branches. Each tip tapers to a point. It is very dark red in colour.

Furcellaria lumbricalis

Red algae

There was a rich red algal flora at Kinish Narrows East totalling 74 species and a further 12 taxa identified to genus only. This was considerably more diverse than the red algae of Kinish Narrows West.

The most common species of the understorey were *Audouinella* spp., *Ceramium rubrum, Ceramium* spp., *Chondrus crispus, Dumontia contorta, Gelidium spinosum, Hildenbrandia* spp., Lithothamnia, *Lomentaria articulata, Mastocarpus stellatus, Membranoptera alata, Osmundea pinnatifida, Plumaria plumosa* and *Polysiphonia lanosa.*

Many of these seaweeds occurred on all the Sherkin shores and some appeared to be specialised in terms of the habitat they occupied. *Catenella caespitosa* mostly occurred on the upper shore. The presence of *Rhodothamniella floridula* reflects the accumulation of sand in small pockets through which the plants grow and thrive. *Membranoptera alata* occurred mostly in the lowest station on kelp stipes and *Plumaria plumosa,* which tends to grow on vertical rock surfaces, occurred within small areas at Kinish Narrows East.

Green algae

Twelve species of green algae were recorded plus a further 6 taxa identified to genus only. The common species were the ephemeral dark green, wiry *Cladophora rupestris,* gut weed *Enteromorpha* spp. and sea lettuce *Ulva lactuca.*

Species recorded in very few years were *Bryopsis plumosa, Derbesia marina* and *Spongomorpha arcta.*

LICHENS

Although there was very little development of the lichen flora, a total of 13 species was recorded, eight of which were the commonly occurring *Caloplaca marina, Lecanora atra, Lichina confinis, L. pygmaea, Ramalina siliquosa, Verrucaria maura, V. mucosa* and *Xanthoria parietina.* Those found in relatively few years included *Anaptychia fusca, Cladonia* spp., *Ochrolechia frigida* and *O. parella.* At both the Kinish Narrows sites, *O. parella* was more frequently recorded than *O. frigida.*

ANIMALS

A total of 137 taxa of animals were recorded of which 114 were identified to species level.

An extensive cover of algae on the lower shore provides a damp and sheltered habitat for animal colonisation. Sponges were present, but not in large amounts, and confined primarily to the commonly occurring breadcrumb sponge *Halichondria panicea* and *Myxilla incrustans.*

Cnidaria likewise were not particularly diverse. The common beadlet anemone *Actinia equina* was the only anemone species recorded frequently (almost every year), with occasional records of *Anemonia viridis, Sagartia elegans* and *Urticina felina.* Hydroids mainly comprised sea fir *Dynamena pumila,* though there were occasional records of *Clava multicornis* (on the wrack *Ascophyllum*), *Coryne muscoides* and *Obelia geniculata.*

Like Kinish Narrows West, the Kinish Narrows East site had several polychaete worm species, including the three *Spirorbis* species *S. inornatus, S. rupestris* and *S. spirorbis* and three species of polychaete worms *Amphitritides gracilis, Cirratulus cirratus* and *Cirriformia tentaculata.*

Several species of crabs and amphipods occurred, though none so regularly as the common shore crab *Cancer pagurus.* These included the spider crabs *Hyas araneus, Inachus* spp. and *Macropodia tenuirostris,* the swimming crab *Necora puber* and the pea crab *Pinnotheres pisum.*

A total of 39 mollusca taxa were recorded, including several species of nudibranch

(*Acanthodoris pilosa, Archidoris pseudoargus, Facelina auriculata, Limacia clavigera* and *Onchidoris bilamellata*). The two cowries which occur in Ireland were both found here (*Trivia monacha* and *T. arctica*) and the bivalve *Chlamys varia.* The saddle oyster *Anomia ephippium* was recorded several times in the 1980s, but only twice in the 1990s.

The lower shore algae were rich in encrusting sea mats and sea squirts, with 14 bryozoan taxa and 15 tunicate taxa.

Bryozoans included three species of *Alcyonidium* (*A. diaphanum*, *A. gelatinosum* and *A. hirsutum*), together with *Cellepora pumicosa*, *Electra pilosa*, *Flustrellidra hispida* and the orange rock-encrusting *Umbonula* spp.

Highlight on Polychaete Worms (Annelids)

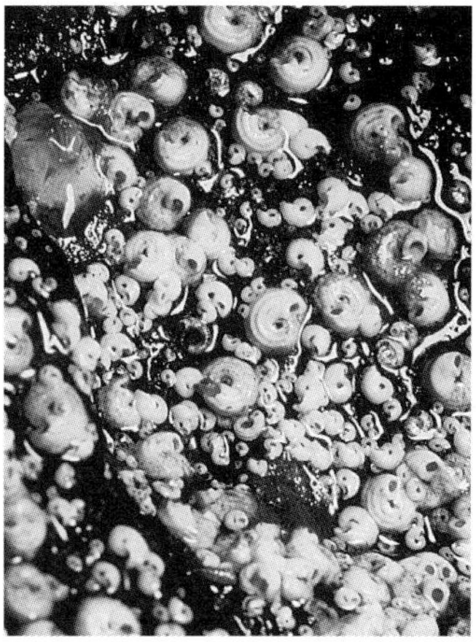
Coiled Tube Worm – *Spirorbis* spp.

Of the huge number of polychaete worm species, very few are found on rocky shores. The majority are adapted for burrowing in sediment and moving through the sediment/water interface. A few build calcareous tubes to house their soft bodies and can therefore colonise hard surfaces of rock, boulders and pebbles. These are the spirorbid and serpulid families that include the calcareous tubeworms *Spirorbis* and *Pomatoceros*. At Kinish Narrows East three species of *Spirorbis* occurred: *S. inornatus, S. rupestris* and *S. spirorbis*. The sheltered nature of the shore allows also the accumulation of small pockets of muddy sand amongst the lower shore crevices where the terebellid and cirratulid worms, *Amphitritides gracilis*, *Cirratulus cirratus* and *Cirriformia tentaculata,* were found. Other species such as *Lanice conchilega* and *Sabellaria alveolata* build tubes of mucus and/or sand grains. *Lanice conchilega* (the sand mason worm) occurred in small numbers in Kinish Narrows West, while *Sabellaria* was only found at Horseshoe Harbour. Large reefs of *Sabellaria* can run from the lower shore downward but none have been found so far on Sherkin.

Highlight on Sea Squirts (Chordates)

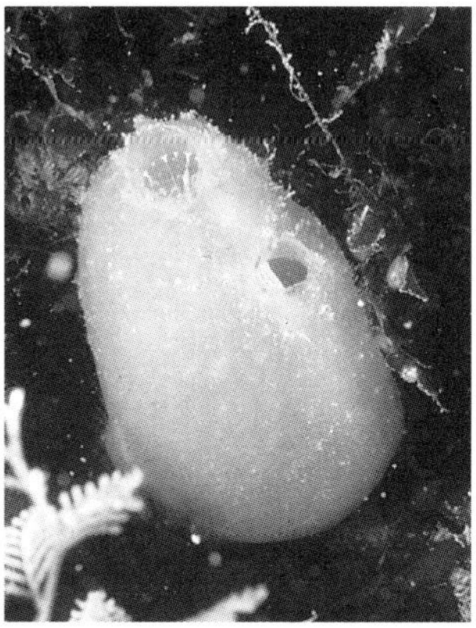
Sea Squirt – *Ascidiella aspersa*

Sea squirts, with their very simple sac-like bodies are classed as Chordates because their larval forms possess a notochord – a rudimentary form of backbone. A sea squirt feeds on organic particles in the sea water, which flows into the body through an inhalent siphon and out through the exhalent siphon. It is classed as a filter feeder. The position of these siphons varies between species and is therefore a useful identification feature. Sea squirts can be solitary or form colonies where the individuals are embedded in a "jelly" in a species-specific pattern; for example the "daisy" pattern of *Botryllus schlosseri* and the double lines of *Botrylloides leachi*. Kinish Narrows East was the richest of the seven Sherkin shores for solitary sea squirts which were mainly found at the lowest stations. The most frequently recorded species were *Aplidium* spp., *Ascidia mentula*, *Ascidiella aspersa*, *A. scabra*, *Botryllus schlosseri, Ciona intestinalis*, *Clavelina lepadiformis*, *Dendrodoa grossularia* and *Sidnyum turbinatum*. All of these are much more common sublittorally where they frequently colonise the surfaces of large rocks.

Species analysed for Kinish Narrows East, their place in the food chain and the shore ecology (Predatory pathway ——► Grazing pathway ••••••►)

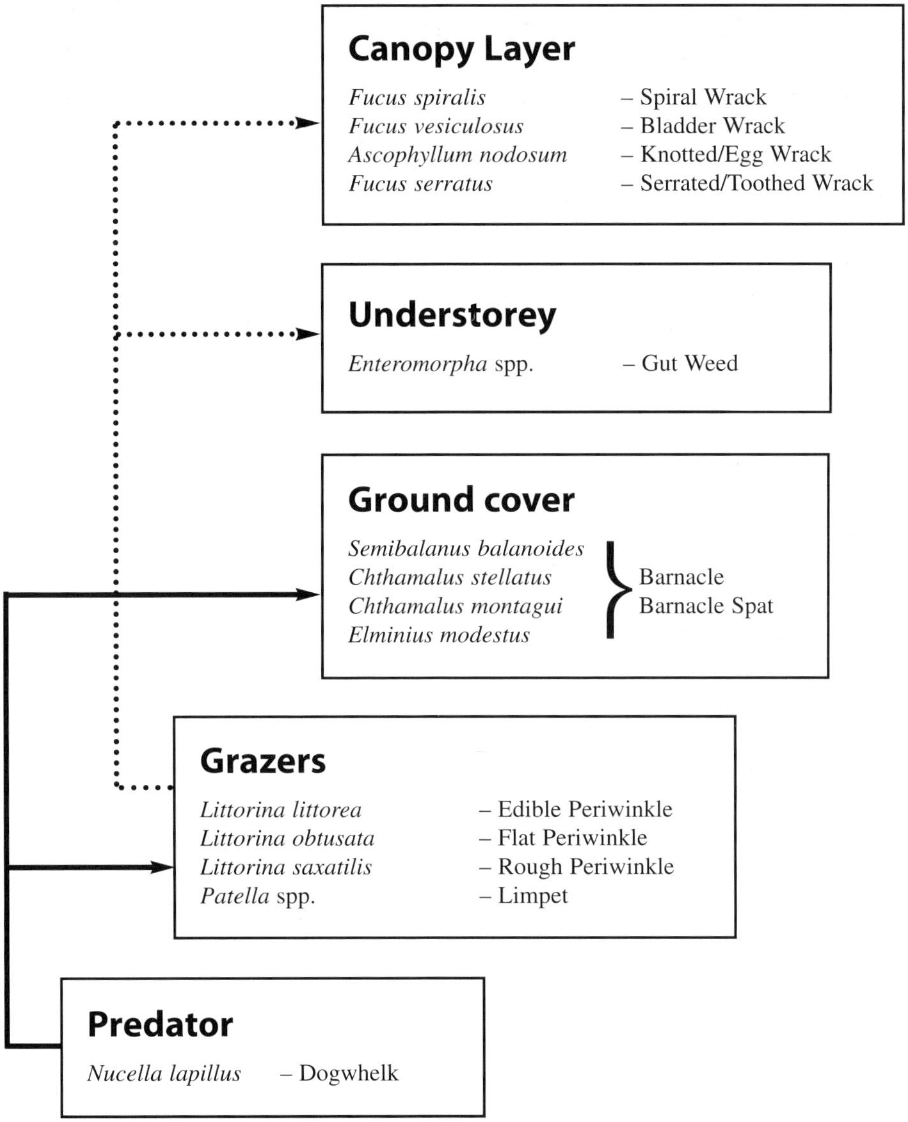

KINISH NARROWS EAST

CANOPY LAYER

Spiral Wrack
Fucus spiralis
Casfheamainn

Spiral Wrack *Fucus spiralis* occurred over a wider range on the shore than perhaps would be expected. It was present at every station except station 1 and the majority of plants were at stations 8 and 9.

F. spiralis cover was fairly constant during April, May and June, but showed a clear decline in July and August, followed by a large increase in September. The decrease from May through to July may represent the loss of young sporelings through grazing. Surviving sporelings then began to increase in cover during August and September, but growth declined again in October.

During the early years of the survey *Fucus spiralis* cover was usually low (< 1% per quadrat), and sometimes unrecorded (1981, 1983). After 1994, cover was usually higher and reached a maximum level of 5.3% in 1998. The previous year however had been a year of sparse cover (< 0.5% in 1997), furthermore the dense cover of 1998 was not sustained and fell back to less than 1% in 1999 and 2000.

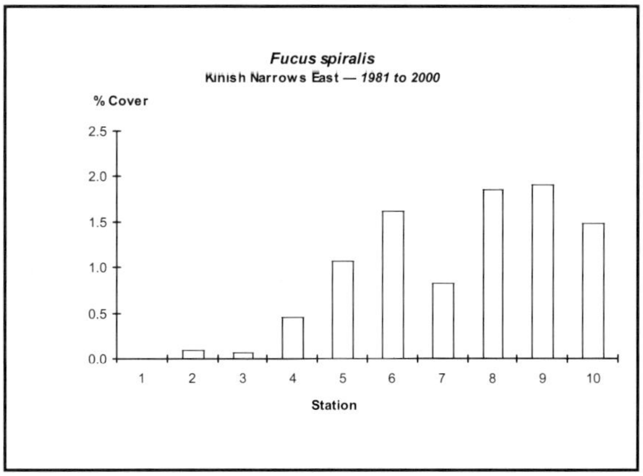

Figure 7.4

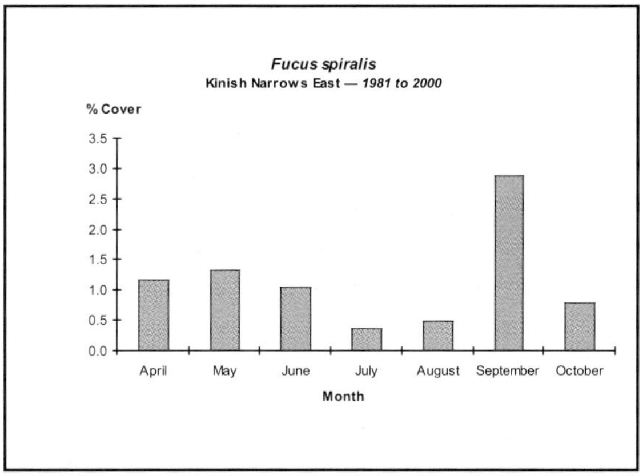

Figure 7.5

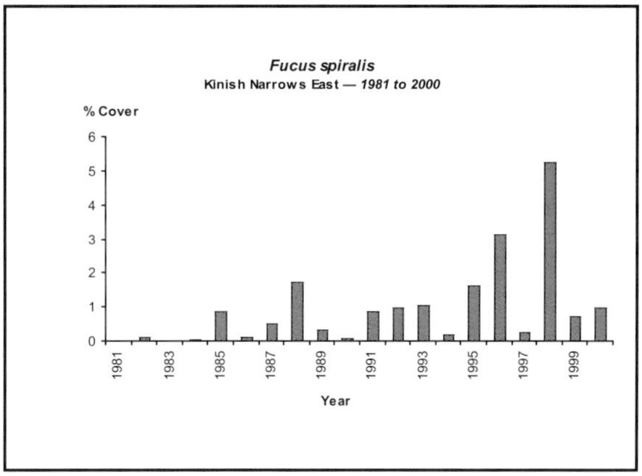

Figure 7.6

KINISH NARROWS EAST

CANOPY LAYER

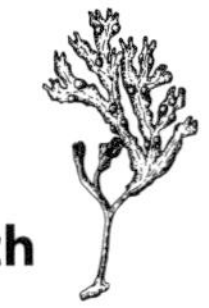

Bladder Wrack
Fucus vesiculosus
Feamainn bhoilgíneach

At Kinish Narrows East, bladder wrack *Fucus vesiculosus* occupied a wider zone than at Kinish Narrows West, being relatively dense at stations 6–10, reaching its maximum cover (21% per quadrat) at station 7 on the middle shore.

Seasonal growth increased from 8.6% in April to about 12.7% in October.

Variation in density after 1981 appeared to occur in three distinct cycles. There was a rise and fall from 1981–89, peaking in 1986 (20.9%). A second rise and fall occurred from 1989–95, with a smaller peak of 10% in 1991 and there was a steep rise in cover from 1995–99 (16.6%) which declined dramatically to 5.5% in 2000.

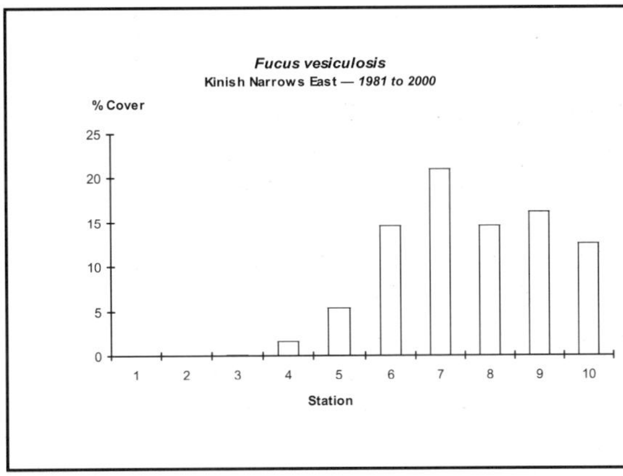

Figure 7.7

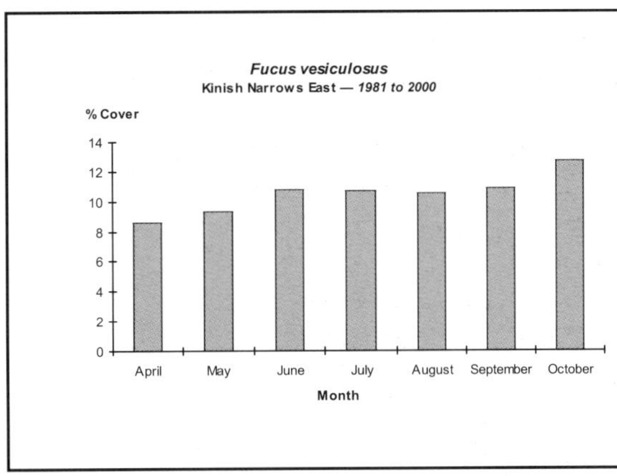

Figure 7.8

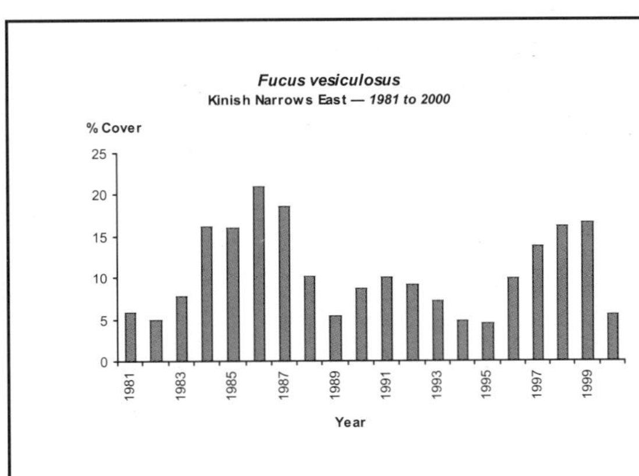

Figure 7.9

KINISH NARROWS EAST

CANOPY LAYER

Knotted/Egg Wrack *Ascophyllum nodosum* Feamainn bhuí

Knotted wrack *Ascophyllum nodosum* occurred on the lower shore between stations 7 and 10, but was only relatively dense at station 8, where it formed 15% per quadrat of the rock cover.

Seasonal variation was small. Monthly values ranged between 2% and 3–4% and there was no significant difference between months.

At Kinish Narrows East *Ascophyllum nodosum* showed a trend of decreasing cover from 1981–93. Exceptions to this were 1988 and 1990 when cover rose to 5.5% and 6.2% respectively. From 1993 *Ascophyllum* virtually disappeared from the shore.

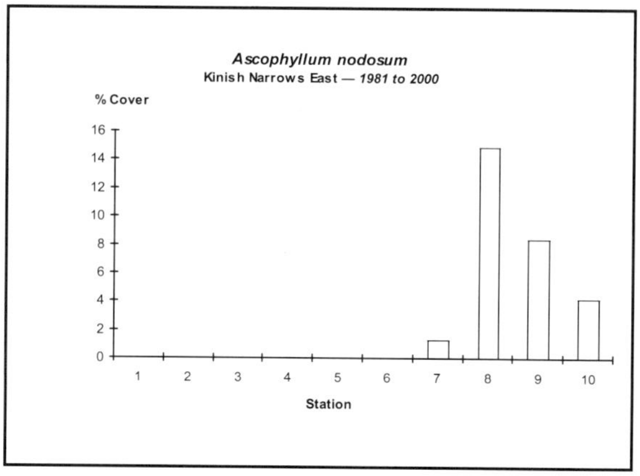

Figure 7.10

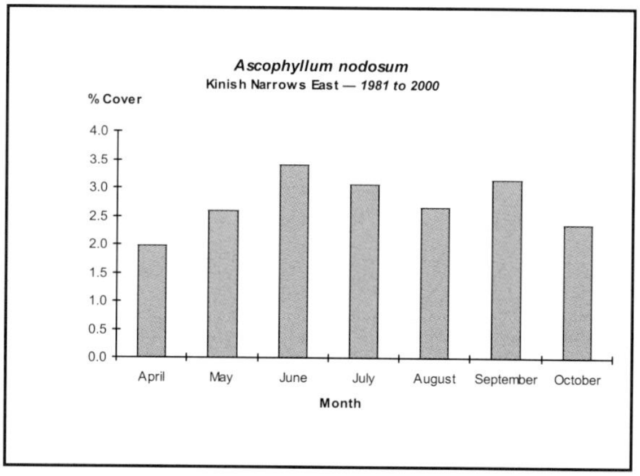

Figure 7.11

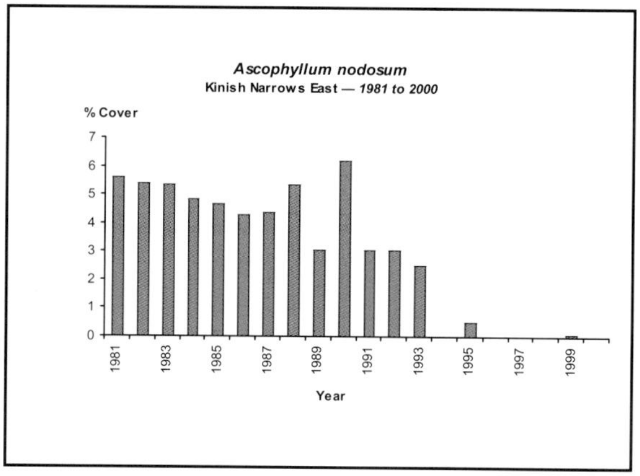

Figure 7.12

KINISH NARROWS EAST

CANOPY LAYER

Serrated/Toothed Wrack
Fucus serratus
Míoránach

Found on the lower middle and lower shore at stations 7–10, *Fucus serratus* co-existed with *F. vesiculosus* but was the dominant fucoid at station 9 and below.

Abundance of *Fucus serratus* jumped from May (4.3% cover per quadrat) to June (6.2%) and decreased slightly over the remaining months.

Species abundance has varied over the years with an overall increase in cover from 1981 until 1989, followed by a decrease in cover to almost no plants at all in the years 1995–2000.

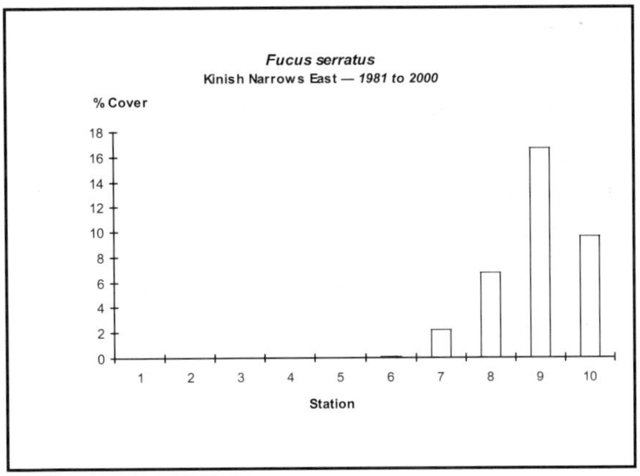

Figure 7.13

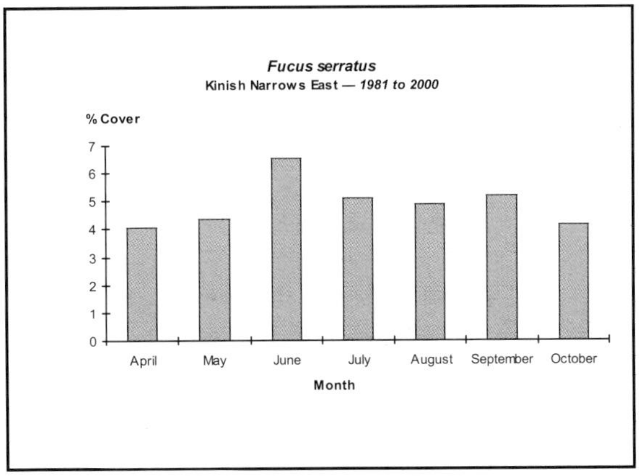

Figure 7.14

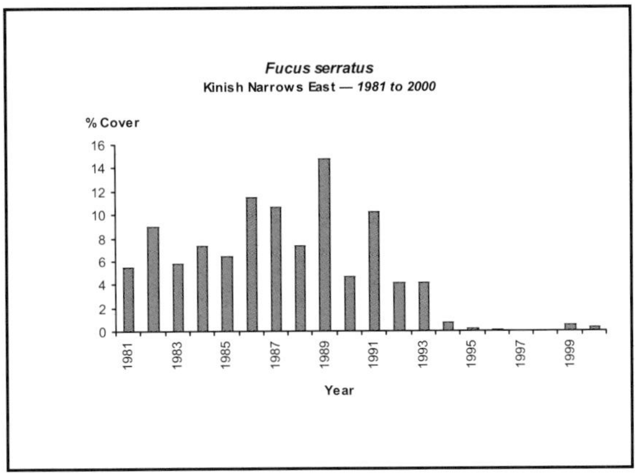

Figure 7.15

KINISH NARROWS EAST

UNDERSTOREY

Gut Weed
Enteromorpha spp.
Líneáil ghorm

Although recorded in all stations, the proliferation of this hollow seaweed, *Enteromorpha* spp., occurred on the middle and lower shore with a peak at station 10, where it reached just over 5% cover per quadrat.

A few plants were always found in April, but there was a massive increase in cover from < 1% in April and May to 3% in June. Thereafter there was a steady decline until October.

Density fluctuated year by year, and 1986 saw an almost fourfold increase in cover over the shore as a whole. It is possible to group the smaller variations of other years into three periods: 1981–84, 1985–91 and 1992–2000. The years 1996–2000 could also be viewed as an overall decrease from the maximum cover recorded in 1996.

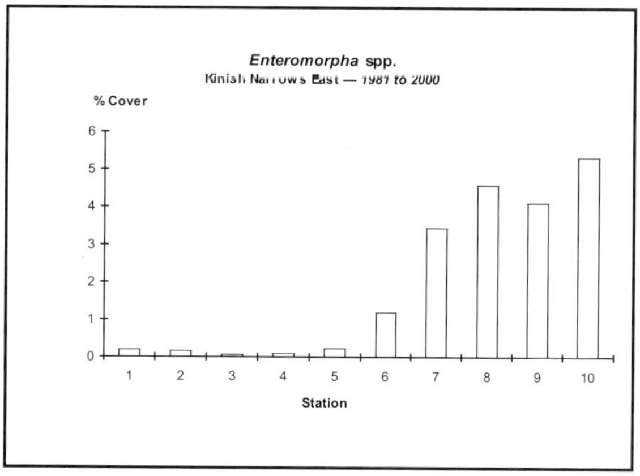

Figure 7.16

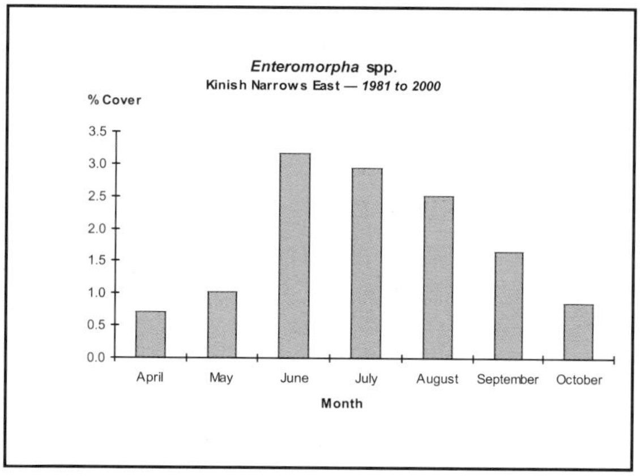

Figure 7.17

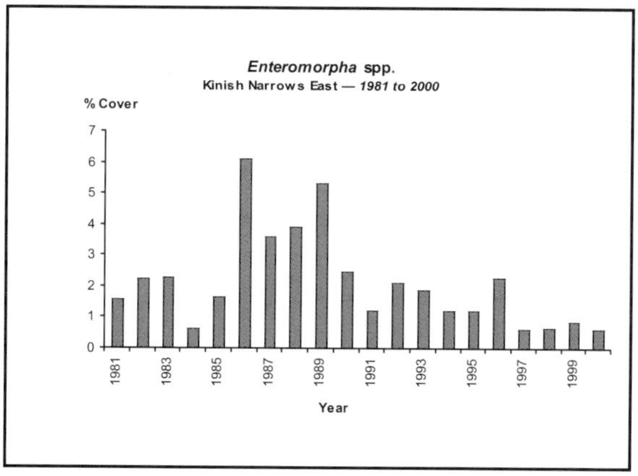

Figure 7.18

KINISH NARROWS EAST

GROUND COVER

Barnacles

Semibalanus balanoides
Chthamalus stellatus
Chthamalus montagui
Elminius modestus
Giúrainn

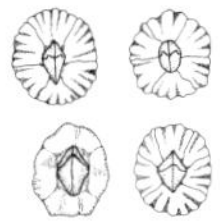

At Kinish Narrows East barnacles occurred in every station, but the population distribution was centred around station 6 (50% cover per quadrat), where it was co-dominant with fucoids.

Percentage cover increased from 20.1% in April to 30.0% in August. In September and October there were small decreases.

At the beginning of the survey (1981) the population was small (8%) and throughout the 1990s the area of shore occupied by barnacles was never more than 23%. This figure differs widely from the barnacle population during 1982–90, when density ranged from 24.6% to 55.8% cover. Thus after the population crash in 1991, barnacles never regained their dominance on the shore at Kinish Narrows East.

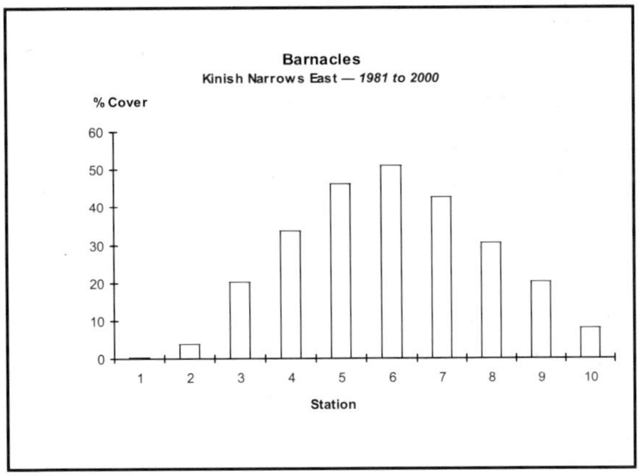

Figure 7.19

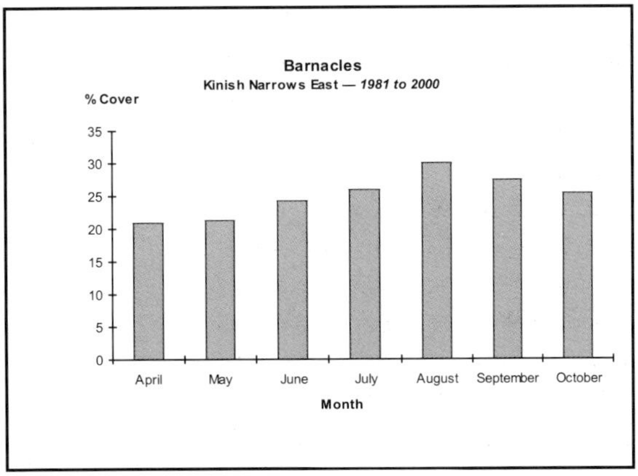

Figure 7.20

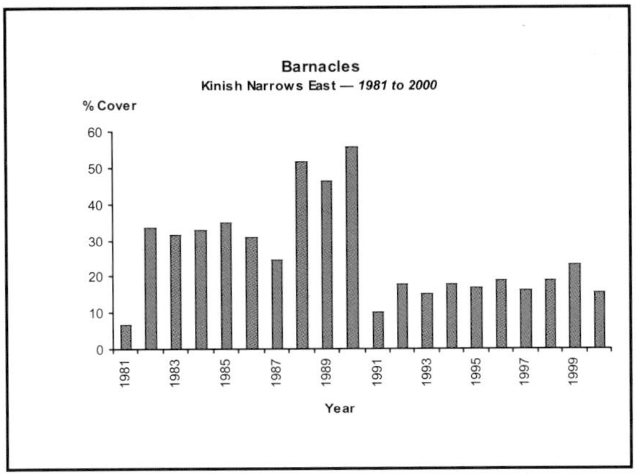

Figure 7.21

KINISH NARROWS EAST

GROUND COVER

Barnacle Spat
Síol giúrainn

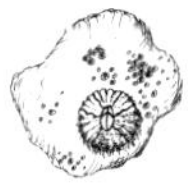

Juvenile barnacles settled mainly between stations 4 and 10, with a peak in spat numbers at station 6. There were however records from practically all stations. Peak spat numbers coincided with the middle shore peak in adult barnacle number.

The large increase in spat numbers in May (to 48/dm^2) showed that the main settlement of barnacle larvae was due to *Semibalanus balanoides*. Decreasing numbers were recorded throughout the summer; then in September there was a small peak in numbers (to 26/dm^2) caused by the later settlement of *Chthamalus* spp. spat.

Settlement was frequent but was not recorded every year; no spat were present in 1984 and 1985, and very low numbers of spat were found in 1999. Mean annual density generally varied from 10/dm^2 to 60/dm^2, but in 1986 the highest density of 150/dm^2 was recorded. The second highest number recorded in 1997 fell far short of this at around 73/dm^2.

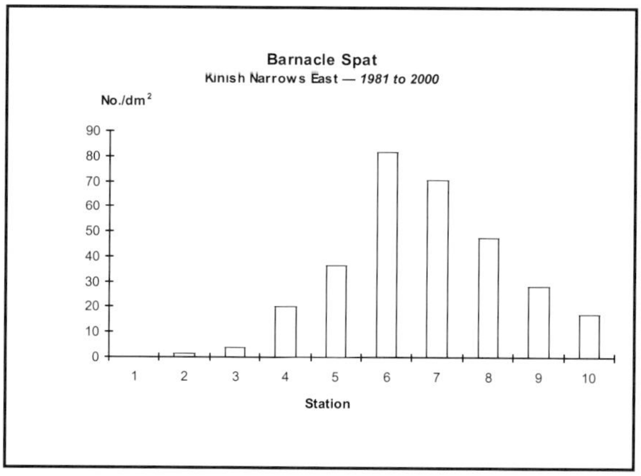

Figure 7.22

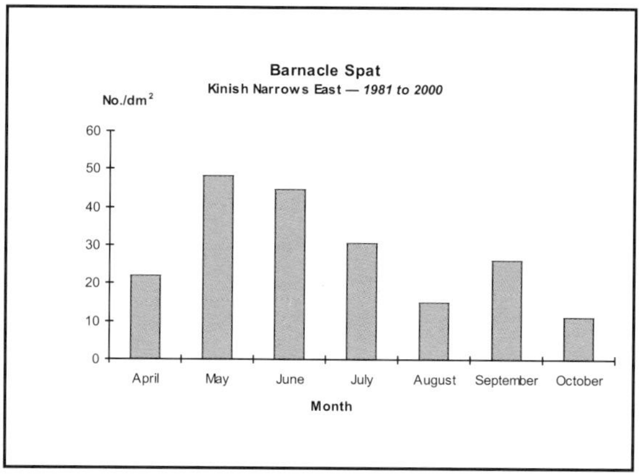

Figure 7.23

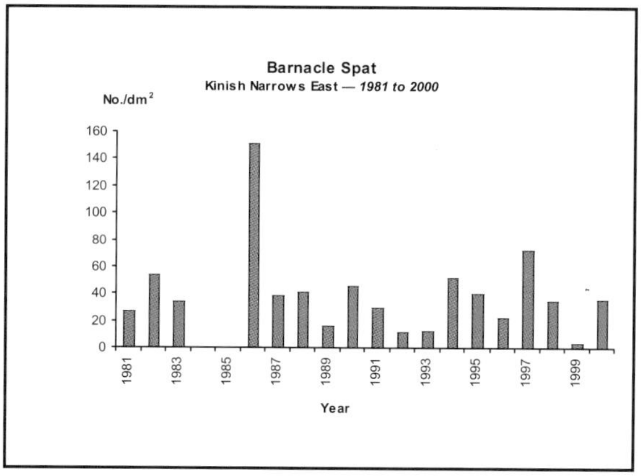

Figure 7.24

KINISH NARROWS EAST

GRAZERS

Edible Periwinkle
Littorina littorea
Gioradán

The Edible periwinkle *Littorina littorea* was found in every station at Kinish Narrows East, albeit in small numbers. The band of highest density (0.55 per quadrat or greater) was from station 4 to station 7. Outside this zone only occasional individuals were found.

In contrast to the flat periwinkle *Littorina obtusata,* numbers were higher at the start of the season in April (0.44 per quadrat), and declined steadily until October (0.22 per quadrat).

The average annual density showed considerable rise and fall over the years. The pattern of general increase in density from 1982–88 was broken by the unexpectedly large peak during 1984. After 1988 there was a trend of decrease for four years. An increase in numbers in 1993 was followed by a further five years of decrease until 1999, when the population rose again dramatically.

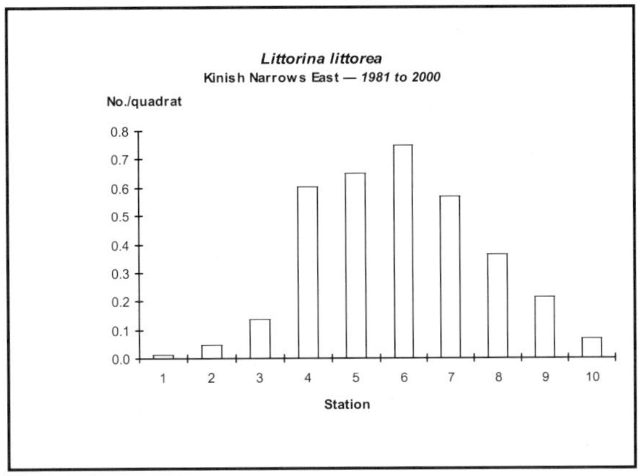

Figure 7.25

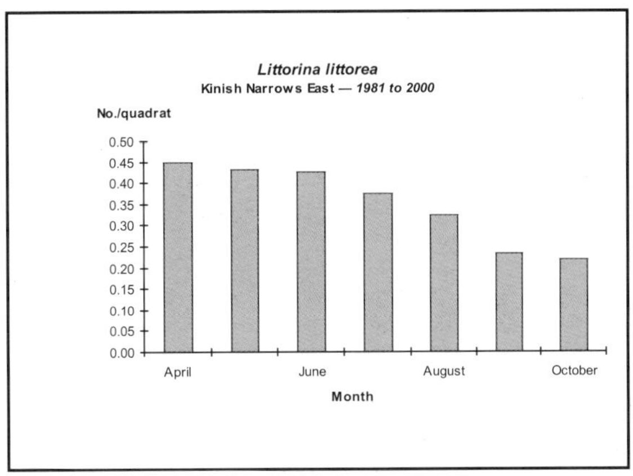

Figure 7.26

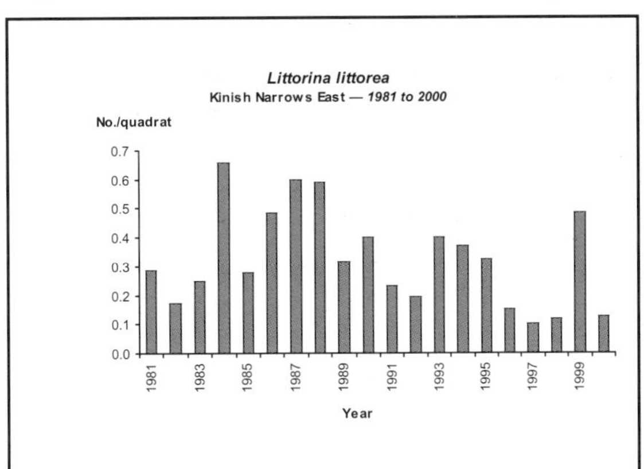

Figure 7.27

KINISH NARROWS EAST

GRAZERS

Flat Periwinkle
Littorina obtusata
Faocha leathan

The flat periwinkle *Littorina obtusata* was concentrated on the lower middle and lower shore between stations 7 and 10, with the maximum density reaching approximately 8 per quadrat at station 9. This distribution was where the majority of the wracks were found – *Fucus vesiculosus* and *F. serratus* contributing greatly to the habitat.

Numbers seemed to increase steadily from April throughout the summer up to August, then decrease slightly in October. The largest difference was found between the April and May numbers.

Annual variation was present, but irregular over the 20 years. There were three cycles of population change. The first (1981–90) and the third (1995–2000) both had a relatively gradual build up of *Littorina obtusata* numbers followed by a fairly steep decline; whereas the middle cycle (1991–94) showed a short-lived increase in numbers and a more gradual decline.

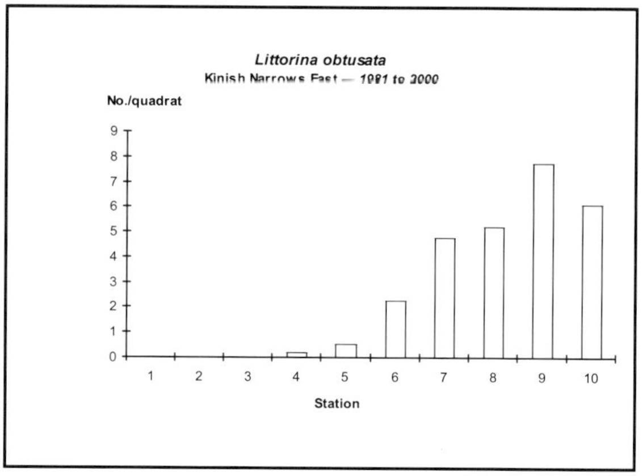

Figure 7.28

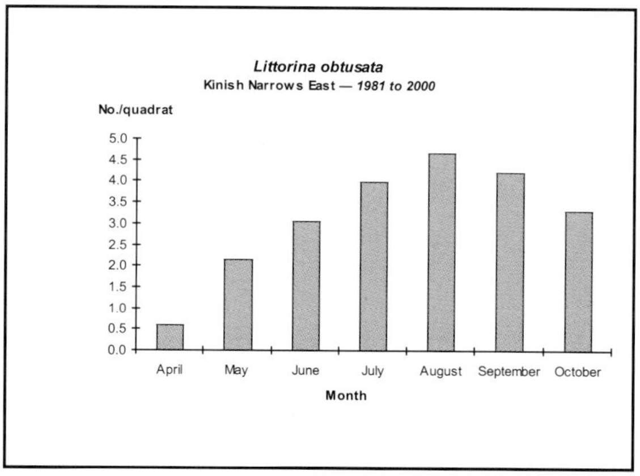

Figure 7.29

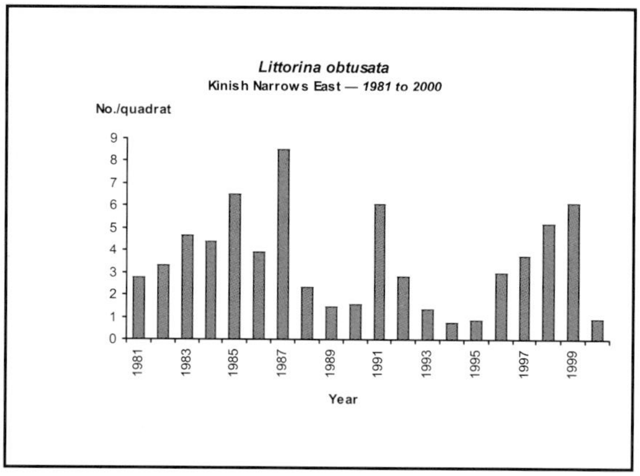

Figure 7.30

KINISH NARROWS EAST

GRAZERS

Rough Periwinkle
Littorina saxatilis
Faocha gharbh

The rough periwinkle *Littorina saxatilis* was found mainly on the upper shore, with the highest density present at stations 3 and 4. Occasional animals occurred in all other stations.

Seasonal variation was present but erratic, with a large increase in numbers between August and September.

There were two trends of increase from 1981–87 and a general trend of increase from 1991–1999. However the state of the population cannot be assessed from 1988–1990 due to inconsistent data (see p. 34). Maximum population numbers were never sustained for more than a single year, and tended to decrease for one or two years before rising again. Maximum population numbers were higher in the 1990s than in the 1980s.

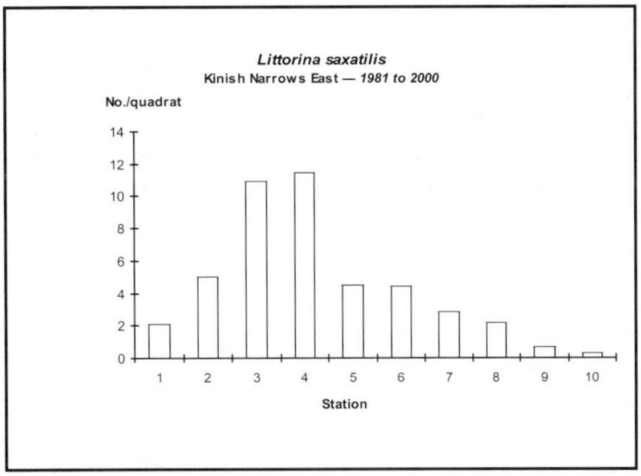

Figure 7.31

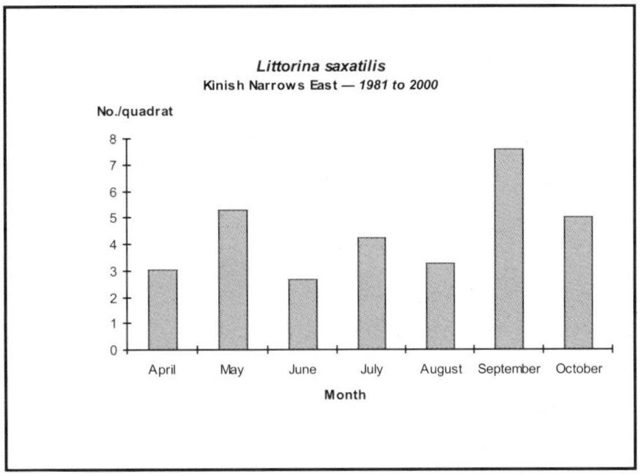

Figure 7.32

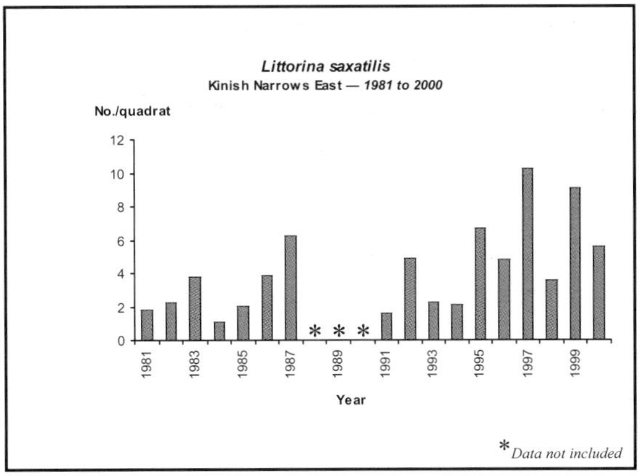

Figure 7.33

KINISH NARROWS EAST

GRAZERS

Limpet
Patella spp.
Bairneach

Limpets *Patella* spp. were present in every station other than the highest. Limpet numbers increased from station 2 to station 6 in the middle shore (50 per quadrat), then decreased steadily throughout the lower shore to 10 per quadrat at station 10.

Numbers were very steady throughout the year at approximately 25 per quadrat.

Annual variation was evident and irregular. A steady decline in numbers was observed from 1981–86 (31 individuals per quadrat down to 15 per quadrat). This was followed by small fluctuations, but an overall trend of increase to reach 31 per quadrat again in 1994; then a decrease in density from 1995–98. There was a marked increase during 1999 (31 per quadrat) and the number in 2000 was not significantly different from this.

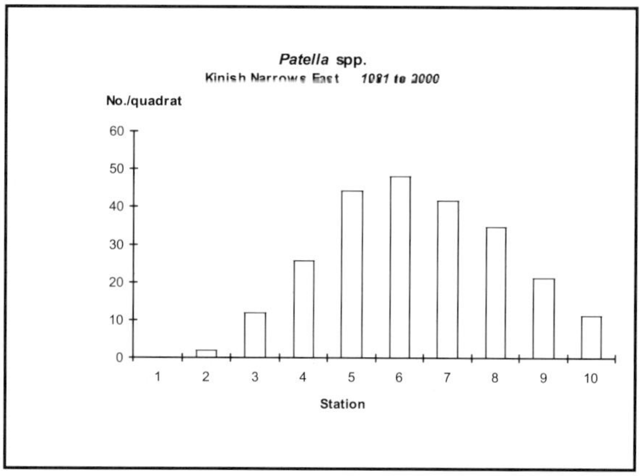

Figure 7.34

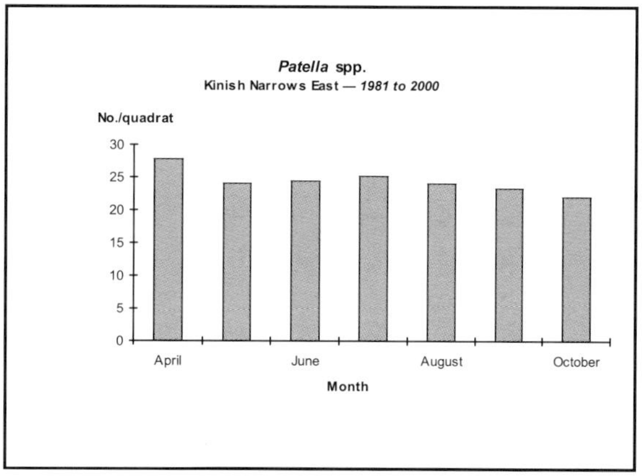

Figure 7.35

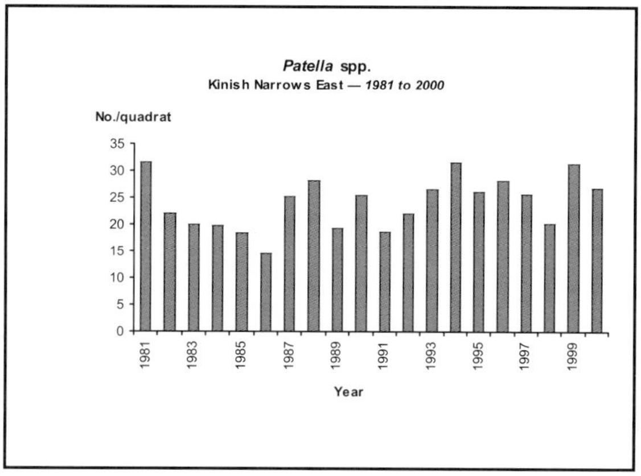

Figure 7.36

KINISH NARROWS EAST

PREDATOR

Dogwhelk
Nucella lapillus
Cuachma chon

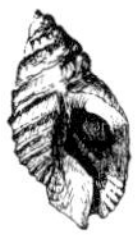

The dogwhelk *Nucella lapillus* was found at stations 4–10 inclusive, with maximum numbers occurring at station 8. Density was generally low however, with the maximum being only 0.65 per quadrat.

Numbers varied between 0.23 per quadrat and 0.51 per quadrat over the season, following a rise in the population from April to May.

Over the 20-year period, dogwhelk density showed a three-fold fluctuation, from a minimum of 0.15 in 1981 to a maximum of 0.45 animals per quadrat in 1987. The long-term trend was one of population increase during the period 1981–87 and of decline during 1993–2000. Density in the intervening years 1988–1992 was quite variable.

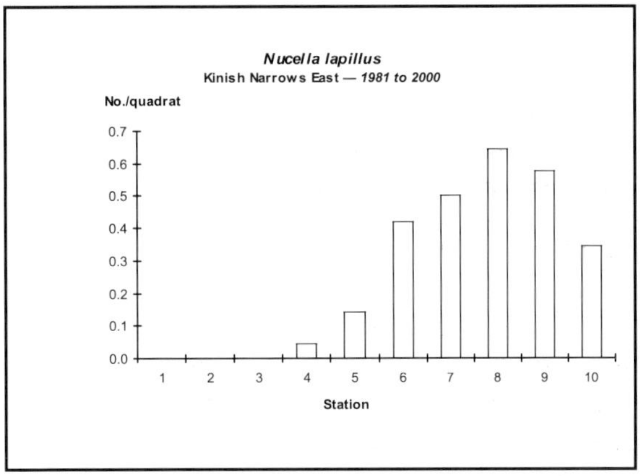

Figure 7.37

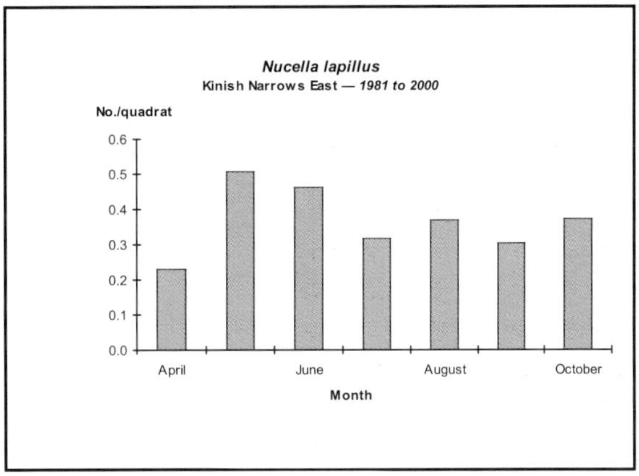

Figure 7.38

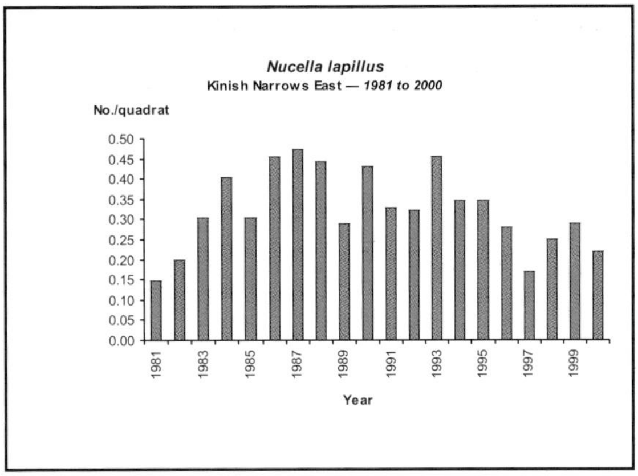

Figure 7.39

Trends for Kinish Narrows East 1981–2000

Of the 12 species analysed for Kinish Narrows East, all showed variation in abundance over the 20 years.

On the upper shore, the population of rough periwinkle *Littorina saxatilis* was much larger in the 1990s than the 1980s, with a general trend of increase in numbers from 1991–99 but a fall in 2000. Spiral wrack *Fucus spiralis* was sparse but more common in the late 1990s than earlier.

On the middle shore the barnacle domination of the 1980s was replaced by the wrack *Fucus spiralis* when the barnacle population crashed in 1991. The best spatfall of barnacles occurred in 1986 when the adult population was dense and increasing. Limpet *Patella* spp. numbers showed only small variance, with the largest fall in numbers occurring between 1981 and 1982 and the largest rise between 1998 and 1999. The edible periwinkle *Littorina littorea* population peaked in 1984 and 1999. Excluding the 1999 peak, there was a general decrease in numbers throughout the 1990s.

On the lower shore, fucoid cover varied, with bladder wrack *Fucus vesiculosus* being richer in the late 1980s and late 1990s but less common in the intervening eight years of 1988–96. Knotted wrack *Ascophyllum nodosum* generally declined from 1981–93, despite its peak in 1990. It was then very sparse from 1994 onwards. Serrated wrack *Fucus serratus* was much less abundant in the 1990s than the 1980s, as was gut weed *Enteromorpha* spp. There was a larger population of the flat periwinkle *Littorina obtusata* in the 1980s than the early 1990s, although the population increased again in the late 1990s. Dogwhelks *Nucella lapillus* increased throughout most of the 1980s and generally declined from 1993–2000.

KINISH NARROWS WEST

VISUAL DOMINANTS

The shore at Kinish Narrows West was visually very similar to that of Kinish Narrows East, having a rich algal development on the middle and lower shore and being dominated by barnacles on the upper shore.

ALGAE

Kinish Narrows West had a total of 112 taxa recorded, which was 20 fewer than at Kinish Narrows East. Ninety were recorded to species level.

Brown algae

Twenty two species of brown seaweed were recorded for Kinish Narrows West. A further four taxa were identified to genus only. As well as the dominant fucoids and laminarians, the frequently recorded but smaller plant species were *Chorda filum, Cladostephus spongiosus,* Ectocarpaceae, *Elachista fucicola* and *Leathesia difformis. Scytosiphon lomentaria* was found on the shore occasionally, but recorded in fewer years than at Kinish Narrows East.

Red algae

A total of 54 species of red algae were recorded for Kinish Narrows West, together with a further 11 taxa recorded to genus only.

The most frequently recorded were more or less the same as found at Kinish Narrows East. They were *Audouinella* spp., *Catenella caespitosa, Ceramium rubrum, Ceramium* spp., *Chondrus crispus, Dumontia contorta, Gelidium* spp., *Hildenbrandia* spp., Lithothamnia, *Lomentaria articulata, Mastocarpus stellatus, Membranoptera alata, Osmundea pinnatifida, Plumaria plumosa* and *Polysiphonia lanosa.* All others were only recorded occasionally.

Species found at Kinish Narrows East but unrecorded from Kinish Narrows West included *Aglaothamnion hookeri, A. roseum,* and *Antithamnionella spirographidis. Calliblepharis* and *Callithamnion* were uncommon, but present on both shores.

Green algae

Fourteen species of green algae were recorded, with a further seven taxa identified to genus level only. The regularly recorded species were *Cladophora rupestris, Cladophora* spp., *Enteromorpha intestinalis* and *Ulva lactuca.*

Highlight on Brown Seaweed Species

Sheltered shores

While knotted wrack *Ascophyllum nodosum* is a common and characteristic species of sheltered shores, there is a special ecological variant associated with extremely sheltered conditions, for example at the heads of sea lochs and marine inlets. Called *A. nodosum* ecad. *mackayi*, it was looked for but not found at Kinish Narrows or other sheltered shores on Sherkin. The plant is free-floating and is not attached to the rocks by any holdfast.

Knotted Wrack
Ascophyllum nodosum

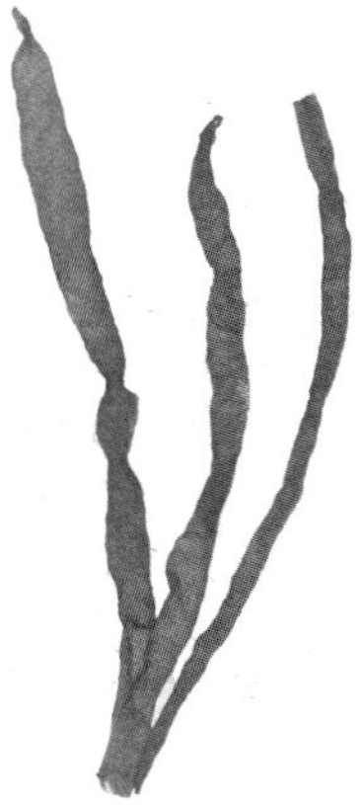

Asperococcus fistulosus

Epiphytic browns

Several species of brown seaweed, for example *Spongonema tomentosum* and *Halopteris filicina,* grow epiphytically on the stipes and fronds of larger fucoids and kelps. By contrast, the strange globular body of *Leathesia difformis* is associated with smaller seaweeds.

Many smaller brown seaweeds grow on a range of substrates which includes other seaweeds, e.g. *Asperococcus fistulosus, Scytosiphon lomentaria, Stictyosiphon tortilis* and *Stilophora tenella. Cladostephus spongiosus,* with its whorled spiny branchlets, grows on coralline algae.

LICHENS

Like Kinish Narrows East, Kinish Narrows West had a very compressed splash zone – but 13 species of lichen were recorded. *Caloplaca marina, Lecanora atra, Verrucaria maura* and *Xanthoria parietina* were recorded every year. *Lichina confinis, L. pygmaea* and *Verrucaria mucosa* were recorded most years, while *Ochrolechia parella* and *Ramalina siliquosa* were less frequently recorded. *Anaptychia fusca, Caloplaca thallincola, Haematomma ventosum* and *Ochrolechia frigida* were only seen in one or two years. *Caloplaca ferruginea* was recorded at Kinish Narrows East in 1999, but was unrecorded from Kinish Narrows West. However *C. thallincola* was recorded in two years at Kinish Narrows West but never at Kinish Narrows East.

ANIMALS

A total of 127 animal taxa were recorded of which 106 were recorded to species level.

The breadcrumb sponge *Halichondria panicea* and *Myxilla incrustans* were recorded most years, with fairly frequent records of *Hymeniacidon sanguinea*.

Annelida were quite diverse, with six species of calcareous tubeworm recorded: *Hydroides norvegica, Pomatoceros triqueter* and four spirorbids – *Spirorbis inornatus, S. rupestris, S. spirorbis* and *S. tridentatus*. While *Pomatoceros* was common, *Hydroides norvegica* was recorded in one year only – 1982. In pockets of mud at low water the burrowing polychaetes *Amphitritides gracilis, Cirratulus cirratus* and *Cirriformia tentaculata* were found. Similar pockets support small numbers of the sandmason worm *Lanice conchilega,* which was recorded twice.

Thirty taxa of mollusca were recorded; the shore was rich in topshells (*Gibbula cineraria* and *G. umbilicalis*) and records of the thick topshell *Osilinus lineatus* were made in several years. The dominant grazing species of periwinkles and limpets, together with dogwhelks, were present every year; banded whelks *Hinia incrassata* and

Highlight on Crabs (Crustaceans)

Hermit Crab - Pagurus bernhardus

Within the various crab families there is wide-ranging variation of their basic segmental body plan, usually in the specialisation of the legs. The first pair of legs bearing the pincers is usually short but can be much elongated as in the long-clawed porcelain crab species *Pisidia longicornis.* The fifth pair of walking legs is tiny in the porcelain crabs and flattened into a paddle in the swimming crabs (*Liocarcinus depurator* and *Necora puber*). Carapace shape varies from the almost triangular body of the spider crabs, through the well-known oval shape of the edible crab to the round body shape of the tiny pea crab *Pinnotheres pisum.*

At one extreme of body development, hermit crabs are a specialist group. They have retained a relatively large abdomen with a very thin exoskeleton. A hermit crab is therefore very vulnerable to predators and adopts empty mollusc shells to protect itself. The common species of Ireland and Britain show an asymmetrical development of the pincers with the right pincer being larger. Hermit crabs and spider crabs especially are often camouflaged. Hermit crabs may have sponges and anemones on their borrowed shell, while spider crabs have pieces of seaweed attached to the shell. Two species of spider crab, *Hyas araneus* and *Macropodia tenuirostris*, occurred at Kinish Narrows.

Sea Mat – *Membranipora membranacea*

Highlight on Sea Mats (Bryozoans)

Sea mats (also called moss animals) are colonial animals, each living in an individual capsule. Some are tufted, e.g. *Crisia* spp., and have a similar growth form to branched algae, but the majority encrust rocks or algal stipes and fronds. Many are eaten by nudibranchs and isopods, e.g. the preferred food species of *Acanthodoris pilosa* is known to be the bryozoans *Alcyonidium hirsutum*, *A. gelatinosum* and *Flustrellidra hispida* (Todd, 1981). Both Kinish Narrows West and Kinish Narrows East were rich in sea mats, because of the wave-sheltered environment.

On Sherkin the common species were *Alcyonidium gelatinosum*, *A. hirsutum*, *Electra pilosa*, *Flustrellidra hispida* and *Umbonula*. More rarely recorded were *Bowerbankia*, *Cellepora hyalina*, *Crisia* spp., *Mucronella*, *Schizoporella* and *Scrupocellaria*.

Many species settle on specific hosts, e.g. *Flustrellidra* and *Alcyonidium* are found on *Fucus serratus*, *Bowerbankia imbricata* on *Ascophyllum*, *Membranipora membranacea* on kelp fronds.

H. reticulata were present most years. The edible periwinkle *Littorina littorea* was more common on the middle shore at Kinish Narrows West than at many of the other Sherkin shores. Nudibranchs such as *Onchidoris bilamellata* and the sea lemon *Archidoris pseudoargus* were occasionally found.

There was a wide range of crustacea with several crab species at low water, *Cancer pagurus*, *Carcinus maenas*, *Hyas araneus*, *Necora puber*, *Macropodia tenuirostris*, *Pagurus bernhardus*, *Pinnotheres pisum* and *Pisidia longicornis*. Amphipods were not common but species recorded included the skeleton shrimp *Caprella linearis* and *Dynamene bidentata*.

Bryozoa were rich and broadly similar in composition to those found at Kinish Narrows East. *Alcyonidium gelatinosum* and *A. hirsutum* were frequently recorded; however *A. diaphanum*, which was found at Kinish Narrows East, was unrecorded here. Species which occurred at Kinish Narrows West but not Kinish Narrows East included *Celleporella hyalina* (which was recorded once in 1984), *Crisia* spp. (1983), *Flustra foliacea* (1988 and 1997) and *Mucronella coccinea* (1991).

Tunicates were also well represented, albeit by fewer species than found at Kinish Narrows East. *Ascidia mentula* and *Ascidiella aspersa* were not recorded at Kinish Narrows West, though found at Kinish Narrows East; but *Morchellium argus* (not found at Kinish Narrows East) had a single record for 1997. The most commonly occurring tunicate species at both the Kinish sites was *Botryllus schlosseri*.

Species analysed for Kinish Narrows West, their place in the food chain and the shore ecology (Predatory pathway ——► Grazing pathway ••••••►)

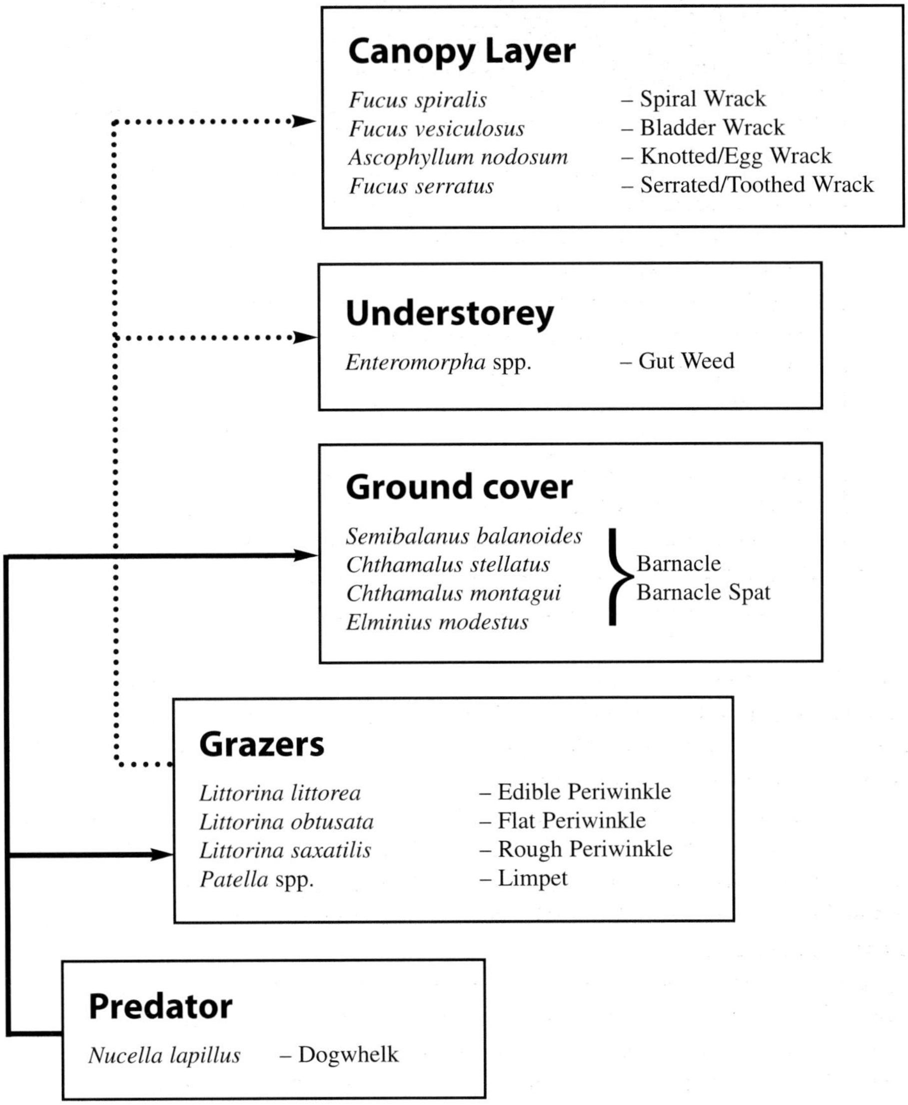

KINISH NARROWS WEST

CANOPY LAYER

Spiral Wrack
Fucus spiralis
Casfheamainn

Spiral wrack *Fucus spiralis* was widely distributed on the Kinish Narrows West shore, but growth was fairly sparse. There were two distinct peaks in distribution, at station 2 (2.2% cover per quadrat) and station 6 (1.5%).

There was very little seasonal variation from April to October. Cover in August was relatively high, and fell off considerably in September.

Fucus spiralis density fluctuated at a low level for all but two years when it rose to 5% (1993) and 3% (1996). There was no similarity with the variation of this species at Kinish Narrows East.

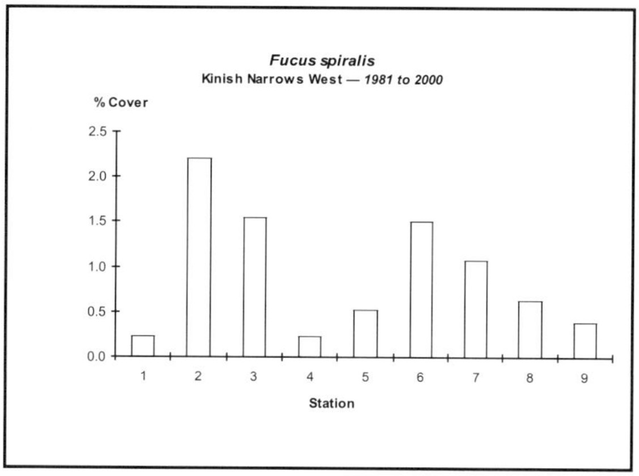

Figure 7.40

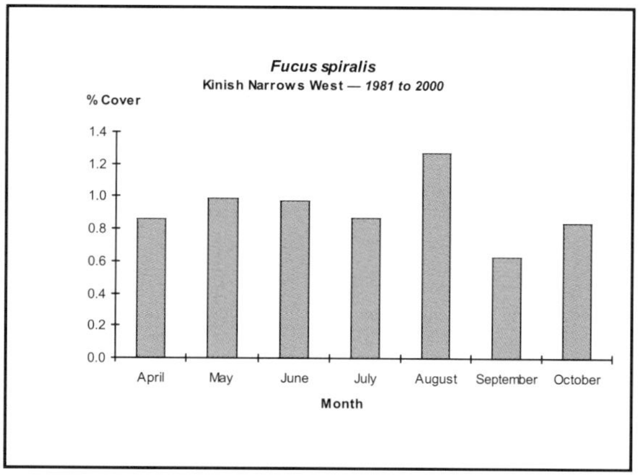

Figure 7.41

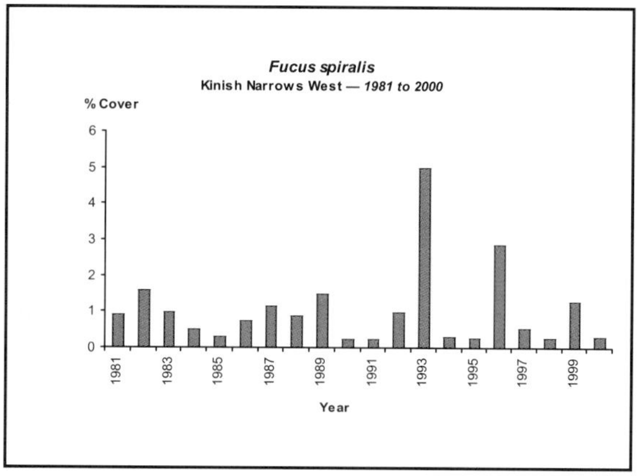

Figure 7.42

KINISH NARROWS WEST

CANOPY LAYER

Bladder Wrack
Fucus vesiculosus
Feamainn bhoilgíneach

Bladder wrack *Fucus vesiculosus* was distributed on the middle and lower shore primarily at station 6, 7 and 8, where it occupied 18–21% cover per quadrat.

The species was fairly constant throughout the spring and summer but showed an increase in October.

Variation over the 20-year period was irregular but distinct. From low levels in 1981–84, there was a marked cycle of increase and decline between 1984–90, with the peak occuring in 1986 (22.6% cover). This was followed by a second moderately large increase in 1991, and from then on there were nine years of steady decline. This can be summarised as showing three distinct phases of abundance.

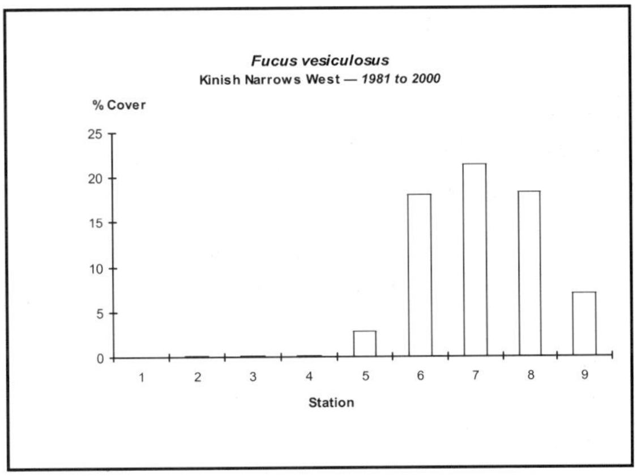

Figure 7.43

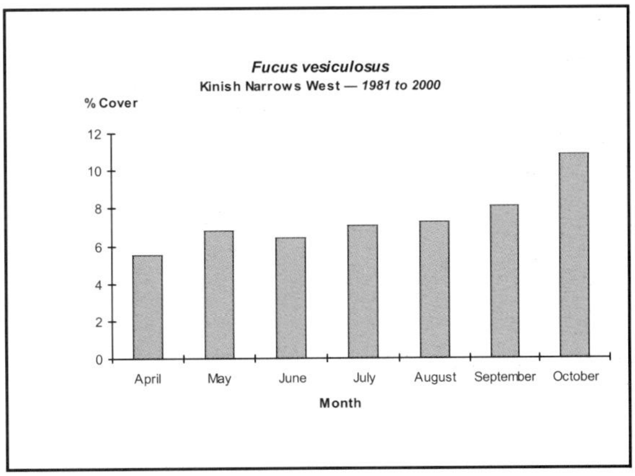

Figure 7.44

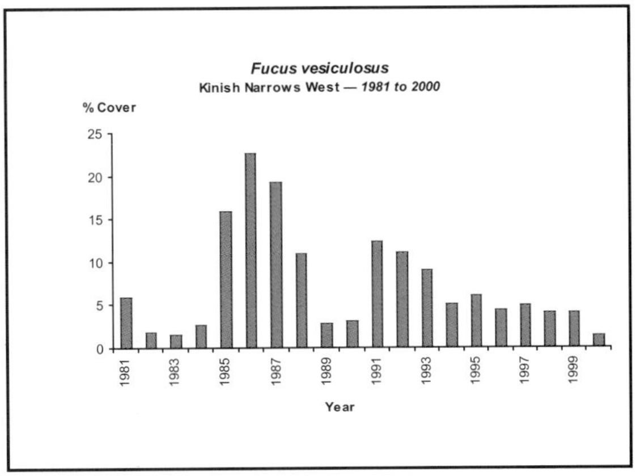

Figure 7.45

KINISH NARROWS WEST

CANOPY LAYER

Knotted/Egg Wrack
Ascophyllum nodosum
Feamainn bhuí

Although knotted wrack *Ascophyllum nodosum* was present at stations 5–9, it was not a dominant canopy species, and only accounted for 6% cover per quadrat when at its maximum at station 8.

Percentage cover remained the same for most of the year, but a small decrease occurred in September.

There was an overall steady decrease in *Ascophyllum nodosum* cover at Kinish Narrows West from 1981–96 and none was recorded at all during 1997. Low levels (< 1%) were present in 1998, 1999 and 2000. Two years in particular, 1989 and 1991, did not conform to this decreasing trend and showed peaks of 3–4%.

It is interesting to note that across the narrows at Kinish Narrows East, knotted wrack peaked in different years, 1988 and 1990.

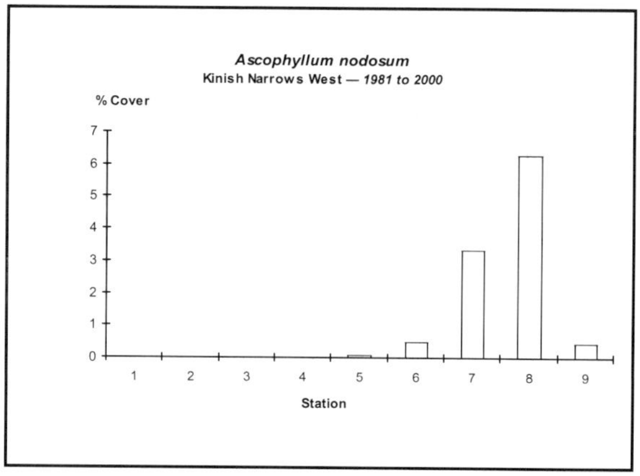

Figure 7.46

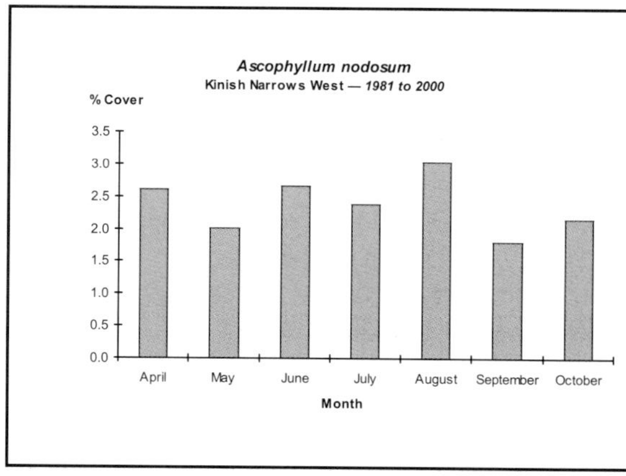

Figure 7.47

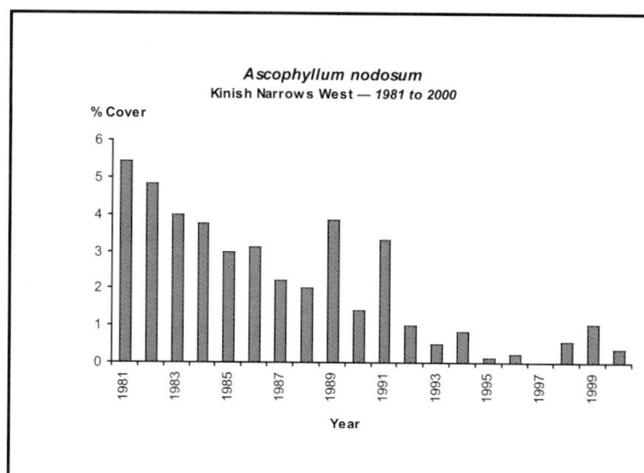

Figure 7.48

KINISH NARROWS WEST

CANOPY LAYER

Serrated/Toothed Wrack
Fucus serratus
Míoránach

At Kinish Narrows West serrated wrack *Fucus serratus* was recorded from the three lowest stations (7–9), with its maximum cover at station 9 (24% per quadrat).

There was no seasonal variation.

Long-term variation was broadly similar to that shown by bladder wrack *F. vesiculosus*. After the first three years of decline, serrated wrack cover increased from 1983 to its maximum of 7% in 1988. A general trend of decline then proceeded up to 2000, although there were occasional years of small increase within this trend (1991, 1993, 1994 and 1997).

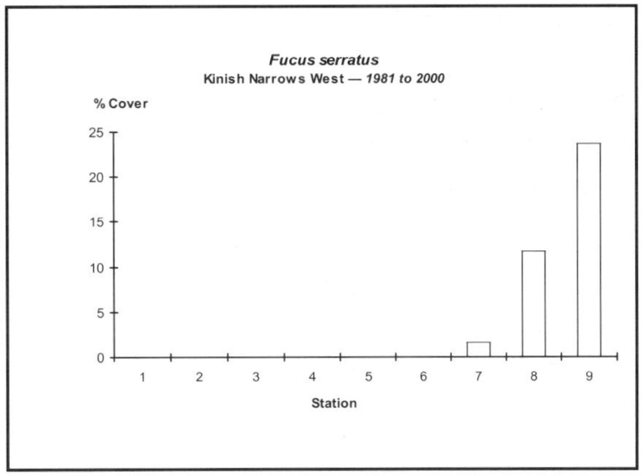

Figure 7.49

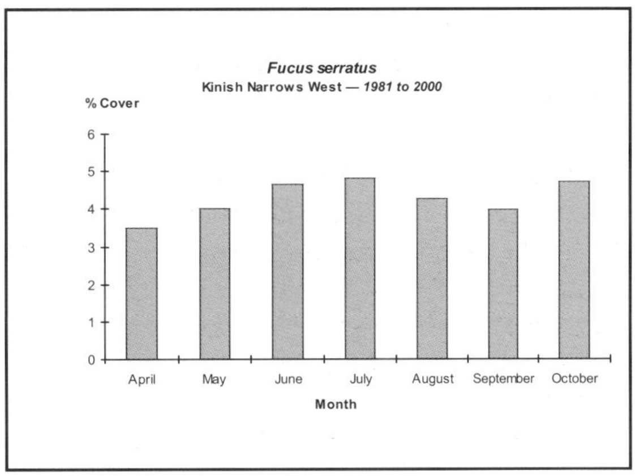

Figure 7.50

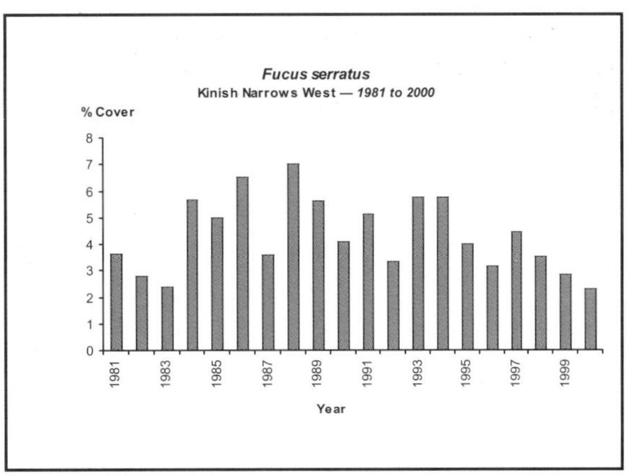

Figure 7.51

KINISH NARROWS WEST

UNDERSTOREY

Gut Weed
Enteromorpha spp.
Líneáil ghorm

At Kinish Narrows West, gut weed *Enteromorpha* spp. had two discrete distributions on the upper and lower shore, with maximum densities at station 2 and station 8.

There was a small increase in cover from April to June, and a decline in cover at the end of the summer from August to October.

Over the years *Enteromorpha* density fluctuated from its highest in 1988 (11.6% cover per quadrat) to its lowest annual level of 2.3% in 1997. Between the years 1985 and 1998 (both being years when *Enteromorpha* cover was low) there was an overall trend of increase in cover from 1986–88, followed by a general trend of decline. However within this general trend there were two intermittent years of high cover (1994 and 1996). In 1997–2000, recorded levels were low.

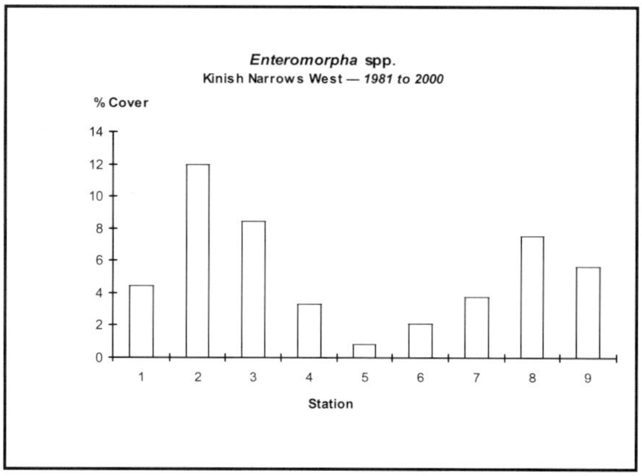

Figure 7.52

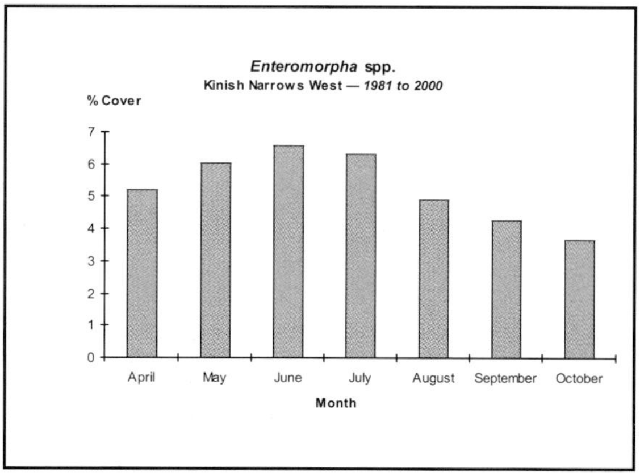

Figure 7.53

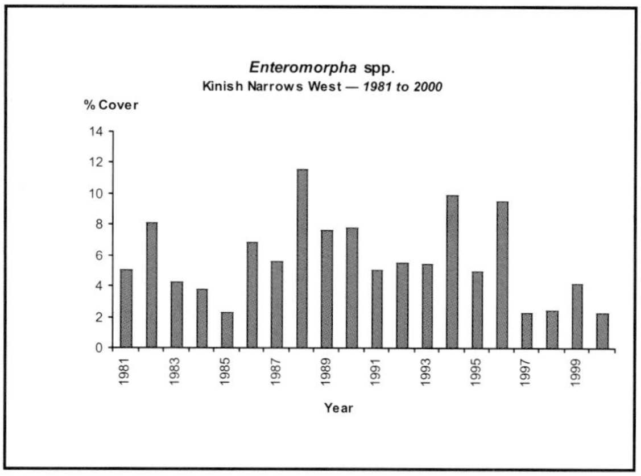

Figure 7.54

KINISH NARROWS WEST

GROUND COVER

Barnacles

Semibalanus balanoides
Chthamalus stellatus
Chthamalus montagui
Elminius modestus
Giúrainn

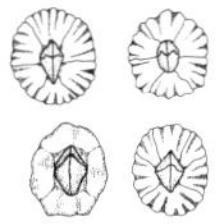

Barnacle cover was low at the two highest stations on the Kinish Narrows West shore; the main distribution was on the middle shore where the maximum percentage cover (68% per quadrat) occurred at station 5.

Barnacle cover showed a steady seasonal increase from 19% cover per quadrat in April to 41% cover in October.

The pattern of annual variation was very similar to barnacle variation at Kinish Narrows East. Percentage cover was generally higher between 1982 and 1990 than 1981 and 1991–2000. Both sites experienced a small loss of cover in 1987 and a large population crash in 1991.

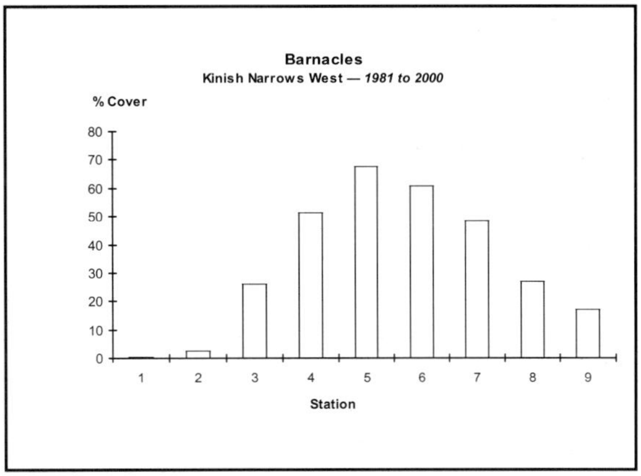

Figure 7.55

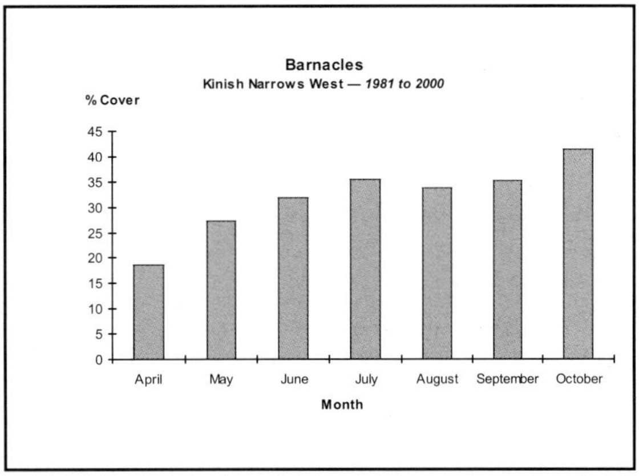

Figure 7.56

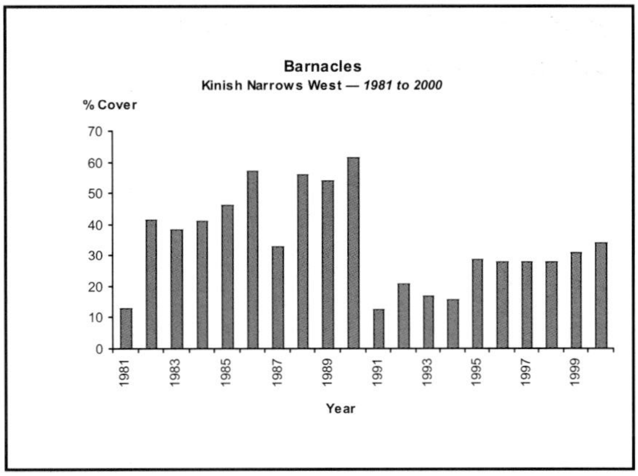

Figure 7.57

KINISH NARROWS WEST

GROUND COVER

Barnacle Spat
Síol giúrainn

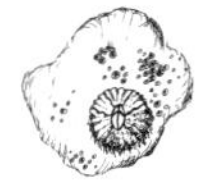

Barnacle spat settled most densely on the middle shore, with peak numbers occurring at station 5 (90/dm^2) which coincided with the densest cover of adult barnacles.

Spat and juveniles were evident every month, but there was a marked increase in May when *Semibalanus balanoides* settled. The expected September peak of *Chthamalus* spp. did not occur, but a small increase in August probably comprised early *Chthamalus* settlement.

No spat were recorded in 1984, 1985 and 1990. Adult barnacle density was relatively high in each of these years, indeed 1997 was a year of maximum cover at Kinish Narrows West. In other years the density of spat varied between 10 and 95/dm^2 and rose to the highest recorded density of 175/dm^2 during 1997. However this high density of spat did not appear to have any effect on the adult population cover the following years (1998 and 1999), which remained consistently low.

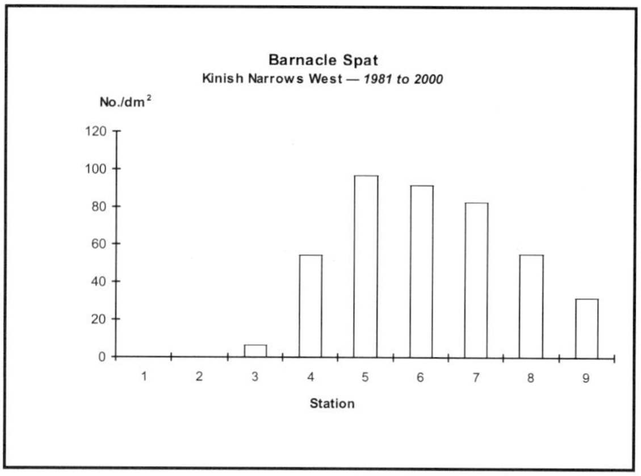

Figure 7.58

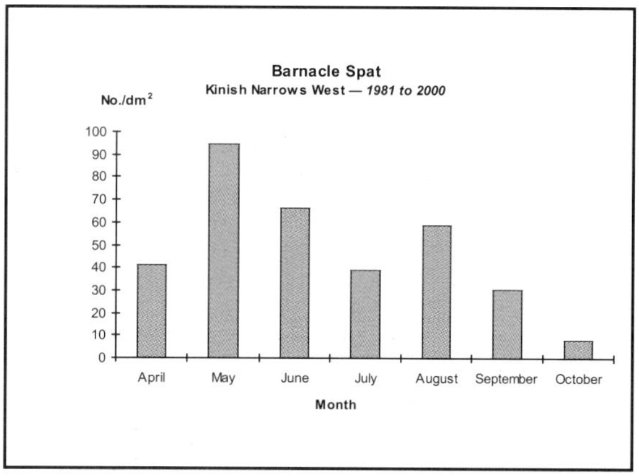

Figure 7.59

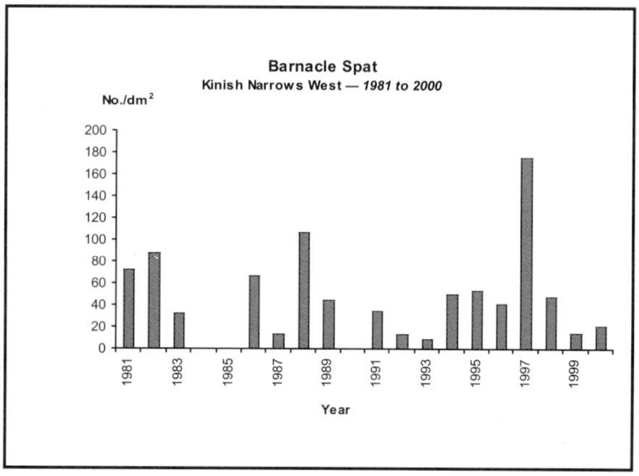

Figure 7.60

KINISH NARROWS WEST

GRAZERS

Edible Periwinkle
Littorina littorea
Gioradán

The edible periwinkle *Littorina littorea* had two distribution peaks on the shore – station 2 (1 per quadrat) and station 7 in the middle shore (1.5 per quadrat).

There was no apparent seasonal variation, as numbers remained within the range 0.7–0.9 per quadrat.

Over the 20 years, *Littorina littorea* abundance varied considerably around an overall 20-year mean of approximately 0.6 per quadrat. However in two years density was significantly lower than this (1992 and 1994). Higher than average densities were recorded in several years – mostly earlier than 1989. The general trend has been one of decline between 1981 and 1994, and a six-year period of overall increase during 1995–2000.

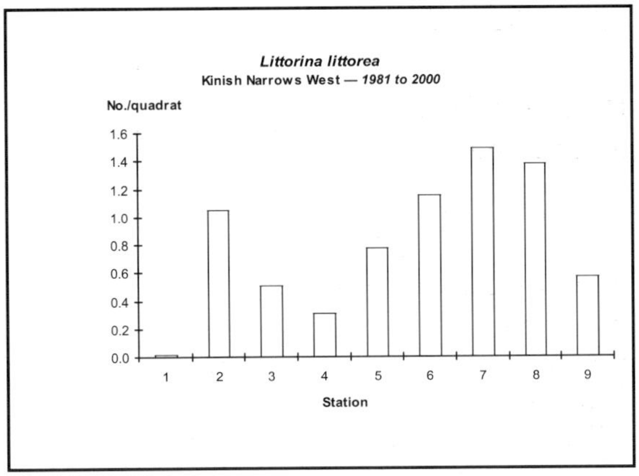

Figure 7.61

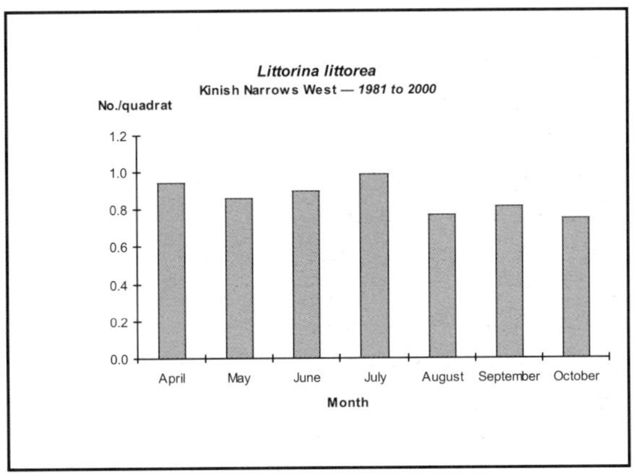

Figure 7.62

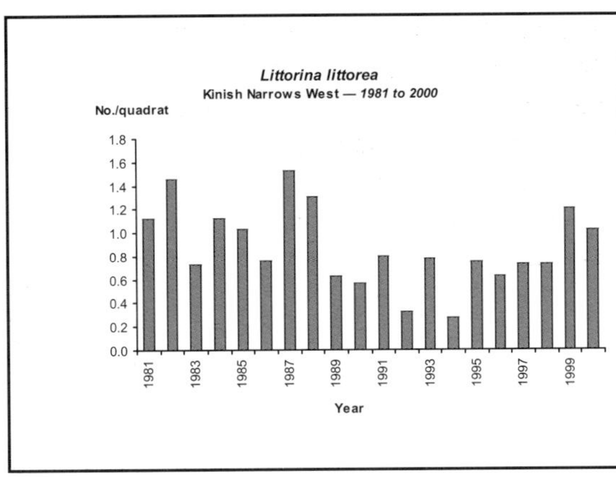

Figure 7.63

KINISH NARROWS WEST

GRAZERS

Flat Periwinkle
Littorina obtusata
Faocha leathan

The flat periwinkle *Littorina obtusata* was found primarily on the lower shore. Highest numbers occurred at station 8 (9.4 per quadrat).

Littorina obtusata numbers were relatively high in the spring (4.2 per quadrat in April), but numbers were very much reduced during May, June and July. Numbers doubled in August and remained generally high in September and October.

Annual variation was limited, with numbers of usually < 6 per quadrat. 1987 was an unusual year in showing a huge increase to 12.5 per quadrat, and it is interesting to see that this population increase was not sustained through the winter of 1987–88. However it must be emphasised that data collection in these years was good (see p. 34). By contrast it is unfortunate that the population size between 1985 and 1987 cannot be assessed; *Littorina obtusata* was present on the shore but data are inconsistent as a dm^2 count was made. The last ten-year period (1991–2000) recorded a trend of population reduction when numbers steadily reduced from 6 to 1.25 per quadrat.

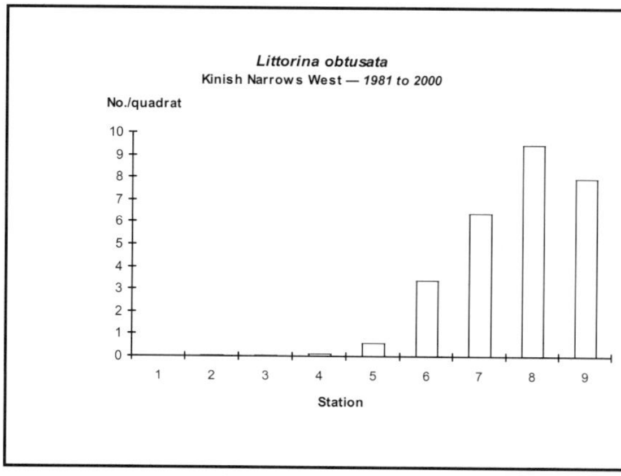

Figure 7.64

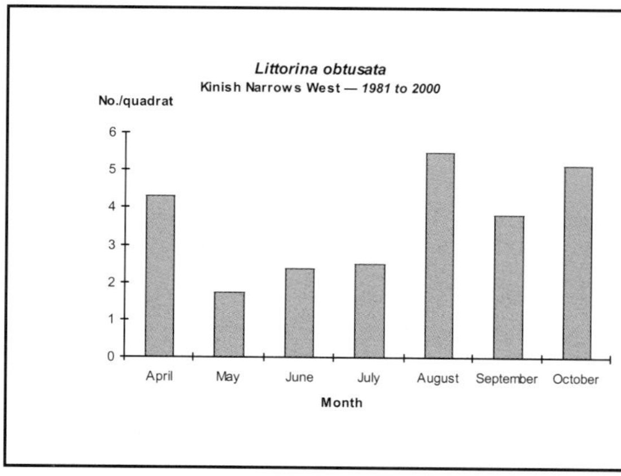

Figure 7.65

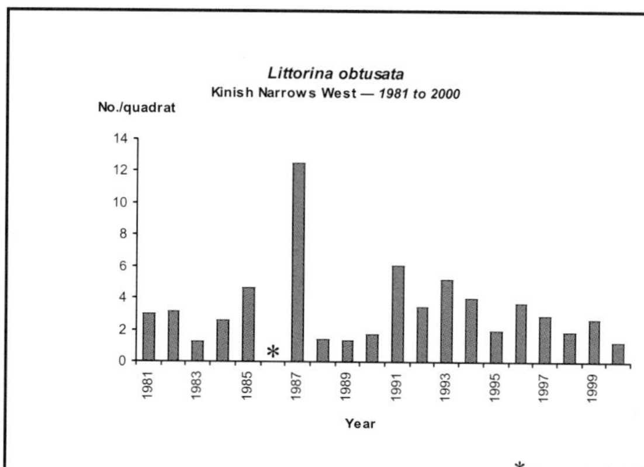

Figure 7.66

KINISH NARROWS WEST

GRAZERS

Rough Periwinkle
Littorina saxatilis
Faocha gharbh

The rough periwinkle *Littorina saxatilis* was distributed over the upper and middle shore with highest numbers (10.4 per quadrat) occuring at station 5. Smaller numbers also occurred on the lower shore.

Seasonal variation was present, with a decline in the population from April to July, and again from August to September. August numbers were much higher (5.16 per quadrat) than those in July (3.0 per quadrat).

The annual population mean showed large variations. Numbers were generally low in the first 15 years and in one year (1986) *Littorina saxatilis* is shown as absent because only a dm^2 count was made (see p. 34). It is therefore difficult to say whether the peak in 1987 (which may be exaggerated due to a similar sampling error) was reached gradually through intermediate densities in 1986, or whether it represents a single year of population increase. A different pattern presented from 1993–2000, with a general trend of increase in population size to reach the 20-year maximum of approximately 12 per quadrat. Numbers fell a little in 2000 and it will be interesting to see whether or not this marks the beginning of a decline.

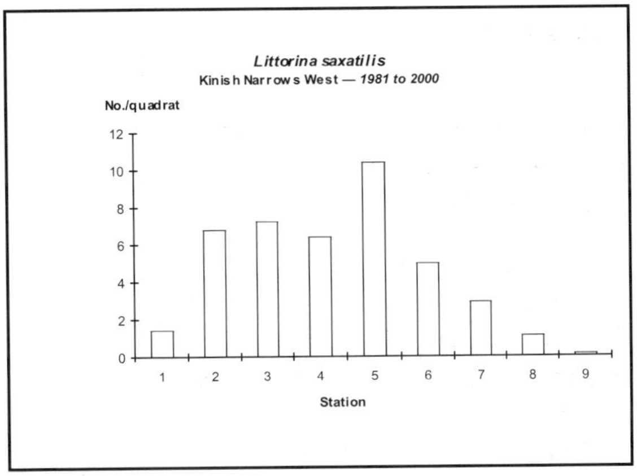

Figure 7.67

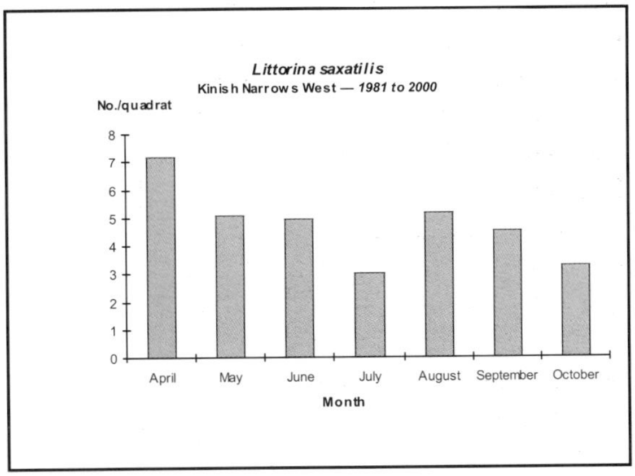

Figure 7.68

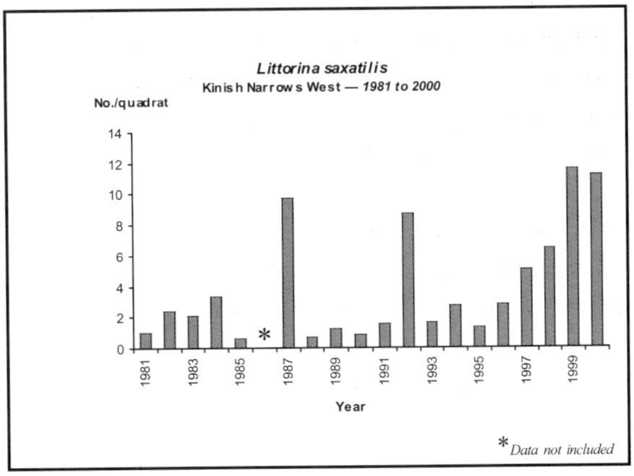

Figure 7.69

KINISH NARROWS WEST

GRAZERS

Limpet
Patella spp.
Bairneach

Limpets *Patella* spp. occurred over most of the shore, but were most dense on the middle shore (stations 5, 6 and 7). Highest density was 45 per quadrat.

There was no seasonal variation in numbers from April to October.

Population numbers were relatively high in the first two years of the survey, but fell in 1983. There were then two periods of slow increase, the first during 1983–90 and the second during 1991–97. After a decrease in numbers in 1998, limpets reached their highest ever population size in 1999. Numbers were slightly reduced in the year 2000. As more data accumulate it will become clear whether the decreases in 1991 and 1998 were significant, or whether the trend from 1983–99 was a single steady population increase.

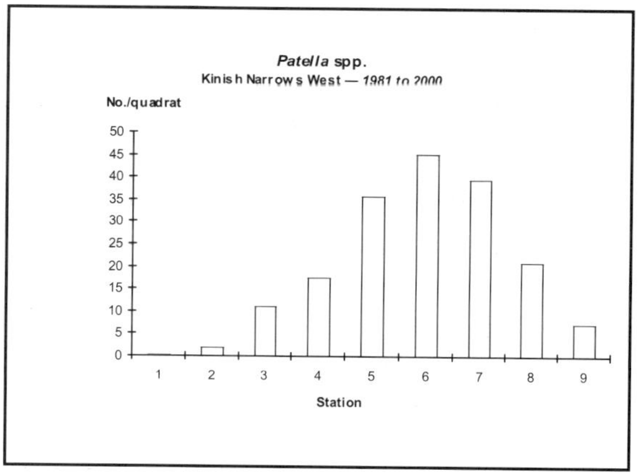

Figure 7.70

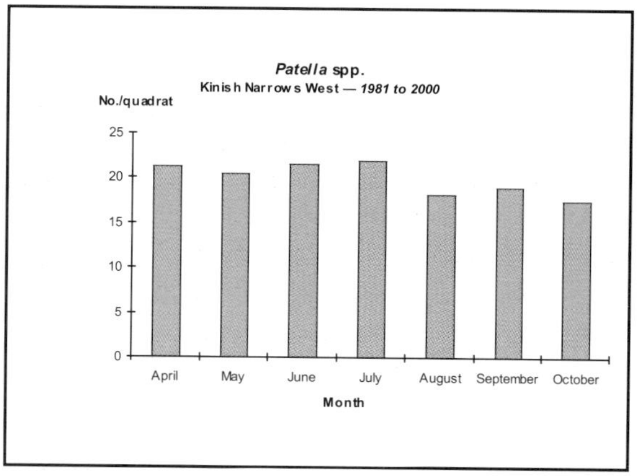

Figure 7.71

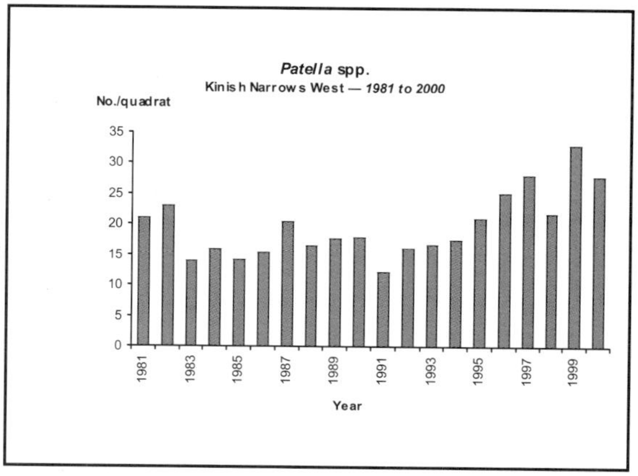

Figure 7.72

KINISH NARROWS WEST

PREDATOR

Dogwhelk
Nucella lapillus
Cuachma chon

Dogwhelks *Nucella lapillus* were found on the middle and lower shore at Kinish Narrows West, with the majority occurring at stations 6–8. Density was generally low with a maximum of just less than 1.8 per quadrat. However this represented three times the density at Kinish Narrows East.

Nucella at Kinish Narrows West showed no seasonal variation.

Annual variation was recorded. The population fluctuated between 1981 and 1985, but from then on there was a general trend of decline to the minimum density recorded in 2000. The 1985 maximum was almost four times as large.

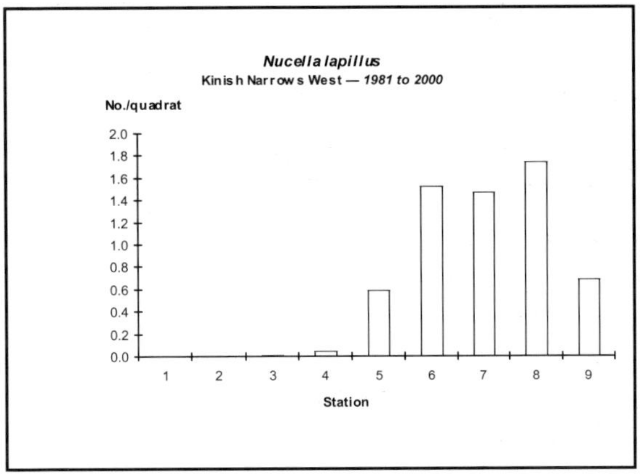

Figure 7.73

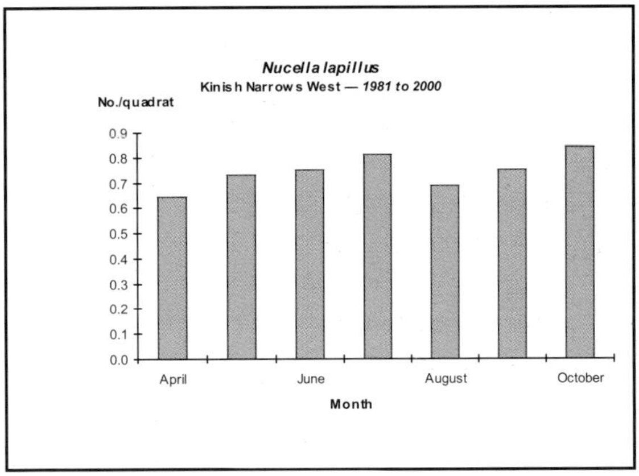

Figure 7.74

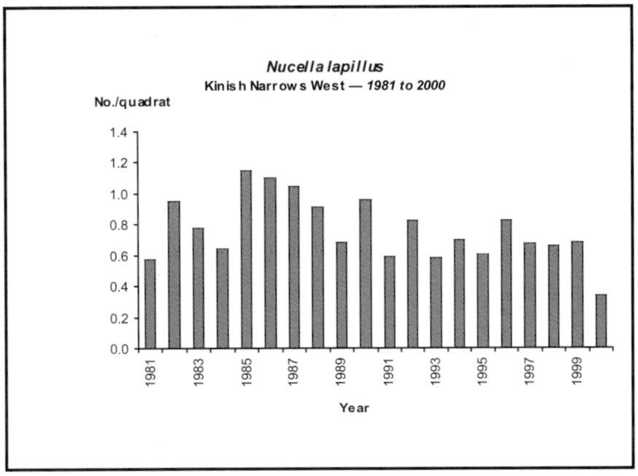

Figure 7.75

TRENDS FOR KINISH NARROWS WEST 1981-2000

Of the 12 species analysed, all showed variation in abundance through the 20-year period.

On the upper shore, the population of the rough periwinkle *Littorina saxatilis* was small for many of the first ten years of the survey. It then increased steadily during 1993–2000. Spiral wrack *Fucus spiralis* remained at a generally low level, with isolated peaks during 1993 and 1996. Gut weed *Enteromorpha* spp. was most common in the middle years 1986–96.

On the middle shore, the barnacle domination of the 1980s was not replaced by any significant increase in seaweed cover when abundance declined in the 1990s. Bladder wrack *Fucus vesiculosus* also declined from 1991–2000, as did knotted wrack *Ascophyllum nodosum*. However, numbers of limpets *Patella* spp., which had increased since their low of 1983, continued to rise in the 1990s. There was no recorded increase in the adult barnacle population following the good spatfall of 1997.

On the lower shore, *Ascophyllum nodosum* and serrated wrack *Fucus serratus* both declined in cover during the 1990s, with *Fucus serratus* having peaked in 1988, and *Ascophyllum nodosum* having shown only isolated peaks in 1989 and 1991 amongst a pattern of general decreasing density. Living among *Fucus serratus,* the flat periwinkle *Littorina obtusata* population, with the exception of 1987, was never large and declined throughout the 1990s. During 1988 when *Fucus serratus* peaked, numbers of *Littorina obtusata* were surprisingly low. The edible periwinkle *Littorina littorea* population was generally smaller during the 1990s than during the first half of the survey. Dogwhelk *Nucella lapillus* numbers were also in general decline during 1985–2000.

KINISH NARROWS EAST AND KINISH NARROWS WEST: SIMILARITIES AND DIFFERENCES

The two Kinish Narrows sites were originally selected with the aim of comparing sites within a similar location that had similar wave exposures but different aspects and different gradients.

Although the number of species was comparable, the species listed are by no means identical. Of the 243 species (plus 54 taxa) recorded at Kinish Narrows East and the 214 species (plus 50 taxa) at Kinish Narrows West, the main differences seen were in red algae, molluscs, crustaceans and bryozoans. Kinish Narrows East was richer in red algae and in molluscs; Kinish Narrows West was richer in crustaceans and bryozoans.

Crustacea recorded only at Kinish Narrows West were the ghost shrimp *Caprella linearis*, the isopod *Idotea granulosa*, the shrimp *Palaemon serratus* and the crabs *Macropodia tenuirostris* and *Pisidia longicornis*. Bryozoans found at Kinish Narrows West but absent from Kinish Narrows East were *Celleporella hyaline, Crisia* spp., *Flustra foliacea* and *Mucronella coccinea*.

At Kinish Narrows East molluscs included three species of nudibranch (*Acanthodoris pilosa, Facelina auriculata* and *Limacia clavigera*) that feed on hydroids and bryozoans. The preferred food species of *A. pilosa* (the bryozoans *Alcyonidium hirsutum, A. gelatinosum* and *Flustrellidra hispida*) were all common at Kinish Narrows East, but also at Kinish Narrows West where these nudibranchs species were not recorded. It is ironic that the number of species of bryozoans was higher at Kinish Narrows West, however total density at each site was equally small and confined to the lower shore stations. Kinish Narrows East had records of five hydroid species as compared with four from Kinish Narrows West, but of these only *Dynamena pumila* was recorded consistently every year at both sites and was likely to be an important food source. The ghost shrimp *Caprella linearis* was found among hydroids and erect bryozoans.

Over the 20-year period 1981–2000, there were both similarities and differences in how the key species varied in abundance. Similar patterns were seen in barnacles and *Littorina saxatilis*, whereas the patterns of variation of *Fucus spiralis, Enteromorpha* spp., *L. obtusata*, *Patella* spp. and *Nucella lapillus* were very different. Fucus *vesiculosus*, *F. serratus*, *Ascophyllum nodosum* and *L. littorea* displayed incomplete similarities.

Species with similar patterns of annual variation

Barnacles: At both sites the barnacle populations were much larger during the 1980s, with a crash in numbers in 1991 and small recovery thereafter. Years of good spatfall differed; the best year for Kinish Narrows East was 1986 – a year not particularly good at Kinish Narrows West; while the best year for Kinish Narrows West, 1997, was also fairly good for Kinish Narrows East.

***Littorina saxatilis*:** Populations of *L. saxatilis* were larger in the 1990's than the 1980s at both sites.

Species with different patterns of annual variation

***Fucus spiralis*:** During the 1980s *F. spiralis* was much more abundant at Kinish Narrows West than Kinish Narrows East. Both sites had large increases in isolated years in the 1990s, but these did not always occur in the same years. In 1996 abundance peaks occurred at both sites, but additional peaks occurred in 1998 (Kinish Narrows East) and 1993 (Kinish Narrows West).

***Enteromorpha* spp.:** Usually present in small quantities at both sites, *Enteromorpha* spp. was more common at Kinish Narrows West. Peaks of abundance occurred in different years – 1986 at Kinish Narrows East, with higher cover (3–6%) being maintained for the four-year period 1986–89. Abundance peaks at Kinish Narrows West were recorded mostly after this time, in 1988, 1994 and 1996.

***Littorina obtusata*:** Population numbers were similar at both sites but the patterns of abundance varied despite two years (1987 and 1991) simultaneously showing density peaks. At Kinish Narrows East there were three cycles of abundance (a third peak occurred in 1999) and the population was stronger in the early 1980s than the late 1980s/early 1990s. This contrasted sharply with the flat periwinkle population at Kinish Narrows West which, with the exception of the 1987 peak in numbers, was low in density throughout the 1980s. A rise in numbers in 1991 was then followed by a gradual decline to 2000.

***Patella* spp.:** The range of population density was similar at both sites, but more annual variation occurred at Kinish Narrows East which showed decrease (1981–86), increase (1986–94) and decrease (1994–98). This contrasted with the steady increase recorded between 1991 and 1997 at Kinish Narrows West.

***Nucella lapillus*:** Dogwhelks were more abundant at Kinish Narrows West (< 1.1 per quadrat) than Kinish Narrows East (< 0.45 per quadrat). At Kinish Narrows East the population increased between 1981 and 1987 and decreased for most of the 1990s (1993–2000), whereas at Kinish Narrows West the population was in decline from 1985–2000.

Species with mixed similarities and differences in annual variation

***Fucus vesiculosus*:** Bladder wrack occupied a similar area of the shore (5–20% cover) at both sites, but cycles of increase and decrease differed. There was similarity during the 1980s when bladder wrack abundance peaked at both sites in 1986 and showed minimum cover in 1981–82 and 1989; but differences were recorded during the 1990s when Kinish Narrows East showed two cycles of rise and fall, whereas Kinish Narrows West showed a rapid climb in 1990–91 followed by continual decline from 1992–2000.

***Fucus serratus*:** While not abundant at either site, the lower shore wrack covered consistently almost twice as much rock area at Kinish Narrows East (4–8% cover) with abundance peaks during 1986 and 1989. 1986 was also a year of peak cover at Kinish Narrows West, but 1984 and 1989 were the other years of higher abundance. At both sites *F. serratus* declined from 1989, but whereas at Kinish Narrows East the species was unrecorded after 1994, at Kinish Narrows West the species was still present at 3–4% in 2000 despite a steady decline from 1989–2000.

***Ascophyllum nodosum*:** For the 13-year period 1981–94 a decline occurred at both sites, but after 1994 a virtual absence of knotted wrack at Kinish Narrows East (present in two out of seven years) contrasted with a consistent but low density (present six out of seven years at < 1% cover) at Kinish Narrows West.

***Littorina littorea*:** Edible periwinkles were consistently more abundant at Kinish Narrows West than Kinish Narrows East. A general trend of decline was evident at both sites but during different years. At Kinish Narrows East during 1984–98 there were three phases of decline, while at Kinish Narrows West a single and prolonged population decrease occurred earlier (1981–94), which was followed by a six-year period of increasing numbers.

Chapter Eight

Natural Variation of Species on the Shore

Our analysis of selected species shows clearly that plant and animal populations on the rocky shore vary over seasons or longer periods of time, or both. A seashore is far from static in composition. This raises many questions, for example: i) how do the sample sites compare with each other? ii) Do the Sherkin Island records illustrate how particular species interact with each other? If there is a good spatfall of barnacles at Poulacurra one year, will the same necessarily be true at Drolain Point or other shores? Are there any apparent environmental cues to species change? Are there any patterns evident in the variation we have recorded and if so, do we see these patterns on each shore? There are so many questions, the task seems impossible, but we have tried to draw together the evidence and look for understanding in the wealth of accumulated data. It must be remembered that the original question posed was: is it possible to record the abundance of organisms at seven sites over at least two decades? The answer to this is unquestionably "yes" and should not be overlooked in the wider discussions that follow.

Seasonality

Algae

At four of our seven sites, Drolain Point, Reenahoe, Kinish Narrows East and Kinish Narrows West, where ephemeral green algae have been investigated, there is distinct evidence of seasonality, a feature also observed in the five-year analysis by Leslie (1986). Figure 8.1 shows distinct June and July peaks of gut weed *Enteromorpha* spp. at three of the above Sherkin sites.

At Reenahoe and Kinish Narrows East, *Enteromorpha* built up rapidly to a June peak,

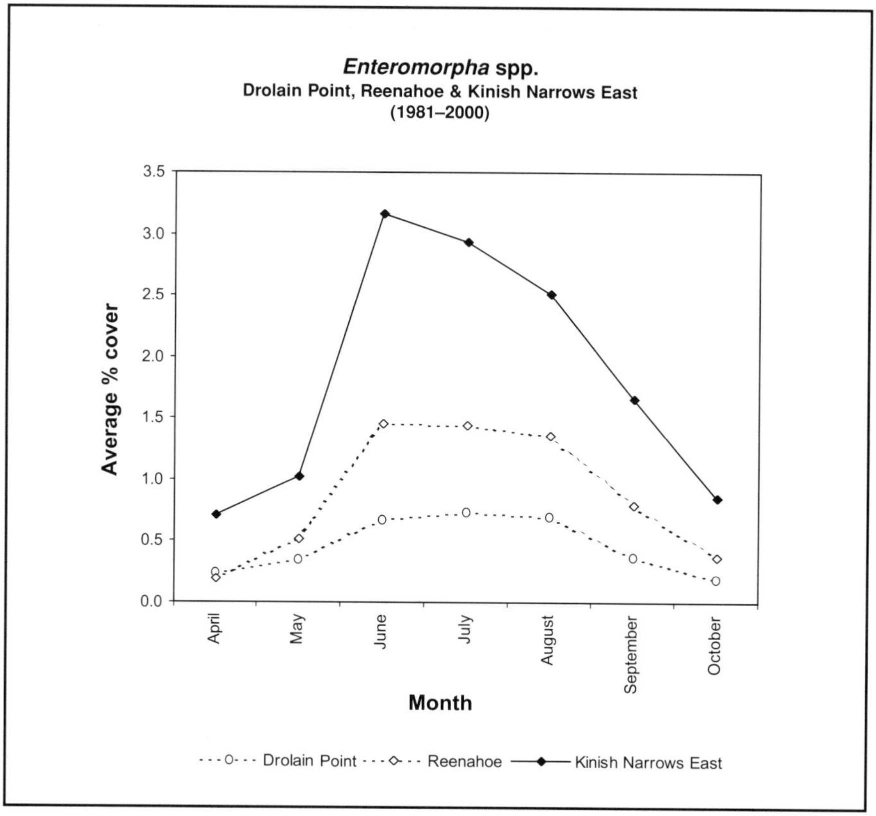

Figure 8.1 Seasonality of the green ephemeral seaweed *Enteromorpha* spp.

and there was almost three times as much cover of green algae in midsummer (June, July and August) as compared to earlier and later in the season. At Kinish Narrows West, although the pattern of a June peak followed by decline was evident, there was significantly more *Enteromorpha* on the shore in the spring (April and May). Thus the rate of growth and increase during June was not so pronounced.

At Drolain Point there seems to be a succession of three taxa of green algae throughout the spring and summer: *Enteromorpha* spp., sea lettuce *Ulva lactuca* and *Cladophora rupestris*. In April, *Ulva* was at its maximum cover. The species then had a second, lower peak in June before decreasing until sampling ended in October. *Cladophora* came to a peak in June, and *Enteromorpha* in July.

At some locations certain red algae showed seasonality also, for example pepper dulse *Osmundea pinnatifida* decreased steadily throughout the summer (April to October) at Horseshoe Harbour; however, this did not occur at Globe Rocks or Reenahoe. Over a five-year subset of the 20-year period, Leslie (1986) found summer minima for *O. pinnatifida* at several sites (Kinish Narrows West, Kinish Narrows East, Globe Rocks, Horseshoe Harbour, Drolain Point). *Lomentaria articulata* is another species which decreased steadily from April to October at Horseshoe Harbour and Reenahoe.

Evidence of seasonality in the canopy layer is sparse. *Alaria* at Poulacurra increased from April to May, then decreased through to October. *Himanthalia* density peaked in different months at each of the three shores where we have analysed the species. At Poulacurra there were two peaks (May and October) which most likely reflect proliferation of "buttons" in the spring and adult frond growth in October. At Drolain Point and Horseshoe Harbour there were summer peaks in August and July respectively. There was very little seasonality recorded in the wracks.

ANIMALS

A few of the dominant animal species also showed seasonality as described below.

Barnacles

The barnacle populations showed seasonal variation at all sites (Figure 8.2).

At Reenahoe and Kinish Narrows West there was a steady increase in barnacle cover from April to October. This might indicate that juvenile recruitment was good and occurred regularly, or it might be a reflection of their occupying more space as a result of steady growth. At Kinish Narrows East there was also a gradual increase in cover until August, but the population then declined in September and October.

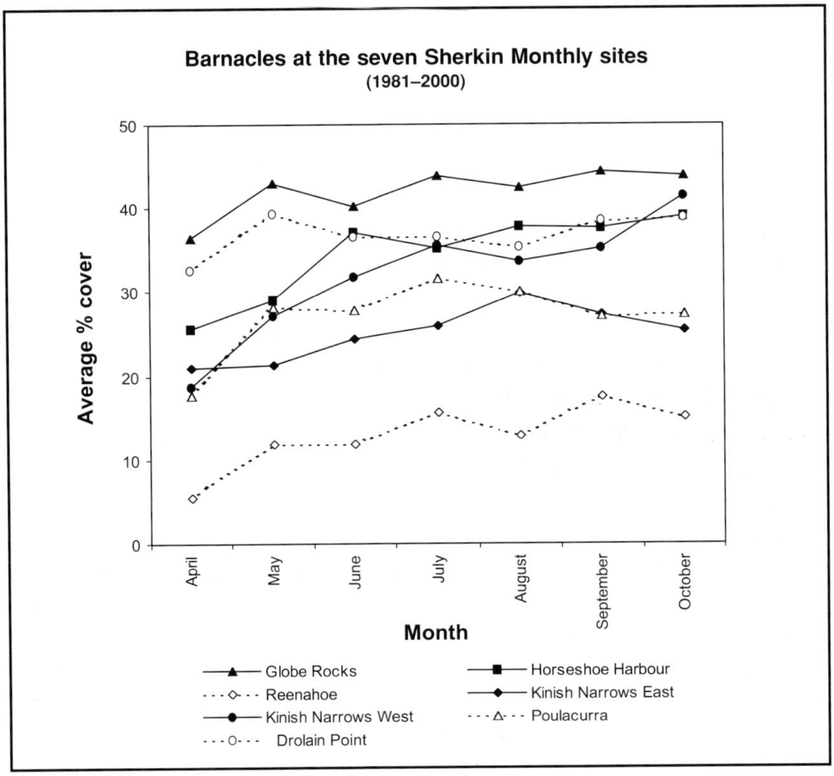

Figure 8.2 Seasonal variation of barnacles.

At the more exposed sites population growth appears to be restricted to early in the season. For example, April to May at Poulacurra, Drolain Point and Globe Rocks and April to June at Horseshoe Harbour. Thereafter, the population sizes were steady at all four sites.

Barnacle Spatfall

Spatfall graphs (pp. 57, 79, 100, 121, 148, 172, 190) show two settlement points which correspond to that of *Semibalanus balanoides* in April/May and *Chthamalus* spp. in August/September. Peak settlement times varied between shores. At Globe Rocks, Reenahoe and Horseshoe Harbour *Semibalanus* settlement took place in April, whereas Poulacurra, Drolain Point, Kinish Narrows East and Kinish Narrows West had maximum settlement during May.

Chthamalus spp. settled during August at Kinish Narrows West and Globe Rocks, a little later (August and September) at Poulacurra and Drolain Point, during September at Kinish Narrows East, and September/October at Horseshoe Harbour. At Reenahoe, no *Chthamalus* settlement peak was recorded

Mussels

Mussels *Mytilus edulis* showed some seasonality over the 20-year period (Figure 8.3). At Drolain Point, although there was no overall increase in density from May to

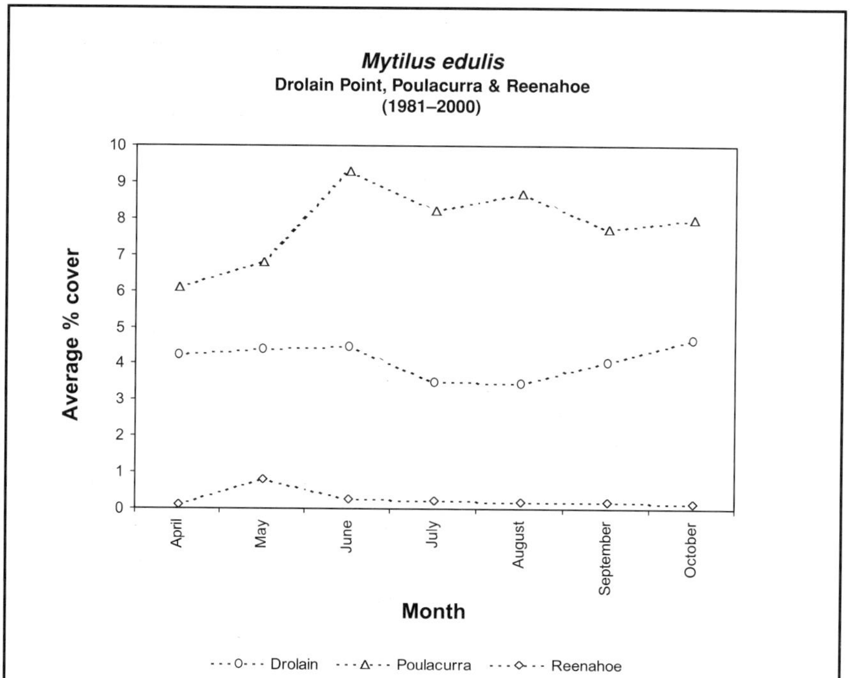

Figure 8.3 Seasonal variation of mussels.

October, young individuals were noted extending the upper edge of the mussel zone on the shore during June and July. There was no change in the location of the overall zone of mussels on the shore, which suggests that juveniles on the upper edge of the adult zone do not survive the winter.

Mussels at Poulacurra showed a steady increase from April until June. This level then declined gradually for the remainder of the season.

At Reenahoe, where mussel cover was much more sparse, a short-lived increase during May was recorded, although this happened primarily in 1982. It was not maintained into the summer and the population was generally steady in size throughout the year.

Flat Periwinkles

The Flat periwinkle *Littorina obtusata* (Figure 8.4) showed fairly consistent increases from low numbers in April to higher summer (July/August) numbers. This was most marked at Kinish Narrows East, Kinish Narrows West and Reenahoe where the populations were larger. At four of the five sites as shown below, numbers then decreased during September, while at Horseshoe Harbour this decline occurred in August. It is very interesting that this early autumn decrease in numbers affected both moderately sheltered and sheltered shores and may well be caused by a migration to

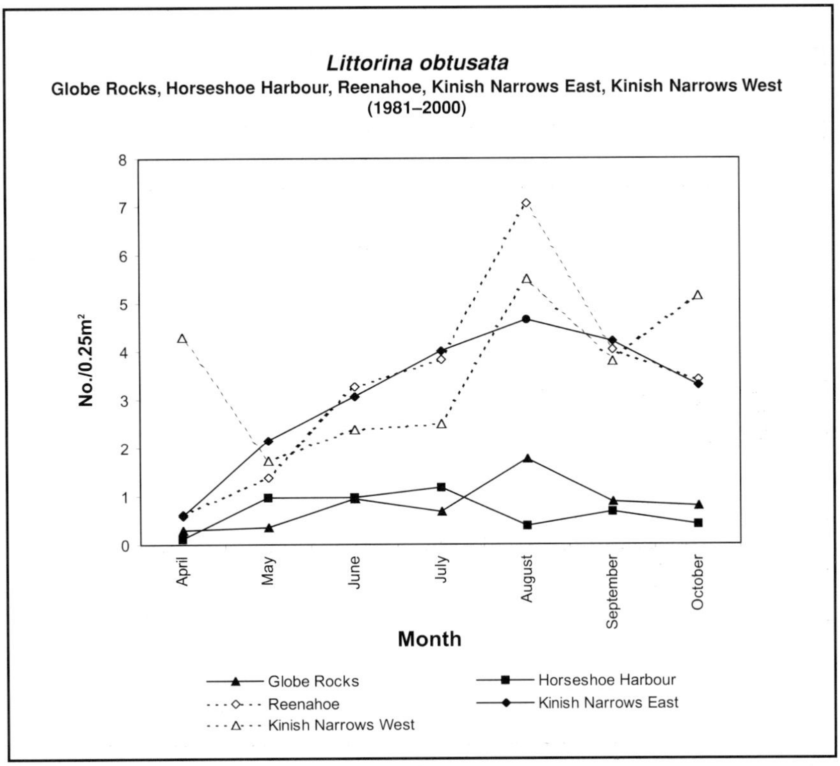

Figure 8.4 Seasonality of the flat periwinkle.

deeper water for the winter. The Kinish Narrows West population subsequently behaved differently from the others and showed rising numbers from September to October. Numbers were also high here in April when sampling began. At Drolain Point, where the population was very small (see p. 81), numbers also rose in August, but the overall pattern was distorted by a single year, 1987, when April numbers were exceptionally high.

Dogwhelks

Abundance of dogwhelks *Nucella lapillus* on the shores showed monthly variation and the patterns observed are fairly consistent. At Drolain Point and Globe Rocks, there were steady decreases from April to October, while at Horseshoe Harbour and Reenahoe numbers increased from April to June, then declined until August and increased again in October. At Poulacurra the increase was from April through to July, thereafter decreasing until October. To avoid being knocked off the rocks by strong seas, dogwhelks migrate down the shore and into rock pools in winter. It is therefore surprising that numbers on the shore were at their highest in April at Drolain Point, an exposed site, just after temperatures begin to rise. Observation at Poulacurra supports the theory of winter downward migration much better.

VARIATION OVER THE 20-YEAR PERIOD

ALGAE

There were particular years when certain species of algae were not recorded. For example, at Poulacurra dabberlocks *Alaria esculenta* was not recorded in 1982, 1989, 1992, 1993 or 1996–2000. It is difficult to suggest reasons for this absence, other than the destructive effects of winter storms. However wind records from the Marine Station show that the preceding winters in each case had below average number of days with gales. For example, in the winter of 1981/82 (November to March) there were only seven days of gales (Force 7 and above). In the winter of 1995/1996 and 1997/1998 there were 15 and 11 days of gales respectively between October and March. These compare with an average of 19 days of gales per winter over the 20 years (1981–2000). Perhaps our data indicate that the species became unviable at Poulacurra. *Alaria* density also declined at three of the Sherkin Annual sites. At one of these it was unrecorded after 1991 and at the other two it was present at much lower abundance in the 1990s.

Fucoids

Table 8.1 summarises how the large brown algae changed in abundance between 1981 and 2000. Channelled wrack *Pelvetia canaliculata* declined in the 1990s at Drolain Point and throughout the 20-year period at Globe Rocks. Likewise thong weed *Himanthalia elongata* and knotted wrack *Ascophyllum nodosum* declined in the 1990s at the shores where the species were recorded.

	Pelvetia canaliculata	*Fucus spiralis*	*Fucus vesiculosus*	*Fucus serratus*	*Ascophyllum nodosum*	*Himanthalia elongata*
Poulacurra						Absent after 1989.
Drolain Point	Thicker in 1980s than 1990s.			Increasing during 1980s. Absent or sparse from 1993–2000 (except 1998).		Absent or sparse 1993–2000.
Globe Rocks	Declined throughout 20 years. Very sparse from 1994.	Generally sparse in 1980s. More common in 1990s.	Sparse until 1997. Fivefold increase between 1997 and 2000.	Declined 1984–1993.		
Horseshoe Harbour		Declined 1984–2000.	Declined 1984–2000.	Declined in 1980s. Remained sparse in 1990s.		Declined in 1990s.
Reenahoe		Increased 1985–1990. Virtually absent 1991-1997.	Increased in late 1980s. Dominant wrack in 1990s in middle shore.	Declined slightly over 20 years.	Dominant on middle shore in early 1980's. Declined and low 1986–2000.	
Kinish Narrows East		More common in late 1990's than earlier.	Less common 1988–1996 than earlier and later.	Declined in 1990s.	Declined in 1990s.	
Kinish Narrows West		Generally low abundance. Isolated peaks 1993 and 1996.	Declined 1991–2000.	Declined slightly in late 1990s.	Declined in 1990s.	

Table 8.1 Major changes in abundance of the large brown algae at the seven Sherkin Monthly sites.

The three wrack species all decreased in abundance at Horseshoe Harbour throughout the 1990s. However different patterns of annual variation were found at the other monthly sites.

Fucus vesiculosus for example, was very sparse at Globe Rocks until 1997, but achieved a fivefold increase in abundance in the period 1997–2000. However this maximum cover was still < 4% as compared to its cover at Reenahoe. Here it was present throughout the 20 years varying from 4–14%, thus offering a considerably larger area of fucoid habitat for exploitation by other species. An increase in *F. vesiculosus* abundance took place at Reenahoe in the late 1980s and the species achieved midshore dominance during the 1990s. Meanwhile at the sheltered Kinish Narrows sites bladder wrack variation was similar to that found at Horseshoe Harbour. At Kinish Narrows East the percentage cover recorded during the first of three cycles of abundance (1982–89) was higher than subsequent values; likewise at Kinish Narrows West the species declined consistently in the 1990s.

Fucus serratus declined at four sites in addition to Horseshoe Harbour – Globe Rocks, Reenahoe, Kinish Narrows East and Kinish Narrows West – but its status at Drolain Point changed in a different manner. Here, although *F. serratus* was unrecorded for many years during the 1990s, the species generally increased from 1982–92. With the exception of 1998 when it did well, it then declined to almost zero cover from 1993–2000. At Kinish Narrows East the wrack reached a maximum abundance in 1989, declined gradually over the next four years and was virtually absent from 1994–2000. At Kinish Narrows West the decline to a minimum of 2% in the late 1990s (1994–2000) was less marked because earlier cover during 1984–94 reached only 5–7%. The decline at Reenahoe in the 1990s was also slight and the figures throughout the 1990s remained above 10%. At Globe Rocks, *F. serratus* was much less abundant in the 1990s than the 1980s, with very low levels in 1992 and 1993. Thus the only site which demonstrates a different story to that of a decline in the 1990s was Drolain Point.

It is interesting to note that a general decrease in a number of species of algae, including fucoids, was recorded at many of the Marine Station's 62 annual sites in Roaringwater Bay in the 1990s. Examples include: *Ascophyllum nodosum, Ceramium* spp., *Chondrus crispus*, *Enteromorpha* spp, *Fucus serratus*, *F. spiralis*, *F. vesiculosus*, *Mastocarpus stellatus*, *Osmundea pinnatifida* and *Pelvetia canaliculata*. Over such a wide area a decline of this magnitude is probably natural in cause.

At some sites however, growth of some of these species (*Ceramium* spp., *Enteromorpha* spp., *Fucus spiralis*, *F. vesiculosus*, *Mastocarpus stellatus*, *Osmundea pinnatifida and Pelvetia canaliculata)* increased in the 1990s, but these occurrences were far fewer.

At several of the exposed Sherkin annual sites brown fucoid algae were unrecorded during many of the 20 years. One can also cite interesting examples from the annual shores over a range of aspects and wave exposure where the dominant species changed:

> On a south-facing semi-exposed shore *Fucus serratus* was the dominant brown alga during 1981–90, then *Himanthalia* was dominant in 1991, but for one year only.

On an east-facing sheltered shore *F. vesiculosus* was the dominant fucoid until 1989, when it was superseded by *F. serratus*.

On a south southwest-facing semi-exposed shore *F. serratus* was the dominant alga on the shore throughout the 20 years, despite its abundance decreasing in the 1990s.

On a north-facing sheltered shore *F. serratus* dominated the shore in the early 1980s; there followed a period when *F. serratus* and *F. vesiculosus* were equally abundant, and this changed to *Fucus vesiculosus* domination in the late 1990s.

Fluctuations in fucoid algae may be related to water temperatures and a warming of the surface water may account for their decline. Sherkin records show surface warming between 1987 and 1995, with subsequent cooling to pre-1987 temperatures.

EPHEMERAL ALGAE

Enteromorpha spp.

At Reenahoe, gut weed *(Enteromorpha* spp.*)* cover was rarely dense, but there were three relatively good years (1987, 1988 and 1994). This prompts the question as to whether any relationship exists between the abundance of ephemeral species and summer air temperatures. Myers *et al.* (1980a) suggest that blooms of *Enteromorpha* are linked with long periods of sunshine which they say prohibits limpet grazing. On Sherkin the sunshine records show that in both 1987 and 1988 the month of May had higher than average hours of sunshine. In 1987 this held true for July and August also, and in 1988 for June.

These observations might lend support to Myers' theory, but contrary data also exist. The following year, 1989, was particularly hot (25.5°C max in July), with two dry periods (May and July) and a period of absolute drought in July. Green algae could have suffered from such extreme conditions and *Enteromorpha* cover was indeed recorded as low (1%) at Reenahoe. However this level of abundance was commonly recorded throughout the 20-year period.

In 1994, the number of sunshine hours was below average for the months of May, June, July and August. There were no dry periods or absolute droughts at all that year, and the maximum air temperature only reached 19.8°C, yet *Enteromorpha* flourished at Reenahoe.

Good years for *Enteromorpha* at other sites were 1988, 1994 and 1996 at Kinish Narrows East, and 1981, 1982, 1987 and 1997 at Drolain Point. Of these years, summer 1981 had a maximum air temperature of 21.3°C and below average sunshine hours, with no dry periods or droughts, while July 1982, May 1997 and July 1997 had above average sunshine. There were also two dry periods and one absolute drought in 1997, and the maximum air temperature was 22.5°C.

Another point of inconsistency between sites occurred in 1994, when *Enteromorpha* was abundant at Reenahoe and Kinish Narrows West, but declined to its minimum recorded value at Drolain Point.

Variation at several annual sites within the area was also recorded (Hunter, 1997). Peaks in *Enteromorpha* occurred in 1987, 1996 and 1997 at three different sites in Roaringwater Bay. All three years coincided with one of the Sherkin site peaks mentioned above, when summer sunshine hours were high and there were dry periods. By contrast, two sites on Whiddy Island in Bantry Bay provide mixed data. One showed a dramatic fall in abundance in 1998, with recovery in 1999, and the other a fall in 1999, with recovery in 2000. Overall, the data are very mixed and do not support Myers' theory.

GROUND COVER

Barnacles

Barnacle populations showed remarkable similarities at our different sites (Figure 8.5 and Figure 8.6). Throughout the 1980s the adult population of barnacles increased at all seven sites. All sites had a dip in population numbers in 1987, followed by increasing and high levels in 1988–90. At all sites a population crash was then recorded in 1991, although this was less severe at Globe Rocks and Drolain Point.

Rates of recovery varied. Reenahoe and Kinish Narrows East showed only a small increase in barnacle numbers after 1991 and maintained a steady smaller population through the 1990s. Numbers at Kinish Narrows West, Poulacurra, Globe Rocks and

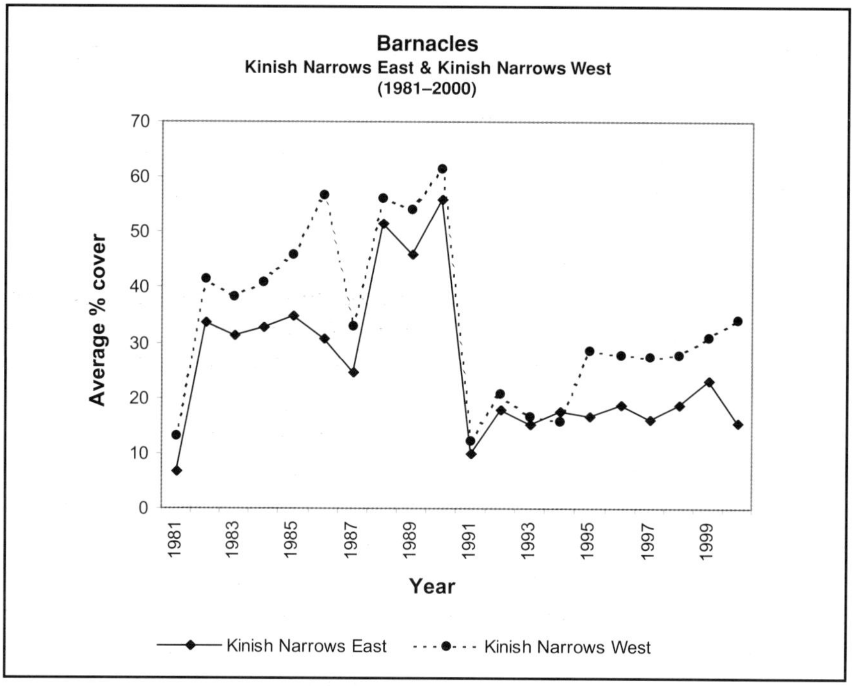

Figure 8.5 Annual variation of barnacles on sheltered shores.

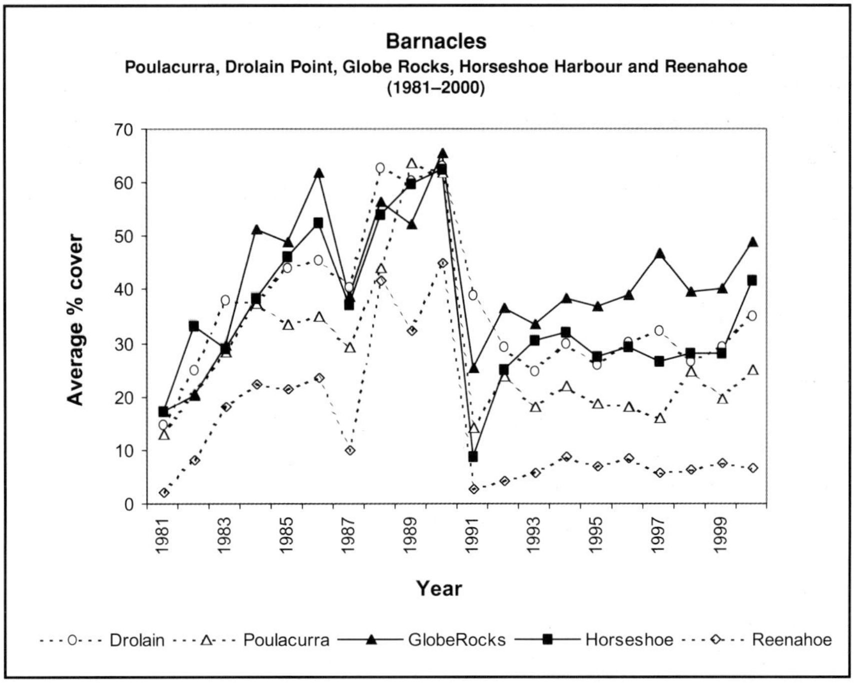

Figure 8.6 Annual variation of barnacles on exposed and moderately exposed shores.

Drolain Point gradually increased to about 50% of the pre-crash population sizes; and Horseshoe Harbour showed the best recovery rate.

It is interesting to see that the pattern of population increase in the late 1980s, followed by a crash in 1991 and a slow but steady increase was also seen in the 19 Sherkin sites which were surveyed annually (Hunter, 1997) and also at sites within Roaringwater Bay and Dunmanus Bay (Clark *et al.,* 1997; Egerton *et al.,* 1998; Clark, 1999; Ratcliff, 1999; Browne *et al.,* 2001a).

Analysis of the climatic data offers no clear suggestion as to why this widespread decline occurred. There was a total of eight days of frost between December 1990 and March 1991 and, although not unusual, it compares with only two days of below zero air temperatures between December 1989 and March 1990. From October 1990 to March 1991 the number of days of strong winds (Force 4 and above) was no different from the same period in 1989/1990, however in March 1991 there were many more days with a northeasterly wind (11 in 1991, two in 1990) and fewer days of southwesterlies (seven in 1991, 18 in 1990). It is difficult to understand how this might affect barnacle populations or cause their demise. It is of course possible that all barnacle populations on Sherkin shores (and in the Roaringwater Bay region) and Dunmanus Bay were of the same age and died from natural old age. According to Connell (1985) barnacles are likely to have a lifespan of 10–12 years (small barnacles) or up to 20 years (large barnacles). However it would be unusual for the numerous and widespread populations in Roaringwater Bay to have such a markedly uniform age structure rather than a mix of age.

In many parts of Britain *Semibalanus balanoides* populations declined on shores during the late 1970s (Hiscock, 1983), and it is interesting that the records for all seven sites show barnacle populations to be at a low point in 1981. Unfortunately, spatfall was not routinely recorded during the development of the Sherkin survey (1975–80). Had this occurred it would have been possible to look at 1979 in particular. In that year settlement was recorded as tremendously successful in several places in west, northwest and northern Britain (Lewis, 1964); however it was a decidedly poor year for populations in northeast Britain, Bantry Bay and the Isle of Man (Hiscock, 1983).

Spatfall

Although spat settlement occurred throughout the barnacle zone, the majority of positive observations of spat and the densest settlement was within the zone of adult presence rather than the upper or lower fringes. The actual density of spat also varied quite considerably between shores; at Globe Rocks for example, it was recorded at a maximum of 470/dm^2 – elsewhere maximum numbers were less than 200/dm^2. Most of the sites usually had an annual spatfall, but each site suffered at least one year where none was recorded. Spatfall of *Semibalanus* is in April/May and *Chthamalus* settles mostly in August/September/October at the different Sherkin sites.

At Drolain Point it is possible that the reasonably good spatfalls in 1989, 1990 and 1991 were a buffer for the 1991 population crash experienced elsewhere, hence the smaller population decline noted here.

The best settlement years varied between shores (Table 8.2) although 1997 was the best year for three sites - Drolain Point, Reenahoe and Kinish Narrows West. At several sites, predominant winds during the main settlement months in best spatfall years were from a direction similar to the open aspect of the shore. For example, Drolain Point is open to the south and southwest, and southwesterly winds were predominant in

	81	82	83	84	85	86	87	88	89	90	91	92	93	94	95	96	97	98	99	00
Poulacurra	-	•	•	•	-	-	-	•	-	•	✓	•	•	•	•	•	•	•	•	•
Drolain Point	-	•	•	-	-	•	•	•	•	•	•	•	•	•	•	•	✓	•	•	•
Horseshoe Harbour	•	•	•	•	-	•	-	✓	•	•	•	•	•	•	•	•	•	•	•	•
Globe Rocks	✓	•	•	-	-	•	•	•	•	•	•	•	•	•	•	•	•	•	•	•
Reenahoe	•	•	•	•	-	•	•	•	•	•	•	•	•	•	•	•	✓	•	•	•
Kinish Narrows E	•	•	•	-	-	✓	•	•	•	•	•	•	•	•	•	•	•	•	•	•
Kinish Narrows W	•	•	•	-	-	•	•	•	•	-	•	•	•	•	•	•	✓	•	•	•

✓ = best year • = present - = unrecorded

Table 8.2 Barnacle spatfall records at the seven Sherkin Monthly sites.

Gillian Bishop and Jenny Baker leading the first marine biology course for industry in 1975.

Eileen Murphy and Audrey on an expedition to the Calf Islands.

The first marine station biologists in 1975; Jacinta Crowley, Pat McCarthy and Gillian Bishop.

John Reilly who, in his boat *Erin*, brought surveyors to the islands in the first year – 1975.

Sr Martin Powell, Pat McCarthy, Jacinta Crowley and Mick Quirke in 1975.

Matt, Eileen, Mark and Robbie, with Molly, the Marine Station's first land transport.

Kitting out the first lab, John Cullinane joins the "bods" in discussion.

Michael Conlon, Manager – Cork County Council, performs the ceremonial opening of the wet lab in 1976.

Jo Elmsworth and Richard Fok-Seang record from a lower shore station in 1982.

1981 rocky shore surveyors Aileen Clements and Simon Walshe.

A cheery smile from Idris Lane en route to a Sherkin sampling site in 1984.

Surveyors racing the advancing tide.

The wet lab in the mid-1980s.

The main pier on Sherkin, looking over to Baltimore.

Thift on the cliff top at Drolain, Sherkin Island.

The Franciscan Abbey, Sherkin Island.

The Marine Station landing stage.

"Bods" of 1983.

"Bods" of 1984.

A sheltered lane in spring, Sherkin Island.

Some vertebrate predators around Sherkin: (clockwise from top right) mink, blenny, grey seal, otter and fulmar.

Sampling at the Fastnet in the late 1990s; Terry Farnell, Jane Clark, Beverly Stubbs, with boatman Michael Murphy.

Early eighties on Sherkin for the young Murphy family (l to r) Michael, Mark, Robbie, Audrey, Matt, Peter, Matty and Susan.

"Bods" in disguise – 1986.

"Bods" of 1987.

"Bods" of 1988.

Off to the islands; Ben Sampson, Mike Robinson and Craig Wheelock, with boatman Robbie Murphy.

Taking part in Sherkin Regatta 1990.

"Bods" of 1992.

"Bods" of 1996.

Unexpected visitors at lunchtime!

Plankton sampling with Lynda Poole, Maria Palfy Gallagher and Geraldine Reid.

The Marine Station's sundial, recording daily sunshine hours.

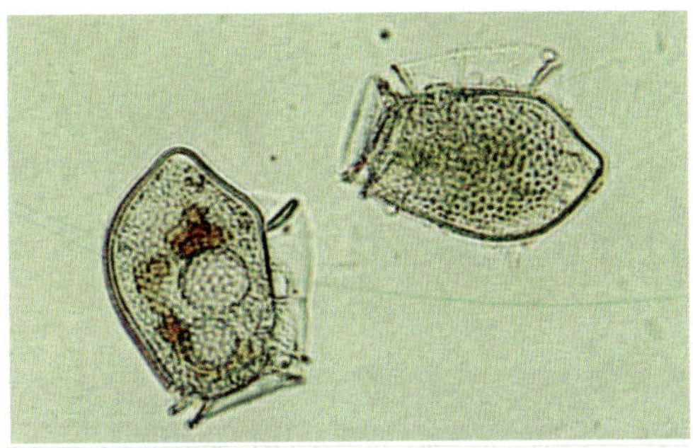

The phytoplankton *Dinophysis acuta.*

The Stephenson's Screen at the Marine Station, recording daily temperatures.

Underwater surveying in Roaringwater Bay.

Waiting for a lift home after a long day's surveying.

"Bods" of 1997.

Terry Farnell shows off a crayfish at an annual Marine Station exhibition in Cork.

Taking time out for a photograph from the annual exhibition in 1999.

Prof. Brian McK Bary donates his collection of scientific papers to Matt at the Marine Station.

Children enjoying one of Audrey Murphy's marine life talks.

"Bods" of 2000.

Outdoor pursuits provided much-needed funding for the Marine Station in the early days.

Fiona Hunter among the Marine Station's thousands of books.

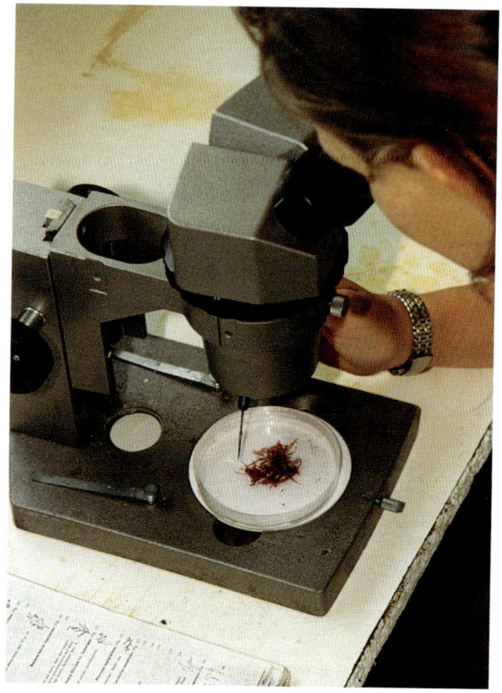

Specimens brought back to the lab for identification.

Computerisation comes to Sherkin in 1990.

The Marine Station has an extensive seaweed herbarium.

Anna Martin identifying and pressing seaweeds.

Levelling a transect with a cross-staff.

Working a transect line.

The specimen collection at the Marine Station.

A labelled, preserved and catalogued specimen.

The Silver Jubilee celebrations, September 2000; Rev. Denis Collin blesses the Jubilee plaque.

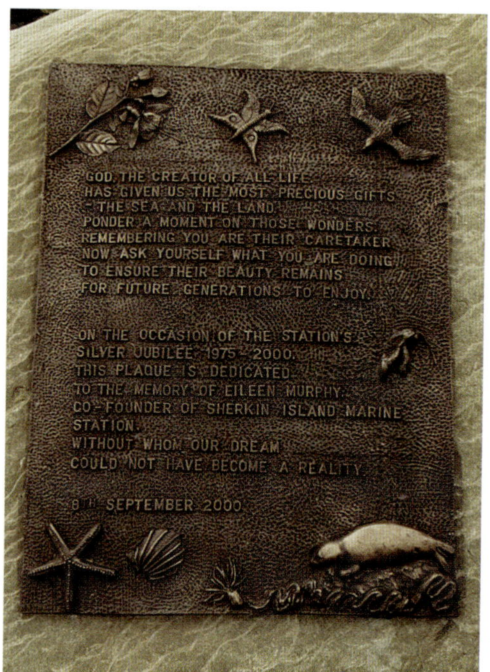

The Silver Jubilee plaque dedicated to the memory of Eileen Murphy.

A contented smile from Matt Murphy.

Site	Best Spatfall Year	Predominant Winds		
		April	May	September
Drolain Point	1997	SW, NE	SW, E	NW, SW, SE
Horseshoe Harbour	1988	SE	SE, SW, W	W
Poulacurra	1991	W, SW	NE, SW	SW, NE
Globe Rocks	1981	E	SE, S, NW	SW
Reenahoe	1997	SW, NE	SW, E	NW, SW, SE
Kinish Narrows East	1986	NE	W	NE
Kinish Narrows West	1997	NE, SW	SW, E	NW, SW, SE

Table 8.3 Relationship between best spatfall and predominant wind directions in years of best spatfall at the seven Sherkin Monthly sites.

April/May and September in 1997. This relationship will be examined in more detail at the Marine Station, comparing wind records more directly and precisely with timing of individual species settlement. From Table 8.3 we see that at Kinish Narrows East and Kinish Narrows West there were northeasterlies in the months and years of best spatfall, but this offers no explanation as to why the years of best spatfall were different in two sites located so closely together. The easterly onshore winds at Globe Rocks coincided with *Semibalanus* spatfall, but not *Chthamalus.* This agrees with the observation that the 1981 settlement comprised *Semibalanus only.*

In 1991 when adult barnacle populations declined (to a marked or lesser degree) at all seven sites, there was recruitment at all sites, and it was particularly good at Poulacurra. The years of 1984 and 1985 are interesting for their poor records of spatfalls, but it is not clear from the climate data whether environmental conditions were responsible in any way. More work will be undertaken at the Marine Station to analyse air temperatures, sea temperatures and wind data in relation, not only to expected settlement times, but to other parts of the reproductive cycle.

It was noted that there were no other unpredictable events in 1984 or 1985 such as red tides or pollution incidents (see p. 17).

Mussels

The common mussel *Mytilus edulis* is an important species in the rocky shore community at our two most exposed sites (Poulacurra and Drolain Point). The consistently small area the species occupied on the other five shores throughout the 20-year survey is a reflection of their more sheltered nature.

Both Poulacurra and Drolain Point showed considerable variation of the mussel populations over the years, and there was some degree of commonality (Figure 8.7). At both sites the population levels were greatly reduced in 1990 and 1991. At Poulacurra this followed a maximum population level in 1989 and a decline in those two years of

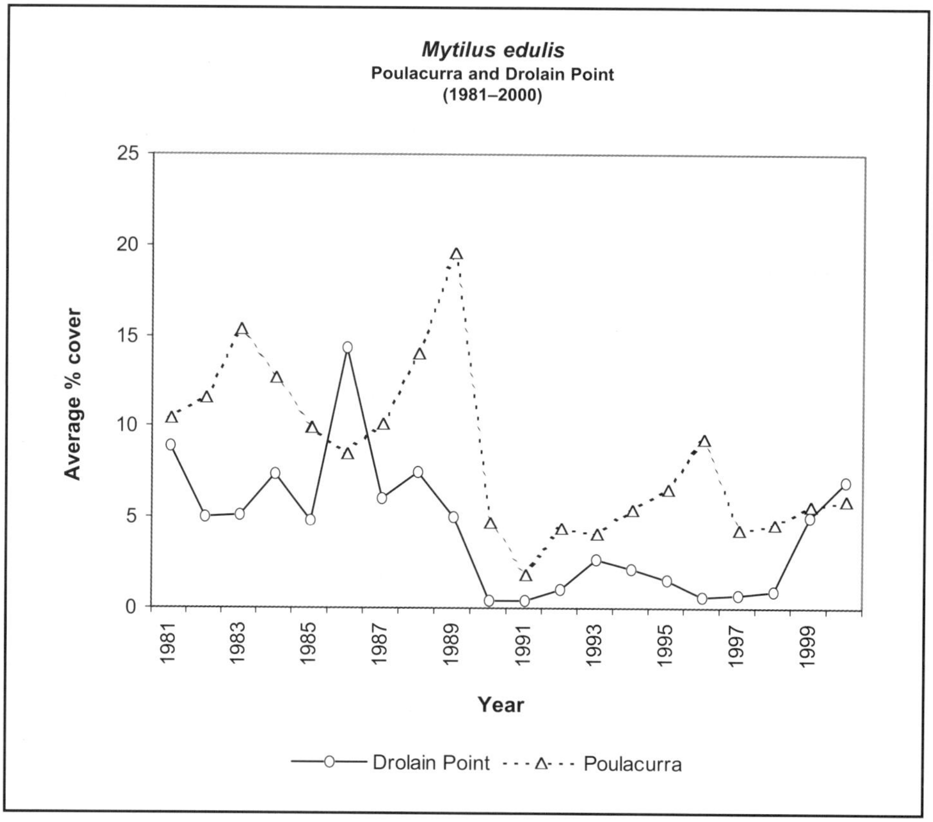

Figure 8.7 Annual variation of mussels at exposed sites.

75%. Whereas at Drolain Point the maximum population size was in 1986 and decline occurred over a five-year period. Neither population has ever recovered to an approximation of those maxima. The populations were both of a similar size in 2000, but whereas Poulacurra recovered quickly between 1992 and 1995, the recovery at Drolain did not occur until 1999 and 2000. Levels between 1990 and 1998 remained fairly consistently low.

Five of the eight sites in Dunmanus Bay, where mussel populations were relatively high in the 1980s, also reported low or absent population levels of mussel in the 1990s (Browne *et al.,* 2001a).

GRAZERS

Limpets

Limpets (*Patella* spp.) are widely recognised as key species in the general biological control of the balance of the animal/plant composition of rocky shore communities. They were present on all seven shores and Figure 8.8 shows annual variation at all sites.

Limpets are relatively long-lived – studies have shown them to live up to ten years (Connell, 1985) – although their lifespan is longer in sublittoral habitats than on the shore (Bowman & Lewis, 1977). Of the selected species analysed at the seven sites, limpets showed the most consistency in population size. This may be partly due to their "homebase" behaviour, although it is not known to what extent other grazers, such as periwinkles, stay within a small area of rock/seaweed, or whether they constantly move to new areas.

The limpet populations at both Drolain Point and Horseshoe Harbour were fairly dynamic, the other five sites showed relative stability after 1983 at 23–30 per quadrat. (In 1982 a good recruitment of juveniles caused numbers to soar to 45 per quadrat at Poulacurra, but this population size was not sustained.) In 1989 and 1998 the number of days of frost was zero and two respectively and limpet numbers increased each subsequent year. This supports the theory that newly settled spat are intolerant of frosts (Bowman and Lewis 1977). By contrast, during 1981 (also a year prior to a peak) the

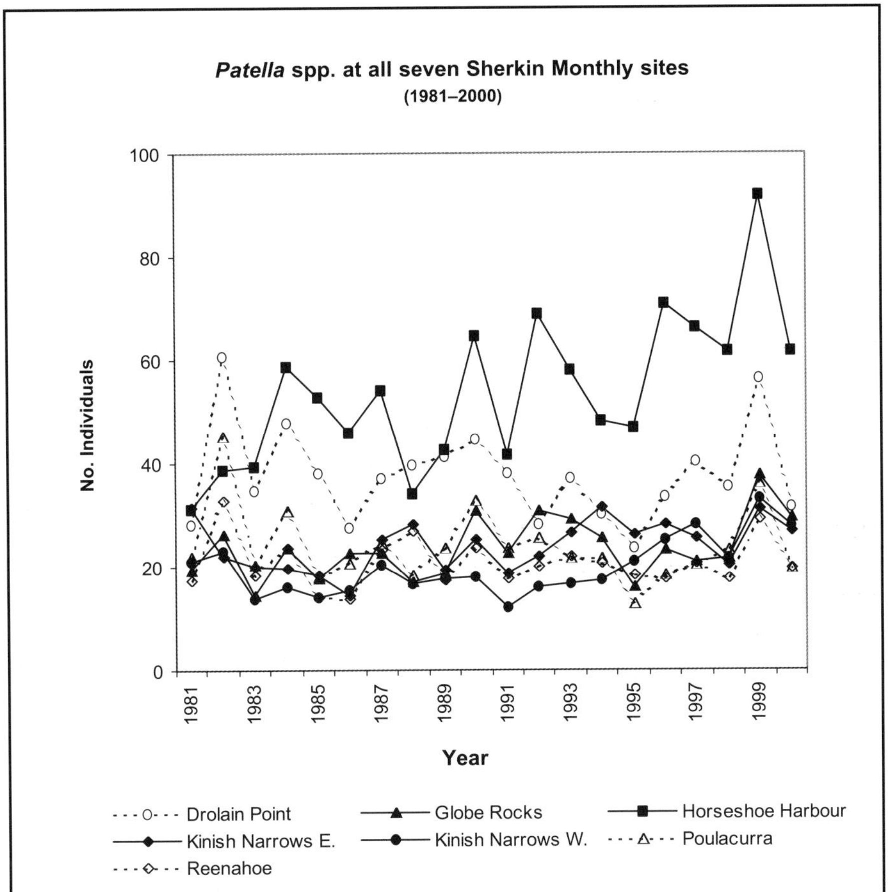

Figure 8.8 Annual variation of limpets at all seven sites.

number of days with air temperatures less than 0°C was fairly high (10), hence the exact timing of the frost days in relation to settlement must be addressed.

The Horseshoe Harbour population generally increased over the 20-year period from a minimum of 30 per quadrat in 1981 to a maximum of 90 per quadrat in 1999. This can only reflect successful juvenile recruitment in the population. Highest densities occurred at the upper limit of the wracks; further down the shore within the main fucoid belt, limpets were present at only 25 per quadrat – a similar density to that found during the low years of the cycles at Drolain Point.

At Globe Rocks, maxima were also recorded in 1982, 1990, 1992 and 1999. The 1999 peak (37 per quadrat) was considerably higher than the earlier peaks, but did not match that of Drolain Point or Horseshoe Harbour.

The limpet population at Reenahoe was very stable for most of the 1990s, with the exception of a rise in numbers in 1999. The 1982 population was elevated but numbers were still lower than those at Horseshoe Harbour, Globe Rocks and Drolain Point.

At Kinish Narrows West, the limpet population was stable during the 1980s at a low density. The population gradually increased in the 1990s from a minimum number recorded in 1991 to a maximum in 1999.

At Kinish Narrows East the pattern is different again. The population seems to fluctuate around an annual mean of about 23 per quadrat. After a year of significantly high density in 1981, there was a general decrease over the next five years until 1986 when the minimum population (14 per quadrat) was recorded. Numbers between 1987 and 2000 fluctuated cyclically with peaks in 1988, 1994 and 1999. It is interesting to note that during 1999, when the population showed peak numbers at all seven sites, there were also peak abundance recorded at 11 of the 19 Sherkin Annual Sites (Jackson *et al.*, 2001).

Flat Periwinkles

The flat periwinkle *Littorina obtusata* was present at six of the seven shores (it was unrecorded from Poulacurra), although the population was minimal at Horseshoe Harbour for most of the 1990s and also at Drolain Point, with the exception of 1987. Certain similarities in population fluctuations at the different sites are evident, and at Globe Rocks, Reenahoe, Kinish Narrows East and Kinish Narrows West, the population fluctuations can be described as cyclical. Although the magnitudes of peaks, troughs and lengths of cycle differ considerably between sites, the years of peak abundance were often coincident.

Globe Rocks showed 3 cycles spanning eight, five and seven years duration.
Reenahoe experienced 4 cycles of six, four, five and six years duration.
Kinish Narrows East displayed 3 cycles of nine, five and six years duration.
Kinish Narrows West showed 3 cycles of three, six and 11 years duration.

Maximum abundance numbers were 2 per quadrat at Globe Rocks and Horseshoe Harbour, 6 per quadrat at Drolain Point, 7 per quadrat at Reenahoe, 8.5 per quadrat at Kinish Narrows East and 12 per quadrat at Kinish Narrows West.

Peaks of the various cycles coincided in:

1983 Globe Rocks, Horseshoe Harbour

1987 Drolain Point, Reenahoe, Kinish Narrows East, Kinish Narrows West

1991 Globe Rocks, Reenahoe, Kinish Narrows East, Kinish Narrows West

1999 Globe Rocks, Reenahoe, Kinish Narrows East

The 1986 peak seen at Horseshoe Harbour was not found at any other site.

Edible Periwinkles

Although present at all seven sites, the edible periwinkle *Littorina littorea* has been analysed for the four sites (Horseshoe Harbour, Reenahoe, Kinish Narrows East and Kinish Narrows West), where it appears to be more important in the shore community. Even here, populations were small.

At Horseshoe Harbour a very sparse population of < 0.5 per quadrat suddenly increased in 1998 to 3.5 per quadrat.

Reenahoe maintained a population of 0.8–1.8 per quadrat and numbers fluctuated greatly, with four peaks (1983, 1987, 1989 and 1997) all followed by a number of years of decline.

At Kinish Narrows West periwinkles declined overall from 1981–94, but then rose each year to 2000. Maximum numbers reached 1.4 per quadrat in 1987.

At Kinish Narrows East periwinkles declined overall from 1984–92 and from 1993–98. Numbers were relatively high in 1999 (0.5 per quadrat). The population was at its most dense in 1984 (0.6 per quadrat). At both these sites it is possible that population numbers were influenced by the harvesting of periwinkles but no figures are available on the years in which collecting took place.

Only two of the population peaks coincided, those at Reenahoe and Kinish Narrows West in 1987.

PREDATORS

Dogwhelks

Dogwhelks *Nucella lapillus* were present on each shore throughout the 20-year period. The populations at Poulacurra, Drolain Point and Horseshoe Harbour were usually larger than those at Globe Rocks, Reenahoe, Kinish Narrows East and Kinish Narrows West.

Despite differences in overall population sizes and patterns of annual variation, there are similarities (Figure 8.9). At five sites (Drolain Point, Globe Rocks, Horseshoe Harbour, Kinish Narrows East and Kinish Narrows West) populations were considerably larger in the 1980s than in the 1990s. At Poulacurra a fall in numbers was not recorded until 1995, although the population was small in the mid 1980s (1983–1987).

The only site where the opposite trend occurred was Reenahoe, where dogwhelks increased during 1993–99.

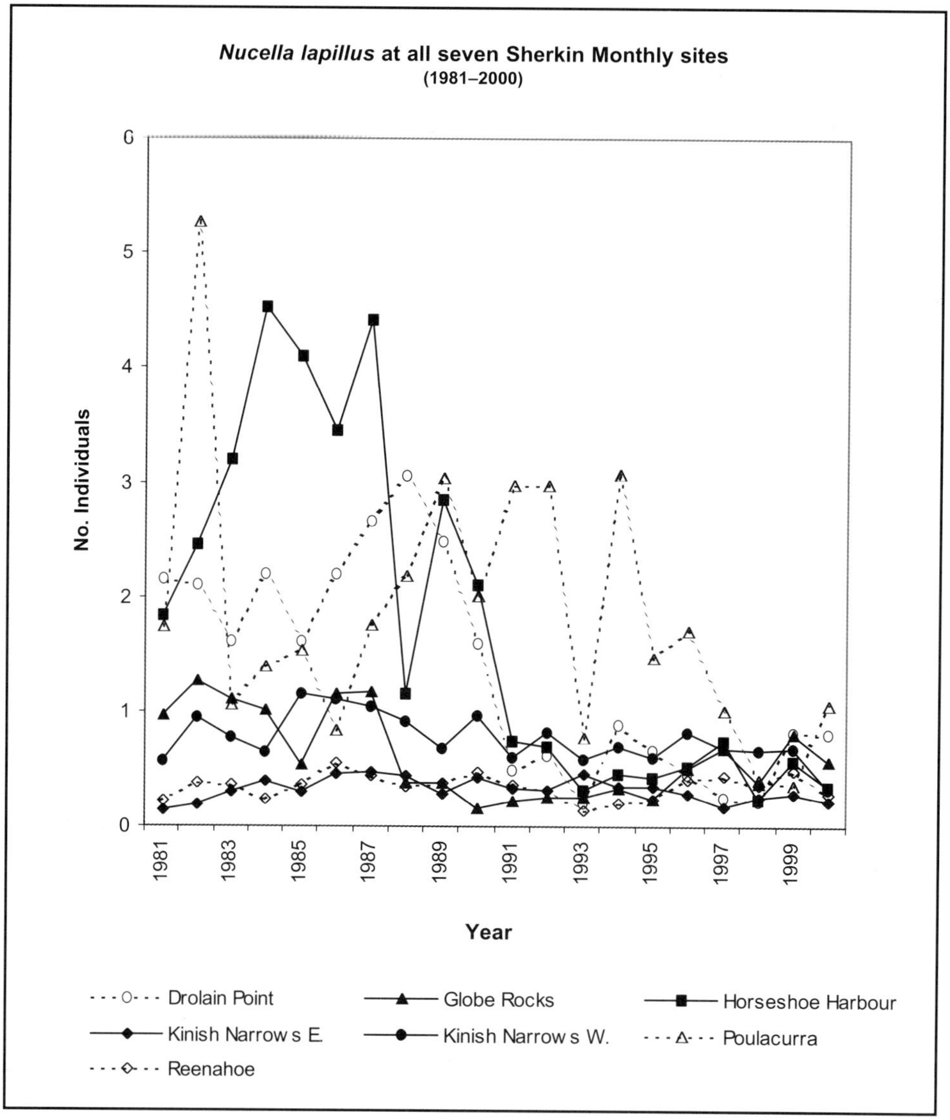

Figure 8.9 Annual variation of dogwhelks.

At Kinish Narrows East loss of whelks from the shore started in 1987 and at Kinish Narrows West it began in 1985. Minimum numbers were recorded at four sites (Poulacurra, Drolain Point, Horseshoe Harbour, Reenahoe) in 1993.

A decline in dogwhelk populations during the 1990s was also recorded at a number of sites surveyed annually on Sherkin (Jackson *et al.*, 2001) and Dunmanus Bay (Browne *et al.*, 2001a).

RELATIONSHIPS BETWEEN SPECIES

Varying abundance of individual algae and animals may be responses in some part to variations in weather, such as extremes of sunshine, air temperatures, storms and wind direction, and we have briefly considered these above. In addition, factors such as food chain relationships and competition for space on the shore are examples of biological controls on the rocky shore. The data from species which live and feed amongst each other have been analysed to see if any related patterns of variation can be identified.

Though there are numerous relationships we could have assessed on the shore we have chose to examine only the following:

Algae – Grazers
- Fucoids/Periwinkles
- Fucoids/Limpets

Ground Cover – competition for space
- Barnacles/Mussels
- *Chondrus crispus/Mastocarpus stellatus/Osmundea*/Mussels

Predator – Prey
- Dogwhelks/Mussels/Barnacles

ALGAE – GRAZERS

Fucoids/Periwinkles

Since the flat periwinkle *Littorina obtusata* lives among the fronds of the wracks, it is not surprising to find that a decline in the algal habitat is followed by a decline in winkle numbers. This was seen in Horseshoe Harbour (Figure 8.10), where combined fucoid density fell from 1981 to 1984 and then remained continuously low to 2000.

Littorina obtusata numbers fell equally steeply between 1981 and 1988, and they remained extremely low (< 1/m^2) throughout a nine-year period 1989–97 when fucoid cover remained less than 2%. There were, however, various population increases (1983, 1986, 1998) which bear no relationship to fucoid density. If the population increases reflect juvenile recruitment, it would appear that there was insufficient fucoid habitat to support them, hence numbers were not sustained into the subsequent years. Also periwinkles have a limiting effect on the growth of fucoid sporelings due to their grazing. Our data suggest that even the minimal periwinkle population size of 1989–97 was sufficient to prevent re-establishment of a rich fucoid canopy. This relationship compounds the situation by the periwinkles destroying the fucoid habitat that it needs for survival.

Fucoids/Limpets

Limpets feed on sporeling algae and also scrape the surfaces of the wracks and rocks to feed on any diatom layer present. Their grazing can weaken the *Fucus* stipes which makes them vulnerable to storm damage by being torn from the shore.

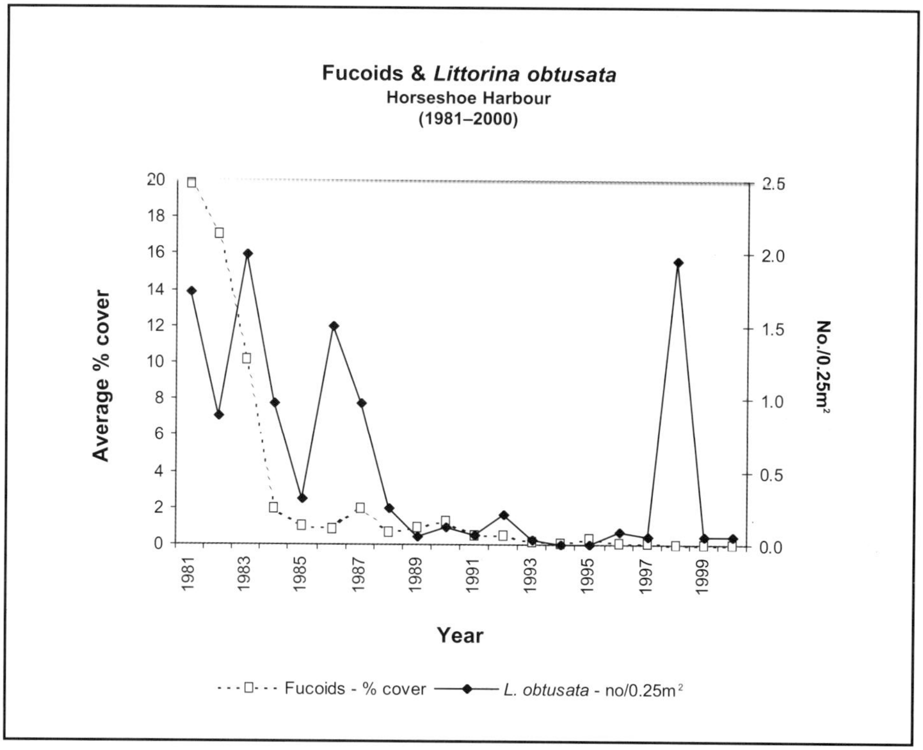

Figure 8.10 Annual variation of fucoids and flat periwinkles.

Fucoids themselves have an influence on whether or not juvenile limpets are able to settle and survive on the shore. While the presence of a fucoid canopy inhibits barnacle settlement (Lewis, 1964; Hawkins, 1981), Hartnoll & Hawkins (1985) have demonstrated that limpet recruitment and survival of juveniles only occurs beneath a fucoid canopy. In algal free areas, recruitment is unsuccessful because the young animals suffer from desiccation.

The relationship between limpets and fucoid abundance has been explored at Reenahoe (Figure 8.11). In general the relationship appears to be direct, but offset in time, similar to that shown by Hartnoll & Hawkins (1985). Fucoid cover increased during six separate periods (1984–86, 1988–89, 1990–91, 1992–93, 1994–96, 1997–98) and, in five of these, limpet numbers decreased (1992–93 being the exception).

In the years when limpet numbers increased (1981–82, 1983–84, 1986–88, 1989–90, 1991–93, 1996–97, 1998–99), fucoid cover decreased in four of these periods (1983–84, 1986–88, 1989–90, 1996–97). The period of limpet increase occurred one or two years after a period of fucoid increase.

When the increase in limpet population was large, fucoid cover was above 25%. It can also be seen that when fucoid cover was less than 25%, limpet numbers stayed between 22 and 30 per quadrat.

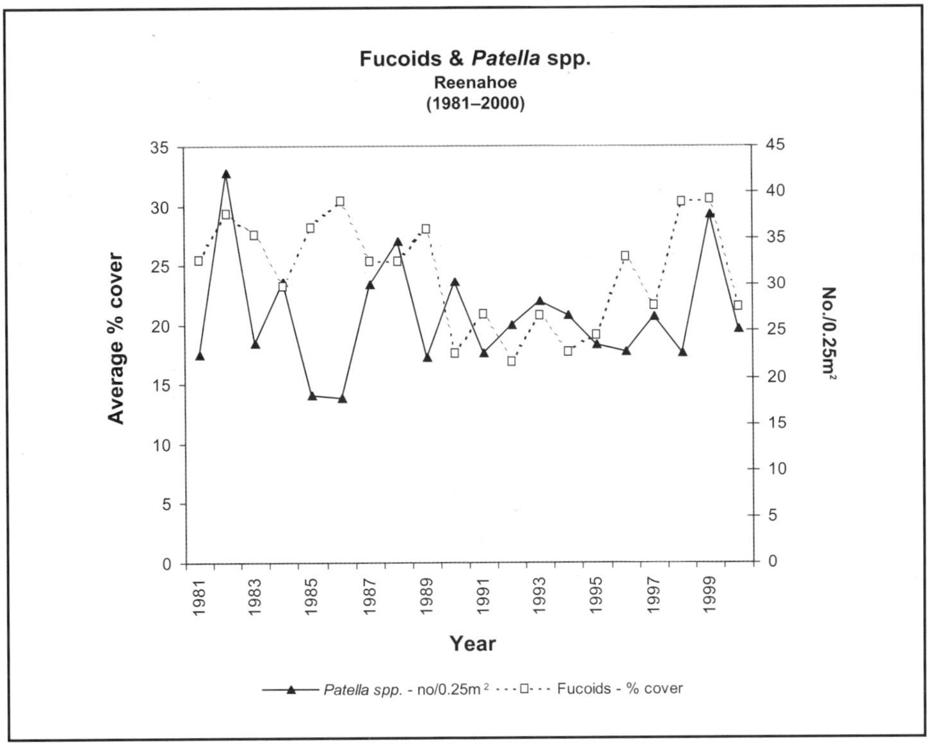

Figure 8.11 Annual variation of fucoids and limpets.

GROUND COVER AND COMPETITION FOR SPACE

Chondrus/Mastocarpus/Osmundea/Mussels

The carrageen seaweeds, *Chondrus crispus* and *Mastocarpus stellatus*, are often found in close proximity to mussels, hence at the two most exposed shores – Poulacurra and Drolain Point – the possibility of a relationship between carrageen and mussels was investigated. There is no feeding relationship between the species since mussels are filter feeders, but a relationship may exist as the two species compete for space. Also, carrageen provides a habitat for juvenile mussel recruitment.

At Drolain Point, *Chondrus* was very sparse or unrecorded apart from the years 1983 and 1989. There is a closer relationship between *Mastocarpus* and mussels. Both species were relatively dense in the 1980s (*Mastocarpus* 1981–92; mussels 1981–89) and sparse thereafter. In 1999 and 2000 mussel cover increased, but there was no associated increase in *Mastocarpus*.

At Poulacurra a summary of percentage cover changes in *Mastocarpus*, *Osmundea* and mussels shows how cycles and peak abundance of *Osmundea* and mussels coincided (1983, 1989 peaks) during the 1980s. Mussel abundance peaked again in 1996, but both *Mastocarpus* and *Osmundea* cover were sparse between 1992 and 2000. No apparent relationship was found to exist between *Mastocarpus* and mussels at this site.

Barnacles/Mussels

On shores where both barnacles and mussels occur, they compete for space on the middle shore where their distributions overlap. It is tempting therefore to assume that a decrease in one species due to predation, old age or loss due to extreme wave action will create a subsequent effect on the density of the other. Since the *Semibalanus balanoides* spatfall usually occurs marginally earlier in the year than that of mussels, any settling barnacles have the advantage of free space being made available during the previous year.

However Figure 8.12 shows clearly that at Poulacurra both species have a fairly similar pattern of variation. Although barnacles occupied significantly more rock space than mussels, both populations increased in abundance between 1987 and 1989. Mussels then decreased significantly during 1990 and 1991, while the widespread barnacle crash occurred in 1991. The abundance of both species then stayed consistently low to the end of the survey period (2000). Prior to 1987, when barnacle cover had increased for three years and then declined slightly, mussels had increased a small amount for two years.

The results at Drolain Point (Figure 8.13) show some similarities to this, but also some interesting differences. While both species experienced population crashes, these happened in different years.

Barnacle density showed an overall increase from 1981–88 and stayed at this maximum cover through 1989 and 1990. In the same period, mussel cover was more erratic, with a very large increase in 1986 and a catastrophic decline over the next four

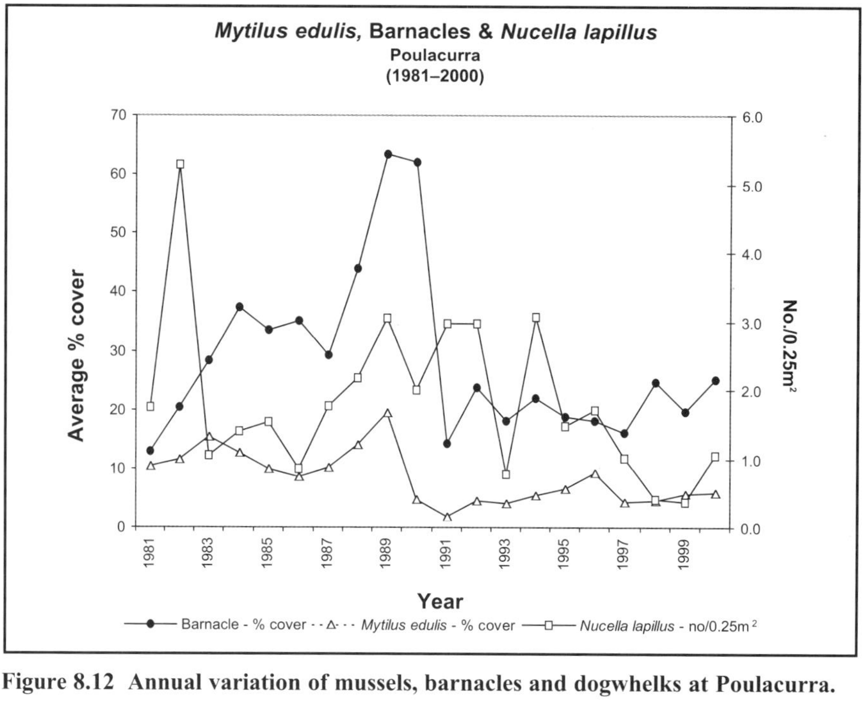

Figure 8.12 Annual variation of mussels, barnacles and dogwhelks at Poulacurra.

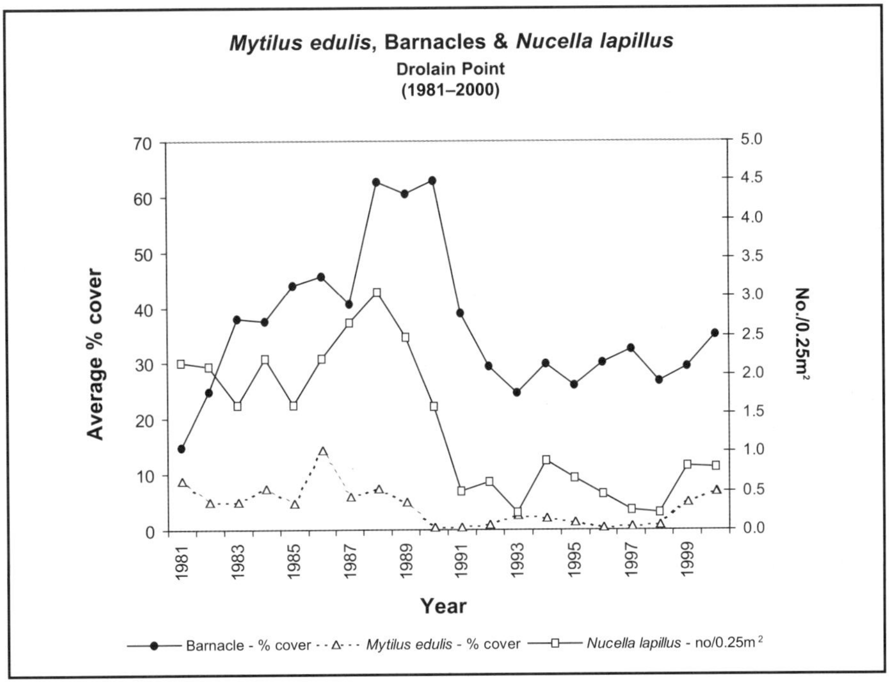

Figure 8.13 Annual variation of mussels, barnacles and dogwhelks at Drolain Point.

years. So although barnacles were able to maintain a high density over three years when mussels were competing less for space, they were unable to sustain this level. Whatever prompted the population to decline in 1991, 1992 and 1993 does not appear to be related to any competition from mussels.

PREDATOR–PREY RELATIONSHIP

Barnacles/Dogwhelks

There is a predator/prey relationship between barnacle and dogwhelks. Simply, dogwhelks eat barnacles. The relationship of these two species has been examined at Globe Rocks (Figure 8.14) and Reenahoe (Figure 8.15). At both sites, barnacles increased from 1981–90 and crashed in 1991 as discussed earlier (p. 208). Percentage cover then gradually increased over the subsequent nine years to 2000.

In the early years at Globe Rocks when barnacles were increasing in cover (1982–1986), dogwhelk numbers were falling (1983–85). 1986 saw an increase in abundance of both species.

Between 1987 and 1988 dogwhelk numbers fell – a year after barnacle density had dropped. While the dogwhelk population remained low (1988–95), barnacles increased (1987–90), then decreased dramatically as part of the widescale crash in 1991. It seems unlikely that this is in any way related to predation. Although dogwhelk numbers rose more

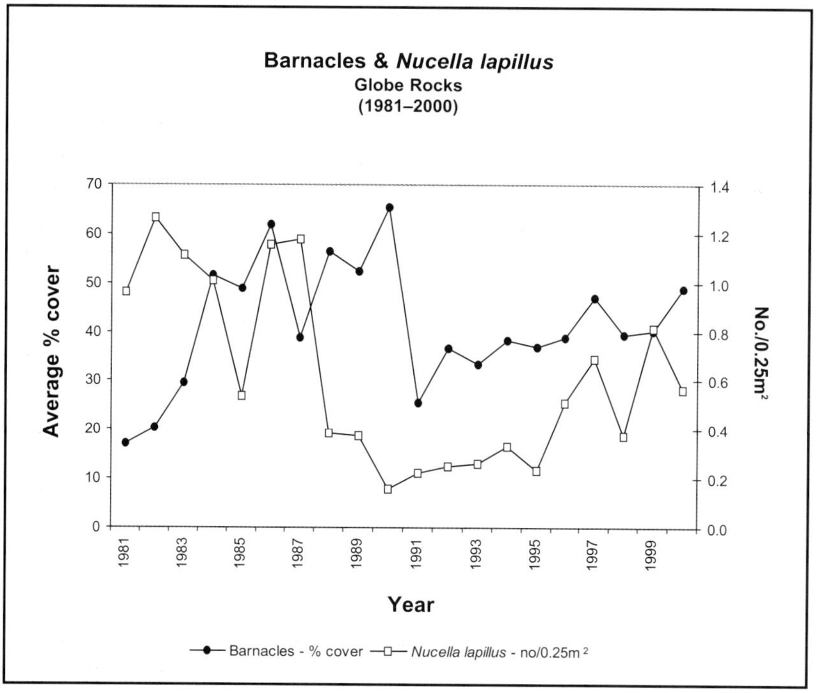

Figure 8.14 Annual variation of barnacles and dogwhelks at Globe Rocks.

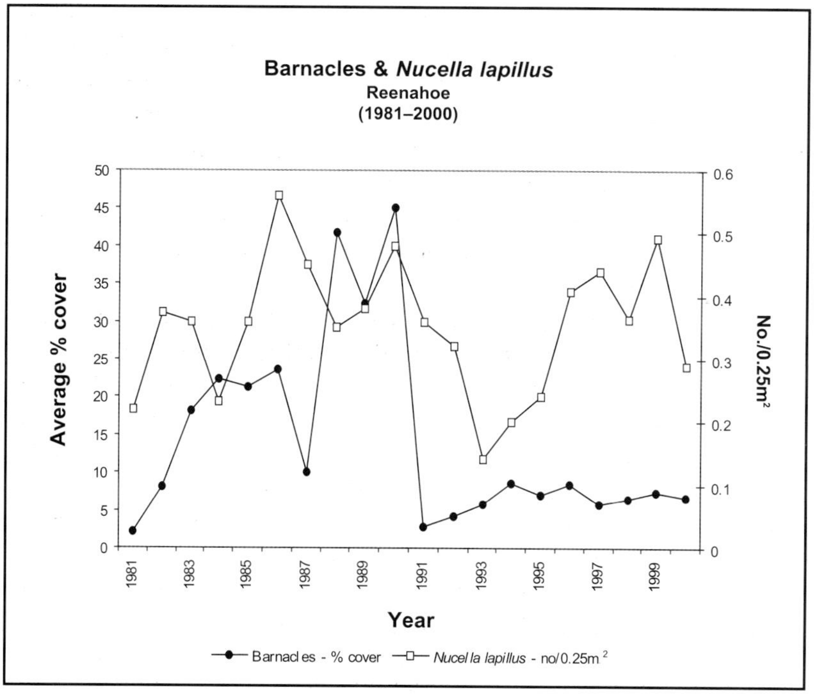

Figure 8.15 Annual variation of barnacles and dogwhelks at Reenahoe.

or less continually throughout the 1990s, the rate of population increase was far greater after 1995. At this time, barnacle cover was sustained at just under 40% and increasing.

The pattern at Reenahoe is broadly similar to that of Globe Rocks. When barnacle cover dropped abruptly in two consecutive years (1986–87), there was a decrease in dogwhelks for the two subsequent years (1987 and 1988). This was also evident after the barnacle population crash of 1990/1991, as dogwhelks continued their downward population trend in 1991, 1992 and 1993. Conversely when barnacles showed a steady increase (as in 1981–86), dogwhelks showed an overall increase despite a fall in numbers in 1984.

At Kinish Narrows East both barnacles and dogwhelks increased throughout the 1980s. When the barnacle population crashed in 1991 from 55% to about 10% cover, dogwhelk numbers decreased a little during 1991 and again in 1992. From 1992–93 they showed a steady increase, then generally declined until 2000, while barnacles remained at a fairly low level of between 15 and 20% cover.

The data as depicted in the figures do not support the idea that dogwhelks influence barnacle abundance.

Barnacles/Mussels/Dogwhelks

Since dogwhelks preferentially prey upon mussels, the relationship of the three animal populations (barnacles, mussels and dogwhelks) has been investigated at the most exposed sites, Drolain Point and Poulacurra, where mussels were most abundant. At Drolain Point, both mussel and barnacle populations showed an increase, decline and recovery (Figure 8.13). However their timings were different, with the mussel decline occurring five years prior to the barnacle crash in 1991. Dogwhelk numbers were at their maximum in 1988, and fell until 1993. It is possible that as dogwhelks increased steadily in 1986, 1987 and 1988, they were responsible for the decline in mussels between 1986 and 1990. After mussels began to decline, perhaps dogwhelks then fed more on barnacles. It is also possible that the decline in mussels was a limiting factor to dogwhelks, causing their numbers to fall. Since dogwhelk numbers declined prior to the barnacle decline, it follows that the predator is not responsible for the crash in the barnacle population.

At Poulacurra (Figure 8.12), it seems likely that the large numbers of dogwhelks recorded in 1982 could not be sustained by the small amount of barnacles and mussels present. This would explain why dogwhelk numbers fell and remained low for the next four years (until 1986). The data do not tell us whether individuals perish through starvation, or migrate to a richer food supply, but the latter is more likely and is a typical characteristic of predators. During 1987–1990 dogwhelk numbers increased (as did mussel cover) and at this time the barnacle population occupied between 30 and 40% of the shore, having increased over the three-year period 1982–84.

All three species increased during 1988 and 1989, and then mussels and dogwhelks both declined, a year before the large barnacle population crash, which was widespread.

Dogwhelk numbers recovered slightly and were sustained for three or four years before falling away significantly. During this fall (1994–2000) barnacles started to increase slightly while mussels sustained a very low level of abundance.

KEY FINDINGS

Throughout the sites and species, one can observe a consistent and conspicuous contrast between population sizes in the first and second decades of the data set. The overall trend was one of decline in many organisms during the 1990s on the Sherkin shores that we examined. Some examples are:

- There was a widespread decrease in fucoid cover during the 1990s.
- *Littorina saxatilis* at Poulacurra was much less abundant in the 1990s than the 1980s, and was also fairly steady in population number from 1992–2000.
- At all seven sites, the barnacle population crashed in 1991 and remained very much lower throughout the 1990s.
- At the two most exposed sites, mussel populations were smaller in the 1990s.
- At all sites dogwhelks populations were smaller during the 1990s.

As recording began in 1981, we have no way of knowing whether the population levels of the 1980s were "normal" or whether they were particularly high. It is equally possible that the low population densities of the 1990s represent the true viability of Sherkin's rocky shore environment.

Perspectives

As the data analysis progressed, it was difficult to accept that the species abundance of so many of those selected for discussion had changed from their 1980s' levels to those of the 1990s. This was compounded by the further population decreases during the 1990s. Clearly, the rocky shore communities of Sherkin are under stress and the populations are in transition as a result of those forces. We would not have seen these changes without the Sherkin data set. The records raise two principal questions. First, what environmental parameters have changed in what ways to induce the precipitous and protracted decline of species that appeared dynamically stable for over a decade prior to the declines? One might argue (with a shorter data set) that the changes are modest in size and might fall within the range of natural variability. The data cover two decades, therefore unless a natural variability cycle covers a longer time frame, we are seeing true change. The second question raised is: are the vacated habitat(s) and species declines being balanced by an increased presence, immigration or colonisation by new species? Simply, how are the abandoned niches being filled? The answer to this question appears to be that they are unfilled and the productivity of Sherkin's coastal community has declined since the late 1980s. The rocky shore data set reveals that a natural environmental event occurred and there is no evidence of a full "recovery". After considering alternative explanations, it appears likely that the changes were induced by the Gulf Stream.

A fall in abundance from 50% to 10% cover or presence would be readily noticeable, possibly even by a casual observer. The Sherkin sampling teams recorded changes in seaweed cover from 10% to 5%, or 5% to 3% and animal changes such as periwinkle declines from two to one per quadrat. Only when several decades of observations are arrayed does a data set enable the researcher a limited insight and the right to provide commentary. The changes reported for the rocky shores of Sherkin Island are real and present a fascinating and disturbing story. Work has started, at the Marine Station, to advance the understanding of the observed species' fluctuations, life cycles and interactions going beyond that presented in this volume. The work is focusing on population and community structure, species functions and needs for survival, all in concert with the effects of climate and habitat change.

Man-induced (anthropogenic) change must not be forgotten. However, with sites such as Poulacurra, exposed to a constant flush by the Gulf Stream, it is difficult to imagine that this is a significant issue. We are nevertheless aware that local harvesting of selected species, such as periwinkles, does occur at more sheltered sites and that the island and surrounding areas have experienced development in both upland and aquatic ecosystems. Local harvesting in the intertidal zone is sporadic, but could account for an occasional discrepancy in the data set. However, using a data set that spans more than two decades allows one to note, but ignore, anomalous data points. This was not necessary. Similarly, development, particularly residential housing, on the uplands surrounding Sherkin Island and on the island itself, might be a pollution source from waste discharges. Sanitary waste management is primarily achieved by septic systems. There is no evidence that sanitary waste disposal is a major regional problem. We believe there are local problems, but would expect that it would take a significant amount of discharge from a large number of individual systems to induce the widespread changes identified. Most importantly, changes caused by organic enrichment would not be manifest as uniform declines in abundance, but rather, enhanced growth of some algae as they benefited from the addition of nutrients. Some animals would benefit from the increased availability of food. We see no evidence of this enhancement occurring. Agriculture has remained a constant presence throughout the period. While the introduction of new or improved farming practices might be a source of change, we are unable to draw any direct relationships at this time.

Finally, the waters of Roaringwater Bay have become the home to a number of aquaculture activities. Shellfish aquaculture requires clean water for food safety and ample supplies of pelagic organisms to feed their crops and sustain the operations. As with local harvesting, those operations do not appear capable of altering regional productivity. Additionally, water circulation within the Bay is such that new sources of water and prey are constantly be made available to the shellfish operations which are located in the sheltered, backwater areas of the Bay. If this were not occurring, the organisms would require a protracted growing period to overcome the limitations of food availability. Discussions with the aquaculturists indicate neither situation is present.

The species list in Appendix 3 and 4 demonstrates the richness of the rocky shores and we have huge amounts of data still to be analysed from the lowest transect stations, only accessible during extreme low water spring tides. Additionally the wealth of data from the annual sites had yet to be interpreted.

The major question has been "Was the crash of barnacle populations in 1991 the most important event of the 20-year period?" The answer again lies in considering the scale and perspective of this event.

When barnacles decline, a food source for dogwhelks is reduced, and dogwhelks are forced to feed more on mussels. Ultimately both food species may decline to a point where they are insufficient to support the dogwhelk population, in which case it will consequently decline and this has indeed been observed on Sherkin. In the absence of their dogwhelk predators, barnacle and mussel larvae settle and survive and new populations grow and thrive until ultimately dogwhelks return to feed on them. This new balance, however, was not evident by the year 2000.

How have the changes identified on Sherkin affected other parts of the marine ecosystem? One might expect other predators, e.g. starfish, crabs or fish, to be affected by the decline of a food source and ongoing analysis of data from lower shore stations may throw light on this. At present we have no records of fluctuating catches from fishermen, and visually we have not perceived major changes in the rocky shore. We have measured fine-scale changes. However fine-scale changes still affect the entire ecosystem as it exists in a dynamic equilibrium, and so ultimately we will become aware of them through the ensuing changes up the food chain or through major visual changes.

Visual changes could include the canopy layer, which at most of the sites reduced a little. However we know from other Sherkin Island Marine Station surveys that there is a rich algal diversity in the understorey. If the canopy were to disappear completely, the algal diversity of the understorey would be likely to decrease and would certainly change in species composition.

THE NEXT 20 YEARS

Natural variation on the shores is indisputable. The populations we have described here do not behave in the same way on each shore, although we have recorded and presented here many similarities of population change. It is a point of great interest that the two sheltered shores, Kinish Narrows West and Kinish Narrows East, display so many differences when they are physically separated by only 55 m of water and have many physical features in common. But hydrodynamics and physical aspect remain potential explanations for the differences. Each shore is thus a system with its own equilibrium, and the many physical and biological variables interact in a way unique to that particular shore. This presents the biologist with many frustrations (but much fascination), especially if there is a desire to model natural systems and to assume predictable sequences of events.

However, it is evident that within each shore we are seeing patterns, and as the Marine Station continues this work, we can only stand to gain a deeper understanding of the interactions and critical factors affecting Sherkin's rocky shores. The analysis and the writing of this book began in 1992 but it is a blessing that it proved to be a longer project than anticipated as our understanding and perspectives have grown and developed as the data set has expanded. The 20-year data set presented here shows unquestionably that the rocky shore is a dynamic environment, and the value of the data increases year on year. Today we realise that working to understand individual species cycles and the dynamics of "connected" species in the rocky shore habitat is not only important in itself, but can contribute significantly to Ireland's examination of long-term data sets with the aim of understanding climate change. An assessment of the distribution status of various intertidal species, which might be affected by such changes, is a useful study for Ireland. There is indeed recognition in Ireland that further long-term integrated ecosystem monitoring is essential (Sweeney *et al.,* 2003). Within the solid framework of data on Sherkin's shores we now plan to interpret the data from the 145 annual sites from Cork Harbour to Bantry Bay. Future work must maintain the high standard of recording and must also include further analysis of our weather data and plankton records, in an effort to define the cues which drive individual species cycles.

The Marine Station has many strengths, not least being the fact that one person has overseen the Station for its existence since 1975. By contrast, we also count the ever-changing team of biologists year on year as an unrivalled bonus; each one bringing interests, skills and opinions which keep the work alive.

BIBLIOGRAPHY

BAKER, J.M., HISCOCK, S., HISCOCK, K., LEVELL, D., BISHOP, G., PRECIOUS, M., COLLINSON, R., KINGSBURY, R. & O'SULLVAN, A.J. (1981) The rocky shore biology of Bantry Bay: a re-survey. *Irish Fisheries Investigations. Series B,* 23: 3–30.

BALLANTINE, W.J. (1961) A biologically-defined exposure scale for the comparative description of rocky shores. *Field Studies* 1 (3): 1–19.

BAKER, J.M. (1987a) The "Kowloon Bridge" Accident, West Cork Shore Survey, 8th–11th January, 1987. *Bulletin of Sherkin Island, No. 6.*

BAKER, J.M. (1987b) The "Kowloon Bridge" Accident, West Cork Shore Survey, 13th–15th March, 1987. *Bulletin of Sherkin Island, No. 7.*

BAKER, J.M. (1987c) The "Kowloon Bridge" Accident, West Cork Shore Survey, 27th–29th April, 1987. *Bulletin of Sherkin Island, No. 8.*

BARNES, H. (1963) Light, temperature and the breeding of *Balanus balanoides. Journal of the Marine Biological Association of the United Kingdom* 43: 717–727.

BARNES, R.S.K. & HUGHES, R.N. (1982) *An Introduction to Marine Ecology.* Blackwell Scientific Publications, UK.

BAXTER, J.M., JONES, A.M. & SIMPSON, J.A. (1985) Rocky shores in Orkney: a long term study. *Proceedings of the Royal Society of Edinburgh* 87B: 47–64.

BISHOP, G. (1998) Twenty Years of Baseline Studies at Sherkin Island Marine Station - What they tell us. *Proceedings of the 14th Annual Environmental Conference, Sherkin Island Marine Station,* pp. 33–39.

BLAKE, P.F. & WALKER, A.J.M. (1980) The effect of the 1980 bloom of *Gyrodinium aureolum* (Dinophyta) on shore invertebrates in Dunmanus Bay and the recovery of populations from previous Red Tides. *Journal of Sherkin Island* 1 (1): 67–74.

BODC (1998). *United Kingdom Digital Marine Atlas. Ver. 3.0.* British Oceanography Data Centre, Birkenhead, UK.

BOLGER-HYNES, E. (1999) A Five Year study from 1995 to 1999 of the Flora and Fauna of the Rocky Seashore of Cork Harbour. Sherkin Island Marine Station (Unpublished report).

BOWMAN R.S. & LEWIS, J.R. (1977) Annual fluctuations in the recruitment of *Patella vulgata* L. *Journal of the Marine Biological Association of the United Kingdom* 57: 793–815.

BROWNE, C., EDWARDS, S., ESCANDELL, M., FALCOUS, K. & JACKSON, T. (2001a). Rocky Shore Survey of Dunmanus Bay 1981–2000. Sherkin Island Marine Station (Unpublished report).

BROWNE, C., EDWARDS, S., ESCANDELL, M., FALCOUS, K. & JACKSON, T. (2001b). Rocky Shore Survey of East of Baltimore 1981–2000. Sherkin Island Marine Station (Unpublished report).

BURROWS, E.M. & LODGE, S.M. (1950) Note on the inter-relationships of *Patella, Balanus* and *Fucus* on a semi-exposed coast. *Report of the Marine Biological Station at Port Erin, Isle of Man* 62: 30–35.

CAMPBELL, A. (1976) *Seashores and Shallow Seas of Britain and Europe (1994 revised edition).* The Hamyln Publishing Group Limited.

CLARK, J. (1999) Bantry, Bay, Cork Harbour and East of Baltimore. Sherkin Island Marine Station (Unpublished report).

CLARK, J., GWENIN, S., NETZER, J., TOMLIN, H. & WADE, T. (1997) The Sherkin Island Marine Station 1997 Rocky Shore Survey of West Cork. Sherkin Island Marine Station (Unpublished report).

COE, K. & SELWOOD, E.B. (1968) The upper Palaeozoic stratigraphy of West Cork and parts of South Kerry. *Proceedings of the Royal Irish Academy* 66B: 113–131.

COLWELL R.K. & FUENTES, E.R. (1975) Experimental studies of the niche. *Annual Review of Ecological Systems* 6: 281–310

CONNELL J.H. (1985) Variation and Persistence of Rocky Shore Populations. In *The Ecology of Rocky Coasts.* Ed. P.G. Moore & R. Seed.

COTTON, A.D. (1912) Clare Island survey: "Marine Algae" *Proceedings of the Royal Irish Academy.* 31(15): 1–178.

CRAPP, G.B. (1973) The Distribution and Abundance of Animals and Plants on the Rocky Shores of Bantry Bay. *Irish Fisheries Investigations. Series B,* 9: 3–35.

CRISP, D.J. (1964) (ed) The effects of the severe winter of 1962–63 on marine life in Britain. *Journal of Animal Ecology* 33: 165–210

CRISP, D.J. & SOUTHWARD, A. (1958) The distribution of intertidal organisms along the coasts of the English Channel. *Journal of the Marine Biological Association of the United Kingdom* 37: 157–208.

CRISP, D.J. & SOUTHWARD, A. (1959) The further spread of *Elminius modestus* in the British Isles to 1959. *Journal of the Marine Biological Association of the United Kingdom* 38: 429–437.

CROSS, T.F. & SOUTHGATE, T. (1980) Mortalities of fauna of rocky substrates in south west Ireland associated with the occurrence of *Gyrodinium aureolum* blooms during autumn 1979. *Journal of the Marine Biological Association of the United Kingdom* 60: 1071–1073.

CROSS, T.F. & SOUTHGATE, T. (1983) An approach to ecological monitoring in the rocky intertidal: a survey of Bantry Bay and Dunmanus Bay, Ireland. *Marine Environmental Research* 8: 149–163.

EBLING, F.J., SLOANE, J.F., KITCHING, J.A. & DAVIES, H.M. (1960) The ecology of Lough Ine VII. Distribution of some common plants and animals of the littoral and shallow sublittoral regions. *Journal of Ecology* 48: 29–53.

EBLING, F.J., SLOANE, J.F., KITCHING, J.A. & DAVIES, H.M. (1962) The ecology of Lough Ine XII. The distribution and characteristics of *Patella* species. *Journal of Animal Ecology* 31: 457–70

EDWARDS, S., BROWNE, C., ESCANDELL, M., FALCOUS, K., JACKSON, T. (2001) Bantry Bay Rocky Shore Report 1995–2000. Sherkin Island Marine Station (Unpublished report).

EGERTON, M. (1998) Comparison of species distribution on selected Sherkin Island Annual Seashore Monitoring Sites from 1995–1998. Sherkin Island Marine Station (Unpublished report).

EGERTON, M. (1999) The Distribution and Abundance of *Elminius modestus*, Darwin, in Cork Harbour 1995–1999. Sherkin Island Marine Station (Unpublished report).

EGERTON, M., DALEY, L., PARTRIDGE, J., DUFFY, S., CLARK, J. & FARNELL, T. (1998) The Sherkin Island Marine Station 1998 Rocky Shore Survey of West Cork. Sherkin Island Marine Station (Unpublished report).

FALCOUS, K., BROWNE, C., EDWARDS, S., ESCANDELL, M., JACKSON, T. (2001) Rocky Shore Survey of Roaringwater Bay 1981–2000. Sherkin Island Marine Station (Unpublished report).

FALCOUS, K., BROWNE, C., EDWARDS, S., ESCANDELL, M., JACKSON, T. (2001) 1995–2000 Rocky Shore Survey of Cork Harbour. Sherkin Island Marine Station (Unpublished report).

GOSLING (1984) The systematic status of *Mytilus gallo-provincialis* in western Europe: a review. *Malacologia* 25: 551–568.

GOSSE, P.H. (1853) *A Naturalist's Rambles on the Devonshire Coast.* J. Van Voorst, London, UK.

GOSSE, P.H. (1856) *Tenby, A Sea-side Holiday.* J. Van Voorst, London, UK.

GOSSE, P.H. (1860) *Actinologia Britannica; A History of the British Sea-anemones and Corals.* J. Van Voorst, London, UK.

GRAHAM, A. (1971) *British Prosobranch and Other Operculate Gastropod Molluscs.* Published by The Linnean Society of London and The Estuarine and Brackish-water Science Association. The Bath Press, UK.

GRAHAM, A. (1988) *Molluscs: Prosobranch and Pyramidellid Gastropods.* Published by The Linnean Society of London. Academic Press London & New York.

GRAHAM, J.R and REILLY, T.A. (1972) The Sherkin Formation (Devonian) of south-west County Cork. *Geological Survey of Ireland*, Bulletin 1: 281–300.

GUPTA, A.S. & KOWALIK, R. (2000) Brittlestar survey 2000. Sherkin Island Marine Station (Unpublished report).

HARTNOLL, R.G. & HAWKINS, S.J. (1980) Monitoring Rocky shore communities: a critical look at spatial and temporal variation. *Helgoländer Wissenschaftliche Meeresuntersuchungen* 33: 484–494.

HARTNOLL, R.G. & HAWKINS, S.J. (1985) Patchiness and Fluctuations on moderately exposed rocky shores. *Ophelia* 24: 53–63.

HAWKINS, S.J. (1981) The influence of *Patella* grazing on the fucoid/barnacle mosaic on moderately exposed rocky shores. *Kieler Meeresforschungen* 5: 537–543.

HAWKINS, S.J. & HARTNOLL, R.G. (1983) Changes in a rocky shore community: an evaluation of monitoring. *Marine Environmental Research* 9: 131–181.

HAYWARD, P.J. & RYLAND, J.S. (1990) *The Marine Fauna of the British Isles and North-west Europe. Volume 1: Introduction and Protozoans to Arthropods.* Clarendon Press, Oxford, UK.

HAYWARD, P.J. & RYLAND, J.S. (1990) *The Marine Fauna of the British Isles and North-west Europe. Volume 2: Molluscs to Chordates.* Clarendon Press, Oxford, UK.

HAYWARD, P., NELSON-SMITH, T. & SHIELDS, C. (1996) *Collins Pocket Guide to the Seashore of Britain and Europe*. HarperCollins Publishers.

HELLER, J. (1975) The taxonomy of some British *Littorina* species, with notes on their reproduction (Mollusca: Prosobranchia). *Zoological Journal of the Linnean Society of London* 56: 131–151.

HINCKS, T. (1868) *A history of the British hydroid zoophytes. Vol I and II.* John Van Voorst, Paternoster Row. London.

HISCOCK, K. (1983) Assessment of Rocky Shore Surveys in Sullom Voe 1976–1981. *Report to the Shetland Oil terminal Environmental Advisory Group from the Field Studies Council, Oil Pollution Research Unit.* Report No. FSC/OPRU/8/83.

HISCOCK, S (1979) A field key to the British brown seaweeds (Phaeophyta). *Field Studies* 5: 1–44.

HISCOCK, S (1986) A field key to the British red seaweeds (Rhodophyta). *Field Studies Council Occasional Publications* 13.

HOLME, N.A. (1963) Some records of sea temperatures in the English Channel in February 1963. *Journal of the Marine Biological Association of the United Kingdom* 43: 701–707

HOLME, N. A. (1967) Changes in the bottom fauna of Weymouth Bay and Poole Bay following the severe winter of 1962–63. *Journal of the Marine Biological Association of the United Kingdom* 47: 397–405

HOWSON, C.M. & PICTON, B.E. (1997) *The Species Directory of the Marine Fauna and Flora of the British Isles and Surrounding Seas*. Ulster Museum and Marine Conservation Society.

HUNTER, J. (1997) The Rocky Shores of Sherkin Island 1987–1997. Sherkin Island Marine Station (Unpublished report).

IRISH NATURALISTS' JOURNAL (1983–1995) Cetacean Notes *Irish Naturalists' Journal* 21–24.

JACKSON, T., BROWNE, C., EDWARDS, S., ESCANDELL, M. & FALCOUS, K. (2001) Sherkin Island Rocky Shore 1981–2000. Sherkin Island Marine Station (Unpublished report).

JAMES, B.L. (1968) The distribution and keys of species in the family Littorinidae and of their digenean parasites, in the region of Dale, Pembrokeshire. *Field Studies* 2: 615–650.

JANCKE (1990) Biological interactions and their role in the community structure in the rocky intertidal of Helgoland (Germany Bight, North Sea). *Helgoländer Meeresuntersuchungen* 44: 219–63.

JENKINSON, I.R. & O'CONNOR, P.P. (1980) The occurrence of the red tide causing organism, *Gyrodinium aureolum* Hulburt (Dinophyceae), round the south and west of Ireland in August and September 1979. *Journal of Sherkin Island* 1 (1): 127–146.

JONES, W.E., BARNETT, E.A. LUMB, C.M. & MACK-SMITH, S. (1981) The Seventh Report of the Coastal Surveillance Unit. *Dept of Marine Biology, University College of North Wales.*

JONES, W.E., BARNETT, E.A., LUMB, C.M. & MACK-SMITH, S. (1982) The Eighth Report of the Coastal Surveillance Unit. *Dept of Marine Biology, University College of North Wales.*

JONES, W.E., BARNETT, E.A., LUMB, C.M. & MACK-SMITH, S. (1983) The Ninth Report of the Coastal Surveillance Unit. *Dept of Marine Biology, University College of North Wales.*

JONES, A.M. & BAXTER, J.M. (1985) The Use of *Patella vulgata* L. in Rocky Shore Surveillance. In: *The Ecology of Rocky Coasts* Eds. Moore, P.G. & R. Seed.

JONES, W.E., FLETCHER, A., HISCOCK, K. and HAINSWORTH, S. (1975) The First Report of the Coastal Surveillance Unit. *Dept of Marine Biology, University College of North Wales.*

JONES, W.E., FLETCHER, A., BENNELL, S., McCONNELL, B. & MACK SMITH, S. (1979) Changes in littoral populations as recorded by long term shore surveillance. In: *Cyclic phenomena in marine plants and animals* Ed. Naylor, E. & Hartnoll, R.G. Pergamon Press, Oxford pp. 93–100.

JUKES, J.B. (1861) Explanations accompanying sheets194, 200, 201, 202, 203, 204, 205 and part of 199. *Memoirs of the Geological Survey of Ireland,*

KAIN J.M. (1975) Algal recolonization of some cleared subtidal areas. *Journal of Ecology* 63: 739– 765.

KENDALL, M.A., BOWMAN, R.S., WILLIAMSON, P. & LEWIS, J.R. (1982) Settlement patterns, density and stability in the barnacle *Balanus balanoides. Netherlands Journal of Sea Research* 16: 119–126.

KENDALL, M.A., BOWMAN, R.S., WILLIAMSON, P. & LEWIS, J.R. (1985) Annual variation in the recruitment of *Semibalanus balanoides* on the North Yorkshire coast 1969–1981. *Journal of the Marine Biological Association of the United Kingdom* 65: 1009–1030.

KITCHING (1987) Ecological studies at Lough Hyne. *Advances in Ecological Research* 17: 115–86.

KITCHING, J.A. & EBLING, F.J. (1967) Ecological studies at Lough Ine. *Advances in Ecological Research* 4: 197–291.

KITCHING, J.A. & THAIN, V.M. (1983) The ecological impact of the sea urchin Paracentrotus lividus (Lamarck) in Lough Ine, Ireland. *Philosophical Transactions of the Royal Society of London,* Series B, 300: 513–52.

KNIGHT, M. & PARKE, M. (1950) A biological study of *Fucus vesiculosus* L. and *Fucus serratus* L. *Journal of the Marine Biological Association of the United Kingdom* 159: 87–90.

KOWALIK, R. & GUPTA, A.S. (2000a) Sublittoral and littoral survey of the flora and fauna of Kinish Narrows, Sherkin Island 2000. Sherkin Island Marine Station (Unpublished report).

KOWALIK, R. & GUPTA, A.S. (2000b) Sublittoral and littoral survey of the flora and fauna of Horseshoe Harbour, Sherkin Island 2000. Sherkin Island Marine Station (Unpublished report).

LAYDEN, S. J. & LANE, I. (1984) Monitoring of the Rocky Shore in Dunmanus Bay, Co. Cork 1981–1984. Sherkin Island Marine Station (Unpublished report).

LEAHY, P. (1980) The effects of a dinoflagellate bloom in 1978 on the invertebrate fauna of the seashore in Dunmanus Bay, Co. Cork. *Journal of Sherkin Island* 1 (1): 119–125.

LEBOUR, M.V. (1947) Notes on the Inshore Plankton of Plymouth. *Journal of the Marine Biological Association of the United Kingdom* 26: 527–547.

LEE, A.J. & RAMSTER J.W. (1981) *Atlas of the Seas Around the British Isles*. Ministry of Agriculture, Fisheries and Food (MAFF), UK.

LESLIE, M. (1986) A five year transect study of marked sites on the shores around Sherkin Island, Co. Cork. 1980–1985. Sherkin Island Marine Station (Unpublished report).

LEWIS, J.R. (1954–55) The ecology of exposed rocky shores of Caithness. *Transactions of the Royal Society of Edinburgh* 62 (3): 695–723.

LEWIS, J.R. (1964) *The Ecology of Rocky Shores.* English Universities Press, London. 323 pp.

LEWIS, J.R. (1975) Long-term ecological survey: practical realities in the rocky littoral. *Oceanography and Marine Biology* 14: 371–390.

LEWIS, J.R. (1977) The role of physical and biological factors in the distribution and stability of rocky shore communities. In: *Biology of Benthic Organisms,* eds. B.F. Keegan, P.O. Ceidigh & P.J.S. Boaden, Pergamon Press, Oxford. pp. 417–424.

LEWIS, J.R. & BOWMAN, R.S. (1975) Local habitat-induced variations in the population dynamics of *Patella vulgata* L. *Journal of Experimental Marine Biology & Ecology* 17: 165-204.

LITTLE, C., MORRITT, D. & STIRLING, P. (1992) Changes in the shore fauna and flora of Lough Hyne. *Irish Naturalists' Journal* 24 (3): 87–95.

LUBCHENCO, J. & MENGE, B.A. (1978) Community development and persistence in a low rocky intertidal zone. *Ecological Monographs* 48: 67–94.

METTAM, C. (1979) Faunal changes in the Severn Estuary over several decades. *Marine Pollution Bulletin* 10: 133–136.

METTAM, C. (1983) An estuarine mudflat re-surveyed after 45 years. *Proceedings 17th European Marine Biological Symposium, Brest, France 1982*. pp.137–140.

MIGUS, S. & MOORE, C. (2002) Rocky Shore Survey of Sherkin Island 1981–2000. Sherkin Island Marine Station (Unpublished report).

MYERS, A. 2002. (Ed.) *New Survey of Clare Island. Volume 3: Marine intertidal ecology.* Royal Irish Academy, Ireland.

MOORE, P.G. & R. SEED (1985) (Eds) *The Ecology of Rocky Coasts.* Hodder and Stoughton.

MOYSE, J. & NELSON-SMITH, A. (1963) Zonation of animals and plants on rocky shores around Dale, Pembrokeshire. *Field Studies* 1 (5): 1–31.

MYERS, A.A., CROSS T.F. & SOUTHGATE, T. (1978) Bantry Bay Survey: First Annual Report. University College Cork, 24 pp.

MYERS, A.A., SOUTHGATE, T. & CROSS, T.F. (1980a) Distinguishing the effects of oil pollution from natural cyclical phenomena on the biota of Bantry Bay, Ireland. *Marine Pollution Bulletin* 11: 204–207.

MYERS, A.A., SOUTHGATE, T. & WILSON, K. (1980b) Bantry Bay Survey, Final Report. University College Cork. (Unpublished) 210 pp.

NELSON-SMITH (1967) Marine Biology of Milford Haven: The distribution of littoral plants and animals. *Field Studies* 2 (4): 435–477.

ORTON, J.H. (1920) Sea Temperature, breeding and distribution in marine animals. *Journal of the Marine Biological Association of the United Kingdom* 12: 339–366.

ORTON (1928) Observations on *Patella vulgata*. Part I. Sex-phenomena, breeding and shell-growth. *Journal of the Marine Biological Association of the United Kingdom* 15: 851–862.

ORTON, J.H. SOUTHWARD, A.J. & DODD, J.M. (1956) Studies on the biology of Limpets. II The breeding of *Patella vulgata* L. in Britain. *Journal of the Marine Biological Association of the United Kingdom* 35: 149–176.

PALMER, H. (1986) Rainfall of Sherkin Island 1973-1984. *Bulletin of Sherkin Island,* No. 5.

POWELL. H. (1957) Studies in the genus *Fucus* L. I. *Fucus distichus* L. emend. Powell. *Journal of the Marine Biological Association of the United Kingdom* 36: 407–432.

RAFFAELLI, D.G. (1982) Recent ecological research on some European species of *Littorina. Journal of Molluscan Studies* 48: 342–354.

RATCLIFF, J. (1999) Changes in the Community Structure of the Rocky Shore in Dunmanus Bay, as indicated by the changing abundance of fourteen selected species. Sherkin Island Marine Station (Unpublished report).

RENOUF, L. (1931) Preliminary work of a new biological station (Lough Ine, Co. Cork, I.F.S.) *Journal of Ecology* 19 (2): 410–438.

REID, D.G. (1996) *Systematics and Evolution of Littorina.* Ray Society, London, UK.

REILLY, T.A. & GRAHAM, J.R. (1976) The Stratigraphy of the Roaringwater Bay area of south-west County Cork. *Geological Survey of Ireland*, Bulletin 2: 1-13.

RODEN, C.M. , RYAN, F. & LENNON, T.J. (1980) Observations on the 1978 red tide in Roaringwater Bay, Co. Cork. *Journal of Sherkin Island* 1 (1): 105–118.

RODEN, C.M., LENNON, H.J., MOONEY, E., LEAHY, P., & LART, W. (1981) Red tides, water stratification and phytoplankton species succession around Sherkin Island, south-west Ireland, in 1979. *Journal of Sherkin Island* 1 (2): 50–68.

ROYAL IRISH ACADEMY (1915). *Clare Island Survey Parts 1-68. Proceedings of the Royal Irish Academy Volume XXXI.* Hodges, Figgis & Co., Ltd. Dublin, Ireland.

RUBIO, A., BLAIR, J., GUPTA, A.S., KOWALIK, R., McCOY, C., PRESTNEY, M., REDMAN, K. & SWAYNE, R. (2000) The occurrence of marine faunal fatality in Dunmanus Bay and Roaringwater Bay, 2000. Sherkin Island Marine Station (Unpublished report).

SCHONBECK, M.W. & NORTON, T. (1980) Factors controlling the lower limits of fucoid algae on the shore. *Journal of Experimental Marine Biology and Ecology* 43: 131–150.

SOUTHWARD, A.J. (1953) The ecology of some rocky shores in the south of the Isle of Man. *Proceedings and Transactions of the Liverpool Biological Society* 59: 1–50.

SOUTHWARD, A.J. (1964) Limpet grazing and the control of vegetation on rocky shores. In Crisp, D.J. (ed) *Grazing in terrestrial and marine environments.* Blackwell, Oxford. pp. 265–273.

SOUTHWARD, A.J. (1976) On the taxonomic status and distribution of *Chthamalus stellatus* (Cirripedia) in the north-east Atlantic region with a key to the common intertidal barnacles of Britain. *Journal of the Marine Biological Association of the United Kingdom* 56: 1007–1028.

SOUTHWARD, A.J. & SOUTHWARD, E.C. (1978) Recolonisation of rocky shores in Cornwall after use of toxic dispersants to clean up the Torrey Canyon spill. *Journal of the Fisheries Research Board of Canada* 35: 682–706.

STEPHENSON, T.A. & STEPHENSON, A. (1949) The universal features of zonation between tidemarks on rocky coasts. *Journal of Ecology* 38: 289–305.

STEPHENSON, T.A. & STEPHENSON, A. (1972) *Life between the Tidemarks on Rocky Shores.* W.H. Freeman and Company. San Francisco. 425 pp.

SWEENEY, J., BRERETON, T., BYRNE, C., CHARLTON, R., EMBLOW, C., FEALY, R., HOLDEN, N., JONES, M., DONNELLY, A., MOORE, S., PURSER, P., BYRNE, K., FARRELL, E., MAYES, E., MINCHIN, D., WILSON, J. & WILSON, J. (2003) *Climate Change – Scenarios & Impacts for Ireland (2000-LS-5.2.1-M1) Final Report.* EPA, Wexford, Ireland.

TAYLOR, S. & HUNTER, J. (1996) A survey of the rocky shores of West Cork 1995–1996. Sherkin Island Marine Station (Unpublished report).

TODD, C.D. (1981) The ecology of nudibranch molluscs. *Oceanography and Marine Biology Annual Review* 19: 141–234.

WOOD, E. (1988) *Sealife of Britain and Ireland.* Immel Publishing, London, UK.

APPENDIX 1:

Seashore Survey Recorders & Contributors
Sherkin Island Marine Station 1975–2000

(Monthly & Annual Rocky Shore Surveys)

Ackland, L.
Adams, R.
Alcock, R.
Anon, J.
Anon, O.
Ashworth, J.
Barker, M.
Baskerville, N.
Beazley, D.
Bellemy, N.
Bennett, A.
Bird, S.
Bishop, G.
Blair, J.
Blake, P.
Bolger-Hynes, E.
Boswell, G.
Bowles, N.
Brockhouse, J.
Browne, R.
Browning, S.
Budd, T.
Challinor, H.
Clark, J.
Clarke, K.
Clements, A.D.
Collier, L.
Collins, D.
Colwell, P.
Coope, C.
Cooper, R.
Coughlan, S.
Cowap, H.
Crowe, W.
Crowley, J.
Cullinan, U.
Cullinane, J.
Cummins, V.
Daley, L.
Duffy, S.
Duncan, K.
Edwards, A.
Edwards, S.
Egerton, M.
Ellis, I.
Elmsworth, J.
Eustace, P.
Farnell, T.
Fennelly, S.
Ferris, J.
Fok-Seang, R.
Foley, T.
Fuchs, P.
Futter, J.
Gaffney, D.
Garwood, R.
Gatland, P.
Gillham, K.
Granville, G.
Gray, J.
Gross, J.
Gwenin, S.
Hall, G.
Harding, M.
Harvey, P.
Hatch, R.
Hearne, D.
Henton-Jones, D.
Higgs, A.
Hill, R.
Holland, C.
Hough, N.
Hubbard, T.
Hunter, F.
Hunter, J.
Johns, R.
Jones, C.
Jones, M.
Kelleher, C.
Kelly, G.
Kelly, S.
Kingston, M.
Kirby, M.
Kroeger, K.
Layden, S.
Lane, I.
Leahy, P.
Leahy, P.
Lennon, J.
Leslie, M.
Lu, T.
Lutyens, B.
MacIntosh, F.
MacLean, L.
Magennis, B.
Malicheck, M.
Markham, D.
Marshall, S.
Martin, A.
McCarthy, J.
McCarthy, P.
McCoy, C.
McDevitt, A.M.
McMahon, P.
Measures, P.M.
Michael, C.
Milliken, W.
Milner, B.
Moffatt, J.
Mountjoy, C.
Moynagh, M.
Mullins, F.
Mundy, R.
Munroe, S.
Murphy, A.
Murphy, E.
Murphy, R.
Murphy, S.
Neary, T.
Netzer, J.
Nikitik, C
Norman, M.
O'Brien, A.
O'Brien, A.
O'Flynn, C.
O'Leary, C.
Oliver, T.
O'Mahony, F.
O'Shea, M.
O'Sullivan, O.
Pagels, P.
Palmer, H.
Parker, T.A.
Partridge, J.
Pater, C.
Phillips, C.
Pittman, S.
Powell, Sr. M.
Prestney, M.
Pritchard, S.
Quirke, M.
Ratcliff, J.
Redman, K.
Reid, G.
Reid, S.
Roberton, E.
Robertson, C.
Roksby, F.
Rooney, C.
Ross, J.
Rubio, A.
Russell, C
Ruttledge, M.
Ryan, S.
Ryan, T.
Sampson, B.
Sen Gupta, A.
Shingles, A.
Shockley, J.
Shreeve, R.
Silvester, P.
Smart, S.
Smith, P.
Smithies, B.
Soroka, A
Squires, K.
Squirrel, N.
Stammers, B.
Stewart, A.
Sunderland, J.
Swayne, R.G.
Tattersall, V.
Taylor, P.
Taylor, S.
Thorp, D.
Tinsley, P.
Tomlin, H.
Tomlin, M.
Torres, E.
Vaughan, D.
Veal, R.
Vinyeta, E.
Waby, P.
Wade, T.
Walker, T.
Walsh, S.M.
Watson, K.
Wheelock, C.
Whelan, P.
White, S.
Whitehead, J.
Whittle, G.
Wickens, J.
Wilkinson, A.
Wood, A.
Wood, J.
Wood, P.
Woodham, A.
Worsfold, T.
Young, M.

APPENDIX 2:

The Plant and Animal Kingdoms of the Seashore

The animal and plant kingdoms are divided in major phyla (animals) and divisions (plants). Each of these categories is then subdivided into three or more levels, according to the similarity of features, until ultimately a unique species is identified. The table below lists only those that are mentioned in this book and is intended as a simple guide for the reader who is new to seashore biology. Hopefully it will help to put these species into perspective but seashore guides and identification keys should be consulted for a more indepth study.

PHYLUM/DIVISION		DESCRIPTION
GREEN ALGAE (Chlorophycota)	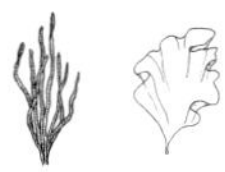	Multicellular algae, often small and delicate; can be finely branched or flat and blade-like.
BROWN ALGAE (Chromophycota)	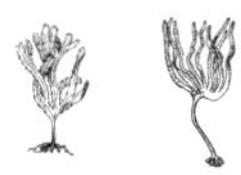	Multicellular algae containing a green brown accessory pigment for photosynthesis; can grow large, e.g. fucoids, or very large, e.g. kelps.
RED ALGAE (Rhodophytcota)	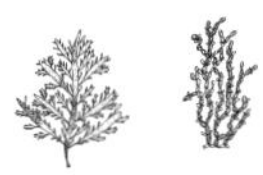	Delicate multicellular algae with a red accessory pigment for photosynthesis; finely branched or flat and blade-like.
LICHEN		Fungi with a symbiotic algal association. Thin covering on rock or with small, upright branches.
SPERMATOPHYTA together with BRYOPHYTA (e.g. grass, flowers, moss)		Higher plants which include gymnosperms (e.g. mosses, conifers) and angiosperms (e.g. deciduous trees, flowers and grasses).
PORIFERA (sponges)		Simple animal colonies whose shape varies from a thin encrusting layer on rocks or seaweeds, to a branching upright, vase-shaped or massive structure. Food is filtered from the water inside the body.
CNIDARIA (hydroids, sea anemones, corals, jellyfish)		Soft-bodied, simple, flower-like animals with stinging tentacles around the mouth.
	ANTHOZOA (sea anemones) 	Carnivorous flower-like animals, occurring as individual polyps, e.g. beadlet anemone, or in colonies, with a hard skeleton, e.g. corals.
	HYDROZOA (sea firs) 	Cnidarians that live in a colony or group, often forming a branching structure of polyps which attach to rocks, seaweed shells.

PHYLUM/DIVISION			DESCRIPTION
PLATYHELMINTHE (flatworms)			Dorsoventrally flattened unsegmented worms, which may be free living or parasitic.
NEMERTEA (ribbon worms)			Unsegmented worms, round in cross section.
ANNELIDA (segmented worms)			Worms with segmented bodies.
	POLYCHAETA (polychaete worms) 		Segmented marine annelid worms with bristle-like structures known as setae, on each segment.
		CIRRATULIDAE 	Sedentary polychaetes that feed on detritus. Prominent red tentacles in the head region.
		SERPULIDAE 	Polychaete worms which secrete calcareous tubes. The fan of tentacles around the head is visible when covered with sea water.
		TEREBELLIDAE 	Tube dwelling segmented worms, in which the body regions are easily differentiated.; many tentacles in the head region.
ARTHROPODA (e.g. crabs, insects (hexapoda), spiders)			Segmented animals with tough exoskeletons and numerous paired limbs; well-developed head.
	CHELICERATA (e.g. spiders) 		Arthropods with two major body regions and four pairs of legs. Front appendages with scissor-like ends. Found occasionally on the shore.
	HEXAPODA (e.g. mites, beetles) 		Arthropods with six legs and three distinctive body parts (head, thorax and abdomen); air breathing. Found occasionally on the shore.
	CRUSTACEA (e.g. crabs, shrimp, lobsters, sandhoppers, sea slaters)  		Segmented body, divided into head, thorax and abdomen; antennae and jaws on the head.
		AMPHIPODA (e.g. gammarids) 	Small crustaceans that have laterally flattened bodies and highly specialised limbs - antennae, walking legs, jumping legs, swimming legs etc.., e.g. sandhoppers.
		IOSPODA 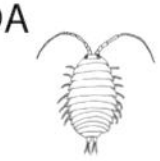	An order of Crustacea that includes woodlice and sea slaters. Flattened from front to back, eyes not stalked.
		CIRRIPEDIA (barnacles) 	Adults very different from other Crustacea. Soft body enclosed in calcareous plates, through which feeding legs emerge at high tide.
		DECAPODA (crabs) 	Head and thorax fused and protect by a hard carapace. Five pairs of walking legs; five pairs of swimming legs.

PHYLUM/DIVISION		DESCRIPTION
MOLLUSCA (chitons, snails, sea-slugs, bivalves and squid)		Soft bodied animals usually protected by a shell. They have an unsegmented body, a well developed head, a radula and a muscular foot. Most have gills.
	GASTROPODA (e.g. snails, whelks) 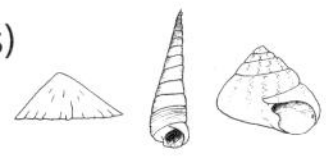	Molluscs with a single usually coiled shell. Move freely on muscular foot in search of food – algal particules.
	BIVALVIA (e.g. mussels, clams) 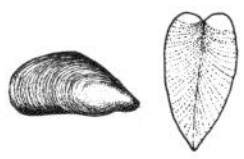	Molluscs with two shells (valves) joined by a strong hinge. Anchored to rocks or burrowed in sand. Sea water is filtered by the body to extract food.
	CHITONA 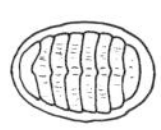	Molluscs with a shell that consists of several plates which lock together. Capable of curling up into a ball.
	NUDIBRANCHIA (e.g. sea hares, sea slugs) 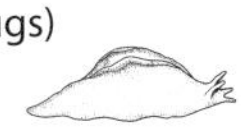	Molluscs that have no obvious shell (hidden or absent) and are often brightly coloured and beautiful; often carnivorous.
BRYOZOA or ECTOPROCTA (sea mats)		Small colonial animals living in individual capsules. Mouth surrounded by tentacles which emerge to filter sea water for food.
ECHINODERMATA (feather stars, starfish, brittlestars, sea urchins)	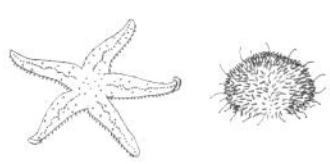	Spiny skinned (though spines may not always be obvious) marine animals which travel on tube feet and have radially symmetrical bodies. The mouth is usually on the underside of the body.
CHORDATA (sea squirts, star ascidians, fish)		Organisms with a single, dorsal nerve cord and a a notochord - a stiff flexible rod of fluid filled cells giving support to the body.
	TUNICATA (sea squirts) 	Live attached to rocks or other organisms. Can be single or colonial; each individual is very simple and passes a current of water through the body to extract food and oxygen.
	OSTEICHTHYES (bony fish) 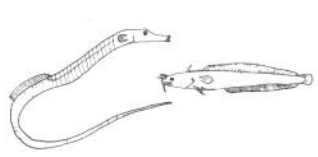	Free-swimming vertebrate animals with a bony skeleton; breathe through gills.

APPENDIX 3:

SPECIES PRESENT AT THE SEVEN SHERKIN MONTHLY SITES 1981–2000

Species present in the period 1981–2000 for each of the seven Sherkin Monthly sites are listed here. All records refer only to species observed within quadrats on the transect lines. We have made no record of species present elsewhere on the shores. Only the stations where data were collected every month are included. (Data from the lower stations, which were not accessed on a regular basis are included in Appendix 4.)

It should be noted that where an animal or seaweed is not identified down to species level in its analysis and graphical presentation, the data used in the graph calculations are a combination of all specific and generic records. For example at Drolain Point (p. 245) the records for *Enteromorpha compressa*, *E. intestinalis*, *E. linza* and *E.* spp are combined in the graphs presented on p.76.

In a very small number of cases the density of a species is so low that it appears as zero on the graph, whereas a presence is shown in this Appendix.

POULACURRA (STATIONS 1–14)

PHYLUM/DIVISION	SPECIES	1981	1982	1983	1984	1985	1986	1987	1988	1989	1990	1991	1992	1993	1994	1995	1996	1997	1998	1999	2000
GREEN ALGAE	*Bryopsis plumosa*				•							•		•							
(CHLOROPHYCOTA)	*Bryopsis* spp.													•							
	Chaetomorpha linum							•		•										•	•
	Chaetomorpha spp.		•										•	•	•	•		•	•	•	
	Cladophora rupestris			•	•	•		•	•	•		•									•
	Cladophora spp.	•	•	•			•		•	•								•		•	
	Enteromorpha compressa			•	•	•				•	•										
	Enteromorpha intestinalis					•				•	•	•				•			•		•
	Enteromorpha linza			•																	
	Enteromorpha spp.	•	•	•	•	•	•	•	•	•	•	•	•	•	•	•	•	•	•	•	•
	Spongomorpha arcta								•	•	•			•							
	Spongomorpha spp.										•	•	•	•	•		•				
	Ulothrix flacca																				•
	Ulva lactuca	•	•	•	•	•	•	•	•	•	•	•	•	•	•	•	•	•	•	•	•
	Urospora spp.				•	•															
BROWN ALGAE	*Alaria esculenta*	•		•	•	•	•	•	•		•	•			•	•					
(CHROMOPHYCOTA)	*Chorda filum*										•										
	Cladostephus spongiosus							•													
	Dictyota dichotoma	•									•	•									
	Ectocarpus siliculosus								•	•				•	•		•				
	Ectocarpaceae	•	•	•	•	•	•				•	•	•	•	•	•	•	•		•	•
	Elachista spp.	•	•							•	•	•		•							
	Fucus spp. sporelings																				•
	Himanthalia elongata	•	•	•	•	•		•		•											
	Laminaria digitata	•	•	•	•	•	•	•	•	•	•	•	•	•	•	•					
	Laminaria saccharina							•	•	•											
	Laminaria spp.		•						•							•	•				
	Laminaria spp. sporelings										•										

POULACURRA (STATIONS 1–14)

PHYLUM/DIVISION	SPECIES	1981	1982	1983	1984	1985	1986	1987	1988	1989	1990	1991	1992	1993	1994	1995	1996	1997	1998	1999	2000
	Leathesia difformis							•	•												
	Pelvetia canaliculata												•								
	Punctaria latifolia				•															•	
	Punctaria plantaginea									•											
	Ralfsia verrucosa		•	•	•			•					•	•		•		•		•	•
	Scytosiphon lomentaria	•	•	•	•	•	•	•		•	•	•	•		•		•	•	•	•	•
	Stictyosiphon tortilis										•										
	Stictyosiphon spp.			•																	
RED ALGAE (RHODOPHYCOTA)	*Aglaothamnion hookeri*																	•			
	Aglaothamnion sepositum			•				•	•					•	•		•				
	Aglaothamnion spp.																			•	
	Audouinella spp.	•	•													•					
	Boergeseniella thuyoides								•				•								
	Brongniartella byssoides								•												
	Callithamnion corymbosum							•													
	Callithamnion tetricum													•						•	
	Callithamnion spp.	•	•	•	•		•	•			•	•	•	•		•				•	
	Catenella caespitosa			•															•	•	
	Ceramium botryocarpum																	•			•
	Ceramium ciliatum															•	•	•	•	•	
	Ceramium echionotum																		•		
	Ceramium flaccidum																		•		
	Ceramium gaditanum				•																
	Ceramium pallidum																•				
	Ceramium rubrum	•		•	•			•	•	•	•		•	•	•	•	•	•		•	•
	Ceramium shuttleworthianum	•	•	•	•	•							•	•	•	•	•	•	•	•	•
	Ceramium spp.	•	•	•	•	•	•	•	•	•	•	•		•		•	•			•	
	Chondrus crispus	•	•	•	•	•		•	•	•	•	•			•						
	Corallina officinalis	•	•	•	•	•	•	•	•	•	•	•	•	•	•	•	•	•	•	•	•
	Corallina spp.															•		•			
	Cryptopleura ramosa									•											
	Dumontia contorta							•	•						•	•	•	•			
	Gastroclonium ovatum			•								•									
	Gelidium pusillum				•																
	Gelidium spinosum			•	•				•	•											
	Griffithsia spp.																			•	
	Heterosiphonia plumosa									•							•				
	Hildenbrandia rubra			•				•		•	•	•		•	•	•	•	•	•	•	•
	Hildenbrandia spp.	•	•	•	•	•	•	•	•	•	•	•	•	•	•	•				•	
	Laurencia obtusa								•		•								•	•	
	Laurencia spp.		•																	•	
	Lithothamnia	•	•	•	•	•	•	•	•	•	•	•	•	•	•	•	•	•	•	•	•
	Lomentaria articulata	•		•	•			•	•	•	•	•	•	•	•		•		•	•	
	Lomentaria clavellosa	•	•	•	•	•						•	•	•	•	•	•			•	
	Lomentaria spp.		•								•										
	Mastocarpus stellatus	•	•	•	•	•		•	•	•	•	•	•	•		•					
	Membranoptera alata							•	•												
	Mesophyllum lichenoides																				•
	Mesophyllum spp.																				•
	Nemalion helminthoides				•			•	•			•			•						
	Nitophyllum punctatum													•							
	Osmundea pinnatifida	•	•	•	•	•		•	•	•	•	•	•	•	•	•	•	•	•	•	•
	Palmaria palmata	•	•		•	•		•	•	•		•		•						•	
	Plocamium cartilagineum							•					•								
	Plumaria plumosa		•											•							

POULACURRA (STATIONS 1–14)

PHYLUM/DIVISION	SPECIES	1981	1982	1983	1984	1985	1986	1987	1988	1989	1990	1991	1992	1993	1994	1995	1996	1997	1998	1999	2000
RED ALGAE (RHODOPHYCOTA)	*Polysiphonia atlantica*																•				
	Polysiphonia brodiei			•	•				•							•		•		•	
	Polysiphonia denudata																			•	•
	Polysiphonia elongata												•	•							•
	Polysiphonia fibrata			•											•						
	Polysiphonia fibrillosa			•																	
	Polysiphonia fucoides																		•		
	Polysiphonia lanosa										•										
	Polysiphonia nigra								•												
	Polysiphonia stricta			•	•	•															•
	Polysiphonia spp.	•	•	•	•	•	•	•	•		•	•			•	•				•	
	Porphyra leucosticta			•																	
	Porphyra umbilicalis	•		•	•	•	•	•	•	•	•	•	•		•	•	•	•		•	
	Porphyra spp.		•	•			•					•	•								
	Pterocladia capillacea								•												
	Pterosiphonia complanata				•																
	Ptilota gunneri							•													
	Rhodymenia pseudopalmata							•													
LICHEN	*Caloplaca marina*													•							
	Caloplaca spp.												•								
	Lecanora atra								•		•		•								
	Lichina confinis						•	•	•	•	•	•								•	
	Lichina pygmaea	•	•	•	•	•	•	•	•	•	•	•	•	•	•	•	•	•	•	•	•
	Lichina spp.											•									
	Verrucaria maura	•	•	•	•	•	•	•	•	•	•	•	•	•	•	•	•	•	•	•	•
	Verrucaria mucosa	•	•	•	•	•	•	•	•		•	•	•	•		•	•	•	•	•	•
	Verrucaria spp.	•																			
PORIFERA	*Halichondria panicea*			•	•	•		•					•								
	Halichondria spp.			•																	
	Hymeniacidon perleve		•									•									
	Hymeniacidon sanguinea				•	•															
	Hymeniacidon spp.	•																			
	Myxilla incrustans							•	•		•	•			•			•			
	Myxilla spp.															•					
CNIDARIA	*Actinothoë sphyrodeta*						•														
	Coryne spp.				•																
	Dynamena pumila							•				•									
	Obelia geniculata			•				•													
	Plumularia setacea		•	•	•																
	Tubularia larynx		•																		
	Actinia equina	•	•	•	•	•	•	•	•	•	•	•	•	•	•	•	•	•	•	•	•
	Anemonia viridis															•			•		
	Aulactinia verrucosa		•		•			•			•	•	•						•	•	
	Cereus pedunculatus		•																		•
	Corynactis viridis			•	•	•															
	Sagartia elegans	•	•	•	•	•	•	•	•	•	•	•	•	•	•	•		•	•	•	•
	Sagartia troglodytes		•	•				•													
	Sagartia spp.			•																	
	Urticina felina	•	•		•		•	•		•	•	•	•								

POULACURRA (STATIONS 1–14)

PHYLUM/DIVISION	SPECIES	1981	1982	1983	1984	1985	1986	1987	1988	1989	1990	1991	1992	1993	1994	1995	1996	1997	1998	1999	2000
ANNELIDA	*Eulalia viridis*	•		•			•	•	•	•	•	•	•	•	•	•	•	•		•	•
	Harmothoe impar											•									
	Hydroides norvegica					•															
	Pomatoceros triqueter		•	•	•			•	•	•	•	•									
	Spirorbis rupestris		•																		
	Spirorbis spp.				•			•	•											•	
CHELICERATA	Acari spp.								•				•	•	•					•	•
HEXAPODA	*Lipura maritima*	•	•	•			•	•	•	•	•	•	•	•	•			•	•	•	•
	Petrobius maritimus												•								
CRUSTACEA	Barnacles	•	•	•	•	•	•	•	•	•	•	•	•	•	•	•	•	•	•	•	•
	Barnacle spat	•	•	•	•				•	•	•	•	•	•	•	•	•	•	•	•	•
	Chthamalus stellatus				•											•					
	Chthamalus spp.	•	•	•	•	•	•	•	•				•	•	•	•	•	•	•	•	•
	Elminius modestus												•			•			•	•	•
	Semibalanus balanoides	•	•	•	•	•	•	•	•				•	•	•	•	•	•	•	•	•
	Verruca stroemia		•		•																
	Cancer pagurus			•																	
	Caprella linearis				•																
	Carcinus maenas			•				•													
	Gammarus spp.		•	•				•	•			•	•	•					•	•	•
	Idotea spp.											•		•						•	
	Ligia oceanica			•			•	•	•	•	•	•	•	•			•	•		•	•
	Talitrus saltator							•													
MOLLUSCA	*Aeolidia papillosa*		•																		
	Archidoris pseudoargus							•													
	Buccinum undatum											•									
	Calliostoma zizyphinum				•																
	Chiton spp.																			•	
	Gibbula cineraria		•		•																
	Helcion pellucidum	•	•	•	•	•		•	•	•	•	•		•							•
	Hinia reticulata																		•		
	Littorina littorea			•	•	•			•	•		•	•					•			•
	Littorina neglecta		•	•	•	•															
	Littorina obtusata										•										
	Littorina saxatilis	•	•	•	•	•	•	•	•	•	•	•	•	•	•	•	•	•	•	•	•
	Littorina spp.	•																			
	Melarhaphe neritoides	•	•	•	•	•	•	•	•	•	•	•	•	•	•	•	•	•	•	•	•
	Modiolus barbatus																		•		
	Mytilus edulis	•	•	•	•	•	•	•	•	•	•	•	•	•	•	•	•	•	•	•	•
	Mytilus spp.			•																	
	Nucella (eggs)	•						•	•	•	•	•	•			•	•	•	•		
	Nucella lapillus	•	•	•	•	•	•	•	•	•	•	•	•	•	•	•	•	•	•	•	•
	Patella spp.	•	•	•	•	•	•	•	•	•	•	•	•	•	•	•	•	•	•	•	•
	Runcina coronata							•													
BRYOZOA	*Bowerbankia imbricata*			•	•																
	Cellepora pumicosa			•																	

POULACURRA (STATIONS 1–14)

PHYLUM/DIVISION	SPECIES	1981	1982	1983	1984	1985	1986	1987	1988	1989	1990	1991	1992	1993	1994	1995	1996	1997	1998	1999	2000
BRYOZOA	*Celleporella hyalina*				•																
	Celleporina spp.		•																		
	Electra pilosa		•	•	•	•		•													
	Flustrellidra hispida							•	•			•									•
	Membranipora membranacea		•		•				•	•											
	Schizoporella unicornis				•																
	Umbonula littoralis					•		•													
	Umbonula spp.							•	•												
ECHINODERMATA	*Asterias rubens*	•		•	•					•											
CHORDATA	*Botryllus schlosseri*		•					•													
	Blennius spp.											•									
	Lipophrys pholis														•					•	•

DROLAIN POINT (STATIONS 1–14)

PHYLUM/DIVISION	SPECIES	1981	1982	1983	1984	1985	1986	1987	1988	1989	1990	1991	1992	1993	1994	1995	1996	1997	1998	1999	2000
GREEN ALGAE	*Bryopsis hypnoides*																	•			
(CHLOROPHYCOTA)	*Chaetomorpha linum*												•	•				•		•	•
	Chaetomorpha mediterranea																		•		•
	Chaetomorpha spp.										•		•	•	•	•		•	•	•	
	Cladophora albida																	•			
	Cladophora laetevirens																	•			
	Cladophora rupestris		•	•	•			•	•	•	•	•	•		•	•		•	•		•
	Cladophora sericea																	•			
	Cladophora spp.	•	•	•	•	•	•			•	•	•	•	•	•	•			•	•	
	Codium tomentosum				•				•	•			•			•					•
	Derbesia marina																	•			
	Derbesia spp.																				•
	Enteromorpha compressa			•	•	•	•			•											
	Enteromorpha intestinalis					•				•		•	•						•		•
	Enteromorpha linza																		•		
	Enteromorpha spp.	•	•	•		•	•	•	•	•	•	•	•	•	•	•	•	•	•	•	•
	Rhizoclonium tortuosum																				•
	Spongomorpha aeruginosa												•								
	Spongomorpha arcta								•	•	•							•			
	Spongomorpha spp.										•	•	•		•		•			•	
	Ulva lactuca	•	•	•	•	•	•	•	•	•	•	•	•	•	•	•	•	•	•	•	•
	Ulva spp.					•							•								
	Urospora spp.				•	•															
BROWN ALGAE	*Alaria esculenta*			•			•	•													
(CHROMOPHYCOTA)	*Ascophyllum nodosum*									•											
	Asperococcus fistulosus					•															
	Asperococcus spp.												•							•	
	Bifurcaria bifurcata															•					
	Dictyota dichotoma	•	•	•	•	•		•	•	•	•	•	•	•	•		•	•		•	•
	Dictyota spp.							•													
	Ectocarpus siliculosus				•			•		•	•									•	
	Ectocarpaceae	•	•	•	•	•	•	•			•	•	•	•	•	•	•	•	•	•	•
	Elachista fucicola								•												
	Elachista spp.		•							•	•			•						•	•
	Eudesme virescens																	•			
	Fucus serratus		•	•	•	•	•	•	•	•	•	•	•	•	•	•			•		
	Fucus spiralis					•				•				•				•	•		•
	Fucus vesiculosus	•	•			•				•			•	•					•		
	Fucus spp.	•		•		•						•				•			•		•
	Fucus spp. sporelings	•	•											•	•	•	•	•	•		•
	Halopteris filicina									•											
	Himanthalia elongata	•	•	•	•	•	•	•	•	•	•	•	•	•	•	•	•	•	•	•	
	Laminaria digitata		•	•	•	•	•	•	•	•	•	•	•	•		•		•	•	•	•
	Laminaria saccharina			•		•	•	•			•				•						
	Laminaria spp.		•		•			•	•		•		•		•	•	•	•		•	
	Laminaria spp. sporelings	•		•															•	•	
	Leathesia difformis		•	•	•	•	•	•	•	•	•	•	•	•		•	•	•	•	•	•
	Pelvetia canaliculata	•	•	•	•	•	•	•	•	•	•	•	•	•	•	•	•	•	•	•	•
	Petrospongium berkeleyi			•							•										
	Punctaria latifolia										•					•				•	
	Ralfsia verrucosa	•	•	•	•			•					•	•	•		•	•	•	•	•
	Scytosiphon lomentaria	•	•	•	•	•	•		•	•	•	•	•	•	•	•	•	•	•	•	•
	Sphacelaria cirrosa	•									•										
	Spongonema tomentosum										•										

DROLAIN POINT (STATIONS 1–14)

PHYLUM/DIVISION	SPECIES	1981	1982	1983	1984	1985	1986	1987	1988	1989	1990
RED ALGAE	*Aglaothamnion hookeri*										
(RHODOPHYCOTA)	*Aglaothamnion sepositum*										
	Audouinella spp.	•									
	Boergeseniella thuyoides				•						
	Callithamnion tetricum										
	Callithamnion spp.			•						•	•
	Catenella caespitosa	•				•					
	Ceramium botryocarpum										
	Ceramium ciliatum				•	•					
	Ceramium diaphanum										
	Ceramium echionotum										
	Ceramium gaditanum						•				
	Ceramium pallidum										
	Ceramium rubrum				•	•	•	•	•	•	•
	Ceramium shuttleworthianum	•	•	•	•	•					
	Ceramium siliquosum										
	Ceramium strictum										
	Ceramium spp.	•	•	•	•	•	•	•	•	•	•
	Chondracanthus acicularis										
	Chondrus crispus		•	•		•	•	•	•	•	•
	Choreocolax polysiphoniae								•		
	Corallina officinalis	•	•	•	•	•	•	•	•	•	•
	Corallina spp.										•
	Cryptopleura ramosa	•									
	Dilsea carnosa										
	Dumontia contorta			•	•			•	•		•
	Gastroclonium ovatum				•	•		•			
	Gastroclonium spp.	•									
	Gelidium pulchellum									•	
	Gelidium pusillum										
	Gelidium spinosum							•		•	
	Gelidium spp.	•		•						•	•
	Gloiosiphonia capillaris	•									
	Griffithsia spp.										
	Halurus spp.										
	Heterosiphonia plumosa										•
	Hildenbrandia rubra				•	•				•	•
	Hildenbrandia spp.	•	•	•	•	•	•	•	•	•	•
	Laurencia obtusa						•		•	•	•
	Laurencia spp.		•					•	•	•	
	Lithothamnia	•	•	•	•	•	•	•	•	•	•
	Lomentaria articulata	•	•	•	•	•	•	•	•	•	•
	Lomentaria clavellosa		•	•	•	•	•	•			
	Lomentaria orcadensis					•					
	Lomentaria spp.					•				•	•
	Mastocarpus stellatus	•	•	•	•	•	•	•	•	•	•
	Membranoptera alata						•				
	Mesophyllum lichenoides			•							
	Nemalion helminthoides	•	•	•	•	•	•	•	•	•	•
	Osmundea hybrida			•		•		•	•		
	Osmundea pinnatifida	•	•	•	•	•	•	•	•	•	•
	Palmaria palmata	•		•					•		
	Phycodrys rubens										
	Plocamium cartilagineum										•
	Plumaria plumosa							•		•	
	Polysiphonia atlantica			•	•						
	Polysiphonia brodiei			•	•	•			•		

PHYLUM/DIVISION	SPECIES	1991	1992	1993	1994	1995	1996	1997	1998	1999	2000
RED ALGAE	*Aglaothamnion hookeri*							•			
(RHODOPHYCOTA)	*Aglaothamnion sepositum*						•				
	Audouinella spp.							•			
	Boergeseniella thuyoides							•			
	Callithamnion tetricum			•	•						
	Callithamnion spp.	•	•								
	Catenella caespitosa								•		•
	Ceramium botryocarpum						•	•	•		•
	Ceramium ciliatum	•		•	•	•	•	•	•	•	
	Ceramium diaphanum							•			
	Ceramium echionotum					•			•		
	Ceramium gaditanum							•			
	Ceramium pallidum						•			•	•
	Ceramium rubrum		•	•	•	•	•	•			•
	Ceramium shuttleworthianum		•	•	•	•	•	•	•	•	•
	Ceramium siliquosum							•			
	Ceramium strictum							•			•
	Ceramium spp.	•	•	•	•	•	•			•	
	Chondracanthus acicularis					•					
	Chondrus crispus	•	•	•			•		•	•	•
	Choreocolax polysiphoniae										
	Corallina officinalis	•	•	•	•	•	•	•	•	•	•
	Corallina spp.			•		•					
	Cryptopleura ramosa										
	Dilsea carnosa										•
	Dumontia contorta	•		•	•	•	•	•	•	•	
	Gastroclonium ovatum										
	Gastroclonium spp.										
	Gelidium pulchellum					•					
	Gelidium pusillum								•		
	Gelidium spinosum								•	•	
	Gelidium spp.			•		•	•				•
	Gloiosiphonia capillaris										
	Griffithsia spp.									•	•
	Halurus spp.	•									
	Heterosiphonia plumosa										•
	Hildenbrandia rubra	•	•	•	•	•	•	•	•	•	•
	Hildenbrandia spp.	•	•	•	•	•					
	Laurencia obtusa					•			•	•	
	Laurencia spp.								•		
	Lithothamnia	•	•	•	•	•	•	•	•	•	•
	Lomentaria articulata	•	•	•	•	•	•	•	•	•	•
	Lomentaria clavellosa	•			•	•					
	Lomentaria orcadensis										
	Lomentaria spp.										
	Mastocarpus stellatus	•	•	•	•	•	•	•	•	•	•
	Membranoptera alata							•			
	Mesophyllum lichenoides	•									•
	Nemalion helminthoides	•	•	•	•	•		•	•	•	•
	Osmundea hybrida				•						
	Osmundea pinnatifida	•	•	•	•	•	•	•	•	•	•
	Palmaria palmata	•	•		•	•		•		•	•
	Phycodrys rubens				•						
	Plocamium cartilagineum										
	Plumaria plumosa		•								
	Polysiphonia atlantica		•	•	•						•
	Polysiphonia brodiei				•	•		•		•	•

DROLAIN POINT (STATIONS 1–14)

PHYLUM/DIVISION	SPECIES	1981	1982	1983	1984	1985	1986	1987	1988	1989	1990	1991	1992	1993	1994	1995	1996	1997	1998	1999	2000
RED ALGAE (RHODOPHYCOTA)	*Polysiphonia denudata*																			•	
	Polysiphonia elongata							•	•				•	•	•					•	•
	Polysiphonia fibrata					•								•	•			•			
	Polysiphonia fibrillosa														•						•
	Polysiphonia fucoides			•				•	•									•			
	Polysiphonia harveyi																		•		
	Polysiphonia lanosa									•						•					
	Polysiphonia nigra			•																	•
	Polysiphonia simulans																		•		
	Polysiphonia stricta					•							•		•						
	Polysiphonia spp.	•	•	•	•	•	•	•	•	•	•	•			•		•		•	•	•
	Porphyra leucosticta												•								
	Porphyra umbilicalis	•	•	•	•	•	•	•	•	•	•	•	•	•	•	•	•	•	•	•	•
	Porphyra spp.			•			•	•		•	•		•								
	Pterosiphonia spp.					•															
	Rhodomela confervoides										•								•		
LICHEN	*Caloplaca marina*	•	•	•	•	•	•	•	•	•	•	•	•	•	•	•	•	•	•	•	•
	Caloplaca spp.					•							•								
	Lecanora atra	•	•		•	•		•		•	•	•	•	•		•	•	•	•	•	•
	Lecanora spp.					•	•					•									
	Lichina confinis	•	•	•	•	•	•	•	•	•	•	•	•	•	•	•	•	•	•	•	•
	Lichina pygmaea	•	•	•	•	•	•	•	•	•	•	•	•	•	•	•	•	•	•	•	•
	Lichina spp.											•									
	Ochrolechia parella								•							•	•		•		•
	Verrucaria maura	•	•	•	•	•	•	•	•	•	•	•	•	•	•	•	•	•	•	•	•
	Verrucaria mucosa	•	•	•	•	•	•	•	•		•	•	•	•	•	•	•	•	•	•	
	Verrucaria spp.	•																			
	Xanthoria parietina	•				•		•		•	•	•	•		•		•				•
BRYOPHYTA	Moss																		•		
SPERMATOPHYTA	*Armeria maritima*	•	•	•	•	•	•	•	•	•	•	•	•	•	•	•	•	•	•	•	•
	Plantago maritima																	•			
PORIFERA	*Halichondria panicea*		•				•	•	•	•	•	•				•		•	•		•
	Halichondria spp.												•								
	Hymeniacidon perleve				•	•		•	•												
	Hymeniacidon sanguinea		•	•																	•
	Hymeniacidon spp.	•	•	•		•	•					•									
	Leucosolenia complicata								•												
	Myxilla incrustans						•	•	•	•	•	•	•	•	•		•	•	•	•	•
	Myxilla spp.							•	•		•	•	•		•	•				•	
CNIDARIA	*Dynamena pumila*				•					•									•		
	Actinia equina	•	•	•	•	•	•	•	•	•	•	•	•	•	•	•	•	•	•	•	•
	Anemonia viridis					•				•		•				•				•	
	Aulactinia verrucosa	•		•	•		•	•		•				•				•	•	•	•
	Cereus pedunculatus	•	•	•	•	•		•			•		•		•		•			•	•
	Sagartia elegans	•	•	•	•	•	•	•	•		•	•	•		•			•		•	•
	Sagartia troglodytes		•	•		•														•	

DROLAIN POINT (STATIONS 1–14)

PHYLUM/DIVISION	SPECIES	1981	1982	1983	1984	1985	1986	1987	1988	1989	1990	1991	1992	1993	1994	1995	1996	1997	1998	1999	2000
CNIDARIA	*Sagartia* spp.					•	•	•		•											
	Urticina felina				•	•				•	•	•	•	•	•	•	•			•	•
NEMERTEA	*Lineus ruber*									•											
	Lineus spp.							•													
ANNELIDA	*Eulalia viridis*	•	•	•		•	•	•	•	•	•	•	•	•	•	•	•		•	•	•
	Hydroides norvegica				•					•											
	Nereis diversicolor				•																
	Pomatoceros triqueter	•	•	•	•	•	•	•	•	•			•	•		•					
	Pomatoceros spp.				•	•															
	Spirorbis spp.		•				•			•	•	•	•	•		•			•	•	
CHELICERATA	Acari spp.								•	•			•	•							•
HEXAPODA	*Lipura maritima*	•	•	•		•	•	•	•	•	•	•	•	•	•	•	•		•	•	•
	Petrobius maritimus							•		•			•	•							•
CRUSTACEA	Barnacles	•	•	•	•	•	•	•	•	•	•	•	•	•	•	•	•	•	•	•	•
	Barnacle spat		•	•			•	•	•	•	•	•	•	•	•	•	•	•	•	•	•
	Chthamalus montagui															•				•	
	Chthamalus stellatus						•														
	Chthamalus spp.	•	•	•	•	•	•	•	•	•			•	•	•	•	•	•	•	•	•
	Elminius modestus			•		•							•	•	•	•			•	•	•
	Semibalanus balanoides	•	•	•	•	•	•	•	•	•			•	•	•	•	•	•	•	•	•
	Amphithoe rubricata												•								
	Cancer pagurus			•						•		•									
	Caprella linearis				•																
	Carcinus maenas	•	•	•	•	•		•							•					•	
	Gammarus spp.						•	•				•	•			•			•		•
	Idotea spp.	•		•			•	•					•	•							
	Ligia oceanica	•	•	•	•		•	•	•	•	•	•	•	•	•	•	•	•		•	•
	Ligia spp.							•													
	Pagurus bernhardus				•																
	Talitrus saltator									•											
MOLLUSCA	*Anomia ephippium*												•								
	Calliostoma zizyphinum		•	•	•	•					•	•			•	•					
	Chiton spp.												•								
	Gibbula cineraria			•													•	•			•
	Gibbula umbilicalis		•		•			•					•					•	•	•	•
	Gibbula spp.										•										
	Helcion pellucidum		•			•				•		•	•	•							
	Hiatella arctica					•															
	Hinia incrassata			•							•						•				
	Hinia reticulata				•														•	•	•
	Hydrobia ulvae				•																
	Lacuna vincta			•																	
	Littorina littorea	•			•			•	•	•		•				•		•	•		
	Littorina neglecta	•	•	•	•	•															

DROLAIN POINT (STATIONS 1–14)

PHYLUM/DIVISION	SPECIES	1981	1982	1983	1984	1985	1986	1987	1988	1989	1990	1991	1992	1993	1994	1995	1996	1997	1998	1999	2000
MOLLUSCA	*Littorina obtusata*		•	•	•			•		•	•	•	•		•	•			•		
	Littorina saxatilis	•	•	•	•	•	•	•	•	•	•	•	•	•	•	•	•	•	•	•	•
	Littorina spp.					•					•										
	Melarhaphe neritoides	•	•	•	•	•	•	•	•	•	•	•	•	•	•	•	•	•	•	•	•
	Modiolus barbatus																		•		
	Mytilus edulis	•	•	•	•	•	•	•	•	•	•	•	•	•	•	•	•	•	•	•	•
	Nucella lapillus	•	•	•	•	•	•	•	•	•	•	•	•	•	•	•	•	•	•	•	•
	Nucella (eggs)							•	•	•										•	
	Ocenebra erinacea					•		•													
	Patella vulgata					•															
	Patella spp.	•	•	•	•	•	•	•	•	•	•	•	•	•	•	•	•	•	•	•	•
BRYOZOA	*Alcyonidium gelatinosum*												•						•		
	Alcyonidium hirsutum		•	•	•								•								
	Alcyonidium spp.									•			•								
	Cellepora pumicosa			•																	
	Celleporina hassallii		•	•	•																
	Electra pilosa		•	•		•	•		•			•	•								
	Flustra foliacea									•											
	Flustrellidra hispida		•		•	•			•			•							•		
	Membranipora membranacea									•			•	•					•		
	Schizoporella unicornis				•																
	Umbonula littoralis						•	•													
	Umbonula spp.					•		•	•				•	•							
ECHINODERMATA	*Asterias rubens*		•	•			•			•		•									•
	Ophiocomina nigra												•								
	Ophiothrix fragilis				•									•							
CHORDATA	*Aplidium proliferum*				•								•								
	Botrylloides leachi										•										
	Botryllus schlosseri								•	•		•									
	Sidnyum turbinatum											•									
	Blennius spp.										•										
	Lipophrys pholis									•	•							•			

GLOBE ROCKS (STATIONS 1–10)

PHYLUM/DIVISION	SPECIES	1981	1982	1983	1984	1985	1986	1987	1988	1989	1990	1991	1992	1993	1994	1995	1996	1997	1998	1999	2000
GREEN ALGAE (CHLOROPHYCOTA)	*Bryopsis plumosa*						•														
	Chaetomorpha linum																			•	
	Chaetomorpha mediterranea																		•		
	Chaetomorpha spp.		•											•	•	•		•	•	•	•
	Cladophora albida																	•			
	Cladophora hutchinsiae																	•			
	Cladophora rupestris			•		•		•	•	•	•	•	•		•			•		•	•
	Cladophora sericea																	•			
	Cladophora spp.	•	•	•	•	•	•		•	•		•	•	•	•	•		•	•	•	•
	Codium tomentosum				•		•	•										•		•	
	Derbesia marina					•															
	Derbesia spp.									•	•										
	Enteromorpha compressa			•	•	•								•							
	Enteromorpha intestinalis		•			•				•			•			•			•		•
	Enteromorpha linza			•																	
	Enteromorpha muscoides																	•			
	Enteromorpha prolifera																				•
	Enteromorpha spp.	•	•	•	•		•	•	•	•	•	•	•	•	•	•	•	•	•	•	•
	Spongomorpha arcta								•		•		•	•							
	Spongomorpha spp.				•					•	•	•	•							•	
	Ulva lactuca	•	•	•	•	•	•	•	•	•	•	•	•	•	•	•	•	•	•	•	•
	Ulva spp.										•		•								
	Urospora spp.					•															
BROWN ALGAE (CHROMOPHYCOTA)	*Ascophyllum nodosum*					•		•	•	•	•	•			•		•	•			
	Asperococcus spp.															•					
	Chorda filum			•																	
	Cladostephus spongiosus		•		•			•			•		•			•		•		•	•
	Dictyota dichotoma																			•	
	Ectocarpus siliculosus								•						•						
	Ectocarpaceae	•	•	•	•	•		•			•	•	•	•	•	•	•	•	•	•	•
	Elachista fucicola		•	•	•	•	•	•	•											•	•
	Elachista spp.	•	•							•	•	•	•	•	•	•	•	•	•	•	
	Fucus ceranoides																				•
	Fucus serratus	•	•	•	•	•	•	•	•	•	•	•	•	•	•	•	•	•	•	•	•
	Fucus spiralis	•		•	•	•	•	•	•	•	•	•	•	•	•	•	•	•	•	•	•
	Fucus vesiculosus	•	•	•	•	•	•		•	•	•	•	•	•	•	•	•	•	•	•	•
	Fucus spp.	•	•										•					•	•	•	•
	Fucus spp. sporelings	•	•						•		•		•	•	•	•	•	•	•	•	•
	Himanthalia elongata														•				•		
	Laminaria digitata	•		•	•	•	•	•	•	•		•			•	•	•				•
	Laminaria saccharina									•		•									
	Laminaria spp.				•										•			•			
	Laminaria spp. sporelings	•	•	•															•		
	Leathesia difformis	•	•	•	•	•	•	•		•						•		•		•	•
	Pelvetia canaliculata	•	•	•	•	•	•	•	•	•	•	•	•	•	•	•	•	•	•	•	•
	Ralfsia verrucosa	•	•	•	•	•							•	•	•			•		•	•
	Scytosiphon lomentaria									•					•		•	•	•	•	•
	Spongonema tomentosum							•								•		•	•	•	
RED ALGAE (RHODOPHYCOTA)	*Ahnfeltia plicata*	•		•	•	•						•						•			
	Audouinella spp.	•	•	•	•	•		•			•	•			•			•	•	•	•
	Calliblepharis jubata														•						
	Callithamnion spp.			•							•						•			•	
	Catenella caespitosa		•	•	•							•	•					•		•	•

GLOBE ROCKS (STATIONS 1–10)

PHYLUM/DIVISION	SPECIES	1981	1982	1983	1984	1985	1986	1987	1988	1989	1990	1991	1992	1993	1994	1995	1996	1997	1998	1999	2000
RED ALGAE (RHODOPHYCOTA)	*Ceramium botryocarpum*																•	•	•		•
	Ceramium ciliatum				•												•	•	•		•
	Ceramium echionotum																		•	•	
	Ceramium flaccidum																		•		
	Ceramium gaditanum														•			•		•	•
	Ceramium pallidum																•	•	•	•	
	Ceramium rubrum	•			•	•	•	•	•	•	•		•		•	•	•				
	Ceramium shuttleworthianum			•			•						•	•	•		•	•	•	•	•
	Ceramium strictum																		•		
	Ceramium spp.	•	•	•		•	•	•	•	•		•		•	•	•	•		•	•	•
	Chondracanthus acicularis		•			•															
	Chondrus crispus	•	•	•	•	•	•	•	•	•	•	•	•	•	•	•	•	•	•	•	•
	Corallina officinalis	•	•	•	•	•	•	•	•	•	•	•	•	•	•	•	•	•	•	•	•
	Corallina spp.															•					
	Cryptopleura ramosa					•															
	Dilsea carnosa																	•			
	Dumontia contorta		•	•	•					•	•						•	•			
	Furcellaria lumbricalis		•						•												
	Gastroclonium ovatum	•																		•	
	Gelidium pulchellum			•													•	•			
	Gelidium pusillum				•	•						•	•	•		•		•	•	•	
	Gelidium spinosum			•	•	•	•	•		•			•	•	•	•	•	•	•	•	•
	Gelidium spp.	•	•		•		•	•		•	•	•		•		•					
	Gracilaria gracilis																	•			
	Halurus equisetifolius											•									•
	Heterosiphonia plumosa						•														
	Hildenbrandia rubra									•		•	•	•	•	•	•	•	•	•	•
	Hildenbrandia spp.	•	•	•	•	•	•	•	•		•	•	•		•	•					
	Jania rubens																				•
	Laurencia obtusa							•	•		•	•						•			
	Laurencia spp.	•	•					•				•									
	Lithothamnia	•	•	•	•	•	•	•	•	•	•	•	•	•	•	•	•	•	•	•	•
	Lomentaria articulata	•	•	•	•	•	•	•	•	•	•	•	•		•	•	•	•	•	•	•
	Lomentaria clavellosa													•				•			
	Lomentaria orcadensis																			•	
	Lomentaria spp.							•													
	Mastocarpus stellatus	•	•	•	•	•	•	•	•	•	•	•	•	•	•	•	•	•	•	•	•
	Membranoptera alata	•	•		•	•	•	•	•	•					•	•				•	
	Mesophyllum lichenoides																				•
	Osmundea hybrida						•	•	•	•		•									
	Osmundea pinnatifida	•	•	•	•	•	•	•	•	•	•	•	•	•	•	•	•	•	•	•	•
	Palmaria palmata	•	•	•	•	•	•	•				•			•	•	•	•	•	•	•
	Plocamium cartilagineum																	•			
	Plumaria plumosa	•	•	•	•	•	•	•	•	•	•	•			•	•		•	•	•	•
	Polyides rotundus																•				
	Polysiphonia atlantica				•								•	•			•	•			
	Polysiphonia brodiei																	•			
	Polysiphonia elongata						•								•			•		•	
	Polysiphonia fibrata														•			•			
	Polysiphonia fibrillosa																		•		
	Polysiphonia fucoides				•	•										•		•		•	
	Polysiphonia harveyi																				•
	Polysiphonia lanosa						•		•	•		•	•		•	•	•	•	•	•	
	Polysiphonia simulans																		•		
	Polysiphonia stricta																	•			•
	Polysiphonia spp.		•	•	•		•	•			•	•	•			•	•			•	•
	Porphyra umbilicalis			•														•		•	

GLOBE ROCKS (Stations 1–10)

PHYLUM/DIVISION	SPECIES	1981	1982	1983	1984	1985	1986	1987	1988	1989	1990	1991	1992	1993	1994	1995	1996	1997	1998	1999	2000
RED ALGAE (RHODOPHYCOTA)	*Porphyra* spp.							•		•			•								
	Ptilota gunneri																•				
	Rhodomela confervoides					•															
	Rhodothamniella floridula		•		•	•											•				
	Rhodymenia pseudopalmata							•													
LICHEN	*Caloplaca marina*			•	•		•	•	•	•	•	•	•	•	•	•	•	•	•	•	•
	Caloplaca thallincola																	•		•	
	Caloplaca spp.							•					•								
	Haematomma ventosum																			•	
	Lecanora atra	•			•	•	•	•	•	•	•	•	•	•	•	•	•	•	•	•	•
	Lichina confinis		•		•		•	•	•		•	•	•	•	•	•	•	•	•	•	•
	Lichina pygmaea				•	•	•	•	•	•	•	•	•	•	•	•	•	•	•	•	•
	Ochrolechia frigida															•					
	Ochrolechia parella							•	•			•			•	•	•	•	•	•	•
	Ramalina siliquosa				•	•	•	•	•	•	•	•	•	•	•	•	•	•	•	•	•
	Ramalina spp.												•								
	Verrucaria maura	•	•	•	•	•	•	•	•	•	•	•	•	•	•	•	•	•	•	•	•
	Verrucaria mucosa	•	•	•	•	•	•	•	•	•	•	•	•	•	•	•	•	•	•	•	•
	Verrucaria spp.		•																		
	Xanthoria parietina				•		•	•	•	•	•	•	•	•	•	•	•	•	•	•	•
	Xanthoria spp.						•														
BRYOPHYTA	Moss												•								•
SPERMATOPHYTA	*Armeria maritima*				•		•	•	•	•	•	•	•	•	•	•	•	•	•	•	•
	Carex spp.											•									
	Festuca rubra									•			•	•							
	Grass						•	•					•		•				•	•	•
	Juncus spp.				•				•		•	•	•	•	•			•			•
	Plantago maritima										•	•	•	•	•					•	
	Plantago spp.											•									
	Spergularia media																			•	
	Spergularia spp.												•								
PORIFERA	*Grantia compressa*																			•	
	Halichondria panicea	•	•		•	•	•	•	•	•	•	•	•	•	•	•	•	•	•	•	•
	Halichondria spp.	•		•				•	•	•					•	•					
	Hymeniacidon perleve	•	•		•	•	•					•	•	•							
	Hymeniacidon sanguinea	•	•	•					•												
	Hymeniacidon spp.	•		•			•										•				
	Myxilla incrustans				•	•	•	•	•	•	•	•	•	•	•	•	•	•	•	•	•
	Myxilla spp.			•	•		•	•	•	•	•	•	•			•				•	
	Oscarella lobularis				•																
CNIDARIA	*Coryne muscoides*			•																	
	Dynamena pumila	•	•	•	•	•	•	•	•	•	•	•		•	•	•	•	•	•	•	•
	Laomedea flexuosa				•																
	Obelia geniculata																	•			
	Actinia equina	•	•	•	•	•	•	•	•	•	•	•	•	•	•	•	•	•	•	•	•
	Anemonia viridis			•		•							•			•					

GLOBE ROCKS (STATIONS 1–10)

PHYLUM/DIVISION	SPECIES	1981	1982	1983	1984	1985	1986	1987	1988	1989	1990	1991	1992	1993	1994	1995	1996	1997	1998	1999	2000
CNIDARIA	*Aulactinia verrucosa*				•																
	Cereus pedunculatus							•													
	Corynactis viridis												•								
	Sagartia elegans				•	•															
	Urticina felina				•	•							•							•	
ANNELIDA	*Cirriformia tentaculata*																			•	
	Eulalia viridis		•					•				•	•	•			•	•		•	
	Nereis spp.			•																	
	Pomatoceros triqueter	•	•	•	•		•	•	•	•						•	•	•		•	•
	Pomatoceros spp.					•				•		•									
	Spirorbis inornatus			•																	
	Spirorbis rupestris		•	•																•	
	Spirorbis spirorbis							•							•	•			•		
	Spirorbis tridentatus			•																	
	Spirorbis spp.	•	•		•	•	•	•	•	•	•	•			•	•	•	•	•	•	•
CHELICERATAA	cari spp.								•			•	•	•	•						•
	Nymphon gracile			•																	
HEXAPODA	*Lipura maritima*	•	•	•				•			•	•	•	•			•	•	•	•	•
	Petrobius maritimus									•											
CRUSTACEA	*Balanus crenatus*			•																	
	Barnacles	•	•	•	•	•	•	•	•	•	•	•	•	•	•	•	•	•	•	•	•
	Barnacle spat	•	•	•			•	•	•	•	•	•	•	•	•	•	•	•	•	•	•
	Chthamalus montagui	•	•	•					•												•
	Chthamalus stellatus	•	•	•			•														
	Chthamalus spp.	•			•	•	•	•	•				•	•	•	•	•	•	•	•	•
	Elminius modestus		•	•	•	•	•	•					•	•	•	•	•	•	•	•	•
	Semibalanus balanoides	•	•	•	•	•	•	•	•				•	•	•	•	•	•	•	•	•
	Verruca stroemia		•	•	•	•															
	Cancer pagurus		•	•	•	•		•			•	•									
	Carcinus maenas	•	•	•	•	•	•	•	•	•	•	•	•	•	•	•	•	•		•	•
	Dynamene bidentata		•																		
	Gammarus spp.							•		•				•		•		•	•		
	Hyas araneus								•												
	Idotea spp.							•					•	•				•			
	Ligia oceanica	•	•	•	•		•	•		•		•	•		•	•	•	•		•	•
	Necora puber								•												
	Pagurus bernhardus		•									•	•								
	Pinnotheres pisum								•												•
	Pirimela denticulata			•								•									
	Porcellana platycheles							•													
	Xantho incisus			•																	
MOLLUSCA	*Anomia ephippium*			•	•	•															
	Archidoris pseudoargus								•												
	Bittium reticulatum								•	•											
	Cadlina laevis								•												
	Calliostoma zizyphinum			•	•	•	•	•	•	•								•	•		

GLOBE ROCKS (STATIONS 1–10)

PHYLUM/DIVISION	SPECIES	1981	1982	1983	1984	1985	1986	1987	1988	1989	1990	1991	1992	1993	1994	1995	1996	1997	1998	1999	2000
MOLLUSCA	*Gibbula cineraria*							•	•		•	•	•	•			•	•		•	
	Gibbula umbilicalis	•				•	•	•		•	•	•	•	•	•	•	•	•	•	•	•
	Gibbula spp.											•									
	Helcion pellucidum	•		•		•		•				•				•				•	•
	Hinia incrassata	•	•	•	•	•						•						•			
	Hinia reticulata			•	•			•				•							•	•	
	Limacia clavigera			•																	
	Littorina littorea	•	•	•	•	•	•	•	•	•	•	•	•	•	•	•	•	•	•	•	•
	Littorina neglecta	•	•	•	•	•															
	Littorina obtusata	•	•	•	•	•	•	•	•	•	•	•	•	•	•	•	•	•	•	•	•
	Littorina saxatilis	•	•	•	•	•	•	•	•	•	•	•	•	•	•	•	•	•	•	•	•
	Littorina (eggs)											•									
	Melarhaphe neritoides	•	•	•	•	•	•	•	•	•	•	•	•	•	•	•	•	•	•	•	•
	Modiolus barbatus																		•		
	Mytilus edulis	•	•	•	•	•	•	•	•	•	•	•	•	•	•	•	•	•	•	•	•
	Mytilus spp.				•																
	Nucella lapillus	•	•	•	•	•	•	•	•	•	•	•	•	•	•	•	•	•	•	•	•
	Nucella (eggs)		•					•				•			•			•			•
	Nudibranch (eggs)		•																		
	Ocenebra erinacea						•	•		•		•									
	Osilinus lineatus										•							•		•	
	Patella spp.	•	•	•	•	•	•	•	•	•	•	•	•	•	•	•	•	•	•	•	•
BRYOZOA	*Alcyonidium gelatinosum*	•	•	•	•	•		•	•						•			•	•	•	
	Alcyonidium hirsutum	•	•	•	•	•			•						•	•	•	•		•	
	Alcyonidium spp.											•					•	•			
	Bowerbankia gracilis												•								
	Cellepora pumicosa	•	•	•																	
	Celleporella hyalina					•															
	Celleporina hassallii			•	•																
	Electra pilosa	•	•	•	•	•	•	•	•	•		•			•	•	•	•	•	•	•
	Flustrellidra hispida	•	•	•	•	•		•	•	•		•			•		•	•	•	•	•
	Membranipora membranacea						•	•	•	•	•					•	•	•	•	•	•
	Schizoporella unicornis				•																
	Scrupocellaria reptans				•																
	Scrupocellaria spp.		•																		
	Umbonula littoralis					•	•	•													
	Umbonula spp.					•	•	•	•	•					•		•	•	•	•	
ECHINODERMATA	*Asterias rubens*				•			•	•												
	Ophiothrix fragilis				•																
CHORDATA	*Aplidium pallidum*				•													•			
	Aplidium proliferum			•	•					•							•	•			
	Aplidium spp.							•					•								
	Ascidia mentula										•										
	Botrylloides leachi	•		•		•										•		•			
	Botryllus schlosseri			•	•	•			•	•			•			•	•	•			•
	Dendrodoa grossularia																•				
	Morchellium argus																	•		•	
	Sidnyum turbinatum											•									
	Blennius spp.										•										
	Coryphoblennius galerita															•					•
	Lipophrys pholis													•				•		•	

HORSESHOE HARBOUR (STATIONS 1–10)

PHYLUM/DIVISION	SPECIES	1981	1982	1983	1984	1985	1986	1987	1988	1989	1990	1991	1992	1993	1994	1995	1996	1997	1998	1999	2000
GREEN ALGAE (CHLOROPHYCOTA)	*Blidingia* spp.																	•			
	Bryopsis plumosa			•																	
	Bryopsis spp.				•													•			
	Chaetomorpha linum	•		•																	
	Chaetomorpha spp.													•	•	•		•		•	•
	Cladophora albida																	•			
	Cladophora laetevirens																	•			
	Cladophora rupestris	•	•	•	•	•		•		•	•	•	•	•	•	•	•	•	•	•	•
	Cladophora sericea														•			•			
	Cladophora spp.	•	•	•	•	•	•		•	•	•	•	•	•	•	•		•	•	•	•
	Codium bursa										•										
	Codium tomentosum	•	•	•	•	•	•	•	•	•	•					•	•	•	•	•	•
	Codium spp.																	•			
	Derbesia marina									•											
	Enteromorpha compressa			•	•	•															
	Enteromorpha intestinalis			•	•	•						•	•						•		•
	Enteromorpha linza			•																	
	Enteromorpha muscoides																	•			
	Enteromorpha spp.	•	•	•	•		•	•	•	•	•	•	•	•	•	•	•	•	•	•	•
	Monostroma grevillei																	•			
	Spongomorpha aeruginosa																				•
	Spongomorpha arcta								•	•	•		•	•							
	Spongomorpha spp.				•							•		•	•						•
	Ulva lactuca	•	•	•	•	•	•	•	•	•	•	•	•	•	•	•	•	•	•	•	•
	Ulva spp.												•								
	Urospora spp.					•															
BROWN ALGAE (CHROMOPHYCOTA)	*Ascophyllum nodosum*	•	•	•																	
	Asperococcus spp.																			•	
	Cladostephus spongiosus					•												•	•		
	Colpomenia peregrina						•														
	Cutleria multifida															•					
	Dictyota dichotoma		•	•	•			•	•	•	•	•	•	•		•	•	•		•	•
	Ectocarpus siliculosus														•			•			
	Ectocarpaceae	•	•	•	•	•	•	•			•				•	•	•	•	•	•	•
	Elachista fucicola	•	•	•	•	•		•													
	Elachista scutulata				•	•															
	Elachista spp.	•	•		•	•				•	•	•	•				•	•		•	
	Fucus serratus	•	•	•	•	•	•	•	•	•	•	•	•	•	•	•	•	•			
	Fucus spiralis	•	•	•	•	•	•	•	•	•			•	•		•					
	Fucus vesiculosus	•	•	•	•																
	Fucus spp.	•		•	•				•				•				•	•			
	Fucus spp. sporelings	•				•							•			•	•		•		
	Halopteris filicina									•											
	Himanthalia elongata	•	•	•	•	•	•	•	•	•	•	•	•	•	•	•	•	•	•	•	•
	Laminaria digitata	•	•	•	•	•	•	•	•	•	•	•									•
	Laminaria saccharina	•	•																		
	Laminaria spp.				•			•			•				•						
	Laminaria spp. sporelings															•					
	Leathesia difformis	•	•	•	•	•	•	•	•		•	•	•	•	•	•	•	•	•	•	•
	Mesogloia vermiculata					•															
	Pelvetia canaliculata	•	•	•	•	•	•	•	•	•	•	•	•	•	•	•	•	•	•	•	•
	Punctaria latifolia																			•	
	Ralfsia verrucosa			•	•	•		•					•	•	•	•	•	•	•	•	•
	Saccorhiza polyschides			•																	
	Scytosiphon lomentaria			•						•		•		•	•		•			•	•

HORSESHOE HARBOUR (STATIONS 1–10)

PHYLUM/DIVISION	SPECIES	1981	1982	1983	1984	1985	1986	1987	1988	1989	1990	1991	1992	1993	1994	1995	1996	1997	1998	1999	2000
BROWN ALGAE (CHROMOPHYCOTA)	*Spongonema tomentosum*	•		•																	
	Stilophora tenella								•												
	Stragularia clavata			•																	
RED ALGAE (RHODOPHYCOTA)	*Aglaothamnion hookeri*			•																•	
	Aglaothamnion sepositum							•	•				•			•	•	•		•	
	Antithamnionella spirographidis																•				
	Apoglossum ruscifolium				•					•	•	•									
	Audouinella spp.		•					•					•	•		•		•		•	
	Calliblepharis jubata		•				•														
	Calliblepharis spp.						•														
	Callithamnion granulatum												•							•	
	Callithamnion tetricum													•							
	Callithamnion spp.		•	•	•				•	•	•	•	•	•		•				•	
	Callophyllis laciniata						•														
	Catenella caespitosa	•	•	•	•	•					•	•	•	•			•	•	•	•	•
	Ceramium botryocarpum																	•		•	•
	Ceramium ciliatum			•	•	•						•	•			•	•	•	•	•	•
	Ceramium echionotum				•																
	Ceramium gaditanum				•												•				
	Ceramium pallidum																			•	
	Ceramium rubrum	•		•	•	•	•	•	•	•	•	•	•	•	•	•	•				
	Ceramium shuttleworthianum	•		•		•						•	•	•	•	•	•	•	•	•	•
	Ceramium strictum								•				•								
	Ceramium spp.	•	•	•	•		•	•	•		•	•	•	•	•	•			•	•	•
	Chondracanthus acicularis	•			•	•						•	•		•	•				•	•
	Chondria capillaris							•													
	Chondrus crispus	•	•	•	•	•	•	•	•	•	•	•	•	•	•	•	•	•	•	•	•
	Compsothamnion spp.		•																	•	
	Corallina officinalis	•	•	•	•	•	•	•	•	•	•	•	•	•	•	•	•	•	•	•	•
	Corallina spp.												•		•	•					
	Cryptopleura ramosa	•	•	•	•	•	•	•		•								•			
	Cystoclonium purpureum											•									
	Dilsea carnosa			•																	
	Dumontia contorta	•	•	•	•	•	•	•		•	•			•		•	•	•		•	
	Erythrodermis traillii			•																	
	Furcellaria lumbricalis									•											
	Gastroclonium ovatum	•	•	•	•		•	•	•		•	•	•		•						
	Gelidium pulchellum			•					•	•							•				
	Gelidium pusillum				•	•						•	•	•				•	•		
	Gelidium spinosum			•	•	•	•	•	•	•	•	•	•	•		•	•	•		•	•
	Gelidium spp.	•	•	•		•	•				•	•				•				•	
	Halurus flosculosus					•													•		
	Heterosiphonia plumosa						•				•		•								
	Hildenbrandia rubra				•	•		•		•	•	•	•	•	•	•	•	•	•	•	•
	Hildenbrandia spp.	•	•	•	•	•	•	•	•	•	•		•	•	•	•					
	Hypoglossum hypoglossoides			•					•												
	Laurencia obtusa							•	•			•		•						•	
	Laurencia spp.																			•	
	Lithothamnia	•	•	•	•	•	•	•	•	•	•	•	•	•	•	•	•	•	•	•	•
	Lomentaria articulata	•	•	•	•	•	•	•	•	•	•	•	•	•	•	•	•	•	•	•	•
	Lomentaria clavellosa				•				•												
	Lomentaria orcadensis														•						
	Mastocarpus stellatus	•	•	•	•	•	•	•	•	•	•	•	•	•	•	•	•	•	•	•	•
	Membranoptera alata	•	•	•	•	•	•	•	•		•	•	•	•	•			•		•	
	Mesophyllum lichenoides		•	•							•	•									•

HORSESHOE HARBOUR (STATIONS 1–10)

PHYLUM/DIVISION	SPECIES	1981	1982	1983	1984	1985	1986	1987	1988	1989	1990	1991	1992	1993	1994	1995	1996	1997	1998	1999	2000
RED ALGAE (RHODOPHYCOTA)	*Nemalion helminthoides*	•													•					•	
	Nitophyllum punctatum							•													
	Osmundea hybrida			•			•		•											•	
	Osmundea pinnatifida	•	•	•	•	•	•	•	•	•	•	•	•	•	•	•	•	•	•	•	•
	Palmaria palmata	•	•		•		•	•		•	•	•	•	•	•	•	•	•	•	•	•
	Peyssonnelia squamaria										•										
	Peyssonnelia spp.	•																			
	Phyllophora spp.			•																	
	Plocamium cartilagineum	•	•	•	•						•	•	•	•	•				•	•	•
	Plumaria plumosa	•	•	•	•	•	•	•	•	•	•	•	•	•	•						
	Polyides rotundus																	•			
	Polysiphonia atlantica								•				•	•	•	•	•	•		•	
	Polysiphonia brodiei																	•	•	•	
	Polysiphonia denudata																		•	•	•
	Polysiphonia elongata									•			•	•	•						
	Polysiphonia fibrata			•														•	•	•	•
	Polysiphonia fibrillosa								•										•		•
	Polysiphonia lanosa							•	•	•		•		•					•		
	Polysiphonia stricta				•								•								
	Polysiphonia spp.	•	•	•	•	•	•	•			•	•	•				•		•	•	•
	Porphyra umbilicalis	•	•	•	•			•		•	•						•			•	
	Pterocladia capillacea									•											•
	Ptilota gunneri	•																		•	
	Rhodomela confervoides								•												
	Rhodothamniella floridula					•															
	Rhodymenia pseudopalmata	•						•													
	Titanoderma pustulatum																	•			
LICHEN	*Caloplaca marina*				•	•	•	•		•	•	•	•	•	•	•	•	•	•	•	•
	Caloplaca spp.												•								
	Lecanora atra				•	•	•	•	•	•	•	•	•	•	•	•	•	•	•	•	•
	Lecanora spp.																	•			
	Lichina confinis				•		•	•			•	•	•	•		•	•	•		•	•
	Lichina pygmaea				•	•	•	•	•	•	•	•	•	•	•	•	•	•	•	•	
	Lichina spp.							•													
	Ochrolechia parella														•	•	•	•	•	•	
	Ramalina siliquosa							•			•										
	Verrucaria maura	•	•	•	•	•	•	•	•	•	•	•	•	•	•	•	•	•	•	•	•
	Verrucaria mucosa	•	•	•	•	•	•	•	•	•	•	•	•	•	•	•	•	•	•	•	•
	Verrucaria spp.	•																			
	Xanthoria parietina						•	•	•	•	•	•	•	•	•		•		•	•	
BRYOPHYTA	*Grimmia maritima*								•												
	Moss												•								
	Schistidium maritimum										•										
SPERMATOPHYTA	*Armeria maritima*				•	•	•	•	•	•	•	•	•	•	•	•	•	•	•	•	•
	Grass																		•		
	Plantago maritima											•									
PORIFERA	*Grantia compressa*			•																	
	Halichondria panicea	•	•	•	•	•	•	•	•	•	•	•	•	•	•	•	•	•	•	•	•
	Halichondria spp.	•	•	•				•	•		•		•								

HORSESHOE HARBOUR (STATIONS 1–10)

PHYLUM/DIVISION	SPECIES	1981	1982	1983	1984	1985	1986	1987	1988	1989	1990	1991	1992	1993	1994	1995	1996	1997	1998	1999	2000
PORIFERA	*Hymeniacidon perleve*	•	•	•	•	•						•	•								
	Hymeniacidon sanguinea								•									•		•	
	Hymeniacidon spp.	•	•	•	•		•										•				•
	Leucosolenia botryoides			•																	
	Myxilla incrustans					•	•	•	•	•	•	•	•	•	•	•	•	•	•	•	•
	Myxilla spp.						•	•			•	•		•			•			•	
	Oscarella lobularis													•							
CNIDARIA	*Dynamena pumila*	•	•	•	•	•	•	•	•	•	•	•	•		•		•	•			
	Obelia geniculata							•													
	Sertularella polyzonias								•												
	Actinia equina	•	•	•	•	•	•	•	•	•	•	•	•	•	•	•	•	•	•	•	•
	Anemonia viridis		•				•	•													
	Aulactinia verrucosa							•													
	Caryophyllia smithii			•																	
	Corynactis viridis			•																	
	Sagartia elegans		•	•	•			•							•						
	Sagartia spp.		•																		
	Urticina felina	•		•				•			•				•					•	
ANNELIDA	*Eulalia viridis*	•	•	•			•	•	•				•	•		•	•	•	•	•	
	Pomatoceros triqueter	•	•	•	•	•	•	•	•	•	•	•	•	•	•	•	•	•	•	•	•
	Pomatoceros spp.						•	•	•											•	
	Sabellaria spp.																			•	
	Spirorbis corallinae		•	•																	
	Spirorbis inornatus	•	•	•																	
	Spirorbis rupestris	•	•	•																	
	Spirorbis spirorbis		•					•	•	•	•	•	•		•					•	•
	Spirorbis tridentatus		•																		
	Spirorbis spp.				•	•	•	•	•	•	•	•	•	•	•	•	•	•	•	•	•
CHELICERATA	Acari spp.								•			•	•	•	•						•
	Pycnogonum littorale													•							
HEXOPODA	*Lipura maritima*	•	•	•				•	•	•	•	•	•	•				•	•	•	•
	Petrobius maritimus						•	•					•	•							
CRUSTACEA	Barnacles	•	•	•	•	•	•	•	•	•	•	•	•	•	•	•	•	•	•	•	•
	Barnacle spat	•	•	•	•		•		•	•		•	•	•	•	•	•	•	•	•	•
	Chthamalus stellatus							•								•					
	Chthamalus spp.	•	•	•	•	•	•	•	•				•	•	•	•	•	•	•	•	•
	Elminius modestus				•	•	•						•	•	•			•	•	•	•
	Semibalanus balanoides	•	•	•	•	•	•	•	•				•	•	•	•	•	•	•	•	•
	Verruca stroemia		•	•	•																
	Cancer pagurus	•	•	•		•										•		•			
	Carcinus maenas	•	•	•	•	•	•	•	•	•	•	•	•	•	•			•		•	•
	Gammarus locusta										•										
	Gammarus spp.		•	•			•	•		•				•		•		•			
	Idotea granulosa						•														
	Idotea spp.	•		•										•						•	

HORSESHOE HARBOUR (STATIONS 1–10)

PHYLUM/DIVISION	SPECIES	1981	1982	1983	1984	1985	1986	1987	1988	1989	1990	1991	1992	1993	1994	1995	1996	1997	1998	1999	2000
CRUSTACEA	*Ligia oceanica*	•	•	•	•		•	•	•	•	•	•	•	•	•		•	•	•	•	•
	Necora puber		•							•											
	Pagurus bernhardus	•	•	•	•	•		•		•	•			•	•						
	Pinnotheres pisum								•	•										•	
	Pirimela denticulata			•								•									
	Pisidia longicornis			•																	
	Porcellana platycheles		•																		
	Sphaeroma rugicauda		•																		
	Talitrus saltator							•													
MOLLUSCA	*Alvania cancellata*							•													
	Anomia ephippium		•	•				•													
	Archidoris pseudoargus										•										
	Bittium reticulatum									•											
	Calliostoma zizyphinum	•	•	•	•	•	•	•	•	•	•		•		•	•	•			•	
	Chiton spp.							•													
	Gibbula cineraria	•	•	•	•	•	•	•	•		•	•	•	•	•	•	•	•	•	•	•
	Gibbula umbilicalis	•	•		•	•	•	•	•	•	•		•	•	•	•	•	•	•	•	•
	Gibbula spp.									•						•					
	Helcion pellucidum	•	•	•	•	•	•	•	•	•	•	•		•			•		•	•	
	Hinia incrassata	•	•	•	•	•	•	•	•	•		•									
	Hinia reticulata		•	•	•			•			•				•						
	Hinia spp.	•			•																
	Hydrobia spp.		•																		
	Jorunna tomentosa																		•		
	Littorina littorea	•	•	•	•	•	•	•	•	•	•		•	•		•	•	•	•	•	•
	Littorina neglecta	•	•	•	•	•															
	Littorina obtusata	•	•	•	•	•	•	•	•	•	•	•	•	•			•	•	•	•	•
	Littorina saxatilis	•	•	•	•	•	•	•	•	•	•	•	•	•	•	•	•	•	•	•	•
	Littorina spp.	•																			
	Melarhaphe neritoides	•	•	•	•	•	•	•	•	•	•	•	•	•	•	•	•	•	•	•	•
	Modiolus barbatus																		•		
	Mytilus edulis	•	•	•	•	•	•	•	•	•	•	•	•	•	•	•	•	•	•	•	•
	Nucella lapillus	•	•	•	•	•	•	•	•	•	•	•	•	•	•	•	•	•	•	•	•
	Nucella (eggs)	•	•	•			•	•	•	•	•	•		•		•	•	•		•	
	Ocenebra erinacea	•		•	•	•	•	•		•	•										
	Osilinus lineatus						•		•									•			
	Patella spp.	•	•	•	•	•	•	•	•	•	•	•	•	•	•	•	•	•	•	•	•
	Tectura virginea												•								
	Trivia arctica				•																
BRYOZOA	*Alcyonidium gelatinosum*	•	•	•		•	•						•							•	
	Alcyonidium hirsutum	•	•	•	•				•							•				•	
	Alcyonidium spp.											•									
	Bowerbankia imbricata				•																
	Cellepora pumicosa	•	•	•																	
	Celleporella hyalina				•	•						•									
	Celleporina hassallii		•	•	•	•															
	Crisia spp.		•	•																	
	Cryptosula pallasiana				•																
	Electra pilosa	•	•	•	•	•	•	•	•			•				•		•	•	•	•
	Flustrellidra hispida	•	•	•	•	•		•	•	•	•	•	•			•	•			•	•
	Haplopoma graniferum				•																
	Membranipora membranacea		•		•		•	•	•	•	•	•	•		•		•			•	
	Schizoporella unicornis				•																

HORSESHOE HARBOUR (STATIONS 1–10)

PHYLUM/DIVISION	SPECIES	1981	1982	1983	1984	1985	1986	1987	1988	1989	1990	1991	1992	1993	1994	1995	1996	1997	1998	1999	2000
BRYOZOA	*Scrupocellaria reptans*				•																
	Scrupocellaria spp.		•																		
	Tubulipora phalangea		•		•																
	Umbonula littoralis					•		•	•												
	Umbonula spp.					•	•	•	•							•	•			•	
ECHINODERMATA	*Asterias rubens*		•	•		•		•	•	•		•	•	•							
	Echinus esculentus	•																			
	Ophiothrix fragilis														•						
CHORDATA	*Aplidium pallidum*				•																
	Aplidium proliferum			•																	
	Botrylloides leachi			•																	
	Botryllus schlosseri			•	•			•													
	Dendrodoa grossularia																•				
	Sidnyum turbinatum											•									
	Lipophrys pholis			•	•									•				•		•	
	Nerophis lumbriciformis								•												
	Nerophis ophidion			•																	

REENAHOE (STATIONS 1–10)

PHYLUM/DIVISION	SPECIES	1981	1982	1983	1984	1985	1986	1987	1988	1989	1990	1991	1992	1993	1994	1995	1996	1997	1998	1999	2000
GREEN ALGAE (CHLOROPHYCOTA)	*Chaetomorpha* spp.									•				•	•	•		•	•	•	
	Cladophora albida																	•			
	Cladophora hutchinsiae																	•			
	Cladophora rupestris	•	•	•	•	•	•	•	•	•	•	•	•	•	•	•	•	•	•	•	•
	Cladophora sericea																	•			
	Cladophora spp.	•	•	•	•	•	•	•	•	•	•	•	•	•		•		•	•	•	•
	Codium tomentosum	•	•	•	•	•			•			•									
	Codium spp.					•						•									
	Derbesia marina								•									•			
	Derbesia spp.									•											
	Enteromorpha compressa			•	•	•		•		•	•			•							
	Enteromorpha intestinalis	•		•		•				•	•								•		•
	Enteromorpha linza									•											
	Enteromorpha spp.	•	•	•	•	•	•	•	•	•	•	•	•	•	•	•	•	•	•	•	•
	Spongomorpha aeruginosa																				•
	Spongomorpha arcta								•	•	•		•	•	•						
	Spongomorpha spp.											•	•	•		•					
	Ulva lactuca	•	•	•	•	•	•	•	•	•	•	•	•	•	•	•	•	•	•	•	•
	Ulva spp.												•								
	Urospora spp.				•	•															
BROWN ALGAE (CHROMOPHYCOTA)	*Ascophyllum nodosum*	•	•	•	•	•	•	•	•	•	•	•	•	•	•	•	•	•	•	•	•
	Asperococcus fistulosus					•															
	Asperococcus spp.				•																
	Chorda filum		•	•							•	•				•		•			•
	Cladostephus spongiosus		•	•	•			•			•		•					•			•
	Colpomenia peregrina		•									•				•					
	Cystoseira spp.												•								
	Dictyota dichotoma	•	•	•	•		•												•	•	
	Ectocarpus siliculosus				•			•								•		•			
	Ectocarpaceae	•	•	•	•	•	•	•		•	•	•	•	•	•	•	•	•	•	•	•
	Elachista flaccida								•												
	Elachista fucicola				•	•	•	•	•											•	•
	Elachista spp.	•	•	•			•	•	•	•	•	•	•	•	•	•	•	•	•	•	
	Fucus ceranoides																				•
	Fucus serratus	•	•	•	•	•	•	•	•	•	•	•	•	•	•	•	•	•	•	•	•
	Fucus spiralis	•	•	•	•	•	•	•	•	•	•	•	•		•	•	•	•	•	•	•
	Fucus vesiculosus	•	•	•	•	•	•	•	•	•	•	•	•	•	•	•	•	•	•	•	•
	Fucus spp.												•								•
	Fucus spp. sporelings	•	•								•		•	•		•	•	•	•	•	•
	Halopteris filicina														•						
	Himanthalia elongata		•	•	•			•		•					•	•		•			
	Laminaria digitata		•	•	•	•		•	•	•	•	•	•	•				•			•
	Laminaria saccharina			•	•		•			•											
	Laminaria spp.			•																	
	Leathesia difformis	•	•	•	•	•	•	•	•	•	•	•	•	•	•	•	•	•	•	•	•
	Pelvetia canaliculata	•	•	•	•	•	•	•	•	•	•	•	•	•	•	•	•	•	•	•	•
	Punctaria latifolia																			•	
	Ralfsia verrucosa			•	•	•		•					•	•				•	•	•	•
	Scytosiphon lomentaria										•	•	•		•						
	Spongonema tomentosum							•		•							•				
RED ALGAE (RHODOPHYCOTA)	*Aglaothamnion sepositum*																	•			
	Ahnfeltia plicata	•	•	•		•	•	•					•					•			
	Audouinella spp.	•	•	•	•	•	•	•			•		•	•	•	•		•		•	•

REENAHOE (STATIONS 1–10)

PHYLUM/DIVISION	SPECIES	1981	1982	1983	1984	1985	1986	1987	1988	1989	1990	1991	1992	1993	1994	1995	1996	1997	1998	1999	2000
RED ALGAE	*Calliblepharis ciliata*																			•	
(RHODOPHYCOTA)	*Calliblepharis jubata*												•								
	Callithamnion spp.			•									•								
	Callophyllis laciniata						•	•													
	Catenella caespitosa		•	•	•	•						•	•	•			•	•	•	•	•
	Ceramium botryocarpum																	•			•
	Ceramium ciliatum																				•
	Ceramium cimbricum																				•
	Ceramium echionotum																		•		
	Ceramium rubrum			•			•		•	•	•			•				•		•	•
	Ceramium shuttleworthianum												•			•					
	Ceramium strictum																	•			
	Ceramium spp.	•	•	•	•	•	•	•		•	•	•	•		•	•	•		•	•	•
	Chondracanthus acicularis		•						•											•	
	Chondria dasyphylla												•								
	Chondria spp.				•																
	Chondrus crispus	•	•	•	•	•	•	•	•	•	•	•	•	•	•	•	•	•	•	•	•
	Choreocolax polysiphoniae																				•
	Chylocladia verticillata									•											
	Corallina officinalis	•	•	•	•	•	•	•	•	•	•	•	•	•	•	•	•	•	•	•	•
	Corallina spp.														•	•					
	Cryptopleura ramosa		•	•		•					•				•			•			
	Cystoclonium purpureum							•		•								•		•	•
	Dumontia contorta		•	•	•	•	•	•		•	•	•	•	•	•	•	•	•	•	•	
	Erythrodermis traillii			•				•					•								
	Erythroglossum laciniatum												•								
	Furcellaria lumbricalis		•	•	•					•	•			•							
	Gastroclonium ovatum		•		•			•		•											
	Gelidium pulchellum			•						•	•						•				
	Gelidium pusillum				•	•						•	•	•	•			•	•	•	•
	Gelidium spinosum			•	•	•	•	•		•	•	•	•	•	•	•	•	•	•	•	•
	Gelidium spp.	•	•	•	•		•		•	•	•	•				•				•	•
	Gracilaria gracilis													•	•						
	Halurus equisetifolius											•									•
	Halurus flosculosus																				•
	Haraldiophyllum bonnemaisonii											•									
	Heterosiphonia plumosa																			•	•
	Hildenbrandia rubra						•			•	•	•	•	•	•	•	•	•	•	•	•
	Hildenbrandia spp.	•	•	•	•	•	•	•	•	•	•	•	•	•	•	•					
	Hypoglossum hypoglossoides						•													•	
	Laurencia obtusa								•		•					•				•	
	Laurencia spp.											•				•				•	
	Lithothamnia	•	•	•	•	•	•	•	•	•	•	•	•	•	•	•	•	•	•	•	•
	Lomentaria articulata	•	•	•	•	•	•	•	•	•	•	•	•	•	•	•	•	•	•	•	•
	Lomentaria clavellosa							•	•			•		•							
	Lomentaria orcadensis																			•	
	Mastocarpus stellatus	•	•	•	•	•	•	•	•	•	•	•	•	•	•	•	•	•	•	•	•
	Membranoptera alata	•	•	•	•	•	•	•		•	•	•	•	•	•	•	•	•	•	•	•
	Mesophyllum lichenoides																•				•
	Nemalion helminthoides														•						
	Nitophyllum punctatum													•							
	Osmundea hybrida		•	•			•			•		•									•
	Osmundea pinnatifida	•	•	•	•	•	•	•	•	•	•	•	•	•	•	•	•	•	•	•	•
	Palmaria palmata	•		•	•	•							•	•	•				•	•	
	Peyssonnelia spp.	•																			
	Phycodrys rubens			•																	
	Phyllophora crispa							•													

REENAHOE (STATIONS 1–10)

PHYLUM/DIVISION	SPECIES	1981	1982	1983	1984	1985	1986	1987	1988	1989	1990	1991	1992	1993	1994	1995	1996	1997	1998	1999	2000
RED ALGAE (RHODOPHYCOTA)	*Plocamium cartilagineum*													•							
	Plumaria plumosa	•	•	•	•	•	•	•			•	•	•	•	•	•	•	•	•	•	•
	Polyides rotundus				•			•		•	•		•								
	Polysiphonia elongata						•		•				•			•					
	Polysiphonia fucoides					•							•								
	Polysiphonia lanosa	•	•	•	•	•	•	•	•	•	•	•	•	•	•	•	•	•	•	•	•
	Polysiphonia nigra																•			•	
	Polysiphonia stricta			•																	
	Polysiphonia spp.	•	•	•	•		•	•	•	•	•					•			•	•	•
	Porphyra umbilicalis					•															
	Ptilota gunneri																•	•		•	
	Rhodomela confervoides					•															
	Rhodothamniella floridula		•		•	•							•			•	•				
	Rhodymenia pseudopalmata				•			•					•								
LICHEN	*Anaptychia fusca*											•									
	Caloplaca ferruginea																			•	
	Caloplaca marina	•	•	•	•	•	•	•	•		•	•	•	•	•	•	•	•	•	•	•
	Caloplaca thallincola																	•		•	
	Caloplaca spp.												•								
	Haematomma ventosum																			•	
	Lecanora atra	•	•	•	•	•	•	•	•	•	•	•	•	•	•	•	•	•	•	•	•
	Lichina confinis	•	•	•	•	•	•	•	•	•	•	•	•	•	•	•	•	•	•	•	•
	Lichina pygmaea	•	•	•	•	•	•	•	•	•	•	•	•	•	•	•	•	•	•	•	•
	Ochrolechia frigida														•	•					
	Ochrolechia parella			•			•	•				•	•		•	•	•	•	•	•	•
	Ramalina siliquosa	•	•	•	•	•	•	•	•	•	•	•	•	•	•	•	•	•	•	•	•
	Ramalina spp.												•								
	Rhizocarpon geographicum									•											
	Verrucaria maura	•	•	•	•	•	•	•	•	•	•	•	•	•	•	•	•	•	•	•	•
	Verrucaria mucosa	•	•	•	•	•	•	•	•		•	•	•	•	•	•	•	•	•	•	•
	Xanthoria parietina	•	•	•	•	•	•	•	•	•	•	•	•	•	•	•	•	•	•	•	•
BRYOPHYTA	*Grimmia maritima*								•			•									
	Moss				•		•	•				•	•	•	•	•	•	•	•	•	•
	Schistidium maritimum									•	•										
SPERMATOPHYTA	*Armeria maritima*	•	•	•	•	•	•	•	•	•	•	•	•	•	•	•	•	•	•	•	•
	Festuca ovina												•								
	Festuca rubra			•						•	•		•			•					
	Festuca spp.										•										
	Grass				•	•		•			•		•	•	•	•	•	•	•	•	•
	Honckenya peploides							•													
	Juncus maritimus											•									
	Juncus spp.								•		•	•		•							
	Plantago maritima													•	•	•	•				
	Sedum anglicum									•	•										
	Spergularia marina						•					•								•	
	Spergularia rupicola								•												
	Spergularia spp.						•			•	•	•	•	•			•	•		•	
PORIFERA	*Cliona celata*									•											
	Grantia compressa		•	•																•	

REENAHOE (STATIONS 1–10)

PHYLUM/DIVISION	SPECIES	1981	1982	1983	1984	1985	1986	1987	1988	1989	1990	1991	1992	1993	1994	1995	1996	1997	1998	1999	2000
PORIFERA	*Halichondria panicea*	•	•	•	•	•	•	•	•	•	•	•	•	•	•	•	•	•	•	•	•
	Halichondria spp.	•		•					•		•		•		•	•	•				
	Hemimycale columella																		•		
	Hymeniacidon perleve												•								
	Hymeniacidon sanguinea	•	•		•	•	•	•	•			•	•		•		•	•		•	•
	Hymeniacidon spp.	•		•								•	•		•				•		
	Myxilla incrustans			•	•	•	•	•	•	•	•	•	•	•	•	•	•	•	•	•	•
	Myxilla spp.						•	•			•		•			•					
	Ophlitaspongia seriata																	•			
	Oscarella lobularis													•		•					
CNIDARIA	*Coryne* spp.				•																
	Dynamena pumila	•	•	•	•	•	•	•	•	•	•	•	•	•	•	•	•	•	•	•	•
	Laomedea flexuosa				•																
	Obelia geniculata																	•			
	Obelia spp.																			•	
	Sertularella polyzonias		•						•												
	Actinia equina	•	•	•	•	•	•	•	•	•	•	•	•	•	•	•	•	•	•	•	•
	Anemonia viridis	•	•	•	•	•	•			•	•	•	•	•		•		•			•
	Aulactinia verrucosa	•	•	•	•	•	•	•							•	•		•			•
	Cereus pedunculatus										•									•	
	Sagartia elegans		•	•		•		•						•	•						
	Sagartia troglodytes							•				•									
	Urticina felina											•					•				
NEMERTEA	*Lineus* spp.								•												
ANNELIDA	*Amphitritides gracilis*		•																		
	Cirratulus cirratus				•																
	Cirriformia tentaculata	•																•		•	
	Eulalia viridis													•		•			•		
	Lanice conchilega																			•	
	Nephtys hombergi							•													
	Perinereis cultrifera										•										
	Pomatoceros triqueter	•	•	•	•	•		•	•	•	•		•	•		•	•			•	•
	Pomatoceros spp.					•	•														
	Spirorbis rupestris																			•	
	Spirorbis spirorbis					•		•		•			•	•	•	•			•		
	Spirorbis spp.	•	•	•	•	•	•	•	•	•	•	•	•	•	•	•	•	•	•	•	•
CHELICERATA	Acari spp.								•				•	•	•						•
HEXAPODA	*Lipura maritima*	•	•	•			•	•	•	•	•	•	•	•	•		•	•		•	•
	Petrobius maritimus	•																			
CRUSTACEA	Barnacles	•	•	•	•	•	•	•	•	•	•	•	•	•	•	•	•	•	•	•	•
	Barnacle spat	•	•	•	•		•	•	•	•	•	•	•	•	•	•	•	•	•	•	•
	Chthamalus montagui					•															
	Chthamalus stellatus												•							•	
	Chthamalus spp.	•	•	•	•	•	•	•	•				•	•	•	•	•	•	•	•	•

REENAHOE (STATIONS 1–10)

PHYLUM/DIVISION	SPECIES	1981	1982	1983	1984	1985	1986	1987	1988	1989	1990	1991	1992	1993	1994	1995	1996	1997	1998	1999	2000
CRUSTACEA	*Elminius modestus*	•	•	•	•	•	•	•					•	•	•	•	•	•	•	•	•
	Semibalanus balanoides	•	•	•	•	•	•	•	•				•	•	•	•	•	•	•	•	•
	Verruca stroemia	•	•	•	•	•	•								•						
	Cancer pagurus	•	•	•	•	•	•	•			•	•	•	•		•		•	•	•	•
	Carcinus maenas	•	•	•	•	•	•	•	•	•	•	•	•	•	•	•	•	•	•	•	•
	Dynamene bidentata		•									•									
	Gammarus spp.						•	•				•	•			•		•	•		
	Idotea granulosa			•																	
	Idotea spp.	•					•											•		•	
	Ligia oceanica		•	•	•		•	•	•	•	•	•	•			•	•	•		•	•
	Pagurus bernhardus	•	•	•	•	•	•	•	•	•	•								•	•	
	Pagurus prideauxi								•												
	Pagurus spp.											•									
	Pinnotheres pisum								•		•									•	
	Sphaeroma serratum																	•			
	Talitrus saltator							•													
	Xantho incisus		•		•																
MOLLUSCA	*Alvania cancellata*													•							
	Anomia ephippium				•																
	Archidoris pseudoargus	•	•		•	•	•	•							•			•			
	Bittium reticulatum								•				•								
	Calliostoma zizyphinum				•									•		•					
	Chiton spp.		•			•					•	•									
	Gibbula cineraria	•	•	•	•	•	•	•			•	•	•	•	•		•	•	•	•	•
	Gibbula umbilicalis	•	•	•	•	•	•	•	•	•	•	•	•	•	•	•	•	•	•	•	•
	Gibbula spp.									•	•										
	Helcion pellucidum		•						•	•		•									
	Hinia incrassata	•	•	•	•	•	•				•	•	•	•	•			•			
	Hinia reticulata		•	•	•			•		•		•				•		•	•	•	•
	Hydrobia ulvae				•																
	Jorunna tomentosa				•																
	Lacuna vincta			•																	
	Lepidochitona cinerea															•					
	Littorina littorea	•	•	•	•	•	•	•	•	•	•	•	•	•	•	•	•	•	•	•	•
	Littorina neglecta	•	•	•	•	•															
	Littorina obtusata	•	•	•	•	•	•	•	•	•	•	•	•	•	•	•	•	•	•	•	•
	Littorina saxatilis	•	•	•	•	•	•	•	•	•	•	•	•	•	•	•	•	•	•	•	•
	Melarhaphe neritoides	•	•	•	•	•		•	•	•	•	•	•	•	•	•	•	•	•	•	•
	Modiolus barbatus																		•		
	Mytilus edulis	•	•	•	•	•	•	•	•	•	•	•	•	•	•	•	•	•	•	•	•
	Nucella (eggs)		•					•		•	•				•		•				
	Nucella lapillus	•	•	•	•	•	•	•	•	•	•	•	•	•	•	•	•	•	•	•	•
	Nudibranch (eggs)																	•			
	Ocenebra erinacea				•		•						•								
	Osilinus lineatus	•							•		•	•	•		•	•		•	•	•	•
	Patella aspera							•													
	Patella spp.	•	•	•	•	•	•	•	•	•	•	•	•	•	•	•	•	•	•	•	•
	Rissoa spp.			•																	•
	Rostanga rubra					•															
	Trivia monacha								•												
BRYOZOA	*Alcyonidium gelatinosum*	•	•	•	•	•			•				•				•	•	•	•	•
	Alcyonidium hirsutum	•	•	•	•	•			•						•	•	•	•	•	•	•

REENAHOE (STATIONS 1–10)

PHYLUM/DIVISION	SPECIES	1981	1982	1983	1984	1985	1986	1987	1988	1989	1990	1991	1992	1993	1994	1995	1996	1997	1998	1999	2000
BRYOZOA	*Alcyonidium* spp.		•									•					•				
	Bowerbankia imbricata		•		•												•				
	Cellepora pumicosa	•	•	•																	
	Celleporina hassallii		•																		
	Electra pilosa	•	•	•	•	•	•	•	•			•	•	•	•		•	•	•	•	•
	Flustrellidra hispida	•	•	•	•	•		•	•	•	•	•	•	•	•	•	•	•	•	•	•
	Membranipora membranacea		•				•	•	•	•	•	•	•	•			•	•	•	•	•
	Schizoporella unicornis				•																
	Scrupocellaria reptans			•	•													•			
	Umbonula littoralis					•	•	•													
	Umbonula spp.					•	•		•				•		•		•	•	•	•	
ECHINODERMATA	*Amphiura brachiata*						•														
	Asterias rubens														•				•		
	Asterina gibbosa										•										
	Ophiocomina nigra						•														
	Ophiothrix fragilis				•								•	•							
CHORDATA	*Aplidium pallidum*				•																
	Aplidium proliferum			•	•	•	•						•								
	Aplidium spp.							•	•							•		•			
	Ascidiella aspersa			•																	
	Ascidiella scabra			•																	
	Botrylloides leachi		•											•							
	Botryllus schlosseri	•	•	•	•	•	•		•	•	•	•	•		•	•		•	•	•	
	Clavelina lepadiformis				•							•									
	Dendrodoa grossularia															•	•				
	Didemnum spp.			•																	
	Morchellium argus																	•		•	
	Polyclinum aurantium			•																	
	Sidnyum turbinatum		•					•													
	Nerophis lumbriciformis																	•			
	Pholis gunnellus						•														

KINISH NARROWS EAST (STATIONS 1–10)

PHYLUM/DIVISION	SPECIES	1981	1982	1983	1984	1985	1986	1987	1988	1989	1990	1991	1992	1993	1994	1995	1996	1997	1998	1999	2000
GREEN ALGAE	*Bryopsis plumosa*			•																	
(CHLOROPHYCOTA)	*Chaetomorpha* spp.													•	•	•	•	•		•	
	Cladophora albida																	•			
	Cladophora rupestris	•	•	•	•	•	•	•	•	•	•	•	•	•	•	•	•	•	•	•	•
	Cladophora spp.	•	•	•	•	•	•	•	•	•	•	•	•	•	•	•			•	•	
	Derbesia marina									•											
	Derbesia spp.									•											•
	Enteromorpha compressa			•	•	•															
	Enteromorpha intestinalis		•			•				•		•	•			•			•		•
	Enteromorpha linza											•									•
	Enteromorpha muscoides																	•			
	Enteromorpha prolifera																				•
	Enteromorpha spp.	•	•	•	•	•	•	•	•	•	•	•	•	•	•	•	•	•	•	•	•
	Spongomorpha arcta								•	•	•										•
	Spongomorpha spp.										•	•		•		•					
	Ulva lactuca	•	•	•	•	•	•	•	•	•	•	•	•	•	•	•	•	•	•	•	•
	Ulva spp.												•								
BROWN ALGAE	*Ascophyllum nodosum*	•	•	•	•	•	•	•	•	•	•	•	•	•		•				•	
(CHROMOPHYCOTA)	*Asperococcus fistulosus*					•	•				•	•									
	Asperococcus spp.				•	•						•									
	Bifurcaria bifurcata					•															
	Chorda filum										•	•				•					
	Cladostephus spongiosus		•	•	•						•										
	Colpomenia peregrina																		•		
	Cystoseira spp.													•							
	Dictyota dichotoma								•					•							
	Ectocarpus siliculosus					•												•		•	
	Ectocarpaceae	•	•	•	•	•	•	•			•	•	•	•	•	•	•	•	•	•	•
	Elachista flaccida									•											
	Elachista fucicola		•	•	•	•		•	•											•	•
	Elachista spp.	•	•			•	•	•	•	•	•	•	•	•	•	•	•	•	•	•	
	Eudesme virescens						•														
	Fucus serratus	•	•	•	•	•	•	•	•	•	•	•	•	•	•	•	•	•	•	•	•
	Fucus spiralis		•		•	•	•	•	•	•	•	•	•	•	•	•	•	•	•	•	•
	Fucus vesiculosus	•	•	•	•	•	•	•	•	•	•	•	•	•	•	•	•	•	•	•	•
	Fucus spp.	•	•														•				•
	Fucus spp. sporelings	•	•		•				•		•		•	•	•	•	•	•	•	•	
	Halopteris filicina									•											
	Himanthalia elongata					•												•			
	Laminaria digitata	•	•	•	•	•	•	•	•	•		•	•	•							
	Laminaria saccharina		•			•	•	•	•	•	•	•	•								
	Laminaria spp.	•	•	•				•			•		•								
	Leathesia difformis	•	•	•	•	•	•	•	•	•	•	•				•	•	•		•	•
	Pelvetia canaliculata	•	•	•	•	•	•	•	•	•	•	•	•	•	•	•	•	•	•	•	•
	Ralfsia verrucosa				•								•	•						•	•
	Scytosiphon lomentaria			•	•	•				•	•	•									•
	Spongonema tomentosum	•									•										
RED ALGAE	*Aglaothamnion hookeri*												•								
(RHODOPHYCOTA)	*Aglaothamnion roseum*			•																	
	Ahnfeltia plicata	•	•	•	•		•				•							•	•		
	Audouinella spp.	•	•	•	•	•	•	•			•	•	•	•	•			•		•	•
	Boergeseniella fruticulosa																	•			
	Calliblepharis ciliata					•		•		•										•	

KINISH NARROWS EAST (STATIONS 1–10)

PHYLUM/DIVISION	SPECIES	1981	1982	1983	1984	1985	1986	1987	1988	1989	1990	1991	1992	1993	1994	1995	1996	1997	1998	1999	2000
RED ALGAE	*Calliblepharis jubata*		•				•						•								
(RHODOPHYCOTA)	*Callithamnion* spp.			•								•		•							
	Callophyllis laciniata							•													
	Catenella caespitosa	•	•	•	•	•		•				•	•	•			•	•	•	•	•
	Ceramium botryocarpum																	•			•
	Ceramium ciliatum					•															
	Ceramium echionotum																		•		
	Ceramium gaditanum													•							
	Ceramium pallidum																•	•			
	Ceramium rubrum	•			•	•	•	•	•	•	•	•	•	•	•	•		•		•	•
	Ceramium shuttleworthianum			•		•							•		•		•				
	Ceramium spp.	•	•	•	•	•	•	•	•	•		•		•	•	•	•		•	•	
	Chondracanthus acicularis		•			•								•	•	•					
	Chondria capillaris							•													
	Chondria dasyphylla													•							
	Chondria spp.				•			•													
	Chondrus crispus	•	•	•	•	•	•	•	•	•	•	•	•	•	•	•	•	•	•	•	•
	Choreocolax polysiphoniae																				•
	Chylocladia verticillata												•								
	Corallina officinalis							•					•								
	Cryptopleura ramosa					•															
	Cystoclonium purpureum					•		•					•								
	Delesseria sanguinea				•																
	Dilsea carnosa						•					•									
	Drachiella spectabilis											•									
	Dumontia contorta	•	•	•	•		•	•	•	•	•	•	•			•		•		•	•
	Furcellaria lumbricalis	•	•				•	•		•		•	•								
	Gastroclonium ovatum											•									
	Gelidium pulchellum			•							•						•	•			
	Gelidium pusillum				•	•		•				•	•	•	•	•		•	•	•	•
	Gelidium spinosum						•	•	•	•				•	•	•	•	•	•	•	•
	Gelidium spp.	•	•	•		•	•	•	•	•	•	•	•	•		•				•	
	Gracilaria gracilis												•	•							
	Grateloupia filicina						•														
	Halurus equisetifolius											•									
	Halurus flosculosus																				•
	Hildenbrandia rubra				•	•				•	•	•		•	•	•	•	•	•	•	•
	Hildenbrandia spp.	•	•	•	•	•	•	•			•	•	•	•	•	•					
	Hypoglossum hypoglossoides								•												
	Laurencia obtusa							•		•		•				•					
	Laurencia spp.																		•	•	
	Lithothamnia	•	•	•	•	•	•	•	•	•	•	•	•	•	•	•	•	•	•	•	•
	Lomentaria articulata	•	•	•	•	•	•	•	•	•	•	•	•	•	•	•	•	•	•	•	•
	Lomentaria clavellosa					•	•					•									
	Mastocarpus stellatus	•	•	•	•	•	•	•	•	•	•	•	•	•	•	•	•	•	•	•	•
	Membranoptera alata	•	•	•	•	•	•	•		•		•	•								
	Nemalion helminthoides	•						•							•						
	Osmundea hybrida			•		•	•	•	•			•		•	•			•			•
	Osmundea pinnatifida	•	•	•	•	•	•	•	•	•	•	•	•	•	•	•	•	•	•	•	•
	Palmaria palmata	•			•	•		•		•		•	•	•				•	•	•	•
	Phyllophora pseudoceranoides			•																	
	Phyllophora spp.			•																	
	Plocamium cartilagineum										•										
	Plumaria plumosa	•	•	•	•	•	•	•	•	•	•	•	•								
	Polyides rotundus		•	•	•		•														
	Polysiphonia atlantica														•						
	Polysiphonia elongata					•							•	•	•						

KINISH NARROWS EAST (STATIONS 1–10)

PHYLUM/DIVISION	SPECIES	1981	1982	1983	1984	1985	1986	1987	1988	1989	1990	1991	1992	1993	1994	1995	1996	1997	1998	1999	2000
RED ALGAE (RHODOPHYCOTA)	*Polysiphonia fibrata*														•						
	Polysiphonia fucoides														•						
	Polysiphonia lanosa	•	•	•	•	•	•	•	•	•	•	•	•	•	•	•	•	•	•	•	
	Polysiphonia nigra												•								
	Polysiphonia stricta					•															
	Polysiphonia spp.	•		•		•	•	•			•	•									•
	Porphyra umbilicalis	•																			
	Porphyra spp.											•									
	Pterocladia capillacea								•												
	Rhodothamniella floridula		•	•	•	•							•				•				
	Rhodymenia pseudopalmata			•																	
	Rhodymenia spp.									•											
LICHEN	*Anaptychia fusca*				•			•	•											•	
	Caloplaca ferruginea																			•	
	Caloplaca marina	•	•	•	•	•	•	•	•	•	•	•	•	•	•	•	•	•	•	•	•
	Caloplaca spp.												•					•			
	Cladonia spp.			•																	
	Haematomma ventosum																			•	
	Lecanora atra	•	•	•	•	•	•	•	•	•	•	•	•	•	•	•	•	•	•	•	•
	Lecanora spp.	•																			
	Lichina confinis	•	•	•	•	•	•	•	•	•	•	•	•	•	•	•	•	•	•	•	•
	Lichina pygmaea	•	•	•	•	•	•	•	•	•	•	•	•	•	•	•	•	•	•	•	•
	Lichina spp.		•																		
	Ochrolechia frigida															•					
	Ochrolechia parella							•	•	•				•	•	•	•	•	•	•	•
	Ramalina siliquosa	•	•	•	•	•	•	•	•	•	•	•	•	•	•	•	•	•	•	•	•
	Ramalina spp.												•								
	Verrucaria maura	•	•	•	•	•	•	•	•	•	•	•	•	•	•	•	•	•	•	•	•
	Verrucaria mucosa	•	•	•	•	•	•	•	•	•		•	•	•	•	•	•	•	•	•	•
	Xanthoria parietina	•	•	•	•	•	•	•	•	•	•	•	•	•	•	•	•	•	•	•	•
BRYOPHYTA	*Grimmia maritima*								•												
	Moss				•			•			•		•	•	•	•	•	•	•	•	•
	Schistidium maritimum																	•			
SPERMATOPHYTA	*Armeria maritima*				•			•	•	•	•		•	•	•	•	•	•	•	•	•
	Festuca rubra															•					
	Grass							•	•							•	•	•	•		
	Plantago coronopus															•		•	•	•	
	Plantago maritima										•			•	•			•		•	
	Spergularia media																			•	
	Spergularia spp.									•											
PORIFERA	*Halichondria panicea*	•	•		•	•	•	•	•	•	•	•	•	•			•	•		•	
	Halichondria spp.	•	•	•				•													
	Hymeniacidon perleve		•	•	•	•			•			•									
	Hymeniacidon spp.	•	•	•		•		•													
	Mycale massa					•															
	Myxilla incrustans			•			•	•	•	•	•	•	•	•	•		•	•		•	
	Myxilla spp.						•	•			•		•	•	•	•					
	Oscarella lobularis															•					

KINISH NARROWS EAST (Stations 1–10)

PHYLUM/DIVISION	SPECIES	1981	1982	1983	1984	1985	1986	1987	1988	1989	1990	1991	1992	1993	1994	1995	1996	1997	1998	1999	2000
CNIDARIA	*Clava multicornis*					•															
	Coryne muscoides			•																	
	Dynamena pumila	•	•	•	•	•	•	•	•	•	•	•	•	•	•	•	•	•	•	•	•
	Laomedea flexuosa				•																
	Obelia geniculata	•						•										•			
	Obelia spp.			•														•			
	Actinia equina			•	•	•	•	•	•	•	•	•				•	•	•			
	Alcyonium palmatum					•															
	Anemonia viridis					•		•			•	•	•		•						
	Sagartia elegans				•				•		•										
	Sagartia spp.								•												
	Urticina felina			•	•	•		•	•	•			•								
PLATYHELMINTHE	*Monocelis lineata*																			•	
ANNELIDA	*Amphitritides gracilis*		•	•																	
	Cirratulus cirratus				•																
	Cirriformia tentaculata								•		•							•		•	
	Eulalia viridis												•	•						•	
	Hydroides norvegica										•										
	Pomatoceros triqueter	•	•	•	•	•		•	•	•	•	•	•	•		•				•	•
	Pomatoceros spp.					•	•	•		•											
	Spirorbis inornatus	•	•	•																	
	Spirorbis rupestris	•	•	•																•	
	Spirorbis spirorbis	•	•	•		•		•		•			•		•	•			•	•	
	Spirorbis spp.	•	•	•	•	•	•	•	•	•	•	•	•	•	•	•	•	•	•	•	•
CHELICERATA	Acari spp.								•				•	•	•					•	•
	Achelia spp.			•																	
	Endeis spinosa				•																
	Nymphon gracile						•	•					•								
	Nymphon spp.			•	•																
	Pycnogonum littorale							•													
HEXAPODA	*Lipura maritima*	•		•			•	•	•	•	•	•	•	•		•		•	•	•	•
	Petrobius maritimus									•											
CRUSTACEA	*Balanus crenatus*		•															•			
	Barnacles	•	•	•	•	•	•	•	•	•	•	•	•	•	•	•	•	•	•	•	•
	Barnacle spat	•	•	•			•	•	•	•	•	•	•	•	•	•	•	•	•	•	•
	Chthamalus spp.	•	•	•	•	•	•	•	•				•	•	•	•	•	•	•	•	•
	Elminius modestus	•	•	•	•	•	•	•					•	•	•	•	•	•	•	•	•
	Semibalanus balanoides	•	•	•	•	•	•	•	•				•	•	•	•	•	•	•	•	•
	Verruca stroemia		•	•	•	•															
	Cancer pagurus		•					•		•	•					•					
	Carcinus maenas	•	•	•	•	•	•	•	•	•	•	•	•	•	•	•	•	•	•	•	•
	Dynamene bidentata		•																		
	Gammarus spp.						•	•		•		•	•			•		•	•		•
	Hyas araneus				•																
	Idotea spp.						•							•				•			

KINISH NARROWS EAST (STATIONS 1–10)

PHYLUM/DIVISION	SPECIES	1981	1982	1983	1984	1985	1986	1987	1988	1989	1990	1991	1992	1993	1994	1995	1996	1997	1998	1999	2000
CRUSTACEA	*Ligia oceanica*	•	•	•	•	•	•	•		•	•	•	•	•	•	•	•	•		•	•
	Necora puber											•									
	Orchestia gammarellus								•												
	Pagurus bernhardus		•	•	•	•	•	•		•											
	Pinnotheres pisum								•		•										
	Talitrus saltator									•											
MOLLUSCA	*Acanthodoris pilosa*							•													
	Anomia ephippium		•	•	•	•		•													
	Archidoris pseudoargus			•																	
	Bittium reticulatum			•						•											
	Calliostoma zizyphinum		•	•	•		•	•		•	•		•								
	Cerastoderma edule		•																		
	Chiton spp.		•	•	•	•										•				•	
	Chlamys varia				•																
	Facelina auriculata				•																
	Gastropod (egg cases)			•																	
	Gibbula cineraria	•	•	•	•	•	•	•			•	•	•	•	•	•	•	•	•	•	•
	Gibbula umbilicalis	•	•	•	•	•	•	•	•	•	•	•	•	•	•	•	•	•	•	•	•
	Gibbula spp.									•						•					
	Helcion pellucidum							•													
	Hinia incrassata	•	•	•	•	•	•	•		•		•	•	•							
	Hinia reticulata		•	•	•			•	•		•	•							•		
	Hinia spp.							•													
	Lepidochitona cinerea			•							•										
	Leptochiton asellus											•									
	Limacia clavigera				•			•													
	Littorina littorea	•	•	•	•	•	•	•	•	•	•	•	•	•	•	•	•	•	•	•	•
	Littorina neglecta	•	•	•	•	•															
	Littorina obtusata	•	•	•	•	•	•	•	•	•	•	•	•	•	•	•	•	•	•	•	•
	Littorina saxatilis	•	•	•	•	•	•	•	•	•	•	•	•	•	•	•	•	•	•	•	•
	Melarhaphe neritoides	•		•	•	•	•	•	•	•	•	•	•	•	•	•	•	•	•	•	•
	Musculus discors				•																
	Mytilus edulis	•	•	•	•	•	•	•	•	•	•	•	•	•	•	•	•	•	•	•	•
	Nucella lapillus	•	•	•	•	•	•	•	•	•	•	•	•	•	•	•	•	•	•	•	•
	Nucella (eggs)	•		•	•		•	•	•		•	•		•			•	•			
	Nucula nucleus			•																	
	Ocenebra erinacea							•			•										
	Onchidoris bilamellata							•													
	Osilinus lineatus				•				•	•		•		•							•
	Ostrea edulis									•							•				
	Patella spat																			•	
	Patella vulgata												•			•					
	Patella spp.	•	•	•	•	•	•	•	•	•	•	•	•	•	•	•	•	•	•	•	•
	Trivia arctica		•										•								
	Trivia monacha							•	•	•											
	Trivia spp.						•														
BRYOZOA	*Alcyonidium diaphanum*							•													
	Alcyonidium gelatinosum		•	•	•	•	•	•	•	•							•	•	•	•	
	Alcyonidium hirsutum	•	•	•	•	•		•		•			•				•	•	•	•	
	Alcyonidium spp.						•		•	•		•	•	•				•			
	Bowerbankia imbricata			•	•	•	•						•	•							
	Cellepora pumicosa		•	•																	
	Electra pilosa	•	•	•	•	•	•	•	•			•	•	•				•			•

KINISH NARROWS EAST (STATIONS 1–10)

PHYLUM/DIVISION	SPECIES	1981	1982	1983	1984	1985	1986	1987	1988	1989	1990	1991	1992	1993	1994	1995	1996	1997	1998	1999	2000
BRYOZOA	*Flustrellidra hispida*	•	•	•	•	•	•	•	•	•	•	•	•	•		•	•	•	•	•	
	Membranipora membranacea	•	•		•		•	•	•	•	•		•	•					•	•	
	Schizoporella unicornis				•																
	Scrupocellaria reptans		•																		
	Tubulipora phalangea		•	•																	
	Umbonula littoralis					•		•													
	Umbonula spp.					•	•	•	•	•			•	•				•	•	•	
ECHINODERMATA	*Antedon bifida*		•							•											
	Asterias rubens									•											
	Asterina gibbosa	•	•	•	•		•	•		•	•			•							
	Ophiothrix fragilis		•				•			•											
CHORDATA	*Aplidium nordmanni*						•														
	Aplidium pallidum			•	•																
	Aplidium proliferum			•			•	•		•				•							
	Aplidium spp.			•	•	•	•	•		•			•								
	Ascidia mentula													•							
	Ascidiella aspersa					•															
	Ascidiella spp.						•														
	Botrylloides leachi						•	•													
	Botryllus schlosseri	•	•	•	•		•	•	•	•		•		•							
	Ciona intestinalis												•								
	Clavelina lepadiformis					•	•	•		•											
	Dendrodoa grossularia		•	•			•	•								•					
	Sidnyum turbinatum			•		•						•									
	Pholis gunnellus					•															

KINISH NARROWS WEST (STATIONS 1–9)

PHYLUM/DIVISION	SPECIES	1981	1982	1983	1984	1985	1986	1987	1988	1989	1990	1991	1992	1993	1994	1995	1996	1997	1998	1999	2000
GREEN ALGAE (CHLOROPHYCOTA)	*Bryopsis plumosa*												•								
	Chaetomorpha linum				•					•											•
	Chaetomorpha spp.													•			•	•	•		•
	Cladophora albida																	•			•
	Cladophora laetevirens																	•			
	Cladophora rupestris	•	•	•	•	•	•	•	•	•	•	•	•	•	•	•		•	•	•	•
	Cladophora sericea																	•			•
	Cladophora spp.	•	•	•	•	•	•	•	•	•	•	•	•	•	•	•	•	•	•	•	•
	Codium tomentosum				•																
	Codium spp.		•																		
	Derbesia marina																	•			
	Derbesia spp.								•												
	Enteromorpha compressa			•	•	•		•		•											
	Enteromorpha intestinalis			•	•	•		•		•		•	•			•	•		•	•	•
	Enteromorpha linza			•																	
	Enteromorpha prolifera																				•
	Enteromorpha spp.	•	•	•	•	•	•	•	•	•	•	•	•	•	•	•	•	•	•	•	•
	Spongomorpha arcta								•	•	•				•						•
	Spongomorpha spp.		•							•		•			•		•				•
	Ulva lactuca	•	•	•	•	•	•	•	•	•	•	•	•	•	•	•	•	•	•	•	•
	Ulva spp.												•								
BROWN ALGAE (CHROMOPHYCOTA)	*Ascophyllum nodosum*	•	•	•	•	•	•	•	•	•	•	•	•	•	•	•	•		•	•	•
	Asperococcus fistulosus					•	•														
	Asperococcus spp.				•																
	Chorda filum		•	•				•	•		•				•	•			•		
	Cladostephus spongiosus			•				•			•	•	•					•		•	
	Colpomenia peregrina															•					
	Dictyota dichotoma				•	•							•								
	Ectocarpus siliculosus				•																
	Ectocarpaceae	•	•	•	•	•		•			•	•	•	•	•	•	•	•	•	•	•
	Elachista flaccida								•												
	Elachista fucicola		•	•	•		•	•	•										•	•	•
	Elachista spp.	•	•			•	•		•	•	•	•	•	•	•	•	•	•	•	•	
	Fucus serratus	•	•	•	•	•	•	•	•	•	•	•	•	•	•	•	•	•	•	•	•
	Fucus spiralis	•	•	•	•	•	•	•	•	•	•	•	•	•	•	•	•	•	•	•	•
	Fucus vesiculosus	•	•	•	•	•	•	•	•	•	•	•	•	•	•	•	•	•	•	•	•
	Fucus spp.					•					•							•		•	•
	Fucus spp. sporelings	•	•					•			•	•	•	•	•	•	•	•	•	•	•
	Himanthalia elongata			•				•							•				•		•
	Laminaria digitata		•	•	•		•			•	•				•				•		•
	Laminaria saccharina				•	•				•		•									
	Laminaria spp.	•			•		•	•							•		•				
	Laminaria spp. sporelings		•			•															
	Leathesia difformis		•	•	•	•	•	•	•	•	•	•	•				•	•		•	•
	Pelvetia canaliculata	•	•	•	•	•	•	•	•	•	•	•	•	•	•	•	•	•	•	•	•
	Punctaria latifolia									•											
	Ralfsia verrucosa			•	•			•						•	•			•		•	•
	Scytosiphon lomentaria			•						•			•		•						•
	Spongonema tomentosum						•	•			•							•			
RED ALGAE (RHODOPHYCOTA)	*Ahnfeltia plicata*	•		•	•		•				•	•	•					•			
	Audouinella spp.			•	•	•	•	•			•		•	•	•	•		•	•	•	•
	Boergeseniella thuyoides			•																	
	Calliblepharis ciliata																	•			

KINISH NARROWS WEST (STATIONS 1–9)

PHYLUM/DIVISION	SPECIES	1981	1982	1983	1984	1985	1986	1987	1988	1989	1990	1991	1992	1993	1994	1995	1996	1997	1998	1999	2000
RED ALGAE	*Calliblepharis jubata*																				•
(RHODOPHYCOTA)	*Callithamnion tetricum*														•						
	Callithamnion spp.			•										•	•						
	Catenella caespitosa	•		•	•	•	•	•				•	•	•				•	•	•	
	Ceramium botryocarpum																				•
	Ceramium ciliatum														•			•		•	
	Ceramium deslongchampii					•															
	Ceramium gaditanum																				•
	Ceramium pallidum																	•			
	Ceramium rubrum	•					•	•	•	•	•		•	•	•			•			
	Ceramium shuttleworthianum					•									•		•	•		•	•
	Ceramium spp.	•	•	•	•	•	•	•	•	•	•	•		•	•	•	•				•
	Chondracanthus acicularis					•									•						
	Chondria dasyphylla					•															
	Chondrus crispus	•	•	•	•	•	•	•	•	•	•	•	•	•	•	•	•	•	•	•	•
	Choreocolax polysiphoniae																				•
	Cryptopleura ramosa			•												•					
	Cystoclonium purpureum							•				•	•								
	Delesseria sanguinea												•								
	Dumontia contorta					•	•	•		•	•					•	•	•		•	
	Erythrodermis traillii												•								
	Furcellaria lumbricalis			•				•					•					•			
	Gelidium crinale					•															
	Gelidium pulchellum			•				•	•	•							•				
	Gelidium pusillum				•	•		•				•	•	•	•	•		•		•	•
	Gelidium spinosum					•	•	•	•	•			•	•	•	•	•	•	•	•	•
	Gelidium spp.	•	•	•		•	•				•	•	•	•		•				•	•
	Gracilaria gracilis					•							•					•			•
	Gracilaria spp.		•					•													
	Halurus equisetifolius																				•
	Heterosiphonia plumosa									•											
	Hildenbrandia rubra							•	•		•	•	•	•	•	•	•	•	•	•	•
	Hildenbrandia spp.	•	•	•	•	•	•	•	•	•	•	•	•	•	•	•				•	
	Laurencia obtusa							•	•	•										•	
	Laurencia spp.		•	•		•			•		•	•								•	
	Lithothamnia	•	•	•	•	•	•	•	•	•	•	•	•	•	•	•	•	•	•	•	•
	Lomentaria articulata	•	•	•	•	•	•	•	•	•	•	•	•	•	•	•	•	•	•	•	•
	Lomentaria clavellosa						•					•				•					
	Lomentaria spp.		•			•			•		•										
	Mastocarpus stellatus	•	•	•	•	•	•	•	•	•	•	•	•	•	•	•	•	•	•	•	•
	Mastocarpus/Chondrus sporeling	•																			
	Membranoptera alata	•	•		•	•	•	•	•			•				•					
	Mesophyllum lichenoides																				•
	Nemalion helminthoides												•								
	Nitophyllum punctatum												•								
	Osmundea hybrida						•	•				•									
	Osmundea pinnatifida	•		•	•	•	•	•	•	•	•	•	•	•	•	•	•	•	•	•	•
	Palmaria palmata					•								•					•	•	
	Phycodrys rubens														•						
	Pilayella littoralis			•																	
	Pleonosporium borreri														•						
	Plocamium cartilagineum					•		•	•									•			
	Plumaria plumosa	•	•	•	•	•	•	•	•	•	•	•	•		•						
	Polyides rotundus				•										•						
	Polysiphonia elongata						•			•		•	•								
	Polysiphonia lanosa	•	•	•	•	•	•	•	•	•	•	•	•	•	•		•	•	•	•	•
	Polysiphonia spp.	•					•		•		•	•			•				•	•	

KINISH NARROWS WEST (STATIONS 1–9)

PHYLUM/DIVISION	SPECIES	1981	1982	1983	1984	1985	1986	1987	1988	1989	1990	1991	1992	1993	1994	1995	1996	1997	1998	1999	2000
RED ALGAE (RHODOPHYCOTA)	*Porphyra umbilicalis*												●								
	Pterocladia capillacea																	●			
	Pterosiphonia parasitica																●				
	Rhodothamniella floridula				●												●				
	Rhodymenia spp.				●																
LICHEN	*Anaptychia fusca*					●									●						
	Caloplaca marina	●	●	●	●	●	●	●	●	●	●	●	●	●	●	●	●	●	●	●	●
	Caloplaca thallincola																	●		●	
	Caloplaca spp.												●								
	Haematomma ventosum																			●	
	Lecanora atra	●	●	●	●	●	●	●	●	●	●	●	●	●	●	●	●	●	●	●	●
	Lecanora spp.	●																			
	Lichina confinis				●	●		●	●	●	●	●		●		●	●	●	●	●	●
	Lichina pygmaea	●			●	●	●	●		●	●	●	●	●	●	●	●	●	●	●	●
	Ochrolechia frigida															●		●			
	Ochrolechia parella					●		●	●							●	●	●	●	●	●
	Ramalina siliquosa				●	●		●		●				●						●	●
	Verrucaria maura	●	●	●	●	●	●	●	●	●	●	●	●	●	●	●	●	●	●	●	●
	Verrucaria mucosa	●	●	●	●	●	●	●	●		●	●	●	●	●	●	●	●	●	●	●
	Verrucaria spp.	●																			
	Xanthoria parietina	●	●	●	●	●	●	●	●	●	●	●	●	●	●	●	●	●	●	●	●
BRYOPHYTA	*Grimmia maritima*								●			●									
	Moss	●			●	●	●	●	●		●	●	●	●	●	●	●	●	●	●	●
	Schistidium maritimum									●	●							●			
SPERMATOPHYTA	*Armeria maritima*	●	●	●	●	●	●	●	●	●	●	●	●	●	●	●	●	●	●	●	●
	Festuca rubra										●										
	Grass												●		●					●	●
	Juncus spp.										●			●	●			●			
	Plantago maritima					●		●	●		●	●	●	●	●	●		●		●	●
	Spergularia spp.								●				●								
PORIFERA	*Halichondria panicea*	●	●		●	●	●	●	●	●		●	●	●	●	●	●	●	●	●	●
	Halichondria spp.	●		●		●	●		●		●		●								
	Hymeniacidon perleve		●																		
	Hymeniacidon sanguinea	●	●		●	●		●	●			●						●			
	Hymeniacidon spp.	●	●	●		●	●					●	●								
	Grantia compressa																			●	
	Leucosolenia botryoides			●																	
	Myxilla incrustans				●		●	●	●	●	●	●	●	●	●	●	●	●	●	●	●
	Myxilla spp.						●		●		●					●		●			
CNIDARIA	*Coryne muscoides*									●											
	Dynamena pumila	●	●	●	●	●	●	●	●	●	●	●	●	●	●	●	●	●	●	●	●
	Laomedea flexuosa				●																
	Obelia dichotoma			●																	
	Obelia geniculata										●				●			●			
	Obelia spp.							●												●	
	Actinia equina	●	●	●	●	●	●	●	●	●	●	●	●	●	●	●	●	●	●	●	●
	Alcyonium palmatum						●														

KINISH NARROWS WEST (STATIONS 1–9)

PHYLUM/DIVISION	SPECIES	1981	1982	1983	1984	1985	1986	1987	1988	1989	1990	1991	1992	1993	1994	1995	1996	1997	1998	1999	2000
CNIDARIA	*Anemonia viridis*	•	•	•	•			•		•			•		•	•			•	•	
	Aulactinia verrucosa																			•	•
	Cereus pedunculatus			•																	•
	Urticina felina							•		•			•								
ANNELIDA	*Amphitrite* spp.							•													
	Amphitritides gracilis		•	•																	
	Cirratulus cirratus				•																
	Cirriformia tentaculata	•														•		•		•	•
	Eulalia viridis																		•		
	Hydroides norvegica		•																		
	Lanice conchilega		•												•						
	Pomatoceros triqueter	•	•	•	•	•		•	•	•			•	•	•	•	•	•	•	•	•
	Pomatoceros spp.					•	•			•	•										
	Spirorbis inornatus	•	•	•																	
	Spirorbis rupestris	•	•	•																•	
	Spirorbis spirorbis	•	•	•		•		•	•	•	•	•		•	•						
	Spirorbis tridentatus		•	•																	
	Spirorbis spp.	•			•	•	•	•	•	•	•	•	•	•	•	•	•	•	•	•	•
CHELICERATA	Acari spp.	•							•			•	•	•	•					•	•
	Nymphon gracile										•					•					
	Nymphon spp.											•									
	Pycnogonum littorale			•																	•
HEXAPODA	*Lipura maritima*	•	•	•		•	•	•	•	•	•	•	•	•		•	•	•	•	•	•
CRUSTACEA	*Balanus crenatus*		•	•														•		•	
	Barnacles	•	•	•	•	•	•	•	•	•	•	•	•	•	•	•	•	•	•	•	•
	Barnacle spat	•	•	•			•	•	•	•		•	•	•	•	•	•	•	•	•	•
	Chthamalus montagui		•	•		•															
	Chthamalus stellatus		•	•	•															•	
	Chthamalus spp.	•	•		•	•	•	•	•				•	•	•	•	•	•	•	•	•
	Elminius modestus	•	•	•	•	•	•	•	•				•	•	•	•	•	•	•	•	•
	Semibalanus balanoides	•	•	•	•	•	•	•	•				•	•	•	•	•	•	•	•	•
	Verruca stroemia		•	•																	
	Cancer pagurus			•	•		•	•							•				•	•	
	Caprella linearis				•																
	Carcinus maenas	•	•	•	•	•	•	•	•	•	•	•	•	•	•	•	•	•	•	•	•
	Dynamene bidentata												•								
	Gammarus spp.			•			•	•				•	•	•		•		•		•	
	Hyas araneus						•		•												
	Idotea granulosa							•													
	Idotea spp.	•												•							
	Ligia oceanica	•	•	•	•		•	•	•	•	•	•	•	•	•	•	•	•		•	•
	Macropodia tenuirostris									•											•
	Necora puber																			•	
	Pagurus bernhardus	•					•	•				•			•						
	Palaemon serratus		•																		
	Pinnotheres pisum								•		•									•	
	Pisidia longicornis					•															
	Talitrus saltator							•		•											

KINISH NARROWS WEST (STATIONS 1–9)

PHYLUM/DIVISION	SPECIES	1981	1982	1983	1984	1985	1986	1987	1988	1989	1990	1991	1992	1993	1994	1995	1996	1997	1998	1999	2000
MOLLUSCA	*Anomia ephippium*		•	•	•	•															
	Anomia ephippium spat							•													
	Archidoris pseudoargus			•			•		•						•						
	Bittium reticulatum							•													
	Calliostoma zizyphinum		•			•	•	•	•		•				•		•	•			
	Chiton spp.			•		•					•	•									
	Gibbula cineraria	•	•	•	•	•	•	•			•	•	•	•	•	•	•	•		•	•
	Gibbula umbilicalis	•	•	•	•	•	•	•	•	•	•	•	•	•	•	•	•	•	•	•	•
	Gibbula spp.					•			•												
	Helcion pellucidum			•								•		•					•		
	Hinia incrassata	•	•	•		•	•	•		•			•	•	•			•			
	Hinia reticulata	•		•	•	•		•	•		•	•	•	•			•	•	•	•	•
	Hydrobia ulvae																			•	
	Littorina littorea	•	•	•	•	•	•	•	•	•	•	•	•	•	•	•	•	•	•	•	•
	Littorina neglecta	•	•	•	•	•															
	Littorina obtusata	•	•	•	•	•	•	•	•	•	•	•	•	•	•	•	•	•	•	•	•
	Littorina saxatilis	•	•	•	•	•	•	•	•	•	•	•	•	•	•	•	•	•	•	•	•
	Littorina spp.	•																			
	Littorina (eggs)											•									
	Melarhaphe neritoides	•		•	•	•		•	•	•	•	•	•	•	•	•	•	•	•	•	•
	Modiolus barbatus																		•		
	Mytilus edulis	•	•	•	•	•	•	•	•	•	•	•	•	•	•	•	•	•	•	•	•
	Nucella (eggs)		•	•	•		•	•	•	•	•	•		•	•	•	•	•	•	•	•
	Nucella lapillus	•	•	•	•	•	•	•	•	•	•	•	•	•	•	•	•	•	•	•	•
	Ocenebra erinacea																		•		
	Onchidoris bilamellata				•																
	Osilinus lineatus							•	•									•	•	•	
	Ostrea edulis			•										•							
	Oyster spat													•							
	Patella vulgata							•													
	Patella spp.	•	•	•	•	•	•	•	•	•	•	•	•	•	•	•	•	•	•	•	•
	Trivia monacha								•											•	
	Turritella communis		•																		
	Venerupis senegalensis						•														
BRYOZOA	*Alcyonidium gelatinosum*	•	•	•	•	•			•	•				•	•		•	•		•	•
	Alcyonidium hirsutum	•	•	•	•	•		•	•				•		•	•		•	•	•	•
	Alcyonidium spp.									•		•	•	•				•			
	Bowerbankia imbricata			•	•													•			
	Bowerbankia spp.																				•
	Cellepora pumicosa	•	•	•																	
	Celleporella hyalina				•																
	Crisia spp.			•																	
	Electra pilosa	•	•	•	•	•	•	•	•	•		•	•	•	•	•	•	•		•	•
	Flustra foliacea								•									•			
	Flustrellidra hispida	•	•	•	•	•	•	•	•	•	•	•	•	•	•	•	•	•	•	•	•
	Membranipora membranacea		•	•				•	•	•	•		•	•	•	•	•	•	•	•	•
	Mucronella coccinea											•									
	Schizoporella unicornis				•																
	Scrupocellaria reptans				•																
	Tubulipora phalangea		•																		
	Umbonula littoralis				•	•	•	•	•												
	Umbonula spp.					•	•	•	•				•	•	•		•	•		•	
ECHINODERMATA	*Antedon bifida*				•								•								

KINISH NARROWS WEST (STATIONS 1–9)

PHYLUM/DIVISION	SPECIES	1981	1982	1983	1984	1985	1986	1987	1988	1989	1990	1991	1992	1993	1994	1995	1996	1997	1998	1999	2000
ECHINODERMATA	*Asterina gibbosa*		•	•	•	•	•			•	•										
	Ophiothrix fragilis			•																	
CHORDATA	*Aplidium nordmanni*						•	•													
	Aplidium pallidum				•																
	Aplidium proliferum			•				•	•				•								
	Aplidium spp.					•	•	•	•									•			
	Botrylloides leachi		•	•										•						•	
	Botryllus schlosseri	•	•	•	•	•		•	•	•	•	•	•	•	•		•	•		•	
	Ciona intestinalis				•								•								
	Clavelina lepadiformis					•							•		•						
	Dendrodoa grossularia			•		•									•	•					
	Morchellium argus																	•			
	Sidnyum turbinatum		•			•						•	•	•	•						

Appendix 4:

Species found at additional lower shore stations at the seven Sherkin Monthly Sites 1981–2000

Data from the lower stations which were not accessed on a regular basis are included in this Appendix (see p. 34). Species are listed which were present only at the lower shore stations for a particular year. However it is not a complete list of species present at the lower stations. If a species occurs higher on the transect, as well as at the lower stations, it will be listed in Appendix 3 only. This Appendix should therefore be read in conjunction with Appendix 3.

Poulacurra

PHYLUM/DIVISION	SPECIES	1981	1982	1983	1984	1985	1986	1987	1988	1989	1990	1991	1992	1993	1994	1995	1996	1997	1998	1999	2000
GREEN ALGAE (CHLOROPHYCOTA)	*Bryopsis hypnoides*																	•			
	Cladophora rupestris																			•	
	Cladophora spp.												•	•							
	Spongomorpha arcta												•								
BROWN ALGAE (CHROMOPHYCOTA)	*Alaria esculenta*									•			•	•				•		•	•
	Asperococcus spp.					•															
	Cystoseira spp.							•													
	Dictyota dichotoma																	•			•
	Ectocarpaceae																		•		
	Elachista fucicola																		•		
	Elachista spp.												•								
	Fucus spp.																				•
	Himanthalia elongata						•														
	Laminaria digitata																	•	•	•	•
	Laminaria spp.												•	•	•			•	•		
	Laminaria spp. sporelings																		•	•	
	Leathesia difformis					•															
	Litosiphon laminariae							•													
	Scytosiphon lomentaria															•					
RED ALGAE (RHODOPHYCOTA)	*Aglaothamnion sepositum*																				•
	Aglaothamnion spp.																				•
	Callithamnion spp.																	•			•
	Ceramium botryocarpum																•			•	
	Ceramium ciliatum					•															•
	Ceramium pallidum																			•	
	Ceramium spp.														•						
	Chondria dasyphylla												•								
	Chondria spp.																•				
	Chondrus crispus												•	•			•	•	•		•
	Delesseria sanguinea												•								
	Gelidium pusillum																		•		
	Gelidium spp.																		•		
	Halurus flosculosus												•								
	Hildenbrandia rubra												•								
	Lomentaria articulata					•	•									•		•			•
	Lomentaria clavellosa						•	•										•			•

POULACURRA

PHYLUM/DIVISION	SPECIES	1981	1982	1983	1984	1985	1986	1987	1988	1989	1990	1991	1992	1993	1994	1995	1996	1997	1998	1999	2000
RED ALGAE (RHODOPHYCOTA)	*Mastocarpus stellatus*						•								•		•	•	•	•	•
	Membranoptera alata													•						•	
	Nemalion helminthoides												•								
	Osmundea hybrida																			•	•
	Osmundea pinnatifida						•														
	Palmaria palmata						•				•		•					•	•		
	Plocamium cartilagineum													•							
	Plumaria plumosa					•					•										
	Polysiphonia brodiei														•		•				•
	Polysiphonia elongata																		•		
	Polysiphonia fibrata																	•	•		•
	Polysiphonia fibrillosa																			•	
	Polysiphonia stricta													•				•			
	Polysiphonia spp.												•	•			•	•			•
	Porphyra umbilicalis													•					•		•
PORIFERA	*Halichondria panicea*						•							•							•
	Myxilla incrustans						•			•			•	•			•		•		•
	Myxilla spp.											•	•								
CNIDARIA	*Anthopleura thallia*														•						
	Coryne muscoides																	•			
	Dynamena pumila													•				•	•		
	Obelia geniculata																	•			
	Aulactinia verrucosa																•	•			
	Corynactis viridis																	•			•
	Haliclystus auricula																				•
	Urticina felina															•		•			•
ANNELIDA	*Pomatoceros triqueter*						•							•	•		•	•			•
	Pomatoceros spp.					•															
	Spirorbis spp.													•				•			
CRUSTACEA	*Cancer pagurus*									•			•								
	Carcinus maenas																				•
	Idotea granulosa							•													
	Idotea spp.												•								
MOLLUSCA	Chiton spp.																	•			
	Gibbula cineraria																	•			
	Helcion pellucidum						•										•	•			
	Hinia reticulata															•				•	
	Littorina littorea																			•	
	Nucella (eggs)													•						•	•
	Nudibranch (eggs)										•										
BRYOZOA	*Crisia eburnea*																	•			
	Electra pilosa						•							•				•			•
	Membranipora membranacea										•		•	•				•	•		
	Mucronella coccinea												•								

POULACURRA

PHYLUM/DIVISION	SPECIES	1981	1982	1983	1984	1985	1986	1987	1988	1989	1990	1991	1992	1993	1994	1995	1996	1997	1998	1999	2000
BRYOZOA	*Umbonula* spp.						•							•				•	•		
ECHINODERMATA	*Asterias rubens*					•		•						•				•	•		
CHORDATA	*Aplidium* spp.													•							
	Botrylloides leachi																	•			
	Botryllus schlosseri																	•			
	Blennius spp.																				•

DROLAIN POINT

PHYLUM/DIVISION	SPECIES	1981	1982	1983	1984	1985	1986	1987	1988	1989	1990	1991	1992	1993	1994	1995	1996	1997	1998	1999	2000
GREEN ALGAE (CHLOROPHYCOTA)	*Cladophora rupestris*													•			•				
	Cladophora spp.							•										•			•
BROWN ALGAE (CHROMOPHYCOTA)	*Dictyota dichotoma*															•			•		
	Elachista spp.																	•			
	Fucus serratus																•	•		•	•
	Fucus spiralis																			•	
	Fucus spp.							•													
	Halopteris filicina								•												
	Himanthalia elongata																				•
	Laminaria spp. sporelings																				•
	Sphaceleria spp.														•						
RED ALGAE (RHODOPHYCOTA)	*Boergeseniella thuyoides*															•					
	Callithamnion spp.															•					
	Ceramium botryocarpum																			•	
	Ceramium echionotum																			•	
	Ceramium gaditanum																•				
	Ceramium spp.																				•
	Chondrus crispus																	•			
	Dilsea carnosa																	•			
	Gastroclonium ovatum																				•
	Gelidium spinosum																				•
	Heterosiphonia plumosa																			•	
	Lomentaria clavellosa													•				•		•	
	Lomentaria orcadensis						•														
	Membranoptera alata																•				•
	Osmundea hybrida																				•
	Palmaria palmata							•						•							
	Plumaria plumosa																	•			
	Polyides rotundus																	•			
	Polysiphonia atlantica															•					
	Polysiphonia denudata																		•		
	Polysiphonia harveyi																				•
	Polysiphonia nigra																	•			
	Polysiphonia stricta																	•			
	Polysiphonia spp.															•					
	Pterosiphonia complanata																			•	
PORIFERA	*Halichondria panicea*													•							
	Hymeniacidon spp.													•		•					
CNIDARIA	*Dynamena pumila*													•							
ANNELIDA	*Pomatoceros triqueter*																	•		•	
	Spirorbis spp.																	•			•
CRUSTACEA	*Idotea baltica*													•							
MOLLUSCA	*Calliostoma zizyphinum*						•											•	•		•

PHYLUM/DIVISION	SPECIES	1981	1982	1983	1984	1985	1986	1987	1988	1989	1990	1991	1992	1993	1994	1995	1996	1997	1998	1999	2000
MOLLUSCA	*Helcion pellucidum*						•	•										•	•		•
	Littorina obtusata																	•			
	Nucella (eggs)															•					
	Trivia monacha																		•		
BRYOZOA	*Alcyonidium hirsutum*													•				•			•
	Alcyonidium spp.													•				•			
	Electra pilosa							•						•				•	•		•
	Flustrellidra hispida							•						•				•			•
	Membranipora membranacea																	•			•
	Umbonula littoralis							•													
	Umbonula spp.																	•	•		
ECHINODERMATA	*Asterias rubens*																	•	•		
CHORDATA	*Botrylloides leachi*						•														•
	Botryllus schlosseri						•							•							
	Morchellium argus																	•			

GLOBE ROCKS

PHYLUM/DIVISION	SPECIES	1981	1982	1983	1984	1985	1986	1987	1988	1989	1990	1991	1992	1993	1994	1995	1996	1997	1998	1999	2000
GREEN ALGAE (CHLOROPHYCOTA)	*Bryopsis plumosa*													•							
	Cladophora rupestris													•							
	Enteromorpha intestinalis											•		•							
	Spongomorpha arcta											•									
	Ulva spp.											•									
BROWN ALGAE (CHROMOPHYCOTA)	*Ascophyllum nodosum*												•	•							
	Chorda filum								•												
	Cladostephus spongiosus											•		•							
	Cutleria multifida												•								
	Ectocarpus siliculosus							•													
	Elachista fucicola											•									
	Himanthalia elongata						•														
	Laminaria digitata												•	•							
	Laminaria saccharina												•								
	Laminaria spp.						•						•	•							
	Leathesia difformis										•										
	Scytosiphon lomentaria													•							
	Sphaceleria spp.													•							
	Spongonema tomentosum										•		•								
RED ALGAE (RHODOPHYCOTA)	*Ahnfeltia plicata*													•							
	Antithamnion cruciatum											•									
	Audouinella spp.						•						•	•							
	Bonnemaisonia asparagoides												•								
	Callithamnion corymbosum							•													
	Callithamnion spp.													•							
	Catenella caespitosa													•							
	Ceramium rubrum													•							
	Champia parvula												•								
	Cystoclonium purpureum												•								
	Furcellaria lumbricalis											•									
	Gracilaria gracilis												•								
	Hildenbrandia rubra										•										
	Hildenbrandia spp.													•							
	Hypoglossum hypoglossoides												•								
	Lomentaria articulata													•							
	Lomentaria clavellosa											•									
	Lomentaria spp.										•										
	Membranoptera alata										•			•							
	Nitophyllum punctatum												•								
	Palmaria palmata												•	•							
	Plumaria plumosa												•	•							
	Polyides rotundus												•								
	Polysiphonia elongata												•								
	Polysiphonia lanosa													•							
	Polysiphonia nigra											•									
	Porphyra umbilicalis														•						
	Rhodothamniella floridula												•								
PORIFERA	*Grantia compressa*												•								
	Halichondria spp.										•		•								

GLOBE ROCKS

PHYLUM/DIVISION	SPECIES	1981	1982	1983	1984	1985	1986	1987	1988	1989	1990	1991	1992	1993	1994	1995	1996	1997	1998	1999	2000
CNIDARIA	*Dynamena pumila*												•	•							
	Alcyonium digitatum				•																
	Sagartia elegans						•	•	•			•									
ANNELIDA	*Eulalia viridis*										•										
	Pomatoceros triqueter											•	•	•							
	Pomatoceros spp.							•													
	Spirorbis spirorbis											•		•							
	Spirorbis spp.												•	•							
CRUSTACEA	*Verruca stroemia*													•							
	Cancer pagurus												•								
	Hyas araneus											•									
	Pagurus bernhardus							•													
MOLLUSCA	*Archidoris pseudoargus*													•							
	Calliostoma zizyphinum											•		•							
	Helcion pellucidum													•							
	Hinia incrassata												•								
	Hinia reticulata										•										
	Littorina (eggs)													•							
	Nucella (eggs)													•							
	Rostanga rubra												•								
BRYOZOA	*Alcyonidium hirsutum*												•								
	Alcyonidium spp.												•	•							
	Electra pilosa												•	•							
	Flustrellidra hispida										•		•	•							
	Membranipora membranacea											•	•	•	•						
	Umbonula spp.												•								
CHORDATA	*Aplidium nordmanni*						•														
	Aplidium spp.													•							
	Botrylloides leachi						•	•					•								
	Botryllus schlosseri						•	•				•		•							
	Dendrodoa grossularia													•							
	Sidnyum turbinatum												•		•						
	Nerophis lumbriciformis							•													

HORSESHOE HARBOUR

PHYLUM/DIVISION	SPECIES	1981	1982	1983	1984	1985	1986	1987	1988	1989	1990	1991	1992	1993	1994	1995	1996	1997	1998	1999	2000
GREEN ALGAE (CHLOROPHYCOTA)	*Bryopsis plumosa*													•							
	Derbesia spp.												•								
	Urospora spp.												•								
BROWN ALGAE (CHROMOPHYCOTA)	*Ascophyllum nodosum*													•							
	Colpomenia peregrina																				•
	Dictyota dichotoma																		•		
	Fucus spiralis																		•		•
	Fucus spp. sporelings													•							
	Laminaria digitata												•	•	•	•		•	•	•	
	Laminaria hyperborea												•								
	Laminaria saccharina						•														•
	Laminaria spp.												•				•	•			
	Saccorhiza polyschides					•															•
RED ALGAE (RHODOPHYCOTA)	*Aglaothamnion hookeri*												•								
	Apoglossum ruscifolium												•								
	Calliblepharis jubata								•				•								
	Calliblepharis spp.					•															
	Callithamnion tetricum												•								
	Ceramium pallidum																				•
	Ceramium rubrum																				•
	Chondracanthus acicularis													•			•	•			
	Cryptopleura ramosa												•		•						
	Dilsea carnosa								•												
	Drachiella heterocarpa												•								
	Dumontia contorta								•												
	Erythrodermis traillii												•								
	Erythroglossum laciniatum												•								
	Gastroclonium ovatum					•											•				•
	Gelidium spinosum														•				•		
	Gelidium spp.													•							
	Gigartina pistillata												•								
	Gracilaria gracilis											•									
	Halurus equisetifolius																				•
	Haraldiophyllum bonnemaisonii												•								
	Nitophyllum punctatum												•								
	Palmaria palmata					•			•												
	Petrocelis cruenta								•												
	Peyssonnelia squamaria								•												
	Plocamium cartilagineum							•													
	Plumaria plumosa																				•
	Polysiphonia elongata								•												
	Porphyra leucosticta												•								
	Porphyra umbilicalis					•															
	Pterocladia capillacea												•	•							
	Ptilota gunneri																•				
	Rhodophyllis divaricata								•												
PORIFERA	*Halichondria* spp.														•						
	Myxilla spp.												•								
CNIDARIA	*Dynamena pumila*													•							

HORSESHOE HARBOUR

PHYLUM/DIVISION	SPECIES	1981	1982	1983	1984	1985	1986	1987	1988	1989	1990	1991	1992	1993	1994	1995	1996	1997	1998	1999	2000
CNIDARIA	*Sertularella* spp.							•													
	Aulactinia verrucosa													•							
	Corynactis viridis					•							•								
	Urticina felina								•				•				•	•			
ANNELIDA	*Spirorbis spirorbis*					•													•		
CRUSTACEA	*Verruca stroemia*																			•	
	Cancer pagurus						•						•	•							
	Caprella linearis													•							
	Galathea squamifera												•								
	Gammarus spp.								•				•								
	Idotea spp.												•								
	Necora puber								•												
	Pagurus bernhardus												•					•			
	Pisidia longicornis					•															
	Porcellana platycheles													•							
MOLLUSCA	*Anomia ephippium*					•															
	Archidoris pseudoargus																			•	
	Archidoris pseudoargus (eggs)																			•	
	Calliostoma zizyphinum											•		•				•			
	Gibbula spp.													•							
	Helcion pellucidum												•			•		•			•
	Hinia incrassata												•	•						•	
	Hinia reticulata																	•	•		
	Hinia spp.																			•	
	Littorina obtusata															•					
	Ocenebra erinacea													•				•			
	Tonicella rubra								•												
BRYOZOA	*Alcyonidium gelatinosum*													•							
	Alcyonidium hirsutum													•	•		•	•	•		
	Alcyonidium spp.												•								
	Celleporina hassallii																	•			
	Crisia spp.													•							
	Electra pilosa												•	•	•		•				
	Flustrellidra hispida													•				•	•		
	Membranipora membranacea													•		•		•			•
	Scrupocellaria reptans																	•			
	Tubulipora phalangea																	•			
	Umbonula littoralis						•														
	Umbonula spp.												•	•	•			•			
ECHINODERMATA	*Asterias rubens*																	•		•	
	Echinus esculentus												•								
	Holothuria forskali												•								
CHORDATA	*Aplidium proliferum*												•	•							

HORSESHOE HARBOUR

PHYLUM/DIVISION	SPECIES	1981	1982	1983	1984	1985	1986	1987	1988	1989	1990	1991	1992	1993	1994	1995	1996	1997	1998	1999	2000
CHORDATA	*Aplidium* spp.												•								
	Botrylloides leachi													•							
	Botryllus schlosseri												•	•							
	Dendrodoa grossularia								•												
	Didemnum spp.												•								
	Morchellium argus																	•			
	Syngnathus rostellatus													•							

REENAHOE

PHYLUM/DIVISION	SPECIES	1981	1982	1983	1984	1985	1986	1987	1988	1989	1990	1991	1992	1993	1994	1995	1996	1997	1998	1999	2000
GREEN ALGAE (CHLOROPHYCOTA)	*Chaetomorpha linum*																				•
	Cladophora spp.																•				
	Codium spp.																				•
	Enteromorpha intestinalis											•	•								
BROWN ALGAE (CHROMOPHYCOTA)	*Cladostephus spongiosus*													•		•					
	Colpomenia peregrina												•								
	Halopteris filicina															•					
	Himanthalia elongata								•				•								
	Laminaria digitata						•														
	Laminaria saccharina							•			•	•	•		•						
RED ALGAE (RHODOPHYCOTA)	*Audouinella* spp.											•							•		
	Calliblepharis ciliata												•								
	Calliblepharis jubata						•														
	Callophyllis laciniata												•								
	Ceramium pallidum																•				
	Ceramium rubrum												•								
	Ceramium shuttleworthianum																•				
	Champia parvula												•		•						
	Chondracanthus acicularis												•								
	Chondria capillaris							•													
	Chylocladia verticillata												•								
	Cryptopleura ramosa												•								
	Cystoclonium purpureum												•								
	Furcellaria lumbricalis							•				•	•		•		•				•
	Gastroclonium ovatum						•						•		•						•
	Gastroclonium reflexum																	•			
	Haraldiophyllum bonnemaisonii												•								
	Heterosiphonia plumosa							•													
	Lomentaria clavellosa												•		•						
	Nitophyllum punctatum												•								
	Palmaria palmata											•						•			
	Phycodrys rubens												•								
	Phymatolithon lenormandii							•													
	Plocamium cartilagineum																				•
	Polyides rotundus						•								•		•				
	Polyneura bonnemaisonii												•								
	Polysiphonia fucoides																	•			
	Polysiphonia spp.											•	•								
	Porphyra leucosticta												•								
	Porphyra umbilicalis											•	•								
	Rhodothamniella floridula													•							
PORIFERA	*Clathrina coriacea*								•												
	Grantia compressa																			•	
	Hymeniacidon perleve											•									
	Hymeniacidon spp.													•			•				
	Ophlitaspongia seriata												•								
CNIDARIA	*Clava multicornis*																•				
	Aulactinia verrucosa												•				•		•		

REENAHOE

PHYLUM/DIVISION	SPECIES	1981	1982	1983	1984	1985	1986	1987	1988	1989	1990	1991	1992	1993	1994	1995	1996	1997	1998	1999	2000
CNIDARIA	*Cereus pedunculatus*												•	•							
	Sagartia elegans						•														
	Urticina felina						•						•								
CRUSTACEA	*Cancer pagurus*																•				
	Dynamene bidentata												•					•			
	Gammarus spp.																				•
	Pagurus bernhardus											•	•				•				
	Palaemon serratus																	•			
	Sphaeroma spp.													•							
MOLLUSCA	*Archidoris pseudoargus*												•								
	Epitonium clathrus											•									
	Helcion pellucidum												•					•		•	•
	Hinia reticulata								•												
	Hinia spp.											•									
	Littorina (eggs)											•									
	Nucella (eggs)												•								
	Rissoa parva												•								
	Trivia monacha												•								
BRYOZOA	*Alcyonidium gelatinosum*						•														
	Alcyonidium spp.												•								
	Callopora lineata																	•			
	Celleporina hassallii																	•			
	Umbonula spp.													•							
ECHINODERMATA	*Asterias rubens*							•													
CHORDATA	*Aplidium proliferum*													•			•	•			
	Aplidium spp.							•	•					•			•				
	Botrylloides leachi																•			•	•
	Botryllus schlosseri							•						•			•				
	Ciona intestinalis												•								
	Clavelina lepadiformis										•										
	Dendrodoa grossularia										•										
	Didemnum spp.										•										
	Sidnyum turbinatum							•													

KINISH NARROWS EAST

PHYLUM/DIVISION	SPECIES	1981	1982	1983	1984	1985	1986	1987	1988	1989	1990	1991	1992	1993	1994	1995	1996	1997	1998	1999	2000
GREEN ALGAE (CHLOROPHYCOTA)	*Bryopsis plumosa*													•							
	Chaetomorpha linum																		•		
	Cladophora spp.																•				
	Spongomorpha spp.																•				
BROWN ALGAE (CHROMOPHYCOTA)	*Ascophyllum nodosum*														•		•	•	•		•
	Cladostephus spongiosus					•							•								
	Dictyota dichotoma												•								•
	Himanthalia elongata													•							
	Laminaria digitata														•			•		•	•
	Laminaria saccharina				•																
	Laminaria spp.														•		•				
	Ralfsia verrucosa																	•			
	Scytosiphon lomentaria												•		•						
RED ALGAE (RHODOPHYCOTA)	*Ahnfeltia plicata*													•	•						
	Antithamnionella spirographidis													•							
	Audouinella spp.															•					
	Boergeseniella thuyoides												•								
	Calliblepharis jubata														•						
	Callithamnion corymbosum								•												
	Callithamnion spp.														•						
	Ceramium deslongchampii																	•			
	Ceramium spp.												•								
	Champia parvula				•								•								
	Corallina officinalis													•	•						
	Cystoclonium purpureum														•						
	Erythroglossum laciniatum												•								
	Furcellaria lumbricalis																			•	
	Gelidium spinosum												•								
	Griffithsia spp.																			•	
	Halurus equisetifolius																				•
	Halurus flosculosus												•								
	Haraldiophyllum bonnemaisonii											•									
	Heterosiphonia plumosa																•				
	Hypoglossum hypoglossoides												•								
	Lomentaria clavellosa				•													•			
	Membranoptera alata														•	•	•		•		
	Mesophyllum lichenoides																				•
	Nemalion helminthoides								•												
	Nitophyllum punctatum												•								
	Palmaria palmata														•		•				
	Plocamium cartilagineum																	•			
	Plumaria plumosa														•	•		•	•	•	•
	Polyides rotundus												•								
	Polysiphonia elongata																			•	
	Polysiphonia fucoides																	•			
	Polysiphonia lanosa																				•
	Polysiphonia spp.															•				•	
	Porphyra umbilicalis														•						
	Ptilota gunneri																			•	
PORIFERA	*Grantia compressa*																			•	
	Halichondria panicea														•	•			•		

Kinish Narrows East

PHYLUM/DIVISION	SPECIES	1981	1982	1983	1984	1985	1986	1987	1988	1989	1990	1991	1992	1993	1994	1995	1996	1997	1998	1999	2000
	Halichondria spp.														•		•				
	Hymeniacidon perleve													•							
	Hymeniacidon sanguinea																•	•			•
	Hymeniacidon spp.													•			•				•
	Myxilla incrustans															•			•		•
CNIDARIA	*Obelia geniculata*																				•
	Actinia equina												•		•				•	•	
	Aulactinia verrucosa												•								
	Cereus pedunculatus												•								
	Sagartia elegans													•							
	Urticina felina														•						
ANNELIDA	*Pomatoceros triqueter*														•		•	•			
CHELICERATA	*Pycnogonum littorale*													•							
CRUSTACEA	*Elminius modestus*								•												
	Verruca stroemia														•						
	Gammarus spp.													•							
	Hyas araneus												•								
	Inachus spp.																	•	•		
	Macropodia tenuirostris													•							
	Necora puber												•								
	Pagurus bernhardus								•				•	•		•				•	
	Xantho incisus																		•		
MOLLUSCA	*Anomia ephippium*												•			•					
	Calliostoma zizyphinum																			•	
	Chiton spp.												•								
	Helcion pellucidum												•								
	Hinia incrassata																	•			
	Hinia reticulata																	•			•
	Hinia spp.																			•	
	Hydrobia ulvae																	•			
	Lepidochitona cinerea														•						
	Nucella (eggs)														•					•	
	Ocenebra erinacea														•						
	Osilinus lineatus																			•	
	Ostrea edulis													•							
	Pododesmus patelliformis													•	•						
	Trivia arctica								•										•		
	Trivia monacha												•	•							
BRYOZOA	*Alcyonidium gelatinosum*												•	•	•						
	Alcyonidium hirsutum													•	•	•					
	Alcyonidium spp.															•	•				
	Electra pilosa														•	•	•		•	•	
	Flustrellidra hispida														•						•

KINISH NARROWS EAST

PHYLUM/DIVISION	SPECIES	1981	1982	1983	1984	1985	1986	1987	1988	1989	1990	1991	1992	1993	1994	1995	1996	1997	1998	1999	2000
BRYOZOA	*Membranipora membranacea*														•	•	•	•			•
	Tubulipora phalangea																	•			
	Umbonula littoralis				•																
	Umbonula spp.														•		•				
ECHINODERMATA	*Asterias rubens*															•					
	Asterina gibbosa																	•			
CHORDATA	*Aplidium proliferum*												•								
	Aplidium spp.													•			•	•			
	Ascidiella aspersa												•	•							
	Ascidiella scabra														•						
	Botrylloides leachi													•							
	Botryllus schlosseri												•			•		•			•
	Ciona intestinalis													•							
	Clavelina lepadiformis														•						
	Dendrodoa grossularia								•						•						
	Lissoclinum perforatum																	•			
	Sidnyum turbinatum														•						
	Pholis gunnellus								•												

KINISH NARROWS WEST

PHYLUM/DIVISION	SPECIES	1981	1982	1983	1984	1985	1986	1987	1988	1989	1990	1991	1992	1993	1994	1995	1996	1997	1998	1999	2000
BROWN ALGAE (CHROMOPHYCOTA)	*Asperococcus fistulosus*							•													
	Bifurcaria bifurcata												•								
	Ectocarpus agg.						•														
	Laminaria digitata							•					•								
	Laminaria saccharina							•													
	Laminaria spp.					•							•								
	Ralfsia verrucosa												•								
RED ALGAE (RHODOPHYCOTA)	*Chondracanthus acicularis*													•							
	Dumontia contorta												•								
	Lomentaria clavellosa							•													
	Palmaria palmata											•									
	Rhodothamniella floridula												•								
PORIFERA	*Myxilla* spp.												•								
CNIDARIA	*Aulactinia verrucosa*												•								
	Sagartia elegans												•								
CRUSTACEA	*Cancer pagurus*								•				•								
MOLLUSCA	*Anomia ephippium*							•													
	Helcion pellucidum							•								•					
	Trivia monacha												•								
ECHINODERMATA	*Asterina gibbosa*							•													
	Ophiothrix fragilis												•								
CHORDATA	*Aplidium proliferum*						•														
	Aplidium spp.												•								
	Ascidiella aspersa												•								
	Botrylloides leachi															•					

APPENDIX 5:

Ballantine's Exposure Scale

(taken from Ballantine, 1961)

Exposure Scale	Criteria
Extremely Exposed	· *Alaria* abundant, with thick 'Lithothamnia' and *Corallina* populations underneath · *Porphyra* band above barnacles; *Fucus vesiculosus evesiculosus* is the only fucoid · Wide supralittoral lichen zone, *Lichina pygmaea* common · *Chthamalus* species abundant, few *Semibalanus balanoides* · *Littorina neritoides** and *L. saxatilis* (small) abundant, other littorinids absent; Topshells absent; Small *Nucella* and *Mytilus edulis* in crevices
Very Exposed	· *Laminaria digitata* starting to replace *Alaria*; Few fucoids, rare *F. v. evesiculosus*, *F. serratus* and *Pelvetia* · Wide supralittoral lichen zone, *L. pygmaea* common · 'Lithothamnia', *Corallina, Mastocarpus* zone at base of mid-littoral · *Chthamalus* still dominant, *Semibalanus* on the increase, *L. neritoides* and *L. saxatilis* common, no other littorinids, Topshells absent; *Nucella* common; *Mytilus* present in crevices
Exposed	· *L. digitata* common; *Alaria* rare or absent; *F. serratus* occasional, other fucoids rare or absent · *L. pygmaea* and other supralittoral lichens common · *Chthamalus* dominates upper mid-littoral, *Semibalanus* dominates lower · *L. neritoides* and *L. saxatilis* common, other littorinids absent, Few *Gibbula umbilicalis* in pools; *Nucella* common; *Mytilus* confined to cracks
Semi-Exposed	· *L. digitata* abundant; *Alaria* absent; Occasional *Pelvetia*, *F. serratus* becoming common, *F. vesiculosus* rare · 'Lithothamnia' and *Corallina* common in pools · Supralittoral lichen zone reduced to a few feet in height · *Semibalanus* now occupies lower 75% of barnacle zone · *L. neritoides* and *L. saxatilis* common, others absent or rare, *G. umbilicalis* occasional to common; *Nucella* abundant; *Mytilus* rare or absent

**Littorina neritoides* now *Melarhaphe neritoides*

Exposure Scale	Criteria
Fairly Sheltered	· *Laminaria digitata* common, *L. saccharina* rare · Definite *Pelvetia* zone, short *Ascophyllum* present, *F. serratus* common forming a definite zone · 'Lithothamnia' and *Corallina* present under fucoids · *Chthamalus* only occupies a very thin zone above *Semibalanus* · *Littorina neritoides* common in supralittoral zone only, *L. saxatilis* common, others occasional in pools or on fucoids, *Monodonta* rare, *G. umbilicalis* common; *Nucella* common; *Mytilus* rare or absent
Sheltered	· *Laminaria digitata* and *L. saccharina* common · *Pelvetia* abundant; *Ascophyllum*, *F. vesiculosus* and *F. serratus* all common to abundant · Thin 'Lithothamnia' and *Corallina* present under fucoids · *Lichina pygmaea* absent, other supralittoral lichens are no more than frequent · *Chthamalus* only at or above the barnacle line, *Semibalanus* dominates zone, sometimes fucoids predominate, *Monodonta* and *G. umbilicalis* common; *Nucella* occasional; *Mytilus* rare or absent
Very Sheltered	· Kelps rare or absent; All fucoids are abundant, lower fucoids overlying 'Lithothamnia' and *Corallina* · Supralittoral lichens absent or rare · *Chthamalus* absent or rare · *Littorina neritoides* absent, other littorinids common or abundant, *Monodonta* and *G. umbilicalis* abundant; *Nucella* occasional; large *Mytilus* specimens common
Extremely Sheltered	· *Laminaria* zone usually absent; 100% cover of all fucoids forming their own zones, some unattached fucoids · Land plants nearly reach *Pelvetia* zone, supralittoral zone scarcely exists · *Littorina neritoides* absent, large *L. saxatilis* common, *L. littorea* and *L. littoralis* abundant · *Monodonta* rare, *G. umbilicalis* common; *Nucella* absent or rare

GLOSSARY

Absolute drought. A period of 15 or more consecutive days to none of which is credited 0.2 mm or more of precipitation.

Aggregate. A term used when two or more closely related species sharing a genus name are mentioned together or cannot be separated. See also Spp.

Algae. Simple photosynthetic aquatic plants which include seaweeds. There are many different types of algae but all of them lack true stems, leaves and roots.

Amphipod. Small crustaceans that have laterally flattened bodies and inhabit a variety of habitats. See Appendix 2.

Annelid. Segmented round worm. See Appendix 2.

Anticline. Geological term for an area of bent or folded rock caused by movement of the earth's crust. It is arch shaped with the youngest layers of rock at the top.

Attenuation. Decreasing strength.

Beaufort Scale. A numerical system used for classifying wind speed, with Beaufort 0 (calm) being winds from 0–1.6 km per hour and Beaufort 12 (hurricane) being winds over 121km per hour.

Benthic. Of or pertaining to the ocean floor.

Benthos. Collectively the organisms living on, in or attached to the ocean bottom.

Biennial. A plant which does not flower in its first year and dies after its second year.

Biological control. An organism used to control the population of another organism by way of a natural relationship. (e.g. Foxes can be introduced and used as a biological control to reduce the rabbit population on which they prey.)

Biomass. The total mass of an animal or plant population or of all organic matter in an area of habitat.

Bivalve. Molluscs with two shells (valves) joined by a strong hinge. See Appendix 2.

Bryozoa. Colonial animals which often encrust solid substrates or algae. Each individual's soft body is contained within a box-like capsule. See Appendix 2.

Bryophyta. Division of plants which are all small and rootless (e.g. liverworts and mosses). See Appendix 2.

Byssus threads. Threads that are produced by some bivalves, enabling them to attach themselves firmly to rocks and other structures, e.g. mussels.

ca. *Circa.* Latin for approximately

Calcareous. Made of calcium carbonate (lime).

Canopy. The area of a plant that extends outside its base (e.g. the leaves and branches of a tree).

Carapace. A shield of exoskeleton covering several segments of the body of some Arthropods (e.g. crabs).

Chart Datum. The standard or baseline from which dimensions are drawn. (e.g. high tide is measured as height above the lowest astronomical tide).

Chelicerata. Arthropods with two major body regions. Front appendages with scissor-like ends. See Appendix 2.

Chiton. Mollusc with a shell that consists of several plates which lock together. Capable of curling up into a ball. See Appendix 2.

Chordata. Organisms with a notochord a stiff flexible rod of fluid-filled cells giving support to the body. See Appendix 2.

Cirratulid. Sedentary polychaete that feed on detritus. Many blood-filled tentacles on a range of body segments. See Appendix 2.

Class. Taxonomic category above order but below phylum or division. A phylum contains one or several classes and a class contains one or more orders.

Cnidaria. Soft-bodied, "flower-like" animals with a ring of stinging tentacles surrounding the mouth. Sea firs, anemones, corals and jellyfish are all cnidaria. See Appendix 2.

Colonisers. Pioneer or initial inhabitants of a new area
Contour. A line on a map or chart connecting places of similar height or depth.
Cross-staff level. The device used in transects to measure elevation change from one transect station to the next.
Crustacea. Aquatic arthropods with many jointed legs. Crabs, prawns, shrimps and barnacles are all crustacea. See Appendix 2.
Datum. Plural of data. Information.
Decimation. Major reduction in population or community (meaning exactly the loss of one in every ten).
Decimetre. One tenth of a metre.
Desiccation. The loss of water from an organism – drying out.
Detritus. Organic material from decomposing organisms.
Diatom. Photosynthetic single-celled microscopic aquatic organisms, which forms the food of many marine animals.
Dinoflagellate. Photosynthetic single-celled microscopic aquatic organism with a cellulose cell wall.
Dry Spell. A period of 15 or more consecutive days to none of which is credited 1.0 mm or more of precipitation.
Ebbing tide. A receding or falling tide.
ecad. A form of plant species showing characteristics imposed by habitat conditions.
Echinodermata. Spiny skinned (though spines may not always be obvious) marine animals which travel on tube feet and have radialy symmetrical bodies. See Appendix 3.
Ecology. The study of the relationships between living organisms and their environment, including physical and biological factors.
Ecosystem. The ecological environment that provides support needed to sustain life.
Ectoprocta. See Bryozoa and Appendix 2.
Ephemeral. Non-permanent. Plants with short life-cycles, often having several generations in one year.
Epifauna. The animals that live on a substrate (e.g. rocks, mud, plants, animal shells).
Epiflora. The plants that live on a substrate (e.g. rock, mud, plants, animal shells).
Epiphytes. A plant which lives and grows non-parasitically on another plant.
Epiphytically. Growing on another plant.
Errant polychaete. A free-living marine annelid worm i.e. not living in a tube.
Eulittoral. Biologically defined (by Lewis, 1964) midshore region of the shore lying between the upper limit of the kelps and the upper limit of barnacles.
Evaporation. The loss of liquid due to its conversion to a gas or vapour.
Exposed shore. A shore that is subjected to considerable wave action.
Exoskeleton. Hard supporting or defensive structures that are external to the body.
Family. Taxonomic category below order and above genus. A family is made up of one or more genera and one or more families make up an order.
Fetch. The uninterrupted distance wind and waves can travel over a body of water.
Filamentous algae. Algae with very fine hair-like branches.
Filiform. Threadlike.
Foliose. Leafy, having a body which can be differentiated into stem and leaves.
Formation. Geological; the assemblage of rock in a specific area
Frond. A leaf-like part of a seaweed.
Fucoid. Sea wrack – the brown algae (Chromophycota) typically found in the littoral zone.
Gammarid. Sub order of the amphipod crustacean that are laterally flattened. See Appendix 2.
Gastropod. Molluscs with either a single, usually coiled, shell or no shell at all. They have a head with tentacles and eyes. See Appendix 2.
Genus. Taxonomic category below family and above species. A family is made up of one or more genera and one or more closely related species make up a genus.
Genera. Plural of genus.

GMT. Greenwich Mean Time. The time at the Greenwich meridian from which all local times around the world are calculated.

Grazers. Animals which browse on crop and eat vegetation.

Gulf Stream. A relatively warm, well-defined ocean current originating north of Grand Bahama Island. It eventually becomes the North Atlantic Current which flows north and eastwards around Ireland's coasts.

Habitat. The place where an organism or community naturally lives or grows.

Hexapoda. Arthropoda with six legs (insects). See Appendix 2.

Holdfast. A structure used by some rootless plants, e.g. algae, to anchor themselves to solid substrates.

Home patch. A location to which an animal returns after feeding expeditions.

Hydrography. The scientific study, description and analysis of the physical elements of oceans, lakes and rivers.

Hydroid. Cnidarians that live in a colony or group, often forming a branching structure of polyps which attach to rocks or seaweed. See Appendix 2.

Immersion. The process of submerging completely or covering something with water.

Infauna. Animals that live within a substrate (e.g. mud or sand).

Intertidal zone. The area of the shoreline between high and low water, subjected to periodic partial or total immersion as a result of the tide.

Isopod. An order of Crustacean that includes woodlice and sea slaters. Body flattened from front to back. See Appendix 2.

Key species. A graphical method of showing the abundance of a species.

Laminarian. A large brown kelp of the family Laminariaceae.

Land-locked. A body of water entirely surrounded by land.

Lichen. A symbiotic association of a fungus and an alga, commonly encrusting rocks in the splash zone. See Appendix 2.

Littoral. The biologically defined (by Lewis, 1964) area of seashore between the upper limit of kelp plants and the upper limit of lichens and periwinkles.

Littorinid. A gastropod mollusc of the family Littorinidae, e.g. periwinkles.

Lower Devonian Period. A period in geological time during the Paleozoic era, extending from 395–345 million years ago.

Maxima. Plural of maximum.

Maximum. The highest value in a set of data.

Mean. Average value. It is calculated by dividing the sum of a set of observations by the number of observations.

Meteorological. Relating to the atmosphere or the weather.

MHWN. Mean High Water Neap (see p. 15).

Micro-algal film. A thin layer of microscopic algae.

Minima. Plural of minimum.

Minimum. The lowest value in a set of data.

Mollusca. Unsegmented coelomate invertebrates with a head and ventral muscular foot – includes sea-slugs, snails, bivalves and squid. See Appendix 2.

Monthly mean. The average value of observations taken over a period of one month.

Nautical miles. A measure of distance. One nautical mile is equivalent to 1.85 km, and one nautical mile per hour is equal to a speed of one knot.

Neap tide. A tide with a small difference in water level between high tide and low tide.

Nemertea. Unsegmented worms, round in cross section, bearing a proboscis inflated by hydrostatic pressure.

Notochord. A stiff, flexible rod of fluid filled cells, which is present in some stage of development of all chodates.

Nudibranchs. A gastropod with no shell, bearing external gills. See Appendix 2.

Old Red Sandstone. Rocks laid down in the Devonian period (395–345 million years ago). It is a red coloured sedimentary rock composed of sand-like quartz grains bound by mud.

Operculum. A plate attached to the foot of some gastropods, e.g. periwinkles, which closes the opening of the shell when the animal withdraws inside. This preserves moisture and protects the animal from predation.

Order. One of seven major taxonomic categories used in the biological classification of living organisms. These categories are (in order of decreasing rank) kingdom, phylum, class, order, family, genus, species.

Osteichthyes. Bony fish, a class of Vertebrata.

Pentamerous. Having a symmetry based on five, or multiples of five.

Perennial. A plant with a multi-year life span.

Pereopod. A walking leg of an amphipod.

Phyla. Plural of Phylum.

Phylum. One of seven major taxonomic categories used in the biological classification of living organisms. These categories are (in order of decreasing rank) kingdom, phylum, class, order, family, genus, species.

Physiological adaptations. Physiological (e.g. metabolic, morphological, or behavioural) adjustment by an organism to environmental demands. This can be a short-term response by an individual, or a result of natural selection acting on a population over a longer period.

Phytoplankton. Microscopic plants, often single celled, which photosynthesise as they drift in the upper water column.

Phytoplankton bloom. A proliferation of phytoplankton in response to an alteration in environmental conditions, and resulting in relatively high concentrations of such organisms in the water column. Temperate waters are characterised by a spring phytoplanton bloom when the surface waters are rich in available nutrients and there is adequate sunlight for photosynthesis. Blooms may also occur suddenly at irregular intervals and the environmental trigger is often unclear. In some cases the water may become visibly discoloured by the organisms or their biproducts. This is commonly known as a "red tide".

Plankton. Generally small, often microscopic, plants and animals that drift freely in the water column, with no more than limited powers of locomotion.

Planktonic larvae. The free-floating young of organisms. Many marine animals have a planktonic larval stage which permits dispersal of a species and, in the case of sessile (fixed to substrate) invertebrates, colonisation of new substrates when the larvae settle.

Platyhelminthe. Dorsoventrally flattened unsegmented worms that may lack a gut; may be free living or parasitic. See Appendix 2.

Polychaete worm. Segmented marine annelid worms with bristle like structures known as setae. See Appendix 2.

Porifera. Sponges. Porifera are simple animals, often colonial, that encrust rocks and other substrates. A current of water is drawn through the body and filtered for food. The soft tissues are supported by a framework of hard spicules. See Appendix 2.

Predator. An animal that hunts and feeds on other animals.

Profile. A graphic representation of observations taken along a horizontal or vertical plane, which may extend over a period of time. A profile can help to visualise, for example, changes in elevation of surface terrain, or the way water temperature changes with increasing depth.

Proliferation. To grow in size or number by vegetative extension or the production of offspring.

Quadrat. A framed area of measurement known as a square (in this study measuring 0.5m x 0.5m), which is placed on the substrate to define the area in which data are collected (see p. 32).

Qualitative. An assessment or record of something, e.g. species distribution in a habitat, which does not collect any precise measurements.

Quantitative. An assessment or record of something, e.g. species distribution in a habitat, which collects actual measurements, e.g. number of animals per sampling unit.

Radula. The "tongue" of a mollusc; a horny strip with teeth on its surface used for tearing food.

Raindays. A day on which 0.2 mm or more of rainfall is measured.

Serpulid. A type of polychaete worm that lives in secreted calcareous tubes.

Sherkin formation. A sub-unit of the sedimentary rock known as Old Red Sandstone.

Sheltered shore. A shore that is relatively well protected from wave action.

Silica. An important and common constituent of many rock types. It is a solid, glassy substance comprising silicon and oxygen. It forms the transparent shells of diatoms, part of the cell wall in many plants and spicules in many sponges.

Spat. The newly settled larvae of sedentary (limited mobility) or sessile (fixed to substrate) marine invertebrates, such as barnacles.

Spatfall. A new settlement of the planktonic larvae of sedentary (limited mobility) or sessile (fixed to substrate) marine invertebrates on a substrate.

Spermatophyta. A group of higher plants that produce seeds and include gymnosperms (e.g. conifers) and angiosperms (e.g. deciduous trees, flowers and grasses).

Spicules. Small pointed processes, either calcareous or siliceous, which form the skeleton in several groups of Porifera (sponges).

Spirorbid. A polychaete worm of the family Spirorbidae which have coiled calcareous tubes.

Splash zone. The area of the shore that is not covered by the tide at any time but is made wet by the spray of breaking waves.

Spongin. A horny, skeletal substance, usually occurring in the form of fibres, which provides a supporting framework for the living cells of many sponges. In some groups spongin fibres occur in combination with spicules.

Sporeling. The early stages of a plant developing from a spore.

Sp. Abbreviation of species (singular). Used where further classification to the species level is not carried out (e.g. *Laminaria* sp.).

Species. A group of very similar organisms potentially capable of interbreeding with one another. Taxonomically, species are grouped into genera (see genus) and divided into subspecies and varieties. In the system of binomial nomenclature the second name refers to the species to which an organism has been assigned, e.g. *Nucella lapillus*, where *lapillus* is the species name.

Spp. Abbreviation of species (plural). Used where a number of species within the same genus are being discussed, e.g. *Fucus spiralis* and *Fucus vesiculosus* may be referred to together as *Fucus* spp.

Spring tides. Those tides with a large tidal range. Spring tides recur over a fortnightly cycle (around the full and new moons) when the gravities of the sun and moon pull in the same direction. Approximately one week of spring tides alternates with one week of neap tides.

Standard error. The standard deviation of the mean. This is calculated to determine sampling error. Sampling error is not an error or mistake due to an observer, rather it reflects the degree to which a mean calculated from a limited number of observations (a sample) is likely to differ from a calculation of the population mean using data from every individual within the population.

Stipe. The supporting "stem" of a seaweed.

Strata. Plural of stratum.

Stratum. A layer, e.g. of rock, considered to be distinct from adjacent layers.

Sublittoral. The area of seabed from the upper limit of the kelp on the shore down to a depth of about 200 metres (the edge of the continental shelf). On the shore it is the area exposed between the upper limit of the kelps and the low water mark of spring tides.

Suspension feeding. A mode of feeding practised by organisms that capture and feed on particulate matter suspended in the water column.

Taxa. Plural of taxon.

Taxon. General term for a taxonomic group, regardless of rank i.e. species, genus, family, order, class and phylum.

Taxonomy. The classification of organisms into similar groups using physical characteristics or genetic relationships.

Terebellid polychaete. Tube-dwelling polychaete worms, in which the body is easily differentiated into two regions: a thorax with eyes and tentacles and a tapering abdomen with reduced appendages. See Appendix 2.

Terrestrial. Living or growing on land.

Tidal cycle. The sequence of a single rise and fall of the tide, e.g. from low-water to high-water to low-water, occuring over approximately 12 hours.

Tidal range. The measured difference between high and low water elevations.

Tide tables. Published data that predicts the time and height of tides at certain locations around the coast. Tide tables are based on solar activity over an 18.6-year cycle.

Transect. An imaginary line or belt imposed across an area to be studied. It is normally positioned across or perpendicular to a suspected environmental gradient, for example the transition from terrestrial to marine conditions found at the seashore. (See page 31.)

Tunicates. A subphylum of Chordata and related to the vertebrates. Sea squirts are one group of tunicates. See Appendix 2.

Turbid. Term used to describe conditions of low water clarity caused by suspended particulate matter.

Turf. A matt-like ground cover of low growing plants (e.g. grasses, mosses mussels or algae). Such assemblages are normally dominated by a single taxonomic group that may physically exclude other plant groups.

Understorey. Plants that occupy space beneath the canopy of taller or more expansive vegetation (e.g. bracken in a deciduous forest).

Wave action. The movement or series of movements of waves which generate a physical force as they break on the seashore.

Wave exposure. The degree of openness of a shore to direct wave action. Wave exposure is one of the criteria used by Ballantine (1961) to rank a shore.

Zonation. Occurrence of a single species or distinct species assemblages in recognisable bands across an environmental gradient (e.g. from the strand line to the low water mark, where a vertical gradient of physical and biological factors influences the distribution of species).

Sherkin Island Marine Station Publications

A Beginner's Guide to Ireland's Seashore. Helena Challinor; Susan Murphy Wickens; Jane Clark; Audrey Murphy (ISBN: 1 87049296 X)

Ireland's Marine Life. A World of Beauty. Edited by Matt Murphy & Susan Murphy (ISBN: 1 870492 75 7)

Ireland's Bird Life. A World of Beauty. Edited by Matt Murphy & Susan Murphy (ISBN: 1 870492 80 3)

The Wild Plants of Sherkin, Cape Clear and adjacent Islands of West Cork. John Akeroyd (editor) Lucy Wright, Karen Clarke, Jennifer Shockley, Nick Rowe, Pat Hatch, Mike Robinson, Beth Milner (ISBN: 1 870492 86 2)

Sherkin Comment
(ISSN: 0791-2447)
Sherkin Comment is a 32-page colour tabloid quarterly publication of Sherkin Island Marine Station, aiming to promote the awareness of our natural resources, their use and protection.

Sherkin Island Marine Station Silver Jubilee Booklet
(ISBN: 1 870492 22 6)

Bulletins of Sherkin Island
No 1: *Marine Research in Ireland* – Matt Murphy
No 2: *The Future of Marine Research in Ireland* – Matt Murphy
No 3: *Marine Science and the Development of Resources in Ireland* – Brian McK Bary (former Professor of Oceanography at University College Galway)
No 4: *Between the Devil and the Deep Blue Sea – the Status of Irish Marine Development* – Owen Sweeney
No 5: *Rainfall of Sherkin Island 1973–1984* – Helen Palmer
No 6: T*he Kowloon Bridge Shore Survey, 8th–11th January 1987* – J. M. Baker
No 7: The Kowloon Bridge Shore Survey (2nd Report), 13th–15th March 1987 – J. M. Baker
No 8: The Kowloon Bridge – Assessment of the Cork Co. Co. clean up of West Cork Beaches – 1987– J. M. Baker
No 9: (Withdrawn)
No 10: Sunshine Records of Sherkin Island 1974–1984 – Helen Palmer (ISBN: 1 870492 85 4)
No 11: Air Temperatures of Sherkin Island 1975–1984 – Helen Palmer (ISBN: 1 870492 90 0)
No 12: Otter Survey of Roaringwater Bay, South West Cork, Ireland, 1990 – Jeremy Wickens (ISBN: 1 870492 60 9)
No 13: Can Irish Aquaculture Help Keep Young People at Home? & The Environment – Double Standards – Matt Murphy (ISBN: 1 870492 56 0)
No 14: Air Temperatures of Sherkin Island 1985–1989 – Trevor Wade
No 15: Rainfall Records of Sherkin Island 1985–1989 – Trevor Wade
No 16: Sunshine Records of Sherkin Island 1990–1994 – Trevor Wade

Distribution Maps
Fauna distribution maps of sea shore monitoring sites in Long Island and Roaringwater Bays, Co. Cork, Ireland, 1975–1982 – by A. L. Martin.
Flora distribution maps of sea shore monitoring sites in Long Island and Roaringwater Bays, Co. Cork, Ireland, 1975–1982 – by K. Squires

Fauna distribution maps of sea shore monitoring sites in Dunmanus Bay, Co. Cork, Ireland, 1978–1982 – by M.J.C. Harding
Flora distribution maps of sea shore monitoring sites in Dunmanus Bay, Co. Cork, Ireland, 1978–1985 – by N. Squirrell

Conference Proceedings
1st International Conference 1985 *Ireland – the Atlantic – Exploitation of its Resources*
(ISBN: 1 870492 10 2)
2nd International Conference 1986 *Norway – the Development of its Fish Farming Industry*
(ISBN: 1 870492 00 5)
3rd International Conference 1987 *Lake, River and Coastal Pollution – Can it be Contained?*
(ISBN: 1 870492 20 X)
4th International Conference 1988 *Domestic and Industrial Waste*
(ISBN: 1 870492 01 3)
5th International Conference 1989 *Can Industry and the Environment Live Together?*
(ISBN: 1 870492 30 7)
6th International Conference 1990 *Sewage Disposal – Where Do We Stand?*
(ISBN: 1 870492 40 4)
7th International Conference 1991 *Management of Landfill Sites*
(ISBN: 1 870492 70 6)
8th International Conference 1992 *Water – Supply & Quality*
(ISBN: 1 870492 16 1)
9th International Conference 1993 *Incineration: The Issues*
(ISBN: 1 870492 26 9)
10th International Conference 1994 *Chemicals – A Cause for Concern?*
(ISBN: 1 870492 51 X)
11th International Conference 1995 *Environmental Protection: The Role of the State*
(ISBN: 1 870492 76 5)
12th International Conference 1996 *Planning Laws: Are they too Severe?*
(ISBN: 1 870492 91 9)
13th International Conference 1997 *Hazardous Waste Management – Industrial & Medical*
(ISBN: 1 870492 02 1)
14th International Conference 1998 *Environmental Impact Studies – Are they Worthwhile?*
(ISBN: 1 870492 07 2)
15th International Conference 1999 *Landfill – The Issues That Must Be Addressed*
(ISBN: 1 870492 12 9)
16th International Conference 2000 *Water – Is its Quality Deteriorating?*
(ISBN: 1 870492 17 X)
17th International Conference 2001 *Infrastructure Development: Can the Environment be Protected?*
(ISBN: 1 870492 32 3)
18th International Conference 2002 *Recycling: Expectation and Reality*
(ISBN: 1 870492 52 8)
19th International Conference 2003 *Tackling Pollution of Coastal and Inland Waters*
(ISBN: 1 870492 72 2)

1st Sherkin Intl. Conference 1987 *The Problems of Toxic Dinoflagellate Blooms in Aquaculture*
(ISBN: 1 870492 15 3)
2nd Sherkin Intl. Conference 1988 *Wild Salmon – Present and Future*
(ISBN: 1 870492 25 0)
3rd Sherkin Intl. Conference 1989 *The Problems of Toxic Dinoflagellate Blooms in Aquaculture*
(No proceedings published)
4th Sherkin Intl. Conference 1990 *Fish Farming – the Other Side*
(ISBN: 1 870492 35 8)

Sherkin Workshop 1990 *Effects of Stocked Salmon & Cage Escapees on Resident Wild Salmon Stocks*
(ISBN: 1 870492 4 55)
May 1991 Conference *The Common Fisheries Policy – Mid-term Review*
(ISBN: 1 870492 55 2)
May 1992 Conference *Reduction, Prevention & Re-use of Waste – An Alternative to Landfill*
(ISBN: 1 870492 11 0)
May 1993 Conference *Maximum Sustainable Yield from Fish Stocks – A Challenge to Fishermen & Managers*
(ISBN: 1 870492 21 8)

Fishing Update No. 1
An occasional publication from Sherkin Comment. A 32-page tabloid newspaper on Canada's East Coast fisheries problems in 1995. Matt Murphy. (ISSN: 0791-2447)

European Contributions to the Taxonomy of Sponges. Edited by W. Clifford Jones
(ISBN 1 870492 05 6)
This book is an outcome of the "Sponge Workshop" held at Sherkin Island Marine Station from 10–17th September, 1983.

The Genus Alexandrium Halim (Dinoflagellata). Professor Enrique Balech
(ISBN: 1 870492 61 7)

Red Tide Newsletter. Volume 1 to 5 (Now in abeyance) (ISBN: 1 870492 06 4)

Special on the Spot Reports
"Salmon Rescue Operation on the Western Norwegian Coast – Algal Bloom – May 1988"
"Algal Bloom – Chile – August/September 1988"

Bird Reports

These reports contain all the information on birds collected by Sherkin Island Marine Station's biologists, over the years.

No. 1. 1985 Compiled by Mike Pollard (ISBN: 1 870492 46 3)
No. 2. 1989 Compiled by R.P. Mundy (ISBN: 1 870492 31 5)
No. 3. 1990 Compiled by R.P. Mundy (ISBN: 1 870492 36 6)
No. 4. 1991 Compiled by Nigel Baskerville (ISBN: 1 870492 41 2)
No. 5. 1992/1993 Compiled by R.P. Mundy (ISBN: 1 870492 66 8)
No. 6. 1994 Compiled by R.P. Mundy (ISBN: 1 870492 71 4)

An Islander Looks Back. Matt Murphy. (Personal reflections)
(ISBN: 1 870492 50 1)

Rocking the Boat. Matt Murphy (Personal reflections)
(ISBN: 1 870492 65 X)

Children's Publications
A to Z of the World Around Us (ISSN: 0791-2447)
Wild Flower Colouring & Guide Book (ISBN: 1 870492 27 7)
Bird Colouring & Guide Book (ISBN: 1 870492 67 6)
Sea Life Colouring & Guide Book (ISBN: 1 870492 62 5)
Nature Diary (ISBN: 1 870492 42 0)